Contents at a Glance

Office 2001 for Mac®: The Complete Reference

Gene Steinberg

Osborne/**McGraw-Hill**
New York Chicago San Francisco
Lisbon London Madrid Mexico City
Milan New Delhi San Juan
Seoul Singapore Sydney Toronto

Osborne/**McGraw-Hill**
2600 Tenth Street
Berkeley, California 94710
U.S.A.

To arrange bulk purchase discounts for sales promotions, premiums, or fund-raisers, please contact Osborne/**McGraw-Hill** at the above address. For information on translations or book distributors outside the U.S.A., please see the International Contact Information page immediately following the index of this book.

Office 2001 for Mac®: The Complete Reference

1234567890 CUS CUS 01987654321

ISBN 0-07-213168-3

Publisher
Brandon A. Nordin

Vice President & Associate Publisher
Scott Rogers

Acquisitions Editor
Megg Bonar

Project Editor
Janet Walden

Acquisitions Coordinator
Alissa Larson

Technical Editor
Pieter Paulson

Copy Editor
Judy Ziajka

Proofreader
Pat Mannion

Indexer
David Heiret

Computer Designers
Tara Davis, Lauren McCarthy,
Melinda Moore Lytle, Kelly Stanton-Scott

Illustrators
Michael Mueller, Lyssa Sieben-Wald

Series Design
Peter F. Hancik

Cover Series Design
Dodie Shoemaker

This book was composed with Corel VENTURA™ Publisher.

About the Author

In 1984 **Gene Steinberg** began to work with the original Apple Macintosh personal computer and never looked back. Over the next few years, Gene finally decided to follow his dream and become a full-time writer, but he also devoted extra time to work as a computer software/systems consultant, partly to provide material for his books and magazine articles. Among those for whom he has provided computer support is best-selling author Tom Clancy.

Gene has written 20 books on computers and the Internet, plus hundreds of articles for industry publications such as *MacAddict*, *MacHome*, *MacUser*, and *Macworld*. His books for Osborne/McGraw-Hill include *Mac OS 9: The Complete Reference* and *Upgrading & Troubleshooting Your Mac*.

He also writes a weekly column, "Mac Reality Check," for *The Arizona Republic's* azcentral.com Web site, and is a contributing editor for CNET.com, the world's largest online technology news service. His computer support Web site, The Mac Night Owl (http://www.macnightowl.com) receives thousands of regular visitors each day.

About the Contributing Author

Grayson Steinberg is a renaissance teenager who tracks tech stocks, writes, produces and acts, plays violin, and builds multimedia presentations in Microsoft PowerPoint. He has written financial columns for *Green Magazine*, a print and online investor's journal and, in his spare time (what little there is of it), he co-authors science fiction novels with his dad.

To my family, who made it possible for me
to realize the impossible dream

Contents

Part I

Getting Started with Office 2001 for Mac

Part II

Getting the Most Out of Entourage

Part III

Putting Word 2001 to Work for You

Part IV

Organizing Your Data with Excel 2001

Part V

Mastering PowerPoint 2001

Acknowledgments

I first started using Office 2001 when it was a mere babe, that is a beta, and I'm grateful to Microsoft's Irving Kwong, former product manager for the Mac Business Unit at Microsoft, for arranging for me to work with a copy early on and for being available for the hard questions. In addition, I appreciate the assistance provided by the helpful folks at Waggener Edstrom Strategic Communications, Microsoft's PR agency, especially Melissa Harris, Linda Siegel, and Karen Sung.

I'm grateful to my friend and agent, Sharon Jarvis, for her able assistance in handling all the business details, so I could concentrate on research and writing.

I would also like to offer my heartfelt thanks to my brilliant son, Grayson, for taking on the difficult tasks of developing chapters on some of the most sophisticated features of Microsoft Excel, such as formulas and charting, and then for putting his multimedia expertise to practice in writing the Microsoft PowerPoint chapters.

Osborne/McGraw-Hill's highly skilled, as usual, editing team attended to delivering the final product you have in your hands. Thanks go to Megg Bonar, Alissa Larson, Janet Walden, Judy Ziajka, and Pat Mannion. I want to give still another thank you to my long-time friend and sometimes co-author, Pieter Paulson, for his careful, exacting technical editing.

Certainly, I could never have done any of this were it not for my beautiful wife and business partner, Barbara, for tolerating the long hours I spent glued to my computer keyboard to finish this book on schedule.

Introduction

When one thinks of Microsoft software, no doubt the focus is on the Windows platform and Microsoft's dominance in the world of personal computing. It may, then, come as a surprise to learn that Microsoft Word actually got its start on the Mac platform, back in the 1980s.

Word was then a fairly simple program to install and use, but over time, as with many programs, it grew in complexity in direct proportion to its growth in features. As part of the Office application suite, it shares its complexity with Microsoft Excel, the spreadsheet program that also leads the pack.

Before developing Office 2001, Microsoft realized that their software had become too complex for many users, and that accessing some of the most useful features involved long trips to arcane dialog boxes to sort out options that were not easy to understand. Their announced goal for the new version was to "simplify difficult tasks," and to achieve that, they developed features such as the Project Gallery, a flexible floating window that serves as the starting point for Office, Excel, and PowerPoint (the slide presentation application), and a floating Formatting Palette. The latter puts many of the most used commands one click away. With power comes simplicity.

Microsoft also made the programs easy to install, almost as simple as the very first Mac programs, by using a drag-and-drop scheme for the basic setup. They put the entire package in a CD box—attractive, distinct, an attention getter. But something big is missing. While previous versions of Office came with thick instruction manuals, all you get with Office 2001 is a six-page booklet. There's not even an electronic manual on the installation CD. If you want assistance in getting up to speed, you are directed to the Help menus or Microsoft's Web site. Thus this book was born.

Office 2001 for Mac: The Complete Reference is meant, first and foremost, to take the place of the manuals that are no longer provided. But more important, this book is designed to take you farther than a traditional manual would take you, so that you discover hidden features and shortcuts that will help you truly harness the powerful features of Office 2001.

Should You Install Office?

My answer is yes, so long as your Mac is a recent model, with enough power and hard disk storage space to handle the programs. Here are the simple requirements:

- **Processor**   You need a Mac or Mac OS–compatible with a minimum clock speed of 120 MHz. The original-generation PowerMacs (with processor speeds from 60 MHz to 80 MHz) will run Office 2001 with almost adequate performance, but you will find it a bit of a struggle if you want to access the most powerful features of the programs.

- **Mac OS Version**   Office 2001 requires Mac OS 8.1 or later, but works best with Mac OS 8.5 or later.

The above requirements can be met by millions of Macs out there, including some of the early generation Power Macintosh models. But if you have an older Mac that isn't up to the task, this may be the perfect time to consider a hardware upgrade.

I don't recommend Microsoft Office 2001 simply because I'm writing a book about it. As a writer, I use Word for all of my work, Excel for my financial data, and PowerPoint when I need to create a presentation for a client. Nearly all of my e-mail and contact information is handled by Entourage, the e-mail and personal information manager application that makes its debut with Office.

Having four feature-packed applications under your control will surely help you take your Macintosh computing to greater heights. It will enhance your productivity by letting you create more sophisticated documents with less work, and time is, to cite the cliché, money.

The Bill of Fare

This is a Complete Reference, and as such, it has a wealth of information that will help guide you through the nooks and crannies of Office 2001. But it's not meant to be read from cover to cover as a novel. As you begin to explore this sprawling application suite, you'll discover areas where you need more information, or just some basic step-by-step guidance to get over a rough spot.

In writing this book, I assume you are reasonably well acquainted with the Mac and the Mac operating system, and that you are adept at mousing around and using menu bar commands, dialog boxes, and Finder features. These are all the tools you need to get the maximum value from this book. In addition, I've organized it into five parts, so you can easily hone in on the most important information.

Part I, "Getting Started with Office 2001 for Mac," introduces you to all the new features of this great application suite. You'll discover the Mac-only capabilities and the new user interface elements that make all of these programs easier to use than ever, and how they work seamlessly with each other. You'll also learn installation strategies, to best install Office so that it meets your needs. From drag and drop to custom, you'll see how installations are done and the impact to your particular setup. You'll also discover the Project Gallery, Microsoft's new feature to simplify difficult tasks and get you going with a complex document without having to spend a long time mastering complex formatting commands.

In Part II, "Getting the Most Out of Entourage," you'll be introduced to the newest member of the Office family. Building from the easy interface of its free e-mail client application, Outlook Express, Microsoft grafted onto it a full-service personal information manager, complete with calendar, reminder capabilities, and the ability to link to messages and files to keep tabs on a project. You'll discover the ins and outs of Entourage in Chapters 5 through 10.

Part III, "Putting Word 2001 to Work for You," focuses on the centerpiece of the Office application suite, Microsoft Word. You'll discover the basics of word processing as well as advanced formatting techniques. Then you'll be guided through the intricacies of the program, including its new table creation tools; the ability to create, import, and edit graphic objects; and how to use styles and macros.

Part IV, "Organizing Your Data with Excel 2001," introduces you to the world of spreadsheets. You'll learn about the makeup of an Excel document, a workbook into which you make worksheets. We'll cover the basics of setting up and creating your first workbook, and then you'll learn how to leverage Excel's ability to do the math for you. You'll discover the Calculator, Formula Palette, and List Manager and how they simplify the management of your data. You'll also learn how to create colorful and informative 2-D and 3-D charts from the very same data.

The final part of the book, Part IV, "Mastering PowerPoint 2001," covers the multimedia component of Office. PowerPoint is mostly known as an application for making slide presentations. But that's only the half of it. The new version of this program also lets you create QuickTime movies, which can be viewed on your Mac, and, in fact, on Windows computers that have QuickTime installed. All in all, there's a tremendous amount of capability built into this flexible program.

How This Book Is Assembled

To make it easier for you to get the information you want, each chapter consists of the following basic elements:

- Lots of background information so you know why something works, and, more importantly, why things may sometimes go wrong.
- Step-by-step descriptions of installation and troubleshooting processes.
- Tips, tricks, and guidelines to help you handle routine installations and complex setups with ease, and to diagnose both the common and very obscure problems you may encounter along the way with Office 2001.

It All Began with a Beta

While a press briefing is useful, you can never tell about a program until you have a chance to give it a test drive. So when Microsoft game me the opportunity to have a look at an early release of Office 2001, I jumped at the opportunity.

Over the next few weeks, as I got more and more acquainted with the application suite, I began to appreciate the power and flexibility of its new features. After you have used the program, I'm sure you will agree. I hope this book will go a long way towards helping you get the most value out of Office 2001, and I welcome your comments and suggestions for future editions—feel free to write me at my e-mail address.

Gene Steinberg
Scottsdale, Arizona
Email: gene@macnightowl.com
http://www.macnightowl.com
http://www.rockoids.com

Part I

Getting Started with Office 2001 for Mac

Chapter 1

Discovering Office 2001

The release of a new version of Microsoft Office is an event, be it for the Mac or Windows platform. The arrival of Office 2001 for the Macintosh is especially significant, because it provides up-front and personal evidence that the world's largest software company is firm in its resolve to deliver top-quality software for our favorite computing platform.

For the new version, Microsoft has gone the extra mile to ensure that ease of use is a primary feature. In the past, the company's programs have been regarded as having huge feature sets buried in arcane menu bar commands and dialog boxes. The learning curve was steep, and huge instruction manuals and comprehensive help menus were needed to get users up to speed.

But even if the information you need is now embedded in the software, the lack of a user manual means that you no longer have a convenient reference to guide you along the way. That's the purpose of this book: to help you harness the power of Office 2001 for the Macintosh and create documents that will allow you to express your creativity and present information in the most productive way.

In this chapter, we'll explore many of the new features of Office 2001.

New Features of Office 2001

The biggest problem in creating a document is just getting started. Which Office program do you use? How do you select the right document format to meet your needs? The following pages list many of the most important new features of Office. You'll find full instructions on how to take advantage of them in the other chapters in this book.

NOTE   *Did you buy the Office applications separately? Excel 2001, PowerPoint 2001, and Word 2001 are available in separate retail packages. You can use the chapters in this book that refer to those programs just as if you had bought the entire Office package in one box (make that CD).*

Introducing the Project Gallery

Microsoft's answer to the dilemma of how to get started is the Project Gallery (see Figure 1-1). This floating palette is sort of a one-stop shopping center that lets you select the kind of document you want to create and then choose from a wide array of templates and wizards to set up that document. You don't even have to specify which application you want to use. Based on the choices you make in the Project Galley, the correct application will be selected and opened for you, automatically. We'll cover this subject in more detail in Chapters 3 and 4.

GETTING STARTED
WITH OFFICE 2001
FOR MAC

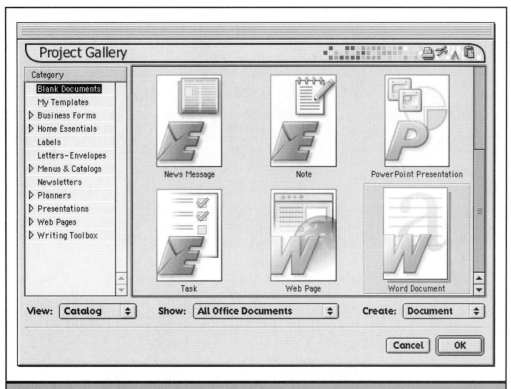

Figure 1-1.   *The Office 2001 Project Gallery is a convenient starting point for creating new documents.*

NOTE   *If you've used AppleWorks 6, you'll find something familiar about the Project Gallery. It resembles the Starting Point feature of Apple Computer's integrated software package.*

The Formatting Palette Simplifies Document Setup

In previous versions of Office, you had to figure out toolbar buttons and pore through a byzantine array of menu bar commands and dialog boxes to handle even the basics of document formatting, such as setting text size and line spacing. With the Formatting Palette (shown in Figure 1-2), this is all simplified greatly. The palette's contents change automatically depending on the Office feature or program you're using, and many of the commands you'll use most are just a click or a pop-up menu away.

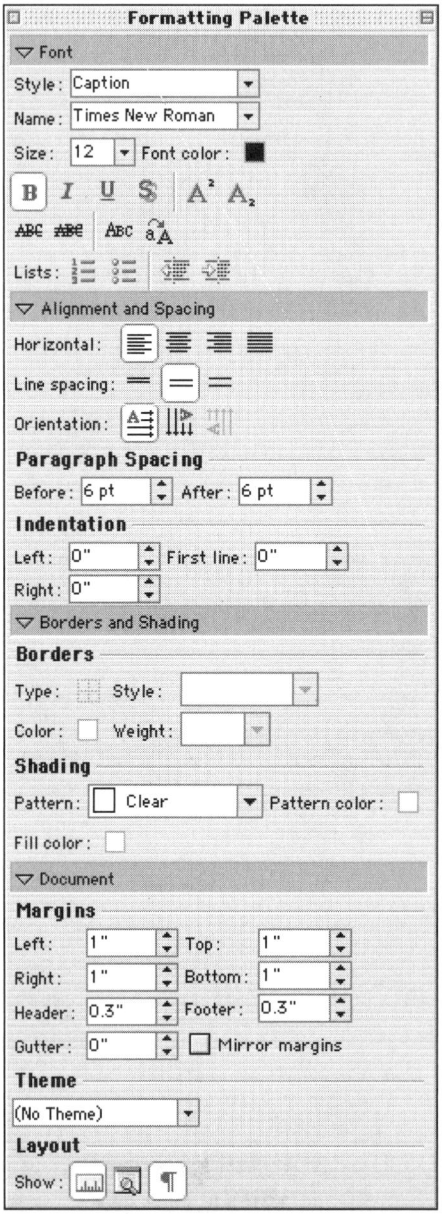

Figure 1-2. *In this example, the Formatting Palette displays many of the Word commands you'll use most often. The choices change if you switch to Excel or PowerPoint.*

Support for New Open and Save Dialog Boxes

Apple's enhanced Open and Save dialog boxes, sometimes called navigation services, are fully supported by Office 2001 (see Figure 1-3). The Shortcuts feature lets you jump right to the desktop, the drives available to your Mac, or networked Macs. A Favorites feature lets you add folders and disks for fast access. Recently accessed documents are also listed.

Introducing Microsoft Entourage

Microsoft's free Outlook Express has been regarded as one of the best e-mail programs, even when compared to a popular commercial alternative, Qualcomm's Eudora. In addition to managing your Internet e-mail accounts and newsgroups, the program has a convenient Address Book feature that stores basic contact information beyond the e-mail address, including phone numbers and physical addresses.

Microsoft took this worthy beginning and melded it with a personal information manager (PIM) and dubbed it Entourage (see Figure 1-4). As you'll learn in Chapters 5 through 10, this new application compares favorably with separate PIM software, but it's also well integrated into the Office application suite.

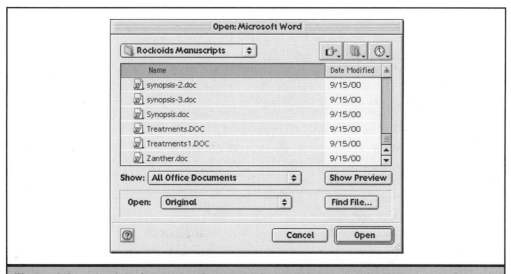

Figure 1-3. *Apple's fancy new Open and Save dialog boxes get full support from Office 2001.*

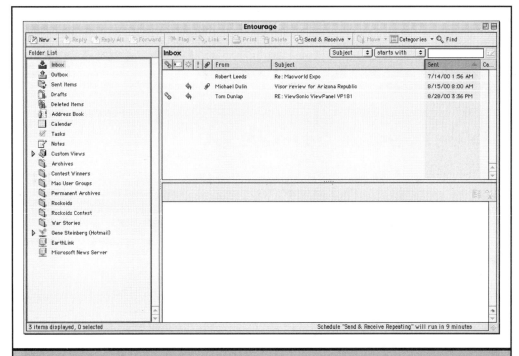

Figure 1-4.   *Entourage is a new e-mail and personal information manager application based on Outlook Express.*

Here are the main features of Entourage:

■ **Easy E-mail Management**   A convenient three-pane window displays e-mail and information category folders, a list of e-mail messages, and the text of the selected message. You don't have to open your message in a separate window, which eases management of messages. This window setup is especially convenient if your Mac has a small monitor.

■ **Smart Address AutoComplete**   When you address a message, Entourage offers to complete the address based on your Address Book contacts and the most recent contacts with whom you've exchanged messages (even if they are not in your Address Book).

■ **Address Book**   In addition to providing basic contact information, such as name, e-mail address, phone number, and location, the Address Book provides an Action button, which you can use to create a new message or even locate the contact by logging onto the Internet and consulting Microsoft's Expedia Web site.

■ **Easy-Access Calendar**   Accessed by a single click from the main window of Entourage, the Calendar (see Figure 1-5) can be used to create new events or tasks and manage existing ones. The Calendar can be published on your Web site or sent as an e-mail attachment to your contacts.

> **NOTE**   *The Calendar automatically resizes itself depending on the size of your document window and the space allocated to the folder list.*

■ **Task Management**   You can build a personal to-do list, where you can enter tasks and set reminders on a one-time basis or for repeating events.

■ **Electronic Sticky Notes**   If your office is cluttered with those paper sticky notes, you'll appreciate the ability to create electronic versions in Entourage. You can write down ideas, recipes, directions to a contact's office and so on.

> **NOTE**   *The Sticky Notes feature of Microsoft Entourage is separate from the feature offered as part of the Mac OS. For one thing, it works only within the program, whereas Apple's Stickies feature puts your notes on the desktop.*

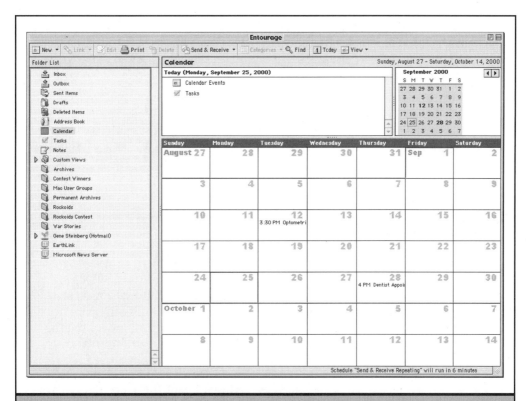

Figure 1-5.   *Entourage's Calendar can be used to enter tasks or reminders, or it can be published on your Web site.*

■ **Electronic Reminders**   You'll see a reminder at the specified time for special events, tasks, or messages that require follow-up. Entourage reminders can be created for Microsoft Office documents that require follow-up.

■ **Custom Views and Categories**   You can organize your personal information the way you want, making it easy to prioritize messages and events and locate the data you need.

■ **Links**   This unique and powerful feature of Entourage lets you attach a link to a message or file, even if that file was created in a program that's not part of the Microsoft Office 2001 suite. This feature allows you to open the linked item without having to perform a special search for it—a real time saver.

■ **Word Text Editor**   Your Entourage messages use some of the same basic editing tools as Word. You can check spelling, apply text formatting, and automatically correct the words you frequently misspell.

■ **Advanced Find**   You wrote a message, but with hundreds or thousands in your archives, how do you find the one you sent to a specific person on a specific day? Entourage's Find feature can search your messages by content or category.

■ **Easy Import of Existing Messages**   Whether you used Outlook Express or a totally different e-mail program, such as Eudora or Netscape Communicator, you can import both messages and address books with a reasonable degree of fidelity. A convenient assistant takes you through the process.

■ **Multiple Users**   With Mac OS 9, Apple introduced systemwide support for multiple users. This allows the owner or administrator of a Macintosh to set up a custom environment for each user. Entourage supports this feature, so each user can have his or her own account information, messages, reminders, and so forth.

Introducing Word 2001

Here, one by one, are brief descriptions of the new features of Word 2001. Following this list is a roundup of the changes in commands as compared to Word 98, so you can see how to access familiar functions with the new version of the program. You'll discover the power of Word 2001 in Chapters 11 through 15.

■ **Templates**   Rather than creating your document formatting from scratch, Word 2001 offers you hundreds of templates to help simplify the process of getting started. A template is simply a document with all the formatting elements in place, ready for you to customize or insert your information. They're defined by category, so you can easily select the ones that apply most to your project. The Value Pack on your Office 2001 installation disk (described in Chapter 2) includes extra templates and clip art for you to install.

NOTE   *If you choose a template or wizard that requires a different application than Word, no problem. Once you've set up your document, the appropriate Office application will be launched if it's not already open.*

■ **Wizard**   Sometimes known as an assistant, a wizard helps step you through the design process, so you can easily build a document or use a particular program feature without having to enter all the formatting information manually. Word 98 offered wizards for such tasks as creating envelopes and labels. The new version adds more sophisticated offerings, for working with such projects as brochures, catalogs, and menus (see Figure 1-6).

■ **AutoCorrect**   Having a powerful Mac at your beck and call isn't enough. What's the good of having all that computing horsepower at hand if it cannot do at least some of the work for you, so you don't have to manually enter every command or function? The new AutoCorrect function still finds and automatically corrects typing errors, such as misspellings and typos, and grammatical errors and so on. But it goes further than the feature in the previous version of Word by using the same dictionary as your spelling checker. Take it from me; this book would have been far more difficult without this feature (I tend to reverse letters when I type really fast, which is most of the time).

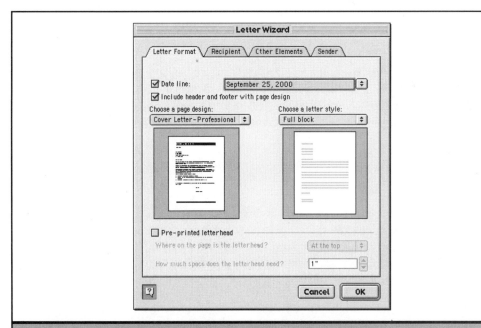

Figure 1-6.   *Use a wizard to guide you through the formatting of the most complex projects.*

■ **Automatic Formatting**   Compared to earlier versions, Word 2001 has a more inspired automatic text formatting feature, which examines document formats that you use for a list item, such as this one, and then applies the same formatting to the next item. In this case, I typed the heading in bold, so Word knew enough to begin the next item in bold as well (even though I was typing in normal text when I ended the previous entry). Word is even clever enough to apply common formats to text entries: for instance, if you regularly place asterisks before and after a word to signify bold. For example, typing *Bold* would yield **Bold**, with the word typed in boldface (without your having to switch back to regular typeface after that word).

■ **AutoComplete**   When you begin to type a word or phrase, Word can recommend how it may be completed, based on the entries in your Entourage Address Book, dates, and entries in the AutoText panel (opened from the AutoCorrect command). When I type **Gen** in my copy of Word, for example, the program comes up with "Gene Steinberg" to complete the entry (of course, your mileage may vary, unless you have some reason to put my name in your Address Book).

■ **AutoSummarize**   This feature allows Word to examine the contents of a document and then provide a summary (see Figure 1-7) based on its analysis. While I would not suggest this as a way for a student to write a report for homework (in case you are a student reading this book), it's a useful way to create an abstract of a complex document to get a sense of the basic subject matter.

■ **Automatic Style Creation and Preview**   In previous versions of Word, you had to manually create a new style based on the formatting of a paragraph. In Word 2001, the style is created for you as you alter the formatting. In addition, styles are updated based on the changes that you make.

TIP   *To see a small preview of the impact of your style, just select Style from the Format menu and click the style's name. Both character and paragraph styles are shown in miniature.*

■ **Letter Wizard**   One of the most common uses of a word processing program is to write letters. In Word 2001, the Letter Wizard takes you step by step through the formatting of the kind of letter you want, be it a formal letter or just a personal note to a friend or family member. What's more, the names of those to whom you've written are stored in a list, along with the contents of your Entourage Address Book. That way, your new letter can be addressed automatically for you. Even your salutation and closings are stored, in case you wish to move beyond a simple "Dear John" beginning and "Cordially" ending.

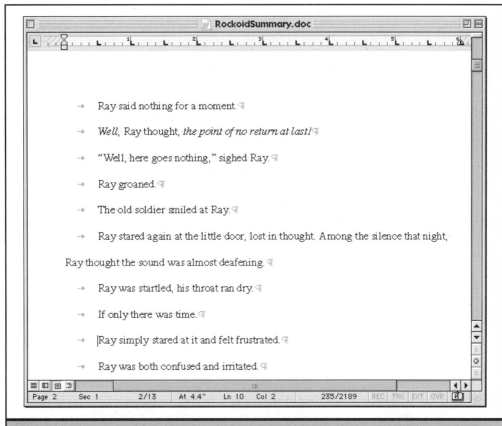

Figure 1-7.   *This is a short summary of a novel written by the author and his son.*

- **Click and Type**   Want to insert a header or footer in your document (such as a book's title or page number)? It's easier with Word 2001: all you have to do is double-click a footer or header in the document where you want to place the entries. This click and type capability is also useful for adding graphics and tables to your document.

- **Checking Spelling and Grammar**   Spelling and grammar checking are tasks where a word processor sometimes falls down on the job. Grammar checking tends to be a little too literal, and spell checkers miss proper names of people, places, and things. Suggestions for grammatical errors are now presented in a more informative, less rigid fashion. In addition, as explained earlier in this section, AutoCorrect has been beefed up to offer near-automatic spell checking and correction of common errors. The result is a cleaner, more error-free document in less time.

TIP   *Just hold down the* CONTROL *key and click a word, and Word will provide a pop-up listing of synonyms in the contextual menu. There's also a Define category, which lists the dictionary definition of the word, as shown here.*

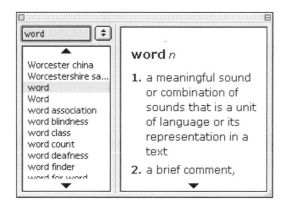

- **New Find and Replace Feature**   Say you want to change the word *scissor* to *knife*. With the previous versions of Word, you also had to seek out several grammatical inflections: for example, you had to replace *scissors* with *knives*, and so on. The new Find and Replace feature intelligently changes all or most of these variations without your having to go through the process several times (which can get to be time consuming on a large document). Remember, the more a computer computes, the easier it is for you to get your work done.

- **Multiple-Language Hyphenation**   You can install multilingual dictionaries in Office, using the Value Pack installer on your Office CD. When Word detects material in your document written in a different language, it will hyphenate accordingly, if document hyphenation is activated (it's activated via the Hyphenation command on the Tools menu).

- **New Table Drawing Tools**   Word's extensive array of illustration tools have been enhanced for tables. Just a click and a drag is all you need to create a boundary around a table or one of the cells within a table. A convenient Eraser tool is on hand to remove any portion of the table, so a portion of the table can be merged. In Word 98, this feature was limited to cells in the same row. Now it works across the board.

- **Nested Tables**   Want to create a table within a table? In Word 2001, you can do it with a click and a drag. Just drag and create your table within a table as easily as you create any other table. We'll cover this subject in more detail in Chapter 13.

■ **Aligning Text**   The text alignment options now include two convenient document layout features. One lets you align text horizontally on a page, and the other lets you align it vertically, aligning the text with the top or middle or setting it justified (which spreads the space between lines to fill your page). These options are similar to the features available on page layout software, such as Adobe InDesign and QuarkXPress.

■ **Rotate Text**   Another convenient page layout feature is the ability to rotate text 90 degrees. Rotation is performed globally, either in your document or in individual table cells or text boxes.

■ **New Table Formatting Options**   In Word 2001, you can now adjust the height of a table by dragging the border of the row up or down, in the same fashion as you can control the width of a column. A move handle lets you place the table elsewhere on a page, and a resize handle lets you alter the size but retain current row and column proportions.

■ **Updated Border Styles**   Included in Word 2001's bag of tricks are 150 brand-new border styles. You can choose from such fancy effects as three-dimensional borders, plus multiple line borders suitable for page layout. In addition, the new Text Border feature allows you to block out text elements, which simplifies the process of adding a special border around a headline.

■ **Shaded Text**   You can now apply a shade or color to just selected letters or words, not just an entire paragraph as before.

■ **Enhanced Drawing Tools**   Although a word processor program isn't the ideal environment for illustration, Word 2001's drawing and graphics tools have been expanded with special three-dimensional effects, shadows, textures, transparent fills, and AutoShapes—a palette of 100 forms that you can use to spruce up your document, as shown here.

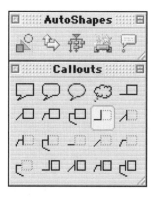

In addition, pictures can be placed in any location in your document, and you can run text around a picture. This gives Word some useful page layout capabilities.

- **Text Boxes**   If you use a page layout program, such as QuarkXPress, the concept of a text box is familiar. It involves putting text in a predefined area or box, which can then be enhanced with artistic effects, rotated, resized, or cropped. You can also link two or more text boxes, so text flows into different columns of a page. This feature makes it easy for you to create a club newsletter or other publication without having to resort to one of those other programs for the task.

NOTE   *Although Word is offering more and more page layout features, it's not meant as a replacement for sophisticated page creation applications such as Adobe InDesign and QuarkXPress. It is useful, however, for smaller, in-house publications and simple brochures, where formatting capabilities and the precision of typography and image placement are not as significant.*

- **Picture Bullets**   A normal text bullet, commonly used for lists (such as in this book), consists of a small, black (or colored) circle. Word's Picture Bullet feature lets you use a picture rather than a type element as a bullet.

- **Clip Gallery**   Organizing your clip art has never been easier than with Word's Clip Gallery. This new feature lets you organize your artwork into a convenient storage area from which you can select and drag and drop images into your documents. What's more, it works with all Office programs, not just Word.

- **Scanner and Digital Camera Support**   You can access TWAIN-compatible scanners and digital cameras, so you can scan a picture directly into Word.

NOTE   *TWAIN is an acronym for "tool without an interesting name," and it allows programs to offer direct access to special software, such as scanning software. Not all scanners and digital cameras support TWAIN. You'll need to consult the documentation for the product, or just check the contents of the TWAIN folder, located in the Preferences folder within the System Folder, to see if drivers for the product are present.*

- **Web Integration**   In previous versions of Word, you could save your documents in HTML format for publishing on the World Wide Web. In Word 2001, the Web authoring features have been greatly enhanced. One important new feature gives you the ability to preview the page before it's saved in the Web browser of your choice—no, it doesn't have to be Internet Explorer (although a copy is included on the Office 2001 CD). In addition, Web pages can be optimized for best display in a browser, thus reducing file size and creating pages that load faster. There are also tools for creating visual effects, editing and optimizing graphics, adding sound and video, and tapping a collection of clip art for special effects and borders.

- **WSIWYG Web Editing**   The WSIWYG (what you see is what you get) feature is similar to what you find in separate Web authoring programs. You can create a Web page with text, pictures, fonts, sounds, and more and never get involved in the raw HTML code on which it's based; you just have to look at the end result, fully formatted (see Figure 1-8). If you like, of course, you can view the HTML source code to perform fine-tuning.

Figure 1-8. *This sample Web page, viewed in Microsoft Internet Explorer, shows how you can produce some sophisticated work with Word's HTML editing features.*

■ **Data Merge Manager**   One particularly useful feature of Word, though difficult to use, is Mail Merge. Word 2001 makes it easier to create form letters, envelopes, labels, and other documents. Using simple drag-and-drop techniques, you can organize your data fields so they show up in the right place. When you're done, you can preview the document before printing to make sure everything is placed correctly.

■ **Expanded Multilingual Support**   If you've earmarked your documents for use around the world, you'll be pleased with Word 2001's ability to handle the requirements for foreign language text. Such elements as special characters, euro styles, special date formats, and Word's powerful formatting tools are customized to meet specific language requirements.

Word Command Changes

With so many changes in the program, it may seem confusing that the basic menu bar commands are essentially the same. Table 1-1 lists the changes and additions that apply to common Word features. This will help you adapt to the new features and the reinvention of old ones.

Word 98	Word 2001
File Menu	
New	Changed to Project Gallery.
Save as HTML	Changed to Save as Web Page.
Edit Menu	
Publishing	Publish & Subscribe is no longer supported.
Insert Menu	
Break	Click command under Break to insert breaks.
Auto Text	Reference Initials, Signature, and Signature Company removed. These commands can be restored by choosing AutoText from the Insert menu and reinserting.

Table 1-1.   *Word Menu Bar Commands Changed for Word 2001*

Word 98	Word 2001
Format Menu	
Style Gallery	Transferred to Theme dialog box.
Tools Menu	
Language	Thesaurus and Hyphenation functions moved to Tools menu.
Mail Merge	Now called Data Merge Manager.
Envelopes and Labels	Split into two commands: Envelopes and Labels.
Preferences	Now where it should be: on the Edit menu.
Table Menu	
Insert Table	Transferred to the Insert menu and renamed Table.
Delete Cells	Choose Delete from the Tools menu and select Cells.
Select Row	Choose Select from the Tools menu and select Row.
Select Column	Choose Select from the Tools menu and select Column.
Select Table	Choose Select from the Tools menu and select Table.
Distribute Rows Evenly	Available under AutoFit.
Distribute Columns Evenly	Available under AutoFit.
Cell Height and Width	Available under Table Properties.
Headings	Changed to Heading Rows Repeat.
Convert Table	Choose Convert from the Tools menu and select Convert Table.
Show Clipboard	Moved to a more logical position, the View menu, and renamed Office Clipboard.

Table 1-1.   *Word Menu Bar Commands Changed for Word 2001* (continued)

Table 1-2 summarizes the commands new in Word 2001 and where to find them.

New Command	Function
File Menu	
New Blank Document	Similar to the New command in Word 98; creates a brand-new, blank document using the default template.
Web Page Preview	Opens your selected Web browser to view Web page.
View Menu	
Contact	Available under Toolbars; used to configure your Entourage Address Book.
Formatting Palette	Displays a convenient floating palette of common commands.
Insert Menu	
Horizontal Line	Available under Picture; inserts a graphic file or horizontal line in your document.
From Scanner or Camera	Available under Picture; inserts a picture directly from your scanner or digital camera.
HTML Object	Allows you to insert objects such as sounds, scrolling text, and form buttons in your Web page.
Format Menu	
Theme	Allows you to create a document based on a preset set of background images, colors, and document styles.

Table 1-2.   *New Commands Available from the Word 2001 Menu Bar*

New Command	Function
Tools Menu	
Dictionary	Accesses the built-in dictionary.
Flag for Follow Up	Works with Entourage to set up a reminder that informs you when it is time to resume work on your document.
Help Menu	
Turn Assistant On/ Turn Assistant Off	Activates or turns off the animated Office Assistant.

Table 1-2.   *New Commands Available from the Word 2001 Menu Bar* (continued)

Introducing Excel 2001

Although Microsoft Word 2001 may get most of the attention, Excel 2001 (see Figure 1-9) has its share of changes that will greatly simplify the often convoluted process of creating a spreadsheet. We'll cover this subject in more detail in Chapters 16 through 19. Here's a brief listing of the changes and improvements:

- **Project Gallery**   As in all other Office applications, the Project Gallery serves as the convenient starting point for creating a new document. You can open a blank document page (known as a workbook in Excel) or choose from a variety of templates and designs.

- **See-Through View**   This feature keeps the color of all selected cells containing colored text the same, rather than reversing the color scheme. This approach is likely to be less confusing.

- **Euroconvert**   This feature offers easy conversion of numbers to euros and European Union (EU) member currencies (the new currency system supported in Europe). It also allows you to convert a figure from one euro currency to another, by way of the euro.

Figure 1-9. *Using Excel, you can create sophisticated spreadsheets and charts in minutes.*

- **Flag for Follow-up** This feature works with Entourage. It allows you to flag your Excel workbooks for later follow-up reminders.

- **Scanner and Digital Camera Support** This feature works with TWAIN-compatible scanners and digital cameras, allowing you to scan a picture directly to Excel. Scanned pictures can greatly enhance the look of your workbooks and charts.

■ **Shared Office Tools**   Because certain features are shared across all Office programs, it's easier to learn how to access and use a program feature.

■ **Border Drawing Toolbar**   This feature lets you draw borders, remove borders, and merge borders, each with a single click. You can also change border styles and colors using this powerful tool.

■ **Calculator**   This feature is a dream come true, especially if math isn't your second language. You can enter figures in the Calculator, and it will automatically come up with the correct formula syntax. Then you can place the figures in any cell in your Excel document.

■ **AutoSum**   The updated version of AddSum includes Average, Count, Max, and Min functions, which makes it easier to create functions.

■ **Four-Digit Dates**   Just in time for the new millennium, this feature lets you specify four-digit, rather than two-digit, years.

■ **Formatting Palette**   As in Word, this little feature places common program features just a click away. The available functions depend on the type of item you've selected, be it a regular cell or a drawing object. The Formatting Palette frees you from long trips through menus and dialog boxes to access many Excel features.

■ **WYSIWYG Font Menu**   This feature is identical to the one available in recent versions of Word. You can now see the actual styles of your available fonts.

```
                          ▲
   Arrus BT Bold
   Arrus BT Bold Italic
   Arrus BT Italic
   Arrus BT Roman
   BernhardMod BT Bold
   BernhardMod BT Bold Italic
   BernhardMod BT Italic
   BernhardMod BT Roman
   BerkeleyFIF BK Regular
   Bookman Hd BT
   Brush738 BT Regular
   BrushScript BT
   CAPITALS
   Carlton LET
   CaslonOpnface BT Regular
   Century Gothic
   Charcoal
   Chicago
   Comic Sans MS
   Cooper Blk BT
   COPPERPLATE GOTHIC BOLD
   COPPERPLATE GOTHIC LIGHT
   Courier
   Courier New
   Cork Ht
   DomBold BT
   Edwardian Script ITC
   Egyptian710 BT
   ENGRAVERSGOTHIC BT REGULAR
   Espy Sans Bold Fonts
   Espy Sans Fonts
   Freetrm710 BT
   FuzelScript
   Gadget
   ✓Geneva
                          ▼
```

This feature can, of course, be turned off as an application preference, or if you have a font menu modifier program already installed, such as Adobe Type Reunion Deluxe or Action WYSIWYG.

NOTE   *A font menu modifier program such as the ones named here does more than just show fonts in their actual styles. It also groups fonts by family to keep menus shorter. Action WYSIWYG also shows fonts divided into columns, to shorten the font menus even more.*

- **Color Picker**   This feature lets you select the colors used in your spreadsheets from the ones available on your Mac. No, it doesn't offer special color palettes, such as Pantone, like page layout programs such as QuarkXPress.

- **List AutoFill**   This is another tool to simplify document formatting. This feature carries over the formats and formulas in lists, so that new items inherit them. For a list to be extended, the formatting and formula properties must show up in three of the previous five rows.

- **Euro Currency Symbol**   Excel 2001 supports new number formats to work with the euro currency symbols.

- **List Manager**   This powerful new feature speeds up the process of sorting, analyzing, and searching for data in your worksheet. You can use it to organize your data for easy viewing.

- **AutoFilter**   Using the choices you make, AutoFilter displays rows of information to help you find specific pieces of data.

- **AutoComplete**   The same powerful feature that is so flexible in Word checks the text you're typing against information already entered in the column. You are then prompted to pick the right text to complete the entry from a list of choices. This feature is a real time saver.

- **Display Units**   This feature is an addition to Excel's powerful charting capability. It helps you shorten numbers by specifying a display unit represented by the number. For example, the number 50 can represent 50,000,000. A label will appear in the chart to indicate that the figure represents millions (or whatever unit you select).

- **Multiple-Level Category Labels**   If a data worksheet contains more than a single heading level, Excel labels the axis of the chart according to the same hierarchical categories as in the worksheet.

- **Web Page Preview**   As in Word, this feature lets you preview your document in your selected Web browser, so you can make sure the Web version looks the way you like.

- **Customize Web Pages**   This feature also mirrors the one in Word. From the Edit menu, choose Preferences, select the General tab, and choose Web Options. In the dialog box that appears, you can give your Web page a title, specify the graphics format and display size, and make other choices to maximize the impact of your page.

- **Manage Files and Links**   A Web page generally consists of text plus a set of linked pictures. All Office programs help you manage all files connected to your Web page, so problems don't occur when visitors to your site attempt to view them.

- **International Web Support**   Office can save Web pages with the correct international text parameters, so users around the world will be able to view your pages in the correct text characters.

- **Full Support for Graphics and Objects**   As with other Office programs, the graphics in your Web page are stored in GIF, JPEG, or PNG format. This allows visitors to your site to view your graphics they way you want.

- **Pivot Table Features**   The PivotTable feature lets you embed reports directly in your worksheets. The new PivotTable Report Wizard simplifies the process for formatting the report according to your needs.

- **Data Selection and Formatting**   This feature is improved in Excel 2001. It lets you carry over existing Excel formatting when you refresh or change the layout.

- **Improved Import and Analysis Features**   In Excel 2001, data can be easily imported into your worksheet from other programs. You can avoid extra steps in typing and formatting the information. Text file data can he handled in the same fashion, retaining formats and formulas.

- **Improved Web Queries**   It's now easier to perform a query, or search, of data on the World Wide Web. The new, improved query function includes sample Web queries to simplify the task of locating data.

- **FileMaker Import Wizard**   One of the missing features of Office for the Mac has been a database program, such as Microsoft's Access, which still remains a Windows exclusive. However, this new Import Wizard lets you retrieve data from Apple's powerful database application, FileMaker Pro.

Introducing PowerPoint 2001

Microsoft PowerPoint 2001 (see Figure 1-10) has progressed way beyond simple online slide shows. As you'll see in the next few pages, it offers new features that let you create powerful presentations. Chapters 20 through 22 cover this subject in detail. In the meantime, here's a list of the new and improved features:

- **Project Gallery**   As in all other Office 2001 applications, the Project Gallery simplifies creation of a new document. Just choose the template or wizard you want, and you'll be able to produce a more professional-looking presentation.

- **Formatting Palette**   As in Excel and Word, the Formatting Palette puts the most commonly used PowerPoint commands at your beck and call in your document.

- **Find and Insert Slides**   Use the Slide Finder to check thumbnail views of slides so you can add the ones you want to your presentation.

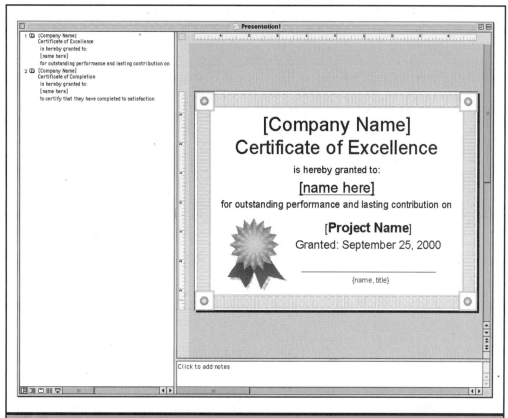

Figure 1-10. *Access new tools to make more professional presentations in PowerPoint.*

- **Easily Access Word Definitions**   The built-in definition dictionary can be used to define and cut and paste a word in your slide.

- **Personalize User Theme**   Apple's Appearance Control Panel is fully supported, so you can change the look of PowerPoint to suit your taste.

- **Euro Currency Symbol**   PowerPoint now provides full support for euro currency values, in case your presentation is designed for viewing in Europe.

- **Multiple Slide Masters**   You can create a series of master slides and titles (not just one), to increase the choices available in your presentation. Masters can also be copied from other presentations, so you can easily give your slides a uniform look and feel.

- **Improved Assistant**   You can now resize and dock the Office Assistant window, so it doesn't occupy too much space on your screen. This is especially useful if your Mac has a smaller display—for instance, if you are using an iMac—and you want to devote as much space as possible to the actual presentation window.

- **AutoFit Text**   Is your text running too long? No problem. PowerPoint's AutoFit feature will resize it to fit.

- **New Normal View**   This new viewing option displays the outline, slide, and notes all at once. Each viewing pane can be sized as you prefer, so you can emphasize the pane that you are giving the most attention. This feature is another boon for users with smaller monitors.

- **Grayscale Output**   Slides can be seen and printed in black and white, not just color. This enhances the results if you're using a regular grayscale laser printer.

- **Native Table Tools**   You no longer have to copy or import tables from other programs. You can use the Draw Table tool to create tables within PowerPoint. Just click the tool and drag to create the tables you want.

- **Graphical Bullets**   As in Word, this feature lets you use a picture, rather than a text character, as a bullet to enhance the look of a slide. PowerPoint offers a selection of bullet clip art, so you don't have to create picture elements from scratch.

- **Numbered Lists**   This is another Word feature that makes its debut in PowerPoint. Just click the List button on the Formatting Palette, and you'll have automatically numbered lists.

- **Flag for Follow-up**   Again you can harness a powerful feature of Entourage 2001. Just flag your presentations for later follow up, and you'll see an onscreen reminder when it's time to return to a project for updating or to send a project to your contacts.

- **Expanded Clip Gallery**   This feature lets you conveniently organize the pictures you use regularly for your presentations. You can place graphics in special categories, add custom keywords, and place the Clip Gallery side by side with your PowerPoint document, so you can easily drag and drop the pictures you need.

- **Graphics and Objects for Web Pages**   When you publish a PowerPoint presentation to a Web site, the pictures are automatically stored in a Web-savvy format: GIF, JPEG, or PNG.

- **Enhanced Graphics Support**   This feature is especially useful if you intend to output a presentation to a film recorder or high-end output device. Exported slide images can be adjusted for size, resolution, and compression for maximum quality for the intended medium.

- **Scanner and Digital Camera Support** As in other Office applications, many scanners and digital cameras with TWAIN drivers can be used to bring a picture into PowerPoint.

- **Animated GIF Support** You can play an animated GIF file in your PowerPoint presentation, which is especially helpful if your presentation is earmarked for the Web.

- **Make PowerPoint Movies** The recipient of your presentation no longer has to have PowerPoint or a viewer program installed. You can save your presentation as a QuickTime movie, providing full control of your presentation via the controls in the player application. This allows your presentations to be seen by anyone using a Macintosh or Windows personal computer with Apple's QuickTime program installed.

> **NOTE** *The latest version of Apple's QuickTime can be downloaded directly from Apple's Web site at http://www.apple.com/quicktime.*

- **Save as Web Page** This feature matches the one in Excel and Word. You can publish your presentation on the Web. The conversion process converts the outline pane to a table of contents of your slides for easier navigation.

- **QuickTime Transitions** Give your presentation a movie-like look and a more fluid flow by adding transitions between slides. The Exit Animations feature also gives you more control over special animation and sound effects.

- **Slide Navigator** Just drag the horizontal scrollbar and view a thumbnail to locate a specific slide in your presentation.

- **Improved Browser Compatibility** Your Web-based presentations can be set up to access the more powerful features of Internet Explorer or Netscape 4.0 or later, yet remain viewable with Internet Explorer and Netscape 3.0.

- **Customizable Web Pages** As in other Office programs, just choose Preferences from the Edit menu, select the General tab, and click the Web Options button. You can use this preference panel to specify Web graphics formats.

- **Automatic File and Link Management** Automatic file and link management facilitates the handling of pictures that are linked to your Web page. Office 2001 applications can also check links and repair broken links to accommodate movement of the main HTML file and graphics to other folders.

- **International Text Encoding** Like all Office applications, PowerPoint is a multilingual program. You can select the text encoding you want so users of foreign language systems can see the presentation with the correct letterforms.

Summary

Although menus and dialog boxes in Excel, PowerPoint, and Word appear reasonably similar to those in Office 98, in fact, vast changes have been made to make Office's powerful features easier to use. This means you can create even complex documents more quickly than ever before.

In the next chapter, we'll explore Office 2001 installation, from the simple drag-and-drop setup to complex, custom installations configured to match your needs.

Chapter 2

Installing Office 2001

In the old days, installing an application on a Macintosh was exceedingly simple. You just placed the application's floppy disk in your Mac's drive and then dragged the program's icon or folder to a convenient spot on your hard drive.

Then you ejected the disk and launched the program. You might, of course, have to personalize the application with your name and perhaps a serial number, but installation couldn't be easier.

As the Mac OS has grown in complexity, so have the programs used on it. Instead of all the files needed to run the program going in a single folder, some now have to go to various locations within the System Folder and elsewhere. As a result, special installer programs have been designed to figure all this out for you; all you have to do is follow a few prompts, and the installation proceeds almost automatically.

Alas, this increased installation complexity has also extended to the process of removing programs. It isn't enough just to drag the application folder to the trash and empty it. There are other files strewn about your Mac's hard drive that need to be exorcised as well. Thus came uninstaller programs to handle the process with various degrees of success.

Do you have just one Mac or a small network, or are you preparing to deploy Office 2001 for the Mac on a large network? Perhaps you have a mixed computing environment, with some computers running the Mac OS, some running Windows, and some perhaps even running a Unix operating system, such as Linux. Where does Office fit into the picture and how should you set up Office 2001 in your specific environment?

In this chapter, we'll cover the whole spectrum of installation options available for Office 2001. One approach isn't necessarily better than the other. It depends on your specific needs, though the simplest approach usually works for most users.

Getting Ready for the Installation

Is your Mac up to the job? Before you attempt to install Office 2001, you'll want to make sure the Mac or Macs on which the suite will be installed meet the system requirements. Older Macs, for example, are going to have trouble. Here are the basic requirements (consider them minimums), in addition to a working CD-ROM drive, of course:

- **Processor**   You need a Mac or Mac OS compatible with a minimum clock speed of 120 MHz. The original-generation PowerMacs (with processor speeds from 60 MHz to 80 MHz) will run Office 2001 with almost adequate performance, but you will find it a bit of a struggle if you want to access the most powerful features of these programs.

■ **Mac OS Version**   Office 2001 requires Mac OS 8.1 or later, but works best with Mac OS 8.5 or later.

NOTE   *As of the time this book went to press, Microsoft was developing a "Carbon-" or Mac OS X–savvy version of Office. If that version isn't available when you read this book, you can safely use the standard Mac OS or "Classic" version under Mac OS X with good performance so long as you have Mac OS 9 installed.*

■ **RAM Needs**   For Mac OS versions prior to 9, you'll need at least 32 MB of RAM, with at least 1 MB of virtual memory. Mac OS 9 and later have more intense memory needs, so the minimum increases to 48 MB of RAM, plus 1 MB of virtual memory. If you want to run more than a single Office program at once, consider adding at least 32 MB to these figures.

NOTE   *Office 2001 applications use much less RAM on your Mac when virtual memory is activated. Unlike the situation with older versions of the Mac OS, activating virtual memory will not have a noticeable impact on system performance unless you have a very small amount of RAM installed (and then it's essential). Virtual memory should be turned off primarily for multimedia-related programs, where there may be compatibility or performance problems.*

■ **Disk Storage Space**   The basic drag-and-drop installation of Office 2001 fills at least 170 MB of space on your hard drive, plus another 5 MB or so for the required system extensions. The Value Pack, mentioned later in this chapter, can consume over 300 MB additional storage space should you opt for all of the components.

CAUTION   *You always should attempt to leave at least 10 percent free space on a drive for printer spooling files and so forth. Otherwise, you run the risk of getting a disk full message.*

■ **Monitor**   Your Mac should have a display capable of 256 gray tones or colors, with a minimum resolution of 640 × 480. Just about any recent Mac display and Mac video circuitry should meet these requirements, so they shouldn't be an issue. The ideal setting is a resolution of 800 × 600, with thousands or millions of colors. That's the standard setting on the iMac, by the way.

■ **Internet Access**   Office 2001 offers Web-based help and tips for the suite, so it's a good idea to have some sort of Internet access available on at least some of the Macs on which Office is installed. A modem with a minimum speed of 14,400 bits per second (bps) is recommended, though it's hard to get decent Net performance if you don't have a 28,000-bps modem or faster.

Drag-and-Drop Installation

For Office 98, the last release of the program suite, Microsoft devised a clever installation technique that gives you the best of both worlds: easy installation for most users, plus custom options if you want to take advantage of extra features (or eliminate some you don't expect to need).

Here's how to install Office 2001 the easy way:

1. Place the Microsoft Office 2001 CD in the Mac's drive. When the CD folder appears on the Mac's drive, you'll see brief text descriptions of the installation folders (see Figure 2-1).

NOTE *Word 2001, Excel 2001, and PowerPoint 2001 are available as separate packages, but the basic installation instructions for the individual programs are essentially the same as described for Office in the following pages.*

2. Click and drag the Microsoft Office 2001 folder to your Mac's hard drive. The most convenient location is the Applications folder, but you can place it anywhere you want.

Figure 2-1. *Before installing Office 2001, check out the text-based directions (they may differ from the ones you see here, as the program gets updated).*

The process of copying of the files will take several minutes, as shown next. How long depends on the speed of your Mac's CD drive. Remember, there are 170 MB of files to be transferred. The Mac Finder will display a rough estimate of the time it takes to install the software, but the estimate may vary considerably as more and more files are copied, so don't take it as gospel.

Click this arrow
to see the names
of the items
being installed →

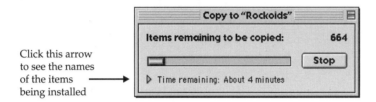

<table>
<tr><td colspan="2">Copy to "Rockoids"</td></tr>
</table>

Items remaining to be copied: 664

[   ]   [Stop]

▷ Time remaining: About 4 minutes

The most convenient location for a software installation is the Applications folder. If you use this folder, you can keep all your programs in one convenient place.

3. When the installation is done, eject the CD.

If you purchased a multi-user license for Office 2001 for your office, you can also perform the installation direct from a network server. Copy the folder to a volume on the network and then have the individual users on the network copy the folder to their own drives. You should have the relevant paperwork from Microsoft to personalize each copy.

4. Locate the Microsoft Office 2001 folder that you've copied to your Mac.

5. Open the folder and double-click the Office 2001 program you want to use first.

6. The first time the program runs, you'll be asked to type your user name and company name (you don't have to enter the latter, if you're just an individual home user), as shown next. Enter the information; then click OK.

Microsoft Office First Run

Type your full name in the box below. You may also specify your
organization. The name(s) you type will be used by the Setup program for
subsequent installations of the product.

Name: Gene Steinberg

Organization: Making The Impossible LLC

[Cancel]   [OK]

7. Enter the 10-digit CD key or serial number at the prompt, as shown next. It should be on the back of the Office 2001 CD case or in one of the documents provided with the software. This number is absolutely required for the programs to run.

That's it. Once the CD key is entered, Office 2001 will go through a self-configuration process taking several minutes. Before the program's startup screen appears, the First Run Installer will launch and place some extensions in the System Folder and a handful of basic fonts in the Fonts folder:

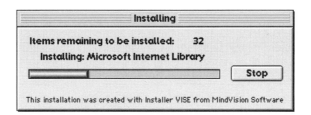

The fonts are used primarily for display of Web sites; they match Microsoft's standard array of Windows fonts and help provide a uniform cross-platform look to a site. The Preferences folder, within the System Folder, gets a new folder called Microsoft, where program settings will be stored.

Depending on the needs of a specific Mac installation, a Restart button may appear. If it doesn't show, don't be concerned. Your Mac won't have to restart to use the new software.

Here's a list of the files placed in the Extensions folder:

- Microsoft Clipboard Library
- Microsoft Component Library

- Microsoft Internet Library
- Microsoft OLE Automation
- Microsoft OLE Library
- Microsoft Structured Storage
- Type Libraries folder

NOTE *If you have also installed Microsoft's Internet Explorer Web browser or some versions of AOL's access software, you may find one or more additional files with a Microsoft or MS prefix in the name. There is no reason to be concerned, and you needn't remove these items. If you have concerns, remove the extra files while the programs aren't running; if they are needed, they will be reinstalled the next time you run those programs.*

After the startup screen of an Office program appears (see Figure 2-2), you're ready to enjoy the power of Office 2001. If you do not intend to customize your installation, you can move right to Chapter 3 (I'm giving you time off for good behavior).

Microsoft's Clever First Run Installer

The typical Mac's System Folder is so complex that it is difficult to figure out just what any particular file does, and whether you can safely remove it.

The clever programmers in Microsoft's Mac business unit came up with a solution: the First Run Installer. If you happen to delete any one of the required extensions by mistake, as soon as you launch one of the Office programs, First Run will be activated automatically, and it will replace the missing files.

Figure 2-2. *Success! One of your Office 2001 programs is now starting.*

Performing a Custom Installation

The easiest procedure is just to follow the drag-and-drop installation process for Office 2001 on your Mac. That way, you can be assured that every element that you need has been properly installed in the right place. However, if you decide you don't need all the Office applications, you can perform a custom installation of the individual components.

Here's how to perform a custom installation:

1. Close all active programs.

2. Turn off virus protection software. If you're using Norton Anti-Virus, it will display a prompt when an installer is launched; just click OK to deactivate Norton Anti-Virus for the Office installation. Otherwise, you'll need to restart your Mac.

CAUTION   *Virus detection software can, by dint of its scanning process, prevent a successful installation of software. If you are concerned about possible virus infections from an installer disk, feel free to scan it first with your virus application before the application is deactivated.*

3. Place the Microsoft Office 2001 CD in the drive.

4. Scroll down the list of contents until you locate the Microsoft Office Installer.

5. Double-click the installer application, which will bring up the dialog box shown in Figure 2-3.

6. Click the Easy Installation pop-up menu and select Custom Install, which brings up the installation window shown in Figure 2-4.

NOTE   *There is no point in running the installer if you intend to perform a standard installation. The drag-and-drop method will get the job done.*

7. Click the installation option you want. You can install each Office application separately. In addition, there are two more installation choices: the Office Tools option includes shared applications, including the spelling checker, fonts, and the Microsoft Graph application; the Converters and Filters package includes components you can use to translate and convert documents in various formats.

NOTE   *Clicking the arrow to the left of any of the options on the installer screen displays a list of individual components, which you can selectively install. But it's best to install the entire collection, because something you need may be omitted if you customize further.*

8. Click the Install button and follow the prompts.

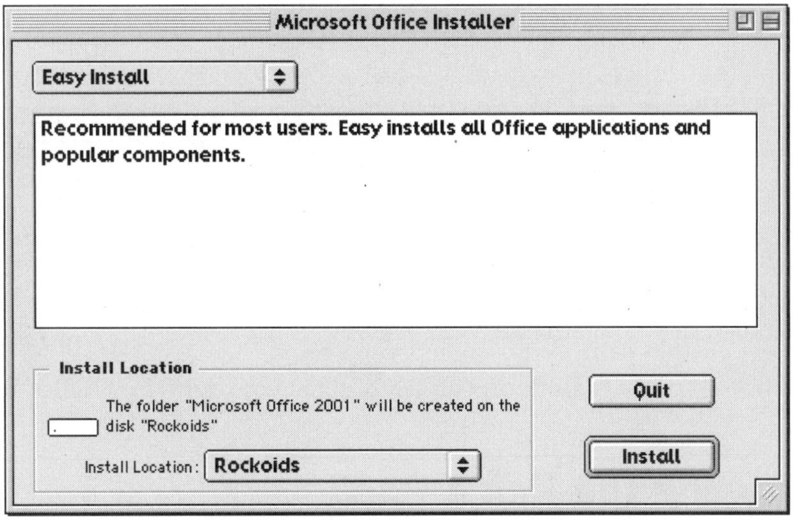

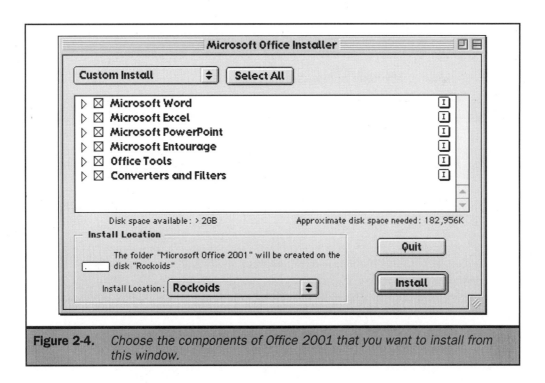

Figure 2-3. *You can use this installer to perform a custom installation of Office.*

Figure 2-4. *Choose the components of Office 2001 that you want to install from this window.*

9. If a restart is necessary, you'll see a Restart button. Otherwise, there will be a Quit button. Click the button that appears.

10. After the installation is complete, open an Office program to complete the installation process.

11. Be sure to enter your user name and company name where requested.

12. Type the CD code from your installation CD at the prompt.

13. After the program suite is personalized, the First Run Installer will run to complete the installation process. At this point, you may see another Restart button that you will need to click to finish. Otherwise, there will be a Quit button. Click the button that appears.

When the setup process is done, you can begin to use your Office 2001 software.

Introducing the Value Pack

Although the drag-and-drop installation of Office 2001 will probably suffice, Microsoft includes a number of additional components on the installation CD, under the title of Value Pack. You can install these items directly, but rather than figure out where they go—other than the fonts, of course, which go in the Fonts folder within the System Folder—just use the installer.

Before you try these optional items, consult the following list of Value Pack components to learn what each component does:

■ **Assistants**   If you've tired of the little animated Mac,

never fear. There are additional cartoonish figures to install.

TIP   *If you cannot stand looking at the animated assistant, just click the close box, and you'll banish the little tyke. It'll wave bye-bye and then vanish. You can restore him via the Turn Assistant On command on the Help menu. You can also CONTROL-click the assistant to produce a menu that lets you modify the assistant and choose various assistant-related options.*

■ **Clip Art**   The standard Office 2001 installation includes a decent collection of artwork, but there's a lot more in the Value Pack. Choose from a collection of clip art, movies, pictures, animated GIFs, and other files.

■ **Equation Editor**   This used to be standard issue with older versions of Office, but now it's an option. Use it to create and place equations and mathematical symbols in your various documents created with Office. The version supplied by Microsoft is a limited-feature version. The full edition of Design Science's Equation Editor can be purchased from the company's Web site: http://www.mathtype.com/msee.

■ **Excel Add-in: Analysis Toolpak**   This Value Pack component provides financial and scientific data analysis capabilities for your Excel worksheets. It's a real time saver.

■ **Excel Add-in: Lookup Wizard**   The Calculator is only one terrific tool to help you create formulas for Excel. The Lookup Wizard can create formulas you can use to find the right data in a list.

■ **Excel Add-in: Set Language**   This feature lets you switch languages for Excel's spelling checker.

■ **Excel Type Libraries**   This add-in is used to convert Excel 5.0 macros written in foreign languages to macros that are Excel 97, Excel 98, Excel 2000, and Excel 2001 savvy. The versions provided are Danish, Dutch, French, German, Italian, Japanese, Norwegian, Portuguese, Spanish, and Swedish.

■ **Fonts**   The Fonts component gives you a cheap way to build a good font library on your Mac. Choose from 53 TrueType fonts, in categories from the simple to the decorative.

TIP   *If you want to sample a font before it's installed, just open the Value Pack folder on your Microsoft Office 2001 CD and then the Fonts folder. When you locate a font suitcase that interests you, double-click it; then click any font inside the suitcase to see what it looks like.*

■ **Genigraphics Wizard**   This service can provide extra capabilities for your PowerPoint presentations. You can get overnight service from this company to convert your files to 35 mm slides and such printed materials as posters.

■ **Handheld Synchronization**   Do you have a Palm or Handspring handheld computer? This component works with Microsoft's Entourage to exchange and synchronize your repertoire of contacts, calendar events, notes, and tasks between your Mac and the handheld device.

■ **Microsoft Query**   This program works with Excel 2001 to access the data from corporate databases and similar files. The program can be used to automatically update Excel whenever the databases are updated—clever!

- **Microsoft Works 4.0 Converter** Before Apple Computer's AppleWorks took over the market in low-cost integrated software, Microsoft Works was one of the more popular suites of its type. It's no longer being updated for the Mac, but if you have documents created in Works 4.0, you'll appreciate this utility. This converter will do a decent job of letting you open your documents in Word 2001.

- **Proofing Tools** If you want to take advantage of the multilingual proofing features of Office, you'll want to install these additional dictionary, hyphenation, and thesaurus files. They come in these languages: Danish, Dutch, French, German, Italian, Japanese, Norwegian, Spanish, and Swedish.

- **Programmability** If you want to get involved heavily in creating macros for your Office 2001 applications, consider installing the Programmability components. They include Visual Basic for Applications, VBA Help, and the Solver add-in for Excel. Office Macros, by the way, can really speed up complex processes. For example, the various text styles used in this book are established by a very neat macro that also displays a handy toolbar that puts each style a click away.

CAUTION *Good things sometimes have downsides. Cross-platform Office macros are ubiquitous and so are viruses that infect them. Fortunately, there are several popular Mac virus programs that will kill these devils; make sure a virus protection program is installed before you run any macros.*

- **Templates** When you open an Office 2001 application, the handy Project Gallery (see Figure 2-5) dutifully lists a number of templates and wizards in various categories. If the offerings don't suit your needs, the additional offerings in the Value Pack are definitely worth consideration.

- **Text Encoding Converter** If you plan on using Office 2001's multilingual features, you need this system extension, which should already be installed with the Mac OS. Since it's required for Apple's current disk file system, HFS+ (also known as Mac OS Extended), it's probably already present in the Extensions folder within the System Folder, and you needn't install it again.

- **Unbinder** The Microsoft Office Binder for Windows combines files from Excel, Word, and PowerPoint. This feature isn't supported on the Mac; if you receive such files, you can use the Unbind utility to separate the files, so you can continue to work on them.

- **Word 97–2001 Converter** If you or one of your contacts is using Word 5.1 or Word 6.0 on a Mac, perhaps because the system is not powerful enough to run Office 2001, use this converter so the person (or you) will be able to read Word 2001 documents.

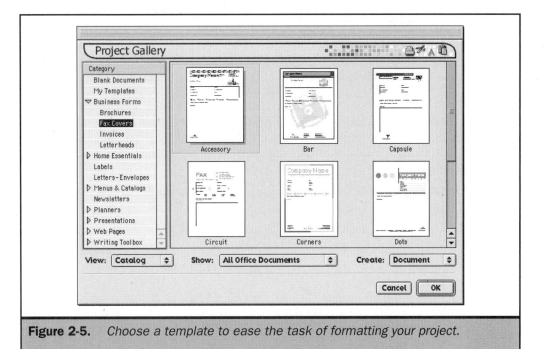

Figure 2-5.   *Choose a template to ease the task of formatting your project.*

CAUTION   *The conversion process isn't perfect. Some features of Word 2001 simply aren't supported on older versions of the program; thus, the formatting will be simplified or altered to conform to the features of the version used to open the document. However, basic text and text formatting should carry over without serious problems.*

- **WordPerfect 5 Converters**   Although WordPerfect, currently published by Corel, is no longer being produced for the Mac, there's a huge installed base of WordPerfect users. These converters allow you to read documents created in WordPerfect 5.0 and 5.1 with reasonable fidelity. You can also save documents in these formats using the Save As command on Word 2001's File menu.

CAUTION   *WordPerfect 5 and 5.1 are fairly old versions of the program (the one shipping as this book went to press is part of WordPerfect Office 8). That means that some advanced formatting features won't carry over, but the basic text ought to be fine.*

Installing the Value Pack

After you've decided which parts of the Value Pack you want to install, the best way to accomplish the task is to let the installer do it for you. You could, if you want, install the pieces separately, but aside from fonts, it would require checking out the proper locations.

Here's what to do next:

1. Quit all open applications.
2. Turn off virus protection software.

If you're using Norton Anti-Virus, you'll see a prompt when the Value Pack installer launches; click OK to turn off Norton Anti-Virus until the Value Pack installation is done. Otherwise, you'll have to restart your Mac after disabling virus protection.

3. Place the Microsoft Office 2001 CD in the Mac's drive.
4. When the window displaying the contents appears, scroll to the bottom of the listings (see Figure 2-6) and double-click the Value Pack folder.
5. With the folder opened, double-click the Value Pack Installer (see Figure 2-7).
6. The installer window will display the Value Pack modules that are available. Just check the ones you want, or click Select All to add the full collection.

The entire Value Pack package fills over 300 MB of hard disk storage space. If free space is at a premium, or if you just don't want to waste what you have, be cautious about which components to select. Finder windows normally display the amount of disk space available.

7. Click Continue to begin the installation.

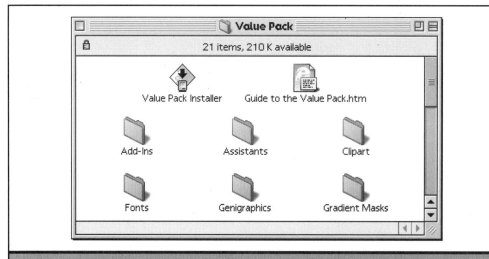

Figure 2-6.   *The short text descriptions show you the basic installation options.*

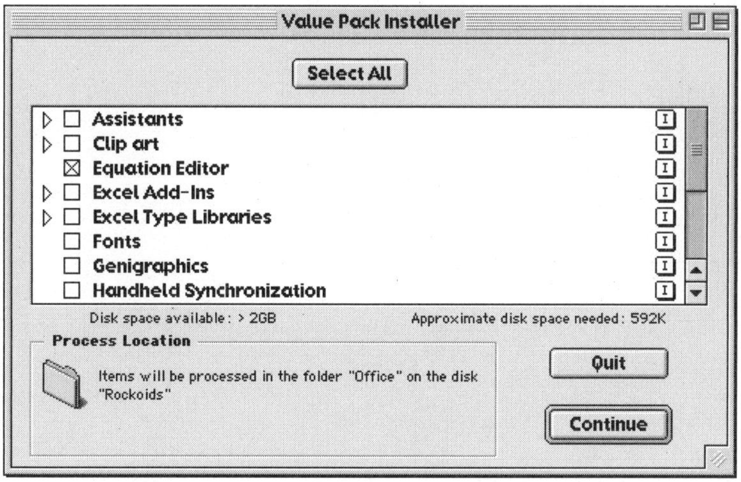

Figure 2-7. *What do you want to install?*

8. During the next few moments, the installer will locate the Office 2001 folder on your hard drive and then install the proper components.

NOTE
If you have more than one copy of Office installed (perhaps you're using an extra for backup), the installer will display several prompts asking which ones you want to use for the installation.

9. When the installation is done, click the Quit button, and then launch your Office 2001 application to begin using the new features.

NOTE
Some installations require a restart before you can continue. Do not be alarmed if the installation application displays a Restart prompt.

Removing Office 2001

If you decide to remove Office 2001 for any reason, you don't have to fret over a complicated removal process. Although there's no uninstall program to sort things out, you can easily remove the essential components of Office without causing any severe difficulties.

Here's what to do:

1. Make sure you've quit all open Office 2001 applications.

2. Locate the Microsoft Office 2001 folder on your Mac's hard drive.

3. Drag that folder to the trash.

4. Empty the trash.

5. Open the System Folder and locate the Preferences folder.

6. Open the Preferences folder and locate the folder labeled Microsoft.

7. Drag the Microsoft folder to the trash.

8. Empty the trash.

9. If you are not using any of Microsoft's Internet applications, any prior version of Office, or AOL version 3.0 or 4.0, go to the Extensions folder within the System Folder.

> **CAUTION** *Current Microsoft Internet applications will invoke the First Run application if you remove the wrong Microsoft extension by mistake, but older versions will not, nor will AOL 3.0 and 4.0, which also use some of these extensions. Thus, it's probably best to leave these files alone if you plan to use any of these programs.*

10. Locate all the items bearing the titles Microsoft or MS in the Extensions folder and drag them to the trash.

11. Empty the trash.

12. If you removed any Microsoft system extensions, be sure to restart your Mac. Now all vestiges of Office 2001 will be gone.

> **TIP** *Microsoft also has an Office removal application that can do the job for you, almost automatically. You can download a copy of this application plus some other handy tidbits from the MacTopia Web site: http://www.microsoft.com/mac/download/default.asp?area=O2001.*

Summary

Installation strategies for Office 2001 for the Macintosh can be as simple as a drag-and-drop procedure or highly complex, depending on your specific needs. This chapter described the options you'll want to consider to get the most out of these terrific applications on your Mac. For myself, I've found that the easiest method works best, but your mileage may differ.

In the next chapter, we'll begin to cover the powerful new features of Office 2001, beginning with the Project Gallery.

Chapter 3

Introducing the
Project Gallery

ometimes it's hard to know just where to begin. You want to create a document
with Office 2001, but you're not certain what program to use. Even if you launch
the correct application, you are in the throes of still another dilemma—just how
do you set up the document to meet your needs?

One of Microsoft's key goals in developing Office 2001 for the Macintosh was to
simplify difficult tasks. In the past, the powerful features of Office applications were
hidden beneath a maze of difficult-to-fathom menu bar commands and multiple-level
dialog boxes.

Microsoft came up with a clever, if not original, solution: the Project Gallery.

Keeping It Simple

Whenever you launch any Office 2001 application—except for Entourage, the e-mail
and contact manager—you'll be greeted by the Project Gallery (see Figure 3-1). This
handy floating palette gives you a convenient way for you to select the type of Office
document you want to create and then get on with the business of making it look as
good as possible.

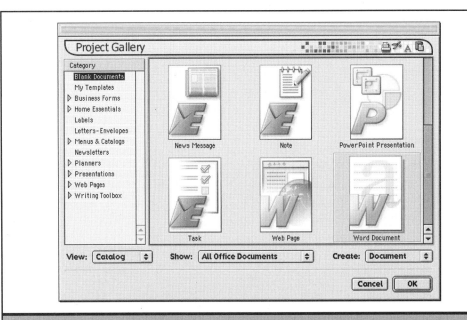

Figure 3-1.   *Use the Project Gallery to get a head start on your document. The icons
at the top right are nonfunctional, by the way.*

NOTE   *Having nonfunctional icons can be confusing, but it's just part of an attempt to provide attractive scenery in Office.*

The Project Gallery is a visual guide that can get you up and running in seconds. It's populated with a healthy collection of special designs, templates, and design wizards in a number of categories. From the Project Gallery, you can select the type of document you want, and the correct Office application will be launched automatically for you. You don't have to concern yourself, for example, with opening PowerPoint to create a slide show if you happen to be working in Word at the time.

Here is a list of the types of documents you can start from the Project Gallery:

- **A Blank Document**   The effect is pretty much the same as when you select New Blank Document from the File menu. A blank document will be opened, ready to be populated with the information you want to enter. The application you're using—Word, Excel, or PowerPoint—determines the screen that you see. In Word, it's a blank document. In Excel, it's a blank worksheet. In PowerPoint, you'll see a blank slide.

- **Document Wizards**   A wizard in Microsoft Office isn't the same as that fellow with the booming voice in a famous 1930s movie. A wizard, sometimes called an assistant, takes you through the steps of creating a brochure, envelope, letter, newsletter, mailing label, or any of a wide variety of documents. As you proceed through the creation process, you just enter the information requested, and the fully formatted document is ready for you to start building your project.

- **Templates**   Once you've spent time creating a unique design, you won't want to have to reinvent the wheel each time you want a document with a similar look. You can choose from a wide array of template designs supplied with Office 2001, or you can take a document that has the right look and save it as a template, so the format can be reused. What's more, those designs aren't set in stone. You can easily customize a design to fit your requirements and then save it as a template , so you can use it again and again. I always use a Word template for my stationery. The template contains a picture, plus several different typefaces to give the design a different look, if not terribly fancy.

NOTE   *A template (called stationery in some programs) is a preformatted document that contains all the elements you need to build a new document, such as letterhead, text styles, pictures, and so forth. A wizard provides step-by-step assistance to help you begin a project.*

In this chapter and the next, you'll step through the basics of working with the Project Gallery. Then you'll learn how to customize the Project Editor so it displays the items you want.

Before we begin, let's take a look at the elements of the Project Gallery (look at Figure 3-1 again).

If the Project Gallery isn't open, choose Project Gallery from the File menu of your Office software to bring it up, or type the shortcut COMMAND-SHIFT-P. If you can't find the Project Gallery, you'll need to reinstall your Office 2001 for the Macintosh software, as described in Chapter 2.

■ **Category**   At the left of the Project Gallery window is a category list. This list divides templates and wizards into distinct, easy-to-recognize topics. Just click a category, and the arrow to the left of its name will expand to reveal the contents.

As you'll see in Chapter 4, you can easily customize categories to display the lists in an easier-to-digest fashion.

■ **Document Preview**   The main part of the Project Gallery displays a miniature preview of the blank document, template, or wizard, so you get a birds-eye view of the contents. Normally, the Project Gallery appears in what's called Catalog view. Another way of viewing the Project Gallery is in List view (see Figure 3-2). This divides the screen into three panes, with the middle showing the name and type of template or wizard. Click any of these items to see an enlarged view of the item in the right pane.

Templates and wizards in Office 2001 for the Macintosh use a special file format. If the format of the document isn't right, the file won't appear in the Project Gallery, even if it's in the correct location. That means you might add a file to serve as a template, but it won't show. You'll learn more about templates as we proceed through this chapter.

Using the Project Gallery to Select a Template

Once you begin to work with the Project Gallery, you may begin to wonder how you got along without it. Let's create a sample document from the generous supply of Office 2001 templates and see the Project Gallery in action.

1. Double-click any Office 2001 application to launch it. If you're already running an Office application, choose New Project Gallery from the File menu or press COMMAND-SHIFT-P (again see Figure 3-1).

2. To start a plain document, click Blank Documents in the Category pane and then choose the graphic representing the kind of document you want. If the Office application you want isn't open, it will be launched automatically, and

Figure 3-2.   *You get a larger preview image when you use the Project Gallery's List view.*

a blank document, worksheet, or slide (depending on which program you're using) will appear on your Mac's screen (see Figure 3-3).

3. To use an existing template or wizard instead, simply click the category in the Project Gallery window. The list will expand to display the items in that category.

NOTE   *You can't resize the Project Gallery window, but you can use the scrollbar or the PAGE UP and PAGE DOWN keys on your Mac's keyboard to see additional entries in a particular category.*

4. Select a subcategory. Figure 3-4 shows Brochures selected in the Business Forms category, which displays a set of predefined templates in various styles.

5. To bring up a template on your Mac, so you can use it, click the preview. Then click OK to open a new document with that style. Figure 3-5 shows the results of selecting the Accessory template.

NOTE   *If you want to create a new template rather than a document, click the pop-up menu under Create at the lower right of the Project Gallery and choose Template.*

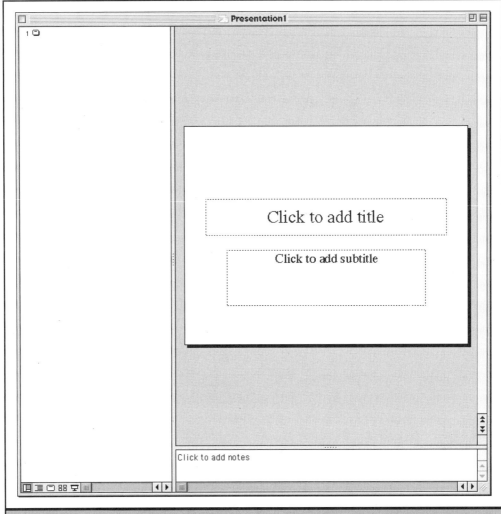

Figure 3-3. *Here's an empty PowerPoint slide, ready for you to begin creating your own presentation.*

6. Once the blank document is on the screen, alter the design to your taste and then fill in the information. In some cases, as you'll see in the pages that follow, a wizard will appear, to help guide you further through the document setup. You can proceed manually or let the wizard assist you.

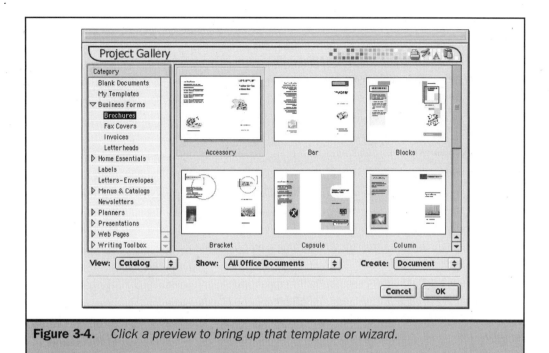

Figure 3-4. *Click a preview to bring up that template or wizard.*

7. If you want to store the result as a new template, choose Save As from the File
menu. In the dialog box that appears, choose Document Template from the
Format pop-up menu, as shown next. Otherwise, your document will be saved
as a regular document using the Office 2001 program in which you're working.

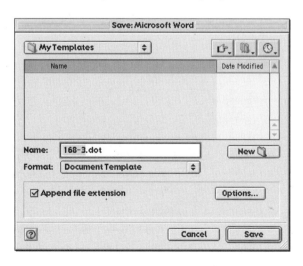

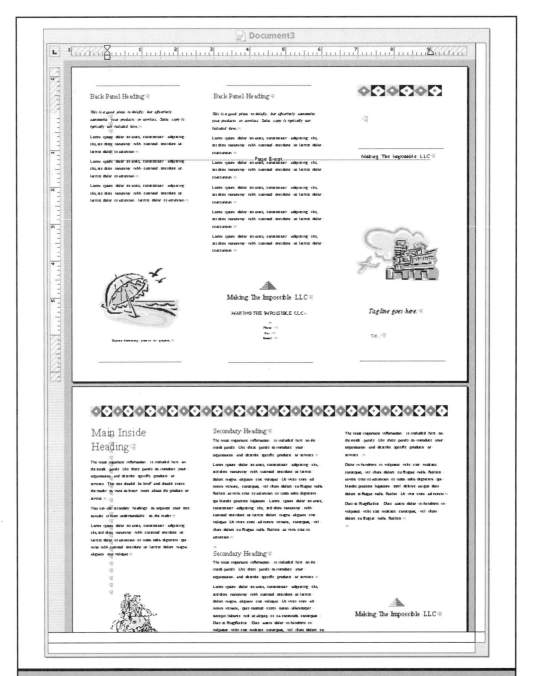

Figure 3-5. *The Accessory template on the Mac screen ready for use*

> NOTE *When you choose to save a document as a template, a different file extension will be appended to the file name, and the Save As dialog box will specify the correct location in your Office 2001 application folder—smart, very smart.*

From here, you can continue to work on your new document. Check the later chapters in this book for hints on creating and customizing documents in the various Office 2001 applications.

Using the Project Gallery to Select a Wizard

A wizard is a step beyond a template. Rather than just producing a formatted sample document on your Mac's display, wizards give you step-by-step instructions on just how to set up your new document; then you're ready to begin.

In the following example, you'll see how to use the Label Wizard to create and format an address label. Using Word 2001's Data Merge feature, as described in Chapter 15, you can create custom preaddressed form letters to an entire mailing list and then print the labels you need to send the letters.

1. Double-click any Office 2001 application to launch it. If you're already running an Office application, choose New Project Gallery from the File menu or press COMMAND-SHIFT-P (again see Figure 3-1).

2. Choose Labels from the Project Gallery window (see Figure 3-6). The Mailing Label Wizard appears, ready for you to select it and then clicking OK to set it in motion.

3. Click OK to bring up the Labels Wizard (see Figure 3-7). If Word isn't already open, it will be launched. When the Labels Wizard appears, a blank Word document will open.

4. The Label Wizard gives you several options for customizing an address label to your taste. Click the Font button to bring up a standard Word font menu, from which you can choose font styling options (see Figure 3-8).

> NOTE *For a simple label, pick a clear font, such as Helvetica or Times, in 10- or 12-point size. The other Font menu options will be described in Chapter 12.*

5. Select the font you want. Then click OK.

6. Click the Options button to bring up the Label Options dialog box (see Figure 3-9).

7. Choose the type of Avery label you want by clicking the label's number; the size of label and page will appear in the Label Information box.

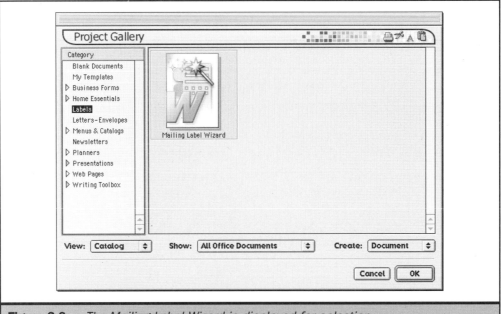

Figure 3-6. *The Mailing Label Wizard is displayed for selection.*

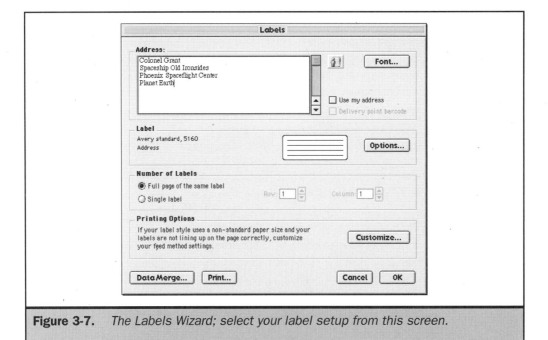

Figure 3-7. *The Labels Wizard; select your label setup from this screen.*

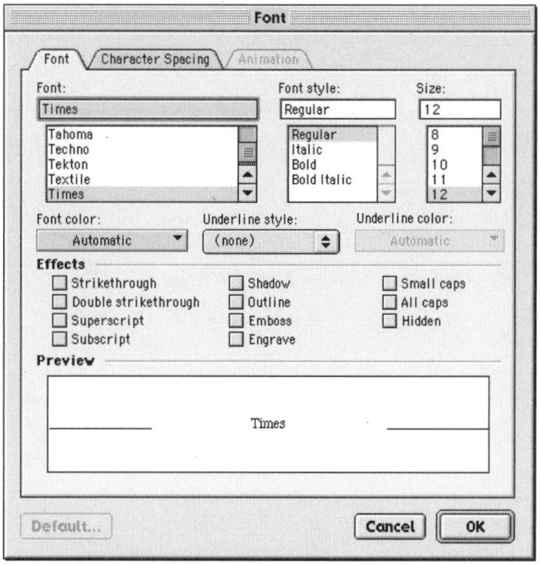

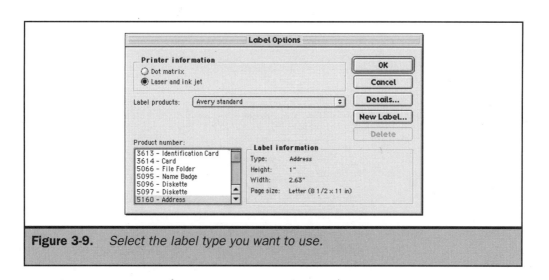

Figure 3-8.   *Choose the font style here. You can use any of Word's flexible font formatting options, but a simple typeface is best for a label.*

Figure 3-9.   *Select the label type you want to use.*

NOTE   *If you're not using a standard laser or ink jet printer, select the Dot Matrix option in the Printer Information box.*

8. When you are done, click OK to return to the main Labels screen.

NOTE   *Microsoft supports a large number of common Avery label designs, as well as designs from other makers, but you're not forced to stick with the predefined labels; you can create a custom label size by clicking the New Label button in the Label Options window.*

9. Do you want the same label repeated, or do you want just a single label? Make your decision by selecting the appropriate option in the Number of Labels box. Click OK.

NOTE   *Avery labels are essentially standard in the industry. Most business supply stores have decent supplies of the common sizes. If you're not sure from the descriptions provided in the Labels Wizard which size suits your needs, take a look at the actual labels themselves to select the ones you want.*

10. This step is optional. If you find that the predefined labels aren't up to the job, you can create your own style. Click the New Label button in the Label Options dialog box (return to Figure 3-9) to bring up the New Custom Laser dialog box (see Figure 3-10). Now construct your own label.

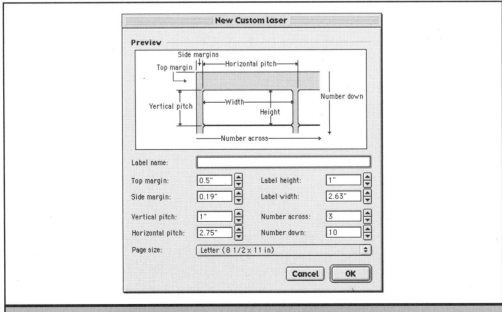

Figure 3-10.   *You don't have to just use Avery labels for your mailings.*

11. Once your custom label has been created, name the label for easier identification later on. Click OK to return to the Label Options screen and click OK again to go back to the main Labels Wizard window.

12. All finished? Just click the OK button on the Labels Wizard screen to see the results of your creativity in that formerly blank document window:

The Labels Wizard's work is done. From here, you can continue to work on your new document or invoke more templates and wizards to create additional documents. Check the later chapters in this book for information on creating and customizing documents in the various Office 2001 applications.

Summary

You no longer have to use guesswork to figure out which Office program to run or to start a document. Whether your project is simple or complex, the handy Project Gallery is your starting point for creating work with a professional level of fit and polish.

In the next chapter, you'll learn how to customize the Project Gallery so it suits your needs. You'll also learn how easy it is to add more templates and wizards.

Chapter 4

Customizing the Project Gallery

In Chapter 3, you learned about one of the most useful features of Office 2001 for the Macintosh: the Project Gallery, which helps you get your document formatted and ready to use without having to spend a lot of time creating a brand-new style.

You discovered one of the key results of Microsoft's extensive surveys of Mac users: that more and more users of Office work in small offices or at home, and the Mac's ease of use and attractive, unique user interface and features are among the reasons they use Macs. The purpose of the Project Gallery, first and foremost, is to simplify difficult tasks.

Once you've become accustomed to using the Project Gallery, no doubt you'll want to stretch its capabilities. That's the purpose of this chapter: to show you how to customize the Project Gallery to exploit its power.

Adding and Removing Project Gallery Templates

When you first open the Project Gallery (see Figure 4-1), you'll be greeted by a simple, default layout and the selection of templates and wizards installed when you set up

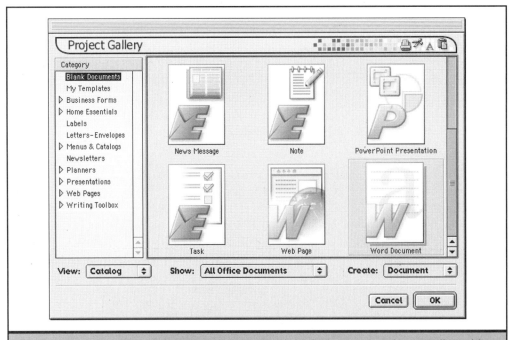

Figure 4-1.   *The Project Gallery's standard look isn't the one you have to live with.*

Office 2001. But you can add or remove items as you wish, so the bill of fare isn't cluttered with items that you will never need.

Here's how to change the Category list:

1. Quit your Office applications (using the Quit command on the File menu), if any are open.

2. Locate the Category list—the list of subjects in which templates are placed. To do that, you have to return to your Mac's desktop, then find and open the Microsoft Office 2001 folder. Inside that folder, find the Templates folder and open that as well.

3. The Templates folder, shown here, contains all the templates and wizards shown in the Project Gallery's Category list. To change the listing, click a specific category to open it; then delete the templates you don't want.

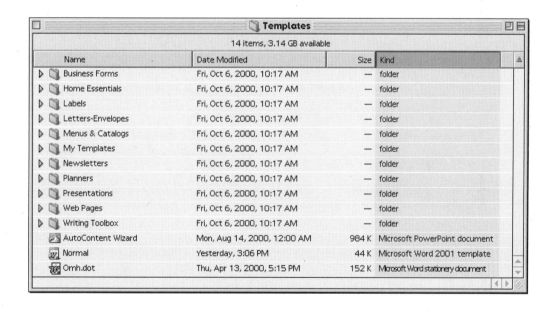

4. You can also create new folders for your templates, using the standard Mac OS New Folder command on the Finder's File menu. Give the folder a name that describes the material you want to place inside:

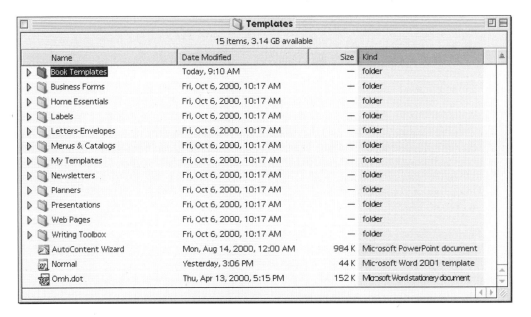

 A new folder will not show up in Office's Project Gallery unless it actually contains templates or wizards in the standard format that the various applications recognize.

5. After you've finished customizing the templates and folders, close the Project Gallery. The next time you start an Office application and open the Project Gallery, you'll see your changes to the folders and templates precisely as you made them (see Figure 4-2).

Customizing the Category List

In addition to making big-time changes in the contents of the Project Gallery, you can go a step further—it's easy to add or remove categories or modify them to suit your needs.

Here's how it's done:

1. Quit all your office applications, using the Quit command on the File menu.

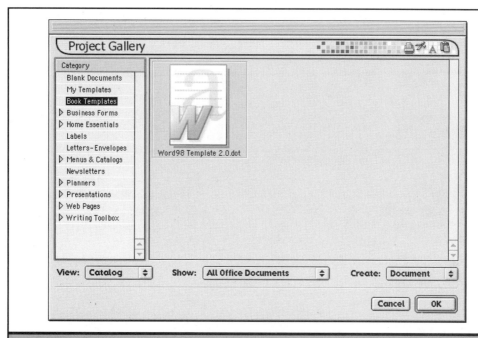

Figure 4-2.   *See how simple it is to alter the Project Gallery's contents?*

2. Locate the Category list—the topic folders where templates are stored. Open the Microsoft Office 2001 folder. Within that folder, find the Templates folder and open that folder as well.

3. To add a category to the Category list, go to the Finder's File menu and choose New Folder.

4. Click the Untitled Folder label and rename the folder to describe the contents you will be storing in it. If, for example, it'll be used for your book manuscripts, that's the name you'd give it. Select and move the templates and wizards that fit the category you've just created into the new folder.

5. Continue the process for each new category you want to add.

6. When you're done, launch an Office application, and the Project Gallery will show the newly added category (see Figure 4-3).

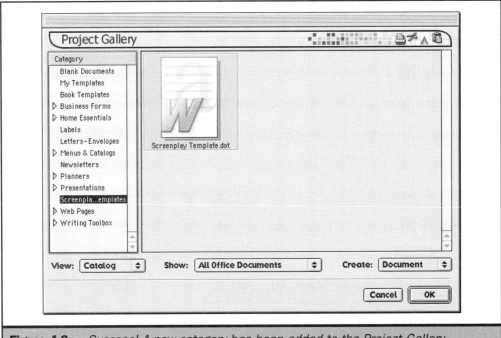

Figure 4-3.   *Success! A new category has been added to the Project Gallery.*

> **CAUTION**   *This note is worth repeating. Don't expect to see your new folder in the Category list unless it contains Office templates or wizards.*

Hiding the Project Gallery

Most users will probably appreciate the presence of the Project Gallery when launching an Office program. But if you don't need it, you don't have to see it. It's not hard to make it disappear. Just follow these steps:

1. Launch any Office application.
2. Go to the Edit menu and choose Preferences.

3. Select the General tab:

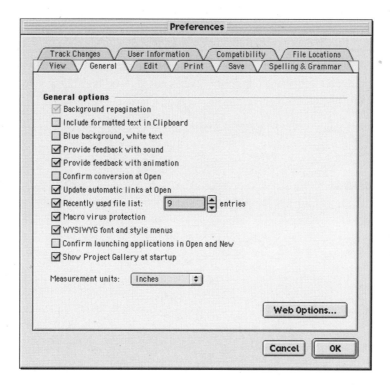

4. Select the Show Project Gallery at Startup check box to uncheck it. The next time you launch an Office application, the Project Gallery will be hidden.

5. To restore the Project Gallery, follow the preceding steps again, this time selecting Show Project Gallery at Startup to turn this option back on.

Using the Project Gallery to Create a Catalog

For many people, one of the great features of a word processor is that you can use it to create a simple brochure, a newsletter, or even a catalog. But creating a catalog can be an awfully complex process, with lots of choices to make depending on the kind of product or service the catalog offers.

Fortunately, the Project Gallery can greatly ease the process of setting up your catalog.

Here's what to do:

1. Launch an Office application to bring up the Project Gallery. If the Project Gallery isn't displayed, choose Project Gallery from the File menu.

The neat thing about Office 2001 is that the right application will be launched when you select a template or wizard, even if a different application is open when you make the selection.

2. Go to the Category list and select Menus & Catalogs. Then click Catalogs (see Figure 4-4).

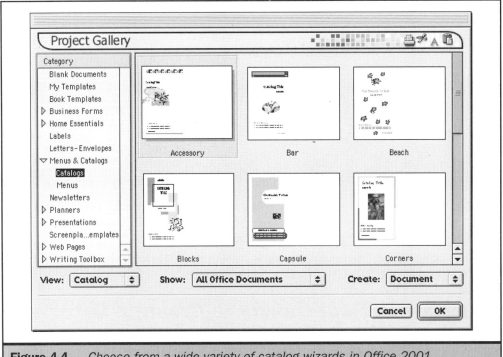

Figure 4-4. *Choose from a wide variety of catalog wizards in Office 2001.*

3. Choose the kind of catalog you want to create by double-clicking the preview icon or selecting the type and then clicking OK. The wizard for that catalog type will appear, as shown here.

4. Fill in the blanks with the requested information to start preparing your catalog. Generally, you'll need to put in the name of your company and contact information and select some check boxes to specify the type of catalog you want.

5. Click the Save and Exit button to finish the wizard. You'll have a brand-new document with the catalog style you wanted, as you can see in the next illustration. From here, you can insert the product information for your company.

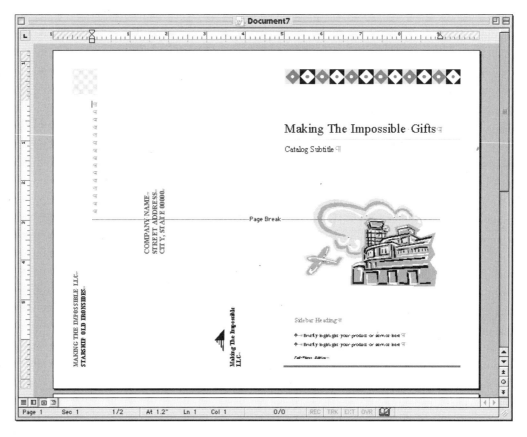

Catalog Wizard missing? Maybe you moved the wizards by mistake? If you cannot locate them, return to your Office 2001 CD and either manually copy the wizards to the appropriate folder, or consider reinstalling Office (but this step will remove the new folders you created in the original Office 2001 folder).

Using the Project Gallery to Create a Brochure

There are few limits to the kinds of documents you can create in an Office application, with professional-grade results. For example, you will learn here how to make a brochure for your business, club, or religious organization.

Here's how to use the Project Gallery for this task:

1. Open an Office application to display the Project Gallery. If the Project Gallery isn't displayed, choose Project Gallery from the File menu.

2. In the Category list on the left side of the Project Gallery, select Business Forms. Then select Brochures, which will produce the set of previews shown in Figure 4-5.

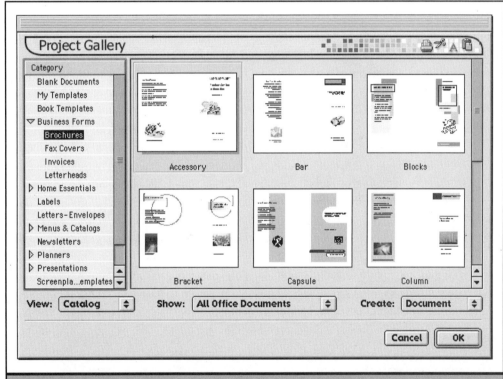

Figure 4-5.   *Here are Project Gallery offerings for a brochure.*

3. Double-click the preview that represents the kind of brochure you want to produce or just select the preview and click OK. This illustration shows the screen when you select the type of brochure.

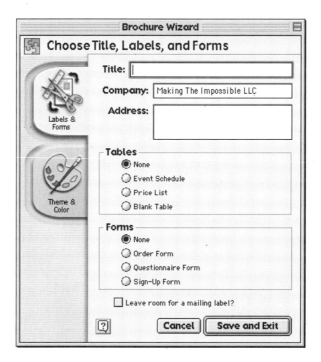

4. The wizard requests information quite similar to what's needed in a catalog. Type your contact information and business name and select the options that specify the kind of brochure you want.

5. Click the Save and Exit button to create a new document with everything ready to roll (see Figure 4-6). You can now finish your brochure, with all the basic document formatting information already in place.

TIP *Once you have set up a new document in the style you want, you can save it as a template, using the Save As command in the File menu. Save the template in the appropriate category folder in the Project Gallery, so you can reuse the style whenever you want.*

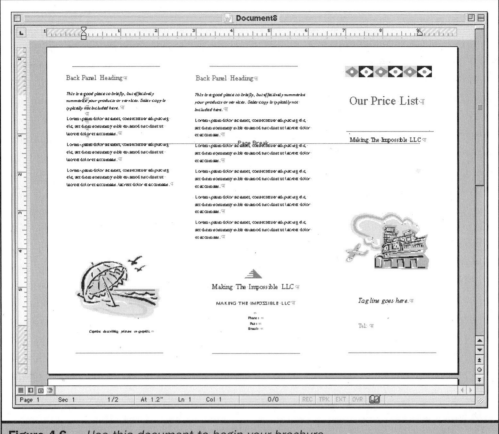

Figure 4-6.   *Use this document to begin your brochure.*

Using the Project Gallery to Create a Menu

Do you run a restaurant or are you preparing a menu for a client? You can use the Project Gallery to create a menu with a minimal amount of preparation. Since a menu can be quite a complicated project to format, this is a useful feature.

Let's apply that ever-clever Project Gallery to this task:

1. Launch any Office application to display the Project Gallery. If the Project Gallery doesn't appear, choose Project Gallery from the File menu.

2. In the Project Gallery, in the Category list on the left side of the window, select Menus & Catalogs.

3. Click Menus to bring up the listing of menu wizards (see Figure 4-7).

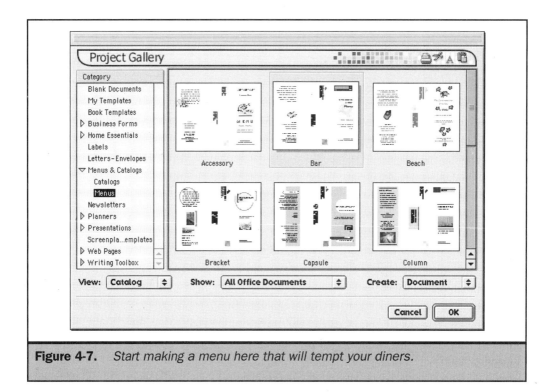

Figure 4-7. *Start making a menu here that will tempt your diners.*

4. Find a menu style you like and double-click its icon to bring up the wizard or just select the preview and click OK. This illustration shows the Menu Wizard when you begin creating your menu.

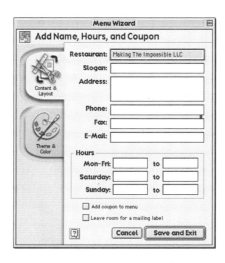

5. Enter the appropriate information in the text fields, select the appropriate
   check boxes, and then click the Save and Exit button. This produces a new
   document with all the information entered, and the basic formatting complete
   (see Figure 4-8). You're now ready to begin your project in earnest, with most
   of the hard work already done for you by Office's Project Gallery.

Adding New Templates and Wizards

Although the standard installation of Office includes a nice selection of useful
templates, and it's easy to add your own, you have another resource for additional
material: the Value Pack.

As mentioned in Chapter 2, the Value Pack on your Office 2001 for the Macintosh
CD lets you populate your Mac's drive with many useful extras, from fonts and clip
art to templates and wizards. To add these components, just follow the simple steps in
that chapter. The next time you launch Office, you'll see that your choices have grown
tremendously. (You can thank me with a free lunch at your new restaurant, after you
create the new menu in Office 2001 on your Mac.)

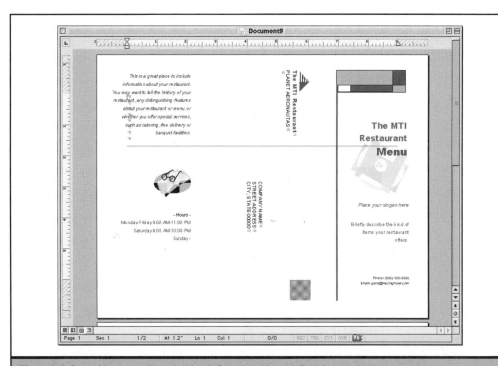

Figure 4-8.   *Now you're cooking! Go ahead and finish your new menu.*

Summary

The Project Gallery is certainly one of the most useful new features of Office 2001. You can use it to select the kind of document you want to create and to format even the most complicated projects with relative ease. What's more, you can customize the contents of the Project Gallery, so you can easily make it do your bidding.

In the next chapter, you'll begin to explore the applications that are part of Office 2001. First you'll learn about a program that Microsoft has called "Outlook Explorer on steroids": Entourage, the combination e-mail program and contact manager that can interact with all the other Office programs to enhance your Mac computing experience.

Part II

Getting the Most Out of Entourage

Chapter 5

Setting Up Entourage

Once there was a neat e-mail program called Outlook Express. It was free, yet offered a powerful set of features that put it in direct competition with the popular commercial alternative, Qualcomm's Eudora. These included a convenient setup assistant to add your user accounts and import data from other e-mail programs; the ability to access e-mail from Microsoft's Hotmail service and synchronize address books with Palm OS desktop organizers from Handspring, Palm, and Sony; and HTML formatting. In addition, the program was capable of sending to and receiving messages from Usenet newsgroups.

NOTE   *Newsgroups are Internet-based message boards where you can read and post statements about all sorts of topics. We'll discuss the topic in more detail in Chapter 10.*

Did I say it was free?

When developing Office 2001, Microsoft took all of the features of Outlook Express, enhanced most of them, and then added a reasonably full-featured contact manager that integrates seamlessly with the rest of the Office programs. For months they looked for a suitable name, but found most of the good ones had already been taken. Finally they came up with Entourage and it stuck.

Getting Set Up in Entourage 2001

When you first install Office 2001, you'll find that Entourage is already present. Nothing extra need be installed. But I'm also assuming here that some of you will opt for custom installation of the various Office applications, so it's possible you've yet to put Entourage on your Mac.

If this is the case, you'll want to read the next section. If not, just skip it and move on to the section that comes after (now how many book writers would tell you to skip a section of their peerless prose?).

A Brief Tour of Entourage

Before we tackle setup of Entourage, here's a brief look at Entourage's ultra-simple user interface. For this discussion, we'll break the main work area into four separate elements. The descriptions that follow are meant to be brief; we'll look at all of these elements in detail in later chapters.

Note that with Entourage, the byword is flexibility. You can adjust many features just the way you like, to meet your specific needs.

The Entourage Window

To simplify the learning curve, you will do most of your work in Entourage from a single, convenient application window, but you can bring up others as needed.

- **Toolbar**   All of the most important functions of Entourage are but a single click away, as you can see next. What you see depends on the program features you are accessing, but this toolbar should help you avoid many trips to the dialog boxes in your day-to-day use of this program.

TIP   *When you hold the mouse over a button, a description of its function will appear on the screen as a tooltip, unless you turn off the ToolTips option in the program's preferences, of course.*

- **Folder List**   Your messages, Address Book, and contact manager items are all stored in handy folders, as shown in Figure 5-1. You can click any folder to see its contents and add storage folders as needed.

TIP   *All of the folders you create can be renamed at any time. Just click once to select a folder and then click a second time to reveal a text box. Now you can change the name. No, a simple double-click doesn't work, and you can't rename default folders, such as the Inbox or Tasks folders.*

- **Folder Contents**   When you click a folder's name, its contents are clearly displayed in a list (see Figure 5-2). You can easily resize, re-sort, or add and remove columns in this list to meet your needs.
- **Message Window**   The messages you have received, sent, or stored appear in the message window (just as shown in Figure 5-3), which you can easily scroll through to read the entire message.

NOTE   *When you select Calendar, Tasks, or Notes, only one window will appear; it won't be divided into separate directory and message windows.*

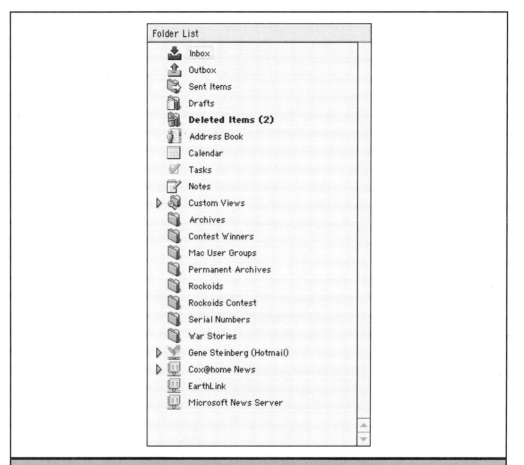

Figure 5-1. *Click a folder's name to see its contents. (This version has many extra folders added by the author.)*

TIP *When you click a message window, you can also scroll through the message with the SPACEBAR.*

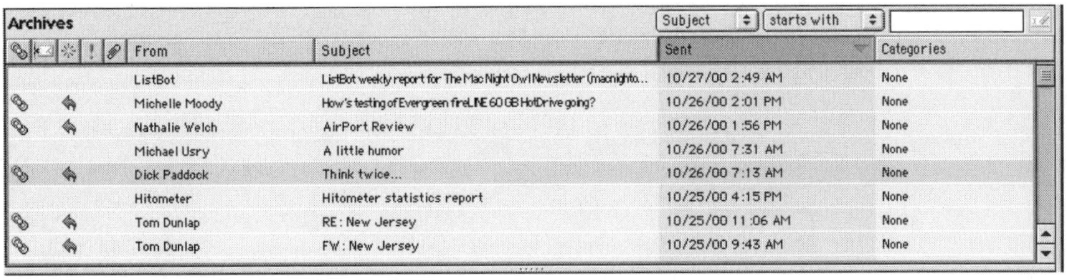

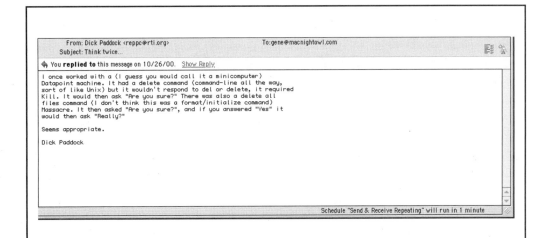

Figure 5-2. *All of your messages and tasks are stored in easy-to-organize folders.*

Figure 5-3. *The messages you see are displayed in this window.*

The Entourage Menu Bar

As with all Mac programs, Entourage provides handy menu bar commands for accessing additional features, beyond those available from the toolbar. Some of the most important commands are described here.

NOTE   *Depending on the message or feature you select, some of the commands displayed are dimmed, and hence not accessible. To show as many commands as possible, I've deliberately accessed some features to make the user options more visible.*

■ **File Menu**   Use this menu, shown next, to open a Project Gallery window, open and save messages, and handle your identities and contact information. You can also print your messages, in case you need a hard copy.

The symbol for the COMMAND key.

TIP   *Many of Entourage's most useful commands are also available from the keyboard. When you see a label that includes the cloverleaf symbol for the COMMAND (or Apple) key, it's the keyboard shortcut you can use to access that particular function. Give it a try and avoid extra mousing around.*

■ **Edit Menu**   Use the menu shown here to copy, save, and transfer text and perform various editing functions on your messages. You can also access your user preferences from this menu.

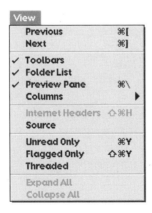

■ **View Menu**   How do you want the interface to appear? You can remove the toolbars, modify the column display, and choose a number of message viewing options here, as shown in the next illustration. One option, Internet Headers, lets you actually trace the route of an e-mail message, which is useful if you want to check the source of an offensive message.

■ **Message Menu**   How do you want to process a message? Do you want to respond to the original sender or to all other recipients? Do you want to follow up later? Do you want to apply an e-mail rule or move the message to a different folder? Entourage message handling, shown here, is sophisticated, but simple to master.

■ **Format Menu**   You have the ability to use HTML formatting for your e-mail messages, and the menu shown here provides various formatting commands, such as font options, background color choices, and more.

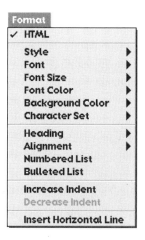

■ **Tools Menu**   The menu shown here lets you run a spell check, choose a user dictionary, and access junk mail and account handling capabilities. Among the more useful features is the ability to automatically insert user signatures and access your accounts on a regular basis.

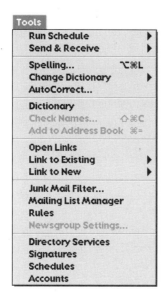

■ **Window Menu**   There are a number of message screens that you can invoke with Entourage in addition to the main window. Choose your options as shown here.

GETTING THE MOST
OUT OF ENTOURAGE

■ **Help Menu**   Need further assistance? Just read the appropriate chapter, but feel free to supplement the information from the handy Entourage Help menu:

> **TIP**   *If the little animated assistant annoys rather than helps you, just choose Turn Assistant Off on the Help menu, and it will be banished (until reactivated, of course, from the same menu).*

Installing Entourage 2001

If you haven't gotten around to adding Entourage to your Mac, just follow the steps here and you'll be ready to configure the program.

> **NOTE**   *I'm not saying you necessarily have to toss out your old e-mail software when you use Entourage. That's entirely up to you. You may, at the very least, want to keep both programs handy until you have a chance to see whether all your old data has been imported correctly. The process may not always be 100 percent perfect.*

1. Place the Microsoft Office 2001 CD in your Mac's CD drive.

2. When the CD's directory appears on your Mac, scroll down to the Office 2001 Installer application and double-click it to launch it.

3. Click the Easy Install pop-up menu at the upper left of the installer window and choose Custom Install. See Figure 5-4 for the list of options.

4. If you have already installed the other components of Office 2001, uncheck everything on the list except for Entourage. Otherwise, add the last two, Office Tools and Converters and Filters. That way, all needed components of Office will be available to you with Entourage.

Microsoft Office Installer

| Custom Install ⬍ | Select All |

▷ ☒ **Microsoft Word**   [I]
▷ ☒ **Microsoft Excel**   [I]
▷ ☒ **Microsoft PowerPoint**   [I]
▷ ☒ **Microsoft Entourage**   [I]
▷ ☒ **Office Tools**   [I]
▷ ☒ **Converters and Filters**   [I]

Disk space available: > 2GB   Approximate disk space needed: 182,956K

Install Location

The folder "Microsoft Office 2001" will be created on the disk "Rockoids"

Install Location: **Rockoids** ⬍

[Quit]

[Install]

Figure 5-2.   *Install individual Office 2001 components from this application.*

5. Normally, the software will go wherever your Office software is present. If you're just installing Entourage, however, you'll want to click the pop-up menu, shown next, that is adjacent to Install Location and specify where you want to place your new software on your Mac. The most convenient location is the Applications folder.

✓ **Rockoids**
Rockoid Two
Rockoid Three
Rockoid Four
Microsoft Office 2001
Select Folder...

6. Once you've selected what you want to install, click the Install button to make it happen.

7. Once the installation is complete, click the Quit button, and you're ready to start using Entourage 2001.

Setting Up Entourage 2001

With the program installed, you're now ready to begin to use it. In this chapter, we focus strictly on initial setup, including importing your e-mail and contact lists from other programs. The next five chapters cover other areas of Entourage's huge feature set.

Establishing Your Initial Account

To use Entourage for the first time, you'll need to create your initial user account. This would normally be your primary e-mail account name. Under normal circumstances, the first time you launch Entourage, a setup assistant will guide you through this process. We'll look at the process separately here, though, in case you want to reconfigure or change things later, but the assistant screens, either way, will be much the same.

Here's how to accomplish this basic setup task:

1. Launch Entourage.

NOTE *If you haven't already used an Office 2001 application, the first time you run Entourage, Microsoft's First Run Installer will kick into action and add several components to your Mac's System Folder. Depending on which files are required, you may have to restart your Mac and then launch Entourage again to continue with the setup process.*

2. Go to the Tools menu and choose Accounts. This brings up the setup screen shown in Figure 5-5.

3. Click the New button, which brings up the Account Setup Assistant (see Figure 5-6).

NOTE *If you want to bypass a setup assistant and just enter everything manually, no problem. Just click the Configure Account Manually button, shown at the bottom of Figure 5-6, and you'll be able to enter everything in two convenient setup dialog boxes, without any help (unless you click Assist Me, which returns you to the Account Setup Assistant).*

4. Enter your name. This is the name that will appear on all of your outgoing e-mail in addition to the actual e-mail address.

5. Click the right arrow and enter the requested information. In this case, it will be you Internet e-mail address. Click the right arrow to continue, and the left (or back) arrow to recheck a setting (see Figure 5-7).

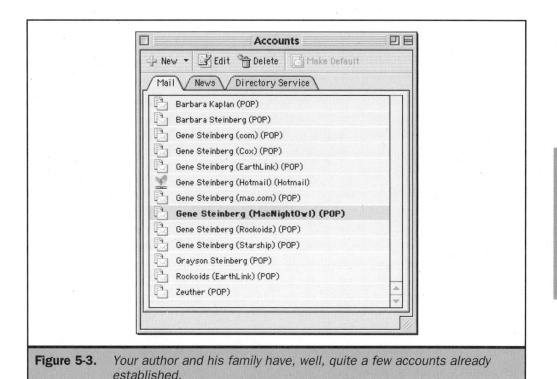

Figure 5-3.   *Your author and his family have, well, quite a few accounts already established.*

CAUTION   *You must enter the server information precisely as required by your Internet service provider (ISP) or e-mail service. Even a single incorrect character will make it impossible for you to make a successful connection.*

6. On the next screen, Internet Mail Logon (see Figure 5-8), enter the user name and password you've established with your ISP or e-mail service. Click Save Password only if you want Entourage to store this entry. If you are concerned about the security of putting a password in the program, don't check this box. If you do not check this box, you will see an onscreen request for the password each time you want to get your messages.

Figure 5-4. *Add your user accounts using this helpful assistant.*

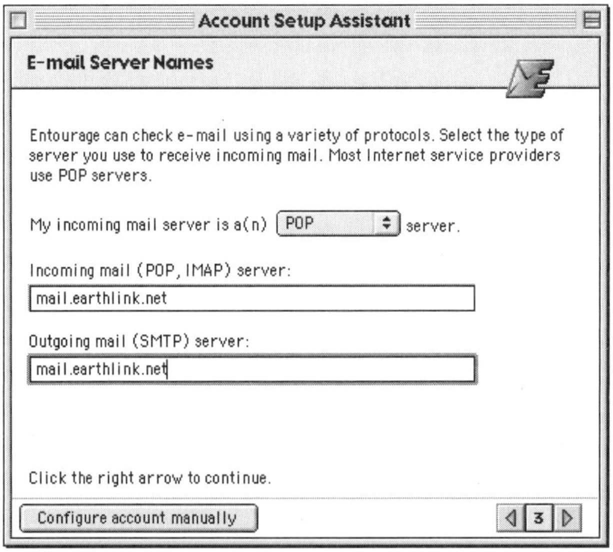

Figure 5-5. *Enter your ISP's incoming and outgoing e-mail server information.*

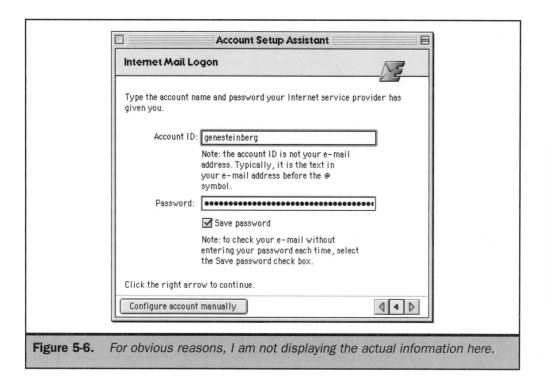

Figure 5-6.   *For obvious reasons, I am not displaying the actual information here.*

7. You're about done now. On the next screen, set a name for the user account (your name or something extra to identify multiple accounts). If you want to include the account in your Send & Receive All schedule (which means that every time you want to retrieve e-mail, this account will be included), check the appropriate box, as shown here:

Using a Strong Password

When you join an ISP, you will normally select both a user name and password. In some cases, the password will be selected for you. You may feel inclined to choose an easy-to-remember password, simply because you don't want to have to struggle with remembering it each time you need to use it or have to locate a piece of paper on which you've written it.

The best approach, though, is to choose your password with care and change it occasionally for added protection. Once you've created a unique password, you'll want to store it in a safe place.

8. Click the Finish button to complete the setup process. The e-mail account will now appear on the Accounts list.

NOTE *You can easily change the information in your account by double-clicking the name in the Accounts window and then entering any necessary changes. This is a quick way to modify an account if you switch ISPs.*

Now that you've entered your initial account, you can follow the same steps to add extra e-mail accounts, as needed.

CAUTION *As of the time this book went to press, there was no way to store or use an AOL or CompuServe 2000 e-mail account in Encourage 2001. AOL and its sister company use proprietary e-mail systems, and a change in the way they set up their services would be needed for you to use Entourage to access these accounts. Do not expect that to happen any time soon, or ever.*

Establishing Your Default Account

Once you've established your user accounts, you'll probably want to specify one of them as the default. The default account is the one that will show up unless you specify otherwise whenever you write a new e-message. Just follow this process:

1. Launch Microsoft Entourage.

2. Choose the kind of account for which you want to create a default account. The options are Mail, News, and Directory Service.

3. Select the name of the account you want to make the default and then click the Make Default button. The result is shown in Figure 5-9.

4. Click the close box in the Accounts window when you're done.

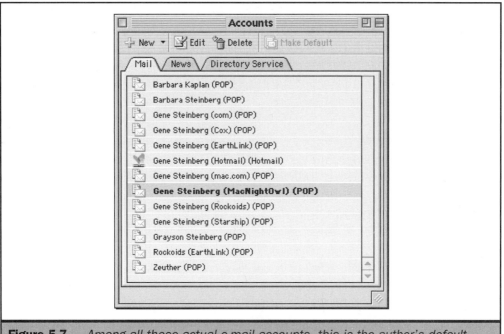

Figure 5-7.   *Among all these actual e-mail accounts, this is the author's default.*

Importing Data from Other Programs

Are you already online? Have you been using another e-mail program (perhaps Microsoft's Outlook Express), or have you been working with a contact manager to organize your business contacts and reminders? Fortunately, Microsoft makes it easy to bring existing information into the application, so you don't have to re-create everything.

Entourage can import such information as stored messages, e-mail contacts, accounts, signatures, and rules (filters) from the following e-mail programs:

- Microsoft Outlook Express (all versions)
- Qualcomm Eudora (all versions)
- Netscape Communicator (limited to version 4.0 or later)
- Claris Emailer (version 2.0v3 only; this was the final released version)

NOTE   *Although you can easily import your messages and address book from Claris Emailer, there is one e-mail feature that you cannot bring over, and that's the ability to send and receive e-mail from AOL and the standard (not "2000") version of CompuServe.*

Additionally, you can easily import such data as contact information, calendar reminders, and tasks from these contact manager programs:

- Now Contact
- Now Up-To-Date
- Claris Organizer
- Palm Desktop

CAUTION   *The process of importing data from another program isn't always perfect. Although you should be able to get most or all messages, address book entries, and PIM data, custom settings or user passwords may not translate correctly. Once you finish importing the data, you should check it against the original program. You may also want to test your user accounts to make sure they work properly.*

When you first launch Entourage, you'll see the Setup Wizard that you can use to enter your user accounts. It will also offer to import the data used in the other programs. But even if you prefer to import the information at a later time, you'll still find it easy to retrieve.

NOTE   *You can also access tabbed information from a text file or from the Windows version of Outlook Express. We'll get to that in the next section.*

To import your contacts, follow these steps:

1. Launch Entourage 2001.
2. Go to the File menu and choose Import, which brings up the Begin Import window (see Figure 5-10).
3. Click the name of the program from which you want to import data.
4. Click the right arrow at the bottom of the dialog box and choose the kind of data you want to retrieve in the Ready to Import dialog box. You can import Messages, Contacts, Accounts, Rules, and Signatures. If you want to change a setting, click the back arrow at any time.
5. To complete the import process, click the right arrow. You'll see a progress bar showing you the progress of the import process.

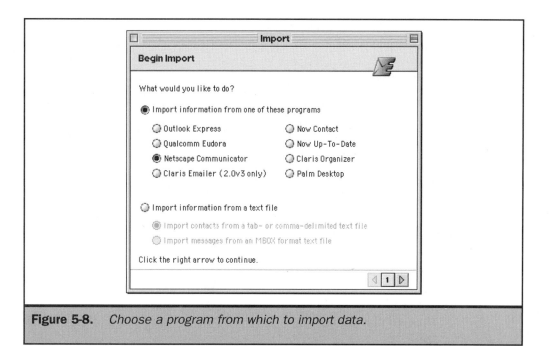

Figure 5-8.   *Choose a program from which to import data.*

NOTE   *Depending on the amount of data you want to retrieve and the speed of your Mac's processor, it may take several minutes or perhaps much longer to access all of the information, so be patient.*

Importing Information from a Text File

For most circumstances, the standard import process should be sufficient for your needs. But what if you are using a PIM or e-mail program not listed, or you want to retrieve contact information from a database (such as FileMaker Pro) or a spreadsheet (perhaps Excel)? How would you manage that task?

Fortunately, with a little patience, you can import the data from these programs as well, simply by first converting the data to text format.

Just follow these steps:

1. Launch the program from which you want to import your data.

2. Use that program's Export or Save As option to convert the data to a text file using tab-delimited or comma-delimited format. You'll want to check the program's documentation to see how to do this.

NOTE *Tab- and comma-delimited files contain data in which one data field is separated from the next by either a tab or a comma.*

3. Launch Entourage if it's not already open.

4. Go to the File menu and choose Import.

5. In the Import Data dialog box, click the radio box labeled Import Information from a Text File and specify whether to use a tab- or comma-delimited text file.

6. In the dialog box that appears, locate and select the text file from which you want to import the data:

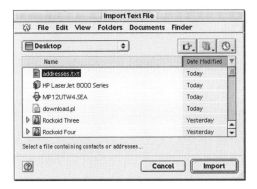

7. Once the file is selected, you see the Import Contacts dialog box (see Figure 5-11). Map or connect the fields so that the data is placed in the correct order. Entourage will attempt to match the data field in the program from which you're importing to its own sequence with a corresponding label. In the Unmapped fields box, specify where any unmapped fields should be placed.

8. If a field is in the wrong sequence, because of differences between your old program and Entourage, you can drag the unmapped field to the proper location.

9. Once you're certain that all the data fields are correctly mapped, click the next or right arrow to verify the information. If it's not correct, click the back arrow and adjust the fields yet again.

TIP *You can reuse field maps over and over again, simply by clicking the pop-up menu in the Map Fields dialog box.*

10. When you are satisfied that all of the data fields are correct, click the Import button to complete the process.

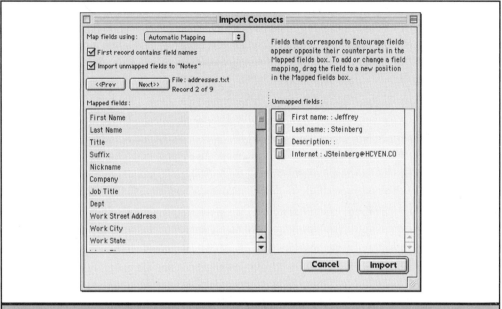

Figure 5-9.   *Use this dialog box to make sure that the data appears with the right label and in the correct order.*

NOTE   *If the source application's own data fields have totally different labels from the ones used by Entourage, you may have to be creative. While Business Phone and Work Phone are obvious equivalents, you may have to leave the unmatched fields under Notes to retrieve all the data successfully. You'll have to then copy and paste that information later on into the right information fields.*

Importing Information from a Windows Computer

One of the great features of Microsoft Office 2001 is its ability to handle files from both Macintosh and Windows computers. You can easily access the data in the Windows version of Outlook Express and bring it into Entourage just by following a few steps very similar to the ones for importing data from a text file.

Start this way:

1. Launch the Windows program from which you want to import your data.

2. Choose the option to export your data into an MBOX-format text file. You will have to check the documentation or help menus for each program. In Outlook Express for Windows, for example, you'll find the Export command in the File menu.

Where's It All Go?

When you first set up Entourage, it creates a series of database files in which all of its external data is stored. The data includes all of your messages, contacts, account information, calendar reminders, and tasks.

The data for the identity of each person who uses Entourage is placed in a separate folder.

Entourage is pretty strict about this: if you move the Microsoft User Data folder (located in the Documents folder) elsewhere, the application won't be able to retrieve it. The only way around this is to create an alias to that folder and place it in your own Documents folder; however, it's just as easy to leave well enough alone.

Since the database files are critical to accessing your stored messages, contacts, and account information, you'll want to make sure that the files are safe. One good way to do this is to make a backup of the entire folder and place it on another drive. You'll also want to update the backup at least once a day or whenever critical information is created in Entourage. Should the worst happen, you'll still be able to retrieve a recent copy.

NOTE   *Another way to transfer the information is via a networked drive, or just e-mail the file to yourself.*

3. Insert the removable media into your Mac's drive.

4. Launch Entourage and choose Import from the File menu.

5. In the Import Data dialog box (refer back to Figure 5-10), select Outlook Express as the program to import from. Select the radio box labeled Import Information from a Text File, and this time specify the option Import Messages from an MBOX Format Text File.

6. Select the file on the removable media.

7. When the file is selected, supply any data mapping information needed; then click Import to complete the process.

Summary

In this chapter, you learned just how easy it is to set up Entourage 2001 with your user data from other applications, e-mail programs, or contact managers.

In the next chapter, you'll proceed to the next step: setting up Entourage to work with most of your e-mail accounts (at least those that support standard Internet e-mail protocols).

Chapter 6

The Ins and Outs of E-mail

W hat do you do when you surf the Internet? Do you check out your favorite Web site, perhaps download a file? One of the most popular pursuits on the Internet is e-mail. Whether it's a message to a friend, a family member, or a business contact, e-mail rules. Even the United States Postal Service uses e-mail for some services.

As you saw in Chapter 5, it's easy to set up your initial user account and import data from other programs. In fact, that may be all you need to get going if you're familiar with Microsoft's free e-mail application, Outlook Express. But Entourage does so much more that you'll want to consider all the many possibilities to help you handle and manage your messages.

In this chapter, we'll discuss the various ways to set up additional user accounts, including Microsoft's free Hotmail e-mail system, and also how to retrieve e-mail with an automated session—all with this clever application.

Creating New Messages

Before we get to setting up additional accounts, let's start with the one you've already established. Once Entourage is running, no doubt you'll want to send a message to someone to test its power.

Your message sending options give you all the control you need. You can simply open a blank message window; enter the recipient's name, the subject, and your text; and send the message right away—or you can just leave the message in your Outbox and send it the next time you connect to your ISP.

If you want to edit your message still further or leave it be until you receive more information (say that document you're working on), you can simply save it as a draft, a good way to plan ahead.

First, let's start with a new message:

1. With Entourage, select Inbox from the Folder list.

NOTE   *No Folder list? To bring it back, go to the View menu and select Folder List. It'll appear in a jiffy.*

2. Click New on the toolbar (or press COMMAND-N), which brings up a blank message screen (see Figure 6-1).

3. Type the address for your message in the To field of the Addressing panel. Your default address will automatically appear in the From field. Entourage's smart AutoComplete feature will bring up a list of possibilities as you type the address (we'll discuss this handy feature in more detail shortly). Feel free to select one of the choices, or just continue typing.

NOTE   *Your default sending address appears the From field. If you have more than one e-mail address, you can access a different one from the pop-up menu adjacent to From.*

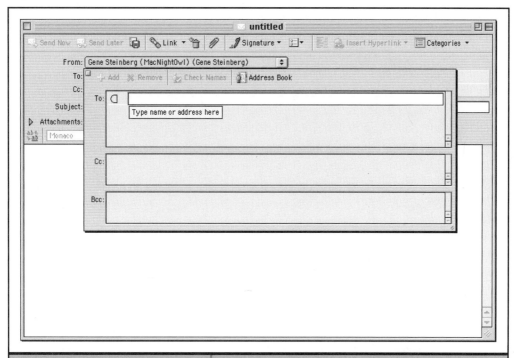

Figure 6-1.   *Start your new message with the address.*

4. If you want to add more names, click the Add button or just separate each name with a comma in a single entry field.

5. Click the Subject text box and give your message a topic. You can leave this box blank if you like, but it's helpful to the recipient if you explain in a short phrase what the message is about.

TIP   *You can quickly move from field to field with the TAB key. Pressing SHIFT-TAB returns you to the previous field. Press RETURN or ENTER to move from the address fields directly to the Subject line.*

6. Click the text box and then type your message. At the end of your message, it's customary to add a signature; we'll get to this again later in the chapter, in the section entitled on "Touring the E-mail Message Window" (also see Figure 6-2).

7. When you're finished typing your message, click Send Now to speed it on its way.

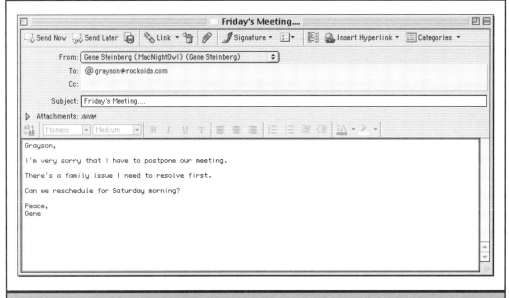

Figure 6-2. *Your completed message is ready to speed on to its recipient via your ISP.*

NOTE

For your message to actually proceed to its recipient, you have to be connected to your ISP. If you're using a cable modem or DSL, you may always be connected; otherwise, you must log in first, and the dial-up process may be triggered by the process of sending or receiving e-mail, depending on how your PPP connection software (Remote Access) is configured.

An Ode to a Correct E-mail Address

It's a sure thing that you've probably reached a wrong number, just because you entered the wrong number on your phone. Just as one digit can get you the wrong party, a single incorrectly entered character in an e-mail address can send your message on to the wrong ISP or the wrong party.

Some e-mail addresses can be extraordinarily complicated—an address may include a long name, plus a domain (location) that's equally difficult to remember. There's plenty of room for mistakes here. Sometimes even a simple address can cause trouble, because it's common for folks to mix up a user name with a person's real name, particularly if the name is very common.

Here's a notable example. My screen name on AOL (the equivalent of a user name with other ISPs) is Gene. The e-mail address for those outside AOL would be gene@aol.com. Now this is a fairly common name, so it stands to reason that mistakes might be made.

Over the last few years, I've received daily e-mails from folks thinking I am their accountant, lawyer, brother, sister, ex-husband, and cheating merchant. I have received get-well e-mail messages, tax returns, photos of one sort or another (don't ask!), and various and sundry greetings, "Dear John" messages, and so on and so forth.

I dutifully write each person, informing them of their mistake (well, actually I have a macro that sets the record straight). Most times they ignore the message, though some are apologetic and others get uppity because I dared suggest they'd made a mistake. Others continue, brazenly, ignoring the corrections and sending me more messages, but eventually they realize that a mistake has been made.

The lesson is be careful and make sure that what you send is going to the right recipient.

Touring the E-mail Message Window

In addition to options for your basic e-mail entries, several options for message handling appear on the message toolbar. You'll want to explore them now or later as you learn more about Entourage and need to access their functions.

Here's a quick look at the various toolbar functions available:

- **Send Now** As soon as you finish writing your message, click this button to send it on its way. If you are not logged into your ISP, this step will usually activate an attempt to connect to the service.

NOTE

I say usually, *because it's a default option in Apple's Remote Access Control Panel. But if the option is turned off, the automatic connection won't take place.*

■ **Send Later**   You'd rather write a few messages first before sending them? No problem. Just click Send Later, and the message will go into the Outbox, but a message sending session won't run at this time.

■ **Link**   This is one of the great contact manager features of Entourage. It allows you to link your message to any of seven categories, including messages, tasks, events, and files. We'll discuss this subject in more detail in Chapter 8.

■ **Attach**   Click the paper clip icon to bring up a Choose Attachment dialog box, shown here, where you can select one or more files to include with your message.

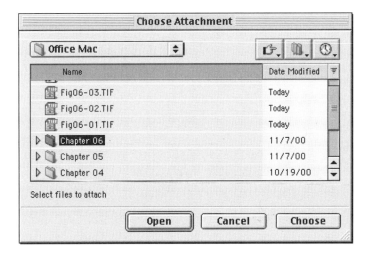

■ **Signature**   You can easily store one or more default signatures from which to select to add at the bottom of your messages. You'll learn more about this feature in Chapter 7.

■ **Options**   Switch to HTML formatting, select priorities, or have your message automatically put in a specific folder after it's sent.

■ **Insert Hyperlink**   This feature works with Microsoft Internet Explorer to allow you to enter a site's address from an open browser Window or Internet Explorer's Favorites or History listing.

■ **Categories**   Give your message a specific category, such as Home, Work, or whatever you choose, to easily identify it for your reference.

TIP   *Not sure what a toolbar icon means? Just hold your mouse over the icon, and a ToolTip will appear that identifies its purpose. This option can be turned off as a program preference, if you decide you'd rather not see the labels.*

Message Sending Options

Entourage is a highly flexible program. You don't have to write and edit e-mail in any prescribed way; you can do it in the fashion that's most convenient for you. After you finish writing a message, you have these choices:

- **Send Now**   Just click this button if you want to send your message to its intended recipient right away.

- **Send Later**   Not logged into your ISP? Or perhaps you want to finish a bunch of messages first. Choose this option. The message will move to the Outbox, along with any other messages that are waiting to be sent.

- **Save as Draft**   If you want to recheck your message at a later time, or if you need to prepare additional material, such as adding a file attachment, click the Save as Draft button instead. The message will be stored in the Drafts folder, where you can access it later.

Message Addressing Options

There are three ways to address your messages in the Entourage Addressing panel, and the choices you make depend on whether a message is destined for one recipient or more than one, and whether you want others to know the names of all recipients.

Here is a list of the options:

- **To**   The main recipients of the message are shown in this category. All recipients will be aware of the names of other recipients in this category.

- **Cc**   Carbon or courtesy copy. This is the list of recipients who are being sent a copy for such purposes as general information or as a courtesy. All recipients will be aware of the names of other recipients in this and the To category.

- **Bcc**   Blind carbon copy. The names of the recipients do not appear at the top of the message (the message header), and hence recipients are not aware of the names of the others in the Bcc category who have received this message.

NOTE

Can't find the Bcc option? It's appears only when you click an addressing category, or when addresses are entered as Bcc. Otherwise, only the To and Cc options are displayed. Confused? Well, it's probably an effort to discourage use of the feature, which can also be used by junk mailers to canvass a large number of anonymous recipients.

The Elements of an E-mail Address

Internet e-mail follows several conventions, and if you follow them just right, you'll always be able to send your messages to the correct recipient.

Let's dissect the e-mail address *gene@macnightowl.com* (it's mine, of course, and your cards and letters are welcomed):

- **Account Name** This is the name at the left of the @, or "at" symbol. In my case, it's *gene*, and in your situation it's whatever e-mail name you've established with your ISP.

- **Domain** The text to the right of the @ symbol is the domain or location of the e-mail server. In my case, *macnightowl.com* is my personal domain (they're sometimes called vanity domains, and lots of companies have them), but it can also be the name of the ISP that handles the recipient's e-mail, such as *aol.com* or *earthlink.net*. The three-letter designation after the dot represents the kind of service: some of the suffixes are *.com* for commercial, *.net* for network, *.edu* for educational, *.org* for organization (often nonprofit), and *.gov* for government. Depending on the service's location around the world, additional two-letter designations may identify a specific country, such as *.au* for Australia, *.ca* for Canada, and *.uk* for United Kingdom.

A number of other options for domain names are being considered, but it really isn't important to know the reason for a specific type of service used by the recipient to address your messages correctly, so long as the right information is entered.

Tips and Tricks for Addressing a Message

One of the most useful features of Entourage is the ability to remember recently-typed e-mail addresses, plus the ones in your Address Book. It's a great time-saver as some e-mail addresses can be, well, complicated.

The feature works like this: When you enter an e-mail address in the To, Cc, or Bcc field, Entourage will consult its listing of names and bring you a pop-up menu with the choices (as seen next). As you continue to type letters, prospects that more closely match your entry will appear.

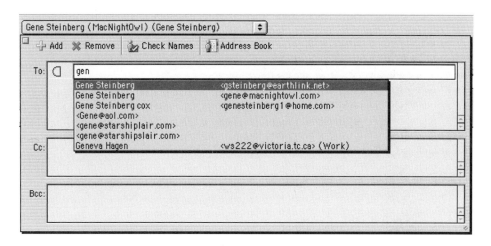

When you see the list, if the name you want is there, just click it to have it automatically placed in the address field.

Here are some additional choices for you:

- **Address Book Entry**   One of the most useful features of Entourage is its Address Book (see Figure 6-3). It serves as the repository for your regular contacts, but it's not just for e-mail addresses. It can be used with the application's powerful contact manager features. We'll discuss the subject of setting up and maintaining your Address Book in more detail in Chapters 7 and 8. For now, just note that you can select your contacts in the Address Book and drag and drop them into the appropriate address categories of an e-mail message.

- **Copy and Drag and Drop**   If the address you want is in another message, just select it and drag and drop it into the appropriate address field, regardless of whether it's To, Cc, or Bcc. Should you want to add more than a single recipient, press SHIFT and select the names you want to add. Then just drag them to the appropriate address field.

TIP   *Another cool way to add multiple e-mail addresses is to copy and paste (or drag and drop) a complete list of names. This procedure will work so long as all entries are separated by commas.*

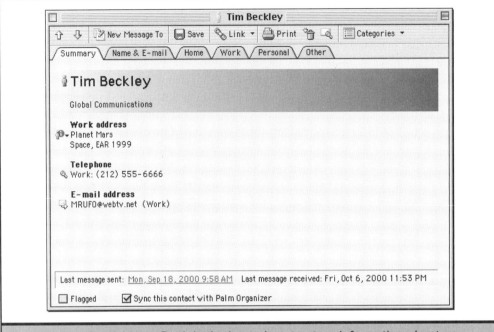

Figure 6-3.   *The Address Book is the best place to store information about your regular online contacts.*

NOTE   *As a practical matter, there's no real difference between copying and pasting and dragging and dropping. The end results are identical. Just do what suits you best in a specific situation.*

■ **Removing an Address**   If you decide that you don't really want to include someone as a recipient of your message, you can easily delete the address. Just select the name, click the Remove button or press DELETE, and it's gone.

CAUTION   *When you address a message, don't put a space between user names; if you do, the first part of the address will be ignored. If a space is required, use an underline instead, such as gene_steinberg. Otherwise, close up the words.*

What If You Don't Know the Address?

As you see, addressing e-mail is simple. You can enter, select, copy and paste, and drag and drop, and your messages will be addressed correctly, so long as the addresses are correctly entered.

If you don't know the address, Entourage can look it up for you via its Directory Services feature. Just follow these steps to perform a search:

1. Open your new e-mail form by choosing New from the File menu or just typing COMMAND-N.

2. Enter the recipient's real name in the appropriate address category, regardless of whether it's To, Cc, or Bcc.

3. Click Check Names, and a directory service will be polled to look for the e-mail addresses for the person you select. If any matches to your request are found, the results will appear in a separate window (we won't show the names to protect their privacy).

4. When you see the results, look them over. If you see the name you want, double-click it to enter the name in the Addressing panel or just drag the name and drop it into the appropriate Addressing panel category.

5. If you want to store the name as a regular contact, click the Add to Address Book button.

CAUTION   *If your intended recipient has a common name, it's very easy to accidentally select the wrong person. If you're not certain the intended recipient is the correct party, you might want to address a carefully worded message in which you ask the person if he or she is indeed the person you want to contact. You'll also want to apologize for the intrusion as folks get plenty of unsolicited e-mail, and you don't want to intrude on their privacy. Also bear in mind that directory services aren't completely reliable or up to date. For example, when I looked for my e-mail address, I found some older, out-of-date ones, but some more recent entries were missing.*

What to Do If the Check Names Feature Doesn't Work

If you click Check Names but don't find the right person, or if you get an error message, you may want to perform the address search using a different directory service. The Check Names function searches only the service selected as the application default, and no one service offers complete or identical results (as we'll discuss in the next section).

Here's how you can conduct a search using additional directory services:

1. With Entourage open, choose Directory Services from the Tools menu (see Figure 6-4).

2. In the left pane, choose a directory service from the list.

3. Enter the name of the person for whom you want to conduct a search in the Search for Name field. If you have only an e-mail address and not a real name and want to verify that you have the right address, use the E-mail field instead.

4. Click the Find button, and the service will be checked to see if a matching name can be found. The results will appear in the bottom pane of the Directory Services window.

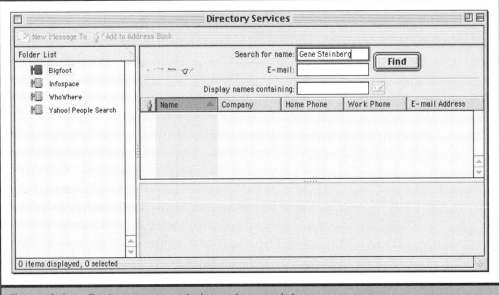

Figure 6-4.   *Begin your expanded people search here.*

5. If you have located a lot of likely prospects, you can use the Display Names Containing field to restrict your search still further.

6. When you've found a likely match, double-click the name to bring up the information, which will show up as a proposed Address Book entry.

7. If you want to send a message to that person, just click the New Message To button at the upper left of the Directory Services window (again see Figure 6-4).

8. To add the entry to your Address Book, click Add to Address Book.

CAUTION   *It is a good idea not to add a proposed recipient's address as an Address Book entry unless you are 100 percent certain the person is the one you want. If you get a confirmation e-mail, you can easily add the name later.*

9. If your search request yields an incorrect result or no result, or if you get a message indicating that your search couldn't be performed, click another directory services site and run your search again.

REMEMBER   *You must be connected to your ISP for the directory search to run.*

10. When your searches are done, click the close box in the Directory Services window to dismiss it.

If you find that one directory service consistently gives you better, more accurate results, you can easily change the default service, so that Entourage searches that site first. Here's how it's done.

1. Go to the Tools menu and choose Accounts.

2. Click the Directory Service tab:

3. The default service will be in bold. Just select another directory service, and click the Make Default button to change the setting.

NOTE

Your mileage may vary, but I have found that Bigfoot yields more consistent and accurate results for my search requests. I recommend that you try it first before choosing another option.

How to Spruce Up the Look of Your Messages

Entourage is a remarkably flexible program when it comes to letting you adjust the look and feel of your messages to suit your tastes or make them look good for your recipients.

Messages are generally formatted as plain text. While plain text may look a bit drab, it has the advantage of being compatible with virtually all ISPs and virtually all computer operating systems. With this format, the person who receives your message won't have to be concerned about missing formatting or links.

You also have the option of sending your messages in hypertext markup language (HTML), complete with text formatting and clickable links. Such messages can contain some of the same formatting as in a word processor, such as multiple fonts and sizes, special alignment, and background colors.

By default, messages are displayed as text for maximum compatibility. In Chapter 7, you'll learn how to customize your e-mail messages.

Receiving Messages

So far, we've focused on how to send a message, but it's quite likely you'll be receiving more messages than you send. In this section, you'll learn how to handle the receive process in a way that suits your working style.

First let's look at the standard ways messages are handled by particular types of e-mail servers.

- **POP** Short for Post Office Protocol. This is the protocol most ISPs (except AOL) use to handle their messages. When Entourage accesses a POP mail server, it transfers the messages to your computer, where they end up in your Inbox. You can also configure Entourage to tell the POP server to leave the messages on the server by using your e-mail account Options tab (available from the Accounts feature on the Tools menu). We'll discuss this in Chapter 7.

CAUTION   *If you choose to leave a message on the server, you may run up against the limits of your ISP. After a certain capacity is reached or after a certain interval set by the service, older messages may be automatically deleted or your e-mail may not arrive because your mailbox is filled. Thus, use this option with care (for example, you may want to use it just when you're on vacation, so you can retrieve the messages a second time when you return to your home or office).*

- **Hotmail and IMAP** Short for Internet Message Access Protocol. IMAP is another method for accessing e-mail where the messages are normally left on the server. Microsoft's free Hotmail service is an example. When you delete a message from Hotmail, it's not just deleted from your Mac, but from the mail server as well. You'll find messages for these two protocols listed in the Hotmail and IMAP folders in Entourage.

The basic process of receiving e-mail is pretty much the same whether you're getting it from a POP or IMAP-based account, but since messages are put in different places in Entourage, we'll look at the two types of accounts separately.

Receiving POP E-mail Messages

Here's how to receive your messages from a standard POP account, such as the ones used by most ISPs:

1. With Entourage open, go to the Tools menu and select Send & Receive.

2. If you want to get a message from just one account, select that account name from the submenu.

3. If you want to get all your messages, choose Send & Receive All.

4. If your account passwords were not saved in your Account setup, you'll see a Password box. Enter your password.

CAUTION   *The Send & Receive All feature functions only with accounts in which you've set up a Send & Receive All schedule or which have been designated as default e-mail accounts. You'll see how to set up message scheduling in detail in Chapter 7.*

5. If new messages have arrived, the titles will appear in bold. Just click a title (see Figure 6-5) to reveal its contents in the lower pane of the Entourage program window.

GETTING THE MOST OUT OF ENTOURAGE

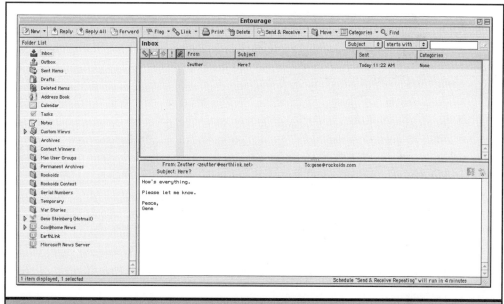

Figure 6-5.   *Aha! E-mail has arrived for your fearless author.*

Receiving Hotmail E-mail Messages

Microsoft's free Hotmail service is a useful tool for managing your e-mail away from the confines of your regular ISP. If you haven't had a chance to check it out yet, just visit the Web site at http://www.hotmail.com (see Figure 6-6). Once your account is established, you can use Entourage to manage the messages.

TIP   *If you want to see just how fast your ISP truly is, try out MSN's Computing Central Bandwidth measurement page. You can access it from the Hotmail home page or this URL: http://msn.zdnet.com/partners/msn/bandwidth/speedtest500.htm. Oh, and by the way, don't do anything while the test is running, and you'll want to run it several times to get the most accurate results.*

Once your Hotmail account has been set up, just follow these steps to get your messages:

1. With Entourage open, go to the Folder list and click your Hotmail account's name.
2. Click the disclosure triangle at the left of the account's name to display the message folders.

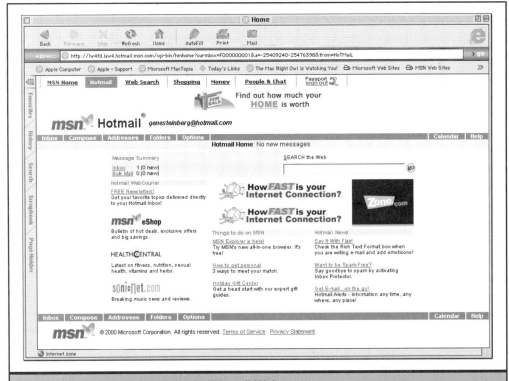

Figure 6-6.   *This is the author's Hotmail Web page.*

3. Click the Inbox to activate the receiving process. You will have to type your password in the Password box if you haven't previously stored it in your Account settings. If you have any messages, they'll appear in your Inbox shortly.

4. If there are new messages, the titles will appear in bold. Just click a message title to bring its contents into the lower pane of your Entourage Window.

Receiving IMAP E-mail Messages

Messages from IMAP accounts are also received in a separate location in Entourage. This helps in the organization of your messages—or the confusion, depending on your point of view, of course.

Here's how to retrieve messages should you have an IMAP account:

1. With Entourage open, click the name of your IMAP account in the Folder list.

2. To see the list of folders in your IMAP account, click the disclosure triangle at the left of the account's name.

3. If you have subscribed to a specific folder for your messages, locate it in the Folder list and click it.

NOTE   *The messages for your IMAP accounts are stored on the server in separate folders. To see the folder's name in your Folder list, you must subscribe to it first, by selecting the folder and then clicking the Subscribe button on the toolbar (the folder doesn't appear otherwise).*

4. If you want to receive your messages in a folder from which you haven't subscribed, first double-click the folder's name in the Folder list. Then click the Subscribe button in the toolbar.

5. Enter your password in the Password box. This box will appear only if you didn't store your password when you set up the account.

TIP   *Do you want to check for new messages? Just click Refresh Message List in the View menu or press COMMAND-L, and the server will be checked for new arrivals. Piece of cake.*

Why Leave Messages on a Server?

While Hotmail and IMAP messages continue to be stored on the mail server even after you retrieve them, the same isn't true for POP messages. When you retrieve them, they are removed from the server and transferred to your Mac's hard drive (so long as that preference option is left at its default setting). Under normal circumstances, this is the best way, because it doesn't clutter up your online mailbox.

But what if you are away from the computer you normally use to receive e-mail and you'd like to be able to see the messages again when you return? Is there an option? Yes, you can change the settings for your POP mail account so that, even when the messages show up in your Inbox, they remain on the server and can be accessed from another computer.

Once you delete a message, it's deleted from the server, if your account is configured in that fashion.

As an alternative, POP accounts can be configured so that only a small part of a large message is retrieved, with the rest left on the server.

If you want to leave messages on the server for your POP accounts, just follow these steps:

1. Go to the Tools menu and select Accounts.

CAUTION   *Your ISP may have established a maximum space and time limit for storing your messages on their server. If the size of your messages exceeds that amount, anyone who tries to send you e-mail may receive a message saying that the mailbox is filled, and hence you won't receive the message. It's a good idea to periodically delete messages to keep the server from becoming overloaded, or just set a preference to have messages automatically deleted after a set interval.*

2. If it's not already selected, click the Mail tab to bring up the list of your accounts.

3. Click an account's name to select it; then click the Edit button.

4. When your account settings are displayed (see Figure 6-7), click the Options tab to bring up a dialog box for the server settings.

5. There are several choices you can make in the Options dialog box, but we'll look at only the Server options here. If you want to leave part of a message on the server, click the check box labeled Partially Receive Messages Over and then click the message size and enter a new figure if you want to change it from the default of 20K.

6. If you want to leave a copy of the entire message on the server, click the second check box, Leave a Copy of Each Message on the Server.

7. If you check the option Leave a Copy of Each Message on the Server, you have two more options. The first, Delete Messages from the Server After, lets you specify the number of days that pass before messages are automatically purged. The default is 30 days, but you can change this value if you get a large number of messages. Select the second option to give the account a separate listing in the Folder list.

8. Once you're finished making the changes you want, click OK to store the settings.

A Look at Message Reading Options

When you receive your messages, they're normally placed in the Inbox. Unless you delete messages or organize them, though, that Inbox can get mighty filled over time,

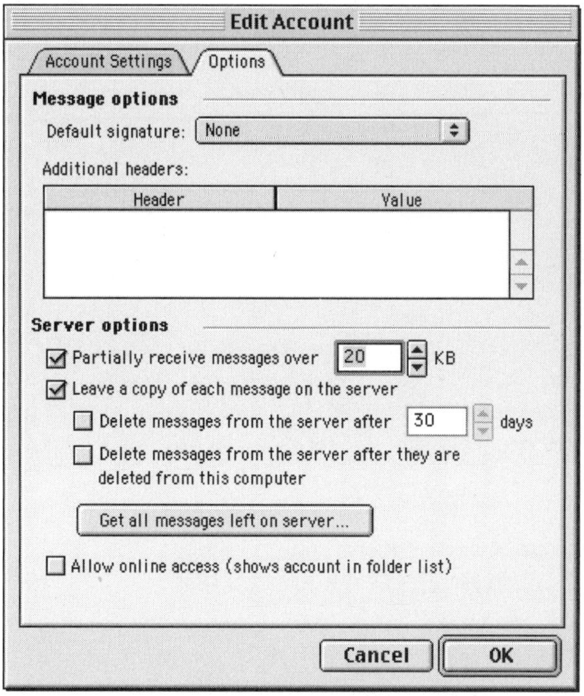

Figure 6-7. *Specify your server settings here if you want e-mail stored.*

so you'll want to consider ways to organize the messages if you want to keep them on hand for later reference.

Here are two approaches to message organization:

■ **Create a Special Storage Folder**   One useful procedure to make sure you can locate messages in specific categories later is to create a folder and drag the messages there. To create a new folder in your Folder list, just choose New from the File menu and select Folder from the submenu or from the submenu next to the New button on the toolbar. Or just press COMMAND-SHIFT-N. When you select this option, a new, Untitled folder will be created. Just click the folder's text field and give the folder a name that defines its contents, such as Business Messages or Archives (to name a couple of examples). Once the folder is set up, just select it and drag the messages you want to store into that folder.

NOTE   *You can also have messages moved automatically to specific storage folders. You'll learn how this can be done in Chapter 7.*

■ **Change the Sorting Order**   By default, messages are stored by date and time received. To change the sorting method, just click a column title in the message folder. Normally, you can sort by the name of the sender (From), the subject, the date sent, and the category. You can pick category labels by choosing Categories on the Edit menu. Messages can also be placed in a special folder and then sorted by these same options.

> **NOTE**   *Entourage provides additional column titles that you can add by choosing Columns from the View menu. These include the date the message was received, to whom the message was addressed, the account name, and the size of the message.*

> **TIP**   *You can easily resize a column title by dragging the mouse to the vertical bar next to a column's name. When the cursor changes to a pair of opposite-pointing arrows, just hold down the mouse button and move the cursor back and forth to resize. You may have to resize other columns to keep the columns from exceeding the size of your message folder window.*

E-mail Problems and Solutions

With millions upon millions of messages being sent each and every day, it's amazing that most, in fact, arrive on the screens of their recipients in seconds. I've marveled how I can e-mail someone on the other side of the world and get a response just a few moments after my message is sent.

On the other hand, it should come as no surprise that sometimes the process just doesn't work properly. A message may go astray, or you may have difficulty sending it in the first place. In this final section of the chapter, we'll cover some common e-mail problems and their typical solutions.

You Cannot Send or Receive Your Messages

You have one or more messages to send, or you're just trying to keep up with the new messages, but when you try to send or receive your e-mail, you get an error message, perhaps telling you that Entourage failed to connect to your e-mail server.

Here are some possible solutions:

■ **You're Not on Line**   Verify that your Mac is really and truly connected to your ISP. It's not unusual for disconnects to occur on a standard dial-up account. It could be the result of a problem at your ISP or with your phone connection. In addition, Apple's Remote Access (or PPP) software may be configured to automatically log you off if you are online but idle for a given period of time. Try logging on again. If Remote Access shows that you're already connected, disconnect and log in again.

NOTE   *If you're using a cable modem or DSL you may have to reset the modem itself, by pressing a reset switch or unplugging and then plugging in the unit and waiting for it to reset itself. Try accessing a Web site or two to verify that you've achieved a successful connection. If you fail to restore your connection, you'll need to contact the ISP directly for assistance.*

■ **Is the Mail Server Active?**   Even if you are indeed connected to your ISP, that doesn't mean that the mail server you're trying to reach is active. Sometimes a mail server is taken down for maintenance. This is true even for the larger ISPs. If this happens, the best thing to do is check with your ISP or network administrator about the situation.

■ **Account Name and Password Correct?**   It's easy to make a mistake, and perhaps you entered the wrong information when you set up an account name. You'll want to recheck, by accessing the Tools menu and selecting Accounts. Double-click the account name you want to check, which will produce the Account Settings dialog box (see Figure 6-8). Recheck your account ID and password information. Since the password is shown as a set of bullets, the best thing to do is just retype the password.

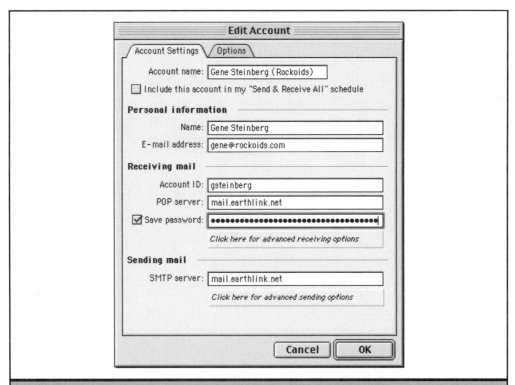

Figure 6-8.   *Recheck your account information in this dialog box.*

NOTE *If nobody else is using your Mac, you can choose the option to save your password in Entourage. But if others use your Mac, you may prefer to enter your password manually when requested, for additional security. You can also use the keychain feature of Mac OS 9 to store your passwords. I cover that feature in another book I wrote,* Mac OS 9: The Complete Reference *(Osborne/McGraw-Hill, 2000).*

■ **Server Name Correct?**   The server name for incoming and outgoing messages must be accurate. While not case sensitive, if even a single character is wrong, you will not be able to send and receive messages. If you're not certain the information is correct, check the documentation from your ISP or access the ISP's Web site or telephone help line to get the right address. Once you are certain the information is correct, access the Account Settings dialog box (as described earlier and shown in Figure 6-8). Correct any incorrect information. In addition, verify that all of your ISP settings are correctly entered in the TCP/IP Control Panel.

■ **Do You Need a Proxy Server?**   In some setups, you may need to enter an e-mail proxy server in your Mail & News Preferences box, which is available from the Edit menu. Your network administrator will have the correct information.

■ **Whoops! Entourage Sent My Message Before I Finished**   If you catch the progress bar while e-mail is being sent and click the Stop All button, you'll halt the process. If you catch it in time, your message will still be in the Outbox.

Hotmail Connection Problems

As explained earlier, you can use Entourage 2001 to connect to your free e-mail account with Microsoft's Hotmail service, but there may be times when you just can't send or retrieve messages. Here's the list of likely problems and their solutions:

■ **Server May Be Busy**   All right; we know it's Microsoft, but that doesn't mean that aren't times when their mail servers will be busy, too. Just try again at a later time and see if the connection works.

■ **Password Correct?**   Check your Hotmail account setup by choosing Accounts from the Tools menu. Double-click the account that represents your Hotmail account and reenter the password. Hotmail expects a password from 8 to 16 characters long. If your password is too short, it won't work. If you want to change the password, access the Hotmail Web site at http://www.hotmail.com and follow the instructions to change a password.

■ **Do You Need a Proxy Server?**   Depending on the requirements of your ISP or local network, you may have to enter a proxy server to access an Internet-based e-mail server. Check with your network administrator or ISP for this information.

In some circumstances, Hotmail won't work with a proxy server. In this event, you will not be able to use Entourage to access the account. You'll have to stick with your Web browser to handle your Hotmail messages.

Summary

E-mail is one of the most important features of Entourage 2001, and its new features extend your ability to communicate and organize your messages to a new level of efficiency.

In the next chapter, you'll learn advanced techniques for organizing your messages, ridding yourself of junk mail, and setting special filters to handle messages in a custom fashion, so that, for example, certain messages will be stored in a specific folder.

GETTING THE MOST OUT OF ENTOURAGE

Chapter 7

Advanced E-mail Techniques

The basic nuts and bolts of writing and sending e-mail are relatively simple. As you saw in the previous chapter, Entourage 2001 is as simple as it is powerful. In just a few minutes, you can configure it to recognize most of your e-mail accounts (except AOL and CompuServe accounts) and then easily retrieve your messages whenever you log onto your ISP.

In this chapter, you'll first take a full tour of all of Entourage's features. Then you'll discover the power of complete e-mail management, including setting schedules for sending and retrieving messages, using HTML to format your documents, storing your custom signature, organizing placement of messages for convenient storage, and handling the ever-present problems of e-mail attachments and junk mail.

A Thorough Tour of Entourage's Commands

So far, you've seen Entourage's browser window, where you handle all your message sending and retrieving chores. You've also been exposed to a very few of the important menu bar commands that let you dig deeper and harness the program's power.

Before going on, we will take a complete tour of all the commands available. Then we'll begin to explore more advanced techniques for preparing and managing messages.

NOTE   *Some folks call me a miracle worker when I fix their Macs, but I cannot make all menu bar commands active at the same time in Entourage, so you'll see some dimmed in the illustrations in this section.*

■ **File Menu**   From commands for opening the Microsoft Office Project Gallery to those for importing, exporting, and printing messages, the File menu commands are pretty standard.

COMMAND key symbol

Notable features are the ability to save an open message as a Web Page and the ability to work offline, so you can continue to write and prepare your messages without actually being logged on to your ISP. This feature is especially useful if your ISP charges you by the hour (and some do offer basic accounts in that form).

NOTE   *The items in a menu preceded by the Command (or Apple) symbol are keyboard shortcuts that you can use to activate the very same features.*

■ **Edit Menu**   At the top of this list are the standard Macintosh Edit menu functions, which you can use to cut, copy, and paste message items.

The Paste As Quotation command lets you paste text in the standard Internet format (with a greater-than sign, or forward triangle, before each line). You can also duplicate and delete messages and create and remove sorting categories. The Auto Text Cleanup option lets you perform some basic text editing functions to selected text. You can also reduce or enlarge text, perform searches of your messages by a variety of criteria, including content, and change Entourage's preference settings.

■ **View Menu**   You can use the View menu to indicate what portions of the Entourage window appear, activate and deactivate column categories, view the source code of HTML text, and prevent display of messages you've already read. The top commands are used for fast navigation.

GETTING THE MOST OUT OF ENTOURAGE

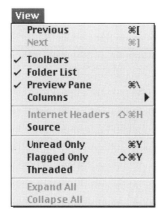

■ **Message Menu**   Do you want to mark a message as read without reading it, mark it as unread so it's title is again listed in bold, forward or redirect a message, or flag a message for later review? These are among the features included in the Message menu.

■ You can also perform such message handling functions is moving messages to another folder, establishing a priority label, or applying a rule you've previously created. Rules provide a useful way to handle both the e-mail you want and the messages you don't want (so-called SPAM e-mail). We'll discuss message rules in "Setting Message Rules" later in this chapter.

■ **Format Menu**   The commands on the Format menu are available only when you choose the option to prepare a message in HTML format. The features are similar to what you might find in some popular Web authoring programs, such as Adobe GoLive and Macromedia Dreamweaver. Once you've chosen to use HTML for a message, you can choose styles, fonts, font sizes, color, heading style, text alignment, and whether to create bulleted or numbered lists.

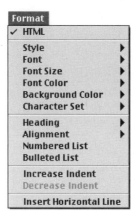

■ **Tools Menu**   From the Tools menu, you can perform such functions as sending and receiving e-mail; running your scheduled e-mail retrievals; spell checking; using Entourage's Link feature; and configuring accounts, schedules, signatures, and various mailing list rules. Chief among the features is the application's handy Junk Mail Filter, which can flag suspected e-mail and even move it to a different folder for later review and disposal.

■ **Window Menu**   Which window do you want open? Normally, you see the main window, but the Window menu lets you display other open windows, including the ones used for Entourage's contact manager feature. Any window can be closed, but this menu (or the keyboard shortcuts listed) lets you bring them to the screen again.

Window	
Main Window	⌘1
Address Book	⌘2
Progress	⌘3
Calendar	⌘4
Tasks	⌘5
Notes	⌘6
Link Maker	⌘7
Error Log	⌘8
Cycle through Windows	⌘~
Progress	
Entourage	
◆ untitled	

TIP   *Under normal use, you'll probably want to keep the progress window open, so you can see if there are any problems with sending and receiving e-mail.*

■ **Help Menu**   You can access Entourage's built-in help features, configure the Help Assistant, and use Microsoft's Web-based help system from the Help menu.

Help
About Balloon Help...
Show Balloons
Turn Assistant Off
Microsoft Entourage Help
Microsoft Entourage Tour
Contents and Index
Help on the Web
Online Registration

Setting Entourage's General Preferences

How often do you change an application's preferences? Most folks never touch the preference panels, but others want to configure each and every setting in a special way. Microsoft has made Office 2001 almost infinitely changeable. If you combine the possibilities, you can specify literally hundreds of combinations of settings to tailor the program to your taste.

However, such flexibility doesn't come at the expense of making the program difficult to use. The preference settings are very easy to specify and equally easy to change back if you don't like the changes you've made.

To be perfectly frank, I change very few of the basic settings on my Office 2001 applications, and you can leave things alone and still use these programs and harness much of their power.

This section covers the general user preference settings you can select, including a few settings you may especially want to consider changing.

To access the basic preferences of Entourage, simply choose Preferences from the Edit menu and General from the submenu, or just press the COMMAND-; (semicolon) key combination. To switch from one preference panel to another, just click the appropriate tab.

After you've made the changes you want, click the OK button to put them in effect. This can be done after all the preference panels have been checked and changed as you prefer. If you want to make no changes at this time, click Cancel instead.

The following sections describe each of the preference panels.

Setting General Preferences

The first tab you encounter, General (see Figure 7-1) covers basic text editing and help features:

- **Double-Clicking in the Folder List Opens a New Window**   If you activate this preference, any folder that's double-clicked opens in a new folder window, in addition to being displayed in Entourage's main window. The default setting is off, because this option adds to window clutter on your Mac.

- **Use Microsoft Office Keyboard Shortcuts for Editing Text**   The default setting is on, making such basic shortcuts as COMMAND-B to switch to bold text consistent across Office applications.

- **When Selecting, Automatically Select Entire Word**   If you click just before or after a word, the entire word is selected. This feature is especially useful for drag-and-drop editing. The default setting is on.

- **Use Smart Cut and Paste**   This useful feature simplifies the process of cutting or copying and pasting text. When you select a word or paragraph and paste it into a new position in that document or another document, you won't find extra or missing word spaces. Smart! This feature is on by default.

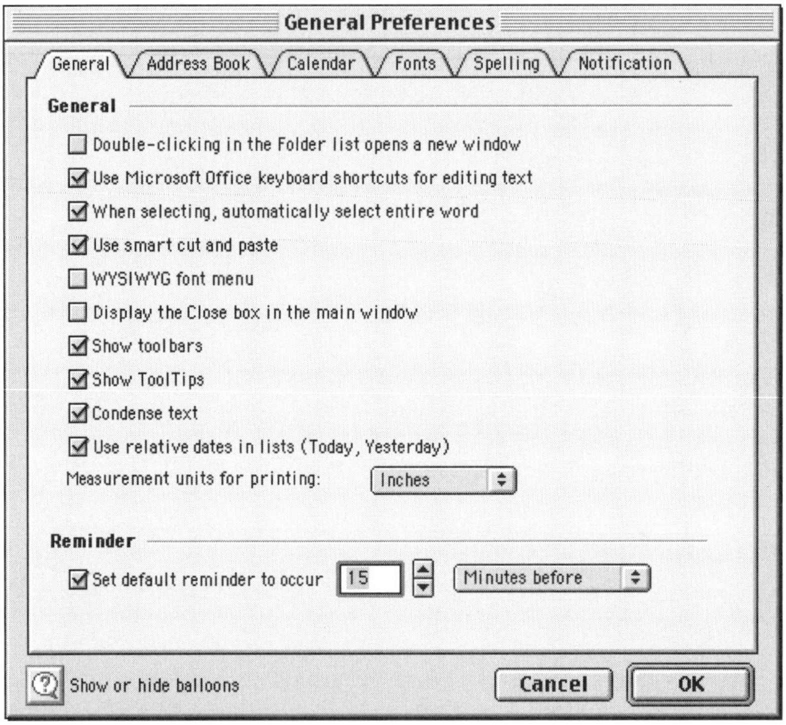

Figure 7-1.   *General preferences for Entourage 2001 give you lots of options for customizing the program.*

■ **WYSIWYG Font Menu**   When your Font menu says Caslon Openface BT, can you visualize how it differs from Copperplate Gothic? You don't have to fret over such things. Just choose the WYSIWYG (what-you-see-is-what-you-get) Font Menu option, and you won't have to guess (it's off by default).

```
▲
Arrus Blk BT Black
Arrus Blk BT Black Italic
Arrus BT Bold
Arrus BT Bold Italic
Arrus BT Italic
Arrus BT Roman
BernhardMod BT Bold
BernhardMod BT Bold Italic
BernhardMod BT Italic
BernhardMod BT Roman
Blackletter444 Regular
Bookman Hd BT
Brush738 BT Regular
BrushScript BT
CAPITALS
Carlton LET
CaslonOpnface BT Regular
Century Gothic
Charcoal
Chicago
Comic Sans MS
Cooper Blk BT
COPPERPLATE GOTHIC BOLD
COPPERPLATE GOTHIC LIGHT
Courier
Courier New
```

■ **Display the Close Box in the Main Window**   Normally, there is no close box, which means that you can dismiss the main Entourage window only by quitting the application. This setup is used to prevent a user mistake, since all of Entourage's core functions are shown in the main window. Click the check box if you want to display a close box.

- **Show Toolbars**   Entourage's toolbars provide easy ways to access the program's major features with a single click. Since these features are also available using keyboard commands (see "The Entourage Menu Bar" in Chapter 5), you can save screen space by turning this option off.

- **Show ToolTips**   When you pause the mouse on a button, text appears in a balloon identifying the button's purpose. This option is turned on by default, and it's a good idea to leave it that way.

- **Condense Text**   If the title text of a folder or message is too long, the text will automatically be condensed (by moving the letters closer together), and ellipses will be added to the end of long titles. The default setting is on. You can expand the main window and individual title windows to avoid the need for this option, since the compressed text doesn't look very pretty, but if your Mac doesn't have a large display, it is probably better to leave the setting on.

- **Use Relative Dates in Lists (Today, Yesterday)**   You don't have to concern yourself about whether yesterday was November 26 or not. The relative date feature, which became a part of the Mac OS Finder with Mac OS 8, is fully supported by Entourage.

- **Measurement Units for Printing**   Most people in the United States talk in feet and inches, but printers talk in picas and points and, outside the U.S.A., people use other measurement systems. Choose the one you want from the pop-up menu. The default is inches.

- **Reminder: Set Default Reminder to Occur**   How long before an event should you be notified about it? Make your choice here. The standard time is 15 minutes, but you can click the number or use the up and down arrows to change this value, and you can even switch from Minutes Before to Hours Before, and so on. If you have to take a long drive to make your appointments, you might want to set the default reminder value to a different figure.

Setting Address Book Preferences

There's not much to configure in your Address Book preferences (shown in Figure 7-2). Let's cover the options:

- **Format Phone Numbers**   What is your local area code? How do you want to display phone numbers? The normal way is to place an area code in parentheses, but if you live in a location outside of North America, you may want to change the default setting to the way phone numbers are specified in your country.

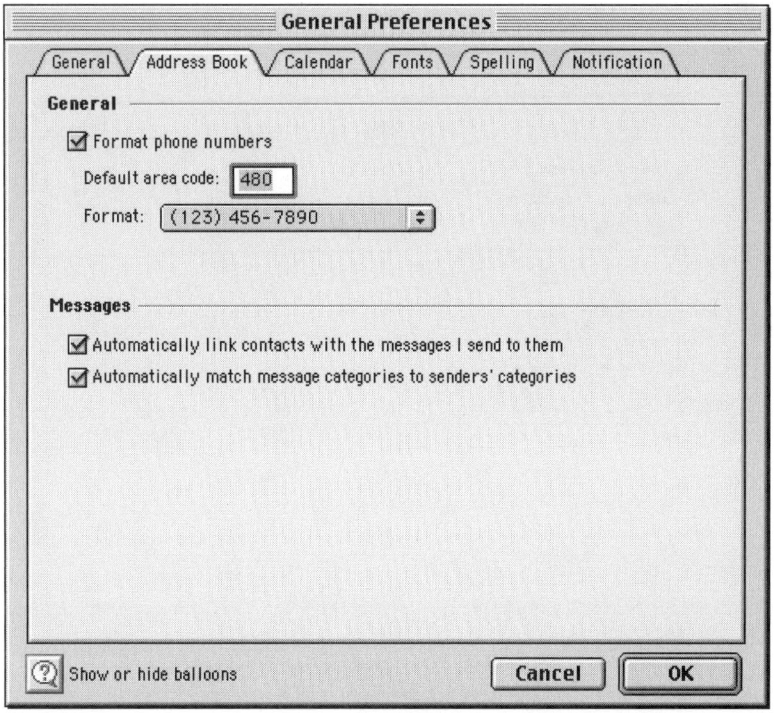

Figure 7-2.   *Choose from a small set of Address Book options here.*

- ■ **Automatically Link Contacts with the Messages I Send to Them**   This option, checked by default, automatically links a contact in your Address Book to the messages sent to that contact. This makes tracking the messages later easier.

- ■ **Automatically Match Message Categories to Senders' Categories**   If your contact is labeled for a business-oriented category, the messages you get from that contact list the same category. This preference is enabled by default.

Setting Calendar Preferences

The Entourage Calendar is where you set up your reminders and tasks. The Calendar preferences (see Figure 7-3) let you configure the way it's displayed.

- ■ **First Day of Week**   Does your work week begin on Monday, or do you prefer a seven-day-a-week setting? Pick your option here.

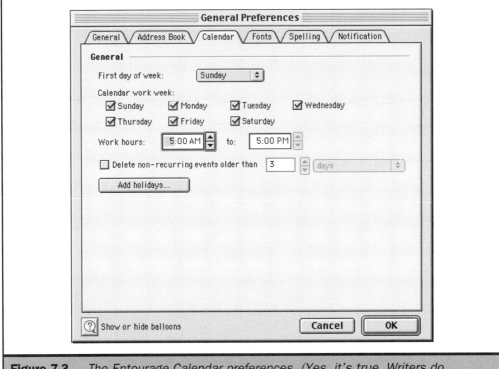

Figure 7-3. *The Entourage Calendar preferences. (Yes, it's true. Writers do sometimes work seven days a week.)*

■ **Calendar Work Week**   Which days do you work? Do you ever take a day off? Check the days here.

■ **Work Hours**   Don't take the work hours shown in Figure 7-3 seriously. Mine are much more intense than that.

■ **Delete Non-recurring Events Older Than**   This option cleans up your Entourage Calendar of outdated events. By default, it's set to three days, when the option is checked. Click the entry or use the up and down arrows to change the value (you can change it only when the preference is checked).

■ **Add Holidays**   Click this button to automatically add holidays that pertain to your country and/or religion from Entourage's default list. After you click the button, you'll see an Open dialog box from which you can select the Holidays option (shown in the following illustration). Then you can check all the holiday events you want to import. When you click OK, they'll be automatically imported into Entourage and included in the Calendar (see Figure 7-4).

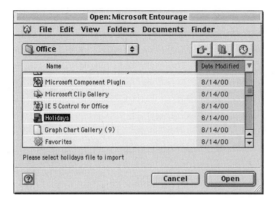

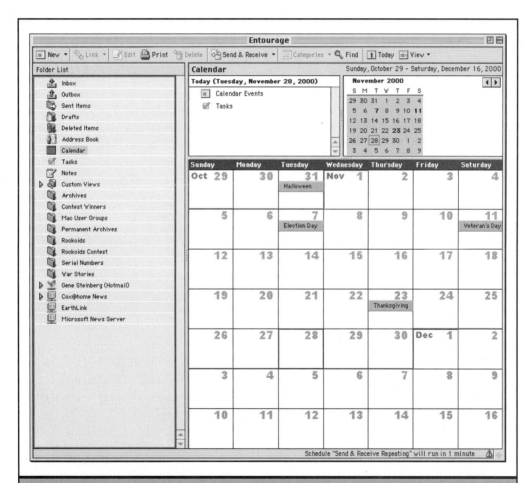

Figure 7-4.   *Here is the result of my holiday choices.*

Setting Fonts Preferences

Which fonts do you want to use for your messages, message window lists, and message printouts? Just click the Fonts tab (see Figure 7-5) and choose fonts and sizes from the pop-up windows. Unless you have a liking for a particular font, you may want to stick with the default settings at the start.

NOTE   *Remember that the font you choose to display a message may not be the font seen by the receiver if the receiver doesn't have the font installed. Regular Mac fonts are specified in Entourage's settings, but if your message recipients use Windows, you may want to choose from such common Windows fonts as Arial, Courier New, and Times New Roman. These fonts are part of your regular Office 2001 installation.*

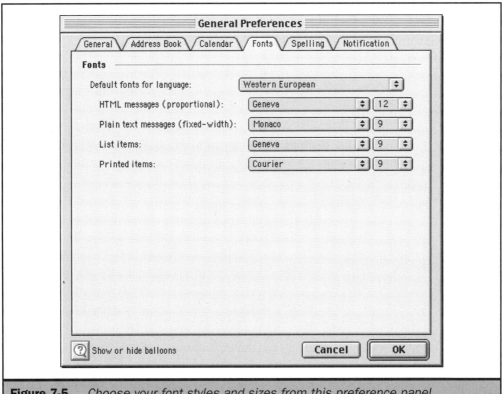

Figure 7-5.   *Choose your font styles and sizes from this preference panel.*

Setting Spelling Preferences

Are you certain you have spelled that word correctly? As with other Office 2001 applications, Entourage 2001 will check each word you type and underline it if it's spelled incorrectly. The Spelling preferences (see Figure 7-6) allow to specify how the spell checking process is handled.

The Spelling preferences available from Entourage are the same as those offered in the other Office 2001 applications.

GETTING THE MOST OUT OF ENTOURAGE

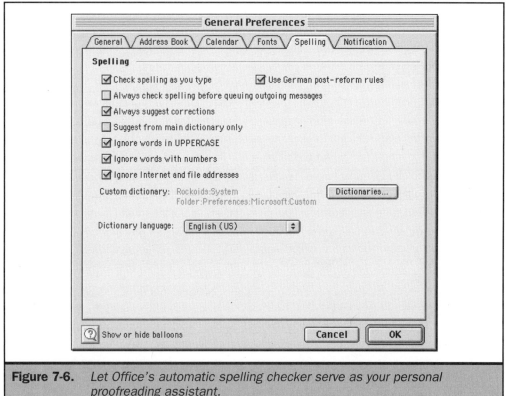

Figure 7-6. *Let Office's automatic spelling checker serve as your personal proofreading assistant.*

■ **Check Spelling as You Type**   By default, this setting is established so that you will not have to fret over the exact spelling of a word. If the word is flagged with an underline, just choose Spelling from the Tools menu, or type COMMAND-OPTION-L to have Entourage help you find the correction. You can use this feature for batch spell checking, too, where you check the entire message for errors in one process.

```
┌─────────────────────────────────────────────────────────┐
│                        Spelling                          │
│  Not in Dictionary                                       │
│  ┌───────────────────────────────┐   ┌──────────────┐   │
│  │ crazieste                     │   │   Ignore     │   │
│  │                               │   └──────────────┘   │
│  │                               │   ┌──────────────┐   │
│  │                               │   │  Ignore All  │   │
│  │                               │   └──────────────┘   │
│  │                               │   ┌──────────────┐   │
│  │                               │   │     Add      │   │
│  └───────────────────────────────┘   └──────────────┘   │
│  Suggestions                                             │
│  ┌───────────────────────────────┐   ┌──────────────┐   │
│  │ craziest                      │   │   Change     │   │
│  │                               │   └──────────────┘   │
│  │                               │   ┌──────────────┐   │
│  │                               │   │  Change All  │   │
│  │                               │   └──────────────┘   │
│  │                               │   ┌──────────────┐   │
│  │                               │   │ AutoCorrect  │   │
│  └───────────────────────────────┘   └──────────────┘   │
│     ┌──────────┐  ┌──────────┐    ┌──────────────┐       │
│     │ Options… │  │  Undo    │    │    Cancel    │       │
│     └──────────┘  └──────────┘    └──────────────┘       │
└─────────────────────────────────────────────────────────┘
```

TIP   *Unsure about the proper definition of a word? Just hold CONTROL and click a selected word to bring up a contextual menu; then choose the Define option. Entourage will consult the Encarta dictionary that's part of Office to find all the related definitions.*

■ **Use German Post-reform Rules**   This option comes into play only if you are handling German-language material and the German spelling dictionary has been installed. Otherwise, you don't need to leave this option checked, though doing so does no harm.

■ **Always Check Spelling Before Queuing Outgoing Messages**   This feature activates the spell checker window when you click the Send Now or Send Later button after finishing your message. This ensures that the message gets a last check before it goes to its recipient. If correct spelling doesn't come easily for you, this is an option you'll want to activate.

■ **Always Suggest Corrections**   When Entourage performs a spell check, this option, normally checked, will automatically list possible corrections. You'll probably want to keep this option on.

■ **Suggest from Main Dictionary Only**   By default, Entourage uses both the regular Office dictionary and your own user dictionary (the one in which you add custom words).

■ **Ignore words in UPPERCASE** With this option checked, Entourage will not check the spelling of words in all caps. This reduces flagging of capitalized titles, which may include proper names and other words not found in the spelling dictionary. You may prefer to turn this off for more extensive spell checking.

■ **Ignore Words with Numbers** Words that consist of mixed letters and numbers will confound a spell checker. The best thing to do is to leave this option checked.

■ **Ignore Internet and File Addresses** File names and the names of Internet sites won't normally fit into the standard spell checker parameters. It's a good idea to check this option, so you don't have to see the strange, inconsistent names of the Internet flagged as incorrect.

■ **Custom Dictionary** You can set up a custom user dictionary that Office applications will use when you need to add extra words. The main dictionary is by no means perfect.

■ **Dictionary Language** Choose your entry from the pop-up menu. The one displayed is normally English (US), unless you perform a custom installation of Word (see Chapter 2) and select a different language.

Setting Notification Preferences

When you receive e-mail, would you like to see or hear a notice, so you know when to check Entourage? The Notification preferences (see Figure 7-7) are normally set with most confirmation notices active.

You can disable the confirmation icon or sounds, depending on your needs. If you're in a busy office and you feel an audible notice would disturb others, you can uncheck the various sound-related choices.

NOTE *The last preference panel you used when you changed settings will be the one opened when you access your user preferences the next time.*

Reviewing Mail and News Preferences

Once you've set your general preferences for Entourage, there are other options you can change: specifically, ones that handle your mail and newsgroup messages.

This section describes Entourage's Mail & News Preferences dialog box. To access this dialog box, choose Preferences from the Edit menu and Mail & News from the submenu, or just press the COMMAND-SHIFT-: (colon) key combination. As with the other user preferences for Entourage, you can leave things at their default settings, and the program will run just fine in most situations, but you may need to configure the software in a special way to handle your particular installation.

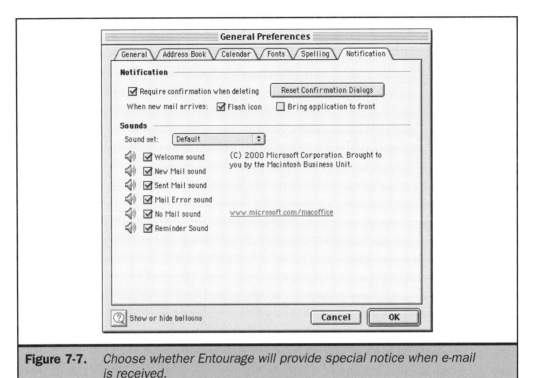

Figure 7-7. *Choose whether Entourage will provide special notice when e-mail is received.*

Just click one of the five tabs to see the panel for the changes you want to make. After you've made your changes, click OK to put them in effect, or click Cancel to restore the settings to the previous configuration.

Setting Read Preferences

The Read preferences panel (see Figure 7-8) specifies the way your incoming messages are displayed by Entourage.

- **After Deleting or Filing an Open Message**   Choose the default option, which is to close the message window. The second option from the pop-up menu opens the next message.

- **Mark Message as Read After Displaying For**   If you get a lot of messages (I receive over 200 e-mails a day and welcome any time-saving measure), you can configure Entourage to automatically mark messages as read after a given interval (3 seconds is the default). I can't imagine why one would want to do this, assuming that most of the messages you get are important and worth reading, but the choice is there.

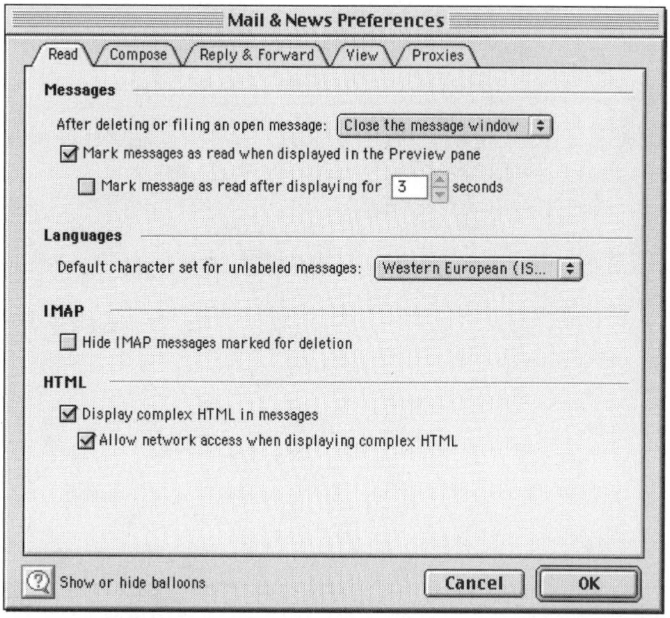

Figure 7-8. *Click a check box to activate a labeled feature.*

- **Default Character Set for Unlabeled Messages**   Choose the language options from the pop-up menu. Western European is the default setting.

- **Hide IMAP Messages Marked for Deletion**   This option essentially provides a convenience. Hiding those messages means you don't have to see the titles again the next time you access your IMAP account. The downside is that you don't have a chance to recheck a message before it's deleted in case you change your mind.

- **Display Complex HTML in Messages**   This option provides one of the more useful features of Entourage's powerful e-mail handling. It allows a message to come through fully formatted with URLs, as appropriate. If you prefer not to deal with such things, just turn the option off, and everything will come through as straight text. The problem, of course, is that you won't be able to click a Web link to access the listed site.

- **Allow Network Access When Displaying Complex HTML**   This setting allows Entourage to retrieve files from the Internet for display in your message. You can turn this off if you'd rather not spend the additional time to get such messages, have security concerns, or are not logged on to your ISP when you access these messages.

Setting Compose Preferences

The various preferences available in the Compose panel (see Figure 7-9) are available to help you when you're writing and sending messages.

- **Automatically Check Names When Sending Messages (Location Manager Aware)**   Entourage's Directory Services feature lets you find someone's e-mail address. However, this option is not checked by default, because those services are not 100 percent reliable in finding someone's address. It's a nice option to have around, but it won't be terribly flexible until the servers themselves are more efficient in what they produce.

NOTE   *Apple's Location Manager, included with recent versions of the Mac OS, lets you specify such things as custom Internet, network, and printing settings for use in a particular location. This enables you to instantly configure your Mac to run in different environments.*

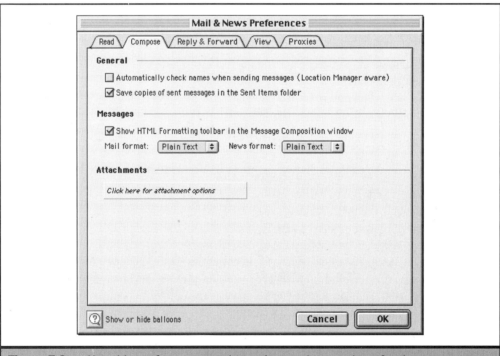

Figure 7-9.   *Use this preference panel to select various options for the messages you write and send.*

- **Save Copies of Sent Messages in the Sent Items Folder** You'll want to leave this option selected, because it makes it easy to check the messages you've sent to others later. Otherwise, a copy isn't made of your messages, which may keep the Entourage message database slimmer, but it will make it difficult for you to check a message you've previously sent.

- **Show HTML Formatting Toolbar in the Message Composition Window** With this option selected, you can change to HTML formatting when you send messages. You can also select whether plain text or HTML formatting is applied to e-mail and newsgroup messages. We'll discuss HTML formatting options in "Using HTML Formatting to Spruce Up Your Messages" later in this chapter.

- **Attachments** One of the most confusing and useful features of an e-mail program is the ability to send and receive file attachments. When you click the button labeled Click Here for Attachment Options, you'll see a dialog box where the options that affect file attachments are set.

You will probably want to leave the default Encode For setting, Any Computer (AppleDouble), since the files you send will then be readable on other computing platforms. You can also choose whether files will be compressed using StuffIt, but that can be a problem for users of other computing platforms (although there is a StuffIt program for Windows). The final options address efficiency and compatibility: whether Cc and Bcc recipients also get the file attachments you send, and whether Windows file extensions will be appended to the file names. If you intend to send files to users of that other computing platform, just check this box (this option is off by default).

Setting Reply and Forward Preferences

How will Entourage work with the messages to which you respond? The Reply & Forward preferences panel (see Figure 7-10) lets you configure those settings. Here the defaults are pretty much the way to go, but we'll look at the options anyway.

■ **Include Entire Message in Reply**   When you respond to an e-mail message, it's customary to quote the message you received, so the recipient knows what you are replying to. With this option checked, the entire message will be quoted.

If you want to quote just selected passages in a message (which is really the best way to handle quoting), select the relevant text and then click the Reply or Reply to All button in a message window. Only the material selected will be quoted.

■ **Use Quoting Characters When Forwarding**   When you forward a message, the original message, normally without alteration, is sent to your new recipient or recipients. With this option checked, quoting characters (the little forward arrows) are placed before each line.

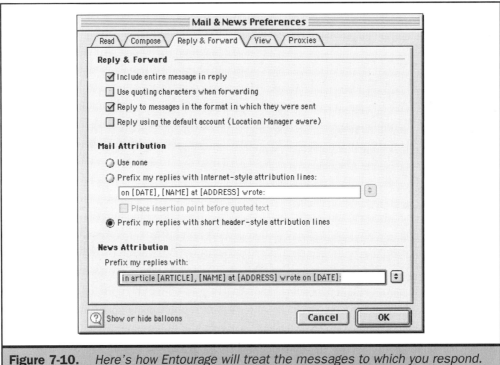

Figure 7-10.   *Here's how Entourage will treat the messages to which you respond.*

- **Reply to Messages in the Format in Which They Were Sent**   This option allows you to automatically use the same text formatting, either plain text or HTML, that was used in the original message. It's a default, and one you'll probably want to leave that way.

- **Reply Using the Default Account (Location Manager Aware)**   You can specify that all messages to which you respond automatically use the default account (rather than the one to which they were sent, if you have several e-mail accounts). Again, the Location Manager feature of the Mac OS will automatically set your Internet-related, printing, and network preferences for a specific locale.

- **Use None**   This is a mail attribution command, and if it is selected, nothing will appear at the top of the message to which you are responding to identify the name of the person to whom you are replying. Normally, this option is left off.

- **Prefix My Replies with Internet-Style Attribution Lines**   As shown in Figure 7-10, the normal way of responding to a message includes the date of the message, the user name, and the e-mail address of the person to whom you're responding. Thus, in my case, a reply might begin, "On 11/27/00 1:09 PM, Gene Steinberg at gene@macnighowl.com wrote:" This is text you can edit; you can select it and change the settings or eliminate a particular category of information.

- **Place Insertion Point Before Quoted Text**   Normally, when you respond to a message, the response is put at the bottom of the message. You prefer the top? No problem. Just enable this option, and the text insertion point will appear at the top of a quoted message for your response.

- **Prefix My Replies with Short Header-Style Attribution Lines**   Despite the name, all this option does is remove the prefix on the e-mail to which you reply and place the insertion point at the top of the message.

- **Prefix My Replies With**   This is strictly a newsgroup setting. In addition to the attribution lines already mentioned, it includes the article number of the newsgroup message. We'll cover this subject in more detail in Chapter 10.

Setting View Preferences

This View preferences panel, shown in Figure 7-11, specifies how messages are displayed when received. Most of the options are best left as they are, but some provide information you may need if you handle a large number of messages or need to trace the source of a message.

■ **Show Unread Messages as Bold**   This default setting is helpful in distinguishing the messages you've yet to read. Otherwise, you can choose the next option.

■ **Show Messages Using These Colors**   Normally, messages are shown in your default colors, with unread messages in bold. This option lets you specify different system colors with which to identify the messages. When you check this option, you'll see default colors. Click the Unread or Read color box to view additional selections.

■ **Show Internet Headers**   The messages you send take a long, circuitous path on their way from sender to recipient. When you select this option, you can just double-click a message to view its travel history. Normally, it's not necessary to see this information, but if you are receiving messages that are offensive to you or need to trace a problem with message receipt, you'll want to check this option so that the messages can be examined more carefully.

■ **Show Attached Pictures and Movies in Messages**   If someone sends you a movie or picture as a file attachment, it will appear in the body of the message. The downside is that the message will take longer to be displayed. If you are concerned about security or about making your Mac vulnerable to possible e-mail viruses, you can switch off this option and view file attachments separately.

■ **Toggle Open Threads That Contain Flagged Messages**   This option is useful for organizing your newsgroup messages. If you've flagged certain messages for later follow-up, the topic folders or threads will open automatically for you.

■ **Show Newsgroups and IMAP Folders Using These Colors**   These options let you display messages and accounts to which you have subscribed in system-related colors. When this option is selected, just click the default color next Subscribed or Unsubscribed to see additional choices.

■ **Color Quoting**   Each quote level, in other words, quoting a quoted message and so on, is displayed in a different color for easy recognition. Click a quote level to select additional color options.

NOTE   *What's that Show or Hide Balloons option about? Since the days of Mac OS 7, Apple has had a convenient, though sometimes annoying, help feature called Balloon Help. If you are uncertain what a preference does, click the little question mark button, and you'll see help text on the item you select. This may be helpful, but since Balloon Help, when activated, inflicts itself on all of your Mac programs and the Finder, you'll want to turn it off after you've used it.*

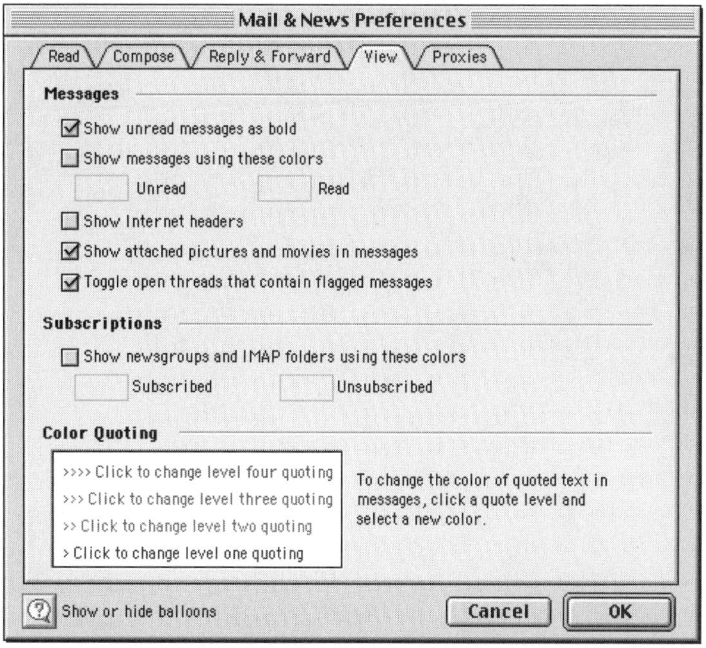

Figure 7-11. *How will messages be viewed? Count the ways.*

Setting Proxies Preferences

The final set of Mail & News Preferences options you can select comes into play only for certain ISPs or a local network with a proxy server, which is essentially a computer that acts as an intermediary between your Mac and other computers on your network and the Internet. When you click the Proxies tab (see Figure 7-12), you can activate a proxy setting for the Web, mail, or a secure server. No settings are listed here, because they will vary by ISP and network administrator. If you're in doubt as to what to do, check with the appropriate parties for advice.

Using File Attachments

One of the important functions of e-mail is sending and receiving file attachments. A file attachment can consist of a family photo, an important document you need for

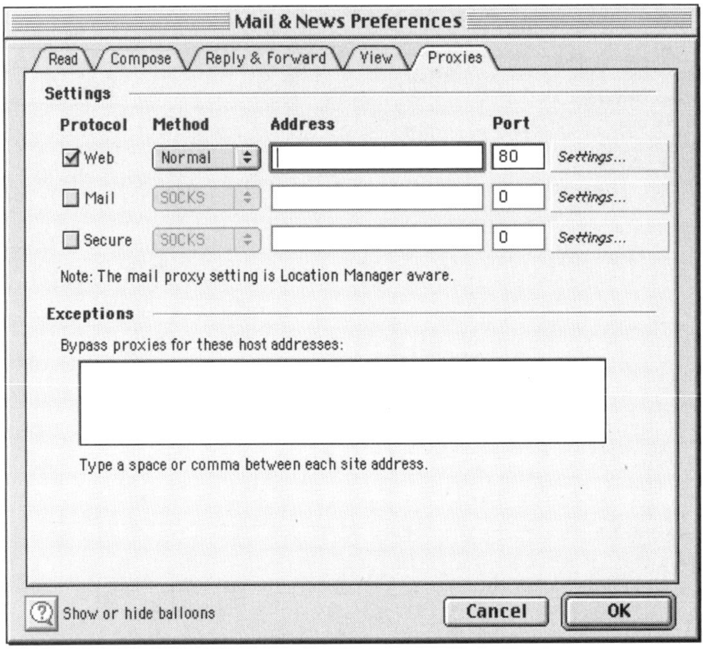

Figure 7-12. *If your system requires a proxy setting to handle e-mail or Internet access, enter the settings here.*

your work, a large page layout file for a publication, or an MP3 music file, but the process for sending and receiving all of these files is pretty much the same.

On the other hand, the subject of attachments is steeped in mystery, and problems often arise when you're trying to send a file properly or work with the files you've received. First we'll discuss the process of sending and receiving these files. Then we'll get to the matter of the files themselves.

Sending File Attachments

Microsoft Entourage makes it easy to send individual or multiple file attachments with your messages. Here's how it's done:

1. Open a new e-mail message window by clicking the New button in Entourage's main window or just pressing COMMAND-N.

2. After you've written your message, click the paper clip icon to bring up the Choose Attachment dialog box.

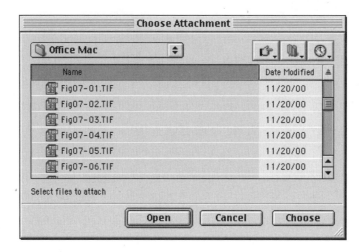

3. In the dialog box, locate and select the files you want to send. If you want to attach more than a single file, hold down the SHIFT key while selecting all the files. You can also select each file separately, which you will need to do if the files are in different locations on your drive or are located on shared drives.

CAUTION   *Do not send multiple attachments to members of AOL and CompuServe 2000. The e-mail systems for these sister services usually have difficulty handling attachments sent in this fashion. Instead, either send a single file with each message or use a file compression program to place all the files in a single archive. See the bulleted item, "Use File Compression with Care," in the "File Attachment Secrets" section later in the chapter for more advice on compressing files.*

4. To add the files to your e-mail message, click Choose. The title of the file will appear next to the Attachments label in your e-mail document window.

5. To see an expanded view of the file attachment window, click the disclosure triangle next to the Attachments label. From here, you can click the Add button to select more files, the Remove button to unattach files (this doesn't delete the files; it just detaches them from this message), and the Find button to search for a file you can't easily locate. The disclosure triangle can be clicked again to collapse the Attachments window.

GETTING THE MOST OUT OF ENTOURAGE

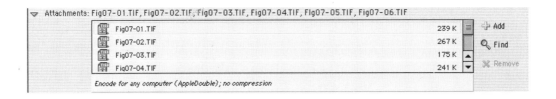

If the file itself is visible on your Mac's desktop or in a folder window when your e-mail window is open, you can just drag and drop the attachment directly into your message. This can be done with one or multiple files.

6. After you have added the file attachments you want, click the Send Now or Send Later button.

Before you send large files with your messages, you may want to check with recipients to determine the size of files they can receive. AOL limits file attachments from users outside the service to 2 megabytes. The limit is 10 megabytes on EarthLink. Your mileage may vary. If the file attachment is too large, the message may arrive without the attachment or not at all; when that happens, there is likely to be no message indicating that the file attachment was omitted.

Receiving File Attachments

If a file you receive has a file attached to it, you'll see a paper clip or attachments icon to the left of the name of the sender (in the From column). Here's how to work with such messages:

1. When you receive an e-mail message with an attachments icon, click the disclosure triangle to the left of the Attachments label to reveal the list of files.

2. If you want to open the file directly, click the Open button in the Attachments window, and the program originally used to create the document, or a compatible program, will be launched. If you have problems opening the file, check the next section for additional advice.

3. If you just want to save a file to your Mac's drive, click the Save button instead of performing step 2.

4. To remove a file attachment from the message window, click the Remove button. This is a good approach if you want to save the message but keep the Entourage e-mail database from growing too large; it can fill many megabytes on your Mac's hard drive if you've received lots of attachments.

File Attachment Secrets

As you can see, sending and receiving file attachments is easy, but preparing the files to send and handling the files that you receive is fraught with pitfalls and uncertainties.

Here are some commonsense file handling suggestions that will help both you and the recipients of your messages:

- **Make Sure Your Recipient Can Use the File**   For someone to read the files you send, the person must have an application that supports the file format. If you're not sure, ask the recipient first before preparing the file to send. If the recipient doesn't have the same application (Windows versions of a Mac application will usually read the same files if the version numbers of the programs are the same), try a more universally accepted format. For a word processor document, save as RTF (rich text format) text, which most word processors can easily read, or HTML text (which limits your formatting options, however). For image files, stick with common formats such as GIF, JPEG, and TIFF, which are usually easily read by many programs on the major computing platforms.

NOTE   *The files you create in Office 2001 are compatible with Office 97 and Office 2000 for Windows and also Office 98 for the Mac. Some special features of Office 2001 may not carry over, but the basic contents of the document should transfer without difficulty.*

- **Use Windows File Extensions When Needed**   It doesn't matter how you name a file for a fellow Mac user, so long as that person has a program that can read the file format. For Windows, you have to spell it out, using the proper three-letter file extension. A Word document, for example, has the .doc suffix. For Excel, it's .xls, and for PowerPoint, it's .ppt. Each of these programs can be set to automatically append the proper extensions in the Save As dialog box.

NOTE   *As you learned in "Setting Compose Preferences" earlier in the chapter, you can configure Entourage to automatically add the proper file extension for most files. I won't say all, as less common file formats may not be recognized.*

- **Use File Compression with Care**   Compressing a file reduces file size, sometimes by a large percentage. It helps you save time sending and receiving files, and this is especially important for large files or when your ISP charges you by the hour. On the Mac, the common compression format, StuffIt, is read by most Mac users, because a StuffIt compression program comes with most recent Macs. But if you intend to send your files to Windows users (or users of both platforms), such files are not normally readable, unless the Windows user gets a copy of the Windows version of StuffIt from the publisher, Aladdin Systems. Rather than put recipients through that process, you may be better off *not* compressing files unless you've made doubly sure the recipient can read them.

NOTE *As a corollary, Mac compression programs can usually read files created in the Zip format used for Windows. If you have StuffIt Deluxe 5.5 or later (the commercial versions of the program), you can use the DropZip utility provided with the software to prepare files for Windows users in their preferred compression format. In fact, that's precisely how I prepared the manuscript and illustrations for this book to send to my publisher.*

TIP *Since there are different versions of StuffIt, and an older version may not read files compressed with a newer one, it may be best to compress files using the .sea, or self-extracting, file format (a StuffIt preference option). That way, the decompression software is embedded in the file itself, and double-clicking it starts the expansion process. You'll also want to prepare files in older compression programs, such as Compact Pro and DiskDoubler, in .sea form.*

■ **Can't Open the File?** If your Mac is not able to open a file attachment, contact the sender and ask what program was used to create it. Even if you don't have the same program, you may be able to use the Insert or Import function in one of your Mac applications to bring up the file on your screen.

■ **Be Cautious of Unexpected or Unsolicited File Attachments** It's a sad fact that there are folks who transfer computer viruses via file attachments. Although most of these viruses infect the Windows platform, there are a few dozen Mac viruses out there as well. In addition, Word and Excel macro viruses are cross-platform offenders. If you receive a file you didn't expect (even if you know the person who sent it), *do not open the file*. Instead, write to the sender to inquire what the file is before you make the decision to open it. Watch out for e-mail from strangers with a subject line such as "Here's the file you expected," because you clearly didn't expect it, and the contents may produce unexpected consequences.

NOTE *Unless a file is opened, a virus in the file cannot infect your Mac. It's important to have up-to-date virus software at hand. Version 7.0 of Norton Anti-Virus from Symantec, for example, is designed to check for e-mail viruses. The program is also bundled with Norton SystemWorks for the Macintosh, which includes Norton Utilities and several other utility programs.*

■ **Watch Out for Virus-Warning Chain Letters**   If you get a message from someone warning about a virus that, in turn, asks you to pass it on to others, ignore the message! Chain letters containing such warnings are usually bogus and alarm folks unnecessarily. In addition, passing on chain letters isn't allowed on most online services, and all you may end up doing is jeopardizing your account with your ISP when you send such material.

Using HTML Formatting to Spruce Up Your Messages

Normally, Internet e-mail goes out as plain text, since the format can be read by all computing platforms, but you are apt to receive HTML formatted messages from time to time. You'll find that they have special text formatting similar to that in a word processor program. In addition, you'll find that they contain clickable links to Internet sites.

You can produce the same messages yourself, simply by using the HTML feature of Entourage. To activate this feature, just click the HTML button at the left of your e-mail message's formatting toolbar, just above the message text window. You can also choose HTML from the Format menu to activate this feature.

NOTE *Depending on the preferences you set for your e-mail, HTML formatting may be activated by default. It can be toggled off in the same way it's turned on, by clicking the HTML button or selecting HTML from the Format menu.*

When you click the button, the formerly dimmed formatting commands will become available, offering the following features, described from left to right:

NOTE   *With HTML formatting activated, the same commands shown on the formatting toolbar are also available from the Format menu. In addition, a Heading command allows you to set headlines in standard Web sizes.*

- **Font**   Choose from any installed font.

CAUTION   *For a recipient to see the message in the same font, the person must have that font, or a similar one, installed.*

- **Size**   Unlike most Mac programs, where sizes are specified in points, such as 10 point or 12 point, HTML font sizes are usually relative. You can choose Medium, Larger, Largest, Smaller, and Smallest.
- **Style**   Choose bold, italic, underscored, or teletype style, or any combination of the four.
- **Alignment**   Choose left, centered, or right alignment.
- **Lists**   You can choose a numbered list, a bulleted list (like this one), or just plain indents for outlines.
- **Font and Background Colors**   Choose the colors with care, so your document can be easily read by its recipients.
- **Horizontal Line**   Use this feature to add a horizontal line in the selected area of your document.

CAUTION   *Don't get carried away. Using multiple sizes, styles, and fonts can provide greater appeal to your message, but if you overdo it, the results may look like a ransom note.*

Creating Online Signatures

When you finish writing a message, no doubt you'll want to sign it. Wouldn't it be nice, though, to have Entourage automatically insert the appropriate signature into your message? You're in luck, because that's exactly what Entourage can do. You can even configure the program to store a custom signature for each online account.

How's how to set up an online signature:

1. With Entourage open, choose Signatures from the Tools menu to display the Signatures window.

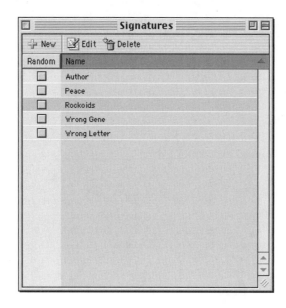

2. Click New to bring up a signature window; then type your signature.

NOTE   *It's customary to keep signatures short and sweet and avoid elaborate formatting. If you're using your account for business purposes, feel free to put in phone numbers, Internet addresses, and other contact information, but limit it to three or four lines.*

3. If you want to format the signature, click the HTML button in the signature window and then choose your formatting, just as described in the preceding section.

4. Click the signature text close box when your signature is finished and then close the Signatures window when you're finished creating online signatures.

5. To delete a signature, select it and click the Delete button.

6. To change an existing signature, select it and click the Edit button.

7. If you want to change signatures at random in your messages, click the Random check box next to the signature. (This technique, which simply puts up a different signature from your list each time you send a message, is most useful if you have a humorous signature.)

Once a signature has been created, it's available from the Signature pop-up menu in your new message window.

Inserting Signatures Automatically

If you always use the same signature for a particular account, you can configure that account so that the signature is automatically placed in the message body.

Just follow these steps:

1. With Entourage open, choose Accounts from the Tools menu.

2. Select the name of the account to which you want to attach a signature and click the Edit button.

3. With the Edit Account dialog box opened, click the Options tab; then choose a signature from the Default Signature pop-up menu.

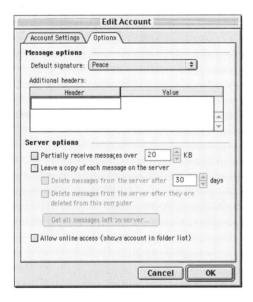

4. Click OK in the Edit Account dialog box to store your settings. Repeat these steps for each account to which you want to append a signature.

Rebuilding Entourage's Database

While some e-mail programs place messages in separate files, Entourage and others (including Outlook Express for the Mac) use single database files to store them all. This helps reduce file clutter, but at times it may also cause problems, particularly if you've deleted lots of messages or the file becomes corrupted due to possible directory damage on your Mac's drive or just a system crash.

The database files are located in a folder called Main Identity. The path is complex. First open the Documents folder on your Mac's startup drive. Then locate the Microsoft User Data folder, which contains the Office 2001 Identities folder. Main Identity is located within that folder. When you open this folder, shown here, you'll see a number of files that contain the messages you've received and saved, plus the various settings you've made to Entourage.

Name	Date Modified	Size	Kind
Database	Wed, Aug 23, 2000, 8:54 PM	448 K	Outlook Express document
Database Cache	Fri, Aug 18, 2000, 6:39 PM	64 K	Outlook Express document
Mailing Lists	Wed, Mar 8, 2000, 11:41 AM	64 K	Outlook Express document
Messages	Wed, Aug 23, 2000, 8:54 PM	704 K	Outlook Express document
Preferences	Wed, Aug 23, 2000, 8:54 PM	256 K	Outlook Express document
Rules	Tue, Mar 21, 2000, 9:56 AM	64 K	Outlook Express document
Schedules	Wed, Aug 23, 2000, 8:54 PM	64 K	Outlook Express document
Signatures	Sat, Dec 11, 1999, 4:36 PM	64 K	Outlook Express document

Main Identity — 8 items, 1.02 GB available

If you have problems running Entourage, particularly after a crash when the program is launched, you can usually fix the problem by rebuilding the database files. This will remove free space in the database and clean up the files. Here's how it's done.

CAUTION: Don't just throw out the files. If you do that, you'll lose all your saved e-mail, your Address Book, and preferences you've set, such as online signatures.

1. Quit all Office programs.

2. Launch Entourage and immediately hold down the OPTION key.

3. When you see a message asking if you want to rebuild the database, choose either Typical Rebuild, which makes basic repairs and compacts the files, or choose Advanced Rebuild, which makes more extensive repairs, but also removes any messages and folder lists you've created for Hotmail and IMAP accounts (meaning you'll have to download them again).

4. After selecting the kind of rebuilding you want performed, click the Rebuild button. You'll see a progress bar indicating the status of the process. This can take several minutes or longer to complete.

5. When the process is done, follow the directions about deleting files labeled Old in your Main Identities folder.

Introducing the Junk Mail Filter

It is ever-present. Just about everyone with an e-mail account receives such things: messages from unknown parties offering special products, work-at-home schemes, low-cost home loans, and the ability to take advantage of one money-making technique or another.

Many of these schemes are likely bogus, particularly if the message comes from a source you don't know. Regardless, the messages are usually annoying. They waste your time and fill your Inbox with material you don't want. Such unwanted messages are known as junk mail (just like regular postal mail of the same category) or *spam*.

NOTE   *Spam is also a well-known lunchmeat of mixed composition from Hormel. Sending mass unsolicited mailings to recipients also garners the same label.*

Fortunately, Entourage 2001 has a feature that helps you minimize e-mail clutter: the Junk Mail Filter (see Figure 7-13).

This marvelous feature examines the messages you receive and classifies those that are suspect as possible junk mail. One common indicator of such a message is an

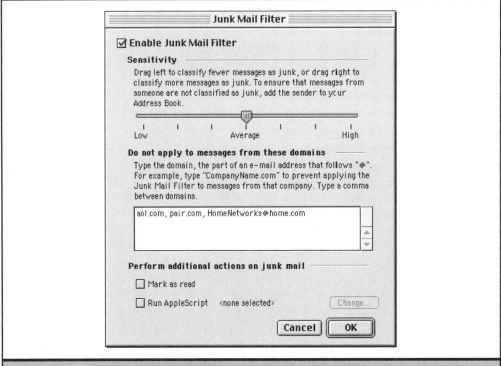

Figure 7-13.   *Use the Junk Mail Filter settings to eliminate clutter in your Inbox.*

apparently forged e-mail address, which is often identified by the use of a domain that differs from the one indicated in the path the message has taken. Another indicator is evidence that the message was relayed from a different e-mail server.

By default, when a suspect message is received, the title of the message receives the color that has been designated for junk mail. By default, it's gray and marked as read.

Here's how to set up this feature:

1. Go to the Tools menu and choose Junk Mail Filter to display the Junk Mail Filter window (again, have a look at Figure 7-13).

2. Click the check box labeled Enable Junk Mail Filter.

3. By default, the sensitivity slider, which determines whether a message may fit into the junk mail category, is placed right in the middle, Average. If you want to change the setting, drag the slider to the left or right.

4. To prevent messages from specific locations from being classified as junk, enter the address or just the domain (the information after the @ symbol) in the box labeled Do Not Apply to Messages from These Domains. Put a comma between each entry.

5. Click the OK button to save your settings.

NOTE   _It's a good idea to start with the default Average setting and see whether it's too sensitive or not sensitive enough. If it flags too few messages as junk, increase the sensitivity setting. If you find that messages that you do not consider junk are being mistakenly classified that way, reduce the sensitivity setting._

Are You a Junk Mailer?

The very idea may be insulting. You are as offended as anyone by junk e-mail, so how could you possibly become an offender?

Do you ever get messages from your friends with a "pass it on" subject? They tell you that if you send it to 10 people, you'll get money in the mail or be eligible for free gifts from Disney or a pair of jeans from the Gap. Such messages are commonly known as chain letters.

Others warn of viruses that will forever taint your computer and vaporize your hard drive. Well, perhaps I am exaggerating, but those messages can become quite outlandish.

True, there are genuine e-mail viruses, but many chain-type warnings are false and alarm folks needlessly. When you forward all such messages, even to recipients that are known to you, it's very likely you are fulfilling the design of the folks who perpetrate such scams. You are the one sending the junk mail.

Besides, chain letters are not allowed on most ISPs. If someone reports your conduct, you face the loss of your account. It's just not worth it. If you find your friends passing on such messages, gently remind them that it's just bad form.

Handling Junk Mail Filter Problems

For most purposes, the default setting ought to be sufficient to protect you from unwanted messages. However, if it's not working the way you want, here are some changes to consider:

- **Junk Mail Filter Doesn't Function**   Are you sure it's on? Choose Junk Mail Filter from the Tools menu and make sure the Enable Junk Mail Filter box is checked. If it is checked, move the sensitivity slider to a higher setting.

- **Junk Mail Filter Mistakenly Labels Messages as Junk**   Perhaps the filter is too sensitive. If you get a number of messages from mailing lists, the Average setting may be too sensitive. Just return to the Tools menu, select Junk Mail Filter, and reduce the sensitivity by dragging the sensitivity slider to the left. You may find it convenient to enter the actual address or just the domain names of the sources of mail you want to receive in the domain box so they're not flagged.

- **Too Few Junk Messages Are Being Flagged**   If the filter just isn't catching junk messages efficiently, you'll want to increase its level of protection. Choose Junk Mail Filter from the Tools menu, but this time move the sensitivity slider to the right to increase the filter's protection.

Additional Junk Mail Filter Actions

Normally, the Junk Mail Filter will simply flag a message with a different color, so you can separate it easily from the normal list of new messages. However, if you prefer to take more drastic action, you have some extra options.

In addition to adjusting the sensitivity slider and specifying domains that you want omitted from the Junk Mail Filter's checking process, there are two check boxes in the setup dialog box you'll want to consider:

- **Mark as Read**   When you check this option, suspected junk e-mail is marked as if you've already read it.

- **Run AppleScript**   Are you adept at AppleScript? Microsoft includes only a handful of predesigned scripts, which are located in the Entourage Script Menu Items folder, located within the Microsoft User Data folder inside the Documents folder. However, you can add your own scripts to increase the program's flexibility.

NOTE   *If you are interested in exploring the possibilities of using AppleScript with Entourage 2001, pay a visit to Microsoft's Web site at http://www.microsoft.com/MAC/products/ office/2001/entourage/applescript_ref.asp. There you'll be able to download a 97-page reference guide to using AppleScript with this program. The guide also includes some sample scripts to get you started.*

You can specify actions to perform on possible junk mail, including marking such messages as read and running an AppleScript. If you want to apply further actions to junk messages, such as filing them in a certain folder, you can create a rule for such actions. Because it is possible for non-junk messages to be mistakenly classified as junk, always review the messages in the junk category before deleting them.

Setting Message Rules

One of the powerful features of Entourage is the ability to apply one or more rules to your messages. This allows you to apply actions to specific messages automatically, as soon as the message is received. That way, you can place messages from specific sources in a particular folder, or even delete the message if it fits into what you regard as the junk category.

You can apply rules to all of your messages, whether incoming or outgoing or from newsgroups, and even establish multiple rules for a single message or different messages. The limit is your needs and your imagination. Since each rule can be instantly modified, you can test and tailor rules to your needs.

To use this feature, first you specify the criteria the message must meet for the rule to be applied. Then you specify the actions taken on messages that meet the criteria.

As an example, we will create a rule to designate that messages from a specific sender are to be deleted. In this case, we are using the rules feature to delete unwanted messages, but you can apply rules even to messages you want to keep.

Here's how to set up this rule:

1. With Entourage open, choose Rules from the Tools menu.

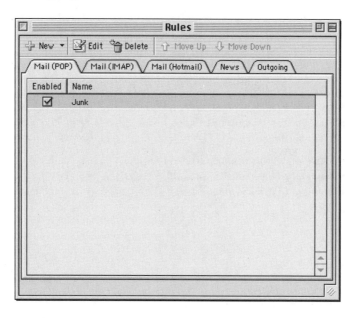

2. Click the tab that represents the kind of account to which you want the rule to apply. There are five to chose from, and the one you select depends on the Entourage feature you want.

3. Click the New button to create your rule.

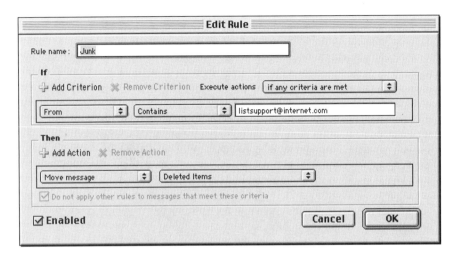

4. By default, one criterion and two pop-up menus will appear in the If category, and one action and two pop-up menus will appear in the Then category. You can click Add Criterion or Add Action to add extra steps to the rule. The Remove Criterion and Remove Action functions will delete the pop-up menus. The available criteria cover every element of your message, including From and To lines, message content, signatures, attachments, dates, message sorting categories, and so on.

5. In the Execute Actions pop-up menu, choose how the criteria are applied. You can specify whether the message must match all or only some of the criteria.

6. Click the left criterion pop-up menu to specify the message or folder category that applies. For this example, I chose From, since I want to delete all messages from a single sender.

7. Click the right criterion pop-up menu to specify which criterion in that message or folder category is applicable and then enter the category in the text field. In this case, I chose Contains and entered the e-mail address in the text field.

8. Now you want to apply actions to the messages that meet the standards. In the Then area, click the leftmost action pop-up menu to tell Entourage how the message that meets the criteria will be handled. In this case, I chose Move Message, but you have all sorts of options, which cover almost every aspect of message handling, including redirecting the message and sounding an alert when such a message arrives.

9. From the right action pop-up menu, choose how the action is completed. In this case, I chose Deleted Items. The choices depend on the action selection you've made.

NOTE *With dozens of possibilities for configuring a rule, you are limited only by your imagination and creativity. Each criterion or action you specify will produce a different set of methods for handling the messages.*

10. Click OK to complete the setup process.

Once a rule has been created, it can be turned off or on in the Rules dialog box. Click New to create more rules and Edit to alter a selected rule.

NOTE *If the rule isn't working as you expect, don't hesitate to use the Edit function to recheck the criteria and actions you've applied. It's easy to make a mistake, and a little testing will usually set things right.*

If you want to remove a rule, select it and click the Delete button.

TIP *You can manually apply rules to messages in a folder simply by selecting one or more of those messages. Choose Apply Rule from the Message menu; then select the rule you want to use from the submenu.*

A Look at Your ISP's Efforts to Fight Spam!

When you want to fight the war against junk e-mail, sometimes you can get help from your ISP. Most have strict rules against sending unsolicited e-mail, and the company will cancel the accounts of proven offenders.

Some take a more proactive stance. AOL, for example, as the largest online service, is a major target for junk mailers. As a result, AOL has taken some junk mailers to court to halt the practice. While junk mail is still prevalent on AOL, it's not as bad as it used to be. Since AOL's e-mail system is not accessible by Entourage, however, this matter is strictly academic.

The second largest ISP, EarthLink, inherited a useful junk mail filtering system when it merged with MindSpring: the Spaminator. When the feature is activated from the service's Web site, it automatically intercepts e-mail reaching the service that meets preset guidelines for junk mail.

The guidelines are largely based on e-mail addresses that appear forged or originate from known junk mail sources. While the Spaminator service stores intercepted e-mail at EarthLink's Web site for inspection, I've yet to find anything that didn't clearly fit the category of spam e-mail.

If your ISP doesn't have such a feature, you'll find Entourage's junk mail filter a useful substitute. It may not be as comprehensive, but it gets the job done.

TIP: One valuable resource for information about fighting junk mail is Paul Vixie's Mail Abuse Prevention System (MAPS), which you can access at http://www.mail-abuse.org/. This nonprofit site contains the IP addresses and names of ISPs that do not block spam, plus known sources of this annoying material. MAPS has also established a legal defense fund to cover the costs of fighting junk e-mail.

Setting an E-mail Schedule

Among the most effective Entourage 2001 features is the ability to send and retrieve e-mail using an automatic schedule. The schedule can be configured in a number of ways, such as automatically signing you on to your ISP before Entourage tries to retrieve a message and then keeping you online after the action is taken.

Here's how to use this very useful feature:

1. With Entourage open, choose Schedule from the Tools menu. This brings up the Schedules dialog box.

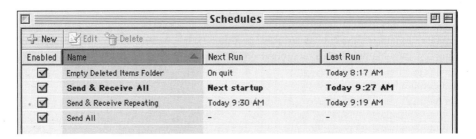

2. To create a new schedule, click the New button, which brings up the Edit Schedule dialog box similar to the one already configured, shown here.

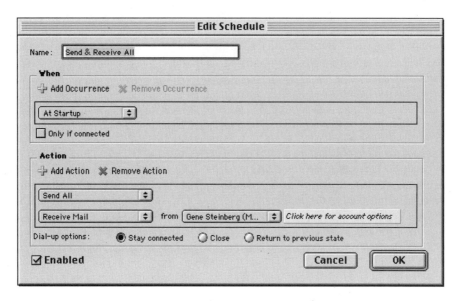

3. In the Name field, enter a description that applies to the kind of schedule you want. The one I used, Send & Receive All, is self-explanatory.

4. In the When category, choose when the schedule will run. It can be, as selected here, At Startup, which is when Entourage is launched, or when the program is quit. You can also set up a repeating schedule, such as every 20 minutes, during which Entourage will perform the actions you will specify.

5. If you want multiple criteria to apply, click the Add Occurrence button to specify another set of events that trigger an action.

6. If you want the schedule to run only when you're logged on to your ISP, select Only If Connected.

NOTE   *If you have an always-on connection via cable modem or DSL, the issue of being connected is basically moot.*

7. Under Action, specify that steps will occur when the schedule criteria are met. In the example shown in step 2, I've specified Send All, to cover all pending messages, and Receive Mail (from a specific e-mail account). You can click Add Action to specify additional e-mail addresses and additional actions taken on those e-mail addresses.

8. If you are connected to your ISP via modem, specify the Dial-up options you want.

9. Before completing your schedule, make sure Enabled is selected, so that the schedule will run as specified.

10. Click OK to store your new schedule.

NOTE   *To change a schedule, just open the Schedules dialog box from the Tools menu, click the schedule's title, and then click the Edit button. The same Edit Schedule dialog box just described will appear, where you can make the changes you want. You can remove a schedule by selecting it and clicking the Delete button.*

Summary

Microsoft Entourage provides an extensive array of options so you can customize your e-mail, giving it a custom look. In addition, there are plenty of ways to organize your Address Book, make sure e-mail attachments are handled correctly, and deal with the ever-present problem of junk e-mail.

In the next chapter, you'll take your e-mail management to the next step, taking full control of your personal information. You'll see how to create reminders and then perform specific actions on your messages and files when the appointed time comes.

Chapter 8

Introduction to the Entourage Contact Manager

Where do you place your personal and business contacts? In a little address or diary book, or perhaps, as your humble author does, on individual sheets of paper that are scattered to the winds whenever the door opens on a windy day? One of the great new features of Microsoft's Entourage is its fully integrated personal information manager. There's a full-featured address book that not only includes the names of your e-mail contacts, but can be configured to handle information about all personal and business contacts, including addresses, phone numbers, e-mail accounts, and even information about family members and custom notes that can include additional information, including directions to that person's home or office.

In addition, you can set up Entourage's full-featured Calendar planner and scheduler to remind you of important events, be they personal or business, and even send automatic e-mail messages to your contacts about special events.

In the following pages, you'll see how easy it is to dispense with those little notepads and let Entourage do your personal organizing for you. We'll get to the Calendar in Chapter 9.

Setting Up and Using the Entourage Address Book

In Entourage, the Address Book can contain an extensive array of information about your contacts, both online and otherwise. You can configure it to include just a person's name and e-mail address, or you can add a host of other information, including phone numbers, street addresses, and even their birthdays.

You can also easily configure the Address Book with special custom fields to reflect additional topic categories, such as thumbnail information you might need about sales contacts, including the kinds of car they own or the last computer they bought from your company, if you're in that business.

If the route to a contact's home or office is complex, you can access a map with illustrated driving instructions, so you won't get lost and miss the appointment. You can send a visual business card (known as a vCard) to introduce yourself, and you can add links to a contact's Web site and link a date, such as the birthday, to your Entourage Calendar.

It's all highly flexible and limited only by your imagination and creativity. What's more, the Address Book is shared with other Office applications, for even greater flexibility.

NOTE   *You'll find, for example, the Address Book listed on the Tools menu of Word 2001, for quick access to your contacts.*

Creating an Entourage Contact

To discover how flexible the Address Book feature is, we'll create a contact, using the Address Book's simple setup menu. Once you've seen how easy the Address Book is to use, we'll look at the rest of the features:

1. Click the Address Book folder in the Folder list.

NOTE   *If the Folder list isn't visible, just choose Folder List from the View menu to bring it back.*

2. With the Address Book displayed, click New, which brings up the Create Contact dialog box.

3. Enter the name and e-mail address of your contact. The pop-up menu can be used to indicate a work, home, or other e-mail address.

TIP   *Press TAB to move forward through the fields and SHIFT-TAB to move backward through the fields.*

4. In the Phone Numbers section, you can enter the contact's home or work phone numbers, and choose another phone category, such as Mobile Phone, from the pop-up menu.

5. The final fields are for the address of your contact. Click the pop-up menu to select which address is being added. The default is Work.

NOTE *We'll get to the More button in the next section.*

6. If you want to put the contact in a special category, click the arrow at the right of the Categories button at the top of the dialog box and choose the appropriate category from the list.

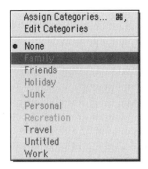

NOTE *You can assign multiple categories to a contact, if you like. That way, the contact can be more easily searched for later.*

7. After your entry is complete, click Save & Close at the top of the dialog box to store the contact. If you want to add more contacts, click Save & New instead.

8. Should you decide you don't want the entry, click the trash icon to delete it. This command is available from all contact information windows.

TIP *You can make a paper copy of your Address Book contacts at any time. Just click a name and click the Print button in the toolbar. To print the entire Address Book, select the folder and click the Print button, without selecting any name. Your printout will be formatted the same as in the preview window and alphabetized. The preview window function is described further in "Previewing a Contact," later in the chapter.*

Advanced Address Book Features

The simple instructions in the preceding section will set up the basic information you need for a contact in your Address Book, but it's by no means all the information you may want to include. There are a number of other information categories you can choose from if you use the expanded Address Book dialog box instead.

Here's how to get started.

1. Click Address Book in the Folder list (make sure the Folder list is active in the View menu if you don't see it).

2. In the Create Contact dialog box, click the More button to display the expanded view (see Figure 8-1).

3. On the Name and E-mail tab, enter the information in the fields. Press TAB to move from one field to the next or SHIFT-TAB to go back to a previous field.

4. To enter an e-mail address, click the E-mail field, and you'll see a blank field for the address, at the left of which will be the default category (Work).

5. If you want to change the category, click its name to bring up the choices.

6. Click the Add button to enter additional e-mail addresses. If you enter more than one e-mail address, you can designate a default entry with the Make Default button. This is the address that will be used for Entourage's AutoComplete feature.

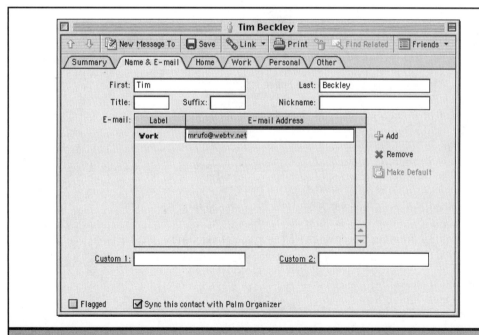

Figure 8-1.   *This is an expanded Address Book dialog box, where you can access all the features.*

NOTE *We'll get to the Custom fields in the next section.*

7. After the entries are complete, click the Home button if you want to add information to that category.

8. On the Home tab, enter the address information and phone numbers, as necessary. You can designate this address or the work address (coming next) as the default.

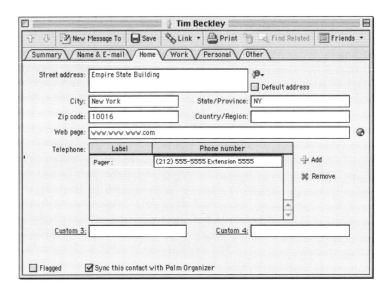

TIP *If you want to find driving directions to your contact, click the "i" icon to the right of the Street Address field. We'll discuss this clever feature in more detail in "Visiting Your Contacts: How to Get from Here to There," later in this chapter.*

9. Feel free to enter the contact's Web page, if you know the URL.

10. Click the Telephone field to enter the first phone number. It will be given the Home category.

NOTE *You can synchronize your contacts with your Palm Pilot or Palm OS–compatible handheld device. You'll learn how later in this chapter, in "Visiting Your Contacts: How to Get from Here to There."*

11. To include more phone numbers, click the Add button. Click the category label to the left of that number to designate the category for that number.

NOTE
You can click the Save button at any time to store your settings and then the close box to dismiss the Create Contact dialog box. You don't have to go through all the tabs to enter information this time, and you can leave any entry field blank if you prefer. A contact can be limited to just the name and e-mail address.

12. When you're finished with Home entries, click the Work tab to continue setting up your contact.

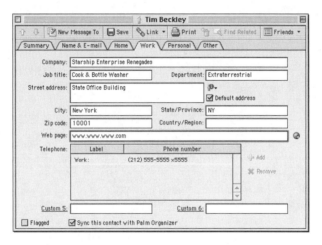

13. Enter the appropriate information in the various text entry fields on the Work tab. The Work tab includes Company and Job Title fields, but the choices are otherwise identical to those on the Home tab.

14. When you've completed your Home and Work entries, you can enter additional information about your contact on the Personal tab. Here you can enter important dates, names of spouse and children, and special interests.

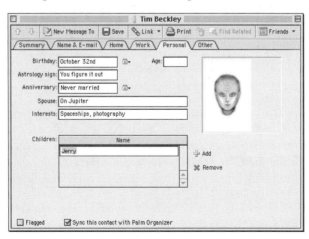

TIP *Any date entered in a field with a miniature calendar icon to its right can be set up as a Calendar entry. You'll learn how to use this feature in Chapter 9.*

15. If you want to include the contact's photo, locate the picture you want to include and drag and drop it into the drag-and-drop image window. It'll show up both here and in the Preview window for this contact.

NOTE *You can include any GIF, JPEG, PICT, or TIFF image. A click of the miniature or thumbnail of the photo will display the full-size image. The image can be replaced at any time with another picture, or you can drag it to the trash icon to remove it.*

16. When the Personal entries are complete, click the Other tab to enter more information about your contact.

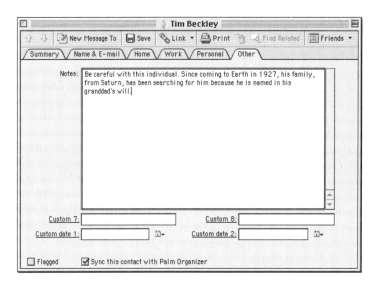

17. When your contact's information is complete, click the Save button and then the close box to dismiss the dialog box.

TIP *Here's a quick way to create a new Address Book contact from a message you've received. Hold down CONTROL and click any message; then choose Add Sender to Address Book from the context menu.*

Reviewing the Contact Toolbar Options

You've seen all the information you can enter on the Add Contact tabs. The toolbar also gives you some additional features you'll want to explore:

■ **Up and Down Arrows** Move to the next or the previous contact.

■ **New Message To**   Launch a new message window preaddressed to this contact.

■ **Save**   Store the information you've entered for your contact. Feel free to click this button regularly while creating or editing your contact, to be sure the information is up to date in case your Mac should crash.

■ **Link**   Link this contact to another Entourage feature, such as a task or Calendar event, or to one or more files.

■ **Print**   Print a copy of this contact's information.

■ **Trash**   Delete the entry.

■ **Categories**   Assign a category for this particular contact from the list of available categories.

Previewing a Contact

One particularly handy feature of Entourage is the ability to preview a contact. This feature enables you to see all the essential information for a contact conveniently displayed on a single screen.

To use this feature, locate the contact you want to check out in the Address Book folder and click it once. The preview will then appear on your screen (see Figure 8-2). After you've finished viewing the contact's information, click the close box to dismiss the preview.

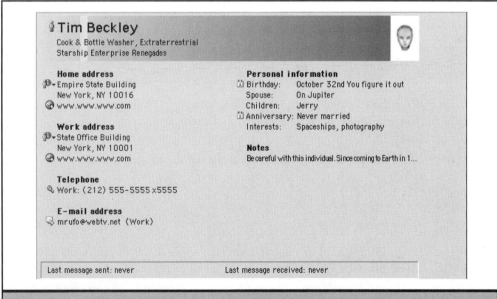

Figure 8-2.   *This is a preview of a typical Entourage contact entry.*

If you want to actually edit the contact, click the person icon to the left of the name to bring up the full Create Contact dialog box.

How to Review Contact Information

While the preview offers all the basic information about a contact in one convenient message window, you'll need to see the completed tabs in the Create Contact dialog box if you want to make changes.

Here's how to bring them up:

1. Locate the contact you want to edit in the Address Book folder.

2. Double-click the listing or choose Open from the toolbar to open any selected contact.

3. Click the tab you want to edit.

4. To see the entire listing, or a summary, on one screen, click the Summary tab.

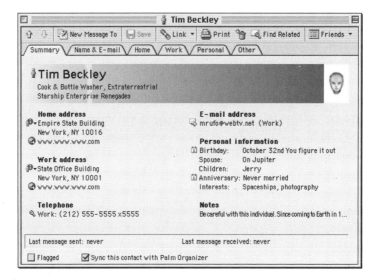

5. To see other contacts, double-click the entries. You can also use the Previous and Next arrows to see other entries.

6. Click the close box to dismiss the dialog box.

Magnifying Phone Numbers

A cool feature of the Address Book is the ability to magnify a phone number listing. This is particularly useful if your phone is some distance from your Mac's display.

To see the magnified view of a phone number, do the following:

1. Locate the contact in your Address Book.

2. Click the entry to see the preview.

3. On the preview screen, click the magnifying glass icon next to the phone number for an enlarged view.

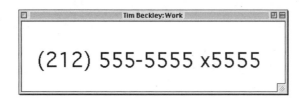

4. Click the close box to dismiss the phone number.

NOTE *Sorry to say, you cannot copy and paste the magnified phone number—nothing is perfect. You can, though, use your Mac to create a screen picture by using the shortcut COMMAND-SHIFT-3.*

Checking Messages Exchanged with a Contact

One of the particularly useful features of Entourage is the ability to track the messages you've exchanged with a contact. This provides a quick way to review your transactions with a client or to refresh yourself on recent gossip you've exchanged with a friend or family member.

This feature uses Entourage's highly flexible Find option to locate the material. Just follow these steps:

1. With Entourage open, locate the contact in your Address Book folder.

2. Click the contact's name to select the contact and bring up the preview.

3. On the Edit menu, choose Find Related Items. Entourage will search its message database for all the e-mail sent to and received from that contact (see Figure 8-3).

4. Click any message to display its contents.

5. When you're done, click the close box to dismiss the search window.

Visiting a Contact's Web Page

Entourage's Address Book has still more features you'll want to use, such as the ability to go right to a contact's Web page. To use this feature, follow these steps:

1. Open Entourage.

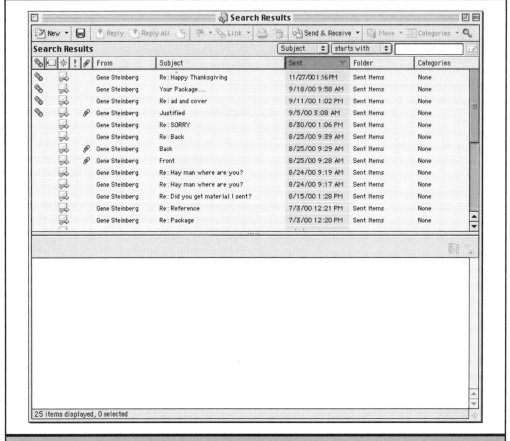

Figure 8-3.   *Entourage locates e-mail exchanged with your contact.*

2. In the Address Book, double-click a contact's name to bring up the full listing.

3. Click a tab that contains a Web page for that contact. You may have one on both the Home and Work tabs.

4. Click the Web icon to the right of the Web Page field. This will bring up that Web page on your chosen Web browser.

5. When you're finished viewing the page, you can quit your browser and close the contact's listing.

Visiting Your Contacts: How to Get from Here to There

As you can see so far, the Entourage Address Book has more features than you might imagine at first glance. Another particularly useful one is the ability to actually view a contact's location on a map and to get driving directions from your location to that contact's home or office.

Here's how:

1. With Entourage open, locate the contact's name and click it to bring up the preview.

2. Click the icon to the left of the address, which will bring up the choices shown here. You can display the contact's location on a map or receive driving directions from your home or work address.

> Show on Map
> Driving Directions from Home
> Driving Directions from Work
> Copy Name and Address to Clipboard

3. To see a map, choose the Show on Map option. Your Web browser will be launched, and you'll be logged on to your ISP if you're not already connected. Then the contact's location will be displayed on an Expedia.com Web page (see Figure 8-4).

4. If you want directions to the contact's location, choose the Driving Directions from Home or Driving Directions from Work option in the menu described in step 2. Regardless of the distance you have to travel, you'll see detailed instructions.

5. To print a copy of these instructions, choose Print from your browser's File menu.

6. Quit your Web browser and close your contact's window when you're done.

CAUTION *Entourage can give you driving instructions only if you've created a contact for yourself in Entourage and entered your home and work addresses. After you've created the listing, select it and choose This Contact Is Me from the Contact menu, which appears when the Address Book folder is selected.*

Using Entourage's vCard Feature

A vCard is an Internet-based business card that displays all the basic information on a contact in one convenient place. To use the feature, follow these instructions:

1. With Entourage open, locate your Address Book in the Folder list.

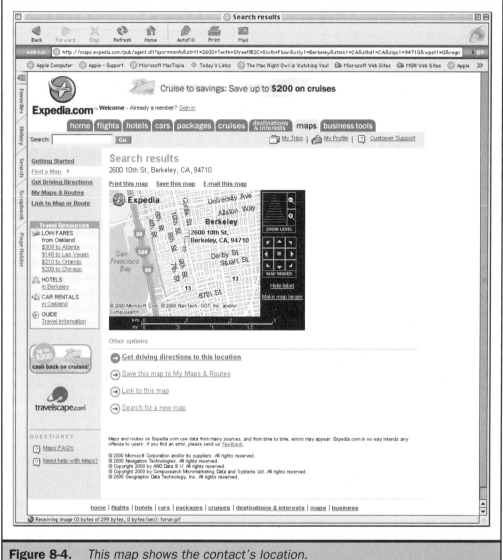

Figure 8-4.   *This map shows the contact's location.*

    2. Click the name of the contact for which you want to see a vCard.

    3. From the Contact menu, choose Forward as vCard and specify the e-mail address to which you want to send the card.

4. When the recipient receives the card, the person will see the very same summary information you have.

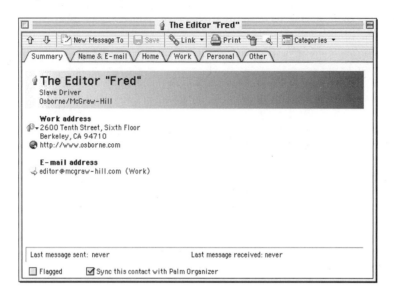

Sending a Message via the Address Book

Ready for one more Address Book feature? All right; here's how you can send an e-mail message to a contact from within the Address Book display.

1. With Entourage running, click the Address Book and locate the contact.

2. Click the contact's name to bring up the preview listing.

3. Click the e-mail icon next to the contact's e-mail address. This will produce a preaddressed message window. From here, just follow the normal rules of setting up e-mail, entering the subject line and message body before you send the message.

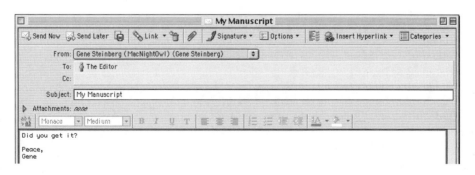

GETTING THE MOST
OUT OF ENTOURAGE

Chapter 6 includes more information about using Entourage's e-mail features.

NOTE   *You can also use the full Create Contact dialog box to access the same feature, by choosing New Message To from the toolbar.*

Tips and Tricks for Creating an Address Book Group

If you have a number of contacts in your Address Book that fit a specific category, you can create an Address Book group that puts them all in a single listing. This is useful for business associates, family members, club members, or a list of the members of your local computing club, to name a few examples.

Each of the names in the Address Book does not even have to have a separate contact entry, though it's better if they do (so you can incorporate all the information you have about that contact in a single location).

Here's how to create a group:

1. With Entourage open, click the Address Book folder.
2. Click the New Group button, which brings up a dialog box where you can insert your entries for the group (see Figure 8-5).
3. In the Group Name text field, give the group a name. You'll probably want to choose something that easily identifies the category into which the contacts all fit, such as In-laws.
4. Click the Add button for each contact you want to add to the group.
5. Type the name of the first group member. If you've already sent messages to that person, or if you've already created a contact for that person, Entourage's AutoFill feature will produce a pop-up menu where you can easily select the proper address.
6. Click Remove to delete any selected entry.
7. After the entries are complete, click Save Group to store the listings.
8. If you want to delete a group, just click the group's name and click the Delete button. Click Delete at the "Are you sure?" prompt to complete the action.

NOTE   *If you prefer that each recipient not see the others' names, click the option Don't Show Addresses When Sending to Group. Perhaps you'd rather not have one relative know another is on the list.*

Address Book Troubleshooting

If you follow the steps presented so far, you should be able to easily configure and use your Address Book. But there may be times when things do not work quite as they should, although those situations should be rare.

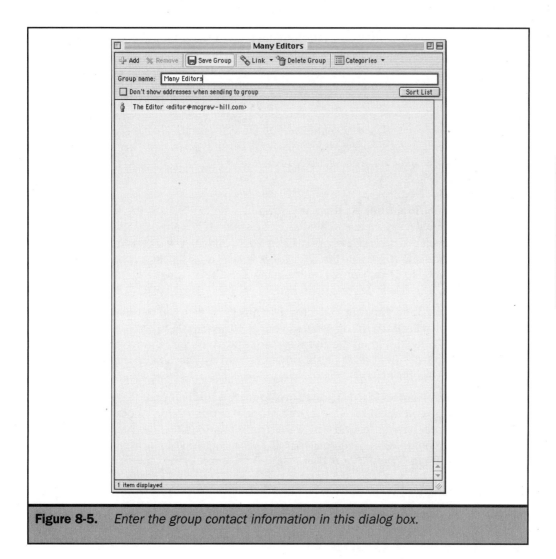

Figure 8-5.   *Enter the group contact information in this dialog box.*

Here are a few potential problems and their common solutions:

■ **Can't Add Contact's Photo**   Entourage will work with any photo format supported by Apple's QuickTime software, which is a standard part of the Mac OS. The usual formats are GIF, JPEG, PICT, and TIFF. If the format isn't supported, you can't add the photo.

NOTE   *The best formats are GIF and JPEG, since the files can be easily read across computing platforms without the recipient having to get additional software.*

■ **Can't Organize Contacts**   All of the contacts you add to Entourage are stored in a single Address Book. You can organize an entry into a category simply by choosing the proper category label. You can also use the groups feature, described in the preceding section of this chapter, to subdivide your list of contacts.

TIP   *You can create a separate Address Book file by creating a new Entourage identity, by choosing the Switch Identity command from the File menu. After you go through the standard setup dialog boxes for the new identity, you'll have a brand-new Address Book that you can configure. You will have to close all other Office applications to create that extra identity, however.*

■ **Individual Identities Appear in Group Messages**   This is the way the program works normally. The name of each member appears in such messages. If you prefer to protect a recipient's privacy, however, you can open the group's dialog box and then click the Don't Show Addresses When Sending to Group check box. That's the equivalent of using Bcc; the recipients do not see the names of the others in the group list.

■ **Can't Rename a Custom Field for a Contact**   When you name a custom field, the name extends to all contacts in your Address Book. When you change the name of a custom field, the change will show up in the other contacts as well. Since there are 10 custom fields, however, you may be able to choose another one for your changes.

■ **Imported Contact List Information Appears Under Contact Notes**   In importing contact information from other programs using a comma- or tab-delimited text file, Entourage uses mapping to match the names of the information fields in the imported file to the ones in your Address Book. If it cannot find a match, it puts that extra information in the Notes category. When you import the contact list, you will see a dialog box where you can manually map the extra fields and reduce the clutter of extraneous information.

Creating and Using Links

An Entourage action doesn't live in a vacuum, all by itself. One of my favorite Entourage features is the ability to link one item to another or, in fact, to any file stored on your Mac. This enables you to access multiple items with a single act, without having to search for messages, tasks, Calendar events, or even individual files.

For example, you can use a link when you schedule a meeting with a business contact who is listed in your Address Book. To prepare yourself for the meeting, you can set up a link to the person's contact information, messages you've exchanged with the contact, files, reminders, and so on. That way, you can be ready for the meeting without having to manually open each file that you just happened to forget to check.

Here's how to use links:

1. With Entourage open, click the item to which you want to add a link, such as a message or Address Book entry.

2. Click the arrow adjacent to the Link button in Entourage's toolbar, which produces the pop-up menu shown here.

NOTE   *You will see the message "No linked items" if a link hasn't been created previously.*

3. Choose a link option. You have the following choices:

- **Open Links**   Open your existing list of Links and link to one of the existing items.

- **Messages**   Whatever category applies to the item selected will appear here, along with a submenu of other items to which links have been attached. The illustration in step 2 shows the Messages category.

- **Link to Existing**   This submenu, shown here, allows you to link to an existing Entourage item, such as a message, Calendar event, task, note, contact, group, or file.

NOTE   *You can link an Entourage item to any file on your Mac or a shared volume, even if the file was created in a program other than one of the Microsoft Office applications.*

■ **Link to New** Use this submenu to apply a link to a new Entourage message, Calendar event, task, note, contact, or group. The action will bring up the appropriate New window.

4. If you link to a file, a standard Open dialog box appears in which you can select the file to which you want to link. When you've selected the file or files for the link, click the Link button to store the setting.

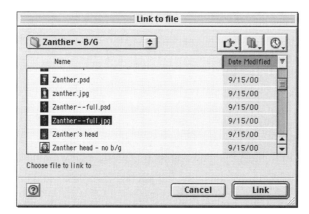

5. Click the close box to complete the link process.

Fast Steps for Removing a Link

After a link has served its purpose or you don't need it any more, you can avoid link clutter by deleting it.

To remove a link, follow these steps:

1. With Entourage open, click the item for which you want to remove the link.

2. Using the arrow next to the Link button, click Open Links from the submenu, or click the Link button to open the link window.

3. Select the item from which you want to remove the link.

4. Click the Remove Link button.

5. Click the close box when you're done.

Adjusting Entourage Panes

The three panes that display information in Entourage are easy to customize to your taste, just by following a few simple steps.

Here are the options that are available:

- **Resizing Panes**   Place the pointer on the divider between panes and, when the pointer changes to a double-headed arrow, click the mouse. With the mouse button held down, drag the divider to a new location. The pane will automatically be resized the way you want. You can resize the pane both horizontally and vertically.

- **Add or Delete a Column**   From the View menu, choose Columns. Then click on the name of the column you want to add or remove. When a column is added, it will be displayed with a check box in the submenu.

- **List Sorting**   It's easy to sort a folder list. Just click a column heading, and the sorting procedure will be changed to sort on that column. You can reverse the sorting order of messages sorted by date simply by clicking the arrow in that category label.

Solving Message Viewing Problems

When you have all your messages organized the way you like, they should be readily accessible. If you can't see them, there are some basic steps you can follow to bring them back again:

- **Check Your Filter**   Perhaps you applied a viewing filter to a message list. If you see the message "Filter applied" next to a name, you will want to remove the filter. Filters may be Unread Only, Flagged Only, or Threaded, all available in the View menu. Deselect each checked filter in turn and see if the messages return.

- **Check Your Rules**   Perhaps you've applied a rule to a specific message category. A rule may automatically delete a message or move it to a different folder. Select Rules from the Tools menu and see which rules may apply. Double-click any rules in the list that seem to apply to see what actions you've specified. You can easily edit or delete rules that mistakenly affect a group of messages.

- **Crossed Out Messages Cannot Be Deleted**   If you have an IMAP account, messages marked for deletion are crossed out in the message list for that account. You can remove the listing for the messages by choosing the option to hide deleted IMAP messages on the Read tab of the Mail & News Preferences window. If you've marked a message to be deleted from an IMAP server, go to the Edit menu and choose Purge Deleted Items. Another option is to set up your e-mail preferences to move automatically deleted messages to the Deleted Items folder.

GETTING THE MOST OUT OF ENTOURAGE

■ **Threaded Messages Don't Sort**   All right; this problem is one not as easily fixed as some of the others. The list of threaded messages, such as the ones in a newsgroup, cannot be sorted normally. You can try using the filtering feature to remove the Subject field and then sort by the From category instead.

Creating and Using Entourage Notes

Sticky notes are everywhere. I've seen them on computer monitors, refrigerators, across desks (and don't ask me where they are found in my office—everywhere is an understatement). A sticky note can be used for questions, ideas, shopping lists—anything that you can commit to pen and paper. You may, as I do, put directions to the home or office of a contact on a sticky note, which is then appropriately stuck to the dashboard of your car.

Entourage lets you create its own brand of notes, which are stored in the application, so you don't clutter your Mac's desktop or physical desktop with this stuff.

To use the Notes feature, just follow these steps:

1. With Entourage open, click the Notes icon in the Folder list (if there's no Folder list, choose View and then Folder List).

2. To create a new note, click New with Notes selected. This brings up a blank note window (see Figure 8-6).

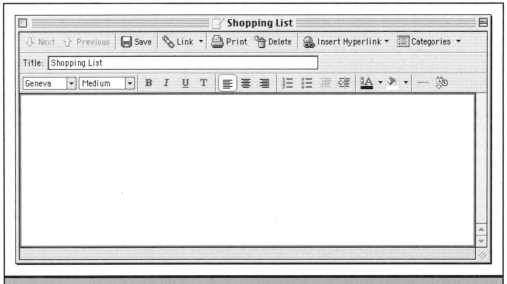

Figure 8-6.   *A note is somewhat like a miniature word processing document.*

3. Enter a title for your note in the Title field.

4. Click TAB to move to the message field and type your note text. You can use the formatting toolbar to give you the same range of formatting options as for a regular message with HTML formatting turned on. Here are the choices:

   - **Typeface**   Click the typeface's name to bring up a list of the fonts stored on your Mac.

   - **Size**   Choose relative font sizes from the size menu.

   - **Style**   Click the buttons for bold, italic, underscored, and teletype text.

   - **Alignment**   Make your note left, centered, or right aligned.

   - **Lists**   Put the contents of the note into a numbered or bulleted list. This does wonders for a shopping list.

   - **Special Formatting**   Give your text or background a custom color or add a horizontal line to your note.

   - **Date and Time**   Automatically insert the current date and time into your note.

5. Click Insert Hyperlink to add a link from your Internet Explorer Web browser to your message. Such links may include the current browser window or your Favorites list or History list (the list of sites you've recently visited).

6. If you want to place your note in a particular category, click the down arrow at the right of the Categories button and select the category you want.

7. When you are finished writing your note, click Save to store it in the Notes folder.

8. If you want to print the note, click the Print button.

NOTE   *Notes can be removed by clicking the Delete button in the Note window or by selecting the note in your Notes folder and pressing DELETE. In either case, you'll need to acknowledge the action by answering the "Are you sure?" prompt.*

9. If you want to edit the note later, open it in the Notes folder by double-clicking it; then make your changes. Click Save again to store your changes.

Using Entourage to Synchronize with Palm Pilot

Do you have a Palm Pilot handheld device or one of the Palm OS models from such companies as Handspring or Sony? You can synchronize your contacts between the Palm device and Entourage. When you synchronize the information, the Entourage contacts, Calendar events, notes, and tasks can be shared between your computer and the Palm device.

NOTE   *Although Palm OS handhelds offer e-mail features, there is, as of the time this book went to press, no way to synchronize your Entourage e-mail with your Palm OS e-mail.*

Here's how to perform the synchronizing operation:

NOTE *To accomplish this task, your Palm handheld must be using version 2.0 or later of the Palm OS. Check the manufacturer's Web site for the updates you need. You also need version 2.6.1 or later of the Palm Desktop software.*

1. Install the Entourage Conduit application. This program is included with the Microsoft Office 2001 Value Pack. We discuss this subject in more detail in Chapter 2.

NOTE *When you install this item, the matching Palm conduits are disabled.*

2. Make sure that your Entourage identity and the user name in your handheld are identical. It doesn't matter which name you choose. You can change your user name in Entourage by selecting Switch Identity from the File menu. In the Identity dialog box, click Rename and then enter your new name.

3. After the Entourage conduit is installed, specify the synchronizing method you want to use and how to handle custom fields in contacts. This is done by launching the HotSync Manager application and then choosing Conduit Settings in the HotSync menu.

4. From the list of conduits, choose Entourage Conduit.

5. Connect the handheld's cradle to your Mac's serial or USB port (which you use depends on the kind of Mac you have and the interface available with your handheld).

6. Click the HotSync button. This will activate the synchronizing operation.

If you have any difficulty with this process, consult the user manual for your handheld.

Cool Keyboard Shortcuts

One artifact of Microsoft's Windows lineage and a benefit to all users of Microsoft software is the liberal sprinkling of keyboard shortcuts. Most important functions can be accessed via one shortcut or another. You'll find many listed as you navigate through the various menu bar commands, but rather than have to remember them all, here's the complete list, by category.

NOTE *It is no coincidence that many of the shortcuts are identical to those in other Office programs or to standard Mac OS conventions.*

Office Assistant

All of the following functions work as advertised, so long as the Office Assistant is active and is visible to you.

CAUTION *You will find many similar keyboard shortcuts as you move from feature to feature in the following listing. They are context sensitive; that is, they depend on which feature is selected to work properly with that feature.*

Shortcut	Function
HELP	Displays Assistant's help search window.
ESC	Cancel an assistant message or tip.

Entourage Function

The following keyboard shortcuts are used to access common functions for Entourage.

Shortcut	Function
HELP	Activates Assistant's help search window.
SHIFT-COMMAND-Q	Switch to another Entourage identity (not Clark Kent).
COMMAND-S	Save a document or item.
OPTION-COMMAND-P	Automatically print one copy of the selected message without changing printer setup options.
COMMAND-Z	Undo the last action.
SHIFT-COMMAND-P	Invoke the Project Gallery.

Entourage Window and Dialog Box

You can use the following keyboard commands when you're within an Entourage window or dialog box.

Shortcut	Function
COMMAND-1	Open the main Entourage window or, if open, make it active.
COMMAND-2	Bring up the Address Book or, if open, make it active.

Shortcut	Function
COMMAND-3	Bring up the progress window or, if open, make it active.
COMMAND-4	Open the Calendar or, if open, make it active. Repeating this keyboard combination will take you through the various Calendar views: Day, Week, and Month.
COMMAND-5	Open the Task list or, if open, make it active.
COMMAND-6	Open the Notes list or, if open, make it active.
COMMAND-7	Open the Link Maker or, if open, make it active.
COMMAND-8	Open the error log (if errors have been logged) or, if open, make it active.
COMMAND-O	Open the feature or folder selected in the Folder list.
COMMAND-; (semicolon)	Bring up the standard General Preferences dialog box.
SHIFT-COMMAND-; (semicolon)	Bring up the Mail & News Preferences box.
COMMAND-~ (tilde)	Move through open windows in Entourage.
SHIFT-COMMAND-~ (tilde)	Move backward through open windows in Entourage.
COMMAND-W	Close the active window.
OPTION-COMMAND-W	Close the currently active window and all other active items and return to the main Entourage window.
TAB	Move ahead through the fields in a dialog box.
SHIFT-TAB	Move backward through the fields in a dialog box.
CONTROL-TAB	Move ahead through the tabs in a dialog box.
SHIFT-CONTROL-TAB	Move backward through the tabs in a dialog box.

Entourage Message List

You can use the following keyboard shortcuts when working with a list of mail or news messages.

Shortcut	Function
COMMAND-N	Begin a new message.
SHIFT-COMMAND-N	Create a new folder.

Shortcut	Function
COMMAND-O	Open the selected message.
COMMAND-\ (slash)	Display or hide the preview pane.
COMMAND-A	Select all the messages in the active pane.
SHIFT-COMMAND-A	Deselect all messages in the active pane.
COMMAND-D	Make a duplicate of the message.
COMMAND-DELETE or DELETE	Remove or delete the message.
COMMAND-Y	Turn the feature to display only unread messages on or off.
SHIFT-COMMAND-Y	Turn the feature to display only flagged messages on or off.
COMMAND-T	Mark the selected messages as read (whether read or not).
SHIFT-COMMAND-T	Mark the selected messages as unread (whether read or not)
COMMAND-L	Refresh the message list for IMAP, Hotmail, and POP accounts.

Entourage Category

You can sort your messages by category for convenience, and here are some keyboard shortcuts to ease the process.

Shortcut	Function
COMMAND-, (comma)	Assign a selected item to a category.
COMMAND-S	Make the selected category the primary category.

Entourage Search

A convenient feature of Entourage is its extensive array of message search options.

Shortcut	Function
COMMAND-F	Find the text in the items.
COMMAND-G	Find the next match to your text search request.
COMMAND-H	Find the next occurrence of the text you've selected.
COMMAND-. (period)	Cancel an operation.
OPTION-COMMAND-F	Display the Advanced Find window.

Entourage Notes

Entourage's Notes feature provides a convenient way to write a short message without having to bring up Microsoft Word. Here are some keyboard shortcuts for this feature.

Shortcut	Function
COMMAND-N	Open a new note.
COMMAND-O	Open the note you've selected.
COMMAND-A	Select all the notes in the active pane.
SHIFT-COMMAND-A	Deselect all notes.
COMMAND-D	Make a duplicate copy of a note.
COMMAND-DELETE or DELETE	Delete the selected or open note.
COMMAND-[	Close the note that's open and reopen the previous note.
COMMAND-]	Close the note that's open and open the next note in the list.

Entourage Tasks

The Tasks feature of Entourage is highly flexible, with plenty of shortcuts.

Shortcut	Function
COMMAND-N	Open a new task.
COMMAND-O	Open the task you've selected.
COMMAND-A	Select all the tasks in the active pane.
SHIFT-COMMAND-A	Deselect all tasks.
COMMAND-D	Make a duplicate copy of a task.
COMMAND-DELETE or DELETE	Delete the selected or open task.
COMMAND-[	Close the task that's open and reopen the previous note.
COMMAND-]	Close the task that's open and open the next note in the list.

Entourage Calendar

The Entourage Calendar does a whole lot more than tell you the day of the week. It also has a number of useful keyboard shortcuts, listed here.

Shortcut	Function
COMMAND-4	Move through Calendar views: Day, Week, and Month.
COMMAND-N	Open a new Calendar event, if Calendar is selected.
COMMAND-O	Open the Calendar event you have selected.
COMMAND-DELETE or DELETE	Delete the selected Calendar event.
COMMAND-Y	Change the view to include today's date.
COMMAND-[	This shortcut has three functions, depending on the Calendar view selected: **Day View** Move to the previous day. **Week and Work Week View** Move to previous week. **Month View** Move to previous month.
COMMAND-]	This one has three functions, depending on the kind of view selected for the Calendar: **Day View** Move to next day. **Week and Work Week View** Move to the next week. **Month View** Move to the next month.

Entourage Address Book

Your Address Book is a full-featured repository of your online contacts, and it also contains phone numbers, physical addresses, and other information. Here are the shortcuts.

Shortcut	Function
COMMAND-N	Open a new contact.
COMMAND-O	Open the contact you have selected.
COMMAND-\ (slash)	Open or hide the preview pane.
COMMAND-A	If the Address Book is active, select all contacts.
SHIFT-COMMAND-A	If the Address Book is active, deselect all contacts.
COMMAND-D	Make a copy of the contact.

Shortcut	Function
COMMAND-DELETE or DELETE	Remove the selected contact.
COMMAND-[	Close the contact that is open and open the previous one.
COMMAND-]	Close the contact that is open and open the next one.

Entourage Message

Here are some handy keyboard shortcuts for your e-mail and news messages; some are complex, performing a variety of functions.

Shortcut	Function
COMMAND-O	Open the message you have selected in a new window.
COMMAND-[	Open the previous message.
COMMAND-]	Open the next message.
COMMAND-=	Enter the sender of the selected message in the Address Book.
SHIFT-COMMAND-M	Moves the selected message to the folder selected from the dialog box that appears when you invoke this combination.
SHIFT-COMMAND- - (hyphen)	Use a smaller size for the text displayed in the open message or preview pane.
SHIFT-COMMAND-=	Use a larger size for the text displayed in the open message or preview pane.
SHIFT-COMMAND-H	Display or conceal Internet header information.
CONTROL-[	Bring up the previous unread message.
CONTROL-]	Bring up the next unread message.
SPACEBAR	Scroll down to the next text screen or, at the end of the message, to the next unread message.
SHIFT-SPACEBAR	Scroll up to the previous text screen.
OPTION-SPACEBAR	Scroll down to the next text screen. If you're at the end of a message, the current message will be deleted, and the next unread message will be opened.

Shortcut	Function
Hold down the SPACEBAR	Scroll slowly and continuously down through a message.
OPTION-COMMAND-[	Delete the current message and open the previous message.
OPTION-COMMAND-]	Delete the current message and display the next one.
CONTROL-OPTION-[	Delete the current message and display the previous unread message.
CONTROL-Option-]	Delete the current message and display the next unread message.
DELETE (DEL)	Delete the open or selected message.
OPTION-COMMAND-DELETE	Delete the open message and close the open message window.

Entourage Threaded Message

Message threading groups news messages in special topic folders. These shortcuts apply to this type of message.

Shortcut	Function
CONTROL-SHIFT-[	Go back to a previous thread in an unread message and read the last unread message.
CONTROL-SHIFT-]	Go to the next thread in an unread message and read the first unread message.
SHIFT-COMMAND-[	Open the last message in the previous message thread.
SHIFT-COMMAND-]	Open the first message in the next message thread.

Entourage New Message

The keyboard shortcuts that follow are used for opening a new message, addressing it, and sending it.

Shortcut	Function
COMMAND-N	Open a new message window.
COMMAND-K	Post the message that's opened.

Shortcut	Function
OPTION-COMMAND-K	Move the open message to the Outbox, where it will be sent the next time you access messages from the mail server.
COMMAND-M	Send all the messages in your Outbox and receive all your new e-mail and news messages.
SHIFT-COMMAND-K	Send all the messages waiting in the Outbox.
COMMAND-S	Save the open message in the Drafts folder.
COMMAND-E	Select one or more attachments to add to the open message.
OPTION-COMMAND-L	Spell check the open message.
SHIFT-COMMAND-C	Check recipient names in the open message from your default Directory Service.

Entourage Message Response

The keyboard shortcuts that follow are used for replying to a message.

Shortcut	Function
COMMAND-R	Reply to the sender of an open message; for a mailing list message, the response goes to the mailing list sender.
SHIFT-COMMAND-R	Reply to all those in the To and Cc message categories.
OPTION-COMMAND-R	Restrict the response strictly to the sender of the message from a mailing list.
COMMAND-J	Forward the opened message to one or more new recipients.
OPTION-COMMAND-J	Redirect the original message to different recipients.

Entourage Message Formatting

The keyboard shortcuts that follow are used for formatting the text in your message, assuming you have the HTML option selected.

Shortcut	Function
COMMAND-B	For HTML messages or signatures, make the selected text bold.
COMMAND-I	For HTML messages or signatures, make the selected text italic.
COMMAND-U	For HTML messages or signatures, underline the selected text.

Office-Type Text Editing

If you activate the option in the Preferences dialog box to use standard Microsoft Office text editing, you'll have the choices listed here. You'll notice that they differ somewhat from standard Mac OS editing keyboard shortcuts.

Shortcut	Function
COMMAND-A	Select all text in a message or folder.
LEFT ARROW	Move the insertion point to the left by one character.
RIGHT ARROW	Move the insertion point to the right by one character.
UP ARROW	Move the insertion point up by one line.
DOWN ARROW	Move the insertion point down by one line.
OPTION-UP ARROW	Move the insertion point to the top of the current or previous screen or to the top of the current selection.
OPTION-DOWN ARROW	Move the insertion point to the bottom of the current or next screen or to the end of the current selection.
OPTION-LEFT ARROW	Move the insertion point to the start of the current or previous word or to the starting point of the current selection.
OPTION-RIGHT ARROW	Move the insertion point to the end of the current or next word or to the end of the current selection.
DELETE	Delete the character to the left of the insertion point or the selected text.
DEL	Delete the character to the right of the insertion point or the selected text. (This key is not available on the standard Apple USB keyboard, which premiered with the iMac.)
TAB	Insert a space to the next tab stop or to every fifth character position.
COMMAND-LEFT ARROW	Move the insertion point to the beginning of the previous word or to the beginning of the text you've selected.
COMMAND-RIGHT ARROW	Move the insertion point to the end of the next word or to the end of the text you've selected.
COMMAND-UP ARROW	Move the insertion point to the start of the previous paragraph.

GETTING THE MOST OUT OF ENTOURAGE

Shortcut	Function
COMMAND-DOWN ARROW	Move the insertion point to the start of the next paragraph.
CONTROL-UP ARROW or HOME	Move the insertion point right to the start of a line or to the start of the selected text block.
CONTROL-DOWN ARROW or END	Move the insertion point to the end of the line or to the end of the selected text block. (The END key isn't available on Apple's standard USB keyboard, which premiered with the iMac.)
COMMAND-HOME	Move the insertion point to the start of a message.
COMMAND-END	Move the insertion point to the end of a message.
PAGE UP	Move the insertion point up one screen (not one page).
PAGE DOWN	Move the insertion point down one screen (not one page).

Mac OS–Style Text Editing

If the Microsoft variation on the keyboard shortcuts theme seems too confusing, no problem. Just turn off the option in the Preferences dialog box that enables standard Microsoft Office-type text editing, and you'll have these choices (and notice that they aren't always different).

Shortcut	Function
COMMAND-A	Select all text in a message or folder.
LEFT ARROW	Move the insertion point to the left by one character.
RIGHT ARROW	Move the insertion point to the right by one character.
UP ARROW	Move the insertion point up by one line.
DOWN ARROW	Move the insertion point down by one line.
OPTION-UP ARROW	Move the insertion point to the top of the current or previous screen or to the start of the current selection.
OPTION-DOWN ARROW	Move the insertion point to the bottom of the current or next screen or to the end of the current selection.
OPTION-LEFT ARROW	Move the insertion point to the start of the current or previous word or to the starting point of the current selection.

Shortcut	Function
DELETE	Delete the character to the left of the insertion point or the selected text.
DEL	Delete the character at the right of the insertion point or the selected text. (This key isn't available on Apple's standard USB keyboard, which premiered with the iMac.)
TAB	Insert a space to the next tab stop or to every fifth character position.
COMMAND-LEFT ARROW	Move the insertion point to the beginning of the previous word or to the beginning of the text you've selected.
COMMAND-RIGHT ARROW	Moves the insertion point to the end of the next word or to the end of the text you've selected.
HOME	Move to the beginning of a message.
END	Move to the end of a message. (This key isn't available on Apple's standard USB keyboard, which premiered with the iMac.)
PAGE UP	Move the insertion point up one screen (not one page).
PAGE DOWN	Move the insertion point down one screen (not one page).

Summary

There's little doubt that Microsoft has done miracles with Entourage. Microsoft started with a wonderful e-mail client and extended it to include capabilities that rival many separate personal information managers.

Now that you've discovered the basics of Entourage 2001's personal information features, you'll want to move to Chapter 9. There you'll take your skills to the next step and learn all the finer points of making this highly flexible application do your bidding.

Chapter 9

The Entourage Calendar

The first part of Entourage's information management capabilities is the ability to build a full-featured contact list containing not just the names of those with whom you communicate via e-mail, but all basic information about the person, including phone numbers, physical address, directions, and personal information that might help you know more about that person.

Another major feature of Entourage is its Calendar planner and scheduler. Not only does the Calendar tell you of the day of the week or upcoming holidays, but it can be used to remind you of important events, be they personal or business, and even to send automatic e-mail messages to your contacts about special events. You can also use this information with Office 2001's Data Merge Manager; we'll cover that subject in more detail in Chapter 15.

In the following pages, you'll see how easy it is to dispense with those little notepads and let Entourage do your personal organizing for you.

Introducing the Entourage 2001 Calendar

Whether you simply want to know what day of the week Christmas will fall on or you need to be reminded of a birthday or business meeting, the Entourage Calendar (see Figure 9-1) is at your beck and call, easy to set up to help you keep track of the events that you need to know about.

Here's a fast look at the important features of the Calendar:

- **Event Planning**   Do you need to schedule events such as your child's birthday party or plan a vacation, business meeting, or appointment with your physician? Events can be set up on a one-time basis or as recurring, depending on your needs.

- **Advance Reminders**   Give up the sticky notes and use Entourage to remind you of important events or even to turn on the TV to catch your favorite program. You can set the warning as far in advance as necessary, so you have plenty of time to travel, get ready, or turn on the VCR and insert a tape.

- **Invitations**   In addition to reminding you of important events, the Entourage Calendar provides support for iCalendar, an Internet calendaring feature. If the folks in your address book have e-mail or personal information manager software that supports this feature, you can use the Internet to send and receive invitations. Once you receive an invitation, Calendar picks up the event automatically, so you're reminded of it at the appointed time. You can, of course, decline the invitation, and you will be notified when the recipients of your invitations accept or decline theirs.

NOTE   *Right now, iCalender is not widely supported by personal information managers. Before writing this book, I consulted the specifications and the product managers for two of the most popular currently available Mac information managers, Power On Software's Now Up-to-Date and Contact And Now Planner, and support for iCalendar is not yet in the cards.*

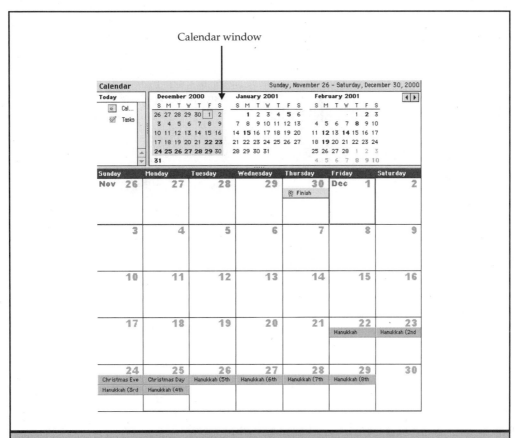

Figure 9-1.   *The Calendar is the centerpiece of Entourage's personal management features.*

- **Holiday Reminders**   Chapter 7 explained how to set up your Entourage 2001 user preferences to include holidays for specific countries and religious beliefs. As your contacts and gift-giving needs expand, you can easily update this list.

- **Publish Your Calendar on the Web**   Internet integration is an important feature of the various Office 2001 applications. You can easily publish your Calendar on the Web. All the hard work is done behind the scenes, as Entourage creates the HTML file and a folder containing all the graphics. Once you've saved your Calendar as a Web page, you can upload it to your Web site or e-mail the file to your regular contacts for viewing on their favorite Web browser (the folks at Microsoft hope it's Internet Explorer, of course).

- **Customize Calendar Display**   You can easily customize the look of the Calendar and have it incorporate your normal work week or work hours.

Choose the format that works best. You can easily view a range of days and upcoming tasks by using the minicalendar in the Calendar window (refer to Figure 9-1), which increases the flexibility of the program (click the right and left arrows next to the minicalendar to change the months displayed).

Setting Up the Calendar

Entourage 2001's Calendar is highly flexible, and you can customize it in a number of ways to reflect your taste or sense of organization.

This section focuses on how you can set up the Calendar to look and work the way you want. In the next section, you'll discover how to set up your Calendar events.

How to Change the Calendar View

By default, the Calendar displays months, but you can change to another view at a moment's notice. Just follow these steps:

1. With Entourage running, click Calendar in the Folder list.

NOTE *No folder list? No problem. Just go to the View menu and click Folder List to bring it back.*

2. On the View menu, choose the viewing format you prefer. These are the choices, with accompanying illustrations, in addition to the standard view:

   ■ **Day View**

   ■ **Week View**

■ **Work Week View**

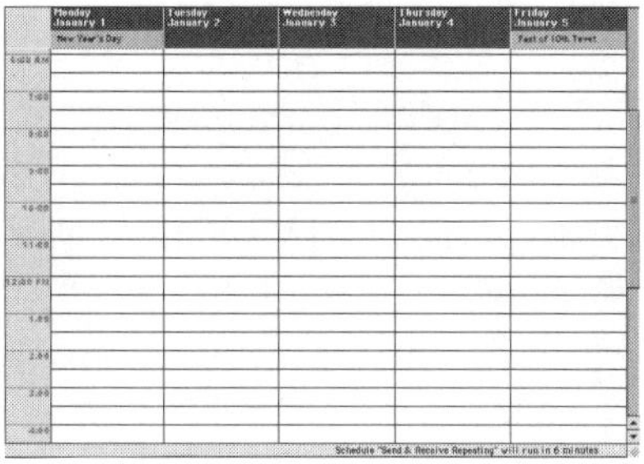

■ **List View**

Using the Calendar to Show a Range of Days

You can also set up the Entourage 2001 Calendar to display a range of days rather than the normal week-by-week view of a conventional calendar.

Here's how to accomplish this task:

1. With Entourage open, click the Calendar in the Folder list.

2. In the minicalendar at the top of the Calendar, click the first day of your range, hold down the mouse button, and move the cursor to the last day of your range. When you release the mouse, the Calendar will display that range of days. Nifty!

NOTE   *You can display up to six weeks when you set a range of days in your Entourage Calendar.*

How to Remove Holidays from the Calendar Display

When you add holidays for a particular religion or country, all the holidays that occur in that religion or country will be put in your Calendar. The preference setting doesn't allow for any greater level of customization. But Entourage can be set to selectively remove certain holidays from the display.

If you want to customize the program in this fashion, here's how:

1. With Entourage open, choose Advanced Find from the Edit menu to display the Find dialog box (see Figure 9-2).

2. You're performing a very narrow search here, so just locate the Calendar Events check box in the Item Types section and make sure the other options aren't checked.

3. In the Criteria section, choose Category from the pop-up menu at the left.

4. Move on to the center pop-up menu and select Is.

5. Your final voyage is to the right pop-up menu, where you select Holiday.

6. Click the Find button. This will bring up the list of holidays that you can remove from the Calendar.

7. Select the holidays that you want to zap from the Calendar and then click Delete; when you are asked to confirm the choice, click Delete again. You can, at this point, also click Cancel and forget the whole process or choose different holidays to remove.

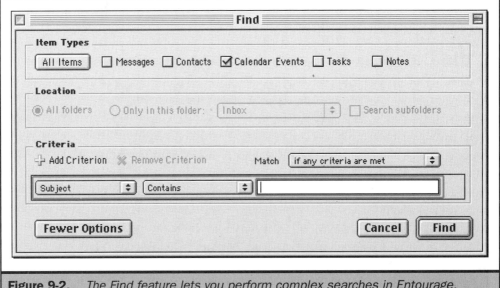

Figure 9-2. *The Find feature lets you perform complex searches in Entourage.*

Creating Events with the Calendar

Now that you have set up the Entourage Calendar to appear in the way you like, it's time to get on with the task of actually creating and storing your events.

Here's how to create a new event:

1. With Entourage open, display the Calendar by choosing Calendar from the Folder list.

2. Click the New button, which brings up a dialog box for setting up a new event (see Figure 9-3).

TIP   *You can accomplish the same thing by double-clicking the appropriate date in the Calendar window.*

3. Enter the event's name or a short description in the Subject field.

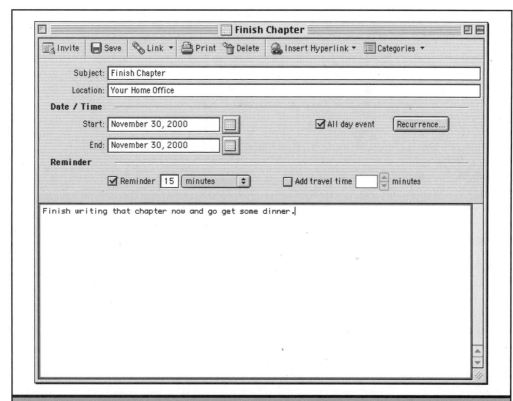

Figure 9-3.   *Fill in the details for your new event in this dialog box.*

4. In the Location field, state where the event is to occur.

Got a further question? Just go to the Help menu and choose Show Balloons. Those little cartoon-like text blocks will appear whenever you point your mouse at an information field in the dialog box. Don't forget to turn Balloon Help off when you're done; otherwise, those annoying balloons will be present throughout your Mac environment.

5. Specify the date and time information for the event. Enter the Start information.

6. If the event is to last throughout the day, select the All Day Event box.

7. If the event will occur on a regular basis, click the Recurrence button and specify in the Recurring Event dialog box how often this event will be repeated.

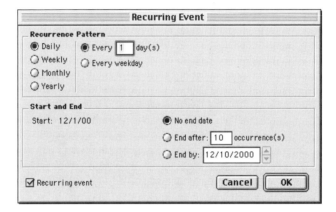

■ Set the frequency of the event by selecting the appropriate buttons and checking the appropriate boxes in the Recurrence Pattern section.

■ If there's a definite end to the recurring event (and I assume there will be), check the appropriate boxes and enter the appropriate beginning and ending dates and times in the Start and End section.

■ Make sure Recurring Event is checked, so the Entourage Calendar will use the information.

■ Click OK to return to the new event dialog box to complete the job.

8. Enter the end time of the event, assuming it's not all day, of course.

9. Specify how far in advance the reminder is to be sent. The pop-up menu allows you to specify minutes, hours, or days.

10. If you want to add travel time, click the Add Travel Time check box and specify the time needed for the trip.

11. Click the text field and enter information about your event.

12. Click the Insert Hyperlink button if you want to incorporate a link to a Web address in your reminder.

13. When you're done, click the Save box to add your event to the appropriate date on the Calendar.

14. Click the close box to dismiss the dialog box.

Here's a fast way to add a new event. With the Calendar in Day, Week, or Work Week view, double-click the start time of the event. Your new event window will appear with the starting information already entered, ready for you to complete.

Receiving a Reminder

At the appointed time, Entourage will sound an audible alert (assuming you haven't changed the notification preference), and the Reminders window will pop up on your Mac's display.

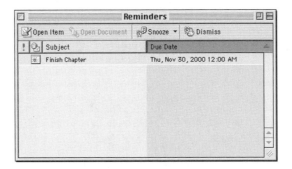

When you see the Reminders screen, you can treat it like an alarm clock. Click Snooze to have it remind you again about the event at the time specified in its pop-up menu, or click Dismiss to send it away for good.

To see the actual event (or events), just click to select it and then click Open Item, or just double-click the event title. The result in this case is what was shown in Figure 9-3.

The reminder that you see can be printed or deleted. You can also have it listed under a specific category, edit it as you see fit, or turn it into an invitation and have it sent to the recipients in your Entourage list of contacts.

Removing an Event

If you decide you no longer want to be reminded of a particular event, just select it in the Calendar and press the DELETE key on your keyboard.

In response, you'll get the typical "Are you sure?" message. Click Delete to trash the message, or click Cancel if you change your mind.

Using the Calendar to Send an Invitation

Using essentially the same techniques as just described, you can send invitations to the folks in your Address Book about an upcoming event.

NOTE   *Don't forget that recipients cannot automatically reply to your invitation and have it automatically added to their calendars unless they have an e-mail or PIM application that supports iCalendar (if they can find one).*

Let's look at the similarities in the following steps:

1. Launch Entourage and then click Calendar in the Folder list.

2. Click the New button, which brings up the dialog box for setting up a new event, or just double-click the appointed date or time on the Calendar.

3. Click the Invite button, which modifies the dialog box so that it includes e-mail address and subject entry fields (see Figure 9-4). Before you continue, take a look at the new buttons at the top of the event dialog box:

   ■ **Send Now**   Speed the invitation on its way.

   ■ **Cancel Invitations**   Click this if you decide not to hold the event.

   ■ **Save**   Use this button to store the event in your Entourage Calendar.

   ■ **Link**   Link this event to another event, an e-mail or news message, a task, a note, a contact, or an Address Book group.

   ■ **Delete**   Deletes the invitation, just as it says.

   ■ **Attach File**   Include one or more file attachments with your invitation.

   ■ **Signature**   Choose a signature from the pop-up menu, assuming you've created one.

   ■ **Insert Hyperlink**   Provide a clickable link to a Web address.

   ■ **Categories**   Choose a category from the pop-up menu or create a new one if you prefer.

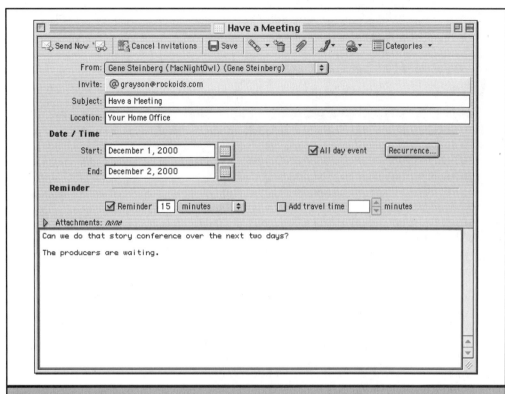

Figure 9-4.   *Take a look at the new options in your event dialog box.*

4. Enter the names of the recipients in the Invite field.

5. Type the subject of the invitation in the Subject field.

6. Enter the appropriate information in the Location field.

7. Enter the date and time information for the event. Begin with the start time.

8. If the event will continue through the day, select All Day Event.

9. If your invitation is for a repeating event, click the Recurrence button and specify how often this event will be repeated. How often the event is repeated is established by selecting the appropriate buttons and checking the appropriate boxes in the Recurrence Pattern area of the Recurring Event dialog box.

   ■ To indicate the end of the event, click the appropriate boxes and enter the appropriate beginning and ending dates and times in the Start and End section.

   ■ Check Recurring Event, so the Entourage Calendar will use the information.

   ■ Click OK to return to the new event dialog box to finish your invitation.

10. If the invitation is not for an all-day event, enter the end time.

11. Specify how far in advance the reminder is to be sent. The pop-up menu lets you specify minutes, hours, or days.

12. If your recipients must travel to attend the event, select the Add Travel Time check box and specify the time needed for the trip.

13. Click the text field and enter the information about your event.

14. Click the Send Now button, which also saves the invitation, to speed the invitation on its way. Now all you have to do is wait for the responses.

NOTE   *If the Invitation window isn't dismissed when you send the invitation, click the Save button and then the close box to get rid of it.*

Changing an Event

When you create an event, it's not set in stone. You can alter it at any time and have the new version take effect immediately.

To edit an event, just follow these steps:

1. Locate the event in your Entourage Calendar and double-click it.

2. Make the alterations you want in the event dialog box.

3. If this event includes an invitation, click the Send Update button to make sure all the recipients of the invitation know that the event has changed (don't send it at the last minute, or you may get more than just accept or decline responses).

TIP   *If all you want to do is change the date and time of the event, make sure your Calendar is displayed in Month, Day, Week, or Work Week view. Then drag the event to the new beginning time in the Calendar, and drag the bottom of the event to the new end time. The change will take effect automatically. You will, however, have to open the actual event if you want to send updated invitations to people on your mailing list.*

Responding to a Calendar Invitation

From time to time, you may receive an invitation from one of your contacts that uses Entourage or another application that supports the iCalendar standard.

If you do get such an invitation (and we hope you will at one time or another), here's the one-click way to respond:

1. When the invitation arrives in your Entourage Inbox, click the invitation's title to view the message.

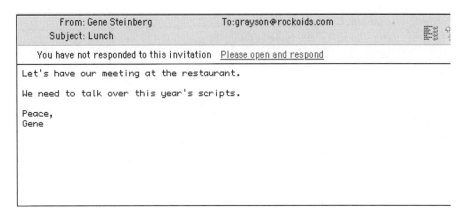

2. Click the Accept, Decline, or Tentative button when you see them in the invitation window.

That's all there is to it. When you click your response, Entourage will send your response to the sender. If you haven't declined the invitation, it will also be added to your calendar.

NOTE *You are not locked in once you accept an invitation. If you change your mind, you can open the invitation again and click Decline instead (or Accept for that matter).*

Adding Dates from a Contact in the Calendar

As you can see, the Calendar's flexibility is limited only by your imagination and creativity. You can, for example, take a date for an event entered in your contact list, such as an anniversary or birthday, and place it in the calendar automatically.
Here's how:

1. With Entourage open, click the Address Book folder to bring up your list of contacts.

2. Double-click a contact's name to display the information for that contact.

3. Click the Personal tab.

4. Click a date; then choose Add to Calendar from the pop-up menu.

5. A standard event dialog box will appear. Enter the particulars about the event.

6. When the event information has been entered, click the Save button to store it and then click the close box. The event will become part of the Calendar.

7. Close the contact window to finish the process.

Storing a Calendar as a Web Page

All Office 2001 programs share features, such as the dictionary and links. One of the most useful features is the ability to save documents as Web pages, completely formatted, for publishing on the World Wide Web. By using this feature, you don't have to use a separate Web authoring program for such chores.

NOTE   *When I describe the ability to store a page in Web format, I'm not dismissing the need to use dedicated Web authoring software. These programs offer additional features that graphic designers and other professionals treasure to create high-grade Web sites.*

Here's how to save your Calendar as a Web page:

1. With Entourage open, click the Calendar in the Folder list to bring it up.

2. With your Calendar displayed, go to the File menu and choose Save As Web Page, to display a setup dialog box (see Figure 9-5).

3. Now you need to customize your Web page. Specify the start and end dates in the Duration section.

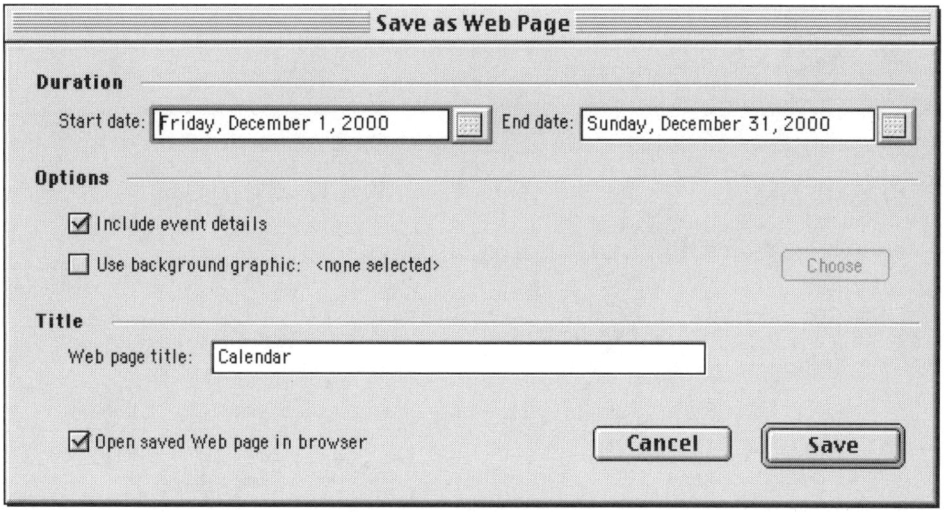

Figure 9-5.   *Configure your Calendar Web page options in this dialog box.*

> TIP   *A quick way to pick a date is to click the little Calendar icon to the right of the Start Date and End Date fields. This will bring up a miniature calendar that you can click to select the date. What you select will appear in the proper Duration field.*

4. In the Options section, select the check box labeled Include Event Details. This will incorporate whatever information you provided in the text field when you set up your events.

5. If you want to enhance the background appearance of your Calendar (a photo is fine), select Use Background Graphic. Then click the Choose button and locate the name of the background image file in the dialog box. Select the background image and click Open to include it along with your Web page (see Figure 9-6).

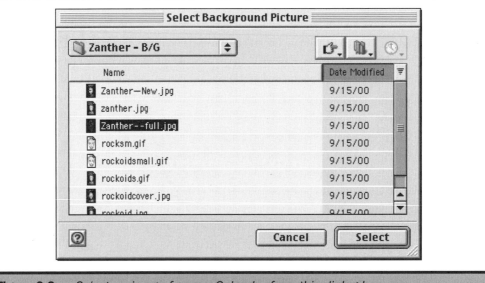

Figure 9-6. *Select an image for your Calendar from this dialog box.*

NOTE *Your background graphic, be it a drawing or photo, must be in GIF or JPEG format to be supported by Web browsers.*

6. Give your Web page a title. You don't have to call it just Calendar.

7. Select Open Saved Web Page in Browser. This enables you to make a final check of the page before you publish it on your Web site or send it to one of your contacts. The result will be similar to what you see in Figure 9-7.

8. Click the Save button and, in the Save As dialog box, locate the folder where you want to put your file.

9. Click Save to store the completed file.

The main file will be created with an .htm file extension (standard for HTML files): for example, Calendar.htm. A companion folder will include all the graphics that accompany the file. To actually access this site, you'd need to enter the domain name of the site in question, followed by a slash and the name of the actual Web file.

NOTE *To cite a personal example, if the domain is http://www.rockoids.com (one of my Web domains), a calendar uploaded to the site and using this file name would be accessed as http://www.rockoids.com/calendar.htm (don't look for a real calendar at this site).*

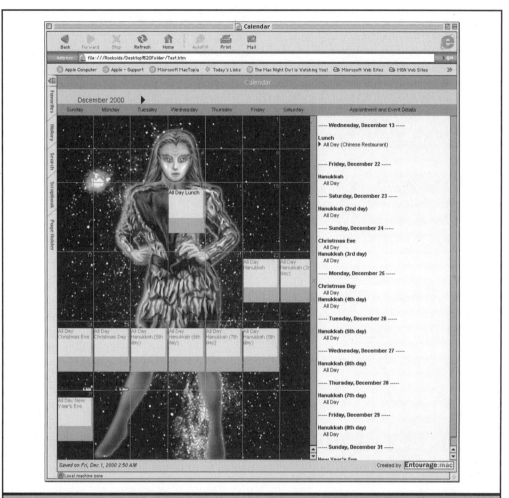

Figure 9-7.   *I'm being a little outlandish here in my choice of background images.*

Making Entourage a Startup Application

One of the nice features of the Mac OS is the ability to make an application launch whenever you boot your Macintosh. That way, you are ready to roll without having to pick and choose the applications you need.

These instructions can apply to any Mac application, but I'm making them Entourage specific here:

1. Locate the Microsoft Office 2001 folder on your Mac's hard drive.
2. Click once on the Entourage application icon to select it.
3. From the File menu, choose Make Alias, or just press COMMAND-M.

Another way to accomplish this is to hold down CTRL when you click the icon and choose Make Alias from the pop-up contextual menu.

4. Locate the Startup Items folder within the System Folder and place the newly created alias inside it. If you want, you can remove the word "alias" from the title (its presence always annoys me for some reason).

From here on, whenever you boot your Mac, Entourage comes along for the ride.

Using Entourage's Search Features

Here is a common dilemma: You've sent and received hundreds or thousands of messages and created a wide range of events. Now you want to find someone's address, a phone number, or some information you placed in a message. What to do?

Entourage offers two highly flexible search features to help you find the information you want in the program's database quickly and easily. Following is a description of the search features and how they differ:

■ **Find** This feature (see Figure 9-8) lets you search for specific text in Entourage. You can look for someone's e-mail address, information in the subject or body of a message, and any event or task you've created.

■ **Advanced Find** Click the More Options button and a feature will be revealed that takes your search a large step further. You can specify various criteria in your search request, such as all the contacts that reside in a particular area of the country, are engaged in a specific application, and so forth. Any item in your Entourage database, including folders, messages, and reminders, can be searched to locate what you want.

If your Mac is configured for Multiple Users (as explained in the next section of this chapter), you're limited in your search to only the information that's contained in the Entourage database under your user name or in user accounts to which you have access.

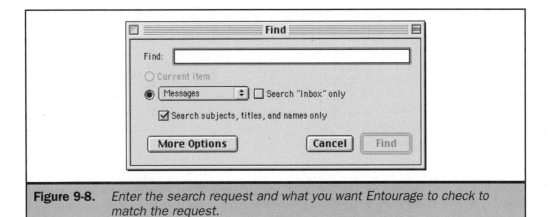

Figure 9-8.   *Enter the search request and what you want Entourage to check to match the request.*

Searching for the Text in a Specific Message

If your search is simple, you'll want to use the basic search feature. Just follow these instructions:

1. Launch Entourage.
2. Open the message in which you want to perform your search.
3. Choose Find from the Edit menu or just press COMMAND-F.
4. Enter the word or phrase you want to locate in the Find text box.
5. Click the Find button to begin your search.
6. If you want to continue searching, press COMMAND-G.

Searching for Text in All Messages, Events, and Tasks

Entourage 2001's search facilities go far beyond a single message. You can use the very same techniques to expand your search to all the information you've stored in the program. Here's how to accomplish the task:

1. Launch Entourage.
2. To bring up the Find window, choose Find from the Edit menu or just press COMMAND-F.
3. Enter the word or phrase you want to search for.

4. Click the All Items pop-up menu and choose the items you want to search. Each category of Entourage information is listed.

NOTE *If you have a folder open during a search request, you'll have the option to search that folder only. Otherwise, the Folder option in the Search window will be dimmed.*

5. If you want to save time and confine your search to subjects, titles, and names only, leave that option checked. If you want to expand your search to the text portions of a message, reminder, or task, uncheck the Search Subjects, Titles, and Names Only box.

NOTE *I haven't forgotten the More Options window. It activates Entourage's Advanced Find feature, which I'll describe in the next section.*

6. Click the Find button to begin your search.

7. You'll see a Search Results window, where you can see the messages that match your request. This window is the same as the regular message Inbox, so you can open, save, print, and apply other actions from this window.

CAUTION *If your Entourage database contains a large number of messages, reminders, and tasks, it will take several minutes to finish your search. If you want to stop a search at any time, press COMMAND-. (period).*

8. Once you've viewed the results of your search, you can close the Search Results window and repeat the preceding steps to conduct a new search.

Using Advanced Find

When you open the Entourage Find window, you'll find a More Options button, which activates many techniques that allow you to refine your searches.

Here is a look at this feature, called, appropriately, Advanced Find.

1. To conduct a more extensive search for information in Entourage, choose Advanced Find from the Edit menu or press COMMAND-OPTION-F. This will bring up the dialog box shown in Figure 9-9.

2. The first section, Item types, is used to specify the types of information you want Entourage to check to find the text you want. By default, all items in the selected folder in Entourage are checked. Feel free to uncheck the ones you don't want to search, as refining your search will get you more accurate results (and take less time to complete).

3. The Location section is dimmed unless you are searching only for messages. Then you can choose which message folder or subfolders to check.

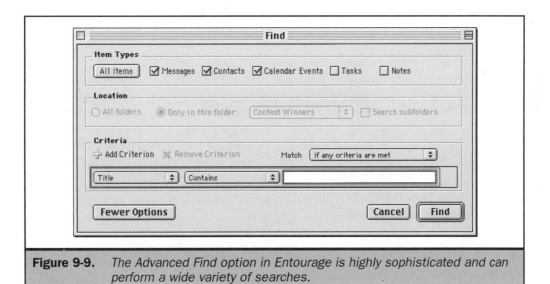

Figure 9-9.   *The Advanced Find option in Entourage is highly sophisticated and can perform a wide variety of searches.*

4. The Criteria section provides the great flexibility of Advanced Find. In the Match pop-up menu, specify how matches to your search requests are handled. By default, Entourage considers text a match if any criteria are met, but you can refine it so that all criteria must be met.

5. Beneath Match, there are two pop-up menus. Click the one at the left and specify what part of the information database is being searched (Title is the first listing).

6. Click the second pop-up menu to refine the content for which Entourage is searching.

7. In the box at the right, enter the word or phrase for which you want to search.

8. If you want to add further conditions to your search, click the Add Criterion button, which will bring up a second group of pop-up menus for you to add search request refinements.

9. You're ready now. Click Find to begin the search. The results of your search will appear in the Search Results window. Be patient if your copy of Entourage has lots of messages to search. The search can take a few minutes to complete.

10. If the search does not find what you want, open Advanced Find again and change your search request.

TIP   *If you decide you'd rather just perform a simple search, click the Fewer Options button in the Advanced Find window to bring up a regular Find window.*

11. If your search request is successful and you want to save the results, keep the Search Results window open. This highly flexible feature keeps you from wasting time trying to reinvent the wheel and having to perform the search all over again. Choose Save as Custom View from the File menu. This will bring up the Edit Custom View dialog box.

12. Give your custom view a name.

13. Click OK.

The search window you've saved will appear under the name you selected in the Custom Views folder of your Folder list. Just click the disclosure triangle to expand its contents, or click it again to collapse the view.

CAUTION   *Don't try to move any of those items from the Custom Views folder to another folder. I tried this, just once, and I experienced a nasty crash in Entourage. I won't say this will happen to everyone, but just be careful.*

Using Entourage with Apple's Multiple Users Feature

In Mac OS 9, Apple introduced a feature that allows the owner or administrator of a Mac system to configure separate environments and access privileges for different users.

Entourage supports the feature, so each user can have his or her own Calendar, contacts, account information, messages, and so on. Only that user or the computer's owner can access the information.

Here's how to set up Entourage for multiple users:

1. Configure the Multiple Users Control Panel (see Figure 9-10) for each user on your Macintosh.

2. Log on to your Mac as the owner or administrator and then launch Entourage.

NOTE   *If you've already set up Entourage for use under your main account name, you'll want to remove the Office 2001 Identities folder with your name in it from within the Microsoft User Data folder inside the Documents folder on your Mac's startup drive. You can then restore that folder later to continue to have it recognize your user information.*

3. When the Entourage Setup Assistant launches, close it without making any entries.

4. Quit Entourage.

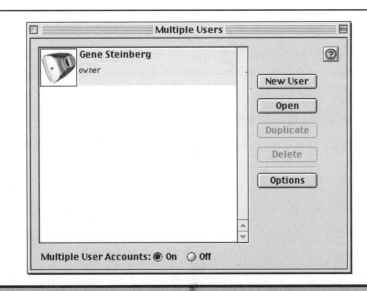

Figure 9-10.   *Apple's Multiple Users Control Panel can be used to configure your Mac for additional users.*

5. Log off.

6. Log on under each user's name and repeat steps 2 through 5.

7. Now we get to the hard part. Log on again as the owner or administrator of the Mac.

8. Locate the Office 2001 Identities folder inside the Microsoft User Data folder within the Documents folder on your startup drive.

9. Place the folders for each user—other then you, since you're the administrator—on the desktop.

10. Look for the Users' folders on your hard drive with the name of each user of your Mac. Locate the Documents folder stored inside each User's folder. Look inside that for a folder called Microsoft User Data, and within that for Office 2001 Identities, and finally for the Main Identity folder. Place the appropriate user's folder inside the corresponding Main Identity folder.

Once you've followed these rather convoluted steps, each user can begin to use Entourage and maintain his or her own personal settings and information. Only those with access to that user's account can open Entourage and view that information.

TIP *If you want to learn more about the Multiple Users feature of Mac OS 9 or later, you'll want to read Chapter 6 of another book I wrote,* Mac OS 9: The Complete Reference *(Osborne/McGraw-Hill, 2000).*

Troubleshooting Calendar Problems

As you can see from the information in this chapter, almost everything related to the Calendar is pretty straightforward. All you have to do is follow the step-by-step setup instructions, and the Calendar should do your bidding precisely as you specify. There are times, though, when you'll find that things just don't work as advertised. This section describes some common problems and what to do about them.

■ **What If a Recipient Can't Respond to an Invitation?** All right; this problem usually has an easy answer, but not an easy solution. For someone to be able to respond to your invitation with an accept or decline message, that person needs to be using e-mail software or a PIM that supports the iCalendar protocol. Otherwise, although the person cannot automatically send you a notice, the recipient can view the invitation and add the event manually and can send you a separate message indicating a response. It's not as easy, but it works.

■ **Something Missing? What If There's No Accept, Decline, or Tentative Button?** Here's the problem: You received an iCalendar invitation. Everything seems all right, but you don't see buttons for Accept, Decline, or Tentative. The usual cause is a cross-platform issue: the sender is using

Microsoft Outlook for Windows. If you get this sort of invitation, you'll need to respond manually. To store the event, click the Save to Calendar button on the invitation's Info bar. The event will be saved as a regular event and put in the Calendar. I suppose this is ripe for an update, but as that newscaster once said, that's the way it is.

Web Page Problems and Solutions

Before we discuss any possible solutions to Web page problems, let me make it perfectly clear, to recall another old phrase, that each Web browser may display a site differently—despite the fact that the publishers of these browsers all claim to adhere to Internet standards. As a result, you may find oddities of one sort or another, such as in the way fonts and artwork are displayed.

In addition, if you have customized a browser to display fonts in a different size or style, you can bet your work won't look the same in someone else's browser where such changes haven't been configured. Sizes and display resolutions for Mac and Windows versions differ, too, although Microsoft Internet Explorer 5 and Netscape 6 use the same settings for both platforms (of course, you can change them, which introduces new disparities).

Here are some hints and tips for getting the pages to display properly, aside from browser variations, of course:

- **Missing Artwork**   Where is the supporting folder? As I said when I described the process of saving a Calendar as a Web page, Entourage will create a folder that contains all the graphic and support files. You should not change the location of the folder or rename it or the supporting files. When you upload the page to your Web site, you'll want to send everything intact. Otherwise, missing artwork will appear as just a small icon, and backgrounds will not be displayed as you intended.

- **Artwork Present But Doesn't Render Properly**   The standard graphic formats for the Web are GIF and JPEG. If the files are in the wrong format or just not named with the appropriate .jpg (for JPEG) or .gif (for GIF) file extension, they won't be recognized. The Web doesn't take substitutes.

NOTE   *All of the Office 2001 applications have the ability to save document pages for the Web. By using these powerful tools, you can create a Web site containing text, spreadsheet data, interactive presentations, and, of course, your Entourage Calendar.*

Summary

Feel free to dispense with Post-it notes and other relicts of the paper explosion. As you discovered in this chapter, it's very easy to configure Entourage 2001's Calendar to handle all of your events and many of your invitations for personal and business gatherings.

Now that you've learned how to exploit Entourage's information management features, the next step is to look at still another of the application's messaging features: newsgroup management. You may not use this feature as often as the others described here, but take a look at Chapter 10 to learn about the sometimes wacky and wild world of Usenet and how to manage your discussions with Entourage.

Chapter 10

A Newsgroup and Mailing List Primer

This book has devoted six full chapters to Microsoft Entourage because it's the new kid on the block as far as Microsoft software is concerned. A large number of features were never part of the software suite previously, and they are worth extensive discussion.

The feature we discuss in this chapter actually arrives pretty much intact from Outlook Express, but it is one not utilized as often as it should be. This is Entourage's news reading feature, the ability to tap into any of tens of thousands of newsgroups, where you can locate informative, entertaining, and infuriating discussions, sometimes from the very same newsgroup.

We'll also talk about mailing lists, a convenient way to receive information about a variety of subjects right in your Inbox, without having to go out and scour numerous discussion groups for that information.

Introducing Usenet Newsgroups

The newsgroup, also known as Usenet, is one of the very oldest Internet features. Short for user's network, it dates back to 1979, the early days of the Internet. At the time, two students networked computers together to exchange information and conduct discussions about a variety of subjects. The technology soon spread to the entire Internet, and today newsgroup messages are managed by thousands of computers, which share the millions of news feeds that travel throughout the Internet.

Newsgroups come in two forms. The most common are unmoderated, which means that nobody manages that newsgroup. Anyone is free to post a message, literally without limit. Of course, that means that some newsgroups can be wild and wooly, and you'll sometimes find messages that may be offensive to you. The other type of newsgroup is moderated, usually by one or more volunteers. Moderators review each and every message sent to the group, determining which to post and which to reject, using either objective criteria or arbitrary ones, or a mix of the two.

Entourage 2001 offers a highly flexible news reading feature, which you can use to locate and subscribe to newsgroups and manage the constant flow of messages. In the following pages, we'll discuss the extensive message management features available to you.

Locating and Accessing Newsgroups

Tens of thousands of newsgroups are available—but first you must locate them. Once you locate a newsgroup, you must subscribe to it to view and post messages.

NOTE
For Entourage to be able to access newsgroups, your ISP must provide newsgroup capability. If your ISP doesn't support newsgroups, you may want to consider using a news-oriented Web site, such as http://www.deja.com, to view and post your messages. Of course, that takes Entourage out of the picture, but it may be your only alterative, other than switching ISPs.

Configuring a News Account

To get started, you need to set up an account for your ISP's newsgroup feature. Just follow these steps:

1. With Entourage open, choose Accounts from the Tools menu.

2. Select the News tab to bring up the dialog box shown in Figure 10-1.

3. Click the New button to set up an account.

4. From the Tools menu, select Accounts.

5. Click the appropriate tab for the type of account you want to set up: Mail, News, or Directory Service.

6. Click New, which will activate the Entourage Account Setup Assistant.

> **TIP**   *If you're used to entering all the information by yourself, just click the Configure Account Manually button and enter the appropriate information in the text entry fields.*

7. In the first Account Setup Assistant dialog box, choose the e-mail account you want to use for direct e-mail responses, along with the name of your company

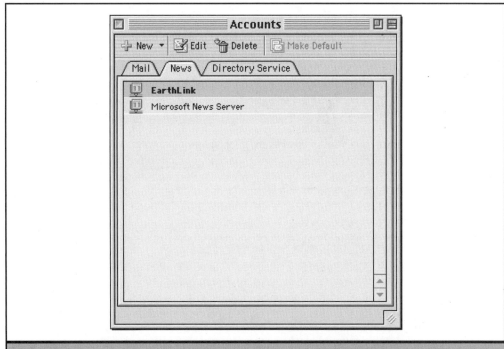

Figure 10-1.   *Use this tab of the Accounts dialog box to edit and configure your various news accounts.*

or organization, if you want to include it (this isn't necessary, of course). When you're done, click the right (or forward) arrow.

8. In the next dialog box, fill in the information specified by your ISP for its newsgroup server.

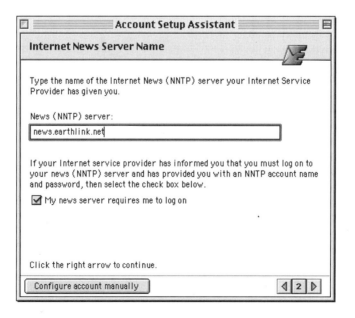

9. If your ISP requires a password for newsgroup access (EarthLink is an example of a service with this requirement), select the My News Server Requires Me to Log On check box. In the next dialog box, specify the user name that you set for that ISP and the password and whether it's to be stored in Entourage.

NOTE *If your Mac is accessed by more than a single user, you may prefer not to have the password stored in the program. If you pick this option, you'll see a password prompt each time you attempt to connect to your ISP's news server.*

10. Click the right arrow to bring up the final setup dialog box. Enter the name under which you want the newsgroup account stored.

11. When you're done, you can click the left (or back) arrow to review your settings. Click Finish to store the new account.

NOTE *You can always edit or remove your e-mail and news accounts simply by bringing up the Accounts dialog box from the Tools menu and selecting the account you want to change.*

Finding Newsgroups

Once your account information has been set up, you will need to have Entourage log on to your ISP's news server and retrieve the list of newsgroups.

Follow these steps.

1. With Entourage launched and running, locate the name of the news server in the Folder list. Select the news server.

2. You'll see a message asking if you want to retrieve the list of newsgroups. Click OK to begin the retrieval process. Over the next few minutes, depending on the speed of your ISP's connection and the number of newsgroups your ISP supports, Entourage will retrieve the entire newsgroups list. This process is needed for you to locate and subscribe to a newsgroup.

NOTE   *If you want to check for newly formed newsgroups from time to time, use the Get New Newsgroups command on the View menu to update the listing.*

3. When the process is done, you'll see the full list displayed. The example shown here is a part of EarthLink's version of a newsgroup listing.

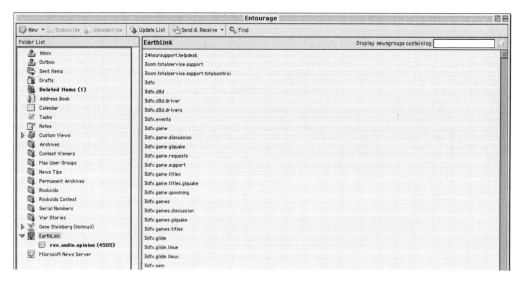

4. There are far too many newsgroups for you to just scroll through the list. To reduce the size of the list, click the Display Newsgroups Containing text field and enter a word or phrase that describes the subject matter you want the newsgroups to discuss. This will reduce the list to those newsgroups that match your request. The example here shows some newsgroups devoted to one of the author's favorite subjects: science fiction (note the "sf" in the Display Newsgroups Containing text field).

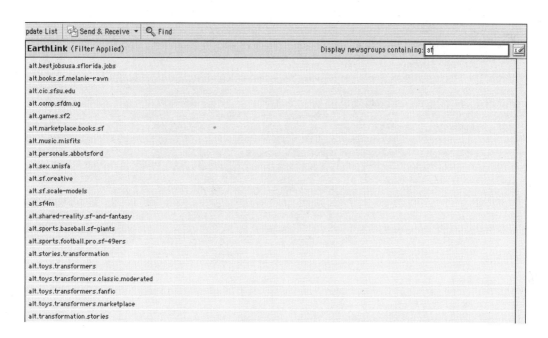

GETTING THE MOST
OUT OF ENTOURAGE

5. When you find a newsgroup to which you want to subscribe, select the newsgroup's name and choose Subscribe from the Edit menu. After you subscribe, you'll be able to access the list of messages and read and respond to them.

NOTE   *To unsubscribe from a newsgroup, simply reverse this process. Select the newsgroup's name and choose Unsubscribe from the Edit menu.*

6. The final step is to restrict your list strictly to newsgroups to which you've subscribed. The 30,000 to 50,000 (or more) newsgroups available from a typical ISP are going to be a bit much. To do this, choose Subscribed Only from the View menu. Much better!

TIP   *If you want to see the full list again to subscribe to additional newsgroups, just choose Subscribed Only from the View menu again to deselect the option and display the full list. It's possible, at this point, that you'll receive a message requesting that you download the full list again, but that doesn't happen very often.*

7. Once you've configured Entourage to handle your newsgroups, click the disclosure triangle next to your ISP's news server folder to see the names of the newsgroups, neatly displayed in a list.

NOTE   *When the headers or titles of the messages are downloaded, you'll see the number of available messages in parentheses next to the newsgroup's name.*

Finding New Newsgroups

Newsgroups are not static. Almost every day of the week, new ones are added. Here's how to check:

1. With Entourage open, click the name of your ISP's news server.

2. Choose Get New Newsgroups from the View menu or choose Update List from the toolbar. Over the next few minutes, the list will be updated.

NOTE   *Unfortunately, you won't see a separate listing of the newly added newsgroups. But when you search for ones that match the topics you specify, there may be additional entries for you to check.*

Reading and Responding to Newsgroup Messages

Now that you've added your news account, you'll want to get started downloading, reading, and posting your messages. When you do, you'll see that they look very similar to e-mail messages coming up in the same windows, with similar subject and message lines.

Here's how Entourage handles newsgroup postings:

■ **Messages Are Displayed by Header**   When Entourage retrieves a list of unread messages from your ISP's newsgroup server, they come in the form of headers, or titles that show such information as the sender, topic, and date sent. They look very much like e-mail messages in most respects.

■ **Only 300 Headers at a Time**   By default, Entourage downloads up to only 300 headers for each newsgroup, out of possibly thousands of available messages. That way, you don't waste a lot of time downloading the message headers (and this can take a long time if your connection to your ISP isn't very fast), and you're not overwhelmed by the sheer number of messages. If you prefer to have a larger number of message headers downloaded, just open the Accounts dialog box from the Tools menu, click the News tab, and select the name of your news server. After you've done this, you'll see the option to increase the number of headers, on the Options tab (see Figure 10-2). Enter the value you want.

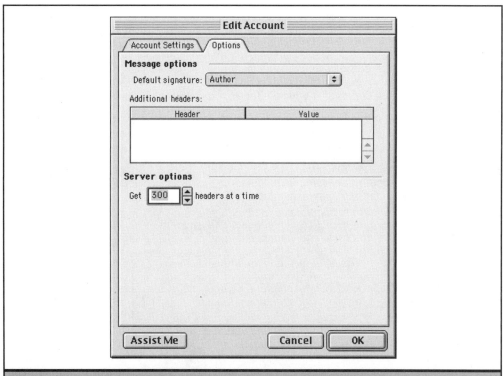

Figure 10-2.   *You can choose to have more message headers downloaded in a single operation.*

You don't have to change message header preferences to see more messages in Entourage. When you're finished reading the first group, just choose Get More News Messages from the View menu, and another batch will be downloaded for you. If you just want to see the newest messages, choose the Refresh Message List command instead (or press COMMAND-L).

■ **Use a Schedule or Message Rules** Another convenient way to organize your messages is to have them accessed on a regular schedule. We discuss that subject in more detail in Chapter 7. You can also follow the instructions in that chapter to set up a message rule that can assign newsgroup messages to a particular category or contact or simply hide the older messages. You'll find that many of the same steps used to configure Entourage for e-mail handling work just as well for newsgroup messages.

Receiving and Viewing Newsgroup Messages

Once you've subscribed to newsgroups that appear of interest and configured Entourage to work the way you want, it's time to get started.

Just follow these steps to receive message headers and read messages:

1. With Entourage open, go to the Folder list and click the news server to select it.

2. Click the disclosure triangle next to the server's name so that it points to download; it will reveal the list of newsgroups to which you've subscribed.

3. Click the name of a newsgroup. At this point, your ISP's news server will be contacted, and a batch of message headers (up to the amount specified as a preference if at least that many are available) will be downloaded. You will see a download progress bar like the one shown here.

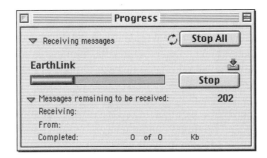

4. The message headers you've downloaded will appear in Entourage's top pane.

rec.arts.sf.fandom			Subject ⬍	starts with ⬍		
✉ ✳ 📎	From	Subject ▲	Sent		Size	Categories
▷ ✉ ✳	mike weber	Re: [OT] Depression Lyrics?	Yesterday 3:38 PM		1 K	None
▷ ✉ ✳	Paul Birnbaum	Re: 13 Myths about the Election	Yesterday 3:17 PM		2 K	None
▷ ✉ ✳	Mary Kay Kare	Re: A tree grows on the IRT	Yesterday 11:33 AM		1 K	None
▷ ✉ ✳	Priscilla H Ballou	Re: ACICIF: Christmas Trees	Yesterday 11:45 AM		2 K	None
▷ ✉ ✳	Vlatko Juric-Kokic	Re: AKICIF: Netscape Newsgroup properties	Yesterday 1:13 PM		4 K	None
▷ ✉ ✳	Omega	Re: AKICIF: Rot	12/4/00 2:23 PM		2 K	None
▷ ✉ ✳	Eloise Beltz-Decker	AKICIF: Song - Meadowlark?	Yesterday 12:19 PM		1 K	None
▷ ✉ ✳	Robert Sneddon	Re: Babies	Yesterday 4:12 PM		1 K	None
▷ ✉ ✳	Lydia Nickerson	Re: Bad Judgment (was something else)	Yesterday 9:00 PM		2 K	None
▷ ✉ ✳	Marcus L. Rowland	Re: Chad ballots getting the OJ treatment	12/4/00 3:43 PM		1 K	None
✉ ✳	Avedon Carol	Re: Circular Argument of the Year	Yesterday 7:29 PM		1 K	None
✉ ✳	Lydia Nickerson	Re: Coming Soon: Lydy in NYC!	Yesterday 8:06 PM		1 K	None
▷ ✉ ✳	Mary Kay Kare	Re: Cooking In Outer Space?	Yesterday 6:38 PM		1 K	None

5. Click a message title, and Entourage will retrieve the actual message from the news server; this may take a moment or two. The message will appear in the bottom pane and has more than a passing resemblance to an e-mail message (see Figure 10-3).

6. To navigate from message to message, press COMMAND-] to move to the next message or COMMAND-[to go back to the previous message.

TIP   *As an alternative, you can scroll through the messages by pressing the SPACEBAR to move from one text screen to the next. At the end of the message, pressing the SPACEBAR will bring up the next message. If the SPACEBAR trick doesn't work, check to see if you have installed a program on your Mac that prohibits adding extra spaces between words. One example of such a program is Casady & Greene's Spell Catcher. Such programs provide this feature because it is bad form to double-space between sentences and punctuation (something you'd do on a typewriter) when you write on a computer.*

7. After you've finished reading the messages (and responding to those that interest you), you can retrieve new postings by choosing Refresh Message List

from the View menu (or pressing COMMAND-L), or you can choose Get More Messages to retrieve a new batch of messages.

8. When you're done with one newsgroup, just click the next to repeat the process of retrieving message headers and viewing messages.

NOTE   *Some newsgroups support a feature called binaries, which simply means that files are attached to the messages. If you access a binary from one of these newsgroups, you'll see the telltale Attachments paper clip icon. It's a good idea, however, to avoid such files, as you have no way of knowing in advance if they are what they're represented to be, and not something that contains a virus.*

A Short Note About Message Threading

Most veterans of newsgroups prefer to view their messages in threaded form. A threaded message means that all those with the same topic are put together. This makes it far easier for you to find messages with the topics of interest. There is incredible clutter in newsgroups, and this is a way to separate the wheat from the chaff.

To sort your messages by threads, simply make sure the Threaded command is checked in Entourage's View menu. If it is not checked, messages will all be separated, even if they are part of the same thread. However, you will have additional sorting options, such as the ability to sort by name and date.

```
rec.arts.sf.fandom                         [ Subject  ‡ ] [ starts with  ‡ ] [                    ] [  ]
  [ ] [ ] [⚹] [🖉] │ From              │ Subject                    ▲ │ Sent              │ Size │ Categories
  ▷ [ ] ⚹         Mary Kay Kare       Re: Cooking In Outer Space?       Yesterday 6:38 PM    1 K    None
    [ ] ⚹         Janice Gelb         DUFF 2001 Reminder!               Yesterday 6:41 PM    1 K    None
  ▷ [ ] ⚹         Patrick Connors     Re: Fandom.com, again             Yesterday 1:11 PM    1 K    None
  ▽ [ ]           Kevin J. Maroney    Re: Flordia Supremes Speak        Yesterday 1:24 PM    1 K    None
    [ ]           Kevin J. Maroney      Re: Flordia Supremes Speak      Yesterday 1:29 PM    1 K    None
    [ ]           David T. Bilek        Re: Flordia Supremes Speak      Yesterday 2:02 PM    1 K    None
    [ ] ⚹         Paul Birnbaum       Re: Flordia Supremes Speak        Yesterday 3:08 PM    2 K    None
    [ ] ⚹         Bob Webber          Re: Flordia Supremes Speak        Yesterday 4:04 PM    1 K    None
    [ ] ⚹         Mary Kay Kare       Re: Flordia Supremes Speak        Yesterday 6:55 PM    2 K    None
    [ ] ⚹         Tony Towers         Re: Flordia Supremes Speak        Yesterday 7:05 PM    2 K    None
    [ ] ⚹         Avedon Carol        Re: Flordia Supremes Speak        Yesterday 7:29 PM    1 K    None
    [ ] ⚹         Bob Webber          Re: Flordia Supremes Speak        Yesterday 8:23 PM    2 K    None
    [ ] ⚹         Alison Hopkins      Re: Flordia Supremes Speak        Today 2:43 AM        2 K    None
```

```
       From: David T. Bilek <DavidBilek@aol.com>        To: rec.arts.sf.fandom
       Subject: Re: Flordia Supremes Speak

On Tue, 05 Dec 2000 11:07:03 GMT, liscarey@mediaone.net (Lis Carey)
wrote:

>DavidBilek@aol.com (David T. Bilek) wrote in
>>Can anyone point out anything specific in the way he handled the
>>case that even hints at partisanship?
>>
>>Besides "my side didn't win", of course.
>
>The fact that he granted very wide latitude in questioning and cross-
>examining witnesses to Bush's attorneys, but was very restrictive with
>David Boies, repeatedly cutting off attempts at cross-examination of
>the Bush campaigns witnesses.
>

I did see Boies getting repeatedly cut off, yes.  Correctly.

For example, he was attempting to grill the plastics expert about
the specific machines used in the contested counties, *after*
stopping, through objections, the Bush lawyer from doing the same.
Similar things happened with one of the other witnesses.

Thats not partisanship, thats the law.

-David
```

Figure 10-3.   *Here is the newsgroup message, ready for you to read and respond to.*

Responding to a Message

After you've spent some time reviewing new messages, no doubt you'll want to send a response. Before doing so, you'll want to read the upcoming section, "A Short Treatise on Proper Newsgroup Behavior." There are a number of rules and conventions or traditions on the Internet that govern online conduct. You'll want to acquaint yourself with them before you get involved. That way, your messages will be accepted more readily, particularly by some newsgroup veterans who, regrettably, don't take easily to newcomers (or newbies, as they are sometimes called).

To reply to a newsgroup message, follow these steps:

1. When you've opened a message that you feel warrants a reply, select the portion of text that you want to quote in your response.

2. Click the button labeled Reply to Newsgroup or press COMMAND-R, which will bring up a message window that contains the name of the newsgroup, the subject, and the quoted text.

NOTE   *If you prefer to write to the message's author directly, choose Reply to Sender. But you should double-check the message to see whether the person posting it has indicated that he or she wants to receive private messages, or whether the e-mail address has been altered to prevent unsolicited messages (something like "nospam" will appear in the address). Under most circumstances, messages meant for the newsgroup should be posted to the newsgroup; reply to the sender only if the person indicates that he or she really wants a personal response. Some will resent it otherwise.*

3. Write your response in the text window (see Figure 10-4).

4. When you're finished writing your message, recheck it for spelling and content.

CAUTION   *It's a good idea to avoid HTML formatting for newsgroup messages. Newsgroups are visited by folks using a number of computing platforms, and it's highly likely that many potential readers will not be able to see your custom text styles.*

5. To send your message right away, click Post Now. If you're not hooked up to your ISP, Entourage will log you on and post the message.

6. If you'd rather post the message at a later time, click the Post Later button instead. The message will be stored in the Outbox to be sent during your next send and receive session.

Posting a New Newsgroup Message

If you want to discuss a matter for which there's no existing message thread, you'll want to create a new topic on your own.

Here's how to do it.

1. With Entourage open, click the name of the newsgroup to which you want to post a message.

2. Double-check the messages to make sure there is no existing topic that might be suitable, and also that the newsgroup is appropriate for the message.

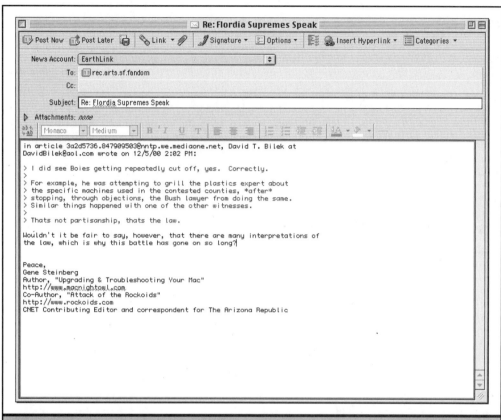

in article 3a2d5736.847909503@nntp.we.mediaone.net, David T. Bilek at
DavidBilek@aol.com wrote on 12/5/00 2:02 PM:

> I did see Boies getting repeatedly cut off, yes. Correctly.
>
> For example, he was attempting to grill the plastics expert about
> the specific machines used in the contested counties, *after*
> stopping, through objections, the Bush lawyer from doing the same.
> Similar things happened with one of the other witnesses.
>
> Thats not partisanship, thats the law.

Wouldn't it be fair to say, however, that there are many interpretations of
the law, which is why this battle has gone on so long?

Peace,
Gene Steinberg
Author, "Upgrading & Troubleshooting Your Mac"
http://www.macnightowl.com
Co-Author, "Attack of the Rockoids"
http://www.rockoids.com
CNET Contributing Editor and correspondent for The Arizona Republic

Figure 10-4.   *This message is ready for a response.*

3. With the newsgroup's messages displayed, click the New button.

4. In the Subject field, enter a subject for your message (this screen will look
   very similar to what's shown in Figure 10-4).

5. Write the message.

6. When your message is complete, you'll want to double-check spelling
   and punctuation.

7. To post the message immediately, click Post Now. Entourage will connect you
   to your ISP if you're not already logged on and then send the message.

8. If you want to send the message at a later time, perhaps after you've written
   a number of messages, click Post Later. The message will be placed in your
   Outbox, ready to go the next time you send messages in Entourage.

GETTING THE MOST
OUT OF ENTOURAGE

A Short Treatise on Proper Newsgroup Behavior

At the start of this chapter, I used the term *infuriating* to describe newsgroups, and that can be an understatement. While many of the messages you will read come from folks who are perfectly decent and will comport themselves in a respectful manner in a discussion group, there are many who use the relative anonymity of a newsgroup to convey a totally different and sometimes obnoxious personality.

Some messages are replete with vulgar language, personal attacks, and all sorts of incendiary comments. Such messages are called *flames*, and if you are one of those being flamed, you are apt to get upset and want to respond in kind. I've been on the receiving end of such messages myself, and it can be downright annoying.

But before you respond in kind, you'll want to think twice before you descend to such behavior. First, whatever you do or say on the Internet reflects on you, not on the other person. You should behave online in a fashion similar to the way you behave with your friends, family, and business colleagues.

A second consideration: The major online services do not cotton to such untoward behavior. While many of those newsgroup flamers belong to ISPs that do not have rules of conduct, or post under false names, you can definitely risk losing your ISP account if you violate its terms. Such terms definitely prohibit online flaming or, in fact, any type of behavior that constitutes a personal attack. Some ISPs, such as AOL, seriously frown on the use of vulgar language.

NOTE   *It is also a good idea not to post personal newsgroup messages from your company e-mail address or network—unless you own the company, of course. Getting involved in a Usenet flame war from a company account can lead to premature career death. Some newsgroup regulars get around this by putting an explicit disclaimer below their signature stating that their views do not represent those of their employer, but it's a good idea to ask your employer before using a company account in this way.*

For all of these reasons, you'll want to be careful in the way you handle yourself when using those message boards. Here is a brief discussion of the general rules of proper online behavior, sometimes known as netiquette:

- **Lurk**   Although this term has connotations of standing in a dark alley watching people go by, in Internet parlance it means hanging out and getting the lay of the land. Before you begin to participate in a newsgroup, you'll want to spend time reviewing the messages, to see the subjects dealt with and the topics that tend to be frowned upon. If the newsgroup has a FAQ (frequently asked questions) document, consult it to learn the mission and purpose of the newsgroup. Once you have spent time lurking in a newsgroup, you'll be ready to begin to participate in the messaging.

- **Don't Oversubscribe**   Depending on your ISP, you may have tens of thousands of newsgroups from which to select. Any one of them may have hundreds or thousands of messages posted each and every day. It is really easy to get overwhelmed with this amount of information, and you won't benefit from poring over messages without time to read or respond. In the beginning, you should join no more than a few mailing lists at a time, and then, as you get accustomed to the routine, you can increase your number of subscriptions.

■ **Be Aware of Your Audience**   Your response to a newsgroup message is a public document, available to anyone with Internet access who chooses to visit that newsgroup. If you prefer to send a personal message to one particular message poster and the poster seems willing to accept e-mail, go ahead and write a personal message. That way, you won't clog the newsgroup with irrelevant chatter that won't interest the audience at large.

CAUTION   *Some newsgroup posters state specifically in the body of their messages that they do not want to receive e-mail. They may use a fake, spam-blocking e-mail address or specify they want responses sent only to the newsgroup. Consider their views carefully before you intrude on their privacy.*

■ **Post in the Correct Newsgroup**   One of the reasons you should lurk for a while is to be fully aware of the subject matter of a specific newsgroup. You would not, for example, talk about your favorite Mac in a group devoted to users of Windows 2000. Well, you could post such a message, but I can tell you that the responses will be a lot more than you bargained for.

NOTE   *There are, in fact, newsgroups that are devoted to advocacy discussions, where Mac and Windows users have it out. One of these, comp.sys.mac.advocacy, has hundreds of messages each day about the benefits of the Mac OS pitted against an equal number of messages stating that Windows Me or Windows 2000 rules.*

■ **Be Polite in Your Responses**   Don't descend to the level of the newsgroup flamer. Be polite and respectful in your responses and don't take attacks personally. To some newsgroup regulars, flaming is nothing more than a game, and they wouldn't think of behaving in that fashion in real, as opposed to Internet, life.

NOTE   *I have actually talked to and met some of the folks who seem to be the most ardent newsgroup flamers, and in real life they are totally different people—usually nice, friendly, with a good sense of humor. But that doesn't apply in all cases, and it doesn't justify the way they behave in those newsgroups.*

■ **Quote Parts of the Message to Which You're Responding**   When you respond to someone's message, it's customary to quote the portions to which you're responding. This is easily done in Entourage, as you merely have to select that portion before clicking the Reply button; the reply will be formatted in the proper fashion automatically. It's not normally good form to quote an entire message, unless it's short and your responses are long and detailed and require that length. When quoting, however, be sure you don't take sentences out of context. If you're not certain, it's better to quote a little bit more material than a little bit less.

CAUTION   *It is especially bad form to quote a long message and then add a short comment, such as "I agree." You might want to quote a sentence that summarizes the message before adding that comment.*

■ **Use a Signature**   Another Internet custom is to use a signature at the end of your message. The signature can include your real name or just an e-mail address. If you include your real name, you can include the address of your Web site or even your particular occupation, if it's appropriate. But try to keep signatures to no more than four or five short lines. As explained in Chapter 7, you can easily add a signature that will appear automatically at the bottom of a message, or even use random signatures, where one of several is chosen for each message.

NOTE   *Another thing to consider is whether or not you should use your real name in your signature. My personal opinion is that you should, so long as you don't put information that would let a casual net visitor figure out in what city or state you reside (unless you're representing a business, of course). There are far too many net visitors who post under fakes names simply for the sake of confusing people and playing practical jokes.*

■ **Be Brief**   There are often dozens or hundreds of messages in a newsgroup daily, and folks have but a limited time in which to trudge through the sheer volume of information. Just express your point and, as they say, get out of the way. Long, convoluted messages are particularly annoying.

■ **Spell Check**   By default, Entourage will flag suspect words. But to be sure your responses are spelled correctly, use the Spelling command on the Tools menu to have Entourage's spelling checker give your message a final check. Remember that your message reflects on you, and it's public, so you'll want to make sure that it is correct before you send it.

NOTE   *Sad to say, some newsgroup flamers think nothing of pointing out spelling and grammatical errors in a message, even without discussing the content. It's rather a dirty way to debate, but it happens—so be sure to double-check your messages.*

■ **Don't Change the Subject for Responses**   Many newsgroup-reading applications, such as Entourage, can sort messages into threads, with a separate folder for each topic. This makes it easy for subscribers to that newsgroup to find relevant messages. You should change the subject only when starting a new message thread, or when a discussion seems to veer off the intended path, in which case you will want to make the subject clear and make sure it truly reflects the topic.

CAUTION *It is against proper etiquette to create a subject title that attacks an individual. Such a title can be considered as much a violation of an ISP's rules of conduct as an actual message that contains a personal attack. If you do find such a topic and you want to respond, you may want to alter the subject to reflect the discussion in a way that doesn't hurt anyone's feelings.*

- **Be Careful About Humor and Emotional Statements** While it may be obvious to you that something is funny, a lot of humor depends on the tone of your voice, your expression, and perhaps your body language. In an Internet message, one normally expresses such sentiments punctuated with an *emoticon*, such as :), to signify a grin ("just kidding folks"). We'll discuss other types of emoticons (some are called *smileys*) in the next section of this chapter.

- **Is the Question Already Answered?** Often I will see someone ask a question in a newsgroup and then read 10 identical responses from different people. Some of this is unavoidable, as it may take hours or even days for messages to show up in newsgroup. But before you answer, see if someone else got there first. Keep the clutter to a minimum.

- **Avoid Courtesy E-mails Unless Requested** You may be tempted to send an e-mail copy of a message as a courtesy, in case the person who asked a question may have missed your response. Think twice before doing so, however. Some people prefer to limit their participation to the newsgroup itself and do not welcome unsolicited e-mail. If the poster, however, indicates that he or she welcomes e-mail messages, go for it.

- **Be Careful About Commercial Postings** If you see someone asking about a product or service you offer, you may be tempted to tell the person in the newsgroup about your business. The rule is: don't do it unless that newsgroup allows commercial messages. Most do not, and the ones that do are carefully identified as commercial, or the flavor of the messages will indicate the kind of content that's acceptable. Otherwise, all you'll end up doing is upsetting people who do not want unsolicited promotions (there's quite enough of that on the Internet already). You won't help your business get more customers.

- **Don't Post Binaries** Except for special newsgroups, clearly identified, binaries (or file attachments, such as photos) aren't allowed. In addition to upsetting the newsgroup regulars, violating this edict may run you afoul of the standards of your own ISP. I've known of folks who posted a binary by mistake and got dropped by their ISP; no amount of protest would get them reinstated.

A Brief Survey of Online Abbreviations and Smileys

How, in a message, do you tell someone you're just kidding, and how do you express an emotion? Skilled writers, particularly journalists and novelists, can handle such chores, but most folks find it difficult to express every emotional nuance with prose. In some cases, there isn't time to do so, especially if you want to respond to a lot of messages. Even professional writers will use shortcuts, such as smileys—a few characters that offer guidance as to the emotional reaction you wanted. Another Internet tradition is the online abbreviation, where several characters signify a short phrase or sentence.

Table 10-1 lists common abbreviations and smileys and their definitions. There are many more, and some can be mighty eccentric. Despite the fact that I love being eccentric, I'll avoid those, however.

Abbreviation	Translation
LOL	Laughing out loud
ROFL or ROTFL	Rolling on the floor laughing
AFK	Away from keyboard
BAK	Back at keyboard
BRB	Be right back
OIC	Oh, I see
IMO	In my opinion
IMHO	In my humble opinion, or in my honest opinion
TTFN	Ta-ta for now
TTYL	Talk to you later
NIFOC	Nude in front of computer. (All right, I said some of these were strange.)
GMTA	Great minds think alike
IHTBHWYG	It's hard to be humble when you're great. (My favorite!)
<g>	Grin
GA	Go ahead
[ ] or { }	A hug, repeated to reflect the degrees of intensity

Table 10-1.   *Common Online Abbreviations and Smileys*

Abbreviation	Translation
:)	Smile
:(	Frown
:/	Ho-hum smile
;)	Winking smile
:D	Smile with a big grin
:*	Kiss
8)	Wide-eyed smile
B-)	Wearing sunglasses
:-*	Just ate a sour pickle
>:-(	Sick and tired of reading this nonsense. (Amen!)

Table 10-1.   *Common Online Abbreviations and Smileys* (continued)

Introducing Internet Mailing Lists

If newsgroups seem daunting to you or perhaps too demanding of attention, there is yet another way to participate in online discussions or receive news about interesting subjects. It's convenient, for you don't have to check a large number of message boards; everything comes right to your Entourage Inbox. It's the mailing list.

Mailing lists are available covering all sorts of subjects, from personal computers and your favorite software or computing platform to alternative lifestyles and UFOs. The way they work is similar. Once you subscribe to the list, you'll receive mailings from a central address containing ongoing discussions, news, and information about a topic, or summaries or digests of interesting messages (see Figure 10-5). Some mailing lists are read-only propositions, such as the ones Apple Computer provides about its various product categories. Others invite interactive discussions, and you may receive anywhere from a few to a dozen messages each day from the participants.

So how do you get involved? Here are some suggestions about joining, leaving, and managing mailing list clutter.

- **Locate a List**   Web sites devoted to your favorite products or subjects are likely to run such lists. Apple's own e-mail newsletters, for example, can be ordered from this site: http://applenews.lists.apple.com/subscribe. One of the major computer magazines, *Macworld*, sponsors some very informative newsletters as well. You can learn about them at http://lists.macworld.com/.

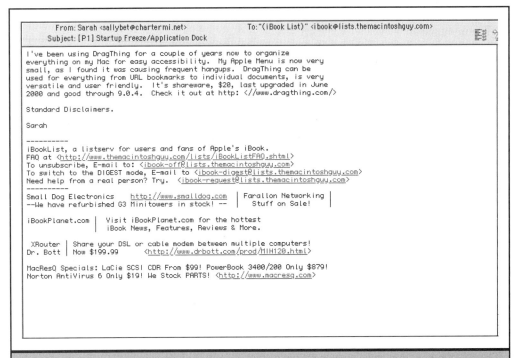

Figure 10-5.   *This is a typical mailing list message received from one of the many lists to which the author subscribes.*

TIP   *One useful source of Internet mailing lists is http://www.liszt.com/. This Web site has a directory of hundreds of mailing lists, and you can even subscribe to several of the ones they run.*

■ **Subscribe**   How do you sign up? That depends. The information about the mailing list will often include a link to take you to the subscription area, where you can enter your own subscription to the list. My own Mac support and information site, The Mac Night Owl (at http://www.macnightowl.com/), has a link right on the home page to order the weekly newsletter. In other instances, you'll need to send e-mail to a specific address, usually with the word *subscribe* or *join* in the subject line.

■ **Learn How to Leave**   Perhaps the mailing list isn't quite what you expected. The discussions or information do not interest you, or you just do not have the time to absorb the glut of information. Many mailings from such lists will have a line at the top or bottom explaining how to get off the list. Often this simply involves sending a message to the address that sponsors the list with an Unsubscribe or Remove command. You also can usually visit the list sponsor's Web site to learn how to get off a list.

■ **Change of Address Suggestion**   A mailing list manager usually doesn't have a way to automatically switch your address for you. If you want to have your mailings sent to a different address, the best way to do this is to unsubscribe or leave the list and then subscribe again using the new address. This may seem somewhat of an inconvenience, but mailing lists are usually run by software that takes commands very literally. You need to follow the specific routine they specify to make the appropriate changes.

■ **Don't Get Overenthusiastic**   With thousands of mailing lists out there, it's easy to oversubscribe. Soon your Entourage Inbox is so cluttered with messages, you hardly have time to handle your regular messages. The best way to start is to subscribe to just a few mailing lists and see how many messages they produce. Build from there, if you feel you can handle more.

■ **Follow Instructions About Responses**   Some mailing lists do not welcome responses, and others contain discussions that are no different in nature from those of newsgroups. Read the information about the mailing list to see if you can participate. If you choose to participate, make sure that your messages are sent from the same e-mail address you used when you subscribed; otherwise, the messages may be rejected.

NOTE   *This requirement can cause confusion if you have a lot of e-mail addresses, as I do. Some mailing lists include a note at the bottom of mailings indicating the e-mail address used when you subscribed. It's definitely welcome information.*

■ **Don't Forget Proper Online Etiquette**   The same rules that apply to newsgroups apply equally when you subscribe to a mailing list. If you choose to respond, follow the same rules of online behavior cited earlier. Mailing list sponsors may even be more rigid or arbitrary in their interpretation of rude behavior, and you can end up losing your access to a list if you don't conduct yourself properly.

Using the Mailing List Manager

Entourage 2001 has a very convenient way for you to manage your mailing lists, so that you can have them sorted in a way that makes it easy for you to view them at your convenience. The Mailing List Manager sets rules that not only handle the messages you receive, but also provide the information you need to contact those who run a list in case you want to leave the list or leave and subscribe under a new name.

Here's how to use this convenient feature:

1. With Entourage Open, choose Mailing List Manager from the Tools menu. This brings up the dialog box shown in Figure 10-6.

2. Click the New button to begin your entry. This will bring up the Edit Mailing List Rule dialog box (see Figure 10-7).

3. Enter the list name in the Name field.

4. On the Mailing List tab, enter the list address. You can locate this address in any mailing from the list or on the source document or site that you used to enter your subscription. Once you've located it, just copy and paste it into the List Address text box.

5. Indicate where messages for this list are to be put. By default, they are placed in your Entourage Inbox, but you can move them to any other mailbox folder, or you can create a new folder for the task.

6. If you like, you can also move messages you've sent to this folder; just check the appropriate box.

7. The next option, Set Category, is used for sorting purposes. Select it to organize messages in a way that's convenient for you to check them out later on.

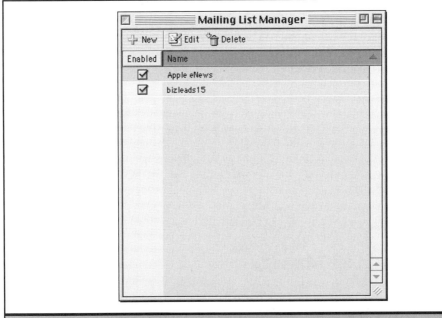

Figure 10-6. *Manage and create mailing list rules from here.*

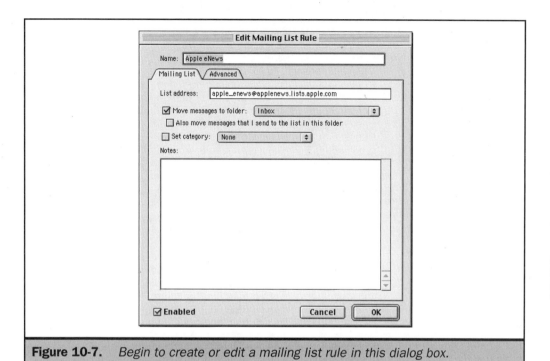

Figure 10-7.   *Begin to create or edit a mailing list rule in this dialog box.*

8. If you want to add some information about the list for later review, just place it in the Notes field.

9. Make sure the Enabled check box is selected to activate the rule.

10. After you've completed the basic setup information, select the Advanced tab to add more steps to your rule for the list (see Figure 10-8).

NOTE   *You do not have to use the Advanced tab to create an effective mailing list rule. The setup information on the Mailing List tab is quite enough to get you started.*

11. In the first section, Other List Addresses, you can enter various contact information for those who manage the list and the list server (if it's managed by a mailing list program).

12. In the next section, Actions on List Messages, you can apply six separate rules to your messages, with a few options. One particularly interesting one is Burst Digests into Individual Messages. Some mailing lists put out a digest mailing,

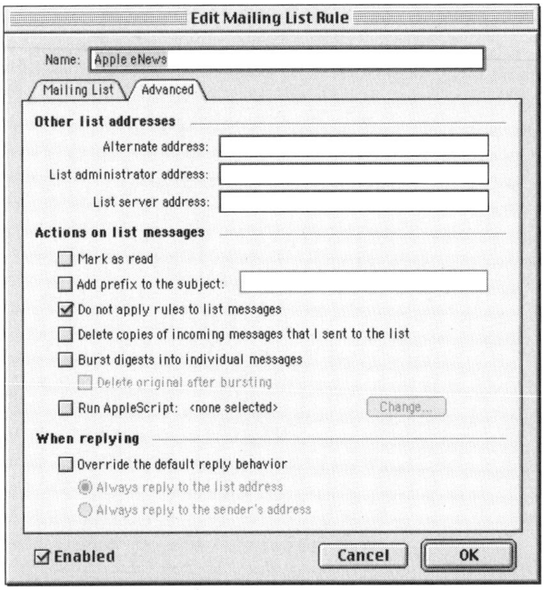

Figure 10-8. *Add more information about the mailing list here.*

which combines separate messages into a single listing. This option separates them for convenience. Here is a description of the options:

- **Mark as Read** Kind of superfluous, if you intend to actually read the messages received from that list.

- **Add Prefix to the Subject** This option lets you conveniently flag a message as from a list, for later viewing. You can add a simple "Mailing List" prefix, for example, to set list messages apart.

- **Do Not Apply Rules to List Messages** This means that other e-mail rules won't apply to this category of messages.

- **Delete Copies of Incoming Messages That I Send to the List** This helps reduce e-mail clutter, as the messages you send won't show up in your Inbox. On the other hand, if you want confirmation that the message was actually received by the mailing list, you may want to keep this option unchecked.

- **Burst Digests into Individual Messages** See the preceding description. You may also want to check the option Delete Original After Bursting so you don't have duplication.

- **Run AppleScript**   If you are adept at writing or using AppleScript, you can create a script to manage your message handling; then check this option, so you can select the script you want to apply.

13. In the final section, When Replying, you can change the response behavior for the list. Normally, when you reply to a list, the response goes to the address handling the list, but you can specify that it go to the address of the sender instead.

14. If you want to edit an existing rule, open the Mailing List Manager, select the name of your list rule, and click the Edit button.

15. To remove a mailing list, select it from the Mailing List Manager dialog box, and click the DELETE key.

16. When your settings or changes are complete, click OK to put them into effect.

Summary

The world of Usenet can be wacky, exciting, and informative, all at the same time. Once you get used to subscribing, reading, and responding to messages, you'll wonder why you've never done it before. In addition, you'll find that an Internet mailing list can bring you a regular repository of fascinating information.

All right; we're done with Entourage, but we're hardly half way into this book, and there is a lot more to explore. In Chapter 11, which begins Part III of this book, you'll discover the ins and outs of the centerpiece of Office 2001: the world's most popular word processor, Word.

Part III

Putting Word 2001 to Work for You

Chapter 11

Setting Up Word 2001

Way back when, there was a simple word processing program that garnered a huge market share on the Mac. It was speedy, reasonably simple to learn, and offered most of the features you'd want in such an application.

Somewhere along the line, simple went out the window, and big and clumsy took over. Word 6 wasn't treated terribly nicely in the Macintosh press. Many regarded it as a clumsy Windows port, and the strong resemblance of the Font dialog box to the one used on that other platform didn't help matters. It also could take over a minute to launch even on a fast Mac and was dog slow in many of its functions.

Microsoft took the hostile reception to heart and managed to beef up performance of Word 6, particularly in the most noticeable areas of application launching and word counting. The interface fixes, however, were reserved for future versions of the program.

Beginning with Office 98, a chastened Microsoft began to make its programs more Mac friendly. This move was accelerated with Office 2001, which has features tailor-made for us, and some are unique to our favorite computing platform.

To Recap

Chief among the new features of Word 2001 is the Project Gallery, described in detail in the first four chapters of this book. Among the features are enhanced templates and wizards (see Figure 11-1). You don't have to concern yourself over how to begin, as Microsoft will guide you there.

The other highly useful feature is the Formatting Palette (see Figure 11-2), which is similar to features offered in other programs, but totally new to Office. It's a context-sensitive palette, which changes to reflect the features you're using, that lets you format text and pictures and perform other functions without having to bury yourself in menus and dialog boxes. In fact, for many Word tasks, you may never have to visit a dialog box at all.

A Look at the Word 2001 Interface

Even if you're familiar with the ins and outs of Word, you'll find changes in Word 2001. Many of these were described in Chapter 1, but by and large they lie beneath the surface, in menus and dialog boxes.

But even on the surface, you'll see that things have changed.

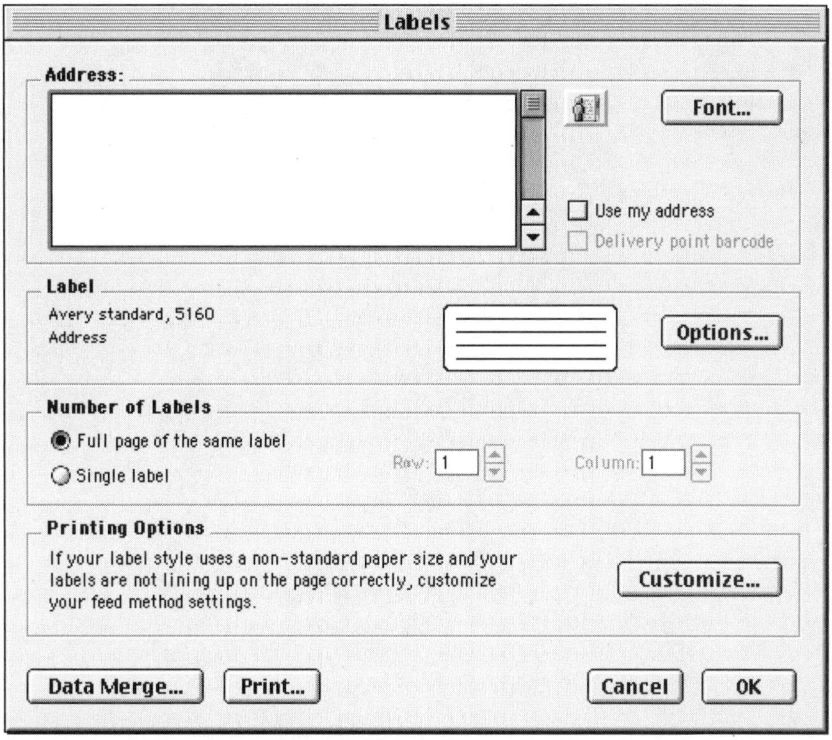

Figure 11-1.   *This is a typical wizard, for creating Labels.*

To start, let's open a new Word document. From here, you can type away as you prefer, or use this information as reference material as you begin to discover the vast power that Word provides.

Let us begin:

1. Double-click Word to launch it.

2. If the Project Gallery appears, as it will unless you've turned off the preference to display it, choose Blank Documents from the Category menu and then Word Document from the thumbnail display. This action will produce a blank Word document, pretty much like the one shown in Figure 11-3.

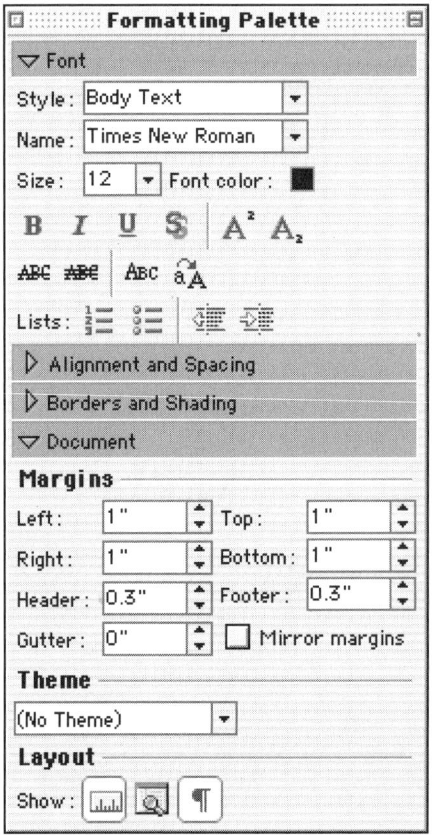

Figure 11-2.   *The Formatting Palette can be collapsed and expanded to give you access to the features you want.*

3. From here, you can click the blinking cursor in the text field of your document and start working, or you can take the time to explore your Word desktop, as follows:

■ **Toolbar**   These buttons provide one-click access to many of Word's most useful formatting functions. As you'll learn later in this chapter, you can customize the toolbar even further to display additional buttons or restrict it to fewer buttons, if you want to save screen space. You can also drag it to a new location on your Mac's desktop.

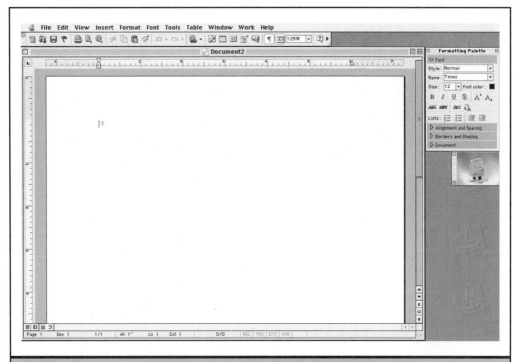

Figure 11-3.   *This is your standard Word desktop. I moved the Formatting Palette and Assistant so you can see everything in a convenient place.*

- **Status Bar**   At the bottom of the work area, Word displays the page number and the location on the page at which the cursor is pointing. At the right of the column character display is Word's clever Live Word Count display. To the left of the slash, Word displays the number of words in the document up to the point of the cursor, and to the right of the slash, Word displays the total number of words in the document.

- **Scrollbars**   The vertical and horizontal scrollbars provide a further visual guide to the size of your document and the location of particular content.

- **Formatting Palette**   As explained earlier, this floating palette offers one-click access to the most popular document formatting commands. It's also context sensitive, which means that the content depends on which Office program you're using and which function. For example, if you were working with a picture in your Word document, the formatting commands displayed would reflect various and sundry picture-related adjustments.

- **Animated Assistant** The little Mac moves and moans and groans in response to the operations you're performing in Word. Yes, you can dismiss this dude by clicking the close box, if you prefer not to have an animated helper guide you along the way (you get used to it after a while).

4. Shortly after you have begun working in your document, choose Save As from Word's File menu, then specify a location and name for the file in the dialog box that appears.

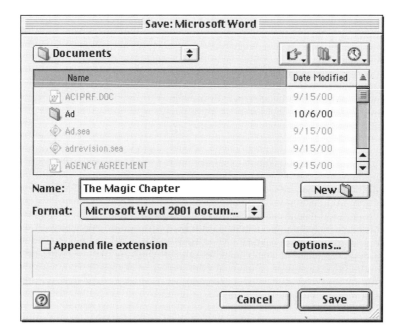

5. Click the Save button to store your document.

6. Continue working on your document, and, every 5 or 10 minutes or so, click Save again, so the contents of your document are continually updated. This way, in case your Mac freezes, or there's a power outage, the contents of your document will be reasonably up to date.

And this is just the beginning. We'll cover more of Word's extraordinary range of features beginning in the next chapter.

Setting Preferences in Word 2001

All Office 2001 applications have an extensive repository of preference options. In fact, they are so extensive that they can be mighty intimidating. Fortunately, you don't have to change any of the settings. You can use Word 2001 and experience the power of this program without altering the factory-issue preferences, but as you continue to work with the program, no doubt you'll find that something doesn't seem quite right the way it is, and you'll want to consider switching something to make the program behave more to your liking.

Here's a look at the various preferences offered in Word 2001, and a suggestion or two on what you might want to change. To bring up the Preferences dialog box, choose Preferences from the Edit menu. Each preference category is identified by a tab. Click a tab to bring up that set of preferences. Actual changes are made by checking or unchecking option boxes or entering new information in text fields.

■ **View Preferences**   How would you like your document pages displayed? The View tab of the Preferences dialog box (see Figure 11-4) gives you a huge number of check boxes, but they are for display only. None of the items you specify here will actually appear when you print your document. The first, under Show, specifies how elements on a page appear. A text boundary, for example, will place a faint rectangle around the text area of a document. ScreenTips, sometimes known as ToolTips, are those little cartoon balloons that pop up when you rest the cursor on a button in a toolbar, the document window, or the Formatting Palette. The second category, Nonprinting Characters, displays faint marks for formatting symbols on a page, so you can keep track of them. My choice is to have all nonprinting characters visible; it's a lot easier to keep track of things that way. The Window options control the various display bars shown in your document window, so you can see the status and position of your document. My favorite, as a writer, is Live Word Count (no; Microsoft didn't create that feature for me, though one of their product managers laughed loudly when I made that very suggestion).

NOTE   *The order in which the Preferences dialog box tabs appear depends strictly on the ones you examined last, so the sequence you see may differ from what is shown here. I am simply covering them in the order in which they appeared when I wrote this chapter.*

■ **General Preferences**   This tab (see Figure 11-5) sets application-wide preferences, such as the use of animation and sound to provide confirmation of some functions, such as saving a document. One particularly valuable feature is the Recently Used File list. This option puts the list on your File menu for fast access to any of the listed documents (regardless of the location of the document).

PUTTING WORD 2001
TO WORK FOR YOU

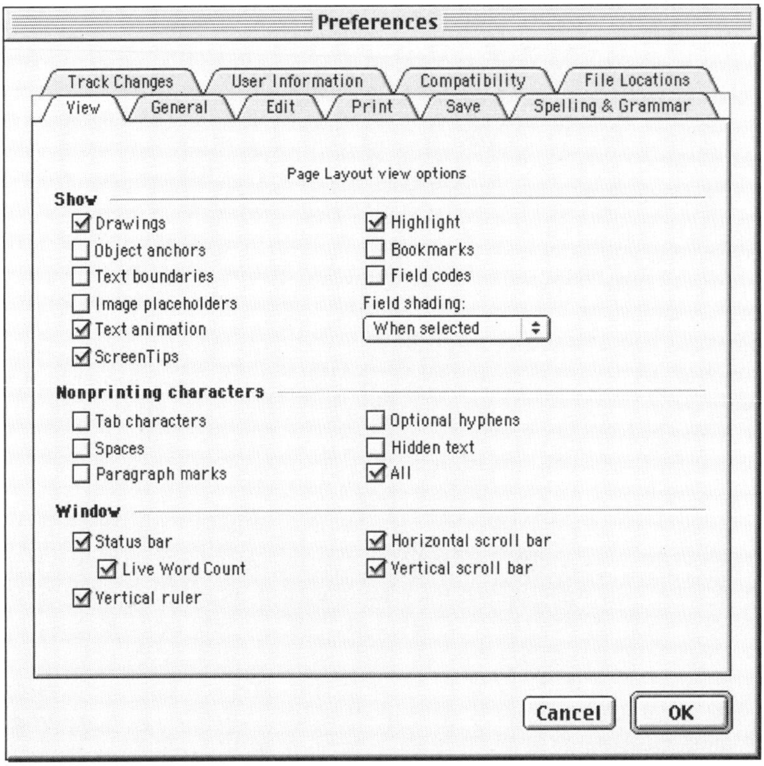

Figure 11-4. *The View tab lets you configure the way your documents are displayed. It has no impact on the actual printing of the documents.*

The Macro Virus Protection feature doesn't protect you from a virus, unfortunately. All it does is warn you about the danger when you open a document to which a macro has been applied. On this tab, you can also specify whether you want the Project Gallery to appear each time you launch the program. If you'd like to see the fonts in their true styles, the WYSIWYG Font Menu option is a plus.

■ **Edit Preferences**   This tab (see Figure 11-6) controls the activation of editing functions. Here you'll find some interesting options in addition to the usual ones. Drag-and-Drop Text Editing, for example, enables you to select and drag text and place it in another position on your existing document, in another Word document, or on your Mac's desktop as a clipping. The option labeled When Selecting, Automatically Select Entire Word, cleverly includes the word spaces when you select a word. As a corollary, Use Smart Cut and Paste eliminates extra word spaces when you paste or drag text into a new position. That's a real time saver.

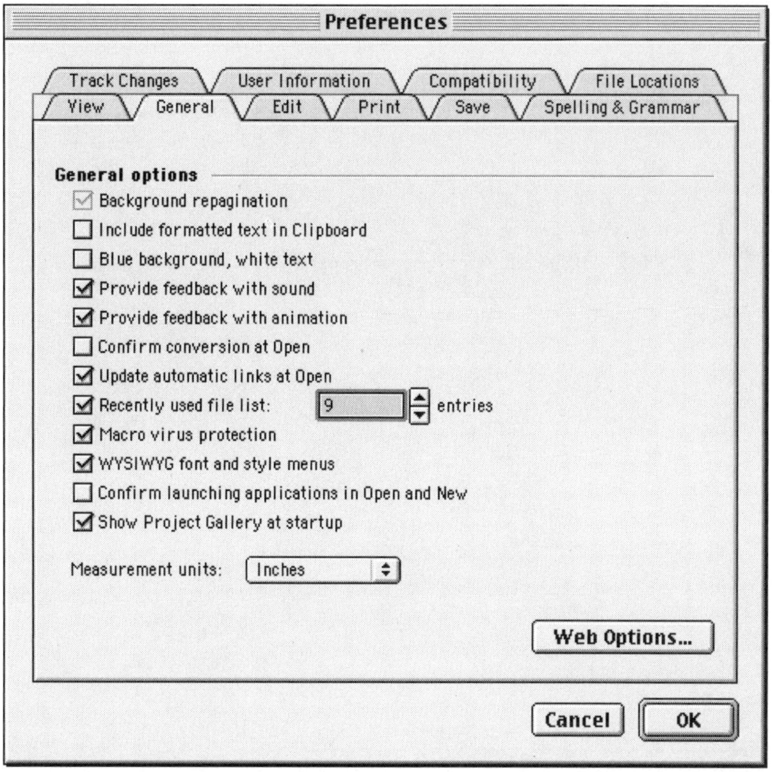

Figure 11-5.   *Choose a number of application-wide preferences from this tab.*

NOTE   *One particularly notable option is, in essence, a throwback to older word processing systems. If Overtype Mode is selected (it's off by default), when you type in an area in which text is entered, the new text replaces what's there, character by character. The normal approach is to just insert the new characters, leaving the old ones unless you've previously selected text to replace. This option might be worth trying, just to see how things were in the old days.*

- **Print Preferences**   The printing preferences you set in Word can specify whether hidden text or comments are displayed. Another option, Fractional Widths, gives you the best print quality with most modern printers, at the expense of the appearance of some of the text on the screen.

- **Save Preferences**   Here are some critical settings (see Figure 11-7), and you'll want to seriously consider the ramifications of each option. The first option, Always Create Backup Copy, is your ounce of protection in case something

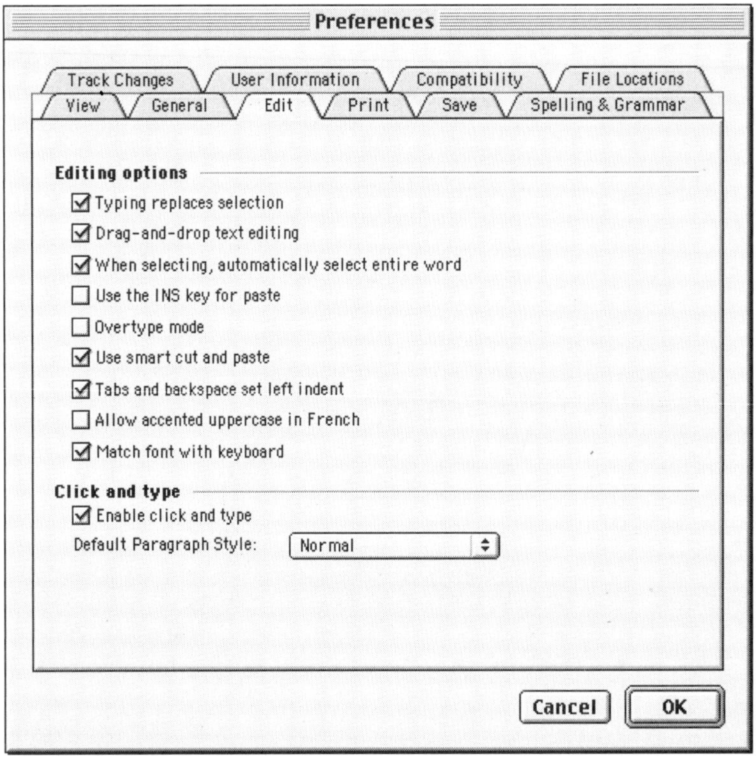

Figure 11-6. *These options control how Word handles text editing chores.*

happens to your original document. Every time you save a document, Word saves the original and a backup, labeled Backup of *<name of document>*. The next option, Allow Fast Saves, speeds up the saving process for big documents but can riddle the documents with extra data and make the file size larger. Another key choice is Save AutoRecover Info Every, with the time specified in the Minutes box. If you choose this option, you can often recover a document that was damaged due to a crash or power failure. The File Sharing Options section allows you to password protect your file.

NOTE *The automatic backup feature for Word is bare bones, and it is not completely effective, since it saves the copy in the same place as the original. It's a better idea to just make extra copies of your documents on another drive on a regular basis, so that you'll have a current copy in the event that the original hard drive fails.*

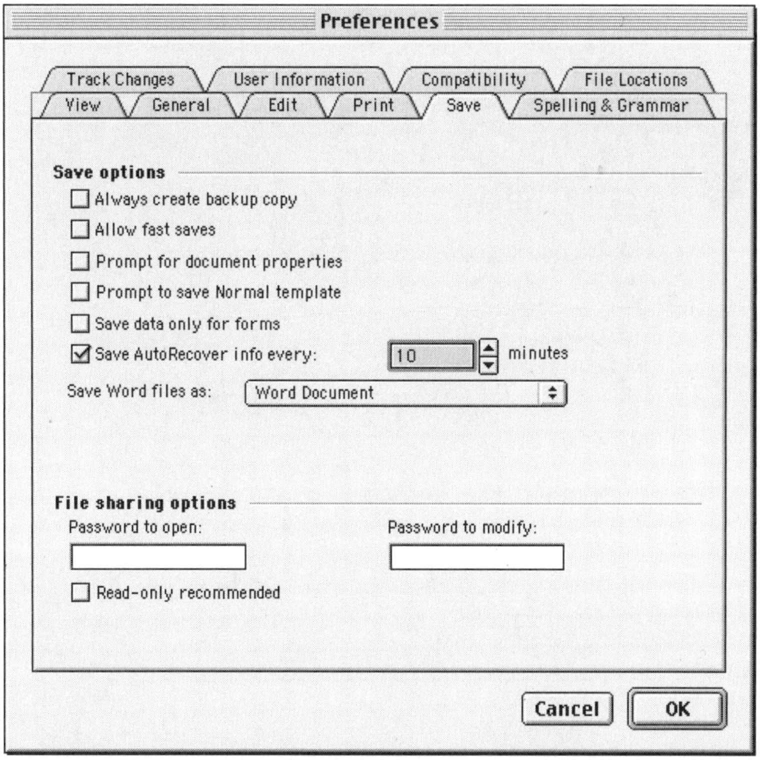

Figure 11-7. *Choose your Save options from this tab.*

■ **Spelling & Grammar Preferences** There are two categories of settings here (see Figure 11-8). The first, under Spelling, controls the way Word's spell checker works. The Check Spelling as You Type option is valuable, because gives you immediate feedback when you misspell a word. You can also specify Custom Dictionary, the location where you store words added to the dictionary (the basic dictionary is not intended to address all possible spelling errors). The Grammar settings mirror some of the Spelling settings. You can also specify the default writing style the grammar checker uses, depending on the purpose of your document. For most purposes, Standard is fine; for personal letters, you may want to switch to Casual.

■ **Track Changes Preferences** If your document is going to undergo a lot of revisions, or if it's being worked on by several writers or editors, you will want to take advantage of Word's ability to show changes being made to the manuscript, so you can see who corrected what, and when. This preference

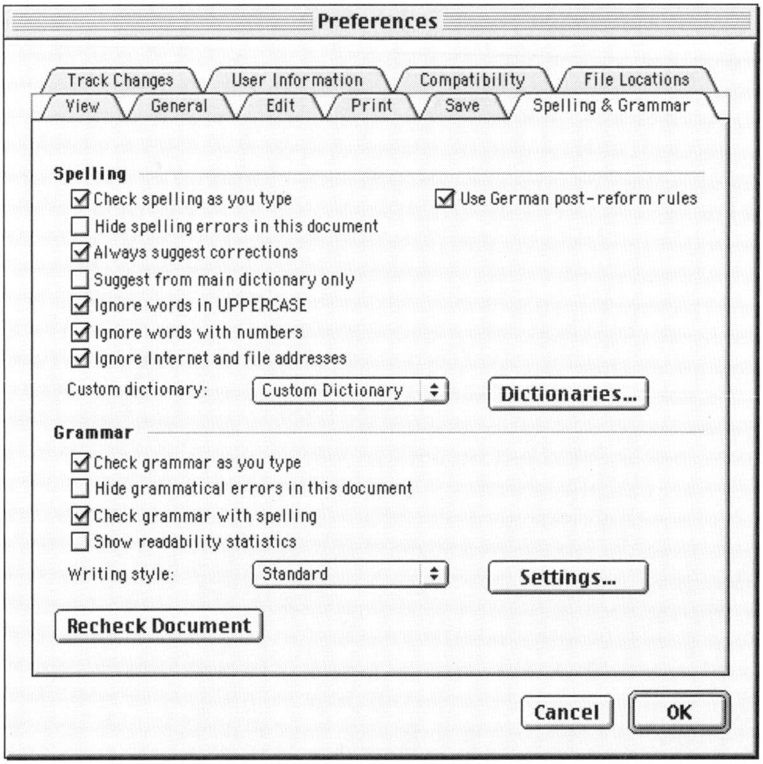

Figure 11-8. *Control Word's spelling and grammar checker settings from this tab.*

setting merely defines how the various types of changed text are displayed on the screen, so you can identify them. When you look over this feature, you'll see the answer to the great secret of how book writers manage to work with their editors during the editing process. It sure beats pen and pencil and little scratch marks on a printed manuscript (though some publishers of novels still prefer pen and pencil and little scratch marks).

■ **User Information Preferences**   Here's where you enter your personal information or the personal information about the primary user of this copy of Word. The information you enter in this tab also becomes a part of Entourage's Address Book.

■ **Compatibility Preferences**   This tab, shown in Figure 11-9, controls how Word works with documents converted from other versions of the program. The settings control the display only and don't affect the final look of that document when it's printed or viewed on another computers.

■ **File Locations Preferences**   This tab (shown in Figure 11-10) specifies the default location for different types of files in Word. It's best to leave these locations set as they are (though you can specify locations for your actual documents), because different settings may cause Word to look in the wrong place for various components needed by the program.

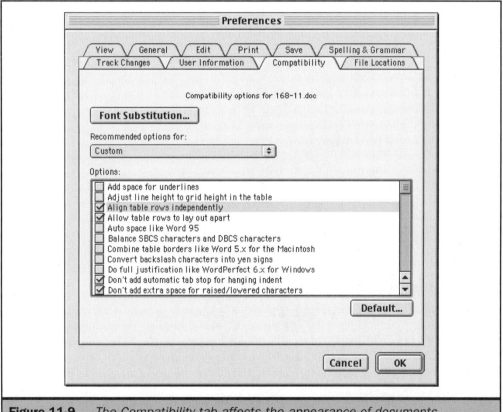

Figure 11-9.   *The Compatibility tab affects the appearance of documents converted from other versions of the program and displayed in the version you're using.*

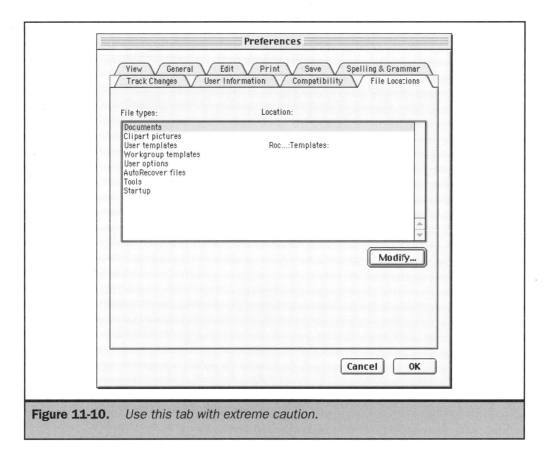

Figure 11-10. *Use this tab with extreme caution.*

Adjusting Word's Toolbars

There are toolbars and there are toolbars, and the one that comes with Word helps you easily access some of the program's most important functions. By default, you get a core collection of buttons, but you can easily add or remove those buttons or add toolbars, depending on the type of information you want displayed.

Customizing Toolbars and Buttons

Have you ever heard of toolbar overload? Well, it's possible to display a huge number of toolbars in Word, each of which offers one-click access to important features of the program. If you choose all of them (see Figure 11-11), you may not have much room left for your document, but you can see the range of flexibility of this application.

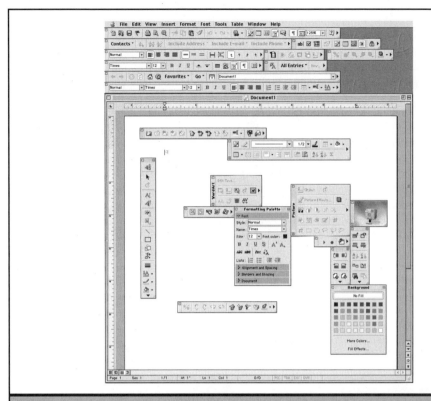

Figure 11-11.   *Here are the standard Word toolbars, displayed at the same time. Who needs room for text?*

NOTE   *Several years ago, when button and toolbar bloat began to infect some word processor programs, someone actually did a mock-up showing a post-year 2000 version of Word with a couple of dozen toolbars that left no more than an inch or two for document content. Art has almost imitated life here; all you need do is make a few custom toolbars and there wouldn't be room for any text at all, but you could at least click to your heart's content.*

Between the single toolbar minimalist approach and the extreme example shown here are lots of possibilities to display and customize toolbars. In addition, you can add command buttons to each toolbar, which gives even more ways to alter the appearance of Word.

In the next few pages, we'll cover some of the basic changes you can make to the program.

The changes you make to the toolbar or buttons are stored as separate settings files in the Microsoft folder, inside your System Folder's Preferences folder. If you delete those files or install Office on a different Mac, you'll have to redo all these changes.

Displaying Additional Toolbars

The example in Figure 11-11 illustrates most of the standard toolbars, except for one, Word for Macintosh 5.1, which simply mimics the one present in that version of the program. Here's how to display or hide a toolbar:

1. From the Tools menu, choose Customize. This will bring up the Customize dialog box.

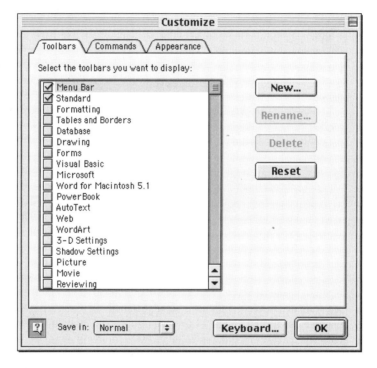

2. If the Toolbars tab isn't displayed, select that tab to bring up the list of choices.

3. Select a toolbar's check box to show or hide that toolbar.

4. If you want to change the toolbar back to the default settings, click the Reset button.

5. When you're finished, click OK or choose another tab to make further adjustments.

Creating a Custom Toolbar

In addition to displaying one of Word's prebuilt toolbars, you can actually create one of your own. Here's how it's done:

1. From the Tools menu, choose Customize.

2. In the Customize dialog box, select the Toolbars tab.

3. Click the New button and give your new toolbar a name.

4. Click OK, and the new toolbar will appear in the Toolbars list.

5. Select the Commands tab, which brings up the repository of command buttons available in the program.

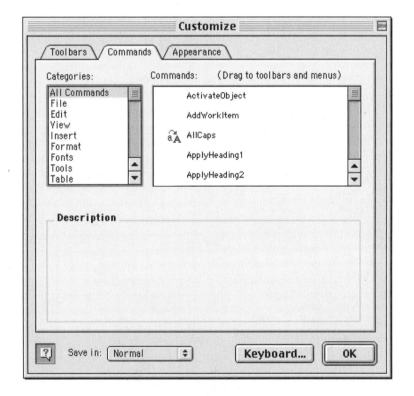

6. Click a category in the Command box, and the commands appropriate to that category will appear in the Commands pane.

7. Drag the command you want to add from the Commands pane to the toolbar.

You can also add commands to menus in the same fashion. Just drag the command to the appropriate menu, and it will appear almost instantaneously.

8. All done? Click OK to store your changes.

9. To delete a custom toolbar, click the Toolbars tab, select the name of the custom toolbar you've created, and click Delete to remove the toolbar.

A press of the Reset button will restore all toolbar settings to the factory-issue defaults.

Changing Word's Appearance

There are yet more options for customizing the look of Word on your Mac. One of these options alters the entire look of Word; another changes the size of command buttons so they're easier to see.

Here's how to make those changes:

1. With Word open, go to the Tools menu and choose Customize.

2. Select the Appearance tab.

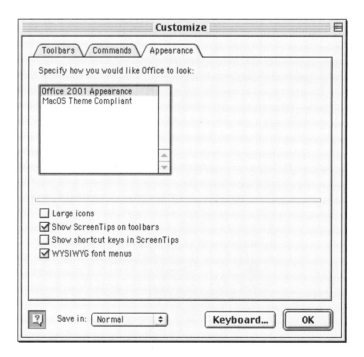

3. Select the Large Icons check box.

4. To change the theme or appearance of your Office software, choose one of
the themes in the display window.

5. Click OK to store your changes.

PUTTING WORD 2001
TO WORK FOR YOU

NOTE

*The settings you make here affect all Office programs. Note that choosing large
command buttons doesn't change the size of ScreenTips or Help screens.*

A Look at Word 2001's Keyboard Shortcuts

As you progress through Word 2001, you'll find it has a liberal sprinkling of keyboard
shortcuts, as do all Office 2001 programs. What's more, as you learn in the next section,
you can customize not only keyboard shortcuts, but toolbar icons as well. This makes it
possible for you to customize the way the program runs precisely to your needs.

I'm assuming, however, that most users will not be changing keyboard shortcuts
(I seldom do). The following sections list the shortcuts that are set by default for Word.

Changing and Resizing Fonts

The following keyboard shortcuts strictly affect font use in Word.

Shortcut	Action
COMMAND-SHIFT-F	Change the font from the Formatting Palette
COMMAND-SHIFT->	Increase the font size
COMMAND-SHIFT-<	Decrease the font size
COMMAND-]	Increase the font size by 1 point
COMMAND-[	Decrease the font size by 1 point

Character Formatting

The following keyboard shortcuts strictly affect formatting of characters.

Shortcut	Action
COMMAND-D	Change the formatting of characters (Font command, Format menu)
SHIFT-F3	Change the case of letters
COMMAND-SHIFT-A	Format letters as all capitals or lowercase

Shortcut	Action
COMMAND-B	Apply bold formatting
COMMAND-U	Apply an underline
COMMAND-SHIFT-W	Underline words but not spaces
COMMAND-SHIFT-D	Double-underline text
COMMAND-SHIFT-H	Apply hidden text formatting
COMMAND-I	Apply italic formatting
COMMAND-SHIFT-K	Format letters as small capitals
COMMAND-= (equal sign)	Apply subscript formatting (automatic spacing)
COMMAND-SHIFT-+ (plus sign)	Apply superscript formatting (automatic spacing)
CONTROL-SPACEBAR	Remove manual character formatting
COMMAND-SHIFT-Q	Change the selection to the Symbol font

Text Format Copying and Viewing

The following keyboard shortcuts strictly affect text formats used in Word.

Shortcut	Action
COMMAND-8 (keyboard, not numeric keypad)	Display nonprinting characters
COMMAND-SHIFT-C	Copy formats
COMMAND-SHIFT-V	Paste formats

Line Spacing

The following keyboard shortcuts strictly affect line space adjustments in Word.

Shortcut	Adjustment
COMMAND-1 (on regular keyboard)	Single-space lines
COMMAND-2	Double-space lines
COMMAND-5	Set 1.5 line spacing
COMMAND-0 (zero)	Add or remove one line space preceding a paragraph

Paragraph Alignment

The following keyboard shortcuts strictly affect paragraph alignment in Word.

Shortcut	Action
COMMAND-E	Center a paragraph
COMMAND-J	Justify a paragraph
COMMAND-L	Left align a paragraph
COMMAND-R	Right align a paragraph
COMMAND-M	Indent a paragraph from the left
COMMAND-SHIFT-M	Remove a paragraph indent from the left
COMMAND-T	Create a hanging indent
COMMAND-SHIFT-T	Reduce a hanging indent

Paragraph Styles

The following keyboard shortcuts strictly affect paragraph styles in Word.

Shortcut	Action
COMMAND-SHIFT-S	Apply a style
COMMAND-OPTION-K	Start AutoFormat
COMMAND-SHIFT-N	Apply the Normal style
COMMAND-OPTION-1	Apply the Heading 1 style
COMMAND-OPTION-2	Apply the Heading 2 style
COMMAND-OPTION-3	Apply the Heading 3 style
COMMAND-SHIFT-L	Apply the List style

Popular Shortcuts

Here are some of the more popular keyboard shortcuts in Word, all in one convenient place.

Shortcut	Action
OPTION-SPACEBAR	Create a nonbreaking space
COMMAND-SHIFT- - (hyphen)	Create a nonbreaking hyphen

Shortcut	Action
COMMAND-K	Insert a hyperlink
COMMAND-U	Make letters underlined
COMMAND-SHIFT-<	Decrease font size
COMMAND-SHIFT->	Increase font size
CONTROL-SPACEBAR	Remove character formatting
COMMAND-C	Copy the selected text or object
COMMAND-X	Cut the selected text or object
COMMAND-V	Paste text or an object
COMMAND-Z	Undo the last action
COMMAND-Y	Redo the last action
DELETE	Delete one character to the left
COMMAND-DELETE	Delete one word to the left
DEL or CLEAR	Delete one character to the right
COMMAND-DEL	Delete one word to the right
COMMAND-X or F2	Cut selected text to the Clipboard
COMMAND-Z	Undo the last action
COMMAND-F3	Cut to the Spike, a feature that lets you store multiple items from different locales so they can be pasted in a single action

Text and Graphic Copying

These shortcuts affect copying and moving of text and graphics.

Shortcut	Action
COMMAND-C or F3	Copy text or graphics
COMMAND-X or F2 (then move the insertion point and press COMMAND-V or F4)	Move text or graphics
OPTION-F3	Create AutoText
COMMAND-V or F4	Paste the Clipboard contents
COMMAND-SHIFT-F3	Paste the Spike contents

Special Characters

These shortcuts are used to activate special characters in Word.

Press	To Insert
COMMAND-F9	A field
RETURN (after typing the first few characters of the AutoText entry name and when the ScreenTip appears)	An AutoText entry
SHIFT-RETURN	A line break
SHIFT-ENTER	A page break
COMMAND-SHIFT-RETURN	A column break or page break (whichever comes next)
OPTION-SPACEBAR	A nonbreaking space
OPTION-G	The copyright symbol
OPTION-R	The registered trademark symbol
OPTION-2	The trademark symbol
OPTION- ; (semicolon)	An ellipsis (three successive dots)

Text and Graphic Selection

The following shortcuts require that you press the SHIFT key as you use the shortcut to select an object.

Press	To Select
SHIFT-RIGHT ARROW	One character to the right
SHIFT-LEFT ARROW	One character to the left
COMMAND-SHIFT-RIGHT ARROW	To the end of a word
COMMAND-SHIFT-LEFT ARROW	To the beginning of a word
SHIFT-END (The END key is not available on all keyboards.)	To the end of a line
SHIFT-HOME	To the beginning of a line
SHIFT-DOWN ARROW	One line down
SHIFT-UP ARROW	One line up
COMMAND-SHIFT-DOWN ARROW	To the end of a paragraph

Press	To Select
COMMAND-SHIFT-UP ARROW	To the beginning of a paragraph
SHIFT-PAGE DOWN	One screen down
SHIFT-PAGE UP	One screen up
COMMAND-SHIFT-HOME	To the beginning of a document
COMMAND-SHIFT-END (The END key is not available on all keyboards.)	To the end of a document
OPTION-COMMAND-SHIFT-PAGE DOWN	To the end of a window
COMMAND-A	To include the entire document
COMMAND-SHIFT-F8 and then use the arrow keys; press COMMAND-. (period) to cancel selection mode	To a vertical block of text
F8-arrow keys; press COMMAND-. (period) to cancel selection mode	To a specific location in a document

Table Selection

The rules change when you select items in a table. Here are the results.

Shortcut	Action
TAB	Select the next cell's contents
SHIFT-TAB	Select the preceding cell's contents
Click in the column's top or bottom cell. Hold down SHIFT and press the UP ARROW or DOWN ARROW key repeatedly.	Select a column
COMMAND-SHIFT-F8 and then use the arrow keys; press COMMAND-. (period) to cancel selection mode	Extend a selection (or block)
SHIFT-F8	Reduce the selection size

Extending the Selection

You can use these shortcuts to extend the selection of text.

Shortcut	Action
F8	Turn extend selection mode on
F8 and then press the LEFT ARROW or RIGHT ARROW key	Select the nearest character
F8 (press once to select a word, twice to select a sentence, and so forth)	Increase the size of a selection
SHIFT-F8	Reduce the size of a selection
COMMAND-. (period)	Turn extend selection mode off

Cursor Movement

You don't even have to move the cursor with your mouse with Word. Here are the options.

Shortcut	Moves Cursor
LEFT ARROW	One character to the left
RIGHT ARROW	One character to the right
COMMAND-LEFT ARROW	One word to the left
COMMAND-RIGHT ARROW	One word to the right
COMMAND-UP ARROW	One paragraph up
COMMAND-DOWN ARROW	One paragraph down
SHIFT-TAB	One cell to the left (in a table)
TAB	One cell to the right (in a table)
UP ARROW	Up one line
DOWN ARROW	Down one line

Shortcut	Moves Cursor
END (The END key is not available on all keyboards.)	To the end of a line
HOME	To the beginning of a line
COMMAND-PAGE UP	To the top of the window
COMMAND-PAGE DOWN	To the end of the window
PAGE UP	Up one screen (scrolling)
PAGE DOWN	Down one screen (scrolling)
COMMAND-PAGE DOWN	To the top of the next page
COMMAND-PAGE UP	To the top of the previous page
COMMAND-END (The END key is not available on all keyboards.)	To the end of a document
COMMAND-HOME	To the beginning of a document
SHIFT-F5	To the location of the insertion point when the document was last closed

Inserting Paragraphs and Tabs in a Table

You can use these shortcuts to add material in a table.

Shortcut	Inserts
RETURN	New paragraphs in a cell
OPTION-TAB	Tab characters in a cell

Searching Text

Word's powerful Find feature is activated by the following commands.

Shortcut	Action
COMMAND-F	Find text, formatting, and special items
COMMAND-OPTION-Y	Repeat the find operation (after closing the Find and Replace window)
COMMAND-H	Replace text, specific formatting, and special items
COMMAND-G	Go to a page, bookmark, footnote, table, comment, graphic, or other location

Shortcut	Action
COMMAND-OPTION-Z	Go back to a page, bookmark, footnote, table, comment, graphic, or other location
COMMAND-OPTION-HOME	Browse through a document

Document Viewing

There are three ways to view a document and three shortcuts to handle these functions.

Shortcut	Action
COMMAND-OPTION-P	Switch to print layout view
COMMAND-OPTION-O	Switch to outline view
COMMAND-OPTION-N	Switch to normal view

Document Reviewing

You can use these keyboard shortcuts when reviewing and adding comments to your document.

Shortcut	Action
COMMAND-OPTION-A	Insert a comment
COMMAND-SHIFT-E	Turn change tracking on or off
HOME	Go to the beginning of a comment
END (The END key is not available on all keyboards.)	Go to the end of a comment
COMMAND-HOME	Go to the beginning of the list of comments
COMMAND-END	Go to the end of the list of comments

Footnotes and Endnotes

Word offers a highly flexible range of shortcuts for working with footnotes and endnotes in your document.

Shortcut	Action
COMMAND-OPTION-F	Insert a footnote
COMMAND-OPTION-E	Insert an endnote

Working in a Field

An additional range of shortcuts are available to work within a text field in Word.

Shortcut	Inserts
CONTROL-SHIFT-D	A DATE field
COMMAND-OPTION-SHIFT-L	A LISTNUM field
CONTROL-SHIFT-P	A PAGE field
CONTROL-SHIFT-T	A TIME field
COMMAND-F9	An empty field

Press	To
F9	Update selected fields
COMMAND-SHIFT-F9	Unlink a field
SHIFT-F9	Switch between a field code and its result
OPTION-F9	Switch between all field codes and their results
OPTION-SHIFT-F9	Run GOTOBUTTON or MACROBUTTON from the field that displays the field results
F11	Go to the next field
SHIFT-F11	Go to the previous field
COMMAND-F11	Lock a field
COMMAND-SHIFT-F11	Unlock a field

Document Outlining

Word's outlining feature is cherished by many business users, and there are plenty of shortcuts to use with this feature.

Outline View Shortcuts	Action
CONTROL-SHIFT-LEFT ARROW	Promote a paragraph
CONTROL-SHIFT-RIGHT ARROW	Demote a paragraph
COMMAND-SHIFT-N	Demote to body text

Outline View Shortcuts	Action
CONTROL-SHIFT-UP ARROW	Move selected paragraphs up
CONTROL-SHIFT-DOWN ARROW	Move selected paragraphs down
CONTROL-SHIFT-+(plus sign)	Expand text under a heading
CONTROL-SHIFT- –(minus sign)	Collapse text under a heading
CONTROL-SHIFT-A	Expand or collapse all text or headings
CONTROL-SHIFT-L	Show the first line of body text or all body text
CONTROL-SHIFT-1	Show all headings with the Heading 1 style
CONTROL-SHIFT-N	Show all headings up to Heading n

Data Merge

These keyboard shortcuts are used to harness the power of Word's Data Merge feature.

Shortcuts When Using Data Merge Manager	Action
CONTROL-SHIFT-N	Merge a document
CONTROL-SHIFT-M	Print the merged document
CONTROL-SHIFT-E	Edit a data-merge data document
CONTROL-SHIFT-F	Insert a merge field

Window Navigation

These shortcuts manage document windows in Word.

Shortcut	Action
COMMAND-W	Close the active document window
COMMAND-F6	Switch to the next Word document window
COMMAND-SHIFT-F6	Switch to the previous Word document window

Dialog Box Navigation

You can use these shortcuts to move within a dialog box in Word.

Shortcut	Action
CONTROL-TAB or CONTROL-PAGE DOWN	Move to the next tab in a dialog box
CONTROL-SHIFT-TAB or CONTROL-PAGE UP	Move to the previous tab in a dialog box
TAB	Move to the next option or option group
SHIFT-TAB	Move to the previous option or option group
Arrow keys	Move between options in the selected list or between some options in a group of options
SPACEBAR	Perform the action assigned to the selected button; select or clear the check box
RETURN	Perform the action assigned to the default button in the dialog box
COMMAND-. (period) or ESC	Cancel the command and close the dialog box

Toolbar Navigation

You can move around toolbars from the keyboard, too, in Word.

Shortcut	Action
CONTROL-TAB or CONTROL-SHIFT-TAB	Select the next or previous toolbar
RIGHT ARROW or LEFT ARROW (when a toolbar is active)	Select the next or previous button or menu on the toolbar
DOWN ARROW (when a menu on a toolbar is selected)	Open the menu
RETURN (when a button is selected)	Perform the action assigned to the button
RETURN (after entering a value in a text box)	Accept that value
RETURN (when a drop-down list box is selected)	Select the option you want
Arrow keys	Move through options in a menu or drop-down list

Function Keys

Ever wonder what you can do with those function keys on your Mac? In Word, there are plenty of options available, as F1 through F12 are fully populated with shortcuts.

Shortcut	Action
F1	Undo the last action
F2	Cut text or graphics
F3	Copy text or graphics
F4	Paste the Clipboard contents
F5	Choose the Go To command (Edit menu)
F6	Go to the next pane or frame
F7	Choose the Spelling and Grammar command (Tools menu)
F8	Extend a selection
F9	Update selected fields
F11	Go to the next field
F12	Choose the Save As command (File menu)
SHIFT-F2	Copy text
SHIFT-F3	Change the case of letters
SHIFT-F4	Repeat a Find or Go To action
SHIFT-F5	Move to a previous revision
SHIFT-F6	Go to the previous pane or frame
SHIFT-F7	Choose the Thesaurus command (Tools menu, Language submenu)
SHIFT-F8	Shrink a selection
SHIFT-F9	Switch between a field code and its result
SHIFT-F10	Display a contextual menu
SHIFT-F11	Go to the previous field
COMMAND-F2	Choose the Print Preview command (File menu)
COMMAND-F3	Cut to the Spike
COMMAND-F4	Close the window

Shortcut	Action
COMMAND-F6	Go to the next window
COMMAND-F9	Insert an empty field
COMMAND-F11	Lock a field
COMMAND-SHIFT-F3	Insert the contents of the Spike
COMMAND-SHIFT-F4	Repeat a Find or Go To action
COMMAND-SHIFT-F5	Edit a bookmark
COMMAND-SHIFT-F6	Go to the previous window
COMMAND-SHIFT-F7	Update linked information in a Word source document
COMMAND-SHIFT-F8	Extend a selection or block (then press an arrow key)
COMMAND-SHIFT-F9	Unlink a field
COMMAND-SHIFT-F11	Unlock a field
OPTION-F3	Create an AutoText entry
OPTION-F6	Go to the next window
OPTION-F7	Find the next misspelling or grammatical error. The Check Spelling as You Type check box must be selected (Tools menu, Options dialog box, Spelling & Grammar tab).
OPTION-F8	Run a macro
OPTION-F9	Switch between all field codes and their results
OPTION-F11	Display Microsoft Visual Basic code
OPTION-SHIFT-F6	Go to the previous window
OPTION-SHIFT-F7	Open or close the dictionary
OPTION-SHIFT-F9	Run GOTOBUTTON or MACROBUTTON from the field that displays the field results

A Quick Way to Change or Add Keyboard Shortcuts

You aren't locked into the voluminous number of keyboard shortcuts that are available in Word. Any one of them can be customized with a different range of keyboard commands.

Here's how to accomplish the task:

1. Choose Customize from the Tools menu.

2. On any tab of the dialog box, click the Keyboard button, which brings up the Customize Keyboard dialog box shown in Figure 11-12.

3. Click in the Categories pane, to display the commands available in that category.

4. Click a command, and you'll see the present shortcut displayed in the Current Keys pane.

5. In the Press New Shortcut Key text field, type a new shortcut. You'll be warned by Word if the shortcut already exists.

6. When you're satisfied with your shortcut, click the Assign button to store the change.

7. If you want to remove a shortcut, click the Remove button instead.

CAUTION   *There is no "Are you sure" prompt when you remove a keyboard shortcut, so carefully choose the ones you delete.*

8. When your changes are done, click OK to store the settings.

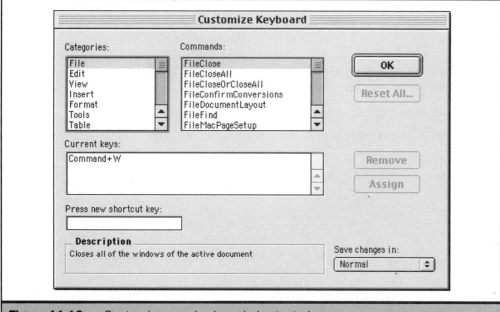

Figure 11-12.   *Customize your keyboard shortcuts here.*

If you make a mistake or just want to restore the keyboard shortcuts to the factory defaults, press the Reset All button, and the changes will be made almost instantaneously.

Reference: Word's Limits

Considering the extraordinary number of features in Word, are there any limits at all? Indeed there are, although you probably won't be stretching those limitations any time soon, except for specialized purposes. But here is a list so you know where you can push the envelope.

Category	Limits
Number of open windows	Limited by the memory applied to the program or the memory available on your Mac
Maximum file size	32 MB
Number of words in custom dictionaries	10,000
Maximum custom dictionary file size	366,590 bytes
Length of bookmark names	40 characters
Number of bookmarks per document	16,379
Length of AutoText entry names (including spaces)	32 characters
Number of AutoText entries per document template	Limited by template file size and/or available memory
Number of AutoText entries per document template	32,000
Number of global AutoText entries	Limited by template file size and/or available memory
Length of style names	255 characters
Number of styles per document or template	10,000
Number of fields per document	32,000

Category	Limits
Number of general switches in a field	10
Number of field-specific switches in a field	10
Number of nesting levels for fields	20
Number of subdocuments in a master document	255
Number of columns in a table	63
Number of newspaper columns	45 (the number of columns is affected by page size and margin settings)
Number of tab stops set in a paragraph	64
Minimum page height	0.1 inch
Maximum number of cascading style sheets linked together	11
Maximum page height	22 inches
Minimum page width	0.1 inch
Maximum page width and table width	22 inches
Number of custom toolbars	Limited only by the memory available to the program or to your Mac
Number of custom toolbar buttons	Limited only by the memory available to the program or to your Mac
Number of characters per line	768
Minimum font size	1 point
Maximum font size	1,638 points (22 inches)
Number of fonts per document	32,767
Amount of space between characters	1,584 points
Distance text can be raised or lowered	1,584 points
Maximum number of colors in color palette	256

Summary

Microsoft Word has justifiably become the industry-standard word processing program, even on the Mac. In this chapter, you began to set up word to perform its tasks in the way you like. You stepped through the creation of a basic document, to get a feel for the program.

In the next chapter, you'll learn the fundamentals of word processing, and you'll be introduced to Word's Formatting Palette, which offers simple one-click access to all of the program's important features.

Chapter 12

The Elements of Word Processing

What is word processing and how has it changed through the years? Back before there were such things as personal computers (let alone Macs), there were dedicated word processing devices and typewriters with little computers that let you store your document for editing. Once the document was stored, you could play it back and insert, remove, or move words from one location to another. You might even have a small selection of typefaces with which to spruce up your material.

This was a huge step away from the simple typewriter with only an eraser or Liquid Paper to make changes.

There is, of course, no comparison between Microsoft Word 2001, with its huge number of features, and those little word processing programs of yore. The options for creating and editing text are enormous, and it also includes a growing array of drawing and picture processing tools. Combine these with the capabilities for creating multicolumn documents, tables, and special effects, and the only limit to what you can do with your document is your imagination.

In the preceding chapter, you learned how to set up Word 2001 to work in a fashion that suits your needs. You were even presented with a reference guide showing the huge number of keyboard shortcuts and how easy it is to change those shortcuts and customize Word's ubiquitous toolbars and command buttons.

In this chapter, you'll learn the basics of word processing: how to create documents, format text, and access some of the program's more advanced document processing features.

A Short Tour of Word's Menu Bar

To get you accustomed to the layout of Word, the next few pages will take you through all the menus, so you can see where the commands you need reside. In this and the next three chapters, you'll discover how to harness the power of all these functions.

■ **File Menu** In addition to providing commands to create, open, and save documents in various ways, the Word 2001 File menu offers several other notable options.

```
┌─────────────────────────────────────────────────────────┐
│ File                                                      │
├─────────────────────────────────────────────────────────┤
│   Project Gallery...                            ⇧⌘P       │
├─────────────────────────────────────────────────────────┤
│   New Blank Document                             ⌘N       │
│   Open...                                        ⌘O       │
│   Open Web Page...                                        │
│   Close                                          ⌘W       │
├─────────────────────────────────────────────────────────┤
│   Save                                           ⌘S       │
│   Save As...                                              │
│   Save as Web Page...                                     │
│   Versions...                                             │
├─────────────────────────────────────────────────────────┤
│   Web Page Preview                                        │
├─────────────────────────────────────────────────────────┤
│   Page Setup...                                           │
│   Print Preview                                           │
│   Print...                                       ⌘P       │
├─────────────────────────────────────────────────────────┤
│   Send To                                         ▶       │
│   Properties...                                           │
├─────────────────────────────────────────────────────────┤
│   1 Rockoids:Documents:Office Mac:Chapter 12:168-12.doc   │
│   2 OfficeMac.doc                                         │
│   3 Rockoids:Documents:CNet:LCDs.doc                      │
│   4 Rockoids:Desktop Folder:Zicam                         │
│   5 Rockoids:Documents:CNet:FireWire_CD-RWs.doc           │
│   6 Rockoids:Documents:CNet:MacOSXHelp2.doc               │
│   7 Rockoids:Documents:Mac OS X Book:Chapter 03:Chap3.doc │
│   8 Rockoids:Documents:Rockoids Manuscripts:Zanther.doc   │
│   9 Rockoids:Documents:Office Mac:Chapter 11:168-11.doc   │
├─────────────────────────────────────────────────────────┤
│   Quit                                           ⌘Q       │
└─────────────────────────────────────────────────────────┘
```

One, Versions, allows you to save multiple states, or *versions*, of the very same document in a single file. That way, you can easily move between versions for editing or updating. The Properties command stores a summary and the names of the people who have worked on a document; this feature is especially convenient in workgroup situations, where a number of people are reading or modifying a document. The Send To option can be used to forward your document as an e-mail attachment or to use your document as the basis of a PowerPoint presentation. The bottom of the File menu lists your most recently opened documents; Word will display the names of up to nine files.

■ **Edit Menu**   Word's Edit menu has the standard array of Mac OS copying and pasting functions, plus a few extras that we will discuss in the next few chapters.

Notable among these is the ability to paste text as a hyperlink; these hyperlinks work like hyperlinks on a Web page, except that you can also link to a page within your document or in another Office document or a picture file. Your Word preferences are also available from this menu.

■ **View Menu**   You can view a Word document in several way, and these options are shown in the View menu.

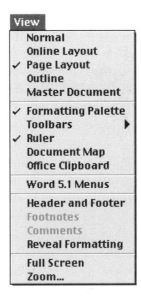

The Page Layout view, for example, lets you see a page fully formatted with page breaks. The Document Map shows the heads and subheads and provides immediate one-click access to various portions of your document. Among the notable features are the Office Clipboard, which offers 10 separate storage places for text and pictures, and the Word 5.1 Menus feature, which makes Word 2001 more closely resemble what some regard as the very best version of this program.

■ **Insert Menu**   As you assemble your document, you will, no doubt, be adding pictures and other elements. The Insert menu is also used to place special text elements, such as page numbers and the date and time (as calculated by your Mac's clock), QuickTime movies, pictures from your scanner or digital camera, and a number of other items. The ability to create an index or table of contents is particularly useful if you are creating a long document, such as a book or company manual.

PUTTING WORD 2001 TO WORK FOR YOU

■ **Format Menu**   What's the size of your document page? How should paragraphs and text be formatted. Do you want to change the background color or paragraph styles or add multiple columns and special borders and shading? The Format menu includes all of these features. However, you're likely to find that the Formatting Palette, described in detail later in this chapter, takes care of most document formatting tasks, and that you won't need to visit this menu very often.

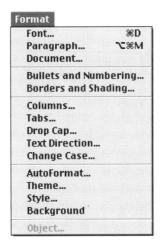

■ **Font Menu**   This is just your typical Macintosh Font menu. If you check the appropriate preference, you'll see a WYSIWYG display, showing you what the font really looks like. Otherwise (unless you use a special font menu modifier program), you'll just see a list.

NOTE   *In case you're wondering, a font menu modifier program will not just show fonts in their true styles, but will also group them into font families for easier access. Such programs include Adobe Type Reunion and Action WYSIWYG.*

■ **Tools Menu**   This menu provides access to features that help you process your document, including spell checking, grammar checking, and checking word count.

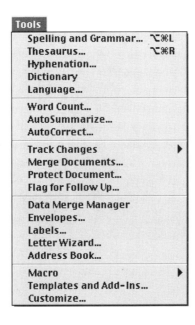

If your document is being revised frequently, perhaps by a workgroup, you can track changes and compare and merge different versions of the same document. The other powerful features in the Tools menu allow you to create letters, envelopes, and labels; update your Address Book; and create powerful macros to automate many of the functions of Word.

■ **Table Menu** You can create a highly sophisticated table in Word 2001 simply by putting a few numbers into a dialog box or clicking and dragging a table shape in your document. Word helps you figure it all out from there. The Table menu also has some other nifty features, such as AutoFit, which lets you automatically adjust text to fit on a page or balance multiple columns (so everything lines up properly). The Sort feature lets you reorganize blocks of text alphabetically or by other sequences you specify.

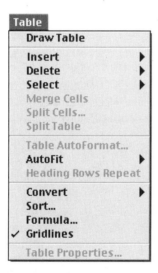

■ **Window Menu** How would you like to view your document? Would you like to see different portions at the same time or split the document into separately accessible halves, so you can easily edit and view different parts? You can also use the Window menu to switch among the Word documents that you have open.

■ **Work Menu** The Work menu provides a great way to access the files on which you regularly work. Just open the menu and choose Add to Work menu, and the document will always be available for fast access (assuming that you haven't deleted the original, of course).

NOTE *If you want to delete a document from the Work menu, just press COMMAND-OPTION- - (hyphen), and the mouse cursor will turn into a minus symbol. Select the document in the Work menu that you want to remove, and it will be deleted from the menu (but the actual file will remain intact).*

- **Help Menu**   Access all of Word's help information from this menu. The available help resources are not just limited to the help text in Word. You can also access Microsoft's Web site for additional information via this menu (but you have to be connected to your ISP at the time to bring it up).

Using the Formatting Palette

One of the handiest features of Office 2001 is the Formatting Palette (see Figure 12-1), which gives you one-click access to many of Word's functions, without having to take a trip to a menu or a dialog box. Although you might like keyboard shortcuts, compared to the chore of memorizing those dozens and dozens of keystrokes, a mouse-click is downright easy. What's more, this palette is context sensitive. The version you see here is strictly for formatting text and documents.

NOTE   *Whenever you activate a function by clicking an icon on the Formatting Palette, the icon will be outlined by a white square to show that it's in use.*

In the next few pages, we'll discuss the various features of the text version of the Formatting Palette. When we get to Word's graphics handling and creation features, in Chapter 14, you'll see the Formatting Palette in another guise.

NOTE   *To expand the Formatting Palette to see a specific set of formatting commands, just click the disclosure triangle next to its label. Click again to collapse it. Whenever you launch Word, just the Font panel of the Formatting Palette appears.*

- **Font Panel**   Select fonts, sizes, and styles from this panel. You can also use it to select text styles and list options, such as numbered lists, bulleted lists, and indents for Word's highly sophisticated Outline feature. To access a feature, just click it. Any item with a down arrow will produce a menu of options when the arrow is clicked, but some allow you to manually enter your choices (such as font size, style name, and so on).

NOTE   *Where's the Formatting Palette? If it's not on the screen, go to the View menu and select Formatting Palette. If you're displaying the Standard Word toolbar, there's also an icon for the Formatting Palette (next to the Zoom feature). If you're not sure what a palette icon does, just hold the mouse cursor over it, and a ScreenTip will shortly appear that will explain its purpose.*

- **Bullets and Numbering Panel**   Where is it? To show you the context-sensitive nature of Word, this option shows up only when you're working in a bulleted or numbered list. Otherwise, it's not available. You can choose bullet styles, the size of the indent, and, for a numbered list, the style and the number at which the list starts.

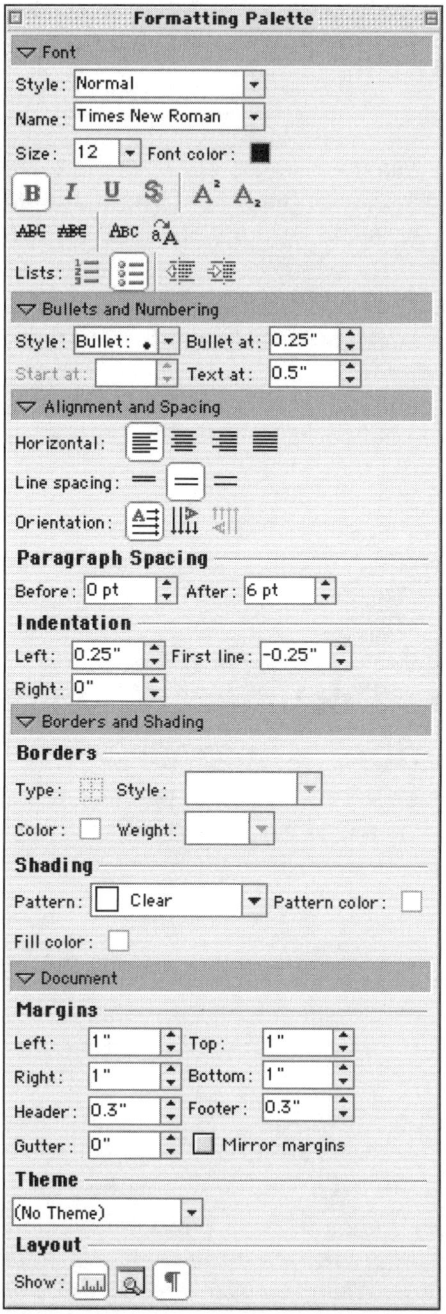

Formatting Palette

▽ Font

Style: Normal ▾

Name: Times New Roman ▾

Size: 12 ▾   Font color: ■

B *I* U̲ S̶   A² A₂

A̶B̶C̶ A̶B̶C̶   Aᴮᴄ aA̶

Lists: 𝟏 ☰   ☷   ⫶   ⫶

▽ Bullets and Numbering

Style: Bullet: • ▾   Bullet at: 0.25" ⬍

Start at: ⬍   Text at: 0.5" ⬍

▽ Alignment and Spacing

Horizontal: ☰ ☰ ☰ ☰

Line spacing: ═ ☰ ═

Orientation: A⊟ ⫿⊞ ⫿⊟

Paragraph Spacing

Before: 0 pt ⬍   After: 6 pt ⬍

Indentation

Left: 0.25" ⬍   First line: -0.25" ⬍

Right: 0" ⬍

▽ Borders and Shading

Borders

Type: ▦   Style: ▾

Color: ☐   Weight: ▾

Shading

Pattern: ☐ Clear ▾   Pattern color: ☐

Fill color: ☐

▽ Document

Margins

Left: 1" ⬍   Top: 1" ⬍

Right: 1" ⬍   Bottom: 1" ⬍

Header: 0.3" ⬍   Footer: 0.3" ⬍

Gutter: 0" ⬍   ☐ Mirror margins

Theme

(No Theme) ▾

Layout

Show: ▦ 🔍 ¶

Figure 12-1.   *This is the Formatting Palette with all elements expanded, so you can see all of its features in one place.*

- **Alignment and Spacing Panel** Here's where you format your paragraphs. There are options for paragraph alignment, fixed line spacing of one or two lines, text orientation, and paragraph spacing and indentation. The First Line feature lets you specify a fixed indent for the beginning of a paragraph or for a list.

- **Borders and Shading Panel** Here's where you can begin to apply extras to your Word text. Add a decorative border to a block of text or a table and choose the style and the thickness of the border. The Shading option lets you apply a decorative pattern to the background of your document and to apply a color to the pattern.

- **Document Panel** Create the basic design of your document from this Window. Choose the margins and where headers and footers will appear. The Theme option can be used to apply a fixed set of background elements for a document, such as a particular style to bullets or specific colors for the backdrop or lettering. The final option, Layout, lets you specify three types of views of your document. The fist shows a document ruler, which is useful for formatting paragraph indents; the second, Document Map, divides your document into twin panes, with clickable links to headlines; and the third hides or shows formatting symbols that are there for guidance only, since they don't print, including symbols for the spaces between words and paragraph endings.

Creating a New Document: Choices, Choices, and More Choices

Depending on your experience with Word and your needs for a specific document, you can begin a new document in any of five ways. Here are your choices, with a few very personal observations regarding which might be best for you and why. Once we cover the choices, we'll go through the steps of creating and working in a new document and then the steps for saving and editing that document.

- **Blank Document** This is the option you'll often use: you start a blank document and then populate it with formatting instructions, text, and graphics. Nothing is formatted for you in advance, aside from the default document dimensions.

- **Web Page** Should your Word document be doing duty on a Web site, you'll want to format it as a Web page from the get-go. You will find that your format options are strictly limited to the requirements of the World Wide Web.

- **Wizard** Wouldn't you rather have Word figure out how to set up your new document? A wizard guides you through every step of formatting a document for a specific purpose. When you install Word, you'll find prebuilt wizards that help you create a letter, label, envelope, brochure, newsletter, catalog, and more.

Once the basic formatting is done, you just have to fill in the spaces with text and pictures, and you're ready to view and print it.

- **Template**   Once you've created a document with a complex range of document formatting, you may want to use it again and again for a specific range of projects. When you save a document as a template, all of the information, be it a company letterhead or the design for the club newsletter, is already there. You can select from Word's existing templates in the Project Gallery, you can modify one of the templates for your own use, or you can create a template from scratch.

- **Copy of an Existing Document**   This is my lazy way out, or a better idea, depending on your point of view. All you need to do is open an existing document and then save it under a new name (or make a copy of the original) and then change it the way you want.

CAUTION   *If you use this last alternative, you'll want to make sure you make a duplicate of the document or save it under a new name before you make any changes. Otherwise, you may alter the original document by mistake.*

Creating a New Document

Now that we're past the preliminaries, it's time to step through the process of creating a new Word document from scratch, from opening, to formatting, and finally to spell checking and printing. As you move through the next few chapters, you'll see there are many ways to expand your options when you create a Word document. You might say we are only scratching the surface here.

Typing and Word Processing: A Big Difference

If you're used to working on a typewriter, no doubt you'll have to get used to some new ways of doing things when you begin to type on a computer. Some of the things you took for granted, such as pressing Return after each line, no longer apply.

Here are the basic changes to which you'll need to become accustomed:

- **Break Lines Only After Paragraphs**   On most typewriters, other than the automatic kind that sport some limited word processing capabilities, you end lines manually, pressing the Return key each time. On a computer, you let the words wrap (flow from line to line automatically) and press RETURN when you end a paragraph. If you break each line, when you change fonts or sizes, the lines will either be too short or too long (in which case you get extra line returns, long lines, followed by short ones).

- **Don't Add Extra Spaces Between Punctuation** On a typewriter, except for certain models with proportional spacing, it is customary to add a second space between sentences, and sometimes after all punctuation. On a computer, just one space is necessary (although you might add an extra space for a better look in a monospaced font, such as Courier, a process typographers sometimes call "French" spacing). It may take a bit of time to get used to, but your documents will have a far more professional look.

- **Use Smart Quotes** On a computer, there are special keys for real, curly quotation marks and apostrophes. Word's AutoCorrect feature is set to change straight quotation marks to curly, or "smart," quotes by default. You don't even have to remember the keystrokes.

NOTE: There are exceptions to the smart quotes rule. Some older e-mail programs, or just older versions, don't recognize smart quotes, but this is nothing for you to be concerned about in Word.

Starting a New Word Document

Since we're starting a document from scratch, we'll only make a fast trip to the Project Gallery for this section and then move on. If you want to see how the Project Gallery can simplify the process of creating a brand-new Word document using templates and wizards, read Chapters 3 and 4.

NOTE
In the following example, we will be discussing a number of document formatting features that you can leave at their default settings. You don't have to change document size and margins, for example, if the default settings are satisfactory for your needs.

1. Double-click Word to launch it.

2. When the Project Gallery appears, click the Word Document icon to open a blank Word window (see Figure 12-2). The screen shown here is based on the default settings in Word. If you've changed any program preferences, some elements may look different, but the end result will be the same insofar as producing a new blank document is concerned.

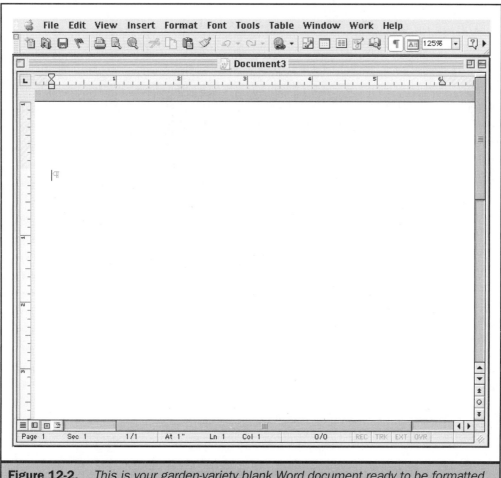

Figure 12-2. *This is your garden-variety blank Word document ready to be formatted.*

3. To set the page size, choose Page Setup from the File menu and specify a paper size from the Paper pop-up menu in the box that appears.

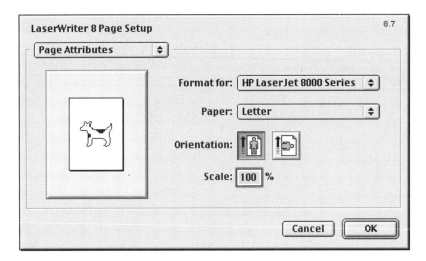

The choices shown here are for a standard laser printer. If a different page size is selected, your blank document will change to reflect the new size (this may take a few seconds to happen).

NOTE *Depending on the kind of printer and printing software you have, the Page Setup dialog box will be different. The page sizes you can select are limited by your output device. Just about every printer designed for the North American market will support 8-1/2 by 11 inch and 8-1/2 by 14 inch paper. Documents from Europe often use the A4 size (8.27 by 11.69 inches).*

4. Go to the Formatting Palette and click the Document arrow to specify page margins.

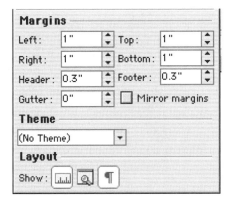

You can click the up and down arrows in each field or just manually enter the value. The margins you select here affect the amount of white space around your text. If your document will have headers and footers (a title at the top and the page number at the bottom, for example), you can specify the amount of space between the top or bottom of your page and that information. You can also adjust the space between columns for multiple-column documents.

PUTTING WORD 2001
TO WORK FOR YOU

TIP   *If you want the left and right margins to be identical, select the Mirror Margins option.*

5. Once margins are specified, it's time to check your text formatting. By default, Word sets your text style as Normal, but what normal is depends on your needs (you'll learn how to change that setting in Chapter 13). For this example, on the Font panel, choose the Normal style and choose Heading 1 from the list of available styles. A default style for this heading will be activated.

Heading 1	☰ ¶ 16 pt
Heading 2	☰ ¶ 14 pt
Heading 3	☰ ¶ 13 pt
Normal	☰ ¶ 12 pt
Default Paragraph Font	☰ a

6. Type your headline and press the RETURN key.

NOTE   *How'd that happen? Yes, when you pressed RETURN, the style changed back to Normal. This is one of the cool features of Word's Style options. You can set up a style to switch to a different style when you end a paragraph; in this case, Heading 1 is designed to change to Normal when you press RETURN.*

7. Now it's time to format your text. On the Font palette, select the pop-up Name menu and choose another font from the menu. You can use any font available on your Mac, but you'll want to check the sidebar, "Picking the Right Font for Fun and Profit," later in the chapter, for guidance.

8. After you've selected the font you want to use for your text, click the Size menu on the Font panel and pick a different font size, if the one you're using isn't what you want.

9. After selecting a size, you can begin to type your document. First, though, you'll want to name your document and specify a default location for it. This isn't a premature step, because if something were to happen to your Mac (such as a crash or power outage), all the work you've done will be lost unless you've made a copy of your document. So the next step is to choose Save As from the File menu (or just press COMMAND-S). This will bring up the standard Save dialog box.

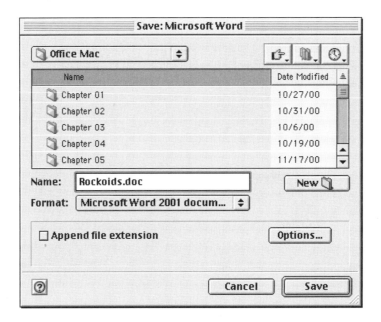

10. Name your document and specify a location for it on your hard drive. The name should be something that will clearly identify the document when you look for it later.

> NOTE
>
> *The best possible location for a file is probably your Mac's Documents folder. Even if you didn't create one, it was put there for you when you installed Office 2001. You can put your documents elsewhere, of course, but this approach keeps things simple, at least until you become accustomed to working in Word.*

11. Click the Save button to store your document. All the work you've done so far will be saved with your document.

CAUTION   *As you continue to work on your document, it is a good idea to save it again every 5 or 10 minutes. This way, you will always have a current or recent version should something happen to your Mac before you're finished. Word's preferences have a Save AutoRecover feature, which will attempt to reclaim a damaged document in the event of corruption caused by a crash, but regular saving is the best protection against losing something in your document.*

Choosing Font Styles

After you've been working on your document, no doubt you'll want to emphasize a point in some fashion. There are several ways to do this, depending on the kind of document you have. Fortunately, many of the styling options are available directly from the Font panel; they're listed here:

- **Font Color**   If you intend to make a color printout of your document, you might want to apply a specific color to a headline. To do that, just select the text and click the square to the right of Font Color. You'll see a palette of colors from which to select.

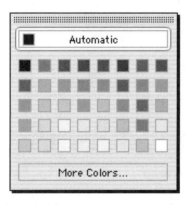

Click the More Colors button for extra choices. Then just click the color you want. To change back to the original color, select it again from the Font Color menu or use the Undo command on the File menu.

- **Font Style**   For emphasis, click the Bold button, and for titles, click Italic. Click both buttons for bold italic text. Other style options include underlined and shaded text, plus superscripts, subscripts, strikethrough, and double strikethrough. Small caps is sometimes used for titles and abbreviations or to start a paragraph in a section in a document, particularly in a book.

■ **Lists**   If you are listing or emphasizing specific points, as is done in this book, you'll want to use a list. A numbered list is generally used for steps (such as the steps used in the previous section to show you how to work in a brand-new document). A bulleted list is used to show specific items that may fit into a particular category, such as the bulleted lists you are reading in this section. The other options on the Font panel control indentation for outlines.

Options for Text Alignment

The normal layout of text in your new Word document is flush left, which means that the margin for the text is aligned on the left; it is ragged on the right, because the number of characters in each line differs.

> NOTE   *These settings can be changed paragraph by paragraph, if you like. They remain in effect until you select a new setting.*

To change text alignment, display the Alignment and Spacing panel of the Formatting Palette. Here are your choices:

> NOTE   *The suggestions I'm making here are intended to be nothing more than rough guidelines. When it comes to creating a document that meets a specific need, rules are often meant to be broken.*

■ **Horizontal: Centered**   This setting is good for headlines, captions, and similar brief text. All the lines are centered, and it's not terribly suitable for long passages of text.

■ **Horizontal: Flush Left**   The left margin is aligned, and the right is ragged. This is the standard format for text.

■ **Horizontal: Flush Right**   The right margin is aligned, and the left is ragged. This alignment also is not necessarily good for long passages of text, but for headlines, captions, and advertising material, for instance, it may be ideal.

■ **Horizontal: Fully Justified**   The text is aligned on both the right and left, and the last line is flush left, unless it's long enough to fill the line. This is the alignment used in many books and magazines. An example is shown here.

Justified: This is the way it's done in books and magazines. The text is aligned on both the right and left, and the last line is flush left, unless it's long enough to fill the line.

Options for Paragraph Spacing and Indentation

Normally, the space between a paragraph is exactly the same as the space between lines. For various reasons, such as to separate sections in a document, you may want to put some extra space between paragraphs or indent the first line of each paragraph to make long text blocks easier to read. Another reason to use an indented paragraph is to make a long quotation stand apart from the rest of the material; this format is commonly used in reference books.

The Indents and Spacing tab, shown in Figure 12-3, of the Paragraph dialog box (chose Paragraph from the Format menu) is where you change these settings. Indentation can be specified, separately, from the left and right margins. You can also specify a first-line indent, which makes it easier for readers to separate one paragraph from the next.

Options for Line Spacing

On a typewriter, you have such options as single-spacing, double-spacing, and sometimes the halfway point, a space and a half, between lines. The very same options are available to you on the Alignment and Spacing panel of Word's Formatting Palette.

For regular text, single spacing is fine. For manuscripts meant for publication in another form, the other two options may be preferable.

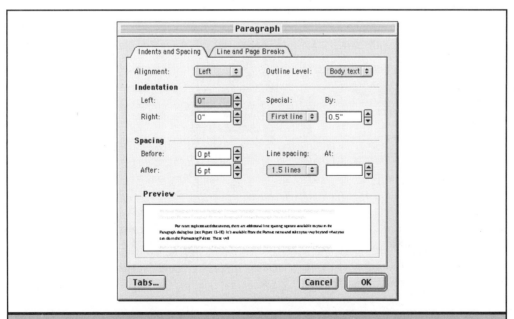

Figure 12-3. *This dialog box has additional paragraph indent and line spacing options should you want to venture beyond the Formatting Palette.*

For more sophisticated documents, additional line spacing options are available to you on the Line and Page Breaks tab of the Paragraph dialog box. These options give you controls way beyond those on the Formatting Palette.

NOTE   *For more information on paragraph indentation and paragraph and line spacing, see "Reference: A Review of Word's Paragraph Dialog Box" at the end of this chapter.*

Options for Borders and Shading

If just plain old text seems just too mundane for you, you'll be pleased to know that Word lets you set off your text elements, such as tables, with borders, and you can also apply shades and patterns behind your text for additional special effects.

The examples you see in this book are the special text elements, such as Note and Caution text. The titles are shaded to make them stand out from the rest of the material. The publisher also indents the text and uses italic so you can easily distinguish these elements from the regular text.

To apply shading to a text block, follow these steps:

1. Click the text block or paragraphs to which you want to apply shading.

2. On the Borders and Shading panel of the Formatting Palette, click the Pattern pop-up menu to specify the intensity of the shade or the type of pattern you want.

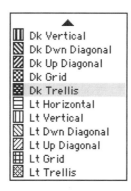

3. After a pattern or shade is selected, click the Pattern Color square to apply a color to the pattern.

4. You can also apply a fill color, which affects the solid background. The result will look something like this.

> He passed up the spicy details of the latest lurid political scandals and haphazardly turned pages until a single small headline atop page three caught his eye. He stared at it for a long moment, long-dormant memories pouring forth into his mind.

You may also need to apply colors to your text to set it off properly from the background. White or red text, for example, is readable on a black background.

Picking the Right Font for Fun and Profit

Your Macintosh no doubt shipped from the factory with a couple of dozen or so fonts. Fonts normally come in two distinct types. One is serif, where the tops and bottoms of a character have little fittings or stems (called serifs). A notable example is Times or a minor variation, Times New Roman. The other type is sans serf, which does not have fittings or serifs. Common sans serif typefaces are Helvetica and its Microsoft variation, Arial.

Normally, serif faces are ideal for text and formal headlines, and sans serif for flashy headlines and short text, such as an ad. But for every rule there are exceptions, and if you look at printed pieces, you'll see plenty of variation.

A third type of font is a script font, which is designed to mimic, in a rough fashion, your handwriting (but not mine, since you'd never be able to read the font). Script faces are ideal for special messages or invitations.

There are thousands of font families, and each family comes in various style variations, such as bold or italic. There are also thicker versions, sometimes called extra bold, and thinner versions, sometimes called, for want of a better word, thin. With so many fonts, how do you select the right one? Answering this question would take an entire book, but the rule is to keep it simple. Use only a small number of fonts for the text and headlines in your document. Too many fonts look amateurish or give your document a "ransom note" look.

The size of a font is generally specified in points. There are approximately 72 points to the inch (approximately because the old printer's specification, 72.27 points to the inch, is seldom used in the world of desktop publishing).

For a good-looking document, you'll want to pick a text style that isn't so large as to be overwhelming and not so small as to be hard to read. By default, Word sets fonts in 12 points. Headlines may be 18 points, 24 points, or if you want a really large banner headline, 48 points or larger.

If you decide to move beyond the limited range of fonts that comes with your Mac, you'll find some extra fonts in your Office 2001 Value Pack, on the installation CD. You can also buy font collections from such companies as Adobe and Bitstream. In addition, many graphics-oriented programs, such as Adobe Illustrator and Macromedia FreeHand, come with nice font collections at no extra charge.

Spelling and Grammar Checking Your Document

As you continue to type your Word document, you may notice a red squiggly line beneath a word. That's Word's interactive spell checker at work, checking each word you type against its built-in dictionary to make sure it is spelled correctly.

However, that's just the starting point. You can harness Word's AutoCorrect feature to automatically correct many words in your document as you type them, to simplify the process.

Once your document is finished, you'll want to give it a once-over with the spelling and grammar checkers just to make sure your document is as perfect as you can make it.

NOTE   *Spell checking a document is no substitute for reading it carefully. Spelling and grammar checkers don't understand context and may not recognize a word that is spelled correctly but used the wrong way. Feel free to veto any suggestions by the spell or grammar checker that seem strange to you.*

Here's how to finish the process:

1. When your Word document is finished, choose Spelling and Grammar from the Tools menu or just press COMMAND-OPTION-L. Either way, you'll see the Spelling and Grammar dialog box.

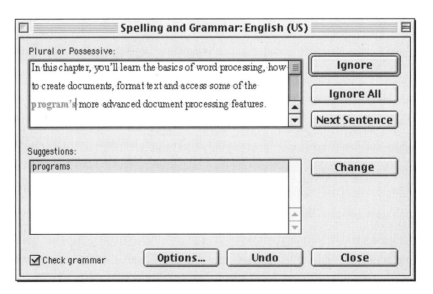

2. As you progress through the spelling and grammar checking process, you can click Change to correct a flagged word with one of the suggested substitutes or Ignore if you want to leave the word as is. Ignore All will bypass all subsequent occurrences of the same term, so Word won't ask you about it again.

3. If you see a word that's flagged as suspect but which you know is correct, you can click the Add button in the Spelling and Grammar window to add the word to your custom dictionary. This is the dictionary Word uses to store exceptions.

4. If you make a mistake and want to revert to the previous version of a term, click Undo.

NOTE   *The Options button will deliver the standard Word Spelling and Grammar Preference dialog box that you configured in Chapter 11.*

5. When you're finished, the Spelling and Grammar dialog box will leave the screen. You can also dismiss it by clicking the Close button.

TIP   *Don't want anyone standing over your shoulder suggesting changes in grammar? No problem. Just uncheck the Check Grammar box in the Spelling and Grammar dialog box, and Word will no longer check that element of your document.*

Printing Your Document

When you have completed your first Word document, you'll want to read it over to make sure it is correct. At any time during the process, you can use Word's editing tools to delete or add text and other elements.

When your document is finished, the next step is to print it. All you need to do is follow these steps:

1. With your Word document open, choose Print from the File menu or press COMMAND-P. This produces a Print dialog box that contains the various print options available to your Mac's printer. The one shown here is for a typical networked laser printer.

PUTTING WORD 2001
TO WORK FOR YOU

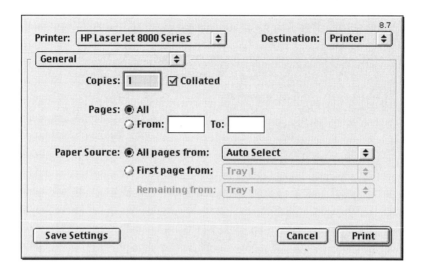

2. If you want to print your entire document, just click the Print button.

NOTE   *If you'd like to see exactly how your page will appear when printed, click the Print Preview button on the toolbar (or choose the Print Preview command on the File menu) instead. You'll see the entire page with headers and footers, and you can change the view size to reflect the approximate size of the finished piece. You can close this viewing window to work on your document again or click the Print button to get your paper output.*

3. If you want to print only a selected portion of your document, select the From radio button in the Pages area and specify the pages you want to print. Then click Print.

Your computer and printer will begin the output process. If your Mac's background printing feature is active, after a few moments you can return to working on the same document, or you can start a new document.

NOTE   *Background printing is not available for all printers, and when it is active (it's a selection in the Chooser), you may find that your Mac's performance suffers somewhat while the document is being processed. The performance hit is especially noticeable if you're using an inkjet printer that uses your Mac's processor during the print process and this applies to most such products.*

Reference: A Review of Word's Font Dialog Box

The choices for font styling on the Formatting Palette don't represent all the options available to you. There are many more ways to specify and modify the look of fonts in Word—in fact, Word enables you to handle your font library in a vast number of ways, limited only by your creativity and imagination.

Here are some of the features that Word's Font dialog box offers. You can easily switch among the options by clicking the appropriate tab in the dialog box.

NOTE *If you used previous versions of Word, such as Word 98, these dialog boxes will be very familiar to you. That's because they are essentially unchanged from the older version.*

■ **Font Tab**   To explore the font options, choose Font from the Format menu or press COMMAND-D. This will deliver the dialog box shown in Figure 12-4. The first tab, Font, lets you choose the font, style, and size from three adjacent lists. The second row on the tab lets you choose the font color and underline style and color. In each case, you choose from pop-up menus to make a selection. You can also apply a number of special effects to your type beyond the bold and italic level, and even combine them to produce a custom effect. The Preview window delivers a sample of your changes, both in font selection and styling.

TIP *By default, Word selects a specific font and style, usually 12-point Times. If you prefer a different default font, just select it in the Font dialog box, click the Default button, and then click OK. From here on, new documents will use your selected font as the default.*

■ **Character Spacing Tab**   The spacing options on this tab (see Figure 12-5) are a basic set of the sort of controls available in a full page layout program. You can scale a font, making the characters wider or narrower, to create a specific effect. You can also reduce or increase the amount of space between characters and move characters above or below the baseline. The Kerning for Fonts option lets you reduce the amount of space between such character combinations as *T* and *o*, for a better look. If you select this option, you can then specify the point size at which the kerning is activated.

NOTE *Word isn't meant to replace a dedicated page design program, such as Adobe InDesign or QuarkXPress. Those two programs and others offer a much finer level of control over the way text is displayed. But for simple publications, Word's options may be all you need.*

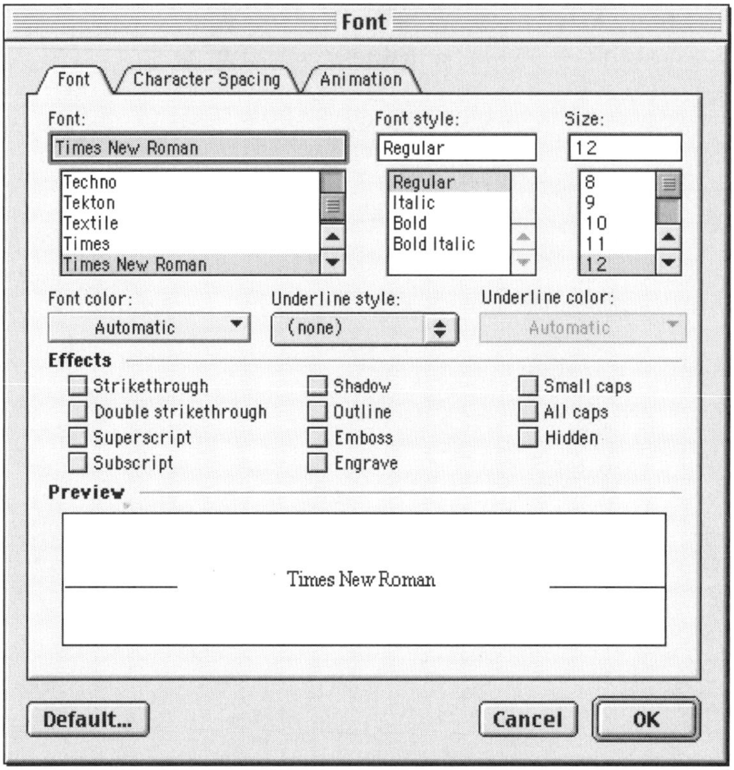

Figure 12-4. *Select and modify the look of fonts on this tab.*

- **Animation Tab** Word also provides a set of animation options that you can apply to your text (see Figure 12-6). You can make the background of text blink or shimmer, for example. Such effects may be nice if you are saving your Word document as a Web page, but otherwise, the results may be more irritating than decorative.

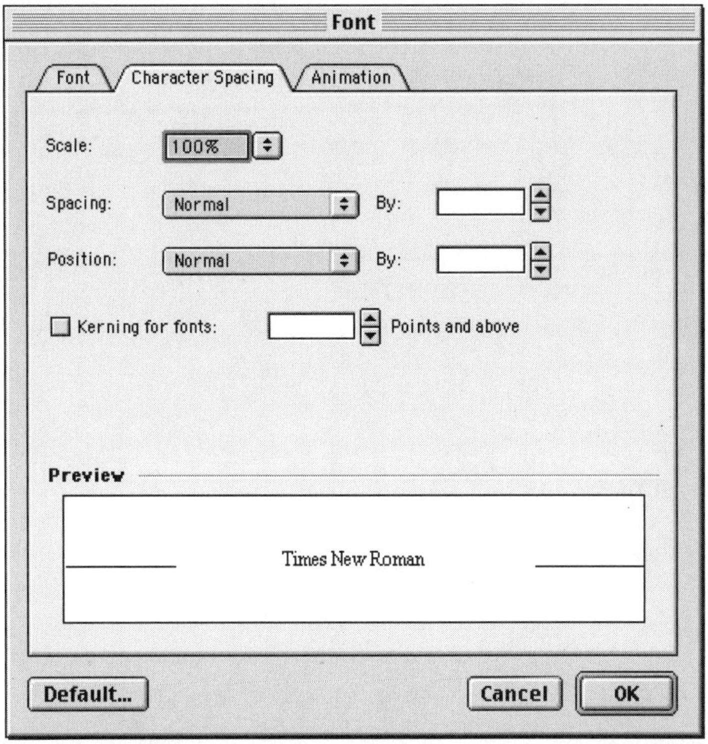

Figure 12-5. *Choose from a basic set of character spacing options on this tab.*

At every step of the way, the Preview box shows you the impact of your changes, so you can easily experiment with different choices to see which work best. The changes you make will affect the selected text, or the next text to be typed in the document, if no text is selected.

If you decide not to make any changes, click Cancel. Otherwise, click OK to put the changes you want into effect.

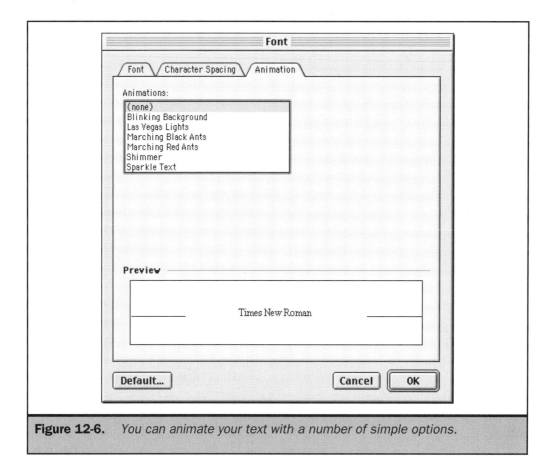

Figure 12-6. *You can animate your text with a number of simple options.*

Reference: A Review of Word's Paragraph Dialog Box

You can apply a host of additional paragraph spacing options in Word's Paragraph dialog box beyond the simple ones available on the Formatting Palette. This is part of the design goal of Word: giving you the ability to handle the most common chores from the palette, and reserving the dialog boxes for more sophisticated chores.

Here is a look at the Paragraph dialog box options available in Word. To bring up this dialog box, choose Paragraph from the Format menu or press COMMAND-OPTION-M.

■ **Indents and Spacing Tab** This tab, shown previously in Figure 12-3, expands just a little the basic commands available from the Formatting Palette. You can specify alignment and outline level options here, too, as well as various types of indents for your document. The Special menu offers two indentation choices:

First Line, to create a paragraph indent, and Hanging, to make the first line in a list extend farther to the left than the subsequent lines. The biggest difference between this dialog box and the Formatting Palette, though, is the flexibility of line spacing adjustments. Instead of just the typewriter-like spacing between lines, you can specify the space—called leading in the printing business—in points. All the entries you make here can be entered directly, or you can use the up and down arrows to move through preset numbers.

NOTE *When you specify the space in points, the figure should be equal to or greater than the point size of the font you're using. In some cases, reduced or negative leading may look nice, but usually it just puts the lines too close together.*

■ **Line and Page Breaks Tab** The Line and Page Breaks options (see Figure 12-7) control the way pages are broken and the criteria used to make a page break. In the normal course of things, you'll want to keep Window/Orphan Control selected. This setting prevents a single line of a paragraph from appearing on a page. Instead, the page will break at the top of that paragraph, and that larger chunk of text will move to the next page. The Keep Lines Together option tells

PUTTING WORD 2001
TO WORK FOR YOU

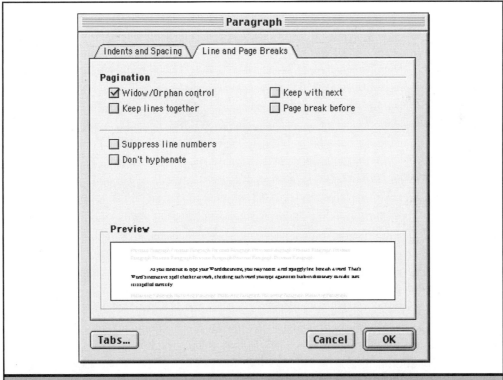

Figure 12-7. *This tab configures page flow in Word 2001.*

Word not to break a page within a paragraph (unless the paragraph is too large, of course, to fit on one page). The Keep with Next option tells Word to keep the current and following paragraphs on the same page, and the Page Break Before option creates a new page before the paragraph on which you're working. By judicious use of these options, you can set up some automatic formatting. For example, you can specify that a particular style of heading for a document always begins a new page, as you might want for a book chapter.

Summary

Word processing and page layout are kissing cousins. Many of the same document design ideas can be expressed with both types of programs. Over time, Word has gained more and more desktop publishing features, and, in many situations, you may not need any other type of program to prepare newsletters and other publications.

In the next chapter, you'll learn about Word's options for tables, headers, and footers. You'll also learn how to create your own Web site using Word.

Chapter 13

Advanced Word Processing Techniques

Now that you've created your first documents in Word, you might hunger for some ways to make Word do more. These days, a word processor does far more than just move words around and perform spelling and grammar checking. Microsoft Word 2001 offers a host of page layout features and table creation features that let you take your document way beyond the ordinary.

In this chapter, you'll learn to create tables, use Word's Click and Type feature, add headers and footers to your documents, and create and apply styles.

In addition, you can save your documents for publishing on the World Wide Web, without having to use a dedicated Web authoring program, while still being able to print the document in the usual way—you get the best of both worlds.

What's a Table and Why Do I Need One?

If you've ever used a regular typewriter, no doubt you know the procedure of lining up material in columns by moving the tab lever or button; more sophisticated electronic typewriters let you adjust text alignment for each tab position. That same feature is available in Word, but Word also offers something far more flexible: tables.

Creating a table, short and simple, is roughly equivalent to placing a number of blocks of text and pictures, called *cells*, and distributing them in rows and columns on your document page. The simplest table can just line up columns of text, but by adding borders and shading, plus graphics and by resizing the cells themselves, you can create all sorts of fascinating page layouts.

A table consists of a number of elements that, when used judiciously together, create a variety of effects and layouts. Word's flexible table creation tools put all of these features at your beck and call without your having to learn a new programming language or use complex commands.

Here's a quick overview of the pieces of a table:

- **Cells** The table cells are the individual boxes formed by the intersection of rows and columns. Cells contain the text or graphics, or both, presented in the table.

- **Rows** When you align a group of cells together horizontally, they make up a row. A table can consist of a number of rows, sometimes spanning several pages in your document.

- **Columns** All the cells that line up vertically are organized as columns.

- **Border** The line that surrounds the table is its border. You have a fair amount of flexibility in choosing the type of line and thickness to achieve the desired effect. A border can be placed around cells or around the entire table, or both.

- **Shading** You can shade the cells of your table and apply different colors to your text and graphic elements.

- **Cell Spacing and Margins** To make your table easier to read and to organize your information, you can put extra space between cells. You can also add padding, which is space around the text within a cell to make the text easier to read or to achieve a desired design effect.

- **Nested Tables**   A nested table is a table within a table. This is a new feature of Word 2001.
- **Easy Table Resizing**   Tables have move and resize handles so you can use your mouse to resize tables. You'll find this is a useful page layout tool.

Creating Word Tables: The Simple Way

You don't have to fret over complex commands to create a quick table. In fact, you can start the process in just a few seconds. Just remember that the number of columns is the number of cells from left to right along the page, and the number of rows is the number of cells from top to bottom. You'll be pleased to know that whatever you set now can be changed later, by adding or removing columns and rows, so all you have to do to start is take an educated guess.

Here's how to begin:

1. With Word open, click the position in your document where you want to insert a table.

2. Choose Insert from the Table menu and select Insert Table from the submenu. You can also click the Insert Table button on the Standard toolbar.

3. In the Insert Table dialog box (see Figure 13-1), enter the number of columns and rows in the Table Size area. You can move the up and down arrows to change the settings or just type the values in the text fields.

4. In the AutoFit Behavior area, you can specify an initial column width (Auto or a specific measurement), or select either of two other AutoFit options. AutoFit to Contents resizes the columns based on the material in the cell, and AutoFit to Window bases the width on the document size.

5. If you want a more elaborate format for your table, with rules and shading and other features, click the AutoFormat button, to display the Table AutoFormat dialog box (see Figure 13-2).

6. Scroll through the Formats list to find a suitable format. The Preview window at the right will display the style.

7. In the Formats to Apply area, indicate which elements of the format you want to use. Unchecking Borders, for example, will remove any borders from your table.

> NOTE   *Even after you select a format for your table, you can manually change any element of that design later. Nothing you pick here is set in stone, but it can be a useful starting point.*

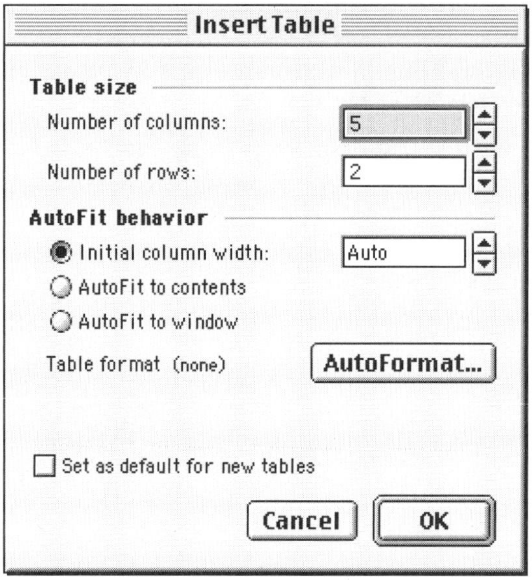

Figure 13-1. The simple road to a Word table begins here.

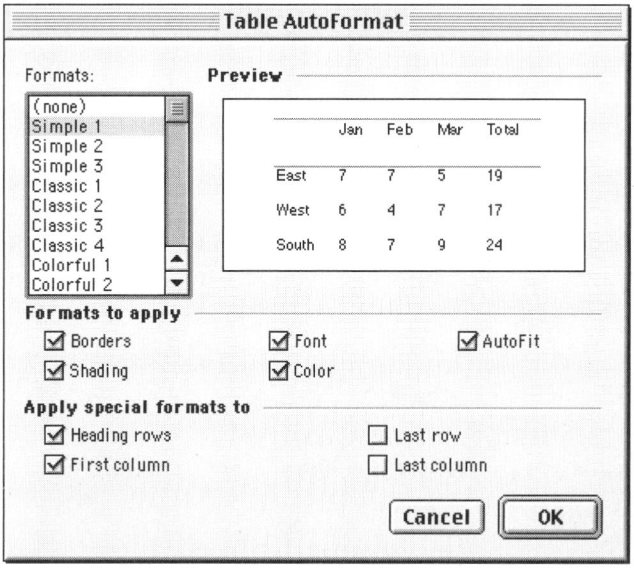

Figure 13-2. Select from a number of prebuilt table formats in this dialog box.

8. In the Apply Special Formats To area, specify whether you want a special design for heading rows, the first or last column, or the last row.

9. When your AutoFormat design is set, click OK to return to the Insert Table dialog box. The format you selected will be listed next to Table Format.

10. If you want to use this style as the beginning point for all of your tables, select Set as Default for New Tables.

11. Click OK to produce a blank table formatted to your specifications in the location of the document that you specified.

12. Enter your information; you can press the TAB key to move from cell to cell, row after row, and SHIFT-TAB to move back.

NOTE   *Whenever you move from one cell to the next using TAB or SHIFT-TAB, any text in the cell you've accessed will be highlighted and can be deleted by your next keystroke.*

Customizing Your Simple Table

Your basic table isn't a fixed commodity. You can add and remove cells and rows and resize your table as necessary with a few keystrokes here and there. Let's look at the possibilities.

Adding Table Rows and Columns

To add rows or columns, or both, to your table, follow these instructions:

1. Locate your table and select the number of rows and columns to match the ones you want to insert. So if you want to add two rows via this method, select two rows.

2. From the Table menu, select Insert; then choose the action you want to take from the submenu. You can also access this menu by clicking the arrow to the right of the Insert Table button on the Tables and Borders toolbar.

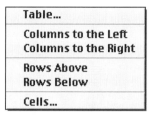

You can add columns to the left or right of, and rows above or below, your selection. Select the Cells command to display the Insert Cells dialog box, which can be used to shift cells and insert rows and columns.

TIP   *Here's an instantaneous way to add a row at the bottom of a table. When you're at the end of the table, press the TAB key. A new row will be created automatically.*

Resizing Your Table

Earlier in this section, you learned how to set the AutoFormat options for a table, so the width of the table cells would be resized automatically based on the cell contents, or the cells would be sized according to the width of your document.

TIP   *If you want to resize a column or row to a specific size, click the column or row. From the Table menu, choose Table Properties. Then click the Column or Row tab and specify the size changes you want.*

You can also manually resize a table to fit your needs. Follow these steps:

1. To resize the entire table, hold the cursor at the upper-left or lower-right corner of the table, until the resize handle (square) appears. Drag the handle down and to the right to make the table larger, and up and to the left to reduce its overall size.

2. To change the size of individual cells, place the cursor on a table border or boundary until the cursor changes to a double-headed arrow. Drag back and forth (or up and down) to the size you want. Here is an example of a typical table, and one with the column widths altered.

⌗	⌗	⌗	⌗	⌗	⌗	⌗

⌗	⌗	⌗	⌗	⌗	⌗	⌗

> **TIP** *If you do not see the move or resize handles, go to the View menu and choose either Page Layout or Outline view.*

Reviewing the Table Resizing and Display Options

In addition to dragging the mouse or changing the table properties, there are other ways to check the size and to resize your table (and there's no need to hold a ruler to your Mac's display).

> **TIP** *One convenient way to format your tables is to use the Tables and Borders toolbar. Check out the next section for information on how to bring it up and the features it includes.*

Here's a look at the available options (in addition to the ones already described):

- **Displaying the Column Width or Row Height**   Position the mouse cursor on a table or column border and hold down the OPTION key. You'll see the actual measurements of the cell or row in the horizontal or vertical ruler (as appropriate). As you resize, you'll see the values change.
- **Making Columns and Rows the Same Size**   With the Tables and Borders toolbar displayed, select the table and click the Distribute Columns Evenly button or Distribute Rows Evenly button.
- **Breaking a Table Across Pages**   Select the row you want to move to the next page and press COMMAND-ENTER.
- **Keeping a Table from Breaking Across Pages**   With the table selected, choose Table Properties from the Tools menu and then click the Row tab. Uncheck the Row to Break Across Pages check box.

■ **Repeat Table Headings When a Table Spans More Than One Page** Select the row or rows that contain the headings (including the first row of the table) and then choose Heading Rows Repeat from the Table menu.

NOTE *If you insert a manual page break in a table, the heading won't be repeated. Also, you must use the Page Layout view to see the repeating headings.*

Activating the Tables and Borders Toolbar

Many of the most powerful table creation features are available on the Tables and Borders toolbar, but it's not displayed automatically in Word. Fortunately, you can display it easily.

Just follow these steps:

1. Choose Customize from the Tools menu.

2. Select Tables and Borders from the list of available toolbars.

3. Click OK to bring up the toolbar on your Word desktop (see Figure 13-3).

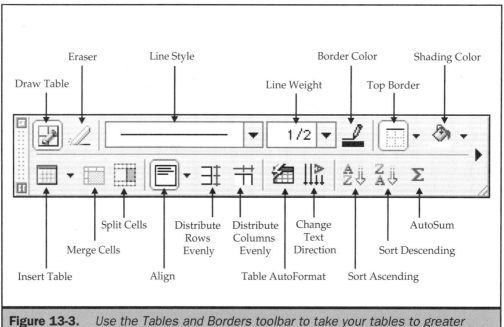

Figure 13-3. *Use the Tables and Borders toolbar to take your tables to greater heights of sophistication.*

The Tables and Borders toolbar gives you these additional features (described from left to right, top to bottom); just click the appropriate button:

- **Draw Table**   Click this button to bring up a pencil tool that lets you draw a table in your document from scratch and add extra cells. This feature is also available on the Tools menu.

- **Eraser**   Use this tool to erase cells and other elements of your table. This tool is used for cell merging (as you'll see shortly).

- **Line Style**   Choose the lines used as borders within cells and around your table.

- **Line Weight**   Adjust the thickness of the border lines. The measurements are specified in points, with the minimum being one-half point.

- **Border Color**   Choose a color for your border from the standard colors or with the color picker, using various color schemes.

- **Top Border**   Specify a border for the top of your table. Click the down arrow at the right of this tool to bring up various designs.

- **Shading Color**   Use the paint bucket to apply fill colors inside your table.

- **Insert Table**   This is the very same feature that's available on the Tools menu; click it to insert a table.

- **Merge Cells**   Use this tool to combine multiple cells into a single cell. The same command is available on the Table menu.

- **Split Cells**   This tool splits one cell into multiple cells. When selected, it brings up the Split Cells dialog box, where you can specify the number of cells and rows you're creating. The same command is also found on the Table menu.

```
┌───────────────────────────────────┐
│ ▤▤▤▤▤▤▤▤ Split Cells ▤▤▤▤▤▤▤▤    │
│                                   │
│  Number of columns:  [10    ] ▲▼ │
│                                   │
│  Number of rows:     [2     ] ▲▼ │
│                                   │
│  ☑ Merge cells before split      │
│                                   │
│         [ Cancel ]  [  OK  ]     │
│                                   │
└───────────────────────────────────┘
```

- **Align**   How will the text be aligned in your table? Click the down arrow at the right of this button to get the options, which include various top-, center-, and bottom-aligned configurations.

- **Distribute Rows Evenly**   Click this button to allot each row in your table the same amount of space.

- **Distribute Columns Evenly**   Click this button to allot each column in your table the same amount of space.

- **Table AutoFormat**   This button delivers the same dialog box that's available from the Table menu.

- **Change Text Direction**   This button rotates the text 90 degrees clockwise. The function is similar to that of the Text Direction command on the Format menu.

- **Sort Ascending**   This button sorts the selected rows by the specified order; it's based on the Sort command on the Table menu.

- **Sort Descending**   This button sorts the selected rows by the specified order; it's based on the Sort command on the Table menu.

- **AutoSum**   Click to calculate the sum of the numbers in a column or row.

Changing the Space Between Cells

Normally, when you create a table, the cells are placed adjacent to one another, without any space between them. You can change that setting by following these steps:

1. With your table selected, choose Table Properties from the Table menu. This brings up the Table Properties Dialog box shown in Figure 13-4.

2. Select the Table tab if it isn't already selected.

3. Click the Options button to bring up Table Options dialog box.

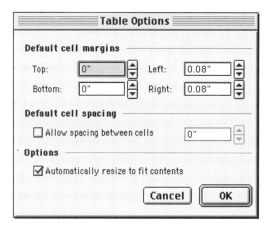

4. In the Default Cell Spacing area, select the Allow Spacing Between Cells check box and then specify a setting in the text field. You can use the up and down arrows to move through fixed sizes.

5. After you've made your changes, click OK in this dialog box and in the Table Properties dialog box to go back to your table.

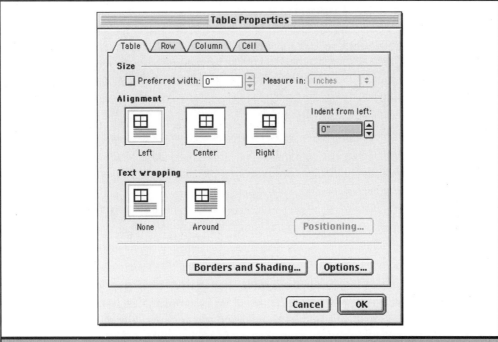

Figure 13-4.   *This dialog box is used to configure a number of different features of your tables in Word 2001.*

Merging Multiple Cells into a Single Cell

Another feature of Word is the ability to merge one or more cells into a single cell. This feature is tailor-made to create headings that extend across several columns.

Here's how you accomplish the task:

1. With Word open, bring up the Tables and Borders toolbar (choose View, then Toolbars, and then Tables and Borders).

2. Click the Eraser button. The cursor will change to an eraser.

TIP   *When you combine table cells for a heading, you can also use the Text Direction command to rotate the text, if needed, for your particular document.*

3. Drag the eraser across the cell dividers that you want to delete.

NOTE   *Another way to accomplish this task is to select the cells you want to combine and click the Merge Cells button on the Tables and Borders toolbar. Word is like this; it gives you several ways to accomplish the same task.*

Splitting a Cell into Multiple Cells

Perhaps you want to do the reverse: split a single cell into many cells (I sound like a biologist here). To do that, follow these steps:

1. With the Tables and Borders toolbar present, click the Draw Table button, which changes the cursor to a pencil.

2. Drag the pencil cursor horizontally, from the top to the bottom of a cell, to create new cell borders.

> **NOTE** *Don't be concerned about exact dimensions. You can easily click the borders to resize them after the cells are divided. Hold down the OPTION key when you resize to see the exact dimensions.*

3. If you want to perform this operation on more than one cell, select them, click Split Cells on the toolbar, and then specify the number of cells you want to create.

Splitting a Table into Two Parts

After creating a table, you may discover that it really would work better split into two separate tables. Fortunately, you don't have to go through any elaborate cutting and pasting process. Just follow these steps:

1. Click the row that will become the first row in the second table: that is, the location where you want to split the table.

2. Choose Split Table from the Table menu, and you're done. (Didn't I tell you that it was easy?)

Copying and Moving Table Contents

Word's table features allow you to easily move table contents to other cells. You can do so by using your regular Word editing features.

> **NOTE** *To move or copy text from one cell without changing the formatting of the destination cell, select just the text and not the end-of-cell mark (which is visible only when you have the option to display nonprinting characters activated as a Word View preference) of the source cells, rows, or columns. To change both the contents and formatting of the destination cell, select the text and the end-of-cell mark of the source cells, rows, or columns.*

1. To move the selected material, drag it to the new location.

2. To copy the material, hold down the OPTION key while dragging it.

NOTE

Our ever-vigilant technical editor, Pieter Paulson, reminds me that you can always use the copy or cut and paste features from the Edit menu, but dragging and OPTION-dragging is easier.

Deleting Tables or Parts of a Table

The process of deleting an entire table is similar to that for deleting any other material in your Word document. Follow these steps:

1. Click the table to select it; then press the DELETE key on your Mac's keyboard.

2. If you want to delete just some of the cells, rows, or columns, select the material.

3. From the Table menu, select Delete; then choose the appropriate option from the submenu: Cells, Columns, or Rows.

TIP

Here are other ways to delete elements of your table. You can select the cells in a single column and press DELETE. You can select cells in adjacent columns, and press DELETE; you'll see the Delete Cells dialog box, where you can specify what you want to do.

Creating Word Tables: The Complex Way

The steps described so far can be used to create not just a simple table, but to format a simple table so that it has the properties of a more complex table.

To create a complex table from the very beginning, follow these steps:

1. With the Tables and Borders toolbar displayed, click the Draw Table button. The cursor will change to a pencil.

2. With the pencil, draw a rectangle, by dragging the cursor down diagonally from the upper-left corner to the lower-right corner of your table.

3. When the table outline is complete, use the pencil to draw the lines representing the columns and rows inside the rectangle.

4. If you make a mistake, simply click the Eraser button and use that tool to delete the lines.

5. When your table structure is complete, follow the instructions in the preceding section to refine the spacing between your cells and rows.

TIP

If you want text wrapping supported in your table, hold down the OPTION key while you're drawing it. Word's drawing features are discussed in Chapter 14.

6. Click a cell and begin typing or inserting text or graphics.

Creating a Nested Table

Beginning with Word 2001, you can create a nested table, or a table within a table. This feature offers all sorts of fascinating design possibilities that you can adapt to your particular needs.

Here's how to create a nested table:

1. With the Tables and Borders toolbar displayed, click the Draw Table button. The cursor changes to a pencil.

2. Position the pencil cursor at the location in a cell where you want to insert another table.

3. Follow the same process as described in the preceding section to create a new table. Draw the table, starting with a rectangle, dragging the mouse downward diagonally from the upper-left corner to the lower-right corner.

4. Draw the lines for columns and rows inside your newly created table. The end result will look roughly like this:

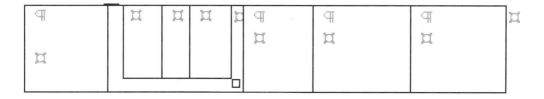

5. Click a cell in the main or the nested table to populate it with text and pictures.

Techniques for Changing Text to a Table

Suppose you are working on pieces of text that you later decide to change into a table. Do you need to start from scratch? No, because Word lets you convert that text to a table just by making a few simple preparations. All you have to do is follow these steps:

1. Place a separator to show where columns and rows should begin within the text. Normally, you enter a comma to define columns, and enter a paragraph mark to define rows, but you can use a different character as the separator if you prefer, as you'll see shortly.

2. Select the text that you want to convert to a table.

3. From the Table menu, choose Convert; then select Convert Text to Table. This brings up the Convert Text to Table dialog box.

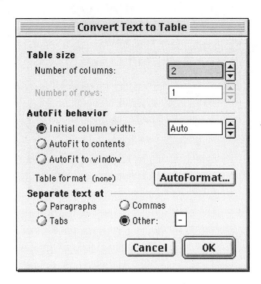

4. In the Separate Text At area, select the separator character you want or specify one of your own choice.

5. Set the Table Size and AutoFit Behavior options as you prefer. These choices are the same as those available to you when you create a table from scratch, as described earlier. The text will be converted to a standard Word table that can be configured in the same way as any other Word table.

Going Back Again: Changing a Table to Text

Despite the claim that you can never go home again, you can not only convert your Word text to a table, but you can also convert your Word table to text. Here's how to do it:

1. Go to the table in your Word document and select the rows, columns, or the entire table that you want to convert to regular paragraphs.

2. From the Table menu, choose Convert and select Convert Table to Text to display the Convert Table to Text dialog box.

3. Select the separator characters you want to insert to substitute for the boundaries of your table columns.

4. Click OK to perform the conversion.

Solving Your Word Table Problems

The setup instructions for creating and formatting Word tables are straightforward enough, but sometimes you'll run into problems simply because there are so many features and options. In this section, we'll look at some of the common problems with tables and their solutions.

- **Table Column Resizes as You Type** The standard setting is for columns to resize to accommodate your text and graphics, so as you type, the column size changes. If this isn't what you want, select the table and select Table Properties from the Table menu. On the Table tab of the dialog box, click Options. In the Table Options dialog box, uncheck the option labeled Automatically Resize to Fit Contents.

- **Table Size Doesn't Change to Fit Window** Make sure your table is set to fit to the size of a document window. If it is, switch to the Online view to see the change.

- **Line Count Is Off After Inserting a Table** This is a Word quirk (yes, this program has a few quirks, too). Whenever a table is split into more than one part because of a page break, the line count may be off. Sorry, but that's the way it is.

- **Text Is Hidden Inside the Table Cell** Perhaps the indents you set for your text are inappropriate. Click the Alignment and Spacing button on the Formatting

Palette and adjust the indentation settings. If there's nothing wrong with the paragraph indent, make sure that you haven't specified a row height that's too small for your text. You can check this by accessing the Table Properties dialog box from the Table menu. Select the Row tab and make sure the Row Height Is option is set to At Least and then specify a height to accommodate the size of the text.

■ **Gray Borders on Tables Won't Print** You may be seeing gridlines (positioning marks) and not an actual border. To print a border in a table, you must actually add one. (If you prefer not to see those gridlines, go to the Table menu and uncheck the Show Gridlines option.)

■ **Table Cuts Off at the End of the Page** Have you applied text wrapping to the table? It's easy to miss this option, particularly if your table is long enough to encompass more than a single page. To fix the problem, choose Table Properties from the Table menu and select the Table tab. Click None in the Text Wrapping area.

■ **Table Won't Resize to Match New Document Margins** Why this doesn't happen is a good question, as the politicians say—but it doesn't happen automatically. When you change page margins, you must also go back and change the width of the table to match.

■ **My Table Snaps to the Left or Right When I Try to Move It** Your table can be mighty stubborn under some circumstances. If you're in Online Layout view and text wrapping has been employed, this problem may occur. To set things right, switch to the Normal or Page Layout view. If you're creating a Web page, you need to turn off the text-wrapping feature (available under Cell Options on the Cell tab of the Table Properties dialog box).

■ **Table Borders Don't Appear on Every Page** This may happen if your document is divided into sections. To get the borders to show up on all pages in your document, go to the Format menu and choose Borders and Shading. Select the Page Border tab and in the Apply To area, select Whole Document.

■ **Page Border Is Not Visible** Be sure that you are using Page Layout view. Other viewing options will not display borders.

■ **Page Border Doesn't Move When I Change Margins** You need to revisit the Borders and Shading dialog box on the Format menu, select the Page Border tab, and click the Options button. Under Options, select Margin in the Measure From pop-up menu. Then take a deep breath!

■ **Borders Don't Print** Is it you or your printer? Probably the latter. With a few exceptions, printers cannot handle edge-to-edge printing. To fix the margin for the borders, bring up the Borders and Shading dialog box from the Format menu. Select the Page Border tab and click the Options button. Look for the margin settings and adjust the settings to provide a big enough margin from the edge of the page to your borders.

TIP *If your printer's documentation isn't available or doesn't list the maximum page borders, check the Page Setup box (available from the File menu). In a standard PostScript laser printer's Page Setup box, just click the image of the dog within a page to see the actual borders. Another way to check is to print a rectangle that covers the full width of your page and shade it with any color. Look at the printed output to measure the precise dimensions.*

Using Word's Click and Type Feature

One notable feature of Word 2001 is usually found in graphics or page layout programs. The feature is called Click and Type, and it lets you insert text, graphics, and tables in a blank portion of your document without having to specify a page boundary or create a text frame. All you have to do is double-click the area and insert your material.

For example, here's how you would insert a title and author for a document:

1. On a blank page, double-click the area where you want to insert the title (perhaps at the center or upper right of the page, for example).

2. Type the title.

3. To insert the author's name, double-click the area where you want to put the name. The bottom center, right, or left would all work fine. Then type the name.

4. When you're finished with your title page, the result may look something like this:

Attack of the Rockoids

By Gene Steinberg & Grayson Steinberg

A Click and Type Reference

The Click and Type feature is, as you can see, remarkably easy to use. But it doesn't work in all cases, and there are a few things you'll want to double-check before you use it.

Here's the short list:

- **Where Click and Type Won't Work**   You cannot use the Click and Type feature in multiple columns, in bulleted and numbered lists, to the left and right of indented text, or to the left or right of images with text wrapping at the top or bottom. You also must be in Page Layout view to access the feature. It's not available in Normal, Outline, or Print Preview view.

- **Check Your Default Paragraph Formatting**   If you insert text via Click and Type below a paragraph, it will use the default paragraph style you specified in your Word Preferences dialog box, on the Edit tab. You can change that default formatting at any time by revisiting the dialog box and picking a different style from the ones available. Text formatting can, of course, be modified from the Formatting Palette.

Creating Headers and Footers

One valuable use of the Click and Type feature is to create headers and footers for your documents. Using it, you can easily place your document's title and author's name or company logo at the top, the page numbers and date at the bottom, or any combination thereof.

Word's header and footer features are very flexible. You can insert a special header and footer on the first page or part of your document, and another on subsequent pages or sections. If you're preparing a book or company manual, for example, you can even have different headers and footers on left and right pages, just as in a regular printed book.

First we'll discuss the ways to create headers and footers; then we'll look at various ways to customize them.

1. With your Word document open, double-click the top or bottom of the page, beyond the regular text area, or choose Header and Footer from the View menu. Either action will deliver the Header and Footer toolbar (see Figure 13-5). The options available include the following:

   - **Insert Page Number**   Use the page number criteria specified from the Page Numbers submenu of the Insert menu to number the pages in your document automatically.

   - **Insert Number of Pages**   This button inserts both the current page number and the total number of pages, using the format 1 of 32, meaning page 1 out of 32 total pages.

   - **Format Page Number**   This option specifies how page numbers appear— for instance, as regular numbers or roman numerals or whether page numbers include a chapter number (2-7 would be page 7 of chapter 2)— and the starting page number (numbering doesn't have to begin at 1).

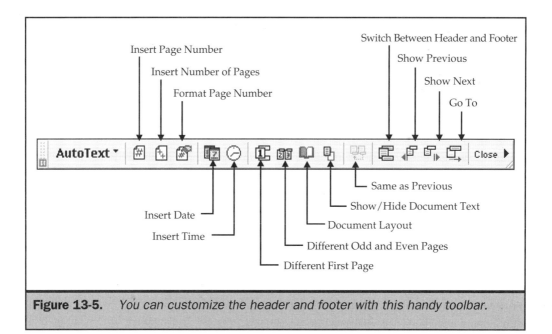

Figure 13-5. *You can customize the header and footer with this handy toolbar.*

■ **Insert Date** This option inserts the current date, as set in your Mac's Date & Time Control Panel, in your header or footer. This date will change dynamically each day if you choose Update Automatically in the Date and Time dialog box, available from the Insert menu.

■ **Insert Time** This button inserts the time as set in your Date & Time Control Panel. You can set this to update dynamically as for Insert Date, to reflect the actual time when the document is opened.

TIP *Mac clocks are frequently off, by seconds and sometimes by much greater amounts. Since Mac OS 8.5, Apple has added the Use a Network Time Server feature. Click that button in the Date & Time Control Panel, and you can configure your Mac to automatically or manually synchronize its own inaccurate clock with Apple's clock or that of another network time server (of course, you need Internet access to make this work).*

■ **Different First Page** Use this option to set up a first-page header and footer that differ from the ones used in the rest of the document.

■ **Different Odd and Even Pages** Just as in a book, you can place, for instance, the title on the left page and the author's name on the right.

■ **Document Layout** How will headers and footers be situated on your page? Specify the distance from text margins, how sections in a document are handled, and so forth.

- **Show/Hide Document Text**   The text in your document normally appears as a faint backdrop when you're using the Header and Footer viewing option. You can hide that text if you want (but, as some people say, why?).

- **Same as Previous**   Pick up the settings of your previous header and footer when creating a new one.

- **Switch Between Header and Footer**   This does just what the title implies.

- **Show Previous**   Click this button to go to the previous header or footer.

- **Show Next**   Click this button to move to the next header or footer.

- **Go To**   Click this button to move to the header or footer.

2. Click the header area and enter the title, date, and other items.

3. Switch to the footer and place the appropriate material there, such as the page number, file name, and so forth.

TIP   *If you want to create different sets of headers and footers in your document, perhaps to reflect a chapter or article change, insert a section break to divide your document (it's accessed by choosing Break from the Insert menu). That way, you can have a unique set of headers and footers (even first-page headers and footers) for each part.*

4. When your headers and footers are complete, click the Close button to return to your regular document text, or double-click the text area to accomplish the same result.

NOTE   *By default (don't you just love application defaults?), Word puts text and graphics left aligned in a header or footer. If you want an item center aligned, press the TAB key. To right align the material, press the TAB key twice.*

Inserting Chapter Numbers and Titles Automatically

You can divide your document into chapters and have Word increment the numbers of the chapters automatically. This will definitely ease the formatting of your document.

NOTE   *You can, of course, do this manually, but Word makes it easy enough that you might as well go with the flow and let the program do it automatically.*

Here's how to perform this task:

1. Insert a section break at the start of each chapter. This is done by choosing Break from the Insert menu and then selecting the appropriate section break from the submenu. There are break commands for new pages, new columns, and four types of sections. The latter set of commands can create a new section on the next page, the same page (continuous), or the next even or odd page.

You also have to apply one of Word's built-in heading styles (specifically, Heading 1 through Heading 9) to the chapter number and chapter title.

Don't feel constrained in your creativity by having to stick with a built-in heading style, since you can easily modify the styles to suit your needs.

2. From the View menu, select Header and Footer, or double-click the header or footer in your document.

3. From the Insert menu, choose Cross-Reference, which brings up the dialog box shown here.

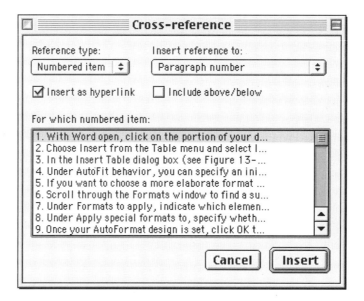

4. From the Reference Type pop-up menu, choose Heading.

5. From the For Which Heading list, select the heading that contains the chapter number and title information.

6. Click the Insert button and then close the dialog box.

7. Repeat this process for each chapter.

Here's the good part: if you decide to change a chapter number or title in your document, press F9, and Word will automatically update the header or footer when either is selected. If you are modifying a chapter heading, just remember to type new text ahead of the existing text before the older text is deleted.

Creating Unique First-Page Headers and Footers

Often you will want a different header and footer—or none at all—on the first page of a document or document section. To accomplish this task, follow these steps:

1. Click the first page or select the section or sections for which you want to insert a first-page header.

2. Choose Header and Footer from the View menu or double-click a footer or header.

3. With the Header and Footer toolbar displayed, click Document Layout, which produces the dialog box shown in Figure 13-6.

4. Select the Layout tab and select the Different First Page check box.

5. Click OK.

6. As needed, move to the First Page Header or First Page Footer area to make your changes.

7. Click Close to return to your document text.

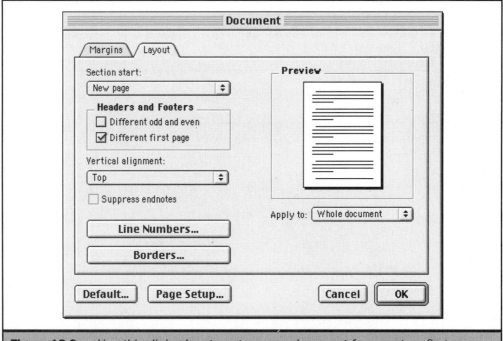

Figure 13-6.   *Use this dialog box to set up your document for a custom first-page header and footer.*

Changing the Position of Headers or Footers

By default (there's the "D" word again), Word puts a one-half inch space between the text area and your headers and footers, but this setting can be changed as needed.

To accomplish the task, follow these steps:

1. From the View menu, choose Header and Footer, or double-click a header or footer whose margins you want to change.

2. Click the Document Layout button on the Header and Footer toolbar.

3. Select the Margins tab, which brings up the dialog box shown in Figure 13-7.

4. Enter the distance from the top of the page to the top of the header in the Header box.

5. Enter the distance from the bottom of the page to the bottom of the footer in the Footer box.

6. To change the distance from the text in your document to the header or footer, go to the vertical ruler at the left of your document window and move the cursor to the margin boundary at the top or bottom. The cursor will change to a box with an arrow at the top and bottom. Drag the margin at the top or bottom up or down as needed.

7. Click Close on the Header and Footer toolbar to return to your regular text.

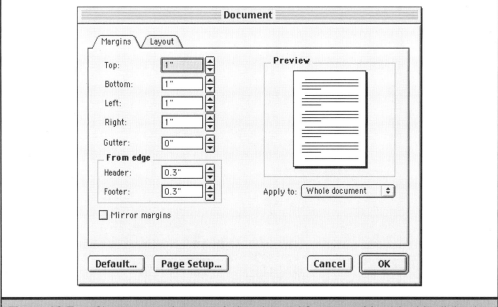

Figure 13-7. *Change your document's header and footer positions in this dialog box.*

Using Word Styles

When you format the text in your Word document, you'll be adjusting a number of elements. You may pick a font, a style, a size, an alignment option, and so on, and you may add some space before or after a paragraph, or indent the first line or even an entire text block to make it stand out from the other paragraphs in your document.

As you progress through your document, you might make other changes, perhaps for a title, a quotation, a byline, and on and on. Word's Styles feature lets you set up the formatting you want just once and then easily apply that style to your document without having to, well, reinvent the wheel over and over again.

When you installed Word, the program came with some prebuilt styles. When you first start typing in a document, for example, the Normal style comes into play. This is the standard text style that's set up for your program. If you click the Style pop-up menu on the Formatting Palette, you'll see the Style dialog box (see Figure 13-8), which lists the styles that came with the program.

Styles are one of the most popular features of Word. (As I wrote this book, I used a number of special styles from my publisher, to ensure that the text and captions appear in the right format.)

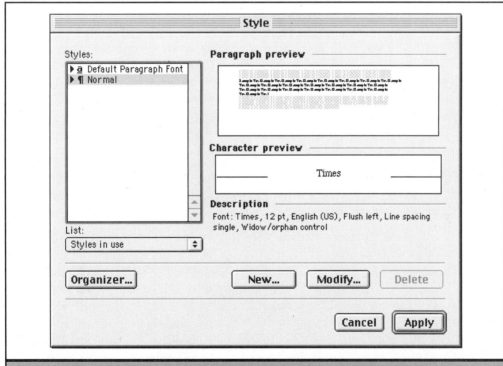

Figure 13-8.   *Pick a standard style for your document in this dialog box.*

There are two types of styles. Paragraph styles apply to the entire paragraph, and character styles affect only specific text within the paragraph. An example of a character style is a bold or italic phrase within regular text.

Using Styles in Word

A fast way to get started using styles is just to work with the ones that are already available as standard issue in your documents. To use one of these styles, follow these steps:

1. Click any part of the paragraph to which you want to use a style.

2. Go to the Formatting Palette and select the Style menu.

3. From the menu, select the style you want. The paragraph's formatting will be changed to reflect the style you've selected and the Formatting Palette will reflect the changes.

4. To modify text to which a style has already been applied, just follow steps 1 through 3.

Creating a New Style

Having a few fixed styles can help when you create a simple document, but they won't be sufficient if you want to use a specific typeface, size, style, alignment, and set of indents. The quickest way to get the style you want is to modify an existing one. For instance, if the text style is 12-point Times, flush left, and you prefer 14-point Helvetica, justified, you can easily create a brand-new style with the changes you want.

Here's how to accomplish the task:

1. To change the text style to 14-point Helvetica, justified, adjust all the text properties on the Formatting Palette to reflect this style.

2. When you've modified the style the way you want, choose Style from the Format menu to bring up the Style dialog box.

3. Click the New button, which will produce the New Style dialog box just as shown, more or less, in Figure 13-9.

4. Make sure the changes you made are reflected in the Description field below the Preview window.

5. If the format isn't quite what you want, click the Format button to display a menu of standard document formatting options; select the type of formatting you want to change and then make the changes.

Font...
Paragraph...
Tabs...
Border...
Language...
Frame...
Numbering...

You do not have to specify every single element of your text properties in a style definition. If you plan on making individual character changes in paragraphs, such as occasionally adding italics or underscores, don't include formatting that may affect those changes. You can also create extra styles that involve just minor formatting changes, for greater flexibility in handling your text properties.

6. When the format is as you want, give it a name in the Name text field. Choose a name that identifies the style as clearly as possible, such as BodyText, Subhead, and so on. Also specify whether the style is for a paragraph or character style. The choice you make affects the options you can use; character formats don't affect such properties as text alignment, list format, paragraph spacing, borders, and shading.

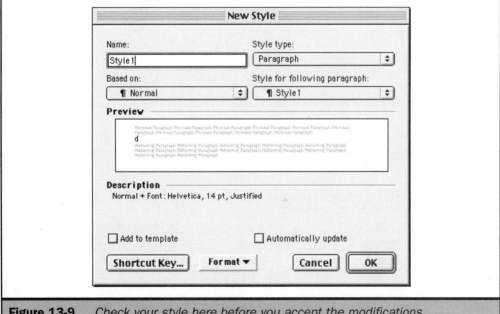

Figure 13-9. *Check your style here before you accept the modifications.*

When you apply a paragraph style, any text within that paragraph will be updated to reflect the change. A character style affects only the selected text; it's used to change such properties as typeface, style, and size.

7. Select a style from the Based On pop-up menu to specify the source style on which you're basing the one you're creating (the current style will be selected by default).

8. To automatically switch to a different style when you press the RETURN key to end a paragraph, use the Style for the Following Paragraph option. This feature is especially useful for headings or paragraphs that are used only at the start of a passage of text.

You can see a glimmer of your format in the Preview screen, although it may be too small to give you anything more than a hint of how the actual text looks.

9. If you want to automatically update the style based on changes you make to a paragraph, select the Automatically Update check box at the bottom right of the New Style dialog box. If you want the document's template to include the style, select the Add to Template check box.

When you create or change a style used as the basis for other styles, any changes made to that base style will also apply to the other styles derived from it.

10. When your style is completed, click OK in both the New Style and Style dialog boxes to store the style.

You can also create a shortcut key to trigger a style change. To activate that feature, click the Shortcut Key button in the New Style dialog box and then select the style to which you want to apply the shortcut. When you press the shortcut key combination, which is limited to modifier keys plus a single character, you'll see whether that combination is already in use. If it isn't, click the Assign button to store the keyboard shortcut. Now whenever you want to apply that style, all you have to do is press the shortcut key.

Modifying an Existing Style

Once you've created a brand new style it's quite easy to modify it should you find that you want to format your document differently. Just follow these steps:

1. Make sure that the option to have a style automatically updated based on the changes you make is selected in the New Style dialog box (as explained in the previous section).

2. Make sure that the style you want to modify is applied to the paragraph where you're going to make your alterations.

3. Change the paragraph properties of the style as you like to reflect the way you want to format your document.

NOTE   *When you make those changes, the style used for that paragraph is updated, too, which means that all text in your document based on that paragraph is also altered in the same way. If you don't want your changes applied this way, don't use the automatic update feature.*

Manually Changing a Style

If you don't have the automatic update option selected, you can manually change a style without going through too many hoops. Here's how it's done:

1. Select the paragraph or text for which you want to change the style.

2. Choose Style from the Format menu.

3. Click the Modify button, which will produce the Modify Style dialog box. (The Modify Style dialog box looks very much like the New Style dialog box shown earlier, in Figure 13-9.)

4. Click the Format button and make the changes you want to your style. As in the New Style dialog box, there are separate commands for each type of style attribute: Font, Paragraph, Tabs, Border, Language, Frame, and Numbering.

5. After changing the formatting the way you want, recheck all other parameters for your style, such as the name, style on which this style is based, and the style for subsequent paragraphs. Then Double-check the description to see that it is correct.

6. Check Add to Template to include the style in the template used for your document.

7. Check Automatically Update if you want to styles updated automatically from now on.

8. If you want to change or add a shortcut key, click the Shortcut Key button and make the additions or changes you want. Then click Assign to store the keyboard shortcut addition or change.

9. Click OK to save the changes to your style and then OK in the Style dialog box to finish the process.

TIP   *You can use the Style Gallery to see how the available styles affect your document. Choose Theme from the Format menu and click the Style Gallery button. There you can select any of the available styles from the list and see the preview update to show the effect of the style in your document.*

PUTTING WORD 2001
TO WORK FOR YOU

Deleting Styles

If you decide that you no longer need a specific style, you may just want to remove it, so you don't have to scroll through useless styles to change your document. Here's how it's done:

1. From the Format menu, select Style.

2. In the Styles dialog box, select the name of the style you want to remove.

3. Click the Delete button.

CAUTION *When a style is deleted, it's removed from the document's template, and all paragraphs that were formatted with that style are changed to the Normal style. This reformatting has no effect, of course, if no paragraphs in your text used the style that you deleted. You cannot delete the Normal style or the standard headings styles.*

Troubleshooting Problems with Word Styles

You might think, from the information about styles just presented, that making styles work ought to be a fairly uncomplicated process. But there are enough variations in the way styles are created that problems can arise.

Here are some common style-related problems and their solutions:

■ **Style Changes Unexpectedly** As mentioned earlier, there is an automatic updating option for styles. Whenever you make changes to the text to which the style applies, the style definition itself changes. If that's not what you want, go to the Format menu, choose Style, select the style you want to change, and then click Modify in the Styles dialog box. Turn off the check box to automatically update styles. Another possible cause of an unexpected change in a style is that the source style or the one on which your style is based has been changed. Follow the steps to modify a style to make sure that you haven't changed the source style or, if you have, to reverse the changes. A third possible cause is that the template on which you based your document has been altered. We'll discuss templates in detail in Chapter 15, which also covers mail merge and Word macros.

■ **Character Formats, Such as Bold or Italic, Change When a Style Is Applied**
The best way to handle this is to do the local character formatting after you've
applied the style. The style may have character formats that override the ones
you've applied to the paragraph.

■ **Template Doesn't Change After the Style Gallery Is Altered**   Document
templates aren't affected when you transfer styles from other templates to
your document. If you want to use a different template with your document,
go to the Tools menu and choose Templates and Add-ons. Then click the Attach
button to change the template, or the Add button to apply more than a single
template style to your document.

■ **Different Paragraphs with the Same Style Look Different**   It's possible that
you've applied local formatting to the various paragraphs. To remove the local
or manual formatting, select the entire paragraph, including the paragraph
mark (if the option to show hidden characters is set in Word's preferences).
Then press COMMAND-OPTION-Q. If you want to just remove the formatting
from individual characters in the paragraph, select the characters and press
CONTROL-SPACEBAR.

■ **Style List Doesn't Display All Styles**   Most Word problems have solutions
that aren't terribly exotic. If you want to see all of the styles that are available
on the Formatting Palette, hold down the SHIFT key when you click the Style
menu. To see all the available styles in the Style dialog box, display the List
pop-up menu and choose All Styles. Otherwise, only the styles currently in
use are displayed.

■ **Can't Redefine Normal Style**   When you apply a style to text, modify text
formatting, and then reapply the style using the Style dialog box, Word
displays a dialog box that offers you the choice of either modifying the style
with the new formats or just reapplying the original style. It's your choice how
to handle this symptom, but it does let you re-engage whatever style you've
selected, Normal or otherwise.

Saving Your Word Document as a Web Page

In addition to printing and e-mailing your Word documents, you can easily format them to appear as pages on the World Wide Web, without having to go through hoops or use complex document formatting. You don't need a trip to a dedicated Web authoring application, and you don't have to reinvent the wheel to use your document for different purposes.

Here's how to save your document in Web format:

1. Open the Word document you want to publish on the Web.

2. From the File menu, choose Save As Web Page, which will produce a Save As dialog box.

3. Before saving your document, you'll probably want to configure some options for the page. Click the Web Options button in the Save As dialog box.

4. In the Web Options dialog box, select the General tab if it's not already displayed; then give your Web page a title and enter some keywords, so the page can be found by search engines.

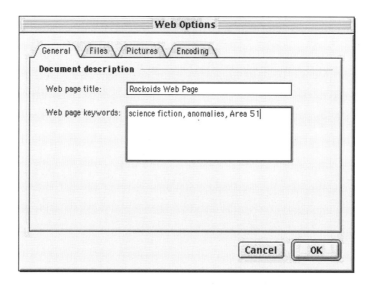

5. Select the Files tab to configure such options as whether to update links when the document is saved (definitely recommended and the default setting) and whether to save only display information in HTML format (as opposed to the entire file).

6. Select the Pictures tab to specify whether PNG is an allowable file format (it's a better version of GIF supported by more recent versions of Web browsers) and also to specify the target monitor size and resolution.

```
╔══════════════ Web Options ══════════════╗
║  ╱General ╲╱ Files ╲╱ Pictures ╲╱ Encoding ╲        ║
║  ┌─ File formats ──────────────────────────┐ ║
║  │  ☐ Allow PNG as an output format            │ ║
║  │                                              │ ║
║  └──────────────────────────────────────────┘ ║
║  ┌─ Target monitor ────────────────────────┐ ║
║  │  Screen size:   [1024 x 768 – 15" and 17" monitors, laptops ▲▼] │ ║
║  │  Pixels per inch:  [72  ] [▲▼]               │ ║
║  └──────────────────────────────────────────┘ ║
║                              [ Cancel ] [  OK  ]   ║
╚══════════════════════════════════════════╝
```

The Screen Size pop-up menu lists the display sizes affected by the resolution you set. You should pick a resolution that you expect most of your site visitors to use. Although the figure shown here specifies 1024 by 768 as the default, you might prefer 800 by 600, which is a standard size for small displays, such as the one on the iMac or iBook.

7. The Encoding tab specifies the text language options. You can leave this alone, unless your target audience uses a foreign language.

8. Click OK to store the option settings.

9. Give your Web page a title. By default, it will be the name of your document, plus the .htm extension so that the file is recognized by Web browsers.

PUTTING WORD 2001
TO WORK FOR YOU

NOTE *If this is to be your home page, however, choose index.htm instead, since most Web hosting facilities require that title for the first or introductory page of a Web site.*

10. Click Save to store your document.

11. To see what the resulting page looks like before it's uploaded or published on the Web, choose Web Page Preview from the File menu. This action will open the page in your normal Web browser (see Figure 13-10), so you can double-check that everything looks all right.

Summary

In this chapter, you flexed your muscles. You learned many ways to spruce up your Word 2001 documents as well as how to create a Web page from a regular word processing document. You also discovered how to exploit Word's flexible table-making tools and to use styles and headers and footers.

In the next chapter, you'll be introduced to a number of ways to create and insert graphics into your document. Even if you find drawing a straight line difficult, you'll find there are many ways to exploit Word's graphics features without being a professional graphic artist.

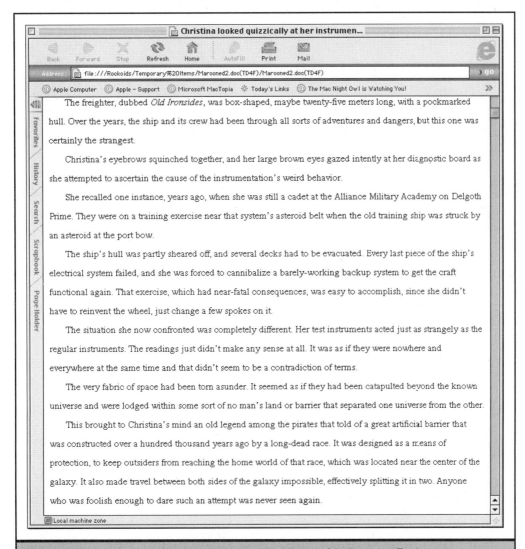

Figure 13-10.   *A sample page as viewed in Microsoft's Internet Explorer.*

Chapter 14

Using Word for Graphics

In previous chapters, you saw how Word's supremely powerful text editing capabilities, table creation tools, and style sheets can give a great deal of luster to your documents. But, as the old saying goes, pictures are truly worth a thousand words. Whether you want to use photos, drawings, or illustrations you create directly in Word, you'll find that this program has a lot more up its virtual sleeve than you might expect.

This chapter focuses extensively on Word's various drawing tools and also on its ability to handle graphics created in other programs. In addition, the ability to run many scanners and digital cameras from within Word gives you a wide range of additional capabilities.

Reference: A Look at Word's Graphics Features

Word 2001 lets you work with two types of graphics in your document. The first are the drawing objects that can be created within the program. These can be AutoShapes, or the curves and lines that you draw. In addition, you can use a companion program that's part of your Word installation, WordArt, to create various types of drawings. Any of these drawing objects can be modified with colors, borders, patterns, and special effects via Word's convenient Drawing toolbar.

The other types of graphics you can use are the pictures you insert into Word from another file or from a scanner or digital camera. These pictures can also be enhanced using Word's built-in editing capabilities, so with a little imagination and some effort, you have at hand a great variety of enhancements to spruce up your documents.

Here's a brief look at the kinds of graphic features available in Word. In the course of this chapter, you'll learn how to use these features to best advantage:

NOTE   *As extensive as Word's graphic capabilities might be, the program is not intended as a replacement for a dedicated illustration program, such as Adobe Illustrator, Deneba Canvas, or Macromedia FreeHand. But for many purposes, Word may be more than sufficient to meet your expectations.*

- ■ **AutoShapes**   The easiest picture objects to work with are the ones that have already been drawn for you. Word has a nice collection of AutoShapes, in such categories as basic shapes, flowchart elements, stars, banners, and callouts that you can mix and match and modify as necessary. The best thing about this feature is that you don't have to draw a complex shape from scratch. You may already have what's needed.

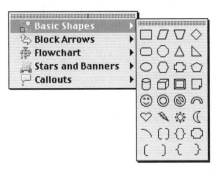

PUTTING WORD 2001
TO WORK FOR YOU

TIP   *Want to keep some of the tools with submenus around for later use? Word's tear-off menu feature can help. Just drag a submenu from the Drawing toolbar, and it will become a floating window, in effect taking on a life of its own.*

■ **WordArt**   Wouldn't you like to create a special text effect for a headline, Web banner, or company logo—and not have to work on it for hours? It's very possible with WordArt (see Figure 14-1). WordArt is a flexible tool that can help you create a special text effect in just seconds. Using the Drawing toolbar and another font, you can easily configure this special effect in a variety of ways.

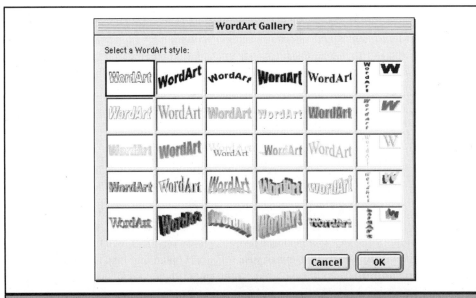

Figure 14-1.   *Choose a design for your logo from this list.*

NOTE *WordArt is slightly reminiscent of an extremely flexible Mac graphic program, TypeStyler. If you like the concept and want to extend your creativity, you can get a 60-day trial version of this terrific program. Just visit the company's Web site at: http://www.typestyler.com.*

■ **Text Boxes**   Normally, the text in your document fits into the area you defined when you set your document margins. But you can also create a *text box*: a totally separate frame into which you can insert picture captions, labels, and other bits and pieces of text. These text boxes are highly flexible; you're not just limited to a square or rectangle. You can even use the AutoShape feature to give your little text block a striking appearance.

■ **Clip Art**   This is either a good starting point or a good ending point, depending on your needs. Clip art is a set of professionally designed picture files that may include drawings and photos. Word comes with a good set of pictures that you can use to enhance your documents, or you can buy clip art from your software dealer. Such pictures range from simple line images and maps to complicated drawings of people, places, and things, which you can insert and then modify to put your own stamp on your document. Word includes a set of clip art in its Clip Gallery, and the Value Pack includes additional selections.

■ **Imported Pictures**   As you'll see in the next section, Word supports a variety of popular graphic formats, so you can easily insert pictures created from other programs into your Word document. The Picture toolbar that comes with Word then lets you perform some simple editing of the pictures, to fix problems or enhance their appearance. You can also wrap text around a picture to give a professional look to your document.

■ **Scanned Artwork**   If you have a scanner hooked up to your Mac, you can also scan the images directly into Word, if your scanner supports the feature. This saves you a trip to another program to perform that task. In addition, the Picture toolbar, described later in this chapter, offers a reasonable set of features that allow you to edit scanned artwork and eliminate such problems in a photo as red eye and scratches.

■ **Borders**   Word automatically creates a border when you create a drawing. But you can also add borders to other graphics and to text boxes and tables. The Drawing toolbar also offers a number of ways to configure a border; for instance, you can select the type of line and thickness, and you can use the color features to spruce up borders for your specific needs.

■ **Fills**   A fill is a shade or color that you apply to the material inside a drawing object or text box. You can select from patterns or textures or use a picture for a different type of effect.

■ **Shadows**   When you apply a shadow to a drawing object, even to text, placing a sort of after-image behind it, you give the object a multidimensional appearance.

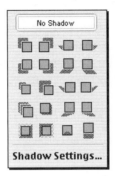

■ **3D Effects**   One step beyond the shadow is the 3D effect, a feature of the Drawing toolbar that truly gives sparkle to drawing objects by adding depth and surface reflections. You cannot, however, apply both a shadow and 3D effect to the same item.

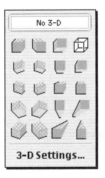

■ **Color Editing**   In addition to fixing flaws in a picture, you can edit to improve color accuracy. For example, if someone's face has a greenish cast because the photo was shot indoors, you can remove the "space alien" effect by adjusting the color balance.

■ **Picture Effects**   One way to give a photo a new look is to make it resemble a painting or a sketch. This can be done using the Picture Effects feature on the Picture toolbar.

■ **Transparent Colors**   This feature is particularly useful if you want to publish your Word document on the Web. You can use the Set Transparent Color feature on the Picture toolbar to make background images transparent, so they show through the page.

An Overview of Supported Graphics Formats

It would be nice if graphic files were all in a single format. But the computing world thrives on diversity, which can definitely lead to unending confusion, since some picture formats are designed for only one computing platform.

Using the graphics filters in QuickTime and Word's own repository of translation filters, though, Word can support many of these formats automatically, behind the scenes, so you don't have to figure out what format is being used and whether your system can read it.

Here's the list, along with a brief description of the purpose of each format:

- **Device Independent Bitmap (DIB)**   This is a bitmap file format that is commonly used on the Windows platform.

- **Encapsulated PostScript File (EPSF or EPS)**   This file format contains PostScript information within the file. As a result, the image can be scaled without any loss in print quality, and it will reproduce at the maximum resolution of which the printer is capable. Such files are ordinarily created by professional illustration programs, such as Adobe Photoshop and Macromedia FreeHand.

- **Enhanced Windows Metafile (EMF)**   This is a version of the Windows Metafile format. It includes both vector (object-oriented) and bitmap information.

- **FlashPix (FPX)**   This picture format incorporates picture information in several formats, so you can access images at various resolutions.

- **Graphics Interchange Format (GIF)**   Originally created by CompuServe, this file format is capable of producing decent, but not stellar, picture quality, and it's commonly used for Web-based artwork or for pictures sent by e-mail.

- **Joint Photographic Experts Group (JPEG or JPG)**   This high-quality image format uses compression to reduce file size. At its maximum quality setting, a JPEG image can be almost indistinguishable from the original, but the file size may be but a fraction of the original.

- **Macintosh Paint (PNTG or MAC)**   This is the original Mac format for paint graphics.

- **Macintosh Picture (PICT or PCT)**   This is the native Mac format for bitmapped graphics.

- **Photoshop Document (PSD, 8BPS)**   This is the native format for files created in Adobe Photoshop.

- **Portable Network Graphics (PNG)**   Some folks refer to this format unofficially as "PNG, not GIF," because this format was created as a successor to GIF, providing superior quality without requiring users to pay royalties to the creator of the original format. It isn't widely used, however.

- **QuickTime Image Format (QTIF)**   This format is used for images created with Apple's QuickTime software.

- **Silicon Graphics Incorporated (SGI)** This format was originally created for use with Silicon Graphics workstations.

- **Tagged Image File Format (TIFF or TIF)** This is a platform-independent, high-resolution bitmap image format. It's widely used in the publishing industry, but file sizes can get mighty large, particularly for full-color photos. It's not atypical to see a TIF file larger than 25 MB.

- **Truevision Graphics Adapter, or Targa (TGA)** This format is used for images processed with Truevision's line of video-capture hardware.

- **Windows Bitmap (BMP)** This is the Windows counterpart to the Mac PICT format.

- **Windows Metafile (WMF)** See the discussion earlier of the Enhanced Metafile Format for a more complete description.

Inserting Pictures from Other Files or the Clip Gallery

After reviewing the many options for placing artwork in your Word document, you're ready to begin. Fortunately, the recognition and conversion of files occurs behind the scenes, so you don't have to necessarily know which format is which. If Word recognizes the format, it'll show up in the Choose a Picture dialog box.

First, we'll cover Word's Clip Gallery (see Figure 14-2). Here is a list of the various features:

- **Category** This is the listing of the topics into which the artwork is divided.

TIP *A piece of artwork can appear in multiple categories, if you like, just click the Properties button. Select a picture, then click Properties, and then select the Categories tab. Check the categories in which you want the picture to appear.*

- **Search** Rather than pore through dozens of topics for the clip art you want, you can just enter a word or phrase that describes what you want and click Search, and you'll see the available prospects.

- **Show** You can choose All Pictures, All Sounds, or All Movies, as needed.

- **Import** Use this option to add items to the Clip Gallery. (The Clip Gallery is explained in the next section.)

- **Online** You can launch your default Web browser (the one selected on the Internet Control Panel) and select from a huge collection of online clip art at Microsoft's Web site.

- **Insert** Just click to place the selected picture where the cursor is situated in your document.

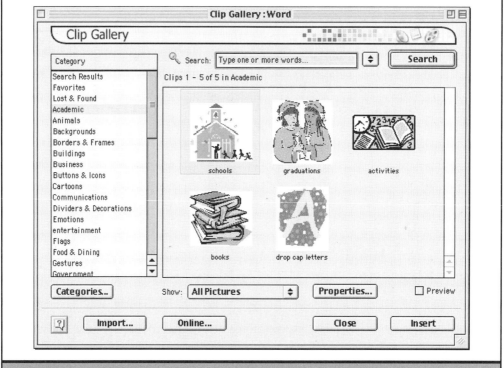

Figure 14-2.   *Word's Clip Gallery is a convenient repository of pictures for your Office documents.*

Inserting Clip Art in Your Document

Here's how you insert clip art in your Word document. We'll use a picture from the Office 2001 Clip Gallery.

1. Click the area in your Word document where you want to put the clip art.

2. From the Insert menu, select Picture and then choose Clip Art from the submenu. If the Drawing toolbar is visible, you can also click the Insert Clip Art icon on the toolbar.

3. Select a category that you think may contain appropriate clip art. If you don't see a suitable category, enter a word or phrase that matches the topic in the Search text field and click Search; available clip art will appear.

4. When you see the clip art you want, click the image to select it.

5. Click Insert, and the image will appear at the cursor position in your Word document.

> TIP
>
> *·If the picture is available on your Mac's desktop or in a folder while you're working in a Word document, you can also drag and drop it where you want it in the document. Of course, the picture has to be in a supported format for this little trick to work.*

Inserting a Picture in Your Document

If you want to insert a picture file instead of clip art, follow these steps:

1. With your Word document open, click the area where you want to insert a picture.

2. From the Insert menu, choose Picture; then select From File from the submenu or click the Insert Picture icon on the Drawing toolbar.

3. In the Choose a Picture dialog box, locate the picture you want to place in your Word document.

4. Click the Insert button, and the picture will appear at the selected location in your Word document.

> NOTE
>
> *Normally Word will embed the actual image in your document. This can simplify file handling, at the expense of creating a file that is very large. You can, however, select the Link to File option in the Choose a Picture dialog box. Then Word will store only a preview to the file; the file itself remains separate. You have to remember to send both files if you're shipping the file to another Mac or to another location via e-mail.*

Adding Items to the Office Clip Gallery

When you install Office 2001, a number of clips are included for the Clip Gallery, and the Value Pack offers more selections for you. Over time, though, you may come across other clip art that you'd like to have on hand, so you can have quick access to these clips.

To add files to the Clip Gallery, follow these steps:

1. If the Drawing toolbar is open, click the Insert Clip Art icon. Otherwise, from the Insert menu, choose Picture; and then choose Clip Art from the submenu.

2. Select a category in the list in the Clip Gallery; this is the category to which the clip will be added.

3. Click the Import button, which will bring up the dialog box in which you can select the file to import (see Figure 14-3).

4. Locate the disk or folder that contains the file you want to include in the Clip Gallery. Then select the clip that you want to store.

5. Select the option you want. You can place a copy of the clip within the Clip Gallery, move the original to the Clip Gallery, or add an alias (a link) to the original file.

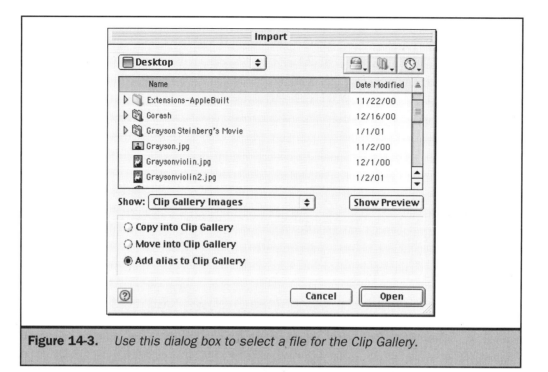

Figure 14-3. *Use this dialog box to select a file for the Clip Gallery.*

6. Click the Import button, which will produce the Properties dialog box (see Figure 14-4).

7. Type a short description of the clip in the Description text box.

8. Click the Categories tab and select the categories in which you want the clip to appear. You can choose as many categories as you like.

NOTE   *If there isn't a suitable category, click the New Category button and create one.*

9. Click the Keywords tab and type a word or phrase that will allow you to easily search for the clip later.

10. Click OK to complete the process.

Troubleshooting File Import Problems

There are so many file formats to deal with that inevitably, from time to time, you will encounter problems in locating files or in the way files appear or print after they are placed in your document.

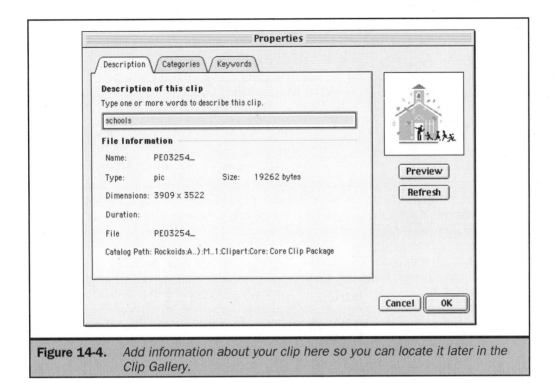

Figure 14-4. *Add information about your clip here so you can locate it later in the Clip Gallery.*

The following list covers the most common problems you might encounter and the usual solutions.

■ **Error Messages Appear When Trying to Insert a Picture**   There are several solutions, depending on what sort of file you're trying to insert. Word, for example, doesn't support TIFF files with multiple alpha channels. If you are trying to insert such a picture, use a graphics program to reduce the number of alpha channels to one, and then try again. When it comes to JPEG files, if the picture is using the JPEG Tagged Interchange Format (JTIF) or the Cyan-Magenta-Yellow-Black (CMYK) format, you need QuickTime 4.0 or later to handle the file. Since the latest version of QuickTime will support more graphics formats, you'll want to have the latest version in any case. You can get a copy from Apple's Web site at http://www.apple.com/quicktime.

NOTE   *If the error message you see consists of a red X or a blank box when the picture is inserted, your system may be running out of memory. First close any other Word documents; then close all other applications you're running. You may also want to give Word more application memory with the Finder's Get Info command.*

■ **Inserted Picture Can't Be Edited** Some picture formats limit your editing options. For example, if you insert a metafile, a type often found among clip art, the Set Transparent Color feature on the Picture toolbar and the Rotate and Flip features on the Drawing toolbar won't work. The solution is to convert the picture to a bitmap. This can be done by selecting the picture and then clicking the Color Adjustment icon. Choose a thumbnail that comes close to the original and click Apply.

> **TIP** *If you have a picture that is in the wrong format for Word, here's a great solution: use GraphicConverter. This shareware program supports dozens and dozens of image file formats. I never go without it; in fact many of the illustrations you see in this book were processed or edited with that program. You can download a copy directly from the publisher's Web site, at http://www.lemkesoft.com/. If you like it, please don't forget to send the author the shareware fee.*

■ **What's Wrong with This Picture?** Did you resize the photo? If you did, you need to make sure the aspect ratio is correct; otherwise, the horizontal or vertical dimension may be out of whack. During the resize process, Word attempts to smooth the rough lines of a picture, which may create a fuzzy look. You can reduce the impact of this processing like this: Select the picture to be resized. Then click the Format Picture icon on the Picture toolbar. In the dialog box that appears, click the Size tab and then select Lock Aspect Ratio and Relative to Picture Size.

> **NOTE** *If your Mac's monitor is set to 256 colors, pictures can take on a somewhat grainy look. Where possible, use thousands or millions of colors, even though the screen refresh process is likely to be slow on an older Mac.*

■ **Why Is There a Text Box Instead of an EPSF Picture?** For you to see a preview of an EPSF picture that you've inserted, you have to save it with a TIFF or PICT preview (WMF previews aren't supported). This is the normal selection in some image editing programs, and it's an option in others. Regardless, the image will print properly on a PostScript printer.

■ **Printouts of EPSF Pictures Are Fuzzy or Blocky** The only way you can output an EPSF picture at full resolution is to use a PostScript printer, or to use PostScript software to output to a non-PostScript printer, such as one of the popular inkjet printers.

> **NOTE** *If you have one of those low-cost inkjet printers, you're not out of luck. There are some PostScript applications that help. One is Stylus RIP, from Epson, which works on many of that company's products. Another product comes from Birmy. But such programs can be slow and memory intensive. If you do need to print PostScript graphics, you may be better off buying a real PostScript printer; some of the more costly inkjets have such capabilities built in.*

- **EPSF Preview Looks Fuzzy or Blocky**   As discussed previously, for you to see an image in your document, the EPSF file has to be saved with a TIFF or PICT preview. Some programs offer the ability to save with a higher quality preview, which will help reduce this effect. Regardless, the image will still print properly so long as a PostScript output device is used.

- **Why Won't the Animated GIF Animate?**   This is normal. Whether you use Word or Excel, only the first frame of an animated GIF will appear. You can see an animated GIF only in PowerPoint, in Slide Show view, or in your Web browser.

- **Only the First Page of a Fax Appears**   Alas, there is no simple solution for this. The only way for you to see all pages of your fax is to save each page separately and then insert each page separately into your document. In addition, regardless of what you do, the image quality is likely to be quite poor, because of the typically low resolution of a fax.

- **Why Don't MacPaint Pictures Show Up in the Dialog Box?**   Try this solution. Add the .pntg suffix to the end of the file's name. That usually works in situations where the file doesn't appear in the list.

- **Windows Users See the QuickTime Logo Rather Than a Picture**   This simply means that QuickTime needs to be installed. The Windows version of QuickTime is available via the same Web site as the Mac version: http://www.apple.com/quicktime. QuickTime is required to support these formats: FlashPix (FPX), Photoshop Document (PSD, 8BPS—unless Photoshop is installed, of course), QuickTime Image Format (QTIF), Silicon Graphics Incorporated (SGI), and Targa (TGA).

- **Windows Users Don't See Transparent Areas**   This is a place where the Mac version does more than the Windows equivalent. Office for the Mac uses clipping paths to store a picture's transparency information. The solution at this point is for you to convert your pictures to PNG format in a graphics program and then insert them once again into your document. Then the Windows version won't have a problem.

NOTE
The presence of some exclusive Mac-only features in Office 2001 has been a huge crowd pleaser during public presentations of the program. Whenever a Microsoft representative is heard using the term "only on a Mac," cheers arise from the audience of the Mac faithful.

Using Word's TWAIN Import Feature

Once upon a time, engineers came up with a standard that allowed users to acquire scanned images in a number of programs. For want of a better term, they called it TWAIN: a "tool without an interesting name."

PUTTING WORD 2001
TO WORK FOR YOU

If you have a scanner or camera that supports TWAIN or has an Adobe Photoshop plug-in, you stand a great chance of being able to use TWAIN to bring your image directly into your Word document.

Here's what you do:

1. Make sure that your scanner or digital camera is hooked up to the Mac and the software is properly installed.

> **NOTE** *If you haven't used your scanner before, it's a good idea to do a trial run with your scanner's regular software just to make sure it works properly. That way, you can tackle any problems at their source before using Word.*

2. Place your artwork in the scanner bed or turn on your digital camera.

3. With your Word document open, put the cursor in the location where you want to insert the picture.

4. From the Insert menu, choose Picture; then select From Scanner or Camera from the submenu. This will bring up the Insert Picture from Scanner or Camera dialog box.

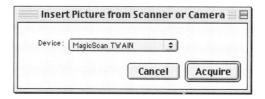

5. Select the pop-up menu and choose the input device you're using. If you see several selections for scanning software, use the one with the TWAIN label first (it's more likely to be compatible).

6. Click Acquire. At this point, your scanner or digital camera software will be launched (see Figure 14-5 for one example).

7. Follow the usual steps to preview and adjust your picture and then use the scan or download function to bring the image into Word. In the next few moments, the scanning or download process will begin, and the picture you scanned should appear where you placed the cursor in your document.

8. With the image on your screen, click the Picture toolbar that appears to adjust the image quality. The following features are available:

> **NOTE** *If the Picture toolbar is not visible, from the Tools menu, choose Customize and then select the Picture Toolbar check box to display it. The available functions will be active when a picture is selected.*

9. Make your adjustments to the picture as described in "Using the Picture Toolbar" later in this chapter.

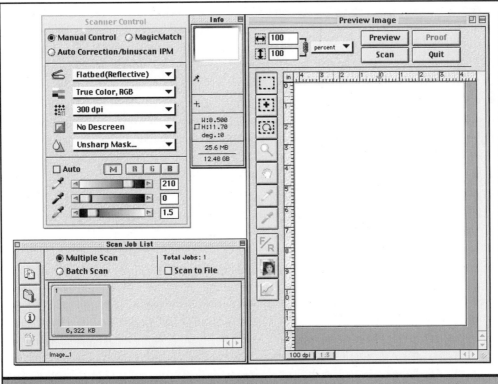

Figure 14-5. *This example uses Umax MagicMatch software, which comes with many of that company's scanners.*

Troubleshooting Word's TWAIN Feature

The process of acquiring a picture in Word is quite straightforward, but it's possible that you'll encounter a problem along the way. The following list presents a few possibilities that should cover most of the issues. You may have to seek outside help for some of these problems, but in most cases there is a solution you can implement.

■ **Nothing Happens or an Error Message Appears When You Try to Use a Scanner**   For you to use the Acquire feature in Word, your scanning software must be properly installed. In addition, the software for your scanner needs to be compatible with TWAIN or must include one or more plug-in files for Adobe Photoshop. If you aren't certain that your scanner meets this requirement, check the documentation. You will be hard pressed to find a scanner that doesn't support either of these technologies, and usually both.

NOTE   *I never say never, because I encountered one scanner that simply wouldn't work with Office 2001's TWAIN feature on one of my Macs, a Blue & White Power Mac G4 upgraded with a G4 processor card. The scanner, a Umax PowerLook 1100, uses the Firewire port, and it worked fine with other software (it's a terrific scanner, but rather costly), but Word never recognized it. But when I set up the same system on a regular Power Mac G4, it worked. So nothing is ever certain in this crazy computer world.*

- **Scanning Speed Is Slow**   The speed of the scanner depends on a number of factors, and you can't control all of them. It may indeed be that your scanner is slow. Some scanners are multiple-pass devices, which means that there are three scans for color. It may also be that you've chosen a resolution that's too high for your needs, which means that the scanner's optics have to move more slowly to capture the extra detail. The best thing to do in any case is to check the instructions that came with your scanner. You may have only a bare-bones manual, but check your installation CD and see if there's something more detailed about tweaking the scanning drivers.

- **Scanner Captures Too Much or Too Little**   You may simply need to crop the image. Usually you can drag a selection rectangle around the image to fine-tune the cropping. Dragging one edge or the other allows you to resize the rectangle. If you're not sure how this is done, check the instructions for your scanning drivers.

- **Scan Quality Is Poor**   Once you crop your image, you can use the scanning software's automatic exposure function to get a decent scan. If that doesn't work, see whether the scanner has any image editing controls (most do) that will allow you to adjust brightness, contrast, and other elements to get a better scan. You can do some minor image touch-ups in Word, but the scanning software will likely offer more features.

- **Mac Freezes When You Try to Scan**   More than likely this is caused by that old bugaboo in the software world: a conflict of some sort. The first thing to do is to see if you can use your scanning software with the image software that came with the unit. Some come with Adobe Photoshop; others with Adobe PhotoDeluxe or a similar program. Regardless, you'll want to make sure that you can get your scanner to work normally. If not, try the instructions or contact the manufacturer for assistance. Don't be surprised if a simple software update is all you need to get rolling.

Using the Picture Toolbar

Although Word isn't designed to be an image editing or illustration program, its built-in tools can handle many tasks for which you might sometimes consider another program. This means that you can get more of your work done within Office.

As with image editing software, Word offers a set of tools for performing a variety of simple editing chores for a picture. You access these tools from the Picture toolbar (see Figure 14-6).

To bring up the Picture toolbar, just follow these steps:

NOTE *Even if the Picture toolbar isn't displayed, it will usually show up when you select a picture.*

1. From the Tools menu, choose Customize.

2. Select the Picture Toolbar check box.

3. Click OK, and the toolbar will appear. Since it's a floating toolbar, you can drag it to any convenient spot on your screen.

Here's a look at the features available on the Picture toolbar:

■ **Format Picture**   Click this icon to bring up another dialog box (shown in Figure 14-7). It has five tabs, but the ones you can use depend on the kind of object you're adjusting. The Colors and Lines tab has fairly obvious functions. The Size tab lets you rotate and scale your images. The Layout tab is used for aligning the picture and specifying whether text will wrap around it and how. The Picture tab is used for cropping the image (on the basis of distance from the edges) and making simple color adjustments. The Text Box tab functions only when a text box is the selected object.

■ **Picture Effects**   Click this icon to bring up a dialog box that lets you apply some really cool special effects to your pictures. The following

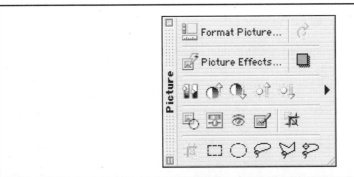

Figure 14-6.   *This handy toolbar is used to edit the pictures you insert into Word.*

Format Picture

| Colors and Lines | Size | Layout | Picture | Text Box |

Crop from

Left: `0"`   Top: `0"`

Right: `0"`   Bottom: `0"`

Image control

Color: `Automatic`

Brightness: `50 %`

Contrast: `50 %`

Reset

Cancel   **OK**

Figure 14-7.   *Use the Format Picture dialog box to handle borders, scaling, cropping, text wrapping, and basic color and brightness settings.*

illustration shows a sample of a regular photo with a little enhancement. The options can be used to give a photo the texture of a painting, a pen and ink drawing, or a canvas, or lots of other fascinating textures. You can also adjust the degree of each effect to provide a more subtle result.

■ **Free Rotate**   This feature isn't available for all images, but when it is, it lets you do precisely what's described. If the image style doesn't work with the feature, it will be dimmed.

- **Image Control**   Click the icon to bring up a pop-up menu that lets you choose among Automatic, Grayscale, Black and White, and Watermark.

- **More Contrast and Less Contrast**   These features mirror the options available in the Picture Effects dialog box, but these give you direct access. Just click the icon to change the setting by a step. The labeled effect increases or decreases with each click.

If you go too far with one of these effects, no problem. Just take advantage of Word's multiple undo feature on the Edit menu or type COMMAND-Z *repeatedly to bring the picture back to its original form or one changed less drastically.*

- **More Brightness and Less Brightness**   These icons work the same as the contrast icons. Click once to change the effect a small amount, and multiple times to increase or decrease the effect. You may prefer the sliders in the Picture Effects dialog box if you want more precision.

- **Set Transparent Color**   If the image format supports this feature, you can create a transparent color background.

- **Color Adjustment**   The Color Adjustment dialog box, shown in Figure 14-8, makes it easy to preview color changes before you put them into effect. Select

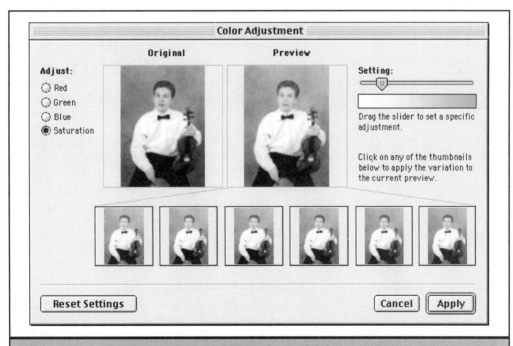

Figure 14-8.   *The Color Adjustment dialog box offers an easy path to color settings for a picture.*

PUTTING WORD 2001 TO WORK FOR YOU

the color you want to adjust (or the saturation setting) and move the slider to the adjustment you want. You can compare the original with the preview at any time to see the effect of your changes.

A quick way to put a color change in effect is just to click one of the six thumbnail images that matches the change you want. It will show up right in the Preview window.

- **Fix Red Eye**   Red eye is the typical artifact of a camera flash that's a bit bright; your subject appears to have a bright red pupil (it's not necessarily the result of being up too late or having one too many). Just select the photo and click the Fix Red Eye icon on the toolbar, and the effect will be reduced, and sometimes eliminated completely.

- **Remove Scratch**   This option slightly softens the resolution in your picture, but it also reduces minor scratches in the photo.

- **Crop**   Just click the Crop icon, which changes the cursor to an angled bar and a pointer. Then drag the mouse to produce new boundaries for your photo.

- **Selection Tools**   The bottom row of the toolbar contains various selection options, from Rectangle to Overall selection, to various types of lassos (useful for odd-sized pictures).

- **Tools Submenu**   Click the right arrow to bring up four additional tools. These are Insert Picture; Line Style, used to configure border styles; Text Wrapping, which determines how text flows around a picture; and Reset Picture, which restores the settings to the ones present when the picture was inserted.

Why Can't You Expand the Toolbar?

All Word toolbars can be conveniently moved around your screen to whatever location is comfortable for you. You can also reshape the toolbar by clicking the size bar and dragging it. However, you will notice that there's a down arrow at the end of many toolbars that offers access to additional functions.

Why can't you enlarge the toolbar to accommodate the extra tools? That's a good question, and I have no good answer. I've reported the issue to Microsoft, and perhaps by the time you read this book, they will have addressed it with an update to this program. Then again, maybe Microsoft believes that the extra tools are not likely to be used very often, so they were left in a submenu so your screen isn't cluttered with extra stuff.

Using the Drawing Toolbar

In addition to being able to make a reasonable variety of adjustments to pictures, you can create a variety of drawings in Word. These features can be activated from the Drawing toolbar (see Figure 14-9). This toolbar contains a variety of easy-access tools

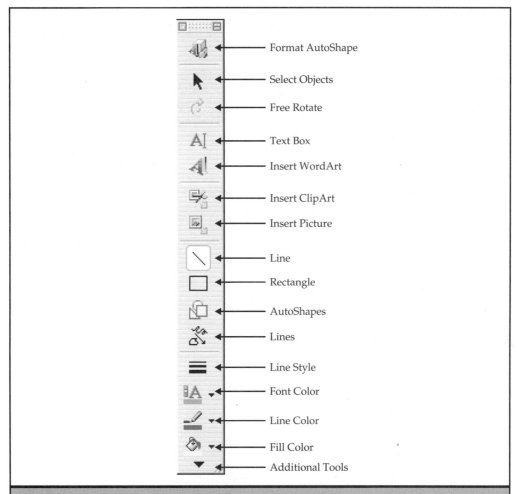

Format AutoShape

Select Objects

Free Rotate

Text Box

Insert WordArt

Insert ClipArt

Insert Picture

Line

Rectangle

AutoShapes

Lines

Line Style

Font Color

Line Color

Fill Color

Additional Tools

Figure 14-9. *Word's drawing toolbar can help you create and edit illustrations.*

for applying special effects, borders and shading, rules, and other features and for creating a variety of drawings.

As with the Picture toolbar, you bring it up this way:

1. From the Tools menu, choose Customize.

2. Select the Drawing Toolbar check box.

3. Click OK, and the toolbar will appear in its default location at the left side of your display. You can, as with the Picture toolbar, drag it to where you want.

Here is what the toolbar offers:

■ **Format AutoShape**   Click this icon to display a dialog box (shown in Figure 14-10) that lets you make some adjustments to the selected drawing object. The Format AutoShape dialog box is the Format Picture dialog box in a different guise. There are settings for lines, arrows, drop shadows, and 3-D effects. An Arrange command lets you stack drawing objects to create a desired effect; you can move

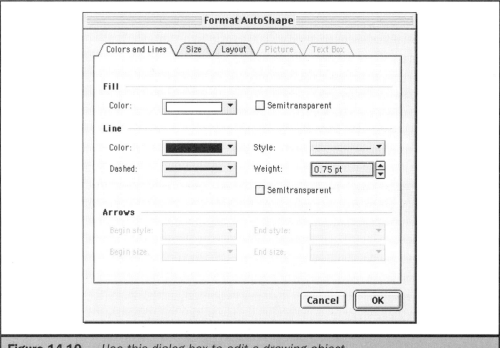

Figure 14-10.   *Use this dialog box to edit a drawing object.*

items in front of or behind other objects. The Group command lets you work with several objects as a single object. Align or Distribute lets you evenly align pictures. You can also rotate or flip objects and configure an invisible drawing grid (see Figure 14-11) that can be used to space objects using a fixed margin.

- **Select Objects**   Before you edit a drawing object, it has to be selected. You can accomplish this result by just clicking the object.

- **Free Rotate**   Use this tool to spin the object around and visually situate it as you like.

- **Text Box**   Use this tool to draw a text box, which is useful for placing titles, labels, or captions on a fixed area of a page. If you are preparing a small brochure, it also helps with precise positioning of text.

- **Insert WordArt**   Use this tool to bring up the WordArt dialog box, which lets you reshape and redesign your text in a variety of ways.

- **Insert ClipArt**   This tool brings up the Office 2001 ClipArt Gallery.

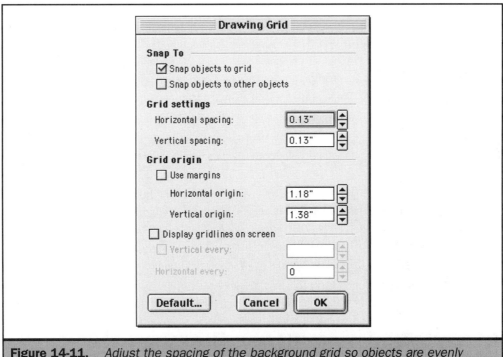

Figure 14-11.   *Adjust the spacing of the background grid so objects are evenly spaced in your document.*

■ **Insert Picture**   This feature is used in the same way as the command on the Insert menu: to insert a picture from a file into your document.

■ **Line**   This tool draws a straight line at any angle in your document. You can use multiple straight lines, of course, to add different shapes.

■ **Rectangle**   Use this to draw a rectangle or, with the SHIFT key held down, a square in your document. The rectangle is drawn by clicking the tool and then the appropriate place in your document and then dragging down and to the right.

TIP   *You only need be approximate when drawing a rectangle. When you double-click the object, the Format AutoShape dialog box will appear, where you can specify the exact dimensions.*

■ **AutoShapes**   This is that fancy command, described earlier in this chapter, that lets you insert a variety of prebuilt drawing objects.

TIP   *What's that icon stand for? No problem. Just hold the cursor over it, and you'll see a ToolTip that displays the label.*

■ **Lines**   This multiple-purpose tool lets you create lines, arrows, and object-oriented graphics in various shapes. We'll discuss these in more detail later in this chapter.

■ **Line Style**   Use this tool to set the thickness and style of lines.

■ **Font Color**   Use this tool to apply a color to your text.

■ **Line Color**   Use this tool to apply a color to the lines you draw.

■ **Fill Color**   Choose a color for the fill placed inside an object.

■ **Additional Tools**   When you click the arrow, a pop-up menu appears that offers additional tools. These tools are essentially the same ones available from the first icon, Draw, such as line styles, plus shadow, 3D, and AutoShape. Two additional tools also are included. The Arrow tool draws an arrow in your document, and the Oval tool (which works the same as the Rectangle tool) produces an oval or, when you hold down SHIFT, a circle.

NOTE   *As with the Rectangle tool, when you double-click with the Oval tool, the Format AutoShape dialog box will appear so you can enter precise dimensions.*

A Primer on Using Word's Drawing Features

Armed with Word's extensive array of drawing and picture editing tools, you have a wide array of options with which to create and edit pictures for your documents. In this section, you'll learn ways to get the most from these features.

Creating AutoShapes, Ovals, and Squares

Consistency is a hallmark of Word's drawing tools. Basically the same instructions apply for creating an AutoShape, an oval, or a rectangle.

Here's what you do:

1. Display the Drawing toolbar (use the Customize menu as described earlier).

2. Click the AutoShapes icon.

3. Select a category on the AutoShapes menu and then click the shape you want to insert into your document.

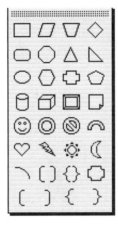

4. If you want to insert an AutoShape with the default size, just click the document, and the shape will appear at full size.

5. After you've placed a shape on the page, you can double-click the shape, and the Format AutoShape dialog box will appear. Select the Size tab for options to make the shape's dimensions more precise (see Figure 14-12).

TIP *You can insert a drawing object with identical width and length simply by holding down the SHIFT key while dragging the shape on your document. When you follow this step, an oval becomes a perfect circle, and a rectangle becomes a square.*

6. If you want to create an oval or rectangle, click the appropriately shaped tool.

NOTE *Where's the oval toolbar? It appears only when you click the arrow at the end of the Drawing toolbar to see the rest of the tools. The version of Office 2001 I used when writing this book didn't allow me to extend the toolbar to show it all in one window.*

7. With the oval or rectangle tool selected, click your document and drag the cursor down and to the right to create your drawing.

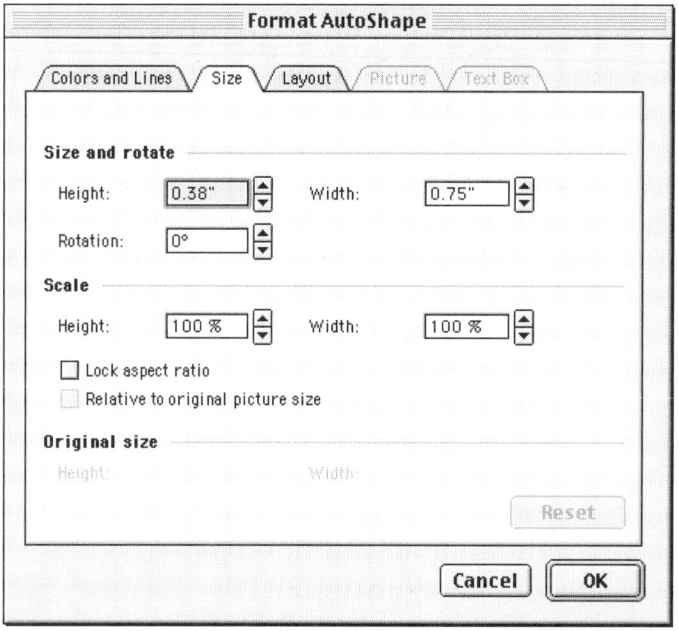

Figure 14-12. *Use this dialog box to ensure precise dimensions.*

8. If you want to edit your drawing, click the drawing to select it; then use the appropriate buttons on the Drawing toolbar.

> NOTE *When you double-click a drawing object, the Format AutoShape dialog box will appear, which lets you customize the size, set the way text wraps around the object, and add fill colors and effects and lines.*

Creating Lines

If you just want to draw a straight line, you don't have to worry about having a steady hand, since Word does most of the work for you.

Here's how you create a line in Word:

1. On the Drawing toolbar, click the Line icon (represented by a single angled line). The cursor will become a crosshair (vertical and horizontal lines crossing each other).

> NOTE *There is a separate tool on the Drawing toolbar called Lines, which is used to create one of several drawing objects. Fortunately, its icon is different enough so that the confusion is restricted only to the name.*

2. Drag the cursor to draw a line on your document's page.

You can constrain the line to 15-degree increments by holding down the SHIFT key as you drag across the page.

3. Release the mouse when the line is approximately the width you want.

4. If you want to increase the line's size at both ends, hold down the OPTION key as you drag either end point of the line.

5. After you draw a line, you can adjust its width and thickness or add arrows to either or both ends by double-clicking it, to bring up the Format AutoShapes dialog box. There, you can make the changes you want.

Creating Curves and Freeform Objects

You do not have to draw a complete oval or circle in Word. You can also draw part of a curve or a freeform object, which gives you greater flexibility in adding objects of various shapes and sizes to your drawings.

Here's how to accomplish the task:

1. Click the Lines (not Line) icon on the Drawing toolbar.

2. In the little window that pops-up, click the Curve or Freeform icon.

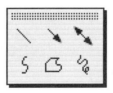

3. Click your document at the place where you want your drawing object to begin.

4. Move the mouse and then click at each place where you want to add a point in the object. This is the point at which you can put a curve into the line when using a the Curve tool.

5. Double-click the curve to complete the process.

If you want to actually close the curve, click near the starting point.

6. If you want to change the size of a curve or freeform object, click any point in the curve (they're known as size handles) and drag the mouse to the new shape. These changes can be made over and over again to fine-tune the size and shape.

> NOTE *To change the actual shape, click the Draw icon on the Drawing toolbar and choose Edit Points from the pop-up menu. Click any of the solid points to reshape the object.*

7. To make exact changes to the size and thickness of the object, double-click it to bring up the Format AutoShape dialog box. There, you can click the appropriate tab to make your changes.

8. Click OK in the Format AutoShape dialog box to complete the process.

Making Objects Line Up

Once you've created your drawings, you're likely to have a collection of different objects that are spread haphazardly across your page. But what do you do next? How do you line them up so that they appear in the form you want?

Fortunately, Word has various alignment features that let you place the objects precisely in relationship to each other. Here's how these features are used:

1. To align the drawing objects horizontally or vertically, select the objects you want to align, by holding down the SHIFT key and clicking each object.

2. Return to the Drawing toolbar, click the Draw icon. From the pop-up menu, choose Align or Distribute, then select the appropriate placement from the pop-up menu, shown here:

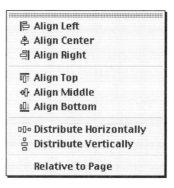

> NOTE *The first three alignment commands determine how the ends of the objects are aligned to each other (at the left, center, or right). The second three adjust the top, middle, and bottom alignment of objects. The final group of commands controls distribution of objects, horizontally, or vertically, by an equal distance or on the basis of the size of the page.*

After you've selected the appropriate alignment or distribution, the command will take effect immediately, and the menu will be dismissed. The result will be similar to what's shown here. The objects at the left show their approximate placement before the operation, and those at the right show their placement after they were aligned using one of the commands.

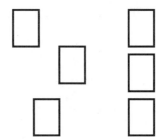

Stacking Objects

You can create a variety of special effects with Word's drawing tools by stacking objects. Some neat effects can be created, for example, by putting circles on top of each other, but spacing each a short distance apart. You can also create a variety of effects by stacking different shapes. You may, however, sometimes need to change the stacking order to achieve the kind of image you want.

To change the stacking order, follow these steps:

1. Click the object that you want to rearrange.

2. Click the Draw icon on the Drawing toolbar and choose Arrange.

3. Select the appropriate operation from the submenu. You can bring the selected object to the front of the stack or send it to the back. There are commands to bring the object forward or send it backward one layer or to move it in front of or behind text.

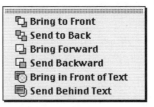

NOTE   *To stack pictures above or below text, you must first change the text wrapping style, in the AutoShapes dialog box, from Inline with Text to another style.*

Wrapping Text Around Graphics

One of the neat effects you'll want to use in your documents is text wrapping, which places text around a graphic. Word lets you adjust the layout in a number of ways, using the Format AutoShape dialog box.

Here's how to set text wrapping to your taste:

1. Double-click the Word graphic, which displays the Format AutoShape dialog box.

2. Click the Layout tab, which presents two categories of text wrapping options (see Figure 14-13).

   - **Wrapping Style** Choose how you want the text to wrap around the graphic. Text can appear inline, which means that the graphic appears on the same line as the text, or around the graphic, either with the Square setting, which shapes the text in a rectangle (or square) around the graphic, or Tight, which makes the text wrap closely to the shape of the graphic. You can also place text in front of or behind the graphic.

   - **Horizontal Alignment** Specify how the graphic is aligned on your document. Choose from the standard Left Align, Center, and Right Align options, or click the Other button for other options (which we'll get to in a moment).

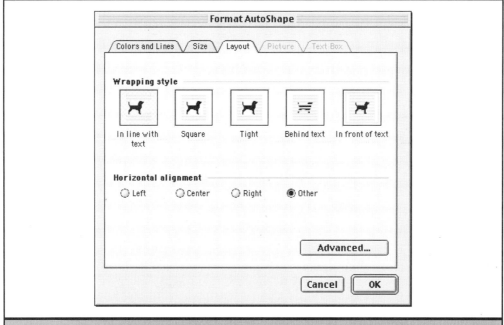

Figure 14-13. *Choose your text wrapping options by clicking the appropriate graphic.*

3. If you want to fine-tune the spacing of the graphic as it relates to the text, click the Advanced button in the Layout dialog box, which brings up the dialog box shown in Figure 14-14.

4. If you want the graphic to stay in an exact position, select Absolute Position in both the Horizontal and Vertical areas and specify whether the position relates to the column, paragraph, line, margin, or document in the pop-up menus.

5. To specify just the alignment of the graphic relative to your document or column, select the appropriate radio button.

6. After these choices are made, look at the Options category to pick the final options. More likely, the Move Object with Text check box will be selected already; it makes the object travel with the text as your document setup and content changes. Use the Lock Anchor option to keep the graphic in its present position, regardless of the text that wraps around it. Use Allow Overlap if you want graphics with the same wrapping style to overlap.

7. Click OK to save your settings.

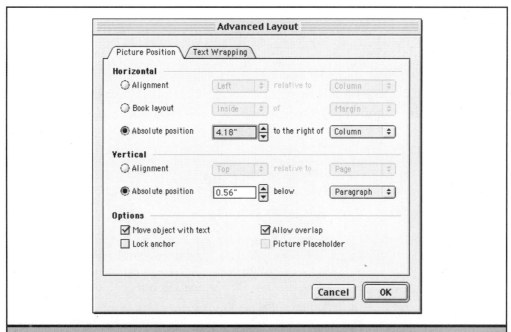

Figure 14-14.   *Choose the positioning of your graphic here.*

PUTTING WORD 2001 TO WORK FOR YOU

Rotating a Drawing Object

You can easily rotate objects freely or to a fixed degree to create the desired effect. Here's how:

1. If you want to rotate an object by a fixed amount, double-click the object to bring up the Format AutoShapes dialog box.

2. On the Size tab, enter the number of degrees of rotation in the Rotation text field or use the up and down arrows to select a preset figure.

3. Click OK to rotate the object. The following illustration shows before and after versions of a rectangle that's been rotated 22 degrees.

4. If you want to freely rotate an object to any angle, click the Free Rotate icon on the Drawing toolbar. Drag a corner of the drawing object in the direction in which you want to rotate. Click outside the object to disengage the rotation setting.

NOTE *If you hold down the SHIFT key while rotating, you can constrain the rotation to 15-degree angles. If you want to rotate the object around the handle to the opposite end of the one selected, hold down OPTION instead.*

Making Areas of a Picture Transparent

If you want to put a transparent area in a picture, perhaps a background that you don't want visible, you'll find that it's easy to accomplish in Word.
Here's how to do it:

1. Select the picture.

2. With the Picture toolbar displayed, click the Set Transparent Color icon (unless you've reshaped the toolbar, it's the icon on the left in the fourth row down).

3. Click the color that you want to make transparent.

NOTE *You can set transparent colors for any imported picture that doesn't have transparency information in the file. You can make only one color transparent, so if the area contains more than a single color, you won't be able to gain the transparency you want unless you use a separate image-editing program. In addition, if you try to set a transparent color in an animated picture, the animation will be lost.*

Selecting Picture Areas

Depending on the shape of the picture that you want to edit, you can select a picture in different ways. One is just to click the object, but there are other options.

Selecting a Picture Area with a Specific Shape

Here's how to select a picture area with a specific shape:

1. Click the picture to select it.

2. With the Picture toolbar open, click the Rectangle or Oval Marquee tool, as needed.

3. Click and drag the shape you want to select, cut out, or apply an effect to.

4. To remove the area, click the Cutout icon on the Picture toolbar. If you want to apply a special effect to the selected area, click Picture Effects and then choose the effects you want to apply.

Selecting a Picture Area with a Lasso or Polygonal Lasso

To select a picture area with a lasso or polygonal lasso, follow these steps:

1. Select the picture you want to use.

2. With the Picture toolbar displayed, click the Lasso tool for a Scribble shape or the Polygonal Lasso tool for a Freeform shape.

3. Drag the pointer around the area you want to select; then click the beginning point to complete the selection.

NOTE *If it's a freeform shape, you'll need to click in small bits around the area to make a precise selection.*

4. Apply the effects you want to the selected area from the Picture toolbar, or use the Cut Out tool or icon to remove the selected area.

Adding Figures or Captions to Drawing Objects or Pictures

Word's flexible document editing options allow you to add captions and figures to your drawings or pictures. When you add a numbered caption, Word will number subsequent captions you create in sequence.

Here's how it's done:

1. Click the area where you want to insert the caption.

2. If you need to create a text box, click the Text Box icon on the Drawing toolbar and move the mouse to the width of your caption.

3. If you want to specify exact dimensions, double-click the text box and use the Format Text Box dialog box to enter the values you want.

4. Choose Caption from the Insert menu and then, in the Caption dialog box, enter the first number, such as Figure 1, so that Word knows that you want to automatically number captions.

5. Type the rest of your caption; then click OK to place it in the text box.

6. Use the Formatting Palette to change the formatting of your caption.

Troubleshooting Word Graphics

If you've used a drawing or paint program before, you'll find that Word's drawing tools behave similarly enough that you won't need to spend a lot of time learning how they're used. But even if you haven't used a Mac to draw before, you should be able to become proficient in short order.

But if things don't look as they should, there are usually some straightforward solutions:

- **Text Doesn't Fit Inside AutoShape or Text Box** You have two possible solutions. You can just select the text and choose a smaller size from the Size column of the Formatting Palette. You can also just make the object larger. Click the object to select it and then draw out the size handles to resize the object. If you double-click the object, you can use the Format AutoShape dialog box to resize to precise new dimensions.

- **Text Box or AutoShape Can't be Moved** First make sure you have actually selected the object. You'll know it can be moved when the cursor changes to a hand.

- **Drag-and-Drop Editing Won't Work** The ability to drag and drop objects or text to new locations is one of the great features of Office. If it doesn't work, first make sure that the cursor is over the selected text or object when you try to move it. If that doesn't work, check Word's Preferences (in the Edit menu), click the Edit tab, and then make sure that the Drag-and-Drop Text Editing check box is checked.

- **Cannot Rotate or Flip Text** To rotate the text in a text box or on a page or an AutoShape, first click the text. From the Format menu, choose Text Direction and select the left or right Orientation option. If you use the Rotate or Flip command available from the Draw dialog box on the Drawing toolbar, only the object itself, not the text, will change direction.

- **Picture Colors Won't Change** By some chance, did you group the graphics, combining them into a single object? If so, select the object, click Draw on the Drawing toolbar, and choose Ungroup from the menu and try again.

- **Ungroup Command Won't Work with Imported Pictures** This is not a bug, but a feature, as some say. Bitmap, GIF, and JPEG objects cannot be ungrouped and changed to regular drawing objects. The only way you can perform such modifications is to open the object in an image editing program, such as Adobe Photoshop, and perform all the work there.

- **Can't Control Freehand Drawing** It takes a while to get used to drawing on a computer. But there are ways to make it easier. First, try using the Zoom feature (on Word's standard toolbar or the View menu) to increase magnification to, say, 200 percent. Another way to make the process simpler is to slow down the mouse tracking speed. This is done by choosing Mouse from the Control Panel folder (it's conveniently available from the Apple menu). Then slow down tracking speed to about half your normal setting and see if you get more precise control.

- **Can't Align Freeform Objects** If the tried and true doesn't work, here's an alternative: Select the object, hold down the OPTION key, and press the arrow keys to move the object in one-pixel increments. If you've selected the option to snap objects to a grid, you can turn off the feature by holding down the COMMAND key as you drag the freeform object.

- **Can't Rotate Objects** The ability to flip or rotate a picture is confined to drawing objects. You can try converting the object to a drawing object by choosing the Ungroup command on the Draw menu (available from the Drawing toolbar) and then the Regroup command. If that won't work, you will have to edit the object in a separate image editing or illustration program.

- **Colors in Drawing Objects Are Distorted or Dithered** The colors you add in Word are best viewed at 100 percent. If you've used the Zoom feature to view at another magnification, the image may be off. You should also set your Mac's display to show 256 or more colors (thousands of colors is better if this setting is available). This is a setting in the Monitors Control Panel, and just about all recent Macs and graphic cards can get you that figure or better.

- **Drawing Objects Aren't Visible** First check your document view setting to make sure that Normal, Outline, or Master Document isn't selected on the View menu. Use the Page Layout viewing option instead. If the object still doesn't appear, choose Preferences from the Edit menu. Click the View tab and then make sure that the Image Placeholders check box isn't selected, since this will prevent display of drawing objects.

- **Graphics Aren't Present in Printed Document** From the Edit menu, choose Preferences. Click the Print tab and make sure that the Drawing Objects check box has been selected; otherwise, graphics won't print. Another possibility is that your Mac is low on available memory, so all elements of your Word document aren't being displayed. First try quitting Word and then all other active applications. When you launch Word again, try printing the same document. If that doesn't work, quit Word again. Then click once on the Word icon to select it and choose Get Info from the Finder's Edit menu. Select Memory from the Show menu and increase the listed preferred memory allocation by 2,000K to 5,000K (but make sure that your Mac has enough available RAM, as shown in the About This Computer box on the Apple menu, before making a change). Launch Word again. If that doesn't work, try restarting your Mac. Finally, choose Preferences from the Edit menu and click the View tab. Clear the following view options by clicking the appropriate check boxes to remove the check mark: Image Placeholders, Status Bar, Vertical Ruler, Horizontal Scroll Bar, and Vertical Scroll Bar. Each of these elements consumes some portion of Word's available memory and unchecking the view options may give Word a little "breathing space."

■ **Can't Locate Correct Import Filter for Graphics**   First make sure that you indeed have the correct import filter. To check this, from the Insert menu, select Picture; then choose From File from the submenu. Look at the listing of available filters in the Show box. If the filter you want isn't there, consider reinstalling Office, to make sure the proper filters are available (review the instructions in Chapter 2). If you don't have the right filter, use a separate image editing or drawing program and save it in one of the formats Word can handle. Then you should be able to import the graphic.

■ **Graphics Have Disappeared**   No, they probably haven't vanished. Double-check that the option to display graphics is on. From the Edit menu, choose Preferences and click the View tab. Make sure that the Image Placeholders check box isn't checked, since this will inhibit display of graphics.

■ **Only Part of an Imported Graphic Appears**   No mystery: you probably just need to make sure that the line spacing set for the place where the picture appears is large enough to accommodate the image. This can be set in the Alignment and Spacing area of Word's Formatting Palette, by clicking a line spacing icon; the single-line spacing option ought to be enough.

■ **Inserted Object Isn't Visible**   First check your Preferences settings, available from the Edit menu. Click the View tab and make sure that Image Placeholders isn't checked. If that doesn't work, look at the view settings in the Preferences dialog box. Make sure the Drawings check box is selected. Also make sure that your View setting is Page Layout, Online Layout, or Print Preview. Other viewing options won't display graphics.

■ **Can't Keep Drawing Object on Same Page as Text**   If you're using a text box, group the two items, so they travel together. In addition, make sure that the anchor for a text box is adjacent to the text itself. If you're using a text box to add a caption to a drawing object, be sure to select the actual object before choosing Caption from the Insert menu. In addition, the anchor for the caption must be connected to the same paragraph as the anchor for the drawing object.

■ **Can't Move Paragraph Without Moving Drawing Object**   Quite possibly the anchor for the drawing object is locked to the one that applies to the paragraph you want to move. To fix this, choose the appropriate function from the Format menu, such as AutoShape, Object, Picture, Text Box, or Word Art. Select the Layout tab and then click the Advanced button; then select the Picture Position tab in the Advanced Layout dialog box (pause for a deep breath). Uncheck the Move Object with Text and Lock Anchor check boxes.

■ **Text Won't Wrap Around Graphic**   Check whether the correct text wrapping style has been chosen. Double-click the graphic to bring up the Format AutoShape dialog box. Click the Layout tab and make sure that the correct wrapping style is chosen. This ensures accurate wrapping around unusual shapes. You'll want to use the Freeform tool for complex shapes that you want to look as smooth as possible, or the Oval or Rectangle tool as needed. If the shape is ragged, text wrapping is not likely to be accurate.

- **Watermark Makes Text Illegible**   A watermark should be a backdrop to your text. The best way to fix a too-dark watermark is to lighten it. If it consists of text, you can use the Font Color icon on the Formatting Palette to choose a lighter color. If it's special effect text that you created with WordArt, choose WordArt. Then click the Colors and Lines tab and change to a fill color with a lighter shading. If you want to lighten an object made using the Drawing toolbar, double-click the object to bring up the Format AutoShapes dialog box and choose a different fill color from the Colors and Lines tab. You may be able to lighten an imported graphic by using the Picture or Object command on the Format menu. Again use the Colors and Lines tab to make the change. With an imported Picture, double-click it; then make sure that the Picture tab in the Format Picture dialog box is selected. Under Image Control, click the pop-up menu next to Color and choose Watermark. This will set a reasonable brightness level for the picture—one that shouldn't overshadow the text above it.

- **Watermarks Don't Appear on All Pages in a Document**   The only way you can repeat watermarks from page to page, without actually manually inserting them on each page, is to put them in the headers or footers.

Summary

Word's powerful graphics features may save you a trip to a dedicated illustration program for many tasks. In addition, the ability to work with many scanners and digital cameras can greatly extend your ability to bring additional content into your documents.

The next chapter covers some fairly deep subjects, in particular using the Data Merge Manager and creating macros. In the past, both features were difficult to master and exploit, but Word 2001 has simplified many functions, and you will find new and easier ways to handle such chores.

PUTTING WORD 2001 TO WORK FOR YOU

Chapter 15

Data Merge Manager and Macros

A s you've learned so far, Microsoft Word 2001 is suited for all sorts of documents. You can create simple memos or letters and complicated multicolumn documents with section breaks and headers and footers, and you can use Word's powerful drawing tools to both create and edit graphics for your document.

In this chapter, we cover what are probably the most arcane of Word's features (but not difficult to master): the Data Merge Manager and macros.

Using the Data Merge Manager

The Data Merge Manager is the outgrowth of the original Mail Merge feature of older versions of Word, which allowed you to create a boilerplate text or form letter and then bring in the names and addresses of recipients and create customized letters for each one. Businesses use this procedure to reach customers or prospects with customized messages that make the letters seem as if they were written for that person. Perhaps you've received them yourself.

The Data Merge Manager (see Figure 15-1) isn't limited to the creation of form letters or other business documents. You can print labels, envelopes, or database listings by following the instructions in this chapter.

The power of this feature is in how well it guides you through the process, so that you can organize all the data you need and then merge it into your boilerplate document.

Preparing for a Data Merge Operation

Let's get going. First there are several processes you need to go through to set up your data merge operation. They are listed here:

- **Create Your Boilerplate Document**   The first thing you'll want to do to prepare for your data merge operation is to set up the document it's based on.

- **Access Your Data Source**   The material you use for your data merge operation consists of names, addresses, and so on. You can use a spreadsheet, such as one you create with Excel; a database file, such as one made with FileMaker Pro or AppleWorks; a text file; or a Word table that's created using the Data Merge Manager.

- **Create Merge Fields**   These are places in your main document that serve as placeholders for the data from the data source you've selected.

- **Customize the Data Merge Operation**   You can customize the data merge operation to meet specific needs. You may want to reach a set of customers with special interests or who live in certain parts of the country, for instance. You can select just the data that meets your requirements for the merge operation.

■ **Merge the Data** After you've prepared your document and set up your source data, you're ready to perform the merge process. Each record or row from your data source is used to create a separate form letter, envelope, mailing label, or catalog entry. After you've prepared your documents, you can print them directly or collect them into new documents that can be checked and printed at a later time.

The Parts of a Data Merge Operation

All right; we're getting close to the starting gate. First, we'll cover the overall steps you follow in performing a data merge operation, and then we'll go through each process in more detail.

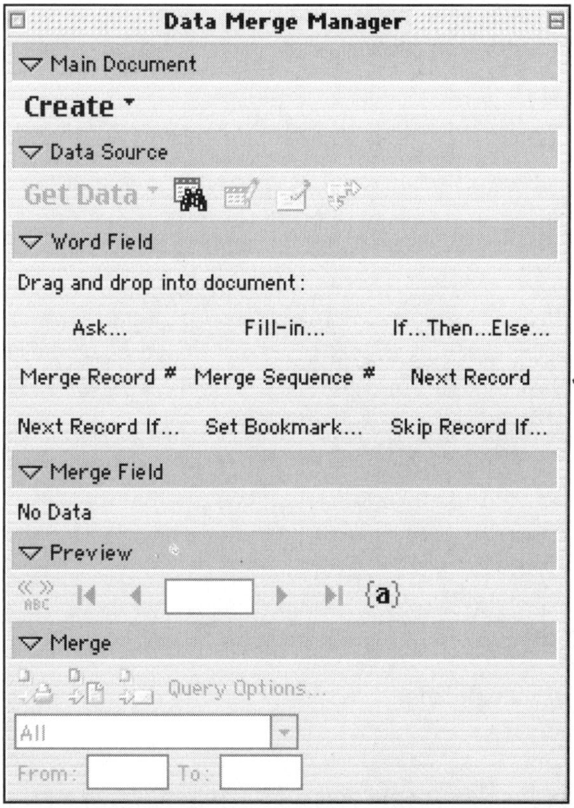

Figure 15-1.   *Word's Data Merge Manager (shown with all categories expanded) simplifies complicated merge steps.*

Using Form Letters

To perform a data merge operation with a form letter, you do the following (as I said, this is the overall view; the details come later):

1. Create a new document or open an existing document that contains your form letter text.

2. Create a new data source. This is the file that contains the names and addresses and other information to put into the form letter. As in a database program, the data source file consists of separate records, equivalent to the rows in a table. Each row contains, for example, the name and address and other information about a specific contact. You can also open an existing data source.

3. Create or open a header source, which is a document that contains the actual names of each field used in the data source, such as Name or City or Zip Code. A header source is especially useful if you're merging data from several different files.

4. Make the final changes in your main document. You can use an existing document style or template to capture basic formatting and then create or update the document with new text. Perhaps you want to extend a sale at your office, or introduce a new product or service that extends or replaces an older product or service; you can use your original document as the basis for your new one.

5. Insert the Word fields into the main document. These are fields that allow you to insert additional information into your document automatically, such as information for a contract or a custom message that applies to customers who live in a specific area or are expected to receive the letter on a certain date.

6. Insert the merge fields. These are the data fields used by the Data Merge Manager to capture information from your data source to place in the document.

7. Check the data and the form letter. Make sure that the letter is what you want, that the data source contains the correct information, and that all fields are correct. The preview operation will help you sort this out.

8. Merge the files. Now you perform the actual data merge operation. Word's Data Merge Manager will sort everything out for you.

Now the devil's in the details.

Reference: A Primer on Data Source Files

The previous section provided a broad overview of the process of performing a data merge operation. As you can see, the process is pretty straightforward, but you'll want to plan a strategy each step of the way to make everything go smoothly.

The first thing you'll want to consider is the data source: the raw information, such as the names and addresses of your contacts, that will be put into your form letters or other documents during the data merge operation.

Here are some things to consider:

- **What Information Fields Do You Need?**   As in a database program, each data record you use must have the same number of fields. There's no mixing or matching allowed—if one field is off, information will end up in the wrong place—so you need to allow the proper number of fields to accommodate all of your information. Perhaps you need to include a business name, the name of an individual and department, and an address with extra lines for room numbers and floors. If your record includes contacts from different countries, you need to add a field for that as well.

> **TIP**   *A quick way to map out your data record is just to type a sample contact that contains all the information you expect to appear in a record. That way, you can be sure that the data source file is set up properly.*

- **Do You Need to Sort the Records?**   Perhaps you want to sort by first name, last name, title, company name, and so on. If you're sorting by name, the first and last names should be in separate fields. When you put more than a single entry into a field, Word can sort only on the basis of all of the information in that field, not a part of it.

- **What About Bar Codes?**   In theory, mail goes more efficiently through the U.S. postal system if you use those bar codes, since the bar code readers at the sorting stations can scan them and properly sort the mail. Word lets you print POSTNET bar codes for mailing labels and envelopes. Just be sure that the delivery address and postal code are in separate fields. The latter is used for that POSTNET code.

> **NOTE**   *Does the POSTNET code really work? The post office says it does, because mail with bar codes can be sorted by machine and not manually. Manual sorting is a labor-intensive process, with more room for error and misdirected or delayed mail; at least that's what they tell me.*

- **Will the Data Source Serve Multiple Purposes?**   Perhaps you'd like to use the data source for mailing labels and the salutation of the form letter. By putting each element of the name, including the title, in a separate field, the process is simplified. You can address your envelope to me, Mr. Gene Steinberg, and then create a form letter that says "Dear Mr. Steinberg," or "Dear Gene," if you want to make it personal (yes, this is how the mailing list firms do their stuff).

- **Keep It to 63 Data Fields**   Are 63 data fields enough? Probably, because it's Word's limit. If you must have more than 63 fields, you will need to create a tab- or comma-delimited text field, or create your data source in Excel or a database program, to get around the limit.

- **Using Separate Header Sources**   Normally the header information, which defines the number of fields, the names, and their order, appears in a separate record at the beginning of the file. There may be times, though, when you want to create a separate data record. One situation is when you're using more than a single data source file. This simplifies the process, because you don't have to create separate header records for each file. You might also want to create a special header source file if the field names in your data source don't quite match the ones you need. So long as the records themselves are in the proper sequence, the difference in the label names in the individual files won't make a difference in the final merge operation.

Header Source Requirements

We're getting closer, but first we'll briefly cover a few of the basic requirements for creating a custom header source file:

- **Match the Field Names with Data Fields**   For the merge process to be accurate, the header source file has to contain the same number of fields as each record in the data source file.

- **Put Them in the Right Sequence**   Be certain that the order of the field names in the header source matches that in the data source. You wouldn't want to see the postal code appear in the field for the city's name, for example.

- **Use the Same Character as for the Text File**   If you're using a tab to separate data fields in the header source file, make sure you've done the same in the data source file. The same is true if you use a comma as the separator character.

- **Match Merge Fields in the Document to the Header Source**   The field names you define in the main document must be the same as the ones in your header source file. If the fields don't match, you need to change one or the other to make them consistent.

Creating a New Data Source Document

Now that you've reviewed the basic steps in this little operation, it's time to get down to the specifics.

First we'll set up a data merge data source, a standard name and address listing, following these steps:

1. Start by creating a brand-new blank document, by choosing New Blank Document from the File menu or the Standard toolbar or pressing COMMAND-N.

2. From the Tools menu, choose Data Merge Manager, which brings up that handy palette you saw in Figure 15-1.

3. In the Main Document section, click the Create button and select the kind of document you want to create from the pop-up menu. The choices are Form Letters, Labels, Envelopes, and Catalogs.

NOTE *Selecting the options with ellipses, such as Labels and Envelopes, will bring up setup wizards that take you through the process of setting up the proper formatting.*

4. In the Data Source section, click Get Data and choose New Data Source from the submenu. This brings up the Create Data Source dialog box shown in Figure 15-2.

5. Check the data fields in the header row list box. If you want to remove a field, select the field name and click the Remove Field Name button.

NOTE *Don't be concerned about removing a field. Next time you want to perform a new data merge operation on another document, all of the fields will be back again.*

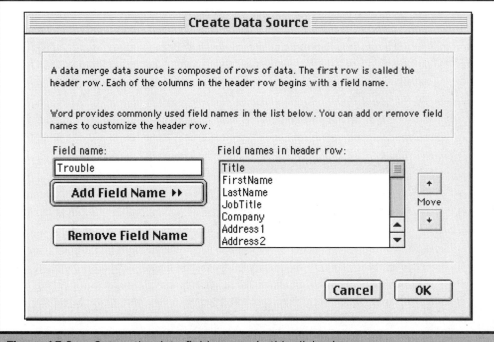

Figure 15-2.   *Set up the data field names in this dialog box.*

6. If the field you want isn't present, type it in the Field Name text box and then click the Add Field Name button.

7. If you want to change the order of fields, select the field name and then click one of the Move arrow buttons (to move the field up or down).

8. Ready yet? Double-check the fields to make sure they are the ones you want.

9. Click OK, which brings up a standard Save dialog box (see Figure 15-3).

10. Give your file a name and specify a location for the file. Now it's time to put the required information into your data records. As you do in a database program, you create a separate record for each name or company in your database.

NOTE   *It's a good idea to keep all documents for your data merge operation in a single folder, so you can easily locate them later.*

11. In the Data Form dialog box, which appears next (see Figure 15-4), type the required information in each text field followed by a RETURN key press. To skip a field, just press RETURN or TAB. Press SHIFT-TAB to move back a field.

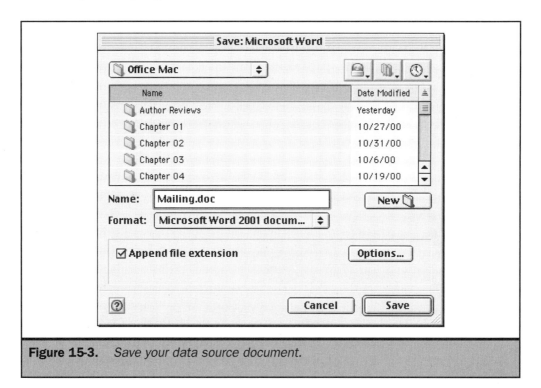

Figure 15-3.   *Save your data source document.*

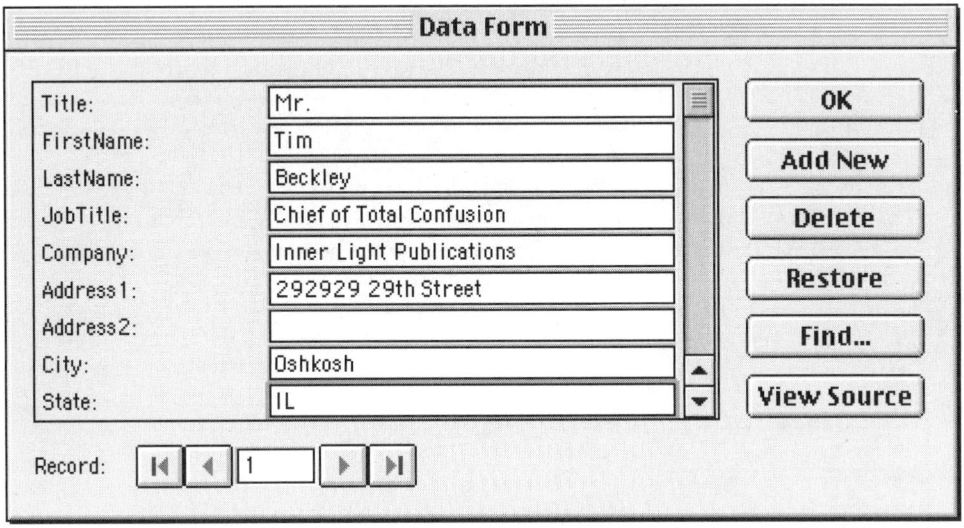

Figure 15-4. *Add the needed information for each entry field.*

12. When you have completed a record, click the Add New button to begin the next record, or just press RETURN.

13. Repeat steps 11 and 12 for each record until you've prepared the last one.

14. If you want to save all changes to your document, click the View Source button to review the raw information you've entered; then choose Save from the File menu or Standard toolbar or press COMMAND-S.

15. To finish the process, click OK.

Accessing an Existing Data Source File

If you just want to use an existing data source document for your data merge operation, follow these steps:

1. With the Data Merge Manager on the screen, click the Get Data button in the Data Source section and choose Open Data Source.

2. In the Open dialog box that you see, select the data file you want to use and click the Open button.

Creating a New Header Source File

As explained earlier, a header source document contains the raw information about fields and is useful if you want to perform a data merge operation using more than one database file.

Here's how to create a header source file from scratch:

1. With the Data Merge Manager open, click the Get Data button, choose Header Source from the pop-up menu, and select New Header Source from the submenu. This brings up the Create Header Source dialog box shown in Figure 15-5.

NOTE   *The resemblance between the Create Header Source and Create Data Source dialog boxes is definitely not coincidental; you perform many of the same setups in both dialog boxes.*

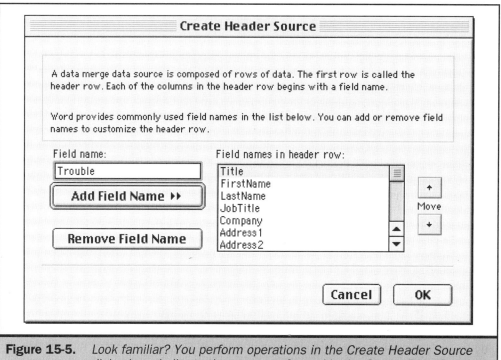

Figure 15-5. *Look familiar? You perform operations in the Create Header Source dialog box similar to those you performed in the Create Data Source dialog box.*

2. Examine the field names in the list box to see if all the ones you want are there. If not, you'll need to change the list.

3. To remove a field, select the field name and then click Remove Field Name.

4. To add a field, type the name of the new field in the Field Name text box and then click the Add Field Name button.

5. To change the order of the fields, select the field name and then click the up or down Move arrow button, as needed.

6. When you've finished the process, double-check the fields to be sure they are what you want; then click OK.

7. In the Save As dialog box, specify a name and location for the header source file.

NOTE   *Once again, putting all your eggs in one basket—in one folder, actually—is a good idea.*

Opening an Existing Header Source File

If you already have a header source file that you want to use for the data merge operation, just follow these steps:

1. With the Data Merge Manager open, click the Get Data Button, choose Header Source from the pop-up menu, and select Open Header Source from the submenu.

2. In the Open dialog box that appears, locate and select the header source file you want to use.

3. Click Open.

Using the Header Record from a Data Source File

You don't have to create a special header source file just to use specific header fields. If you already have a data source document that contains the header information you want, you can access the header record from that file instead (and save a little time and energy).

Here's what to do:

1. With the Data Merge Manager open, click the Get Data button in the Data Source area and select Open Header Source from the submenu. Word will scan the header information and bring it into the program.

2. In the Open dialog box, locate and select the header source file you want to use.

3. Click Open.

Preparing Your Document for the Data Merge Operation

Once your data source files are ready to roll, it's time to return to the main document and get it ready to receive the information.

Here's how to prepare your document for the merge operation:

1. Open and edit your main document and then spell check it.

TIP *When editing a file that will be going to a variety of recipients, use as much boilerplate text as possible, because the more manual intervention you need to enter custom information, the longer and more complex the data merge operation. To reduce the possibility of errors, keep the document as simple as possible.*

2. Click in the document where you want to insert a Word field. The Word fields are the placeholders for custom information that can be entered as your data merge operation proceeds. World fields include the following commands:

   ■ **ASK and FILLIN Fields**   These fields allow you to insert customized notes to clients. For example, the FILLIN field pauses to allow you to manually enter some information, such as a custom appointment time. The ASK feature lets you switch to another bookmarked piece of text to insert it in the document.

   ■ **IF Then ELSE Fields**   The IF field performs an action when a certain preset condition is met. For example, say your business contact is having a wedding anniversary on February 23. If the letter is going out before that date, you, perhaps as the manager of a local restaurant, can invite the contact and spouse to come for dinner and get a free dessert. You can also submit a customized statement should a contact live in a particular zip code, such as a localized offer or a request that the person contact your local office for further information.

   ■ **SET Fields**   The SET field applies a text or number value to a bookmarked file to be inserted into your document. To change the information in the file, all you need to do is alter the information in the Set field.

- **MERGEREC Field**   Use this field to insert a sequential number in your document. You can use it to print, for example, the invoice number in your merged document.
- **MERGESEQ Field**   This field counts the number of data records that were merged into your main document.
- **NEXT Field**   This field tells Word to merge the next available data record into the current document.
- **NEXTIF Field**   This field compares two expressions. If a specific condition, such as a date or location, is met, then the next data record available will be merged into the current document.
- **SKIPIF Field**   This field tells Word to skip a record if a condition is met: for instance, if the record falls in a particular location or timeframe.

3. Click the Word Field arrow, so that it points down and reveals the available fields.

4. Select the Word field you want and then drag the field name into the place where you want it to be inserted in your document.

NOTE   *In some cases, you will have to respond to a dialog box to complete the field insertion process, such as inserting one piece of text to accommodate one situation and another piece of text to accommodate a second situation.*

5. After you've inserted the Word fields, it's time to put the merge fields in place. To do that, click the Merge Field arrow, so that it points downward to disclose its contents.

TIP   *It's a good idea to make sure that field codes are visible, so you can see what you have in your document and confirm, visually, that the right codes are there. Just choose Preferences from the Edit menu, click the View tab, and make sure that the Field Code check box is selected.*

6. Drag the names of the fields you want to the appropriate locations in your document. An insertion point will appear at each location.

Be sure that spaces and punctuation for your document are placed outside of the field labels. If you want to put a merge field on the next line, press the RETURN key. To make the merged information more readable, consider formatting the merge fields in a different font than the rest of the document.

7. After all of the merge fields are in place in your document, save your document. The following illustration shows a sample of a completed merged document announcing a new product.

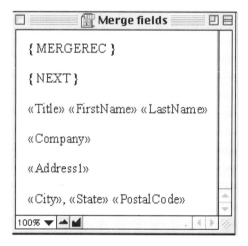

Since computers can freeze at untimely moments, it's a good idea to periodically save your main document during the merge setup process, so you don't lose a complicated field sequence.

Displaying Merged Information in Your Main Document

Once you've set up your merge operation, you'll want to look at your main document to see how the merge affects it. Here's what to do:

1. Open your main document.

2. In the Data Merge Manager, click the View Merged Data icon (the first one) in the Preview area. You'll see the contents of your first data record instead of the merge fields.

3. If you want to check out other data records, click the arrow buttons or just type a record number in the Preview area text field (the Go to Record text box).

You can print the document with the data that you've displayed in the normal way. Just choose the Print command from the File menu or Standard toolbar or press COMMAND-P and click the Print button.

Merging the Data

The preliminaries have taken a while, but now you're ready to actually merge the data. Compared to what you had to do to set things up, this may seem anticlimactic; the Data Merge Manager has made the process far easier than it was with prior versions of Word.

Now let's begin:

1. Before you merge the data (yes, I did say we were going to move beyond the preliminaries now, didn't I), you'll want to see whether or not the records should be sorted. To do that, click the arrow next to Merge in the Data Merge Manager to reveal its contents, which include the options to fine-tune your merge operation.

2. Click the Query Options button.

3. In the dialog box that appears, click the Sort Records tab.

4. Select the data field to be sorted and then select the sort order you want.

NOTE *If you are sorting data records created in another program, you must select all the records you want to sort. Word does this automatically for its own documents.*

5. To merge a single record, click the arrows in the Preview area to display the appropriate record.

6. In the Merge area, choose Merge Data Range from the pop-up menu and then select Current Record.

7. If you want to merge a group of records rather than just one, in the Merge area choose Custom from the pop-up menu.

NOTE *To merge all the records, just leave the default setting, which is All.*

8. Enter the starting record in the From column and the end record in the To column.

9. Click one of the three icons that represent the merge action you want to perform. They are as follows:

   ■ **Merge to Printer**   Choose this option if you want to send the merged information right to the printer.

   ■ **Merge to New Document**   Choose this option if you want to save the information in a new Word document and print it later. If you chose this option, you'll get a finished document containing the data.

   ■ **Merge to E-Mail**   This option merges your material into an Entourage e-mail message to the designated recipients.

Once you've selected your merge option, it will proceed to follow your instructions. At the end of the process, you'll have the merged document, precisely as you specified.

Using the Data Merge Manager to Create Labels

In addition to creating a wide variety of customized form letters with Word's flexible Data Merge Manager, you can also make labels in pretty much the same way.

You'll find that the setup process is remarkably similar to the one for the data merge operation described in previous sections.

Creating Your Main Labels Document

The first part of this process involves setting up a main document formatted with the label design you want. Here's what to do:

1. Choose New Blank Document from the File menu or Standard toolbar or just press COMMAND-N. A new blank document appears.

2. If the Data Merge Manager isn't present, choose Data Merge Manager from the Tools menu to bring up the palette.

3. In the Main Document area of the Data Merge Manager, click Create and choose Labels from the pop-up menu. This produces the Label Options dialog box shown in Figure 15-6.

4. In the Printer Information area, select the kind of printer you're using for the labels.

NOTE   *It may seem surprising that some folks still use dot-matrix printers, but they do provide good handling of labels, even though they are less suited for many other tasks. I still have a client who swears by (and seldom at) his original Apple ImageWriter.*

5. In the Label Products area, select the printer manufacturer from the pop-up menu. Since Avery is the most popular manufacturer in the United States, it's listed by default, but choose whatever kind of label you plan to use (most major companies are shown).

6. In the Product Number list, choose the kind of label you want. If the numbers don't clearly express what you want, look at the Label Information displayed at the right of the list to make sure it's correct.

NOTE   *The label dimensions and type will appear under Label Information as you scroll through the label list. But the easiest thing to do is buy the labels you want first and then simply locate the proper number in the Label Options dialog box.*

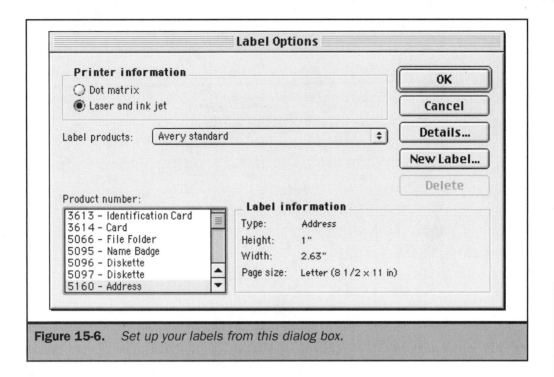

Figure 15-6.   *Set up your labels from this dialog box.*

7. If you're not completely certain how the label will appear, click the Details button, which brings up a dialog with information on all label dimensions. Click OK to close the window.

8. If you can't find a suitable label style, you can make your own. Just click the New Label button in the Label Options dialog box. This will produce a New Custom setup box, as shown in Figure 15-7.

9. Give your label a name and then specify the dimensions and page size.

TIP   *As you create settings for a custom label, keep the actual labels at hand, along with a ruler so you can enter the information as precisely as possible. After doing your data merge operation, test a single sheet of labels to make sure that the figures you entered are correct before you print a large list.*

10. Click OK to store your settings.

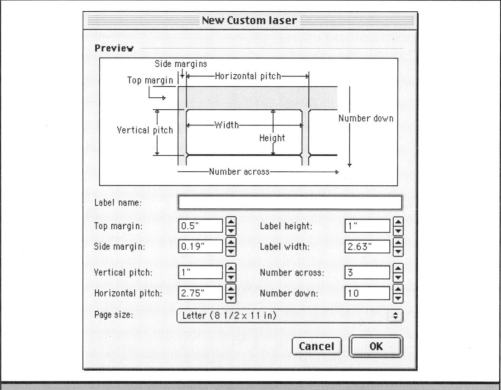

Figure 15-7. *Specify the dimensions of your custom label here.*

Once your labels are set up, review the earlier sections of this chapter, beginning with "Creating a New Data Source Document," to set up your various data source fields and conduct your data merge operation. The steps involved are almost the same, regardless of the type of document.

Putting Postal Bar Codes on Labels

To send your mailing with the maximum possible speed, printing a bar code on the label is a good idea. This is especially true if you're using bulk mailing, which already slows down the shipping process considerably.

Here's how to print a bar code:

1. Set up your data merge operation using the instructions provided earlier.

2. In the Data Source area of the Data Merge Manager palette, click the Edit Labels for Data Merge button (the second from the right).

3. Click the Insert Postal Bar Code option.

4. Choose a field for the zip code data. It should be labeled PostalCode.

5. Select the field for the street address in the Merge Field with Street Address area and click OK. The postal bar code will be displayed in your completed label above the delivery address.

Creating a Main Envelope Document

In the final portion of this tutorial on the Data Merge Manager, you'll learn how to use this powerful feature to print envelopes. Notice the resemblance to the way you handled labels:

1. Start a main document by choosing New Blank Document from the File menu or Standard toolbar or just press COMMAND-N.

2. With the Data Merge Manager palette displayed, click the Create button and then select Envelopes from the submenu. This brings up the Envelope dialog box shown in Figure 15-8.

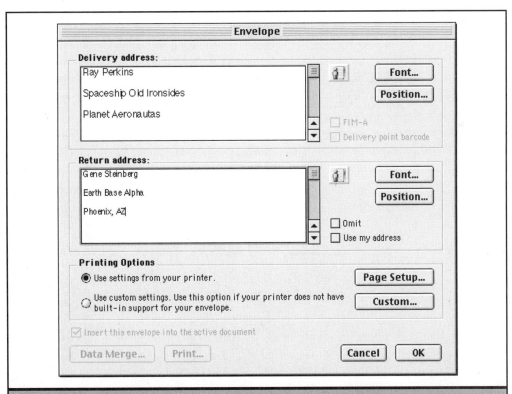

Figure 15-8.   *Normally only the return address will appear in the setup screen, but I've put in a delivery address just to show how it appears in this dialog box.*

3. Click the Font button to specify a type size and style for your envelope. You can format the return and delivery addresses separately.

NOTE   *Click the Delivery Point Barcode check box to include the bar code on your envelope.*

4. To make sure that the names are positioned properly on the envelope, click the Position button, which produces the Address Position dialog box. If you want to specify a distance other than Auto, click the appropriate data field, enter a numeric value, or use the up and down arrows to specify a value.

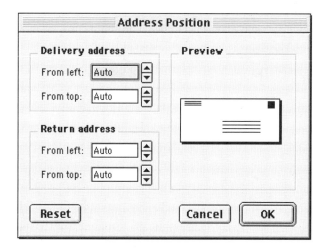

CAUTION   *After accepting an envelope setting, print a sample envelope just to make sure that it looks correct. You wouldn't want to print a few hundred envelopes, only to find that the address is in the wrong position.*

5. Click OK to store the settings.

6. If your printer doesn't have regular support for envelope printing, click the Use Custom Settings button under Printing options and then click Custom to alter the printer setup to accommodate the size of the envelopes you want to use.

7. If your printer does handle envelopes, click the Page Setup button and specify the type of envelope you want to print from the options available.

8. Click OK to store the setup.

NOTE *There is wide variation in how printers are set up to handle envelopes. The best route to take is simply to read the instructions that came with your printer and see what settings need to be made and how envelopes are fed into the unit. Some printers offer optional envelope trays to simplify the process.*

After you have set up your envelope printing options the way you want, review the earlier sections of this chapter, beginning with "Creating a New Data Source Document," to set up your various data source fields and conduct your data merge operation. The steps involved are almost the same, regardless of the type of document.

Creating Macros with Word

So much of what you do on a Mac is the result of manual labor. You save documents, call up dialog boxes, click boxes, enter information in text fields, format tables, add fills and rules to drawing objects, and so on. You have all that incredible computing power under the hood on your Mac, even if it's just a basic iMac, yet it goes to waste if you do everything yourself.

But Word has a feature that will take you on the road toward automating many tasks, and sometimes very complex tasks. It's Word's macro feature. Word's macros take a series of separate program commands and group them together, so you can access them via a single shortcut.

When you create a macro in Word, the program records it as a set of commands in its Visual Basic for Applications software and stores it in a macro for later retrieval. But you don't have to know any programming language to build a macro.

Macros can consist of a single series of connected steps, or a set of separate tasks into which you insert information that's needed to trigger the next set of actions. You create a macro simply by starting the macro recorder and performing the actions you want to store. If you want to allow for user input in your macro, you can insert a pause in the macro.

Once your macros are complete, you can put them on a toolbar or menu or create a shortcut key for fast access. Or you can simply use the Macros command on the Tools menu to access a dialog box of available macros and run the ones you want. In fact, that's just how we hard-working authors write these books for Osborne/McGraw-Hill. We use a special macro toolbar, shown here, which contains the formatting codes needed to make sure the books look just right when the final pages are done.

| H1 H2 H3 H4 | BodyText Normal TextAfter CodeListing Table# Fig# III# SP | PD AQ ABC | Quotes |

Getting Ready to Create a Macro

Before you start creating a macro, you'll want to take a few moments to plan your strategy. Here are some suggestions to make your macro creation process as smooth as possible (but don't worry; you can easily delete a macro that wasn't recorded properly):

■ **Rehearse**   Just as you might rehearse a speech or a part for a play, it's a good idea to take some time to plan out each step and Word command you're going to store in your macro. You can, of course, edit the macro and remove incorrect or unneeded steps, but it's a good idea to try to zip through the process as seamlessly as possible, since it is easier to do it right than to edit later.

■ **Anticipate Word Prompts and Error Messages**   When you create a macro, you need to be ready for possible dialog box and warning prompts. For example, you may perform a delete function that initiates an "Are you sure?" dialog box you have to respond to. You'll want to be sure that your macro takes that possibility into account. As mentioned in the previous paragraph, rehearsing the entire macro process from beginning to end will help you see what sort of interruptions you'll have to consider.

■ **Are You Using the Find or Replace Command?**   If so, you'll want to click More on the Find tab and then All in the Search dialog box. If the macro is searching to the bottom or top of your document, the macro will stop at the end or start of your document with a warning dialog box asking if you want to continue the search. Following the steps described here will avoid that message.

■ **Is Your Macro Content Dependent?**   Before you record your macro, make sure that it doesn't require certain material in a document, such as a word or other contents; otherwise, as the document is edited, or if other documents are used with this macro, the macro won't work, or won't work properly.

■ **Give It a Shortcut**   If you plan on using your macro frequently, consider giving it a keyboard shortcut or putting it on the menu or in a toolbar. That will avoid a trip to the Macros dialog box.

Reference: Using Word's Built-in Macros

Before you build a macro from scratch, you may just want to take a gander at the ones already available in Word. Just open the Macros dialog box and choose Macros in Word Commands from the pop-up menu. You'll find literally dozens of prebuilt macros that can be used to control a variety of simple and more complicated functions.

When you click on a particular macro's name, the purpose will appear in the description field, at least most of the time. Some just list the name of the person who made the macro.

Some of the macros control basic text formatting and commands; others control document formatting, menu bar commands, drawing objects, outlining, and other functions.

Feel free to spend a little time pouring through the list, trying out macros to see how they work. If the end result isn't what you like, the Undo command in the Edit menu will cancel the operation, whatever it is.

Word stores the macros in template files, which are placed in the Templates folder, which you'll find in the Word or Office program folder. These templates are made active in all your documents by making them global templates. You can do that by copying the macros in that template to your Normal, or global, template.

Here's how it's done:

1. Open the document or template from which you want to copy the macros.

2. From the Tools menu, choose Macro and select Macros from the submenu. This brings up the Macros dialog box (see Figure 15-9).

3. With the dialog box displayed, click Organizer. This brings up the Organizer dialog box (see Figure 15-10).

4. Click the Macro Project Items tab if it isn't selected (it usually is when you access the Organizer this way).

NOTE   *The Organizer can also be used to copy styles, AutoText items, and toolbars from one document or template to another using the very same techniques described in this section.*

5. Select the names of the macros you want to copy on the left.

6. Make sure that the Normal (global) template is selected on the right, from the pop-up menu.

7. Click Copy to transfer the macro or macros.

8. To complete the process, click the Close button to dismiss the dialog box.

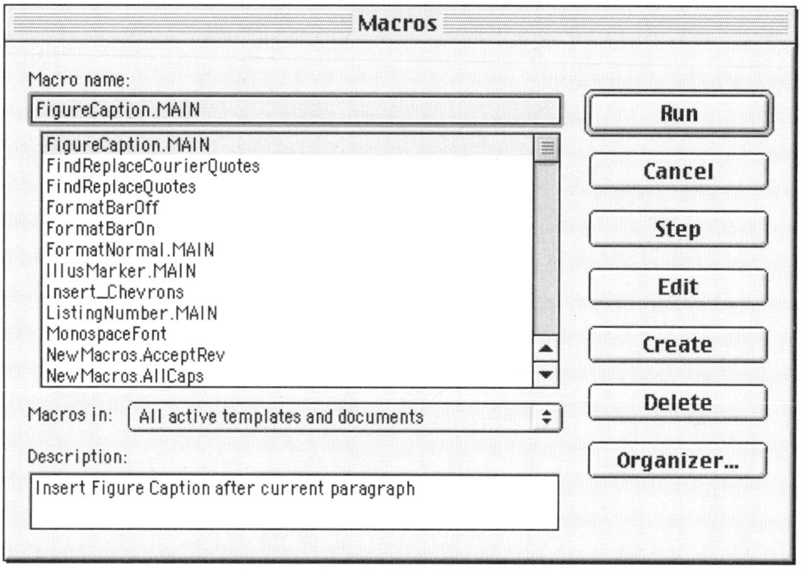

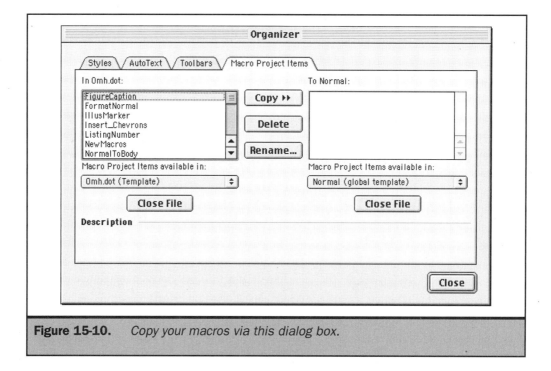

Figure 15-9. *Manage macros from this dialog box.*

Figure 15-10. *Copy your macros via this dialog box.*

Adding a Macro to Your Word Document

You can easily place the macros from a template or another document in a Word document you're working on, without affecting the Normal template (which applied to all of your Word documents). Here's how:

1. From the Tools menu, choose Templates and Add-Ins. This brings up the dialog box shown in Figure 15-11.

2. Click the Attach button and then locate the template you want to add in the dialog box (see Figure 15-12). By default, the menu points to the Templates folder within your Office 2001 folder.

NOTE *If the template isn't there, view the folder on your hard drive to be sure you put the file in the right place. Although you can open a template from another location, it's more convenient to keep all templates in the same place.*

3. When you locate the template, click the Open button to store it in your document, and then click OK to complete the process.

NOTE *As you see (refer back to Figure 15-10), the Organizer dialog box is just a click away if you decide you'd rather just copy the template to your Normal template instead.*

PUTTING WORD 2001 TO WORK FOR YOU

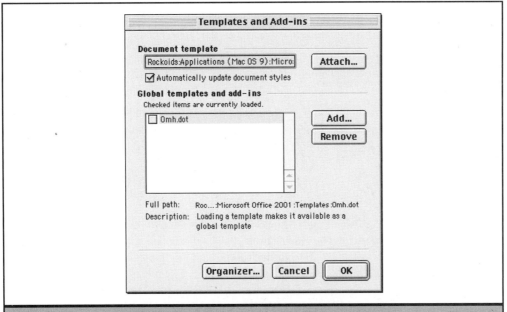

Figure 15-11.   *Manage templates used in your document from here.*

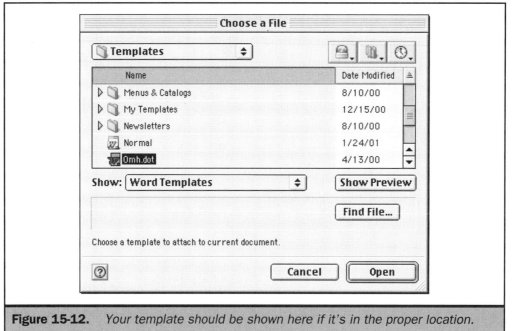

Figure 15-12. *Your template should be shown here if it's in the proper location.*

4. To actually run one of the Macros, return to the Tools menu and choose Macros.

5. In the Macros dialog box, make sure that the pop-up menu listed under Macros In points to the right document.

6. Click the macro's name.

7. Click the Run button to activate the macro and close the dialog box.

Creating a Macro from Scratch

While running a macro that's already been created is surely a time saver, there will be many occasions when you'll find yourself wanting a macro to speed up the particular work you do in Word.

Fortunately, Microsoft has made the process of creating those new macros as painless as programming can be. Here's how it's done:

1. From the Tools menu, select Macro and choose Record New Macro from the submenu.

2. In the Record Macro dialog box that appears, give the macro a name.

```
┌─────────────────── Record Macro ───────────────────┐
│  Macro name:                                         │
│  ┌──────────────────────────────┐    ┌─────────┐    │
│  │ Trouble                      │    │   OK    │    │
│  └──────────────────────────────┘    └─────────┘    │
│  ┌ Assign macro to ─────────────┐    ┌─────────┐    │
│  │                              │    │ Cancel  │    │
│  │    [Toolbars]   [Keyboard]   │    └─────────┘    │
│  │                              │                   │
│  └──────────────────────────────┘                   │
│  Store macro in:                                     │
│  ┌──────────────────────────────────────────┐  ▲▼  │
│  │ All Documents (Normal)                    │      │
│  └──────────────────────────────────────────┘      │
│  Description:                                        │
│  ┌──────────────────────────────────────────────┐  │
│  │ right here in River City.                      │  │
│  │                                                │  │
│  └──────────────────────────────────────────────┘  │
└─────────────────────────────────────────────────────┘
```

NOTE *In naming your macro, try to use no more than a word or two that clearly expresses your macro's purpose, such as FigureCaption, if you are creating a macro that formats a figure caption for pictures in your document. Remember, too, that if you pick a name that's already being used, Word will just replace the old macro with the new one (so you lose the older macro's functionality). You'll want to look through the list first before naming the macro, but you will be warned if you're about to overwrite an existing macro.*

3. Choose the location where you want to place the macro from the Store Macro In pop-up menu. You can store your macro in your open document or any available template.

NOTE *Again, if you want the macro to appear in all the Word documents you create on your Mac, choose the All Documents (Normal) option.*

4. If you want to put the macro on a toolbar or menu or create a keyboard shortcut, click the appropriate Assign Macro button:
   - If you click the Toolbars icon, you'll see a Commands dialog box; select the macro you're creating and then drag it to the toolbar or menu to which you want to assign it.
   - To create a keyboard shortcut, click the Keyboard icon. In the Commands dialog box, select the macro you're creating and click in the Press New Shortcut Key box. Type the keyboard sequence exactly as you want it and click Assign. Word will warn you if there's a conflict with another shortcut. You'll find an extensive list of Word's keyboard shortcuts in Chapter 11.

5. When you're ready to roll, click OK.

6. Now you'll see where that rehearsal suggested earlier will help. Perform through the very actions that you want to record.

CAUTION   *Word's macro editor cannot detect mouse movements or clicks in a document window. If you want to perform a mouse function, you will need to use Word's shortcut keys, so that Word understands the precise action you want to take.*

7. When you're finished creating your macro, click the Stop Recording button on the Macro toolbar that appears on your screen.

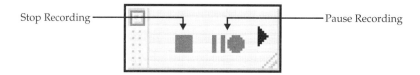

Stop Recording ——————————————————— Pause Recording

Pausing Macro Recording

During the macro recording process, you may find that you need to do something else on your Mac or perform other functions that you don't want recorded in your macro. Fortunately, you don't have to redo the macro; Word has a Pause button to help.

To use it, follow these steps:

1. While Word records your macro, the Macro toolbar will appear. To pause the recording, click Pause Recording button.

2. Do whatever you want to do on your Mac that you do not want recorded as part of the macro.

3. When you're ready to resume recording, click the same button, whose function has now changed to Resume Recording. Smart button!

Editing Macros

Once your macro has been created, you will want to give it a thorough test to make sure it does just what you want without any missteps. Don't be concerned if a complicated macro doesn't work right the first time, because errors do occur, even when you've rehearsed carefully.

The macro isn't etched in stone. You can zap it and try again or try editing it to make corrections or change the name and description.

If you're ambitious and want to learn a little programming, you can try using Word's macro editing tool, the Visual Basic Editor; it's part of the standard Word installation. If you haven't used it before, you will need to spend a little time examining its help menus and learning the lingo.

After you do that, you'll be able not only to test your macros but actually debug them, character by character, to make them perfect; you may even be able to write them from scratch.

To edit your macro, follow these steps:

1. From the Tools menu, choose Macro and then select Macros, which produces the Macros dialog box.

2. Locate the name of the macro you want to edit and select it.

NOTE *If you don't see the macro you want, make sure the correct document or template is selected from the Macros In pop-up menu.*

3. Click the Edit button. This will produce the Visual Basic Editor (shown in Figure 15-13

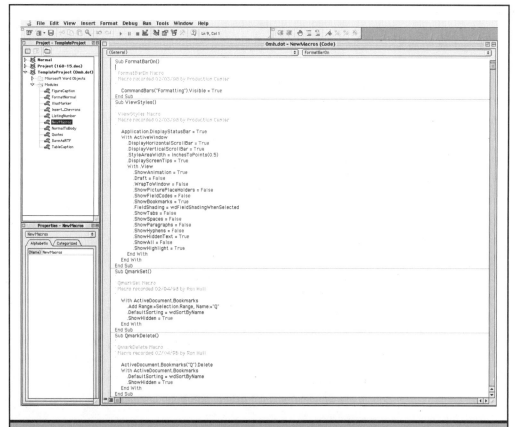

Figure 15-13.   *Visual Basic Editor, Office 2001's programming tool*

4. Use the Debug menu to test your macro and make sure your syntax is correct.

5. When you're finished, quit the Visual Basic Editor and save your work to make sure the changes to your macro are applied.

Removing Macros

Although macros are handy to have when you need them, if your macro is designed strictly for temporary duty, you may want to clear it out when it's no longer needed. To do that, follow these steps:

1. From the Tools menu, choose Macro and select Macros.

2. In the Macro Name list box, select the name of the macro you want to remove.

NOTE   *If the macro you want is not listed, open the Macros In pop-up menu and select the appropriate document or template. If a macro is in a document, that document must be open for the Macros dialog box to list it.*

3. Click Delete and respond "yes" to the "Are you sure?" prompt to remove the macro.

Renaming Macros

As mentioned earlier in this section, it's a good idea to name your macros so that they are easy to identify and so that it is clear to you or anyone else what each macro does. If you need to rename your macro, follow these steps:

1. If the macro applies strictly to a document rather than to a global template, make sure that document is opened in Word.

2. From the Tools menu, select Macro and then choose Macros to open the Macros dialog box.

3. Click the Organizer button.

4. In the list, select the macro you want to rename.

5. Click the Rename button, which brings up the Rename dialog box.

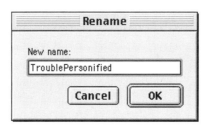

6. Enter the new name for the macro.

7. Click OK to dismiss the dialog box and then close the Organizer window.

Reference: Using Older Macros

If you've upgraded from a previous version of Word, you don't have to do anything special to convert your macros. When you open the template that contains a macro or a document based on that template, or when you attach the template to your document using the Templates and Add-Ins dialog box (on the Tools menu), the macro will be converted to Word 2001 format.

If you see a status bar indicating that your macros are being converted, resave the document template to avoid having to repeat the process again.

 If a macro has been converted to Word 2001, you may have problems running that macro in old versions of Word, such as Word 6 for the Mac and Word 95 for Windows.

Macros created and stored in a Word 98 document do not need to be converted.

Diagnosing Word Macro Problems

Any time you create a macro for a program, you are, in effect, doing a limited amount of programming, even though it's very simple in most cases. But because you are programming, problems may sometimes arise.

Here are some common troubles and the likely solutions:

- **Macro Sometimes Produces an Error Message**   A macro that you create may not run properly in all situations. For example, if you created a macro that needs to search for hidden text in your document, and the Display Hidden Text option is turned off, you will get an error message to that effect. The best thing to do is test your macro when you create it, and also make sure that the Word settings you used when you created the macro haven't changed. You can also try to create macros that don't depend on individual preference settings, if other people will be using your macros; you can't predict what other users' settings might be on their copies of Word.

- **Can't Edit, Record, or Run Macros in Open Document**   Is your document set as read only? If so, the title or file name of the document will show [Read-Only] in the title bar. The solution is to change the file sharing options of the document if you want to edit the macro. This is done in the Preferences dialog box, available from the Edit menu. Click the Save tab to set passwords and read preferences.

Word Macros and Viruses

Over the years, Macintosh virus strains have been rare compared to those that infect the Windows platform—that is, they were rare until macro viruses became prevalent, because the Mac versions of Office can read macros created on the Windows platform, too.

A macro virus can be activated whenever you launch a Word document that contains an infected macro. On the Mac platform, the effects are generally not severe, though they can be downright annoying. One common symptom of a macro virus is the inability to save a document except as a template.

But on the Windows platform, macro viruses can dig down deep and hurt critical functions in the operating system. What's more, even though the effects of macro viruses on the Mac aren't severe, opening an infected file on your Mac and sending it to someone using Windows can propagate the virus.

Word's Virus Warning Feature

Whenever you open a document that contains a macro, Word puts up a warning about it, so you can determine whether you want to open the file with the macros enabled or disabled. Remember: a macro virus, just like any other virus, doesn't do its damage unless you open the document and activate the infected macro.

This is, however, just a caution. It doesn't help you actually beat the virus. For that, you need up-to-date virus detection software.

Antivirus Software Options

There are three well-known commercial programs that can detect and, if you wish, repair infected documents:

- **Norton Anti-Virus (Symantec)**   First known as SAM (or Symantec Anti-Virus Utilities for Macintosh), this program is updated each month (more often if need be) to detect known virus strains and Trojan horses (the latter are programs that appear to be perfectly normal, but are, in fact, harmful). The version shipping when this book was written, 7.0, included the ability to check for e-mail viruses, such as the Melissa virus. It also has a LiveUpdate feature that allows updates to be retrieved automatically from the Internet. This program is also included as part of Norton SystemWorks and Norton Internet Security.

- **Virex (Network Associates)**   This program is also a long-time entrant in the Mac virus detection arena. It offers features fairly similar to Norton Anti-Virus, although the ability to check for e-mail viruses was not in the version shipping when this book was written: version 6.1. There are, however, monthly updates of virus detection strings, so you can be assured that the latest virus strains can be detected and destroyed.

■ **VirusBarrier (Intego)**   This is the new kid on the block, so to speak, but it offers most of the features of the competition, including the ability to check for macro viruses. It is also bundled as part of Internet Security Barrier, which is marketed as a direct competitor to Norton Internet Security.

NOTE   *Virus detection capabilities are also included with MicroMat's TechTool Pro 3, but the version shipping when this book went to press was still not able to detect macro viruses, though this capability is promised for a future version.*

A Brief Look at Other Macro-Creation Options

In addition to Word's powerful macro features, there are other options you can use to automate tasks.

One of these is AppleScript, Apple Computer's free scripting software. Although Word doesn't contain built-in AppleScripts, you can use this program when you want to have Word work with other programs on your Mac and automate repetitive tasks.

Another handy tool is CE Software's QuicKeys. This Mac program has stood the test of time and grown more powerful with each edition. At its core, it will do what a Word macro can do: record a series of steps, either simple or complicated, and then activate them via a single keystroke. It can also work with all of your Mac applications, including the Finder, to create a variety of custom functions. The version available when this book was written, 5.0, also lets you create custom toolbars to activate various macros. It's also integrated with AppleScript, which means that you can use AppleScript functions within QuicKeys. You can learn more about the program and download a limited-time demonstration version from the publisher's Web site at http://www.cesoft.com.

Summary

Word's features for performing data and mail merges and letting you create macros to automate your work greatly add to its capabilities. In fact, this book was formatted using a template created using Word macros. The macros make it easy for the publisher to apply its page layout software to the manuscript and correctly format the pages for the completed book.

That concludes our coverage of Word. Beginning with Chapter 16, you'll learn about Office 2001's powerful spreadsheet application, Excel. You'll start by learning how to set up a basic worksheet and then discover the many uses for this program, both at home and at the office.

Part IV

Organizing Your Data with Excel 2001

Chapter 16

Introduction to Spreadsheets

One of the most popular parts of Office is Excel, an application that lets you store and organize and calculate data in a wide variety of categories. Home users can insert information about household expenses. Business users can track projects, analyze when products are shipped and received, and create account histories.

In addition, Excel can summarize all the information in an easy-access chart, so you can quickly get the information you need.

How Excel Stores Data

The core of Excel is the workbook. This is the document file you create in the program, the one you use to insert and store your data. Each document can consist of a number of pages called worksheets. The worksheet actually lists the data that you enter and edit, and you can analyze the data from one or more worksheets at the same time.

As your workbook expands, each worksheet is identified with a convenient tab at the bottom of the workbook window, so you can easily move from one worksheet to another. In Figure 16-1, you see a sample Excel worksheet, in this case, it's one created by the lab department at CNET to analyze performance of a Mac graphic card.

Customizing Excel to Suit Your Needs

As you see, Excel is an extremely powerful program, one that can provide everything from a simple chart to an industrial-strength spreadsheet that can be used to plot the data in a large business. There are also many ways for you to customize the look and feel of the program.

In this section, you'll learn about Excel's preferences settings. They are available when you choose Preferences from the Edit menu.

NOTE   *The Preferences tab you see depends on the one you opened last time you accessed the feature.*

View Preferences

Excel's View preferences (shown in Figure 16-2) specify the program elements that will appear when you're using Excel. They're listed by category:

- ■ **Show**   These settings determine whether the formula and status bars are displayed. The default setting, and the one I recommend, is to display them.

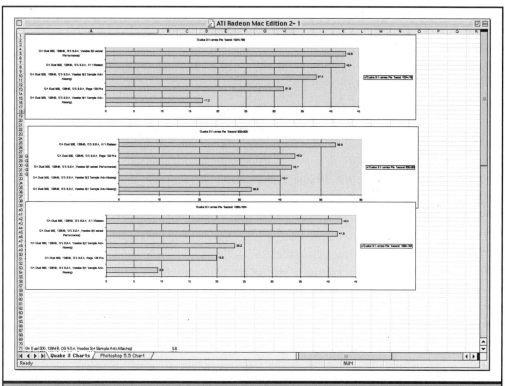

Figure 16-1. *Here's one use of a spreadsheet: to analyze the performance of different products.* (Reproduced with the permission of CNET.)

- **Comments** These settings determine whether comments you add to your spreadsheet are displayed.

- **Objects** Normally, graphic objects will appear in position, but if you have an older, slower Mac and want to maximize screen display speed, you can display placeholders instead. You can also hide graphics, but that may lead to confusion if there are lots of objects in your worksheet.

- **Window Options** These settings control whether such elements as page breaks, formulas, and gridlines (used for cell placement) are displayed. Gridlines are on by default. The remainder of the settings control headers, symbols, scroll bars, and sheet tabs, the latter used to access multiple worksheets in your workbook.

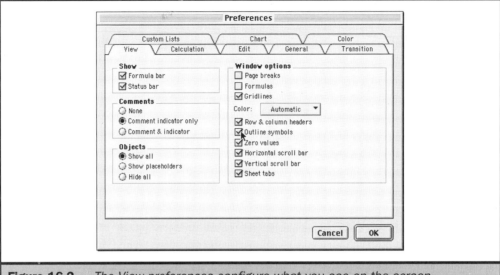

Figure 16-2. *The View preferences configure what you see on the screen.*

Calculation Preferences

The heart of Excel is its ability to do math for you, based on the settings you specify. When you click the Calculation tab in Excel's Preferences dialog box (see Figure 16-3), you'll be able to specify whether calculation is automatic, automatic except for tables, or manual. There are also settings that determine how your Workbook updates information, particularly when the source material is on a network or in a linked file.

Here are the specifics:

■ **Calculation** Decide whether you want Excel to perform calculations automatically, automatically except tables, or only when you specifically ask it to (manually). If you pick Manual, you can choose an additional option, Recalculate Before Save, to have Excel recalculate each time you save your workbook. If you choose Automatic Except Tables, Excel performs calculations automatically except for data tables; when you want to calculate these, you must select calculation manually.

■ **Iteration** *Iteration* refers to the number of times Excel performs an operation in situations involving goal seeking or circular references. If you select this check box, you can specify the number of iterations (set to 100 by default) and the maximum amount of change (set to 0.001 by default).

■ **Calc Now (Cmd-=)** Click this button to recalculate the selected data in your workbook on demand.

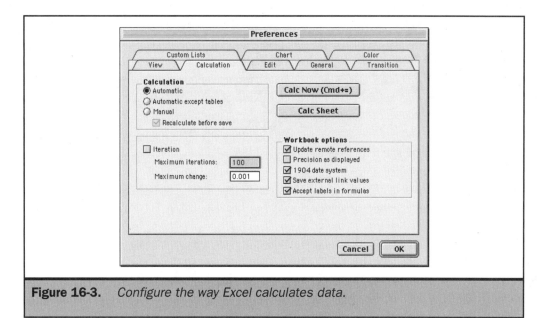

Figure 16-3.   *Configure the way Excel calculates data.*

- **Calc Sheet**   Click this button to calculate your worksheet.
- **Workbook Options**   These check boxes specify how your workbook is handled. Use the Update Remote References option if you are linking to data from another application. The Precision as Displayed option changes the standard 15-digit precision to whatever is being displayed in the cell. The 1904 Date System option changes the starting date to January 1, 1904 (Apple's way), and recalculates the worksheet accordingly, in case you work for a company that uses this method or exchange data with the Windows platform. Use Save External Link Values when your worksheet links to a document in another program. The Accept Labels in Formulas option does precisely what it says it does, in case your worksheet has labels in the columns and rows.

Edit Preferences

Creating a workbook is a combination of entering new data and editing what's already there. The Edit tab in the Preferences dialog box (see Figure 16-4) configures a number of default system settings:

- **Edit Directly in Cell**   This default setting lets you use the cell rather than the text box on the toolbar to enter and edit data (it still shows up in the toolbar, by the way, so you can also work in the old-fashioned Excel way if you like).

ORGANIZING YOUR DATA
WITH EXCEL 2001

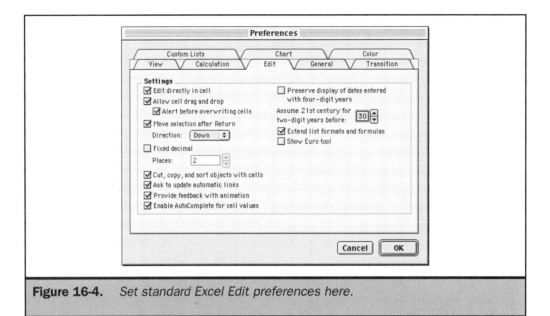

Figure 16-4. *Set standard Excel Edit preferences here.*

- **Allow Cell Drag and Drop**   This setting lets you use the Mac's drag-and-drop feature to move cells from one location to another.

- **Alert Before Overwriting Cells**   If you choose dragging and dropping, you can use this option to display an alert so you don't overwrite an existing cell.

- **Move Selection After Return**   Click the Direction pop-up menu to specify where the selection goes. By default, it's down, to the cell in the column below. The remaining options are right, left, and up.

- **Fixed Decimal**   Specify the number of decimal places in the Places text field for your numbers (the default is 2 if you use this option; otherwise, the default is the number of decimal places supported by the selected number format).

- **Cut, Copy, and Sort Objects with Cells**   This option is a convenience; it keeps objects with their associated cells when you perform these editing functions.

- **Ask to Update Automatic Links**   If the data in your workbook is linked to an external document, checking this option will display a prompt asking if you want to update the external document when you change data in the workbook.

- **Provide Feedback with Animation**   This option is a convenience; it gives you visual feedback by moving the worksheet as you move cells, rows, and columns.

- **Enable AutoComplete for Cell Values**   I always say, let your computer do the work, particularly if it is one of those Mac G4s that Apple's ads place in the "supercomputer" category. Let it do as much work as it can. This option performs the task that is described, automatically completing cell values based on previously entered data.

■ **Preserve Display of Dates Entered with Four-Digit Years**   Normally, if you enter the date 5/15/2001, for example, Excel will convert it to 5/15/01. If you'd rather keep the four-digit format, select this option.

■ **Assume 21st Century for Two-Digit Years Before**   If the four-digit years option is selected, choose the date for which 21st century years are assumed. The default is 30, which means that if you specify 5/15/29, Excel assumes that you mean 5/15/2029; if you enter 5/15/31, Excel assumes that you mean 5/15/1931.

■ **Extend List Formats and Formulas**   This option formats the new items entered to the end of the list in the same fashion as those already in the list.

■ **Show Euro Tool**   This option is needed only if you are creating a workbook that needs to incorporate the euro currency standard. Otherwise, leave it off.

General Preferences

Are you in need of a warning about possible Excel macro viruses? What is the standard font, and where do you place your default documents and startup files? Excel's General preferences (shown in Figure 16-5) set these options plus your user name and a few frills, such as audible feedback for each action you take.

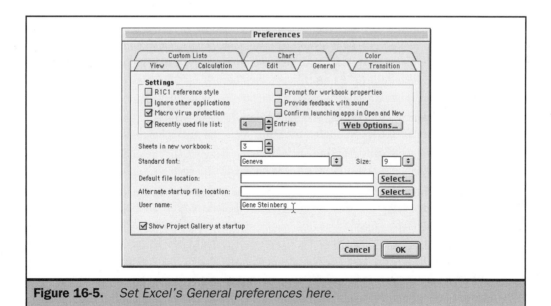

Figure 16-5.   *Set Excel's General preferences here.*

- **R1C1 Reference Style** Use this option to refer to rows (R) and columns (C) by their numbers preceded by R or C.

- **Ignore Other Applications** Checking this option prevents sharing of data with other documents that support Dynamic Data Exchange (DDE).

- **Macro Virus Protection** Actually, this is mislabeled. With the option selected, all you will see is a warning whenever you open an Excel workbook that contains a macro. You can decide whether to run the macro or not, but if you need the processes included in the macro, there's not much choice. You are better off getting good virus software so you needn't concern yourself about the possibility of a macro virus.

- **Recently Used File List** By default, the number of recently opened documents that appear on the File menu is four. The maximum is nine.

- **Prompt for Workbook Properties** This is a reminder to include a summary with your workbook, such as its title, its subject, the author, keywords, and a brief description of the contents.

- **Provide Feedback with Sound** As you perform open, save, and print operations in Excel, you'll hear a faint click. If you like faint clicks, select this option to get a lot of them. If you'd rather not be annoyed, leave it off (the way it is by default).

- **Confirm Launching Apps in Open and New** Select this option to display a confirmation box if an action will open a different application.

- **Web Options** Click this button to see options (see Figure 16-6) for saving your workbook as a Web page; they are quite similar to the ones already present in Word, specifying how linked files are handled, display size, and so on.

- **Sheets in New Workbook** Specify the default number of sheets in a new workbook. The data field lists 3 and the maximum is 255; you can easily add worksheets to your document as necessary up to the limit.

- **Standard Font** Specify the name or open the pop-up menu to select a font installed on your Mac. Geneva, the standard, is a perfectly good font for screen display, but totally unsuited for printing.

- **Size** Specify the default size. In this case, it's 9 points.

- **Default File Location** Specify the path (such as rockoids:documents for a file in the Documents folder on a volume named Rockoids), or click Select to locate a suitable folder. The Documents folder is fine, unless you want to subdivide and group a number of files in a folder within that folder.

- **Alternate Startup File Location** If you want a document or template to automatically open with Excel, you place it in the Excel folder, within the Startup folder, which is located in the Office folder. You can specify another location if you prefer.

Web Options

/ General \ / Files \ / Pictures \ / Encoding \ / Fonts \

Document description

Web page title: | rockoids.chart |

Web page keywords: | |

[Cancel] [**OK**]

Figure 16-6.   *Click a tab to see that set of options.*

■ **User Name**   Enter your name here, if you want, in the text field. By default, it reads the name of the user of your Mac, as set in the File Sharing Control Panel.

■ **Show Project Gallery at Startup**   Specify whether the Project Gallery appears at startup. By default, it does.

Transition Preferences

When you click the Transition tab of Excel's Preferences dialog box (see Figure 16-7), you'll see settings that are not needed unless you are working with other spreadsheet programs in addition to Excel. The Default Save As Type, for example, provides a pop-up menu of various programs and format options, some of which are shown here:

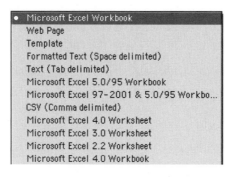

● Microsoft Excel Workbook
Web Page
Template
Formatted Text (Space delimited)
Text (Tab delimited)
Microsoft Excel 5.0/95 Workbook
Microsoft Excel 97–2001 & 5.0/95 Workbo...
CSV (Comma delimited)
Microsoft Excel 4.0 Worksheet
Microsoft Excel 3.0 Worksheet
Microsoft Excel 2.2 Worksheet
Microsoft Excel 4.0 Workbook

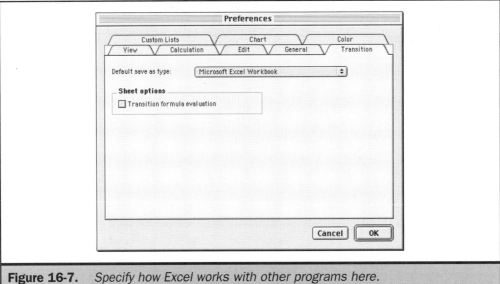

Figure 16-7.   *Specify how Excel works with other programs here.*

Custom Lists Preferences

In Chapter 17, you'll learn how to use lists and the List Manager. The Custom Lists preference tab works in conjunction with those features. It's used to set lists of dates, times, and numerical information for regular use by the program (see Figure 16-8). To put more lists into Excel, click the Add button and then type the material in the List Entries text box, with each entry followed by RETURN. You can also select the lists from a spreadsheet and copy and paste them into the List Entries field.

Chart Preferences

A powerful feature of Excel is its ability to create charts from selected data. This enables you to show your data in a graphical format, so it's easy to examine by you or others. The Chart tab (seen in Figure 16-9) lets you add chart tips that indicate where names and values will be added. The rest of the preferences control the way chart information is plotted when you create a chart. We'll cover this subject in more detail in Chapter 19.

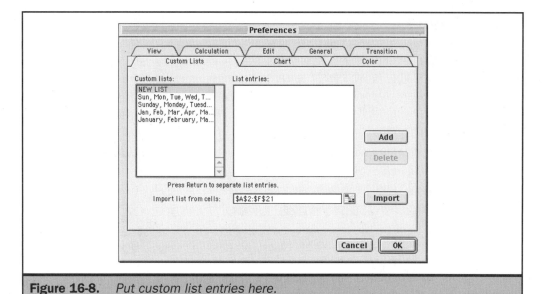

Figure 16-8.   *Put custom list entries here.*

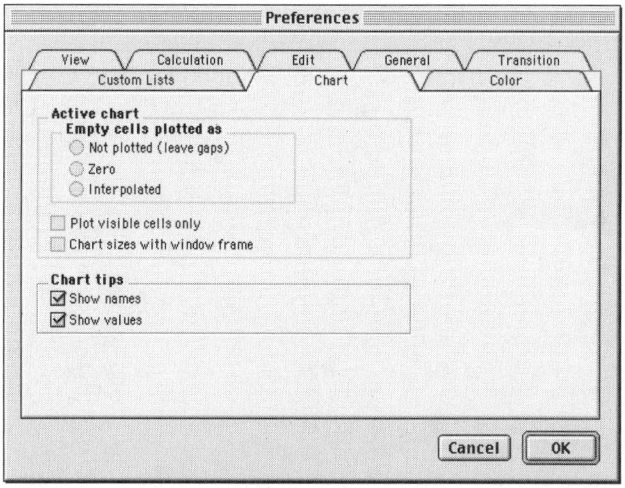

Figure 16-9.   *Specify how your charts are set up here.*

Color Preferences

Although a spreadsheet is often thought of as a drab collection of black-and-white labels and numbers, you can adjust color preferences to greatly enhance them. Using the Color tab (see Figure 16-10), you can choose from the standard colors, or click the Modify button to use color wheels to customize the appearance still further. The Copy Colors From option is used to transfer custom colors from other documents.

NOTE   *Color and font preferences can always be modified in your workbook. You don't have to stick with the defaults. The default settings just make it easier for you to begin a document with the settings you normally use already present.*

Additional Ways to Customize Excel

In addition to the wide range of preferences you can set in Excel, there are other ways you can customize the way your workbooks appear on your Mac's screen and your interaction with the program.

Customizing Startup Defaults

One convenient way to get to work without delay is to have a workbook automatically open when you launch the program. Here is how to make it happen:

1. Quit Excel, if it's running.
2. Locate the Excel Startup folder. To find it, open the Microsoft Office 2001 folder and locate the folder labeled Office. Inside the Office folder, look for the folder labeled Startup. Inside the Startup folder, locate and open the folder labeled Excel.
3. Place the workbook file you want to open (or an alias to it) in the Excel folder. Next time you launch Excel, that workbook will open automatically.

TIP   *If you work on workbooks that are located on a shared network drive or another folder on your drive, you can specify a different location. Just open Excel's Preferences dialog box, select the General tab, and specify an alternate startup file location.*

Creating Custom Templates

You can create custom templates for Excel, using a workbook formatted in the design you like. Save the workbook as a template and place it with your other Office 2001 templates. Chapters 3 and 4 describe how to set up the Project Gallery to recognize and open your templates.

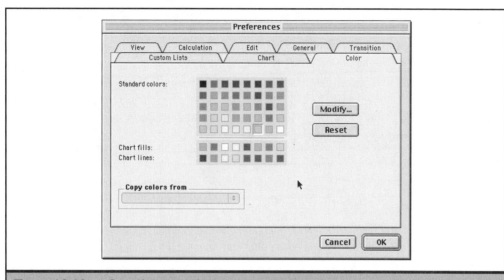

Figure 16-10.   *Specify your default color choices in Excel.*

Hiding Portions of a Workbook

Having a lot of information can make it confusing to see the little pieces of data you need for a specific purpose. For instance, you may want the financial data for a particular quarter for your company, but the spreadsheet shows the full year, with lots of details. You also may want to hide certain sensitive data from outside viewers. Or you just may want a less cluttered workspace, so you can focus on a particular task.

One way to make it easier to view the data you need is to hide parts of the workbook or individual worksheets. That way, the data is not available for viewing and printing, but it's still present in the document when you need it.

To hide parts of a worksheet or workbook, follow these steps:

1. From the Edit menu, choose Preferences.

2. In the Preferences dialog box, select the View tab.

3. In the Window Options section, remove the check marks from any items that you don't want displayed.

4. Click OK to close the Preferences dialog box. You can easily restore the display of the hidden information at any time by revisiting the dialog box.

Hiding Specific Worksheet Elements   To hide only portions of your worksheets, follow these steps:

1. Select the worksheets you want to hide.

2. From the Format menu, choose Sheet and then select Hide from the submenu.

3. To display that worksheet again, return to the Format menu, choose Sheet, and select Unhide. This brings up the Unhide dialog box, where you can specify which worksheets you want to view again.

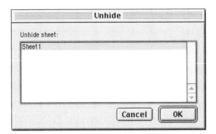

Hiding Rows and Columns   If a worksheet is particularly busy looking, you may want to hide parts of the data for a better view of the contents. Here's how this is done:

1. With the worksheet open, select the rows or columns that you don't want to see.

2. From the Format menu, select Rows to hide selected rows or choose Columns to hide selected columns; and then select Hide from the submenu.

3. To make the hidden items appear again, return to the Format menu, choose Columns or Rows, whichever applies, and then select Unhide from the submenu.

Protecting Documents with a Password

One useful preference setting is password protecting your document. That will help keep unauthorized people from seeing or editing your document.

The simplest way to password protect a document is to use Excel's password protection feature. Here is how to set it up:

1. Open the workbook you want to protect. Choose Protection from the Tools menu and select Protect Sheet, Protect Workbook, or Protect and Share Workbook from the submenu. Here is the dialog box you see when you want to protect your worksheet.

If you want to control the ability of others to share your workbook, choose Protect and Share Workbook from the Protection submenu.

2. Select the features you want to protect. By default, the Protect Sheet dialog box sets protection for your document's contents, objects, and scenarios.

3. Enter a password for your worksheet.

NOTE *Follow the suggestions for choosing a strong password in the chapters covering Entourage in this book (Chapters 5 through 10). The best password is one that includes a mixture of numbers and uppercase and lowercase letters. Don't lose the password, or you won't be able to access the document.*

4. Click OK. From here on, the password must be entered to access the selected contents on the worksheet.

Creating Custom Views in Excel

As you continue to work with Excel workbooks and worksheets, no doubt you'll customize your view settings to see just the information you want, and perhaps you'll also customize your printer settings, so that only the information you require is printed.

Your view settings may include special column widths, display sizes, and window size and position, and you may want to select a specific worksheet, enable special filters, and split or freeze panes to display just the information you want.

To simplify the setup process, you can create a custom view for your entire workbook. That way, you can just open the workbook and get to work rather than waste time customizing it to make it look the way you prefer.

Here's the process:

1. Set up your workbook with the view and printing options you want.

Is Office's Password Protection Robust?

Several years ago, a magazine publisher gave me an unlikely assignment: Would I test the password-protection features of various Macintosh applications and see if they worked? To conduct a thorough test, I called upon an experienced Mac programmer, David Heller, who had worked on a number of commercial applications, such as AutoDoubler and CopyDoubler, and who was quite interested in such matters.

During the course of the test, we found that dedicated security software was usually the most robust and, when the most intense security was put in place, cracking the protected documents would be nearly impossible with the existing technology without years of effort.

The only other applications that passed the test were Aladdin's StuffIt Deluxe, the popular compression program, and Dantz' Retrospect, a backup program.

We haven't put Office 2001 to a similar test, but I recommend dedicated security software as the best means of ensuring proper security for your Mac's sensitive files.

As to Mr. Heller, after he helped me prepare that article, he ended up getting a job for a publisher of security software.

2. Choose Custom Views from the View menu, which brings up the Custom Views dialog box.

3. Click the Add button.

4. In the Add View dialog box, enter a name for the view.

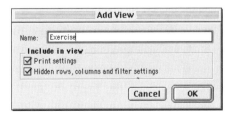

5. In the Include in View section, choose the viewing options you want for that workbook.

6. To get rid of any custom views already created, select them and click the Delete button in the Custom Views dialog box.

7. Click Close to dismiss the dialog box.

CAUTION *The custom views you create are available for use only when the workbook to which they apply is actually open.*

Displaying Your Custom View   Once you've created your custom view, the next time you open your workbook, follow these steps to apply the custom view:

1. With the workbook open, choose Custom Views from the View menu.

2. Select the name of the custom view you want in the Custom Views dialog box.

3. Click the Show button.

TIP *One quick way to bring up a workbook for which you have a custom view is to place the file or its alias in the Excel Startup folder. That way, it will be opened and ready to use each time Excel is launched.*

Touring Excel's Menu Bar

Now that you have Excel configured to run the way you like, let's take a tour of its menu bar, so you get a good handle on the basic commands available. As you progress through this and the next three chapters, you'll learn how to use many of these commands to build comprehensive workbooks and create some very fancy looking charts.

File Menu

The Excel File menu is basically the same as Word's. The notable difference is the Save Workspace command, which saves information on the workbooks you have open, so you can restore the same setup the next time you launch Excel. Excel also lists recent documents opened via the program and includes a number of printing-related commands.

Edit Menu

The Edit menu includes the standard Mac object and text editing commands, plus a Fill submenu you can use to indicate the direction in which you want to extend a selection.

The Clear submenu lets you specify the items in the workbook that you want to remove. When you select Delete, a dialog box appears where you indicate in which direction you want cells, rows, or columns shifted when you delete material.

View Menu

Use the View menu to specify just how your Excel documents appear to you. You can, for example, decide whether the Formatting Palette is displayed and select toolbars, the formula bar, and the status bar. The Comments command lets you insert informational notes with your workbook.

Insert Menu

Use the Insert menu to insert objects and add cells, rows, columns, worksheets, and charts. You can also place a chart within your workbook to really enhance the way information is presented. We'll cover charting in detail in Chapter 19.

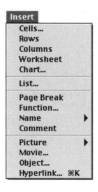

Other Insert functions include the ability to invoke the List Manager (described in more detail in the next chapter) and to insert page breaks, function commands, label names, comments, picture objects (including the ability to acquire images from a scanner or digital camera), movies, and objects from other Office programs. You can also insert hyperlinks, should you want to save your workbook as a Web page.

Format Menu

Use the Format menu to format each element of your workbook for the best look and to present the information in the clearest way. The AutoFormat command lets Excel do the work for you; it will set up workbook formats based on selected cells. The Conditional Formatting command bases a format on whether certain conditions in the selected material are met.

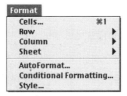

Tools Menu

Open the Tools menu to access various Excel functions. You can bring up the spell checker and dictionary or access the AutoCorrect feature, so that the words you misspell can be fixed nearly as quickly as you mess them up. The Track Changes feature is similar to the one in Word; it allows workgroups to keep tabs on how a workbook changes. Flag for Follow Up works with Entourage to remind you when a project needs revision. The other commands control various functions you'll access while you're using Excel. And you won't want to miss the Calculator option, which greatly simplifies the way you create formulas; it's particularly helpful if you are somewhat math challenged and need a little helper to do the hard stuff.

The Goal Seek adjusts the value of a cell, working with the formula feature. Scenarios are used to project how data might look if a particular situation is met. You'll use the Auditing feature to check your data. As described in Chapter 2, Add-Ins are companion utilities that work with Excel to provide added functions.

Data Menu

How should your data be processed? The Data menu includes the Sort feature, which lets you organize rows of data the way you want. You can also configure tables, filter data, and access the Form feature, which works with the labels on your workbook. If you need to grab data from another program, such as Apple's FileMaker Pro, the Get External Data command will do the job. The PivotTable is an interactive table that eases analysis of data. You will use the Consolidation feature to summarize data from source material and place it in a table.

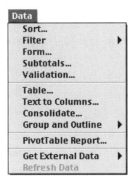

Help Menu

Help is what this book is for, but you also have the Help menu to activate and defeat the animated assistant and access Excel's built-in help. You can also register your Office software and access further assistance on Microsoft's Web site. From time to time, Microsoft provides software updates, workarounds for software problems, and so on.

Window Menu

You use the Window menu to switch among open workbooks, of course, but the most useful features come into play with large workbooks, when you need to see as much data as possible. The Split feature lets you divide the display into separate panes (the default is four), and you can scroll each separately to view the work area. Freeze Panes lets you lock specific panes in one position as you view others.

Creating Your First Excel Workbook

Once Excel is set up to look and run the way you want, no doubt you'll want to create a sample workbook, just to see how it works, or perhaps to begin to insert the data you want to work with in a spreadsheet.

In this example, we'll create a simple household spreadsheet that you might find occasion to use, particularly if you're fighting the battle of the bulge or just want to create a solid exercise regimen so you can keep healthy.

Here's how to accomplish the task:

CAUTION
I am not recommending that anyone follow a specific exercise routine, nor the one I'm using here as an example (this is adapted from one of Microsoft's own user instruction texts). Although my family and I work out regularly, you should consult your physician as to the best exercise course for you. I'm not a doctor or physical trainer, nor do I play one on TV.

1. Launch Excel.

2. Display the Project Gallery (see Figure 16-11) and click the Excel Workbook icon.

3. When your new document is on the screen, double-click the tab labeled Sheet1, which will highlight that name. Type a new name for your worksheet. In this case, type **Exercise Routine**. The tab will expand to accommodate a wider label.

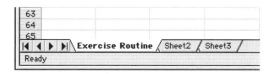

Figure 16-11. *Select a blank workbook to begin your task.*

NOTE

As with the tables you create in Word, the boxes across your worksheet are called cells. Rows are identified by numbers, and columns by letters, so the cell at the intersection of row 4 and column C, for example, is called C4. That's where all that B1, C4, and M7 talk comes from when Excel users discuss their worksheets.

4. To format the text, press COMMAND-A to select all the cells in the workbook.

TIP

You can also select the entire worksheet by clicking the little rectangle in the upper-left corner of the worksheet, just above the numbers and to the left of the letters identifying the rows and cells.

5. Go to Excel's version of the Formatting Palette (see Figure 16-12) and click the Font Size pop-up menu; select 12 (for 12-point type).

6. Navigate to cell A13 (the first column of the row 13) and type **Duration.**

7. Move to cells B3, D3, F3, and H3 and enter **Workout** in each.

TIP

You can press the TAB key to move from cell to cell.

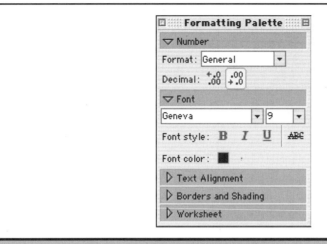

Figure 16-12.   *Excel's Formatting Palette gives you fast access to specific workbook formats.*

8. Since this is a weekly exercise routine, you'll want separate columns for each week of your program, so type **1st Week** in cell C3, **2nd Week** in cell E3, **3rd Week** in Cell G3, and **4th Week** in cell I3. The result should be a worksheet that looks much like the one in Figure 16-13).

9. Aren't we missing something? Yes, the days of the week. So you'll want to create columns for each day. First select column B.

10. From the Insert menu, choose Columns. A new column will appear to the left of the selected column.

11. In the newly created cell B3, type **Day.**

12. To complete the initial setup, we need to add a row to accommodate some additional information. From the Insert menu, choose Rows, if you want to add more rows to the worksheet (they'll appear above the selected row).

Your workbook is almost set up.

Using Excel's AutoFill Function

Using the program's AutoFill feature, information that is part of a series, such as the days of the week, can be put in automatically. As I say, let the computer do the work when you can. Your G3 or G4 (especially the one with two processors) needs the exercise.

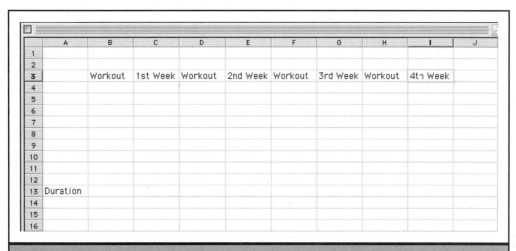

Figure 16-13. *Your work in progress is beginning to shape up.*

Here's how to use AutoFill for your exercise worksheet:

1. With your worksheet open, click cell B5 and type **Monday**.

2. Put the mouse cursor at the lower-right corner of the cell. It will change to an AutoFill handle. Drag the handle downward, and you'll see the days appear on your screen as you move from row to row. When you end in cell B11, you'll have all the days of the week.

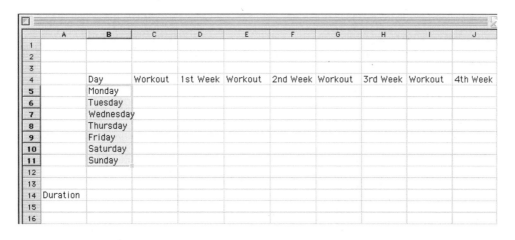

If the entries you make in a cell don't fit, just double-click the boundary at the right of a column heading, and the column will shrink or expand to accommodate the widest entry.

Adjusting Headline Formats

For this weekly exercise worksheet, we've concentrated on the basic setup. You can also make changes to increase the readability of your worksheet, using Excel's extensive formatting options. Just follow these steps to get underway:

1. With your workbook open, go to cell C2 and enter **Exercise Time (in minutes).**

2. From the View menu, select Toolbars and then choose Formatting from the submenu. This will bring up the Formatting toolbar.

We need the Formatting toolbar to provide functions not available in the Formatting Palette.

3. With the Formatting toolbar open, select cells C2 to J2, click Merge Cells and Center on the Formatting toolbar or the Formatting Palette. All the selected text will be centered in the merged cells.

4. On the Formatting Palette, click the Bold icon on the Font tab.

5. With your text now in bold, put the mouse cursor at the lower corner of row 2 and drag the boundary down until you see "Height: 32.00" in the ToolTip. This will give your headline more space in row 2.

6. You'll want to center your headline. To do that, go to the Formatting palette. On the Text Alignment tab, click Center Lines in the Vertical section.

Applying Shading to a Worksheet

I know you're eager to see just how your exercise worksheet is faring, but we have yet another modification to make, purely in the interests of making the worksheet look nicer. Let's apply a shading to alternate rows, to make the spreadsheet easier to read.

1. With your workbook open, select row 5 and choose Rows from the Insert menu.

2. Hold down the COMMAND key and select rows 8, 10, and 12, to select all the rows at once.

3. Click the Borders and Shading pane on the Formatting Palette and then the Fill Color box.

4. Select a color that's suited for your needs. If you have a color printer, you might choose a pastel, so it doesn't overshadow the text. Presto; the alternate rows will have that color. Figure 16-14 shows a sample (I used light gray, because this page isn't going to be printed in color).

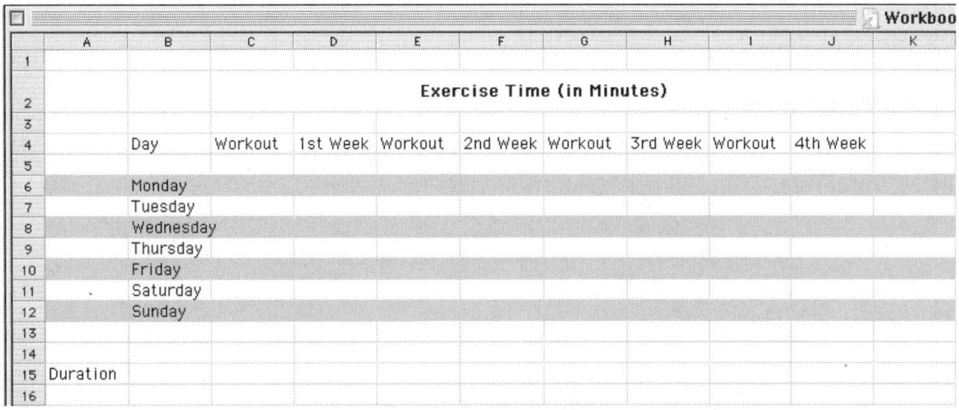

Figure 16-14. *The finished result. Now we have shaded rows alternating with clear ones.*

Keeping Tabs on Your Exercise Routine

Your worksheet is ready to roll. Now you can keep daily tabs on your exercise, so you can be sure you've met your goals. Here's how to enter your data:

1. In column C, enter the exercise activity you performed for each day of the week that you actually worked out.

> NOTE
>
> *As you enter the first letter of an exercise activity, you'll notice that Excel attempts to fill in the balance with a little pop-up AutoFill menu. You would press* ENTER *if you wanted to use Excel's suggestion.*

2. In column D, enter the number of minutes you spent performing that workout.

3. For weeks 2 through 4, repeat steps 1 and 2. Be as accurate as possible.

4. Finally, it's time to save your workbook, so go to the File menu and choose Save.

5. Enter the name of your workbook and the location where you want to save it.

6. Click the Save button.

It All Adds Up

Wait. Don't grab that calculator to see just how much of your week you spent doing your workouts. We'll use Excel's formula function to create an equation that will figure everything out for you. As I said, that's what computers do best.

Here's what to do:

1. Select cell D15, which is the cell where you want to enter the formula for week 1.
2. Click the AutoSum icon on the Standard toolbar and press RETURN.

NOTE   *Excel will create a formula for you, in this case, =SUM(D6:D14), to add up the number of minutes you worked out during the week.*

3. To copy that formula to subsequent weeks, select cell D15 and choose Copy from the Edit menu or press COMMAND-C.
4. Click the cell for next week entry, cell F15, and choose Paste from the Edit menu or press COMMAND-V.
5. Repeat steps 3 and 4 for the remaining two weeks. The finished result, with data already in place, is shown in Figure 16-15.

Excel Keyboard Shortcuts

This section presents all the powerful keyboard shortcuts that you can use to speed your work in Excel. As you saw with Entourage and Word, Microsoft provides a liberal sprinkling of keyboard shortcuts to help you accomplish your tasks.

	A	B	C	D	E	F	G	H	I	J	K
1											
2						Exercise Time (in Minutes)					
3											
4		Day	Workout	1st Week	Workout	2nd Week	Workout	3rd Week	Workout	4th Week	
5											
6		Monday		24		13		33		55	
7		Tuesday		15		22		24		52	
8		Wednesday		24		12		16		35	
9		Thursday		15		15		42		25	
10		Friday		12		16		24		12	
11		Saturday		13		15		14		14	
12		Sunday		14							
13											
14											
15	Duration			117		93		153		193	
16											
17											
18											

Figure 16-15.   *This is the finished product, with data from a sample exercise routine.*

Data Editing

Shortcut	Action
CONTROL-U	Edit the active cell.
ESC	Cancel the entry in the cell or formula bar.
DELETE	Edit the active cell and then clear it, or delete the preceding character in the active cell as you edit the cell contents.
COMMAND-V	Paste text into the active cell (a standard Mac shortcut).
RETURN or ENTER	Complete the cell entry.
CONTROL-SHIFT-RETURN	Enter the formula as an array formula.
CONTROL-A	Display the Formula Palette after you type a valid function name in a formula.
CONTROL-SHIFT-A	Insert the argument names and parentheses for a function, after you type a valid function name in a formula.

Copy Editing

Shortcut	Action
COMMAND-C	Copy the selected material (a standard shortcut).
COMMAND-X	Cut the selected material (a standard shortcut).
COMMAND-V	Paste the selection (a standard shortcut).
CONTROL- - (hyphen)	Delete the selected material.
COMMAND-Z	Undo the last action.
CONTROL-SHIFT-+ (plus sign)	Insert blank cells.

Navigating a Selection

Shortcut	Action
RETURN	Move from top to bottom within the selection (down), or move in the direction that is selected on the Edit tab (Edit menu, Preferences command).

Shortcut	Action
SHIFT-RETURN	Move from bottom to top within the selection (up), or move opposite to the direction that is selected on the Edit tab (Edit menu, Preferences command).
TAB	Move from left to right within the selected material, or move down one cell if only one column is selected.
SHIFT-TAB	Move from right to left within the selection, or move up one cell if only one column is selected.
CONTROL-. (PERIOD)	Move clockwise to the next corner of the selection.
CONTROL-OPTION-RIGHT ARROW	Move to the right between nonadjacent selections.
CONTROL-OPTION-LEFT ARROW	Move to the left between nonadjacent selections.

Using Cells or the Formula Bar

Shortcut	Action
CONTROL-SHIFT-RETURN	Enter a formula as an array formula.
ESC	Cancel an entry in the cell or formula bar.
CONTROL-A	Display the Formula Palette after you type a valid function name in a formula.
CONTROL-SHIFT-A	Insert the argument names and parentheses for a function, after you type a valid function name in a formula.
COMMAND-K	Insert a hyperlink.
RETURN (in a cell with a hyperlink)	Activate a hyperlink.
CONTROL-U	Edit the active cell and position the insertion point at the end of a line.
SHIFT-F3	Paste a function into a formula.
COMMAND-= (equal sign)	Calculate all worksheets in all open workbooks.
SHIFT-F9	Calculate the active worksheet.
= (equal sign)	Begin a formula.

Shortcut	Action
COMMAND-SHIFT-T	Insert an AutoSum formula.
CONTROL-; (semicolon)	Enter a date.
CONTROL-SHIFT-: (colon)	Enter a time.
CONTROL-SHIFT-" (quotation mark)	Copy the value from the cell above the active cell into the cell or the formula bar.
CONTROL-~ (tilde)	Alternate between displaying cell values and displaying cell formulas.
CONTROL-' (apostrophe)	Copy a formula from the cell above the active cell into the cell or the formula bar.
OPTION-DOWN ARROW	Display the AutoComplete list.
CONTROL-F3	Define the name.

Data Formatting

Shortcut	Action
COMMAND-SHIFT-L	Display the Style dialog box.
COMMAND-1	Display the Format Cells dialog box.
CONTROL-SHIFT-~ (tilde)	Apply the General number format.
CONTROL-SHIFT-$ (dollar sign)	Apply the Currency format with two decimal places (negative numbers will appear in parentheses).
CONTROL-SHIFT-% (percent sign)	Apply the Percentage format without decimal places.
CONTROL-SHIFT-^ (caret)	Apply the Exponential number format with two decimal places.
CONTROL-SHIFT-# (pound sign)	Apply the Date format with the day, month, and year.
CONTROL-SHIFT-@ (at symbol)	Apply the Time format with the hour and minute; indicate A.M. or P.M.
CONTROL-SHIFT-! (exclamation mark)	Apply the Number format with two decimal places, the thousands separator, and the minus sign (–) for negative values.

Shortcut	Action
COMMAND-OPTION-0 (zero) or COMMAND-OPTION-RIGHT ARROW, LEFT ARROW, UP ARROW, or DOWN ARROW	Apply an outline border.
COMMAND-OPTION- - (hyphen) or COMMAND-OPTION-RIGHT ARROW, LEFT ARROW, UP ARROW, or DOWN ARROW	Remove outline borders.
COMMAND-B	Apply or remove bold text formatting.
COMMAND-I	Apply or remove italic text formatting.
COMMAND-U	Apply or remove underlining.
COMMAND-SHIFT-_ (underline)	Apply or remove strikethrough formatting.
CONTROL-9	Hide rows.
CONTROL-SHIFT-((opening parenthesis)	Unhide rows.
CONTROL-0 (zero)	Hide columns.
CONTROL-SHIFT-) (closing parenthesis)	Unhide columns.
COMMAND-SHIFT-W	Add or remove shadow on text.
COMMAND-SHIFT-D	Add or remove outline on text.

Navigating in Worksheets and Workbooks

Shortcut	Action
Arrow keys	Move one cell up, down, left, or right.
CONTROL- arrow key	Move to the end of the current data region.
HOME	Move to the beginning of the row.
CONTROL-HOME	Move to the beginning of the worksheet.
CONTROL-END (not available on original USB keyboards that shipped with iMac, G3, and G4)	Move to the last cell on a worksheet, which is the cell at the intersection of the rightmost used column and the bottommost used row (in the lower-right corner), or the cell opposite the home cell, typically A1.

Shortcut	Action
PAGE DOWN	Move down one screen.
PAGE UP	Move up one screen.
OPTION-PAGE DOWN	Move one screen to the right.
OPTION-PAGE UP	Move one screen to the left.
CONTROL-PAGE DOWN	Move to the next sheet in the workbook.
CONTROL-PAGE UP	Move to the previous sheet in the workbook.
CONTROL-TAB	Move to the next workbook or window.
CONTROL-SHIFT-TAB	Move to the previous workbook or window.
F6	Move to the next pane in a workbook that has been split.
SHIFT-F6	Move to the previous pane in a workbook that has been split.
CONTROL-DELETE	Scroll to display the active cell.
CONTROL-G	Display the Go To dialog box.
COMMAND-F	Display the Find dialog box.
COMMAND-G	Repeat the last Find action (same as Find Next).
TAB	Move between unlocked cells on a protected worksheet.

Data Outlining Keys

Shortcut	Action
CONTROL-8	Display or hide outline symbols.
CONTROL-9	Hide the selected rows.
CONTROL-SHIFT-((opening parenthesis)	Unhide the selected rows.
CONTROL-0 (zero)	Hide the selected columns.
CONTROL-SHIFT-) (closing parenthesis)	Unhide the selected columns.

Working in Print Preview

Shortcut	Action
Arrow keys	Move around a page when zoomed in.
PAGE UP or PAGE DOWN	Move by one page when zoomed out.
CONTROL-UP ARROW or CONTROL-LEFT ARROW	Move to the first page when zoomed out.
CONTROL-DOWN ARROW or CONTROL-RIGHT ARROW	Move to the last page when zoomed out.

Selecting Cells with Special Characteristics

Shortcut	Action
CONTROL-SHIFT-* (asterisk)	Select the current region around the active cell (the current region is an area enclosed by blank rows and blank columns).
CONTROL-/ (forward slash)	Select the current array, which is the array that the active cell belongs to.
COMMAND-SHIFT-O (the letter O)	Select all cells with comments.
CONTROL-\ (backslash)	Select cells in a row that do not match the value in the active cell in that row (the row starting with the active cell must be selected).
CONTROL-SHIFT-| (pipe symbol)	Select cells in a column that do not match the value in the active cell in that column (the column starting with the active cell must be selected).
CONTROL-[	Select only cells directly referred to by formulas in the selection.
CONTROL-SHIFT-{	Select all cells directly or indirectly referred to by formulas in the selection.
CONTROL-]	Select only cells with formulas that refer directly to the active cell.
CONTROL-SHIFT-}	Select all cells with formulas that refer directly or indirectly to the active cell.

Shortcut	Action
COMMAND-SHIFT-Z	Select only visible cells in the current selection.

Selecting Cells, Columns, or Rows

Shortcut	Action
CONTROL-SHIFT-* (asterisk)	Select the current region around the active cell (the area enclosed by blank rows and blank columns).
SHIFT- arrow key	Extend the selection by one cell.
CONTROL-SHIFT- arrow key	Extend the selection to the last nonblank cell in the same column or row as the active cell.
SHIFT-HOME	Extend the selection to the beginning of the row.
CONTROL-SHIFT-HOME	Extend the selection to the beginning of the worksheet.
CONTROL-SHIFT-END (not available on original USB keyboards that shipped with iMac, G3, and G4)	Extend the selection to the last cell used on worksheet (at the lower-right corner).
CONTROL-SPACEBAR	Select the entire column.
SHIFT-SPACEBAR	Select the entire row.
COMMAND-A	Select the entire worksheet.
SHIFT-DELETE	Select only the active cell when multiple cells are selected.
SHIFT-PAGE DOWN	Extend the selection down one screen.
SHIFT-PAGE UP	Extend the selection up one screen.
CONTROL-SHIFT-SPACEBAR	When an object is selected, select all objects on a sheet.
CONTROL-6	Switch among hiding objects, displaying objects, and displaying placeholders for objects.
CONTROL-7	Show or hide the Standard toolbar.
F8	Turn on selection extension using the arrow keys.

ORGANIZING YOUR DATA
WITH EXCEL 2001

Shortcut	Action
SHIFT-F8	Add another range of cells to the selection. Or use the arrow keys to move to the start of the range you want to add; and then press F8 and the arrow keys to select the next range (whew!).

Using Excel's Toolbars

Shortcut	Action
OPTION-F10	Make the toolbar active.
TAB or SHIFT-TAB (when a toolbar is active)	Select the next or previous button or menu on the toolbar.
CONTROL-TAB or CONTROL-SHIFT-TAB (when a toolbar is active)	Select the next or previous toolbar.
RETURN	Perform the action assigned to the selected button.

Using Document Windows

Shortcut	Action
COMMAND-TAB	Switch to the next program.
COMMAND-SHIFT-TAB	Switch to the previous program.
COMMAND-W	Close the active workbook window.
COMMAND-F5	Restore the active workbook window size.
F6	Move to the next pane in a workbook that has been split.
SHIFT-F6	Move to the previous pane in a workbook that has been split.
COMMAND-F6	Switch to the next workbook window.
COMMAND-SHIFT-F6	Switch to the previous workbook window.
CONTROL-F5	Restore the window size.
CONTROL-F10	Maximize or restore the workbook window.

Shortcut	Action
COMMAND-CONTROL-SHIFT-3	Copy the screen image to the Clipboard.
COMMAND-CONTROL-SHIFT-CAPS LOCK	Copy the image of the active window to the Clipboard. (After pressing and releasing the key combination, click the window you want as picture.)

Using Dialog Boxes

Shortcut	Action
TAB	Move to the next text box.
SHIFT-TAB	Move to the previous text box.
CONTROL-TAB or CONTROL-PAGE DOWN	Switch to the next tab in the dialog box.
CONTROL-SHIFT-TAB or CONTROL-PAGE UP	Switch to the previous tab in the dialog box.
RETURN	Perform the action assigned to the default command button in the dialog box (the button with the bold outline—often the OK button).
ESC	Cancel the command and close the dialog box.

Working with Data Forms

Shortcut	Action
DOWN ARROW	Move to the same field in the next record.
UP ARROW	Move to the same field in the previous record.
TAB	Move to the next field you can edit in the record.
SHIFT-TAB	Move to the previous field you can edit in the record.
RETURN	Move to the first field in the next record.
SHIFT-RETURN	Move to the first field in the previous record.
PAGE DOWN	Move to the same field 10 records forward.
CONTROL-PAGE DOWN	Move to a record.

Shortcut	Action
PAGE UP	Move to the same field 10 records back.
CONTROL-PAGE UP	Move to the first record.
HOME or END (END key not available on original USB keyboards that shipped with iMac, G3, and G4)	Move to the beginning or end of the field.
SHIFT-END (not available on original USB keyboards that shipped with iMac, G3, and G4)	Extend the selection to the end of the field.
SHIFT-HOME	Extend the selection to the beginning of the field.
LEFT ARROW or RIGHT ARROW	Move one character left or right within the field.
SHIFT-LEFT ARROW	Select the character to the left.
SHIFT-RIGHT ARROW	Select the character to the right.

Using AutoFilter

Shortcut	Action
Select the cell that contains the column label and then press OPTION-DOWN ARROW	Display the AutoFilter list for the current column.
DOWN ARROW	Select the next item in the AutoFilter list.
UP ARROW	Select the previous item in the AutoFilter list.
HOME	Select the first item (Sort Ascending) in the AutoFilter list.
END (not available in original USB keyboards that shipped with iMac, G3, and G4)	Select the last item in the AutoFilter list.
RETURN	Filter the list by using the selected item in the AutoFilter list.

Summary

This chapter discussed the kinds of projects you can create in Excel to help you keep tabs of personal and business information. You also discovered ways to configure Excel to work best in your particular work setting.

In the next chapter, you'll begin to discover some of the more sophisticated features of Excel, starting with the List Manager, which you can use to analyze, search, and sort your spreadsheet data.

Chapter 17

Using Excel 2001's Advanced Features

In the previous chapter, you discovered how to set up Microsoft Excel to do your bidding. From setting preferences to menu bar displays and keyboard shortcuts, you got a glimpse of how easily you can customize the program to look and run as you like. You also got your first taste of making a spreadsheet.

In this chapter, you move deeper into Excel's sophisticated feature set. You'll learn how to extend the kinds of information you put in your worksheets and evaluate that data, and also learn how to harness the power of Excel's new List Manager. We'll also cover printing your finished workbook, and you'll see that doing so isn't quite as simple as with other Mac programs; it takes a little preparation.

Using Lists in Worksheets

All right; so what is an Excel list?

Basically, it's a group of rows in a worksheet that include data that's related. Examples include the list of your contacts or the sales information needed to create invoices. Lists in Excel serve the function of a database. Each row is a record, or a single group of data, and each column represents a field for such information as the name, address, or billing status of a client.

Excel 2001 also provides another way to handle a list, by using a feature called the List Wizard, which works with the List Manager. The List Manager simplifies the work of setting up and managing lists.

Getting Ready to Set Up a List

Before we discuss just how you set up a list in Excel, let's look at some guidelines for this feature. By following these guidelines, you'll avoid troubles later.

- **Use Only One List per Worksheet**   Each worksheet can support only a single list, unless you're using the List Manager. One reason is that filtering and other features for managing your list work on only a single list at a time.

- **Put Related Items In the Same Column**   You'll want to make sure that any items that are essentially the same or similar are always in the same column. You would not, for example, want to have some rows with the postal address in the second column and others with the e-mail address in that same column. Excel won't be able to handle this mixed information.

- **Separate the List from the Rest of the Worksheet**   If you are including other data on your worksheet besides the list, leave a blank row and a blank column between the list and the other information. This makes it easier for Excel to separate the list from the data, particularly if you're going to run sort or filter or automatic summing operations on the data.

■ **Place Important Data Above or Below the List**   Excel requires that you put critical data above or below the list, not to either side of it. The reason is that the data might be hidden when the list is filtered.

■ **Keep Rows and Columns Visible**   Don't hide columns or rows in your list. If you make them hidden, you could, by mistake, delete some data.

■ **Format Column Labels Clearly**   When you create labels for the columns in your worksheet, put them in the first row. Excel will use that information to locate and organize data and create reports. The column labels can be formatted in a variety of ways, by changing font, text alignment, pattern, border, or capitalization style. Differentiating them in these ways makes them stand out from the rest of the data, so they are easy to see at first glance.

■ **Formatting Don'ts**   Don't use blank rows and columns for formatting, because these make it more difficult for Excel to detect and select the proper formats. You should also avoid adding extra spaces for indents; use regular formatting commands instead.

■ **About Extended Formats**   When the automatic formatting function is set in the Preferences dialog box, via the Edit tab, the data you add at the end of a list will match the preceding rows, and formulas will be copied. If you prefer to format manually, though this can add to the complexity of your task, you can turn off this option.

Overview of List Sorting

In the normal scheme of things, the data in your worksheet is sorted in the form in which you type it. But you may sometimes want to change the sort order to provide a better view of specific information, such as to see how sales projections are faring or how each member of your staff has performed.

You can sort data in ascending order by letter or number, or in descending order, if you prefer. Additionally, you can sort on the basis of multiple columns. This means, for example, that a sales report could be sorted first by city or state, and then by the sales staff within that state or the branch office, whatever applies.

You can also create custom sorting schemes, such as sorting months and days according to their calendar order rather than alphabetical order.

Sorting Data in Ascending or Descending Order

To sort your data based on the data in a single column, follow these steps:

1. Click and select the column by which you want to sort.

2. Click the Sort Ascending or Sort Descending button on the Standard toolbar.

Sorting Data Using Two or More Column Labels

If you want to sort the column labels on the basis of two or more columns, do this:

1. Click the cells in your worksheet list that you want to sort.

2. Choose Sort from the Data menu. The Sort dialog box appears.

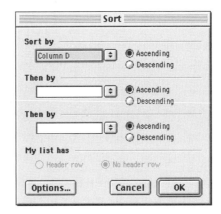

3. From the Sort By and Then By pop-up menus, choose the columns you want to sort.

NOTE   *If you want to sort your worksheet by more than three columns, it's a good idea to sort by the columns that are of lesser importance first and then perform a second sort. An employee spreadsheet, for example, might be sorted by the department in the company, then by title, then by last name, and then by first time. First click the Data menu and select Sort. Then select the column that contains the employee's first name in the first pop-up menu, and select the employee's last name in the next pop-up menu. You'll then want to sort by first name using the Sort By pop-up menu. Then sort by department using the Sort By pop-up menu, and then by title, using the Then By pop-up menu. In other words, you are doing your sort operation in reverse, with the most important sort sequence coming last.*

4. Repeat steps 2 and 3 for each successive sort operation.

Sorting Data by Custom Lists and Other Criteria

Another way to sort your data is by day, date, or a custom list that you've created using Excel's Preferences dialog, on the Custom Lists tab.

Here's how it's done:

1. With your worksheet open, select the range of cells or columns in the list that you are going to sort.

2. Choose Sort from the Data menu.

3. Click the Options button and display the Custom Sort Order pop-up menu.

4. Choose the custom sort order you want from the pop-up menu. You can choose from Normal to any of the sort items that are part of your custom list.

5. Click OK.

NOTE *Only the column specified in the Sort By box will be sorted on the basis of the values present in the column on which you're basing the sort. If you want to sort additional columns, perform each operation separately. Sorting should be done on the least important sort sequence first and the most important sort sequence last.*

Diagnosing Data Sorting Problems

As you can see, creating lists and sorting data entails a lot of choices, and sometimes the information you want will not be displayed in the form you need. In this section, you'll learn some things to check to get a handle on such problems.

- **What's the Default Sort Order?** In sorting the data in your worksheet, Excel has to follow the rules you set. Normally, you'll have Excel sort by numeric or alphabetical order. If you want to sort days and months in chronological order, you need to create a custom sort to address those issues. This can be done using the Custom Lists tab in Excel's Preferences dialog box (settings for days and months are already present).

- **Is Mixed Data Formatted as Text?** If your cells contain both letters and numbers, such as 800a, 800, and so on, you will need to format the entire entry as text. Otherwise, the numbers will be sorted first, and then the numbers with the text. You can set the formatting using Excel's Formatting Palette. Just click Text on the Format pop-up menu, enter the value of the cell by double-clicking the cell, and press the ENTER key.

TIP *Before you enter data from here on, you'll want to format the cell as text before you begin typing the entry.*

- **Format Dates and Times Correctly** In the normal course of events, Excel will handle dates and times as numbers. If Excel recognizes the entry as a date or time, it will use the appropriate format. If Excel doesn't recognize the date or time format, the entry will be formatted as text instead. To make sure date or time formatting is set correctly, choose Cells from the Format menu. Click the Number tab and see how the cell is formatted. If the tab says Text, choose Date or Time, as needed, and click OK. You can now retype the value in the correct format.

- **Don't Hide Columns and Rows to Be Sorted** Excel cannot sort hidden columns when columns are sorted, nor rows when rows are sorted. It will, however, sort hidden columns when rows are sorted, and vice versa. Make sure that you use the Unhide feature in the Format menu to make the cells visible before you sort.

About Excel's List Manager

One of the handy new features of Excel 2001 is the List Manager. This feature enables you to search, analyze, and sort your data in the most efficient way. With the List Wizard, the List Manager can help you analyze the data based on the criteria you set.

What's a List Manager?

The items the List Manager maintains consist of databases of rows and columns in your worksheet. The rows are used as records, and the columns as fields, just as you'd find in a database program, such as FileMaker Pro.

Using the List Manager, you can create a list using data from your Excel worksheet or from data imported using the Microsoft Query utility that comes with Office 2001.

Features of List Manager Lists

Here are some elements of List Managers that help you get a better handle on your data:

- **List Frame**   This feature is used to outline your data. The information inside the frame is part of the list, and the information outside isn't.

- **Row Selector**   This is a feature found in the List toolbar.

- **Separate Column Headings**   Column headings not part of the list are displayed, so your headings aren't sorted by mistake.

- **New Record Row Placed at Bottom of List**   Each new record is placed at the bottom of the list, making it easier to add data to your row. All you need to do is click the new row and type away.

- **More Than One List Allowed in a Worksheet**   Unlike when you handle lists in the standard way, the List Manager lets you create more than one list in a single worksheet, or even a worksheet that contains nothing but a list.

- **Database Functions**   You can use a list as a quasi-database (or a real database for that matter), handling such functions as searching, sorting, and filtering. The List toolbar, created when you run List Manager, lets you locate specific records using the row finder. Lists can be sorted in the standard ascending or descending order, or you can create custom sort orders, as with a regular list.

- **List Names**   When you create a list using List Manager, you can name it any way you want. You can use the name to identify a range of cells or a specific function, formula, macro, or PivotTable.

- **Data Integrity Features**   One of the most important aspects of handling databases is maintaining data integrity. With the List Manager, you can add data validation functionality, such as allowing only 10-digit numbers for a telephone number. Also, if you choose to prohibit duplicate values in your list, you might, for example, prevent the addition of a row with a duplicate social security number.

- **List Object Formatting**   The cells in your list can be formatted exactly as you format the cells in a worksheet. You can add conditional formatting to a list, for example, to make data that meets a certain criterion (such as a city or area code) appear in bold, so it stands out from the pack.

List Manager Guidelines

A little later in this chapter, you'll go through the steps of using the List Manager, but we have to get through some more preliminaries first. Here is how to get the most value from the List Manager:

- **Organizing Lists**   Try setting up only one list in a worksheet. If you want to put more than a single list in the worksheet, position them so you don't hide data from one list while you filter another.

- **Advice for Larger Lists**   If you're going to create a list with more than 50 rows, set up a list sheet for best organization.

- **Don't Put Critical Data to the Left or Right of a List**   If you want to make sure data isn't hidden when you filter a list, put critical data above or below it.

- **Keep Rows and Columns Visible**   Before modifying a list, make hidden rows and columns visible. If they're not showing, you might delete important data by mistake.

- **Avoid Leading or Trailing Spaces**   Don't use extra spaces at the beginning or end of a cell to indent the text. This can throw off sorting and searching capabilities. Instead, indent the text within the cell.

Using the List Manager

All right; we've finished the preliminaries. Now it's time to get down to the actual process of using the List Wizard to set up a List Manager list.

In this section, we'll cover the basic setup process, and then you'll learn how to apply variations of the basic list.

To use the List Wizard, follow these steps:

1. Choose List from the Insert menu. This will bring up Excel's List Wizard (shown in Figure 17-1).

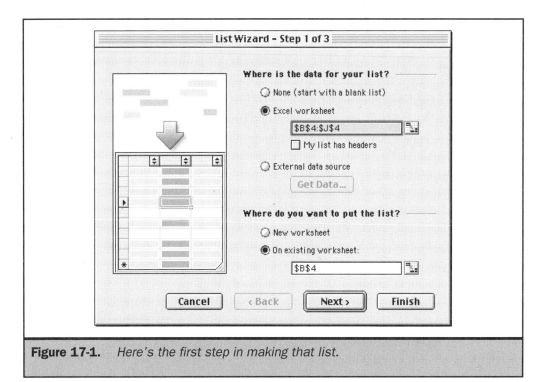

Figure 17-1.   *Here's the first step in making that list.*

2. In the Where Is the Data for Your List? section, you have three categories from which to choose. Click the one that applies to your worksheet:

- **None**   You can use this option to start with a blank list.

- **Excel Worksheet**   The selected area is displayed.

- **External Data Source**   Click the Get Data button to invoke Microsoft Query to manage your external data.

> NOTE   *Microsoft Query isn't a part of the standard Office 2001 installation. To add this utility, you have to use the Value Pack installer on the original CD. Read Chapter 2 to check into installation options.*

3. In the Where Do You Want to Put the List? section, specify whether you want the list placed on a new worksheet or on an existing worksheet.

4. Click Next to proceed to Step 2, which is shown in Figure 17-2.

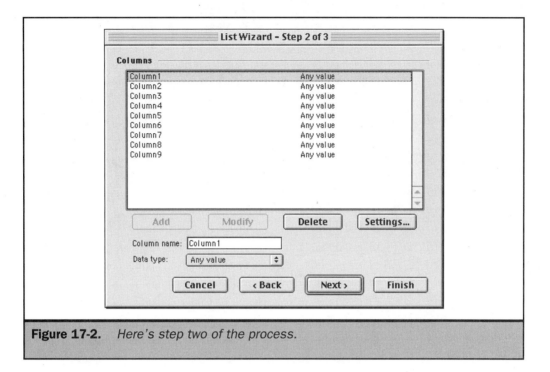

Figure 17-2.   *Here's step two of the process.*

5. Here you can apply a name and data value to the selected column. You can include the name, numbers, currency, or date, for example.

If you have headers in your list, you can select the option to use them in the first step of the List Wizard dialog box.

6. If you want to further customize the columns, select the column and then click the Settings button, which brings up the Column Settings dialog box shown in Figure 17-3. The choices are as follows:

   ■ **Column Name**   Enter a descriptive name for the selected column.

   ■ **Data Type**   Select the kind of data in the column from the scrolling list.

   ■ **Formatting**   Click Formatting to display the Format Cells dialog box (see Figure 17-4), and you'll be able adjust five sets of properties for the cell. The Number tab shows category formats. The Alignment tab sets horizontal and vertical alignment, indents, text wrapping, scaling, and orientation. Click the Font tab to adjust various font-related properties. You'll be able to pick from a number of border styles from the Border tab, and cell shades from the Patterns tab. The Protection tab addresses hidden and locking cells.

Column Settings

Column name:

Column8

Data type:

Any value
Whole number
Decimal
Currency
Counter
Text
List
Date
Time
Calculated Column

Formatting

[Formatting...]

[Conditional Formatting...]

Formula:

☐ Default value:

☐ Unique values only

[Validation...]   [Cancel] [OK]

Figure 17-3. *Customize the column from this dialog box.*

- **Conditional Formatting** Click this option to display a dialog box where you can specify how cell or formula values are handled. This subject is discussed in more detail in Chapter 18. Briefly, if the contents of a cell meet the specified condition, the specified formatting goes into effect when you click the Format button.

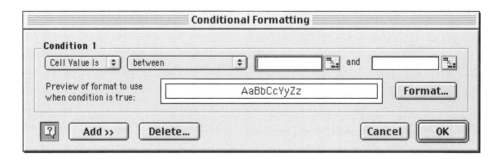

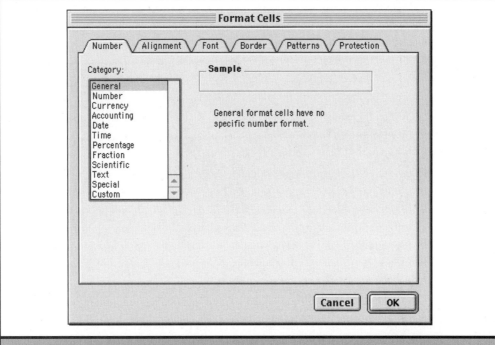

Figure 17-4.   *This dialog box lets you set a number of properties for a selected column label.*

- **Formula (or Source)**   This is one of those context-sensitive features. You enter the range of cells or the formula used for your list, based on the selected cells.

- **Default Value**   This option lists the default value for the selected column.

- **Unique Values Only**   Use this option to allow only unique values in a column to ensure, for example, that a name is not duplicated.

- **Validation**   Select this option to specify what data is valid for a specific cell or range of cells.

7. In the dialog box, enter the name for the column and select the data type from the list; then complete the settings.

8. Click OK to move to the third and final step (see Figure 17-5). Here you will specify whether the AutoFormat option will apply, and how column headers, totals, and list visual displays are handled.

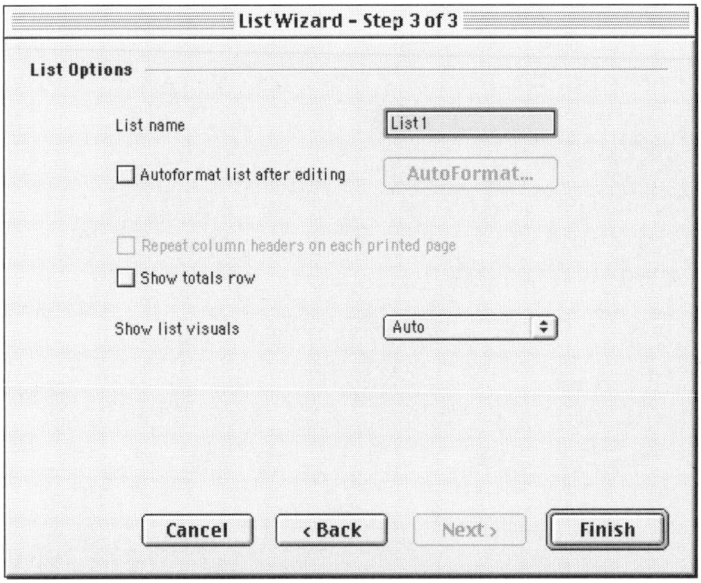

List Wizard – Step 3 of 3

List Options

List name   [List1]

☐ Autoformat list after editing   [AutoFormat...]

☐ Repeat column headers on each printed page
☐ Show totals row

Show list visuals   [Auto ▴▾]

[Cancel]   [‹ Back]   [Next ›]   [**Finish**]

Figure 17-5. *This is the final step in the List Wizard setup process.*

9. When you're done, click Finish to complete the List Manager setup process. You'll see the List Wizard toolbar. This toolbar includes the following buttons:

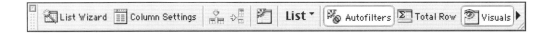

- **List Wizard**   Activate the List Wizard to edit a list you've created or to create another list.
- **Column Settings**   Click this button to bring up the Column Settings dialog box, described earlier.
- **Insert Column**   Add a column to the left of the one you've selected.
- **Insert Row**   Add a column above the one you've selected.
- **AutoFormat**   Bring up the standard array of cell formatting options.
- **List**   Use the pop-up menu to invoke the List Manager, courtesy of the List Wizard, and handle other formatting chores for your list.

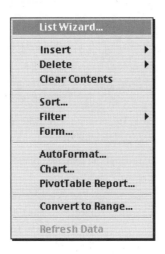

- **AutoFilter**   This feature lets you hide selected parts of your list, so only the data you want to display appears.

- **Total Row**   Click this button to insert a row at the bottom of your list to display totals.

- **Visuals**   Use this button to change the look of your list, to enhance the display of the information.

- **Right Arrow**   The rest of the toolbar is used for row navigation and to add new rows, as needed.

Using PivotTable Reports

If you have a huge amount of data in your worksheet to analyze, you might just want to try a PivotTable report. This is an interactive table that lets you summarize data easily. The features of the PivotTable report allow you to rotate rows and columns to produce various summaries of your data and display different pages or details that apply to your needs.

Why use a PivotTable report? Say you want to compare totals that relate to each other, perhaps related to the sales for your company or the units sold in a particular year. Maybe you want Excel to handle the sort, subtotals, and totals for you in a single, simple operation.

Creating a PivotTable Report

To create a PivotTable report, follow these steps:

1. Open the workbook that contains the data you want to use for the PivotTable report.

2. If the PivotTable report uses data from a database or Excel list, click a cell in the list or the database to get started.

3. Choose PivotTable Report from the Data menu, which will bring up the PivotTable Wizard, shown in Figure 17-6.

4. This is a three-step process. For Step 1, just select the location of your data by clicking the button. You can choose from an existing list or database, an external source of data, multiple consolidation ranges (separate groups of data or lists), or another PivotTable. Click next, which brings up Step 2.

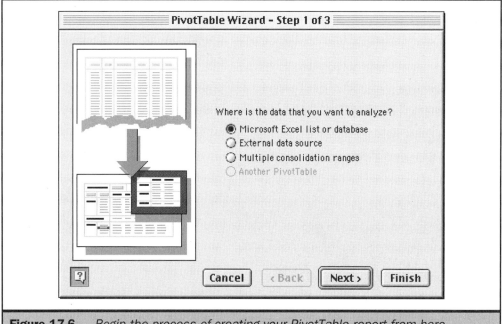

Figure 17-6. *Begin the process of creating your PivotTable report from here.*

5. Indicate the range of cells; the ones selected will appear by default.

6. Click Next to move to the final part of the process, or click Select and locate and open the file that contains the data.

7. Specify whether you want to open the data in a new worksheet or the existing one.

8. To change the layout of the PivotTable, click the Layout button. The dialog box shown in Figure 17-7 appears. As indicated in the dialog box, drag field buttons on the right to the diagram on the left to show how data is to be set up. Then click OK to continue. This takes you back to Step 3.

9. If you want to customize the data display still further, click the Options button to display the PivotTable Options dialog box shown in Figure 17-8. Specify your format and data options from this dialog box. You can have your PivotTable display grand totals for columns and rows, AutoFormat the table, merge labels, preserve formatting, and select page layout options. You can also specify how your data is handled; for example, whether the data will be included with the table layout. Click OK to finish setting up your options.

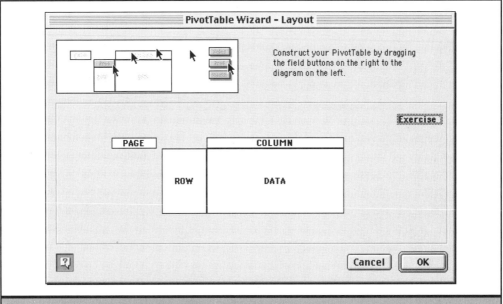

Figure 17-7. *Design your PivotTable from this dialog box.*

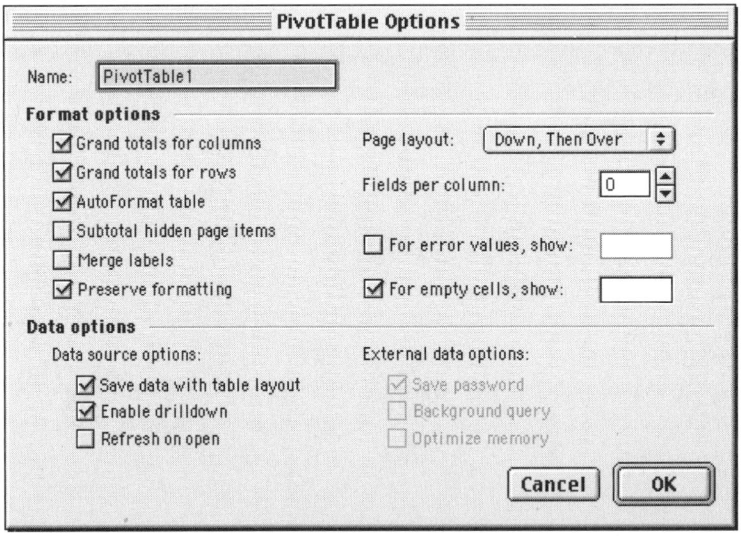

Figure 17-8. *This dialog box offers a variety of ways to configure the PivotTable.*

10. Click Finish to deliver your PivotTable. The following example shows the original data and the PivotTable.

	Source data				PivotTable report			
	A	B	C	D	E	F	G	H
1	Sport	Quarter	Sales					
2	Golf	Qtr3	$1,500					
3	Golf	Qtr4	$2,000		Sum of Sales	Quarter ▼		
4	Tennis	Qtr3	$600		Sport ▼	Qtr3	Qtr4	Grand Total
5	Tennis	Qtr4	$1,500		Golf	$7,930	$2,000	$9,930
6	Tennis	Qtr3	$4,070		Tennis	$4,670	$6,500	$11,170
7	Tennis	Qtr4	$5,000		Grand Total	$12,600	$8,500	$21,100
8	Golf	Qtr3	$6,430					

Using Excel on a Network

Microsoft Office applications are not designed just for the individual user. They are also designed to create documents that can be shared by a workgroup. The Track Changes feature of Word, for example, allows writers and editors and others to examine and keep tabs on the way a document evolves or is edited.

The workbooks you create in Excel are also available for sharing by other users on your network, to cite a frequent situation, so a number of users can manipulate and edit data or just view the information for different purposes.

Here are the ways that Excel lets you share and edit a workbook:

■ **Sharing Workbooks**   You can set up a workbook as shared. This allows users who access the file on a network or by individual distribution to access and enter data and change formatting, formulas, charts, and so on.

■ **Workbook Distribution Techniques**   Once a workbook has been designated as shared, you can make it available for access on a server or individual computer on your network. If you prefer not to share the workbook, or if you need to reach users not part of your network, you can distribute it using other methods, such as on disk or via e-mail.

■ **Merging Changes**   If those who are editing the workbook have separate copies, you can merge all the changes into a single workbook so the editing can be checked and, if appropriate, incorporated into the final version.

NOTE   *If your company is using Microsoft Exchange for its corporate messaging and collaboration system, you can't share the Excel workbook in your Outlook public folder.*

■ **Workbook Sharing Limits**   When you share a workbook on your network, up to 256 users can access the same workbook at the same time. In addition, you can track changes to see who made a change, what was changed, and when. The change history is normally set for 30 days, but it can be specified anyway

ORGANIZING YOUR DATA
WITH EXCEL 2001

you want. In addition, you can protect the workbook, so only those with the proper password and access privileges can gain access and make changes.

Simple Sharing of Your Excel Workbook

The easiest way to share a single workbook is to use Apple's personal file sharing to make it available from the hard drive of a specific user on the network. You can also place it on a shared volume of a network server that all users with access can open.

Here's how to share your workbook:

1. With your workbook open, choose Share Workbook from the Tools menu. This delivers the dialog box shown in Figure 17-9.

2. If you want to merge data from different copies of the workbook and allow simultaneous changes, click the check box. This display will list the users who have access rights.

3. To customize the way the shared workbook is handled, click the Advanced tab. This brings up the dialog box shown in Figure 17-10.

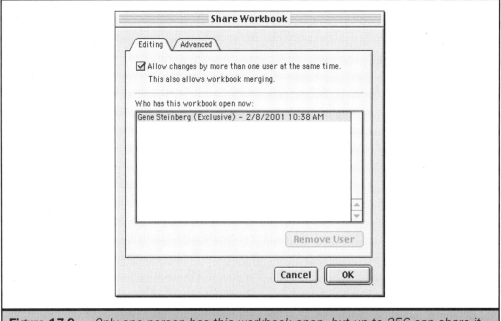

Figure 17-9.   *Only one person has this workbook open, but up to 256 can share it.*

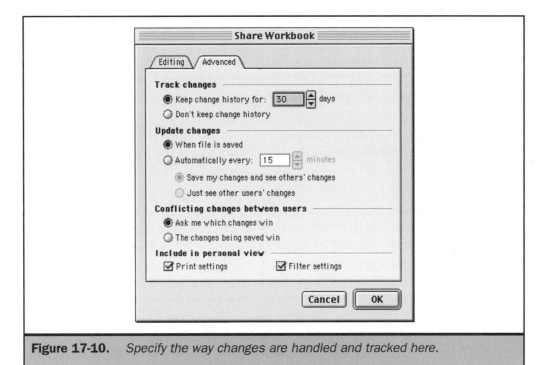

Figure 17-10.   *Specify the way changes are handled and tracked here.*

4. Click the buttons that specify the settings you want. The Advanced Share Workbook dialog box has these options:

■ **Track Changes**   Specify whether you want a change history kept. If you do, the default time period is 30 days, but you can select a different setting, depending on your needs.

■ **Update Changes**   When do you want to update the file with the list of changes? The default time is when the file is actually saved, but you can set Excel to update the file automatically after a given period of time (the default is every 15 minutes). If you choose that option, you can specify whether you want to see the changes of other users only or your changes as well.

■ **Conflicting Changes Between Users**   No fistfights necessary. You can specify whether you want to be asked which changes will "win," or be incorporated, or whether any changes actually saved are incorporated in your workbook.

■ **Include in Personal View** Both print and filter settings can be incorporated.

5. When the settings are complete, click OK to make the workbook shared.

Giving Access to a Shared Workbook

Once you've set up your workbook as shared, you can either distribute copies separately or make it available on the network.

Use the following steps to set up your Mac for file sharing, so others can connect and access the workbook:

1. If your Mac's control strip is available, click the sharing strip and select Turn File Sharing On. Alternatively, you can go to the Apple menu, choose Control Panels, and select File Sharing from the submenu. This brings up the File Sharing Control Panel (see Figure 17-11).

2. Click Start in the File Sharing Control Panel.

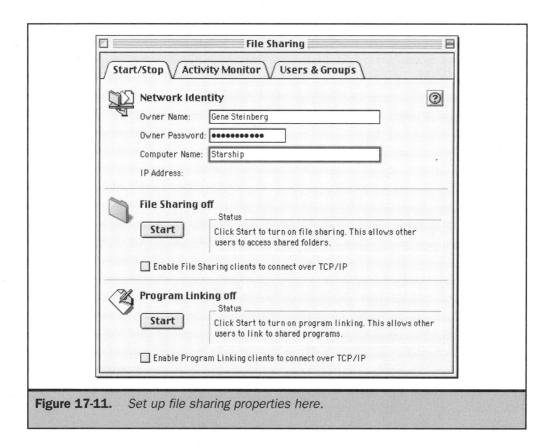

Figure 17-11. *Set up file sharing properties here.*

CAUTION

For file sharing to work, you must specify the Owner Name and Computer Name in the File Sharing Control Panel. It's up to you whether to specify a password, but if you need to limit outside access to your Mac, it's a good idea to specify a password that is a random mixture of numbers and uppercase and lowercase letters, to make it hard to guess. You will, however, want to make the password reasonably easy to recall, or just write it down and put the password in a safe place.

3. Close the File Sharing Control Panel by clicking the close box.

4. To customize the access to your Mac, click the Finder desktop.

5. Select the folder that contains the workbook you want to share.

6. From the File menu, choose Get Info and select Sharing from the submenu. The Office Mac Info dialog box opens (see Figure 17-12).

7. Select the check box labeled Share This Item and Its Contents.

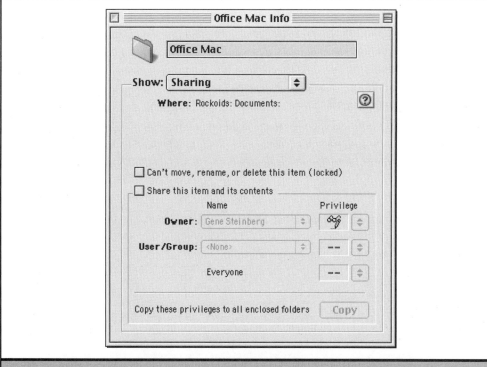

Figure 17-12.   *Adjust access to your shared file here.*

8. Click the pop-up menus to select the access privileges you want to grant.

9. Select any other options you want; then click the close box to finish the setup process.

Removing a User from a Shared Workbook

For whatever reason (I won't pry), you may want to revoke access to a workbook for one or more users. Perhaps the people have left the company or department or are no longer in the loop as far as this document is concerned.

To accomplish this task, follow these steps:

1. Open the shared workbook.

 If you remove a user who has shared a workbook, any unsaved changes made by that user will be lost, so make sure that the user's work is done before completing this process.

2. Choose Share Workbook from Excel's Tools menu.

3. Click the Editing tab.

4. In the Who Has This Workbook Open Now display, select the name of the user you want to remove.

5. Click Remove User.

Unsharing a Workbook

After your project is done, you may no longer want to share the workbook. If you change the workbook's status from shared, all users who have access to it will be disconnected, and the change history will be removed. In addition, you will no longer be able to merge changes from other copies.

Here's how to unshared a workbook:

1. With the workbook open, choose Share Workbook from the Tools menu.

 Confirm that the other users of your shared workbook know that it will no longer be shared and that they have saved their changes and closed the workbook before you proceed.

2. Select the Editing tab.

3. Uncheck the Allow Changes by More Than One User at the Same Time check box.

4. Click OK and then Yes to the warning about the effects on other users to complete the process.

Handling Shared Workbook Conflicts

When a number of workers are involved in editing a single document, there will be occasions where the suggested changes conflict. Perhaps data entered in the same cell will be different, and perhaps other changes, such as a label's name, will be different as well.

Fortunately, Excel offers tools to handle such conflicts, so hassles aren't necessary. Here are the things you can do to resolve conflicts (Excel doesn't handle shattered egos, however):

- **Choose the Changes You Want to Keep** The first thing you should do is make sure that you have selected the option labeled Ask Me Which Changes Win on the Advanced tab of the Share Workbook dialog box. This setting should be made either by you or the person who is managing the final resolution of conflicting changes.

- **Examine All Changes** You will need to be able to review all the changes that have been made and decide which to keep and which to discard.

- **Consult the Change History** The change history incorporated into your workbook allows you to see who changed what and when, to help ensure that the changes you accept are the ones you want.

Tracking Changes in Your Shared Workbook

A fast way to keep tabs on what's been changed is to use the option to track the changes that are made. Here's how:

1. With the workbook open, go to the Tools menu, choose Track Changes, and then select Highlight Changes from the submenu. This brings up the dialog box shown in Figure 17-13.

2. Select the check box labeled Track Changes While Editing.

NOTE *This option will automatically share your workbook without your needing to make a separate visit to the Share Workbook dialog box.*

3. In the When section, indicate when changes will be reflected. The default setting is All, but you can choose Since I Last Saved, Not Yet Reviewed, or Since Date from the pop-up menu.

4. Do not check anything in the Who or Where section.

5. Make sure the check box next to Highlight Changes on Screen is checked.

6. Make sure that List Changes on a New Sheet is selected.

7. Click OK to store your settings.

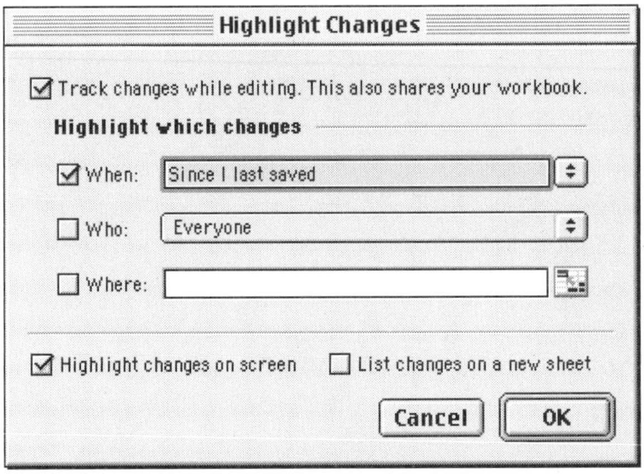

Figure 17-13. Set Excel's ability to track changes here.

You must save the shared workbook for the setups described previously to become available.

8. Look at the History worksheet that appears and examine what has been done to the open workbook.

Putting Limits on Shared Workbook Changes

When a number of workers are handling the same document and suggesting changes, things can get mighty confusing. You may, therefore, want to put limits on the changes that users can make. The result will be some peace of mind, less confusion, and, of course, more efficient handling of changes, because casual alterations won't occur.

Here's how to put limits on changes:

1. With the shared workbook open, go to the Tools menu, choose Protection, and select Protect Shared Workbook from the submenu.

2. If you want to protect the actual structure of your workbook, click the Structure check box. This way, users will not be able to move, delete, hide, unhide, or rename the workbook or add worksheets.

3. If you want to have the windows always open with the same size and position, select the Windows check box.

4. This next setting is a biggie. If you want to keep others from removing the protection elements you've added, enter a strong password (the way I've described it throughout this book) and click OK. In the password confirmation dialog box, retype the password exactly as you first typed it (don't worry; Excel will warn you if you make an error).

NOTE   *Don't forget to use a strong password: a random combination of uppercase and lowercase letters mixed with numbers. Be sure to write it down, because if you forget it, you won't be able to change protection features or access the protected items.*

Merging Changes

If you've distributed separate copies of your workbook rather than network a single copy, no doubt each copy will have a different set of user changes. Eventually, to finalize the document, you'll have to merge those changes. Here's how it's done:

1. Before you send copies of your workbook to other people, activate the Track Changes option for the workbook (on the Advanced tab of the Sharing dialog box), or at least make sure the other users activate it before changes are made.

2. Open the copy of the shared workbook you want to use to create the final or master version, the one that will contain all the merged changes.

NOTE   *The master copy can also contain changes, but the final process will resolve all the conflicts and make the changes necessary to produce a final workbook.*

3. Choose Merge Workbooks from the Tools menu. You may see a dialog box asking if you want to save changes; if so, be sure to click Yes.

4. In the Select File to Merge into Current Workbook dialog box that appears (see Figure 17-14), choose the copy of the shared workbook from which you want to merge changes.

5. Click OK.

6. Repeat steps 3 through 5 for each copy you want to merge. All the suggested changes will now appear in your copy of the workbook.

7. To actually make the changes, choose Track Changes from the Tools menu, and select Accept or Reject Changes from the submenu. Don't forget to click OK at the prompt to save changes to the workbook, if necessary.

8. Select the changes you want to review:

   ■ If you want to review changes made by a specific user, select the Who check box and then select the name of the user from the Who pop-up menu.

   ■ If you want to review changes made by all users at the same time, uncheck the Who check box or select Everyone from the pop-up menu.

   ■ If you want to review changes to the entire workbook rather than to an individual worksheet, make sure the Where check box isn't selected.

9. Accept the setup. Now you'll be able to review the details of the changes in the Accept or Reject Changes dialog box. Be sure to scroll through the dialog box to see the entire change.

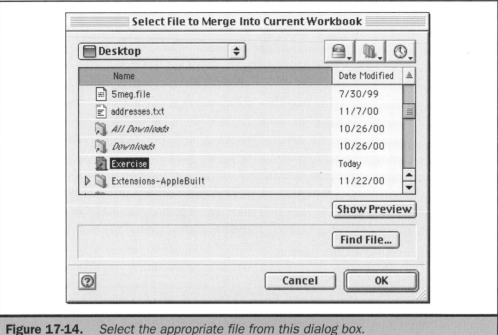

Figure 17-14. *Select the appropriate file from this dialog box.*

10. Click Accept to incorporate a change and Reject to discard it.

> NOTE *You may have to select a value for a cell. If you receive a prompt asking for a value, select the value before clicking Accept.*

11. For each change, repeat steps 9 and 10. You can, if you want, click the Accept All or Reject All buttons to make all the changes at once. Otherwise, you'll need to review each individual change and act upon it before proceeding to the next one.

> NOTE *If you make a mistake, you can consult the History worksheet and undo changes from the Action Type information column. Using this procedure, you can ensure that you have accepted or discarded the correct changes.*

Printing Worksheets in Excel

When you finish working on a document, or even while it's in progress, you are probably accustomed to choosing Print from the File menu (or pressing COMMAND-P) to invoke the Print dialog box and, perhaps, specifying a range of pages to be printed.

In Excel, printing doesn't quite work that way. One reason for this is that a typical worksheet may include separate pockets of data or may span a distance wider or longer than the page sizes your printer can handle. Thus, you have to do a little more work to print your worksheets properly.

In this section, you'll learn how best to set up your worksheet for printing.

■ **Worksheet Viewing Options**   In setting up your worksheet to work properly with your printer, you have three worksheet viewing options. The default is the Normal view. This shows you the raw worksheet, giving you the speediest display of your worksheet. The second option, Print Preview, available from the File menu (rather than the View menu), shows you how the page will look printed and lets you adjust columns and margins for the best possible look. The final viewing scheme, Page Break Preview, available from the View menu, shows you the data that will appear on a particular page and lets you adjust the page breaks and printing area.

NOTE   *With so many printers and printer driver choices available, I can't cover all the options. The best I can say is that you should be mindful of the limitations of your printer and try to tailor your worksheet's printing options to accommodate them.*

■ **Worksheet Formatting: Printing Versus Viewing**   There are a host of worksheet formatting options that you can use in Excel to make your worksheet look better. But it's a balancing act, because what looks good on the screen may not look so good on the printed page. Some of the considerations are fairly simple; for instance, you will need to consider how a worksheet that uses different colors for good screen display will appear when printed by a black-and-white laser printer, where all the intermediate colors appear as shades of gray.

■ **Printing Headers and Footers**   To easily identify the contents of your worksheet, no doubt you'll want to use headers and footers. As with the documents you create in Word, a header appears at the top of a page, and a footer appears at the bottom. But unlike with Word documents, the headers and footers of a worksheet are created in the page setup process rather than in the workbook itself.

■ **Repeating Titles**   In addition to having those running heads and footers, you may also want to have the same row and column labels repeat on each page, to make it easier to figure out which columns and rows stand for what. This setting is also made in the Page Setup box, under your sheet options.

■ **Print Orientation**   As with your other documents, you can print your worksheet in portrait or landscape format. If your document has a large number of columns and you want to get them all in without reducing the size of the printed page, you'll want to choose landscape format. If you have a large number of rows, you'll use portrait format. You can also adjust the layout of your worksheet to accommodate your needs.

- ■ **Fitting Your Printed Page** As mentioned at the start of this section, a worksheet may far exceed the dimensions of the largest paper size available on your printer, and in some cases, it may be smaller. Thus, you will want to adjust the data to fit the printed page. You can reduce or expand the page or adjust margins, adjust page numbering, and center data on the page.

NOTE *When you adjust the page setup for your worksheet, you are not changing the properties of the page itself. You are just configuring printer settings, which affect the printed page only, not what you see on the screen.*

- ■ **Printing Part of Your Worksheet** You can also set a page's print area, to select only part of the page for the printed version. You may find this useful, for example, on a multiyear spreadsheet where you want to confine your data to a single year or portion of that year.

Using Excel's Print Options

Now that you know the basics, let's look at the various print options available for your Excel worksheets and the full workbook. In the next section, you'll learn how to cope with printer-related or setup problems.

Printing All or Part of a Worksheet

Here's how to print all or part of your worksheet:

1. If you want to print just part of your worksheet, select the area you want to print, choose Print Area from the File menu and choose Select Area from the submenu. Select the rows and columns you want to print. Choose Print from the File menu.

TIP *You can change or remove the selected print area by choosing Clear Print Area from the Print Area submenu. Then you can select a new area.*

2. If you want to print only specific pages, choose the pages you want to print in the Print dialog box. Click the radio button that specifies whether you want to print the selected area, the active worksheets, or the entire workbook. Click the Print button and wait for your printer to do its job. Figure 17-15 shows the Print dialog box setup for an Epson inkjet printer.

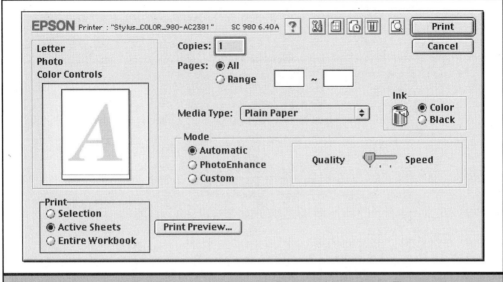

Figure 17-15.   *This Print dialog box is for an Epson inkjet printer. The one you see may differ quite a bit from this one.*

NOTE   *For standard laser printers, you'll need to choose Microsoft Excel from the pop-up menu labeled General to view the options for choosing what to print in your worksheet.*

Another Way to Print a Part of a Worksheet

Excel often offers several ways to do the same thing. In addition to the Print Area command, there are other ways to specify the parts of a worksheet you want to print. Here's another way to print part of a worksheet:

1. With your worksheet displayed, choose Page Break Preview from the View menu.

2. Select the area of your worksheet that you want to print.

3. Hold down the CONTROL key and click anywhere in that selected area to bring up the contextual menu.

ORGANIZING YOUR DATA
WITH EXCEL 2001

4. Choose Set Print Area from the contextual menu.

5. Choose the Print dialog box from the File menu and print your worksheet.

TIP   *Want to add extra cells to the printed document? No problem. For cells that are right next to the selected print area, drag the thick blue border to include those cells. If you want to add cells that aren't adjacent to the print area, select those cells and then CONTROL-click a cell in the newly selected area. Choose Add to Print Area in the contextual menu.*

Making the Worksheet Fit

As explained previously, an Excel worksheet may be a lot larger than the available print area of your printer, and in some cases, it will be smaller. Fortunately, you can easily set up things so that the document will fill the maximum available area of your printer (whatever that is).

To accomplish this task, follow these directions:

1. Click the tab for the worksheet that you want to print.

2. Select the area that you want to print.

3. Choose Page Setup from the File menu.

4. Select the Page tab (see Figure 17-16).

5. Under Orientation, choose the direction the page will print, either Portrait or Landscape.

6. Select Fit To.

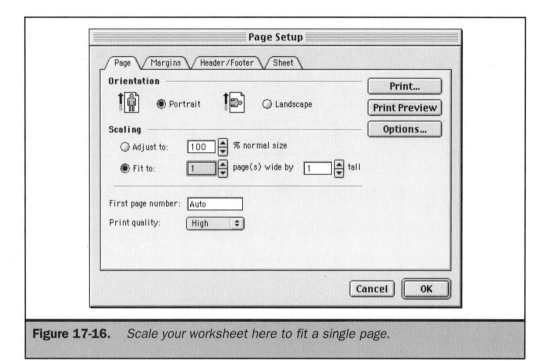

Figure 17-16.   *Scale your worksheet here to fit a single page.*

NOTE   *When you choose Fit To, Excel will ignore any manual page breaks you've made and will scale the selected areas as needed.*

7. In the box adjacent to Fit To, enter **1**, to adjust the size of the worksheet to a single page.

8. In the second box, delete the Tall number.

9. Click the Print button to print a single page based on the settings you specified. Excel will expand the printed area up to 100 percent or reduce it as necessary to fit the maximum available margins of the selected page size.

Getting a Handle on Print Problems with Excel

As you can see, setting up printing under Excel requires rather more attention to detail than with other programs. As a result, you may have some problems from time to time. Here is a list of common problems and their solutions.

ORGANIZING YOUR DATA
WITH EXCEL 2001

■ **Nothing Happens When You Print**   The first thing to do is to go back to the basics. Open the Chooser and make sure the right printer is selected (Excel won't display a Page Setup dialog box if no printer is selected). If there are special setup options for your particular printer, make sure they are selected in the Chooser setup. The second thing to do is to access Page Setup from Excel's File menu and make sure that the proper page size is selected for the workbook you want to print. If you tend to switch often from one paper size to another or to a different paper tray (on printers that offer extra trays), it's easy to forget to switch back. Alas, printers aren't equipped to sort that out for you, except, perhaps, to return to a default setup.

■ **Only a Portion of a Worksheet Prints**   Did you specify a print area for that worksheet? If so, then only that specific defined area will print; Excel is very rigid about that. To see just what might have happened, choose Page Break Preview from the View menu. Look for the area of the worksheet with a blue boarder; that's what's configured to be printed. Should you prefer to print the entire worksheet, you need to clear the print area first. This is done simply by going to the File menu, choosing Print Area, and Selecting Clear Print Area from the submenu. Otherwise, choose Page Break Preview from the View menu and redefine the print area of your worksheet.

■ **Multiple Print Areas Don't Appear on the Same Page**   The normal way of handling worksheets is for Excel to print each selected area on a separate page, if they're not adjacent to each other. There are ways around this, though. One is to hide the columns that separate the areas. You do this by choosing Column from the Format menu and selecting Hide from the submenu. Another way is to hide the rows, if that applies, by choosing Row from the Format menu and selecting Hide from the submenu. Either action (or both if need be) will allow nonadjacent areas of your worksheet to print on the same page, and being on the same page is a great way to get along (that's a bad joke).

■ **Printed Header or Footer Doesn't Look Right**   Excel offers several header and footer formatting options. Select the Header and Footer command on the View menu to see the options and pick a format you like, but there are some things you cannot do. One is to apply colors to the text; headers and footers must be in black and white. If the headers and footers are set up right, make sure the distance from the page margins is sufficient to allow them to print (the margins you need vary from printer to printer). The Margins button, in the Print Preview dialog box, available from the File menu, can be used to make these settings. One more thing: If you'd like to use graphics or linked information at the top of a page, such as a company logo and address, you need to use print titles rather than a header. You can do this in the Page Setup box (available from the File menu) when you click the Sheet tab. Enter the rows that include the logo and address in the Rows to Repeat at Top box.

■ **My Worksheet Must Stay on One Page**   Assuming that reducing your worksheet to one page won't make it too small to read, this is easily done. What you need to do is to reduce the worksheet to a single page. Choose Page Setup from the File menu. Select the Page tab and then click the Fit To button and enter the number **1** in the Page(s) Wide By box or Pages Tall box. Be sure to specify the proper print orientation (portrait or landscape) in the dialog box. Now when you print your worksheet, it'll be sized to fit on a single page.

■ **Where Are My Print Titles?**   Are they missing on some of your printed pages? Excel can print repeated column and row labels only on the pages that include those columns and rows. If you want Excel to print the information on other pages, you'll need to copy the labels to those columns and rows. To do that, first select and copy the column or row labels you want to repeat; then paste them into the additional columns or rows where you want them to print. Then choose Page Setup from the File menu and click the Sheet tab. At the left, select Columns to Repeat, or Rows to Repeat, as needed, and repeat the data that contains the row or column labels.

■ **Where's My Worksheet Background?**   You've gone to the trouble to pick a fancy background pattern for your worksheet, but it doesn't print. Why? Well, if you added the background pattern using the Background command, on the Sheet submenu of the Format menu, forget about it. This feature isn't supported. Instead, you have to add an actual background graphic to the cells. Otherwise, consider using the shading feature to apply an effect that you like.

■ **Why Does Excel Ignore My Page Breaks?**   It doesn't have a grudge against you. More than likely, you've told Excel to reduce the size of a printed worksheet to fit on a single page. Select the Page Setup command from the File menu, select the Page tab, and see if the Fit To option under Scaling is selected. If it is, choose the Adjust To option instead. Now you can split your worksheet into the number of pages you want. Another way to handle this problem is to set a separate page area on each page and select it as a separate range. Excel prints pages that aren't adjacent to each other as totally separate pages.

■ **Columns and Rows Are on the Wrong Page**   To solve this problem, recheck your settings for column widths, row heights, page breaks, and page margins to see if something has gone awry. A page margin that's too large, for example, may force data to appear on another page. You can reduce the page margin in the Page Setup dialog box, chosen from the File menu, by selecting the Margins tab. But be mindful of the limitations of your printer. You'll also want to check Page Break Preview in the View menu for proper page breaks. If page breaks are correct, you may want to scale the worksheet to fit one page; use the Page tab of the Page Setup dialog box. This option will reduce the print size, but it may meet your needs.

NOTE
To get the largest possible printed image, adjust orientation; switch to landscape format to accommodate wider columns on a page or portrait format to make longer worksheets fit better.

Excel Macros Briefly Described

Just like Word 2001, Excel has a macro feature that allows you to record and playback complex steps, even with a single keystroke. As a result, you can simplify creation of very sophisticated workbooks. As you see from the chapters covering Excel, many of the steps involved in performing important functions in the program can get mighty complex.

Before you examine the macro feature further, (it's available in the Tools menu), you'll want to read Chapter 15. The way macros are created in Word is essentially the same as the way they are done in Excel. The only difference of note is that Excel doesn't come with a prebuilt collection of macros. You have to create your own, but once you get used to recording your actions, you'll find that you can get through the task with reasonable speed and be assured of good results most every time.

Summary

From the powerful List Manager to Excel's flexible printing features, Excel offers tremendous power. And the features are accessible; they're not as hard to use as you might expect.

The next chapter will take you to the next level of Excel advanced spreadsheet capabilities. You'll learn how to do the hard stuff, using the powerful Formula Palette and the new Calculator, both of which greatly ease the burden of setting up complex calculations to get the data you want.

Chapter 18

Advanced Spreadsheet Techniques

A
lthough most people probably use Excel just to create and edit simple spreadsheets and may prefer not get into the intricacies of Excel, the program can also be used to create complex mathematical formulas and thus greatly extend your ability to build complex workbooks.

New for Excel 2001 is a feature known as the Calculator, which greatly simplifies the task of creating, editing, and, in fact, understanding formulas in the program. It provides a layout based on an actual hand-held calculator. This feature is the central point from which you'll be creating formulas, and this chapter mainly focuses on how to create formulas, the various types of formulas that are available, and other related subjects.

Formulas

A formula is an equation that performs calculations in a cell. A formula can be created to perform mathematical operations such as addition, multiplication, division, and subtraction. To open the Calculator, select its symbol from the formula bar (it looks like a mini-calculator), which is located under the main toolbar.

When the Calculator is displayed (as shown in Figure 18-1), an equal sign (=) appears in the formula box at the top. All formulas in Excel start with an equal sign.

To create a formula, click the buttons for the numbers and operators (+, −, x, and so on). When these buttons are clicked, the Calculator creates the formula in the formula box and updates the result in the Answer box. For example, if you click 8*4, you will see =8*4 in the formula box and 32 in the Answer box.

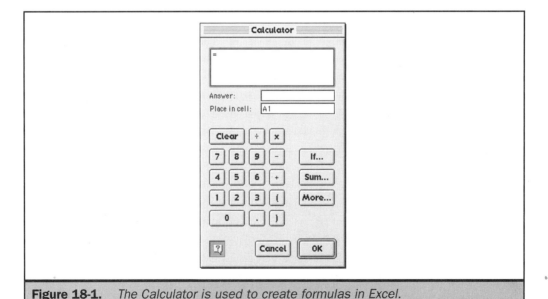

Figure 18-1. *The Calculator is used to create formulas in Excel.*

NOTE   *An operator is a character or symbol that indicates the type of operation performed in your formula.*

When you have finished writing the formula, click OK to enter the formula in the specified cell in the Place in Cell box. The result will then be displayed in the cell, and the formula will appear in the formula bar.

If you want to edit the formula later, select the cell and do one of the following:

- Select the cell and choose Calculator to edit the formula
- Double-click the cell and edit the formula using the keyboard

Creating a Complex Formula

If you want, you can create more complex formulas to take advantage of worksheet functions. The More button on the Calculator lets you create a formula with any worksheet function and will display the Paste Function dialog box (see Figure 18-2), where you can choose the function. Then Excel will display the Formula Palette to allow you to fill in the arguments of the function. When you close the dialog box, the function will be inserted into the formula in the Calculator.

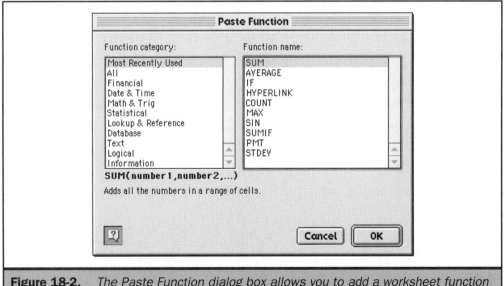

Figure 18-2.   *The Paste Function dialog box allows you to add a worksheet function to a formula.*

Using the Formula Palette

The Formula Palette is a valuable companion to help you handle the various mathematical functions in the program. Here are some of the palette's features:

■ **Entering Formulas**   When you create a formula with a function, displaying the Formula Palette (as in Figure 18-3) will help you enter worksheet functions. When a function is entered into the formula, the Formula Palette will show the name of the function, each of its arguments, a description of the function and each argument, the current result of the function, and the result of the whole formula. To bring up the Formula Palette, click the Edit Formula button on the Formula bar.

■ **Editing Formulas**   The Formula Palette can also be used to edit functions in formulas. To do this, choose a cell with a formula in it and then click the Edit Formula button (which looks like an equal sign) to display the Formula Palette. The first function of the formula and each of its arguments will appear on the palette. The first function can be edited, or you can edit another function in the same formula by selecting the formula bar anywhere within the function itself.

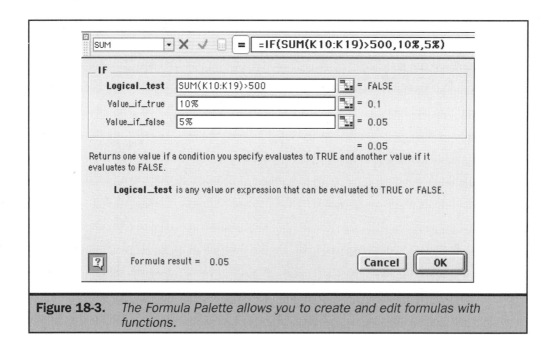

Figure 18-3.   *The Formula Palette allows you to create and edit formulas with functions.*

Other Calculator Functions

The Calculator also offers the following features that expand its usefulness:

- **Referencing Cells in Formulas** A reference identifies a cell or a range of cells on a worksheet and tells Excel where to find a value used in a formula. For example, the reference C1 identifies the first cell in column C. If C1 has the value 195 and you write a formula referring to C1, Excel will use the value 195 to calculate the result. You can also use the Calculator to create formulas that reference cells. Select any cell when the Calculator is displayed, and Excel will automatically insert the cell reference in the formula. You also can click and drag on the worksheet to add a reference to a range of cells. Another supported reference style is R1C1, in which "R" followed by a row number and "C" followed by a column number specifies the location of a cell. This style is especially useful for macros.

- **Checking a Condition with the If Button** You can use the If button (see Figure 18-4) of the Calculator to create a formula that determines whether a condition is true or false. If the condition is true, the formula will return one value; if the condition is false, the formula will return another value. Excel does

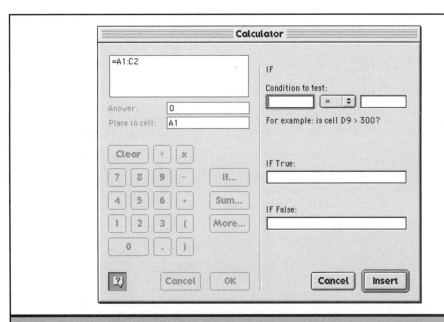

Figure 18-4. *The If function determines whether a condition is true or false.*

this by using the information you provide and converting it into a formula containing the IF worksheet function.

■ **Creating a Total with the Sum Button** Use the Sum button of the Calculator (see Figure 18-5) to calculate the total value of a range of cells that you have selected. The Calculator will use the information provided and transform it into a formula with a SUM worksheet function.

The Calculator also provides the *AutoCalculate* feature, which can show you the total value of a range of cells. When cells are selected, Excel displays the sum of the range in the status bar, which is the horizontal region under the worksheet window (you won't see it if the workbook window is too narrow).

If you can't see the status bar, just select Status Bar from the View menu.

AutoCalculate can also perform other types of calculations for you. When you click the mouse button and hold down the CONTROL key on the status bar at the same time, a contextual menu comes up. You can now find the average of or the minimum or maximum value within the selected range.

■ If Count Nums is selected, the cells that have numbers in them will be counted.

■ If you click Count, AutoCalculate counts the number of filled cells. Whenever you start Excel, AutoCalculate resets to the SUM function.

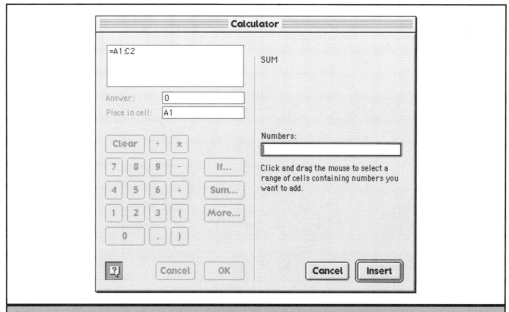

Figure 18-5. *The Sum button finds the total value of a range of cells.*

- The sum of a range of cells can be entered automatically using the AutoSum feature. When the cell where you want the sum to be inserted is selected and you click AutoSum, Excel adds up the columns. To accept this formula, press ENTER.

- To modify the suggested formula, select the range you want to total and press ENTER.

- If your worksheet has several total values created with the SUM function, a grand total can be created for these values using AutoSum.

- If you have a report or list of information and need to calculate subtotals and grand totals, use the Subtotal feature. This allows you to choose the items you want a subtotal for, the values you want subtotaled, and the kind of subtotal you want (such as a sum or an average).

> **NOTE**   *Before you can add a subtotal, you must sort your list by the column for which you want a subtotal. For example, if you want a summary of the number of units sold by every salesperson in a list of people, sales amounts, and the total number of units sold, sort the list by the Salesperson column.*

Use the following steps to create a subtotal:

1. Select a cell from the worksheet, which is where the subtotal will be added.

2. Choose Subtotals from the Data menu to display the Subtotal dialog box.

3. From the At Each Change In pop-up menu, select the column with the groups for which you want subtotals. This should be the same column by which your list was sorted.

4. From the Use Function pop-up menu, choose the function you want to use to calculate the subtotals.

5. In the Add Subtotal To box, select the check boxes for the columns with the values for which you want subtotals.

NOTE *If you want, you can nest subtotals, or insert subtotals for smaller groups within subtotal groups. You also can remove subtotals from a list without changing your original data.*

Array Formulas

An array formula can perform multiple calculations and then give either a single result or several different results. Array formulas act on two or more sets of values called array arguments. Every argument needs to have the same number of rows and columns. Array formulas are created in the same way as other formulas, although you must press COMMAND-RETURN to enter an array.

Here's some additional information about array formulas:

- **Calculating One Result**   Sometimes several calculations most be performed to get a single result. For example, a worksheet shows that a company has operations in Asia and Europe and that each region has five product divisions. To find the average revenue for each product division in Asia in 1999, you'll have to use an array formula.

- **Calculating Several Results**   To use an array formula to calculate several different results, the array must be entered into a range of cells with the same number of rows and columns as the arguments in the array.

- **Array Formula Producing Multiple Results**   When a formula is entered as an array formula, it produces multiple separate results. For example, it might produce three separate results using three sales figures for three months.

- **Array Formula Using Constant Values**   An array formula can be used to calculate a series of values that haven't been entered on the worksheet. Constants can be accepted in the same manner as nonarray formulas, but the array constants have to be entered in a certain format. For example, using the same three sales figures as in the previous example, the sales figures for the next two months can be projected.

Reference: Rules for Array Constants

An array constant can contain the following:

- An array constant can consist of numbers, text, logical values such as TRUE and FALSE, and error values such as #N/A.

- Numbers in array constants can be in integer, decimal, or scientific format.

- Text must be enclosed in double quotation marks—for example, "Rockoids."

- Different kinds of values can be used in the same array constant—for example (2, 7, 8, TRUE, FALSE, TRUE).

- Values in array constants must be constants, not formulas.

An array constant can't contain the following:

- $ (dollar signs), ( ) (parentheses), or % (percent signs)
- Cell references
- Columns or rows that aren't the same length

Applying Conditional Formatting

Use conditional formatting to highlight formula results or other cell values that you want to keep an eye on. Conditional formatting is especially useful if, for example, you're trying to track the difference between the sales forecast and the actual sales reported for a store. Conditional formatting will be applied to cells until it is removed, even if none of the conditions are met and the specified cell formats aren't being displayed.

Use the following steps to apply conditional formatting:

1. Choose the cells that you want to format.

2. Select Conditional Formatting from the Format menu to display the Conditional Formatting dialog box.

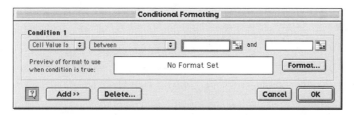

3. To use values in the cells that you selected as the criteria for the formatting, select Cell Value Is in the left Condition box, choose a comparison phrase, and then type a value in the appropriate boxes at the right. You can enter a constant value, or a value that doesn't begin with an equal sign in a formula, or a formula. If you enter a formula, it must be preceded by an equal sign.

4. To evaluate data or a condition besides the values in the selected cells, use the formula as the formatting criterion. From the pop-up menu on the left, select Formula Is and then enter the formula in the box on the right. The formula has to evaluate to a logical value of TRUE or FALSE.

5. Click the Format button.

6. Select the font style, font color, underlining, borders, shading, or patterns you want to apply.

NOTE   *The chosen formats will be applied only if the cell value meets the condition or if the formula comes up with a TRUE value.*

7. Add other conditions by clicking Add and redoing steps 3 or 4 and 5 and 6. Up to three conditions can be defined.

Tips and Tricks

Here are some neat things you can do with conditional formats to enhance the information you can display in your spreadsheet:

- Conditional formats can be copied to other cells. To do this, choose the cells with conditional formats that you want to copy, select Format Painter, and then choose the cells that you want to have the same conditional format. Copy only the conditional formats by choosing the cells that you want to format and include at least one cell in the selection that has the conditional formats you want copied. Select Conditional Formatting from the Format menu and click OK.

- Examine data such as sales results in "a stoplight chart." Choose the data you want and make sure three conditions are defined. Use a red font color or cell shading for cell values less than a defined minimum, yellow for values within a defined range, and green for values greater than a defined maximum.

- If multiple conditions are specified and more than one is true, only the format of the first true condition will be applied.

- If none of the defined conditions is true, the cells will keep their existing formats. These formats can be used for the identification of a fourth condition.

Locating Cells with Conditional Formats

Use the following steps to find cells with conditional formats:

1. Select a cell with the conditional criteria and format you want to locate. If you want to locate any cells on the worksheet with conditional formats, choose any cell.

2. From the Edit menu, select Go To.

3. Choose Special.

4. Select Conditional Formats.

5. Find cells with the same conditional formats by selecting Same, below Data Validation. Locate cells with any conditional formats by choosing All.

Conditional Sum Wizard

The Conditional Sum Wizard summarizes values in a list based on specific conditions. For example, if you have a list with sales amounts for different salespeople, you can use the Conditional Sum Wizard to create a formula that calculates the total sales amount of one person.

NOTE *The Conditional Sum Wizard is an add-in program. If you don't see the command listed on the Wizard submenu of the Tools menu, you will need to install the program from your Office 2001 CD. Chapter 2 covers installation of Value Pack components.*

Follow these steps to use the Conditional Sum Wizard:

1. Select a cell from the list to which you want to apply a conditional sum.

2. Select the Wizard submenu from the Tools menu and choose Conditional Sum.

3. Follow the instructions in the wizard. Figure 18-6 shows one of the wizard screens.

Circular References

A circular reference is a formula that refers back to its own cell, either directly or indirectly. For such a formula to be calculated, every cell involved in the circular reference must be calculated once using the results of the previous iteration. Unless the default settings for iteration are changed, Excel will stop calculating after 100 iterations or after all the values of a circular reference change by less than 0.001 between iterations, whichever comes first.

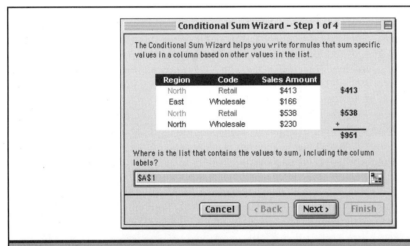

Figure 18-6. *Use the Conditional Sum Wizard to summarize values in a list based on specific conditions.*

■ **Locating Circular References with the Circular Reference Toolbar** Formulas with circular references can't be resolved using normal calculation. When you make a circular reference, Excel displays a message warning you that a circular reference has occurred. If the reference is an accident, simply click OK. The Circular Reference toolbar will then appear, and tracer arrows will point to every cell referred to by the circular reference.

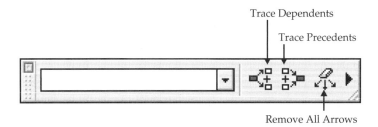

You can use this toolbar to move through every cell in the reference so you can redesign the formulas or logic to end the circular reference (although certain scientific and engineering formulas require circular references).

■ **Changing the Number of Iterations** Certain formulas need circular references, but you may have to modify the number of iterations. Whenever Iteration is turned on, Excel will recalculate the worksheet the number of times defined in the Maximum Iterations box or until the results between calculations change less than the amount defined in the Maximum Change box.

To change the number of iterations, do the following:

1. Select Preferences from the Edit menu and then select the Calculation tab (as in Figure 18-7).

2. Make sure the Iteration check box is selected.

3. Set the maximum number of times that Excel will recalculate by typing the amount of iterations in the Maximum Iterations box. The higher the number of iterations, the more times the worksheet will be recalculated.

4. Define the maximum amount of change between calculation results that is necessary to continue iteration by typing that amount in the Maximum Change box. The smaller the number, the more accurate the result and the more times the worksheet will be recalculated.

Finding Cells That Create a Circular Reference

Excel cannot automatically calculate all open workbooks if one of them has a circular reference. To find the cells involved in the circular reference, use the Circular Reference

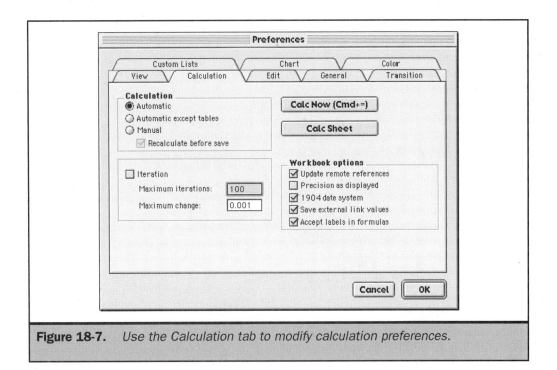

Figure 18-7. *Use the Calculation tab to modify calculation preferences.*

toolbar. The toolbar allows for the movement of each cell in the circular reference so the formulas can be changed as necessary to correct them.

Follow these steps to find the cells:

1. On the Circular Reference toolbar, select the first cell in the Navigate Circular Reference box. To display the bar manually, open the View menu, select the Toolbars tab, and then choose the Circular Reference check box.

2. Review the formula in the cell. If you can't figure out whether the cell is causing the circular reference, select the next cell in the Navigate Circular Reference box.

3. Keep reviewing and correcting the cells until the status bar no longer displays the word *Circular*. Once this happens, you will know that the active worksheet no longer has a circular reference. If the word *Circular* still appears, it will be followed by a reference to one of the cells in the worksheet.

Creating a Formula for Calculating Data on Another Worksheet or Workbook

If you are going to link to a new workbook, make sure the new workbook is saved before the link is created.

Follow these steps to create a formula for calculating data on another worksheet or workbook:

1. In the workbook that will contain the formula, choose the cell in which you want to enter the external reference.

2. Type = (equal sign) if you are setting up a new formula.

> NOTE *If the external reference is being entered in another location in the formula, type the operator or function that you want to have before the external reference.*

3. To set up a link to another worksheet in the active workbook, select the worksheet containing the cells to which you want to link.

4. To create a link to a worksheet in a different workbook, open the other workbook and then select the worksheet containing the cells to which you want to link.

5. Select the cells to which you want to link.

6. Finish the formula. Once you have done this, press the RETURN key.

> NOTE *To update the formula for a worksheet in a different workbook, select a cell in the external data range you want to refresh and then click the Refresh Data button on the main toolbar.*

Date and Time Calculations

Dates are stored as sequential numbers called serial values in Excel. Times are stored as decimal fractions since time is considered a part of a day. Since dates and times are considered to be values, they can be added, subtracted, and included in other calculations. For example, if you want to find out the difference between two dates, you simply have to subtract one date from the other. A date can be viewed as a serial value and a time as a decimal fraction by modifying the format of the cell that has the date or time to General format.

Two date systems are supported by Excel: the 1900 and 1904 date systems. The default date system for Excel on the Mac is 1904, and it is also the date system the Mac has used since the first Mac came out in 1984. To change to the 1900 date system, which was more common during the early days of the PC era (for non-Macintosh computers), choose Preferences from the Edit menu and select the Calculation tab and make sure the 1904 date system check box isn't checked.

The following shows the first date and the last date for each date system and the serial value associated with each date.

1900 Date System
First date: January 1, 1900 (serial value 1)
Last date: December 31, 9999 (serial value 2958465)

1904 Date System
First date: January 2, 1904 (serial value 1)
Last date: December 31, 9999 (serial value 2957003)

Troubleshooting Date and Time Calculations

If you find that your date calculations just aren't coming out properly, you'll want to look at these situations to see if they apply to you:

- **Two-Digit Years**   When a date is entered in a cell and only two digits are entered for the year, the year will be interpreted as follows:

    The years 2000 through 2029, if 00 through 29 are typed for the year   For example, if 2/19/07 is typed, Excel will interpret the date as February 19, 2007.

    The years 1930 through 1999, if 30 through 99 are typed for the year   For example, if 12/23/52 is typed, the date will be interpreted as December 23, 1952.

- **Four-Digit Years**   Type year values as four digits (2001 instead of 01) to be sure that year values are interpreted as you planned. If four digits are entered for the years, the century will be automatically interpreted by Excel.

- **The DATE Worksheet Function**   If it is necessary to change part of a date, such as the year or the month, in a formula, the DATE worksheet function can be used.

- **The TIME Worksheet Function**   If it is necessary to change part of a time, such as the hour or the minute, in a formula, the TIME worksheet function can be used.

- **Display Four-Digit Years by Default**   By default, when you enter dates in a workbook, the dates will be formatted to show two-digit years. The Date & Time Control Panel can be used to modify the default date format to display four-digit years instead of two-digit years.

Use the following steps to display the year in four digits by default:

1. Save any active workbooks and exit the program. Save any open workbooks and quit Excel.

2. Select Control Panels from the Apple menu and choose Date & Time.

3. Under Current Date in the Date & Time dialog box, click the Date Formats button. The dialog box shown in Figure 18-8 appears.

4. Select the Show Century check box under Short Date.

5. Open Excel again.

NOTE   *The manner in which Excel displays four-digit years can also modified using the Preferences dialog box. Select the Preserve Display of Dates Entered with Four-Digit Years check box from the Edit tab. Whenever a four-digit year is entered, Excel will keep the four digits regardless of any previous cell formatting.*

ORGANIZING YOUR DATA
WITH EXCEL 2001

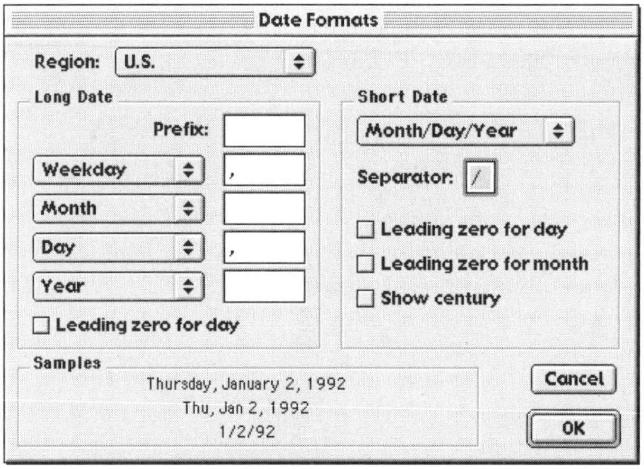

Figure 18-8. *The Date Formats dialog box allows you to change the formats of the dates used in Excel.*

Calculating the Running Balance

Among the useful features for home and business users is the ability to create a checkbook register in Excel for tracking banking transactions. You can build a formula to calculate a running balance as part of a spreadsheet. For example, if the cell F6 has the previous balance, cell D7 has the first transaction's deposit subtotal, and cell E7 has any cash-received amount, you can calculate the current balance after the first transaction by entering the following in F7:

=SUM(F6,D7,-E7)

You should copy this formula into the current balance cell for every new transaction.

Calculation Operators

The following tables summarize the various operators on the Calculator.

Arithmetic Operators   These are used to perform basic mathematical operations such as addition, subtraction, division, and multiplication; combine numbers; and indicate numeric results.

Arithmetic Operator	Meaning	Example
+ (plus sign)	Addition	2+2
– (minus sign)	Subtraction or negation	2–1 or –2
* (asterisk)	Multiplication	2*2
/ (forward slash)	Division	2/2

Arithmetic Operator	Meaning	Example
% (percent sign)	Percent	30%
^ (caret)	Exponentiation	3^2

Comparison Operators   Two values can be compared using the following operators. When this occurs, the result is a logical value: either TRUE or FALSE.

Comparison Operator	Meaning	Example
= (equal sign)	Equal to	A1=B1
> (greater-than sign)	Greater than	A1>B1
< (less-than sign)	Less than	A1<B1
>= (greater-than or equal-to sign)	Greater than or equal to	A1>=B1
<= (less-than or equal-to sign)	Less than or equal to	A1<=B1
<> (not-equal-to sign)	Not equal to	A1<>B1

Text Concatenation Operator   The ampersand (&) is used to join, or concatenate, one or more text strings to create a single block of text.

Text Operator	Meaning	Example
& (ampersand)	Connects, or concatenates, two values to make one continuous text value	**North & wind** make **Northwind**

Reference Operators   Combine ranges of cells for calculations with the following operators:

Reference Operator	Meaning	Example
: (colon)	Range operator, which produces one reference to all the cells between two references, including the two references	**B5:B15**
, (comma)	Union operator, which combines multiple references into one reference	**SUM(B5:B15,D5:D15)**

Intersection Operator   Use a space between a row name and column name to return the value at the intersection of the row and column.

Intersection Operator	Meaning	Example
Space	Returns the value at the row and column intersection	Assume that you have a row labeled Sales, columns labeled Quarter1 and Quarter2, and values 100 and 200 in the respective cells. Typing **=Sales Quarter2** returns the value 200.

Using the Solver to Define and Solve Problems

Excel's Solver is a helpful tool designed to allow you to model data so it can provide you with information on optimal solutions. For example, you can use the Solver to predict what mix of numbers will give you the necessary results for a calculation.

Here's how the Solver is used:

1. Select Solver from the Tools menu to display the Solver Parameters dialog box (see Figure 18-9).

NOTE   *If you don't see the command, you will have to install the Solver add-in from your Office 2001 CD, by running the Value Pack installer (see Chapter 2 for more information).*

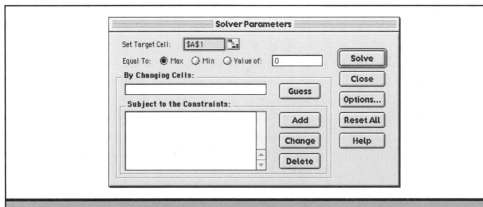

Figure 18-9.   *The Solver can be used to define and solve problems.*

2. Enter a cell reference or name for the target cell in the Set Target Cell box. This cell has to have a formula in it.

3. Select Max to make the value of the target cell as large as possible. Choose Min to make the value of the cell as small as possible. Make the target cell a certain value by selecting Value Of and typing the value in the box.

4. Enter a name or reference for each adjustable cell in the By Changing Cells box, separating nonadjacent references with commas. The adjustable cells must be directly or indirectly related to the target cell. Up to 200 adjustable cells can be defined. If you want the Solver to propose the adjustable cells automatically based on the target cell, click Guess.

5. Add any constraints you want in the Subject to the Constraints box.

6. Click Solve.

7. Keep the values of the solution on the worksheet by selecting Keep Solver Solution from the Solver Results dialog box. Restore the original data by choosing Restore Original Values.

> NOTE   *You can end the entire solution process by pressing the ESC key. At that point, Excel will recalculate the worksheet with the last values found for the adjustable cells.*

Auditing Worksheets

Excel offers tools that allow you to find certain problems on your worksheets. For example, the value you see in a cell may be the result of a formula, or it may be used by a formula that produces an inaccurate result. The auditing commands graphically display, or trace, the relationships between cells and formulas containing tracer arrows. When you audit a worksheet, you can trace the precedents (cells that provide data for a specific cell) or the dependents (cells that depend on the value of a specific cell) of a cell.

Auditing Toolbar

The following list summarizes the options found on the Auditing toolbar (see Figure 18-10).

- **Trace Precedents**   Displays tracer arrows for a cell that provides data for other cells

- **Remove Precedent Arrows**   Removes tracer arrows for the cell

- **Trace Dependents**   Displays tracer arrows for a cell that is dependent on the value of a specific cell

- **Remove Dependent Arrows**   Removes tracer arrows for the cell

- **Remove All Arrows**   Removes both precedent and dependent arrows from all cells

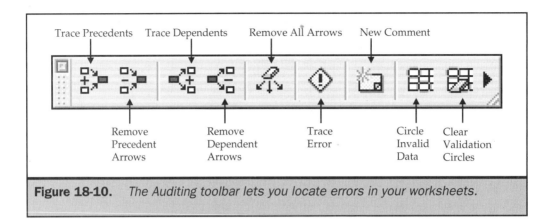

Figure 18-10.   *The Auditing toolbar lets you locate errors in your worksheets.*

- ■ **Trace Error**   Locates all cells providing data to a formula with an error value
- ■ **New Comment**   Adds a comment for the purpose of documenting the structure and data in a worksheet
- ■ **Circle Invalid Data**   Shows cells with values that don't meet the validation rules applied to them
- ■ **Clear Validation Circles**   Removes all validation circles from the active worksheet

Finding Formulas Using the Value in a Specific Cell

Another mathematical feature of Excel is the ability to find formulas based on the value in a cell.

1. Choose Preferences from the Edit menu, select the View tab, and select the Show All or Show Placeholders option in the Objects area (see Figure 18-11).

2. Select Auditing from the Tools menu and then choose Show Auditing Toolbar from the submenu.

3. Choose the cell for which you want to find the dependent cells.

4. Display a tracer arrow for each cell that is dependent on the active cell by selecting Trace Dependents from the Auditing toolbar. Identify the next column of cells dependent on the active cell by selecting Trace Dependents again.

NOTE   *Blue arrows point to cells in the same worksheet that depend on the selected cells. Red arrows point to cells causing errors. If the selected cell is referenced by a cell on another workbook or worksheet, a black arrow will point from the selected cell to a worksheet icon. Double-click an arrow to select the cell at the other end. Double-click the black arrow and then the reference you want to put in the Go To list to choose a dependent cell in another workbook or worksheet.*

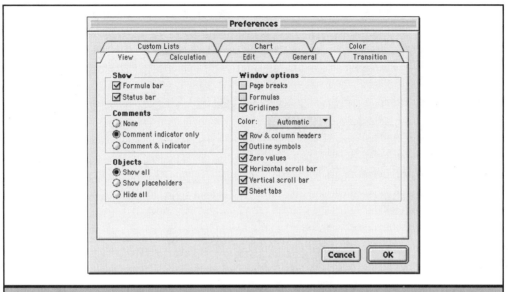

Figure 18-11. *Use the View tab of the Preferences dialog box to select the Show All or Show Placeholders option.*

Finding Cells That Don't Equal the Value of the Selected Cell in a Column or Row

Use the following steps to find cells that match the value of an active cell in a column or row:

1. Choose the range of cells to which you want cells compared.
2. Select Go To from the Edit menu.
3. Choose Special.
4. Select Row Differences to select the cells in the active row.
5. Select Column Differences to select the cells in the active column.

Finding Cells That Provide Data for a Formula

Here's how to find cells that have the data needed for a certain formula.

1. Choose Preferences from the Edit menu, select the View tab, and select the Show All or Show Placeholders option in the Objects area.
2. Select Auditing from the Tools menu and then choose Show Auditing Toolbar from the submenu.

3. Choose the cell containing the formula for which you want to locate precedent cells.

4. Select Trace Precedents from the Auditing toolbar to display a tracer arrow to each cell that directly provides data to the active cell. Identify the next level of cells by choosing Trace Precedents again.

Finding Cells in Another Workbook or Worksheet That Provide Data for a Formula

If the reference you want to find is in a different workbook, you first have to open that workbook. Then do the following:

1. Select Auditing from the Tools menu and choose Show Auditing Toolbar from the submenu.

NOTE   *Before you do this, choose Preferences from the Edit menu, select the View tab, and select the Show All or Show Placeholders option in the Objects area.*

2. Select Trace Precedents from the Auditing toolbar to show a tracer arrow pointing to each cell that provides data directly to the active cell.

3. Double-click the arrow showing the worksheet icon that points to the active cell.

4. Choose the reference you want to go to in the Go To box.

NOTE   *The workbook containing the precedent cell must be open before the cell can be selected.*

Finding Cells That Cause Errors in a Formula

To locate cells that result in errors in a formula, do the following:

1. Select Auditing from the Tools menu and choose Show Auditing Toolbar from the submenu.

NOTE   *Before you do this, choose Preferences from the Edit menu, select the View tab, and select the Show All or Show Placeholders option in the Objects area.*

2. Select the cell with the error.

3. Choose Trace Error from the Auditing toolbar.

Using Range Finder to Find the Cells Referred to by a Formula

The following process describes the use of the Range Finder feature, which locates and modifies references:

1. Double-click the cell with the formula you want to modify. Each cell or range of cells will be highlighted with a different color.

2. Drag the color-coded border of the cell or range to the new cell or range to change the cell or range reference. To include fewer or more cells in a reference, use the drag handle in the lower-right corner of the border.

3. Press the RETURN key once you have finished updating the references. Press COMMAND-RETURN if the formula is an array formula.

Eliminating One or More Levels of Tracer Arrows

The following steps show you how to remove one or more tracer arrow levels from your spreadsheet:

1. Select Auditing from the Tools menu and choose Show Auditing Toolbar from the submenu.

> **NOTE** *Before you do this, choose Preferences from the Edit menu, select the View tab, and select the Show All or Show Placeholders option in the Objects area.*

2. To eliminate the tracer arrows one level at time, begin with the dependent cell that is farthest from the active cell and select Remove Dependent Arrows from the Auditing Toolbar. Click the same button again to get rid of another level of tracer arrows. The same instructions apply for Precedent Arrows (except the button is called Remove Precedent Arrows instead). To remove all tracer arrows from the worksheet, select Remove All Arrows.

Labels and Names

Often worksheets have labels at the top of each column and at the left of each row that describe the data inside the worksheet. You can also use these labels in formulas when they are needed to refer to the related data. In addition, descriptive names that are not labels on the worksheet can be used to represent cells, ranges of cells, formulas, or constants.

Guidelines for Naming Cells, Formulas, and Constants

Here are some basic guidelines to keep in mind when you name cells, formulas, and constants:

- **Characters That Are Allowed**   The first character of a name must be a letter or underscore. All the rest of the characters can be letters, numbers, periods, or underscores.

- **Names Can't Be Cell References**   Names can't be the same as cell references, such as Z$100 or R1C1.

■ **More than One Word Can Be Used**   You can use multiple words, but you cannot use spaces. Underscore characters and periods can be used as word separators—for example, Income_Tax or Third.Quarter.

■ **Number of Characters**   A name can have up to 255 characters.

CAUTION   *If a name defined for a range has more than 253 characters, it can't be selected from the Name box.*

■ **Excel Isn't Case Sensitive**   Names can have uppercase and lowercase letters. Excel doesn't distinguish between uppercase and lowercase characters in names. For example, if you have the label Sales and then create another label called SALES in the same workbook, the second label will replace the first one.

Naming a Cell or Range of Cells

Follow these steps to name one or more cells in your spreadsheet:

1. Choose the cell, range of cells, or nonadjacent selections that you want named.

2. In the Name box at the left end of the formula bar, type the name for the cells.

3. Press the RETURN key.

NOTE   *A cell cannot be named while its contents are being changed.*

Naming Cells Using Existing Row and Column Labels

The following directions describe how you can name cells using the row and column labels you've already created:

1. Select the range you want named, including -the row or column labels.

2. Select the Name submenu from the Insert menu and choose Create.

3. In the Create Names dialog box choose the location for the labels in the Create Names In area; select the Top Row, Left Column, Bottom Row, or Right Column check box.

NOTE   *A name created using this procedure refers only to the cells containing values and doesn't include the existing row and column labels.*

Naming Cells in More Than One Worksheet Using 3-D References

The following instructions demonstrate how to name cells in multiple worksheets using the 3-D references. You'll learn more about the feature itself later in this chapter.

1. Select the Name submenu from the Insert menu and choose Define.

2. In the Define Name dialog box (see Figure 18-12), type the name in the Names in Workbook box.

3. If the Refers To box contains a reference, select the equal sign (=) and the reference and click the Delete button.

4. Type = in the Refers To box

5. Select the tab for the worksheet that will be referenced first.

6. Select the tab for the last worksheet that will be referenced and at the same time hold down the SHIFT key.

7. Choose the cell or range of cells that you want to reference.

Creating a Name to Represent a Formula or Constant Value

The following steps describe how to create a name to represent a formula or constant value in your worksheet:

1. Select the Name submenu from the Insert menu and choose Define.

2. Enter the name of the formula in the Names in Workbook box.

3. Type = (an equal sign) in the Refers to box, followed by the formula or the constant value.

Figure 18-12.   *Use the Define Name dialog box to name cells in more than one worksheet using 3-D references.*

Changing the Name for a Reference, Formula, or Constant

Follow these steps to change the name of a reference, formula, or constant:

1. Select the Name submenu from the Insert menu and choose Define.
2. Choose the name you want to change from the Names in Workbook list.
3. Type the new name for the reference and then click Add.
4. Delete the original name by selecting it and pressing the DELETE key on the keyboard.

Changing the Cell, Formula, or Constant Represented by a Name

Follow these instructions to change the cell, formula, or constant that a name represents:

1. Select the Name submenu from the Insert menu and then choose Define.
2. Choose the name whose cell reference, formula, or constant you want to modify.
3. Edit the reference, formula, or constant in the Refers To box.

Transforming Cell References in Formulas to Names

Use the following steps to transform cell references in formulas to names:

1. Choose the range with the formulas in which you want the references replaced with names. Select one cell to transform the references to a name in every formula on the worksheet.
2. Choose a name from the Apply Names box.

Using Multiple Labels

A single label may not always be sufficient to describe your worksheet or the cells inside it. In this case, you can use the multiple labels feature, which offers the following:

■ **Stacked Labels**   When the columns and rows of a worksheet have labels, those labels can be used in the creation of formulas that refer to data on the worksheet. If the worksheet contains stacked column labels, where a label in one cell is followed by one or more labels under it, the stacked labels in formulas can be used to refer to data on the worksheet. For example, if the label West is in cell R5 and the label Projected is in cell R6, the formula =SUM(West Projected) brings you the total value for the West Projected column.

■ **The Order for Stacked Labels** When stacked labels are used to refer to information, the references occur in the order in which the labels appear, from top to bottom. If cell F5 contains the label West and cell F6 has the label Actual, the actual figures for West can be referenced by using West Actual in a formula. For example, to calculate the average of the actual figures for West, you can use the formula =AVERAGE(West Actual).

Finding What a Name Refers To

These steps show you how to find what a specific name refers to:

1. Select the Name submenu from the Insert menu and choose Define.

2. Choose the name whose reference you want to check from the Names in Workbook list. The Refers To box shows the reference, formula, or constant represented by the name.

TIP   *You can also create a list of the available names in a workbook. Find a region with two empty columns on the worksheet (the list will consist of two columns: one for the name and the other for a description of the name). Choose a cell that will serve as the upper-left corner of the list. Select the Name submenu from the Insert menu and then choose Paste. Choose Paste List from the Paste Name dialog box.*

Importing FileMaker Pro Files Into Excel 2001

Fans of Microsoft Access for Windows may be displeased to see that this application hasn't made its way into Office 2001 for the Mac. But that doesn't mean you don't have the ability to work with data from a database. Since FileMaker Pro rules the roost in this very small product category, and it's also available for Windows, Microsoft has devised a way to bring its data into your Excel worksheet. The feature is called the FileMaker Import Wizard (naturally!).

There are two different ways of accessing your FileMaker Pro files in Excel. The data can be imported to a worksheet, or the FileMaker Pro file can be opened in the program and saved as an Excel file. Both use Excel's FileMaker Import Wizard. In the wizard, you select the fields that need to be included on your worksheet, the order in which you want to display them, and criteria for filtering out unnecessary records. When you import a file, you can also select properties that refresh the worksheet data whenever the file is opened. You also can use the List Manager if you want.

Importing FileMaker Files

To import, open, or refresh files from FileMaker Pro, both that program and Excel 2001 have to be installed on the same computer.

> **NOTE** *If you're copying the file from another Mac or a Windows PC that has both programs, you can then put it on your own Mac as an Excel file.*

1. Launch Excel. Select the Get External Data submenu from the Data menu and choose Import from FileMaker Pro.

2. In the Choose a Database dialog box (see Figure 18-13), find and open the FileMaker file that you want to import.

3. At this point, FileMaker Pro will open, and the FileMaker Import Wizard dialog box (see Figure 18-14) will appear. Choose the fields that you want imported from FileMaker Pro.

4. To import all of the records from the FileMaker file, click Finish.

5. To import only records that match your criteria, click Next (the dialog box that is displayed is shown in Figure 18-15). This dialog box allows you to filter your FileMaker file to import only records that match your criteria. Select from the list of fields to be imported and the list of operators and then enter the value you want to serve as a filter for each criterion. Then click Finish.

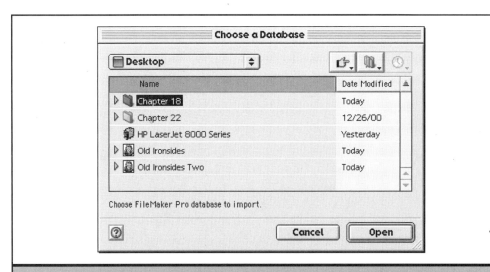

Figure 18-13. *The Choose a Database dialog box lets you import a database from FileMaker Pro.*

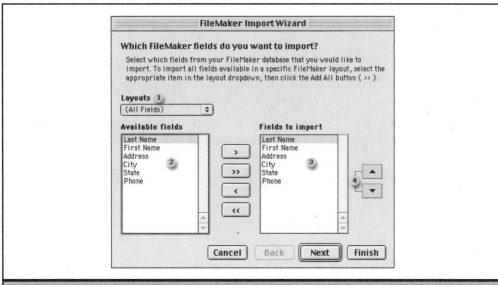

Figure 18-14.   *The FileMaker Import Wizard lets you choose the fields you want imported from FileMaker.*

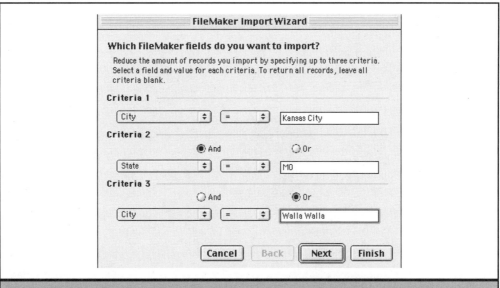

Figure 18-15.   *The Next dialog box lets you set up criteria for importing records from FileMaker.*

NOTE

When multiple criteria are present, records either have to match both criteria (And) or match any of the criteria (Or) to be imported. If you want to import sales figures for NY, NJ, or PA, for example, use the Or option wherever these states are included. In addition, the And and Or operators can be used in combination if, for example, you want a comparison of sales in regions of different sizes, such as a large urban area and a small rural area.

6. After you have finished working with the wizard, the Returning External Data to Microsoft Excel dialog box will be displayed. Here you choose where you want your data to be placed: either on the current worksheet or a new one.

7. Click the Properties button to open the External Data Range Properties dialog box (shown in Figure 18-16), where you can customize a number of the import features. Have the data on your worksheet updated whenever it is opened by choosing the Refresh data on file open check box. This means you won't have to deal with the worry that your data could be inaccurate or out of date.

NOTE

Besides being able to select certain criteria for the importation of your records, this dialog box provides additional options. You can define where you want to put your data and whether you want to be able to refresh the data in the Excel file.

8. If you want to use the List Manager to maintain your data, choose the Use List Manager check box. The List Manager makes it easier to keep multiple lists separate and locate data in lists. Chapter 17 covers the List Manager in detail.

NOTE

If you decide not to use the List Manager, the data will be imported into an Excel worksheet without a list frame.

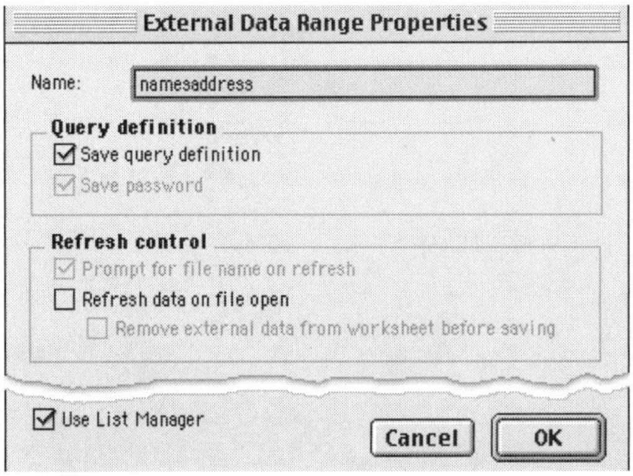

Figure 18-16.   *The External Data Range Properties dialog box allows a number of the import features to be customized.*

9. When you're finished, click the OK button to accept the Properties and then click OK again to finish the import process. At this point, your FileMaker Pro file will be successfully imported into Excel.

Opening a FileMaker Pro File and Saving It as an Excel Workbook

The Open command of Excel can be used to bring your FileMaker Pro files into Excel. Just click the Open button, choose the needed file, and then click Open again. This will bring up the FileMaker Import Wizard. Here you can make the necessary modifications for importing your FileMaker records, as described in the preceding section.

You can also open a FileMaker Pro file by dragging the file onto the Excel icon. When the icon is selected, drop the file. At this point, both Excel and FileMaker Pro will be opened and the FileMaker Import Wizard will appear.

When the Open command or dragging and dropping are used, your list will be opened in a new workbook with one list sheet. A list sheet is a worksheet used as a list. The list sheet and the Excel workbook will have the same name as the FileMaker Pro file.

FileMaker Import Limits

As much as one might like this import process to proceed with total perfection, there are a few limitations:

- The results of FileMaker Pro calculations are imported, but the formulas used in these calculations are not.

- Excel doesn't keep the sorting order of FileMaker Pro. The data will have to be resorted once it is imported into Excel.

- The maximum size of an Excel worksheet is 65,536 rows by 256 columns. If your FileMaker Pro database has more than 65,535 records or 256 fields, only the fields within the maximum size limitation will be imported. The first row of the worksheet is reserved for the field names. (All right, this is a rather extreme example, but one that may exist in some situations.)

- One cell in a worksheet can have a maximum of 32,767 characters. Any FileMaker Pro fields that have more than 32,767 characters are truncated, and only the first 32,767 characters will be imported into Excel.

References

As explained earlier, a reference identifies a cell or range of cells on a worksheet and tells Excel where to find the values or data that you want to use in a formula. References allow you to use data found in different sections of a worksheet in one formula or to use the value in one cell in a number of formulas. Cells on other worksheets in the same workbook, cells in other workbooks, and data in other programs can also be referred to. References to cells in other workbooks are known as *external references*. References to data in other programs are known as *remote references*.

A1 and R1C1 References

A1 and R1C1 are two kinds of references used by Excel.

■ **A1 Reference Style**   The A1 reference style, which refers to columns with letters (A through IV, for a total of 256 columns) and refers to rows using numbers (1 through 65536), is used by Excel by default. These letters and numbers are known as row and column headings. To refer to a cell, enter the column letter and then enter the row number. For example, B12 refers to the cell where column B and row 12 intersect. To refer to a range of cells, enter the reference for the cell in the upper-left corner of the range, a colon (:), and then the reference to the cell in the lower-right corner of the range.

■ **R1C1 Reference Style**   The R1C1 reference style means that both the rows and columns on the worksheet are numbered. This style is good for computing row and column positions in macros.

Absolute and Relative References

Absolute and relative references are two other kinds of references used in Excel.

■ **Absolute References**   If you don't want references to be adjusted when a formula is copied to another cell, you should use an absolute reference, which always refers to a cell in a specific location. For example, if your formula multiplies cell A5 by cell C1 (=A5*C1) and the formula is copied to a different cell, both references will be adjusted by Excel. An absolute reference to cell C1 can be created by putting a dollar sign ($) before the sections of the reference that don't change. For example, add dollar signs to the formula as follows: =A5*C1.

■ **Relative References**   When a formula is created, references to cells or ranges are usually based on their position in relation to the cell with the formula. For example, suppose that cell B6 has the formula =A5, to tell Excel to find the value one cell above and one cell to the left of B6. This is called a relative reference.

When a formula containing relative references is copied, the references in the pasted formula are automatically adjusted so that they refer to different cells in relation to the formula's position. For example, if the formula in cell B6, =A5, is copied to cell B7, the formula in cell B7 will be adjusted to =A6, so that it still refers to the cell that is one above and one cell to the left of the cell that contains the formula, which in this case is cell B7.

■ **Relative Versus Absolute References** Either absolute or relative cell references can be used, depending on the task you want to perform in Excel. If there is a dollar sign before a letter and/or a number, like C2, the column and/or row reference will be absolute. Relative references are automatically adjusted when they are copied, and absolute references are not.

■ **Switching Between Relative and Absolute References** If a formula is created and it is necessary to make an absolute reference relative (or vice versa), choose the cell with the formula in it. Select the reference you want to change from the formula bar and then press the COMMAND and T keys at the same time. Every time COMMAND-T is pressed, Excel toggles through the combinations: absolute column and absolute row (for example, A2), relative column and absolute row (A$2), absolute column and relative row ($A2), and relative column and relative row (C1). For example, if you choose the address C1 from a formula and press COMMAND-T, the reference is transformed to C$1. Press COMMAND-T again, and the reference is transformed to $C1, and so on.

3-D References

Use a 3-D reference if you want data to be analyzed in the same cell or range of cells in a number of different worksheets in a workbook. It has the cell or range reference, preceded by a range of worksheet names. Any worksheets stored between the starting and ending names of the reference are used by Excel. For example, =SUM(Sheet2: Sheet13!B5) adds all the values found in cell B5 on all the worksheets between and including Sheet 2 and Sheet 13.

Use the following steps to create a 3-D reference:

1. Select the cell where you want the function entered.
2. Type = (equal sign), enter the function's name, and then type an opening parenthesis.
3. Select the tab for the worksheet that will be referenced first.
4. Select the tab for the worksheet that will be referenced last and hold down the SHIFT key at the same time.
5. Select the cell or range of cells that are going to be referenced.
6. Finish the formula.

Guidelines for Using 3-D References

Follow these suggestions to use 3-D references in your workbook:

■ Use 3-D references to refer to cells on other worksheets, to define names, and to create formulas using these functions: SUM, AVERAGE, AVERAGEA, COUNT, COUNTA, MAX, MAXA, MIN, MINA, PRODUCT, STDEV, STDEVA, STDEVP, STDEVPA, VAR, VARA, VARP, and VARPA.

- 3-D references can't be used in array formulas.
- 3-D references can't be used with the intersection operator (a single space) or in formulas with implicit intersection.

How a 3-D Reference Is Affected When Worksheets Are Moved, Copied, Inserted, or Deleted

The following examples explain what occurs when worksheets involved in a 3-D reference are moved, copied, inserted, or deleted. The examples use the formula =SUM(Sheet2:Sheet4!B3:B6) to sum cells B3 through B6 on worksheets 2 through 4.

- **Inserting or Copying**   If sheets are being copied between Sheet 2 and Sheet 4, Excel will include in the calculations all the values found in cells B3 through B6 on the added sheets.
- **Deleting**   If sheets are deleted between Sheet 2 and Sheet 4, their values will be removed from the calculations.
- **Moving**   If sheets are moved from between Sheet 2 and Sheet 4 to a location outside the referenced sheet range, their values will be removed from the calculations.
- **Moving an Endpoint**   If Sheet 2 or Sheet 4 is moved to a different location in the same workbook, the calculation will be modified to accommodate the new range of sheets between them.
- **Deleting an Endpoint**   If Sheet 2 or Sheet 4 is deleted, the calculation will be adjusted to accommodate the range of sheets between them.

Opening a Workbook Referenced by a Formula

To upgrade a workbook referenced by a formula in Excel, follow these steps:

1. Open the workbook with the formula that has the external reference. Switch to the workbook that contains the formula with the external reference.
2. Select Links from the Edit menu.
3. Click the Open button.

Updating References to a Workbook That Has Been Moved or Renamed

If you have moved or renamed the references to a workbook, you need to update the references. Here's how:

1. Open the workbook with the formula containing the external reference that points to the workbook that has been moved or renamed.
2. Select Links from the Edit menu.

3. From the Source File box, choose the name of the workbook with a reference that you want to update.

4. Select Change Source.

5. From the Open dialog box, choose the workbook to which you want to refer.

Controlling Calculation

Although Excel will automatically recalculate formulas when the cells the formula depends on are modified, you can choose when and how you want Excel to calculate open workbooks.

To calculate open workbooks manually, just press the F9 key.

NOTE   *If you click the formula bar at the same time the F9 key is being pressed, the value of the formula or the selected part of it will be displayed. To restore the formula to the cell, press the ESC key. Select Undo from the Edit menu to restore the formula if the RETURN key is pressed.*

Changing When a Workbook or Worksheet is Calculated

To change when a workbook or worksheet is calculated, follow these steps:

1. Choose Preference from the Edit menu and then select the Calculation tab.

2. Choose an option from the Calculation area.

3. If any option other than Automatic is chosen, you can calculate all worksheets in every open workbook by pressing the F9 key. If you want to calculate only the active worksheet, press the SHIFT key and the F9 key at the same time.

NOTE   *If there is a formula linked to a worksheet that hasn't be calculated and the link is updated, Excel will display a message saying that the source worksheet hasn't been calculated completely. Update the link with the current value stored in the source worksheet by clicking OK even if the value isn't correct. Click Cancel to stop updating the link and use the previous value you got from the source worksheet.*

Modifying the Precision of Calculations in a Workbook

When the precision of calculations is modified in a workbook using the displayed (or formatted) values, any constant values on the worksheets of the workbook will be changed permanently. If you decide later to calculate with full precision, the original values can't be restored.

If this is what you want to do, follow these steps:

1. Choose Preferences from the Edit menu and select the Calculation tab.

2. Select the Precision as Displayed check box under the Workbook options.

Replacing a Formula with Its Calculated Value

A formula will be permanently removed when it is replaced by its value. If this occurs accidentally and you want to restore the formula, select Undo from the Edit menu immediately after the value is entered or pasted.

To replace a formula with its calculated value, follow these steps:

1. Choose the cell with the formula. If it is an array formula, choose the range with the formula.

2. Select Copy from the Edit menu.

3. Choose Paste Special from the Edit menu.

4. Select Values, under Paste.

Replacing a Portion of a Formula with Its Calculated Value

To replace a portion of a formula using its calculated value, follow these steps:

1. Click the cell that contains the formula.

2. In the formula bar, select the part of the formula that you want to replace with its calculated value. When this portion is chosen, make sure that the entire operand is included. For example, if you are selecting a function, be sure that the entire function name, the open parenthesis, the arguments, and the closing parenthesis are selected.

3. Press the F9 key to calculate the selected part.

4. Press the RETURN key to replace the selected part of the formula with its calculated value. If the formula is an array formula, press the COMMAND and RETURN keys at the same time. Restore the original formula by pressing the ESC key.

Summary

In this chapter, you learned about some of the more advanced spreadsheet functions of Excel, including how to create and edit formulas, audit worksheets, import data from a FileMaker Pro file, use references, and control calculation timing.

In the next chapter, you will learn about some additional advanced Excel functions, including how to set up different kinds of charts and edit them and how to import data from a chart and put it on a Web page.

Chapter 19

Charts and Web Pages

A s you've learned in Chapters 16 through 18, there are a variety of ways you can display information in a Microsoft Excel 2001 spreadsheets. In this chapter, you'll learn about a way to present information that may be the best of all, particularly if you're looking for the maximum impact: charts.

Charts are useful for displaying information visually and make comparisons, patterns, and trends in that data easier for those viewing your data to see. For example, instead of having to analyze several columns of worksheet numbers, your viewers can simply look at a chart of that data to see whether sales are rising or falling over quarterly periods, or whether actual sales match those originally forecast.

In addition, you can create a chart on its own sheet or embed it in a worksheet. You can also publish it on a Web page. To create a chart, you must first enter your data on a worksheet and then select it so Excel's handy Chart Wizard can take you through the process of selecting a chart type and choosing options for that chart.

Chart Reference

There are many components of a chart in Excel. The main ones are described in the following list:

- **Axis Values**   An axis is a line that borders a side in the plotting area, so you get a point of reference for comparisons and measurement. An axis is created from the data on your worksheet. Unless you specify otherwise, the format of the upper-left cell in the value range will be used as the number format for the axis.

- **Category Names**   Column or row headings are used for category names of the axes in the worksheet data. You can decide whether Excel uses row or column headings for these names, or you can simply create different ones.

- **Chart Data Series Names**   The column and row headings can also be used for series names in the data. Series names will be displayed in the chart legend. You can decide whether the row or column headings are used for these names, or whether you want to create new ones.

- **Data Markers**   Data markers that have the same pattern stand for one series of data. Each data marker represents one number on the worksheet.

NOTE *A chart tip (a variation of a ToolTip) that displays the name of a chart item will appear whenever the pointer rests on the item. For example, if the pointer is resting on the legend, the legend chart tip will be displayed.*

Chart Sheets and Embedded Charts

A chart can be set up on its own chart sheet or as an embedded chart in a worksheet. However you choose to configure a chart, it will be linked to the source data on the worksheet, which means that whenever the worksheet data is modified, the chart will be updated to reflect those changes.

Here's a basic overview of chart sheets and embedded charts:

- **Chart Sheets** A chart sheet is a separate worksheet in your workbook with its own name. Use it whenever you want to display or edit large or complex charts separately from the data on the worksheet, or when you want to save space on your screen while you're working on the worksheet.

- **Embedded Charts** An embedded chart is considered to be a graphic object in your Excel document and will be saved as part of the worksheet on which it is created. Use these types of charts whenever you want to show or print more than one chart with the data on your worksheet.

Types of Charts

Microsoft Excel provides many different kinds of charts that you can choose from to give maximum impact to your worksheets. A brief description of each type of chart is provided here:

- **Area** An area chart shows the amount of change over a period of time. In addition, it displays the relationship of parts to a whole by showing the sum of the plotted values.

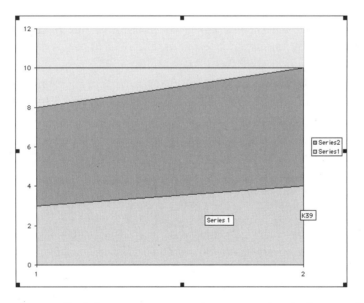

- **Bar** A bar graph defines comparisons between individual items. Categories are vertically organized, and values are organized horizontally, allowing the chart to focus on the comparison of values, so it is easier for you to hone in on the information you need.

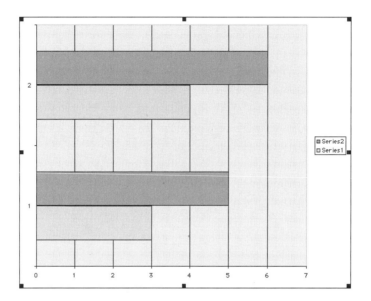

■ **Bubble** A bubble chart is a kind of XY (scatter) chart (see the following discussion of this chart type for more information). The size of the data marker shows the value of a third variable (in addition to x and y). To organize your data, put the x values in one row or column and put their corresponding y values and bubble sizes in nearby rows or columns.

■ **Column** A column chart displays changes in data over a given amount of time or shows comparisons between items. Values are vertically organized, and categories are organized horizontally to make sure that the chart properly displays how data changes over a period of time.

■ **Cone, Cylinder, and Pyramid** These are not actually charts, but data markers that can be used to spruce up 3-D column and bar charts.

■ **Doughnut** A doughnut chart displays the relationship of parts to a whole. It can't have more than one data series. Every ring stands for a data series. Like a pie chart (see later in this list), it breaks down into two or more sections to represent percentages of the whole, such as the percentage of total revenue made in one year from each business line.

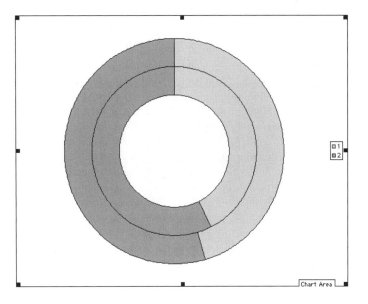

■ Line A line graph displays data trends at equal intervals.

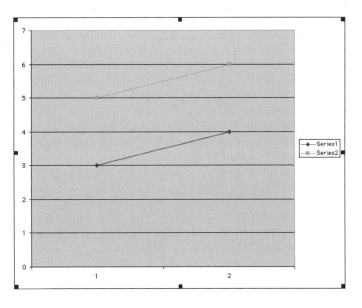

■ **Pie**   Like a doughnut chart, a pie chart displays the proportional size of items that make up a data series to the sum of the items. It displays only one data series and is useful for putting emphasis on an important element.

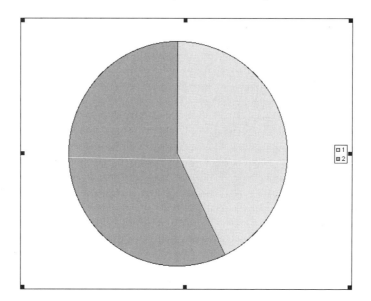

■ **Radar**   In a radar chart, every category has its own value axis coming from the center point. All the values in the same series in the chart are connected by lines.

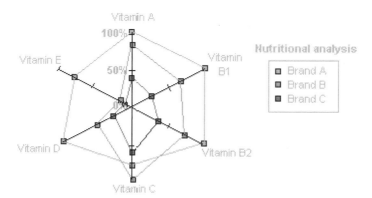

■ **Surface**   It's a good idea to use a surface chart when you're trying to discover the best combinations between two sets of data. Just like a topographic map, colors and patterns point out regions that have the same range of values.

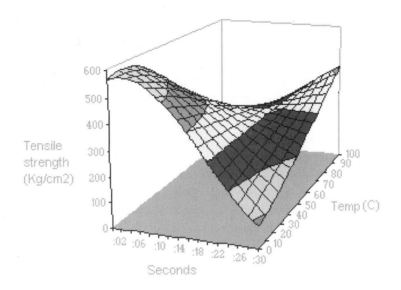

■ **Stock**   This high-low-close chart can be used for the illustration of stock prices. It can also be used to display scientific data, such as changes in temperature. To create this type of chart and similar ones, your data has to be arranged in the proper order, which must be highs and lows, respectively.

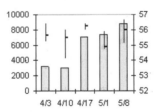

■ **XY (scatter)**   An XY (scatter) chart displays either the relationships between the numeric values in a number of data series or plots two groups of numbers as one series of *x,y* coordinates. This type of chart displays uneven intervals, or clusters, of data and is often used to show scientific data. When your data is organized, make sure *x* values are placed in one row or column, and the corresponding *y* values are put in the adjacent columns or rows.

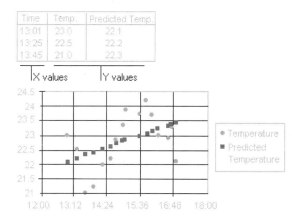

Choosing a Different Type of Chart

Although the standard types of charts will suit many purposes, you may find that you need to modify the style for a better presentation of information or simply to make your chart look nice. You can change the chart type of either a data series or the entire chart for a 2-D chart. Only the entire chart can be modified for bubble charts. Modifying the chart type will affect the entire chart in most 3-D charts. For 3-D bar and column charts, a data series can be changed to the cone, cylinder, or pyramid type.

To select a different kind of chart, follow these steps:

1. Change the type of the entire chart by selecting it.

2. Change the type of a data series by selecting it.

3. Select Chart Type (see Figure 19-1) from the Chart menu.

4. Select the chart type you want from the Standard Types or Custom Types tab.

5. Apply the cone, cylinder, or pyramid chart type to a 3-D bar or column data series by selecting Cylinder, Cone, or Pyramid from the Chart Type box on the Standard Types tab and then choosing the Apply to Selection check box.

NOTE   *If the Apply to Selection check box is cleared, Excel will change the chart type of the entire chart even if just a data series is chosen.*

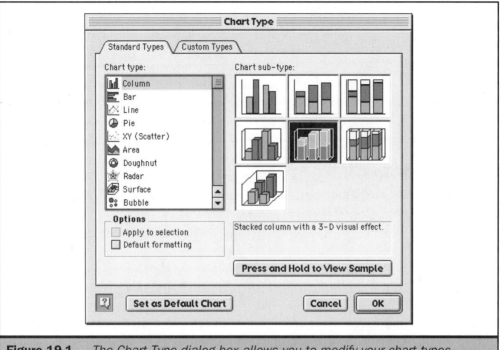

Figure 19-1.   *The Chart Type dialog box allows you to modify your chart types.*

Creating Your Own Chart Types

When you want to create a chart or change the type of a chart, you can choose between a standard chart type and a custom one. If you'd prefer to use a custom chart type, you can select one of the built-in custom chart types or create one of your own. Using a built-in type can save you lots of time compiling your chart, since you don't have to spend extra time setting up a new chart format.

- **Built-in Custom Chart Types**   Microsoft Excel comes with several built-in chart types that are based on standard chart types but include additional formatting and options, such as a legend, gridlines, data labels, a secondary axis, colors, patterns, fills, and placement choices for various chart items. These chart types can be found on the Custom Types tab in the Chart Type dialog box.

- **Creating Your Own Chart Types**   You also have the ability to create your own custom chart types by modifying any of the ones provided by Excel. You even have the ability to share these custom chart types with other users. For example, if you want the same title information to be displayed on all the charts created for your company, you can create a chart with that title, save it as a user-defined custom chart type, and then share it with others in your company to use just as you would a template.

> **NOTE** *Built-in custom chart types are kept in the file Excel Chart Gallery. If you have created your own custom chart types, they will be stored in the file Excel Chart User Gallery as well. Your own charts will have different names from the standard ones found in the Gallery.*

Saving a Custom Chart Type

Once you've created a custom chart, you may want to use it again. Just follow the steps below to save a custom chart type:

1. Select the chart you want saved as a custom chart type.
2. Select Chart Type from the Chart menu.
3. Choose User-defined from the Custom Types tab.
4. Click Add.
5. Type a name in the Name box. If you want a description, type it in the Description box.
6. Click the OK button.

Modifying the Default Chart Type

Use these steps to change the default chart type:

1. Select a chart to bring up the Chart menu.
2. Choose Chart Type from the Chart menu.
3. Select the chart type you want from the Standard Types or Custom Types tab.

> **NOTE** *The Custom Types tab will list the current default chart, the built-in custom chart types, and any custom chart types you've added. A chart can be created with the type, items, and formatting you want and then saved as a custom chart type.*

4. Select Set as Default Chart and then click the Yes button.
5. Close the dialog box without modifying the chart type of the current chart by clicking Cancel.
6. Click OK to close the dialog box and modify the chart type of the current chart.

Using the Selected Chart as the Default Chart Type

Once you've selected a suitable chart design that you want to use again, you can easily make it your default chart type. To use a selected chart as a default chart type, follow these steps:

1. Select the chart you want to use as the default.

2. Select Chart Type from the Chart menu.

3. Choose Set as Default Chart from Custom Types tab and then click the Yes button.

4. If the Add Custom Chart Type dialog box comes up, type a name in the Name box, type a description in the Description box, and then click OK.

Creating a New Chart

Now that you know the ramifications of changing various chart types and setting up defaults for additional use, here's how to create your first new chart.

Follow these steps to create either a chart sheet or an embedded chart:

1. Choose the cells with the data you want in the chart. If you also want the column and row labels to be displayed in the chart, include the cells that have them in the selection.

2. Select Chart Wizard (a picture of a graph) from the main toolbar.

3. Since the instructions in the Chart Wizard will vary from chart to chart, just follow the instructions indicated.

> NOTE
>
> *If there are multiple levels of column and row labels in your worksheet, your chart can be configured to show those levels. When the chart is created, make sure the labels are included for every level in your selection. To keep the hierarchy in place when data is added to the chart, modify the cell range being used to create the chart.*

Creating a Chart in One Step

An even simpler way to make a chart involves just one step, but it's limited to your default chart type. Here's how to create a chart in a single step:

■ Create a chart sheet using the default chart type by choosing the data you want plotted and then pressing the F11 key.

■ Create an embedded chart using the default chart type by choosing the data you want plotted and then clicking the Default Chart button. If this button isn't available, add it to a toolbar. To add a button, follow these steps:

1. Bring up the toolbar to which you want to add a button.

2. Select Customize from the Tools menu and choose the Commands tab. It might be necessary to move the Customize dialog box by selecting either the title bar or dialog border in order to see the tab.

3. Choose the category of the command that you want the button to perform from the Categories list.

4. Move the command you want from the Commands list to the toolbar currently being shown.

> NOTE *When a chart is created using this simple procedure, the default chart type will be used. This is a column chart, unless you have changed it to something else.*

Creating a Chart from Nonadjacent Selections

Although you set up most charts by selecting a series of connected data, there are other methods you can use. Follow these steps to create a chart using nonadjacent selections:

1. Choose the first group of cells that contain data you want in your chart.

2. Hold down the COMMAND key and select any other cell groups you want to include in the chart. While doing this, keep in mind that the nonadjacent selections have to form a rectangle.

3. Select the Chart Wizard from the main toolbar.

4. Follow the instructions in the Chart Wizard.

Changing an Embedded Chart to a Chart Sheet (and Vice Versa)

As explained earlier, you can configure a chart as a separate document or as an object that's part of your original worksheet. Follow these steps to transform an embedded chart into a chart sheet (and vice versa):

1. Select the chart that you want moved or changed.

2. Select Location from the Chart menu. This brings up the Chart Location dialog box.

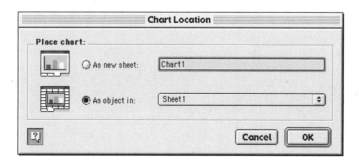

3. To place the chart on a new chart sheet, select As new sheet and type a name for the new chart sheet in the As New Sheet box.

4. To place the chart as an embedded object on a worksheet, select As Object In, choose a sheet name from the As Object In pop-up menu, and click OK. Then drag the embedded chart to where you want it on the worksheet.

Adding Data to a Chart

After you've created your chart, you may need to alter the data as new information is received, or values may need updating. There are many ways to add data to a chart and modify that data. These ways are described in the following sections.

Adding Data to a Chart by Copying and Pasting

Use these steps to add data to a chart by copying and pasting it from a worksheet:

1. Choose the cells with the data you want to add to your chart. If you also want the column or row label for the new data displayed in the chart, include the cell with the label in the selection.

2. Select Copy from the Edit menu.

3. Choose the chart you want to change.

4. Select Paste from the Edit menu to have Microsoft Excel automatically paste the data in the chart. To specify how you want your data plotted in the chart, select Paste Special from the Edit menu and choose the options you want.

```
╔═══════════════ Paste Special ═══════════════╗

  Paste ─────────────────────────────────────
    ● All               ○ Comments
    ○ Formulas          ○ Validation
    ○ Values            ○ All except borders
    ○ Formats

  Operation ─────────────────────────────────
    ● None              ○ Multiply
    ○ Add               ○ Divide
    ○ Subtract

  ☐ Skip blanks         ☐ Transpose

  [ Paste Link ]     [ Cancel ]   [  OK  ]
```

Adding Data to an Embedded Chart by Dragging

Follow these steps to add data to an embedded chart by dragging the data to the appropriate area in your worksheet:

1. Choose the cells that have the data you want added to the chart.

NOTE *The cells must be adjacent to each other on the worksheet. Select the cells that contain the data you want to add to the chart. If you want the column or row label for the new data to be displayed in the chart, make sure the cell with the label is included in the selection.*

2. Point to the border of the selection.

3. Drag the selection to the embedded chart you want to update. If more information is needed to plot the data, the Paste Special dialog box will appear.

NOTE *If you cannot drag the selection, make sure that the Allow Cell Drag and Drop check box is selected. To check this setting, choose Preferences on the Edit menu and then select the Edit tab.*

Adding Data to an Embedded Chart Using Color-Coded Ranges

To add data to an embedded chart using color-coded ranges, you must create the embedded chart from adjacent selections and it must be on the same worksheet as the data used for its creation. Simply follow these steps to make it happen:

1. Type the data and labels you want added to the worksheet in the cells adjacent to the existing data.

2. Choose the region of the chart by selecting the blank area between the chart's border and the plot area.

   ■ To add new categories and data series to the chart, drag the blue selection handle to cover the new data and labels in the rectangle.

   ■ To add only new data series on the worksheet, drag the blue selection handle to encompass the new data and labels in the rectangle.

   ■ To add new categories and data points to the worksheet, drag the purple selection handle to encompass the new data and labels in the rectangle.

NOTE *Modify the range of data plotted in the chart by dragging the border of the color-coded range.*

Modifying the Cell Range Used to Create a Chart

Use the following steps to modify the cell range used to create a chart:

1. Select the chart you want to modify.

2. Select Source Data from the Chart menu and choose the Data Range tab.

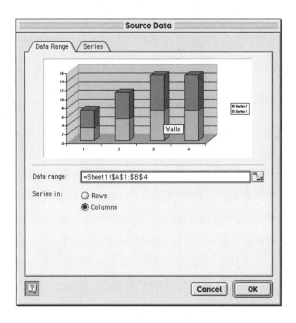

3. Be sure that the entire reference in the Data Range box is selected.

4. From the worksheet, choose the cells that contain the data you want displayed in the chart.

NOTE *If you want the column and row labels to appear in the chart as well, include the cells that contain them in the selection.*

Plotting Data Series from Worksheet Rows Instead of Columns (and Vice Versa)

To plot data series from worksheet rows instead of columns (and vice versa), follow these steps:

1. Select the chart.

2. Select Source Data from the Chart menu and choose the Data Range tab.

3. Choose Series in Rows or Series in Columns.

NOTE *You also can modify the orientation of a data series by selecting By Row or By Column from the Chart toolbar.*

Plotting a Data Series Along a Secondary Value Axis in a 2-D Chart

Two-dimensional (2-D) charts can be used to display a wide variation between the range of values for different data series of several kinds of data (such as price and volume). If you want to do this, one or more data series can be plotted on a secondary value (*y*) axis. The scale of the secondary axis reflects the values of the associated series.

Here's how to accomplish the task:

1. Select the data series you want plotted along a secondary value axis.
2. Choose Selected Data Series from the Format menu and then select the Axis tab.
3. Select Secondary Axis.

Reversing the Plotting Order of Categories, Values, or Series

The plotting order of categories or values can be reversed for most charts, as well as the data series of 3-D charts with a third axis. However, the plotting order of values in a radar chart can't be reversed.

Follow these steps to reverse the order of categories, values, or series:

1. Select the axis for the category values or series whose plotting order you want reversed.
2. Choose Selected Axis from the Format menu and select the Scale tab.

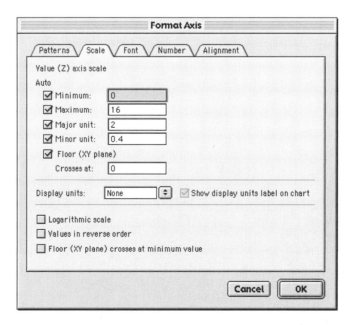

3. Reverse the plotting order of categories by selecting the Categories in reverse order check box. Reverse the plotting order of values by choosing the Values in Reverse Order check box.

> **NOTE**
>
> *To reverse the plotting order of series in 3-D charts, choose the Series in Reverse Order check box, which can be found in the Scale Tab of the Selected Axis command in the Format menu.*

Modifying the Plotting Order of Data Series

To change the plotting order of a series of data, follow these steps:

1. Select a data series from a chart that you want to modify.

2. Choose Selected Data Series from the Format menu and select the Series Order tab.

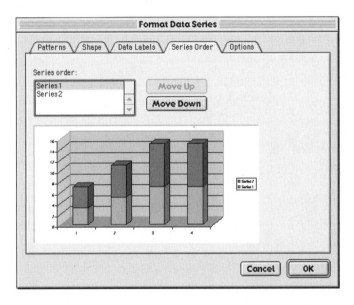

3. Choose the series you want to move from the Series Order box.

4. Select Move Up or Move Down to put the series in the order you want.

> **NOTE**
>
> *Modify the plotting order of data series in surface charts by selecting a legend key and then choosing Selected Legend Key from the Format menu.*

Controlling the Way Empty Cells Are Plotted

How will empty cells be handled? Will they appear in the chart or not? Follow these steps to control the way empty cells are plotted in a chart:

1. Select the chart.

2. Select Preferences from the Edit menu and choose the Chart tab.

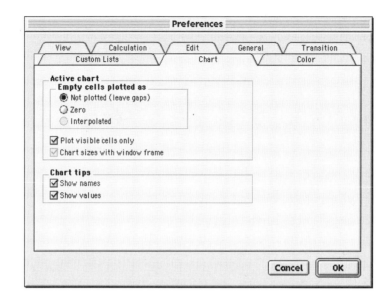

3. Choose any option you want under Empty Cells Plotted As.

Modifying the Points Plotted in a Pie-of-Pie or Bar-of-Pie Chart

A pie-of-pie chart is made when the values of one pie are extracted and used in the creation of a second pie chart. A bar-of-pie chart is created when the data in a pie chart is broken down into a bar graph. Use the following steps to change the points plotted in a pie-of-pie or bar-of-pie chart:

1. Select a slice in the pie that you want to change.

2. Choose Selected Data Point from the Format menu and select the Options tab.

3. Select the options you want.

> **NOTE** *You also can change which slices appear in the pie-of-pie or bar-of-pie chart by dragging. Select a slice or bar from the main chart and then drag it to the pie-of-pie or bar-of-pie chart, or vice versa.*

Modifying Values

The values of a chart are linked to the worksheet from which the chart was created. Whenever the data in the worksheet is modified, the chart will be updated to reflect those changes. Follow these steps to change the values in a chart:

1. Open the worksheet with the data plotted in the chart.

2. Type a new value in the cell that has the value you want to change.

3. Press the RETURN key.

Modifying Values by Dragging Data Markers and Using Goal Seeking

To change the values created from worksheet formulas in 2-D column, bar, pie, doughnut, line XY (scatter), and bubble charts, drag the data marker in the chart and use the Goal Seek feature (we'll get to this shortly).

NOTE   *When the value of a data marker is modified by dragging, Excel also changes the underlying value in the worksheet.*

To modify values, select the data series with the data marker you want to modify and then select the marker:

- If the data marker is a bubble, line, or XY (scatter) data marker, drag the data marker.

- If the data marker is a bar or column data marker, drag the top-center selection handle.

- If the data marker is a pie or doughnut chart data marker, drag the largest selection handle on the outer edge of the data marker.

- If the value of the data marker was generated from a formula, the Goal Seek dialog box will appear. Select the cell with a value that you want to modify and then click OK.

Displaying Visible Worksheet Data

You may want to show and hide details in an outline with subtotals or filter data using specific criteria selected from one of the Filter commands in the Data menu. Whenever data is hidden, displayed, or filtered on a worksheet, the corresponding chart will display only the visible rows and columns.

To display visible worksheet data, do the following:

1. Select the chart.

2. Choose Preferences from the Edit menu and then select the Chart tab.

3. Choose the Plot Visible Cells Only check box.

NOTE   *If you prefer to display all worksheet data in the chart, even if some rows or columns are hidden, clear the Plot Visible Cells Only check box.*

Reestablishing Links Between Number Formats in a Worksheet and a Related Chart

If the number formatting in a chart has been modified, the number formatting will no longer be linked to the worksheet cells. To reestablish those links, do the following:

1. Reestablish number formats for labels along an axis by clicking twice on the appropriate axis. To reestablish number formats for data labels on a trendline label, click the item twice.

2. Choose the Link to source check box on the Number tab.

Adding Text and Labels

You can add and change text and labels in a chart in a number of different ways, as described in the following sections.

Adding a Text Box

To add a text box to a chart, do the following:

1. Select the chart to which you want to add a text box.

2. Select Toolbars from the View menu and choose Drawing from the submenu.

3. Click the Text Box button on the Drawing toolbar.

4. Click the area where you want one corner of the text box to be and then drag until the size of the box is adequate.

5. Type the text you want in the box. The text will wrap inside the box. Start a new line in the box by pressing the RETURN key.

6. After you are done typing, press the ESC key or click outside the text box.

Modifying Category (*x*) Axis Labels

To change category axis labels, do the following:

- Change category (*x*) axis labels on the worksheet by selecting the cell with the label name you want to modify, typing the new name, and then pressing the RETURN key.

- Modify category (*x*) axis labels on the chart by selecting the chart, opening the Chart menu, and selecting Source Data. Then specify the worksheet range you want used as category (*x*) axis labels in the Category (X) Axis Labels box on the Series tab. In addition, you can type the labels you want to use and separate them by commas, as in this example:

  Region A, Region B, Region C

If the label text is typed in the Category (X) Axis Labels box, the category axis text will no longer be linked to a worksheet cell.

Modifying Data Labels

Modify data labels on a worksheet or chart by doing the following:

- To modify the data labels of a worksheet, select a cell with information that you want to change, type the new text or value, and then press the RETURN key.

- Change data labels on a chart by selecting the data label you want to change, which will select the data labels for the entire series, and then click again to choose the individual label. Type the next text or value and press the RETURN key.

If the data label text is changed on the chart, it will no longer be linked to a worksheet cell.

Modifying the Position of Data Labels Automatically

You can change the position of a data label to drag it. This procedure can be used for the placement of all labels in a data series in a standard position on their data markers in 2-D bar, column, and line charts; 2-D and 3-D pie charts; and scatter and bubble charts.

To do this, follow these steps:

1. Select the chart outside the data labels you want to modify. Make sure that Show Labels on the Data Labels tab of the Chart Options dialog box (it can be reached by accessing the Format Data Series dialog box from the Format menu) has been selected.

2. Choose one of the data labels from the series you want to modify.

3. Choose Selected Data Labels from the Format menu and select the Alignment tab.

4. Choose the location you want from the Label Position pop-up menu.

Changing Data Series Names or Legend Text

If you want to change data series names or legend text, use the following steps:

- To modify legend text or data series names on the worksheet, select the cell with the data series name that you want to change, type the new name, and press the RETURN key.

- To modify legend text or data series names on a chart, select the chart, and choose Source Data from the Chart menu.

- Select the data series names you want to change on the Series tab.

- Choose the worksheet cell that you want to use as the legend text or data series name in the Names box.

You also can type the name you want to use. If a name is typed in the Names box, however, the legend text or data series name won't be linked to a worksheet cell anymore.

Linking a Chart Title or Text Box to a Worksheet Cell

Link an existing chart title or text box to a worksheet cell by doing the following:

1. To link a title, select the title. Set up a linked text box by selecting the chart area.

2. Type an equal sign (=) in the formula bar.

3. Choose the worksheet cell with the data or text that you want displayed in your chart. You also can type the reference to the worksheet cell. Make sure the sheet name and an exclamation point are included, as in this example: **Sheet1!F2**.

4. Press the RETURN key.

Rotating Text in a Chart Title or Along an Axis

You can rotate, or angle, text in a chart title or along an axis. To do this, follow these steps:

1. Select the axis or title that you want to format.

2. Choose Selected Axis from the Format menu, if you selected an axis. Choose Selected Axis Title from the Format menu if you selected an axis title. Choose Selected Chart Title if you selected a chart title.

3. Select the Alignment tab.

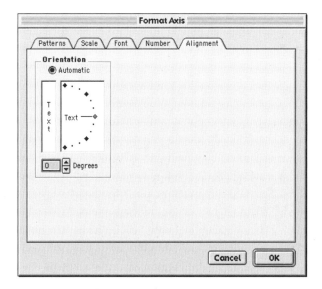

If the Alignment tab isn't displayed, click the Cancel button, select something outside the text you want to format, and redo steps 1 through 3.

4. Rotate text by selecting a degree point or dragging the indicator to the position you want under Orientation.

5. To quickly rotate selected text 45 degrees up or down, select Angle Text Upward or Angle Text Downward from the Chart toolbar.

NOTE *If there is more than one level of category axis labels, only the first level (which is the one nearest to the axis) can be rotated.*

Aligning Text in Chart Titles and Text Boxes

Do the following to align text in chart titles and text boxes:

1. Select the title or border of the text box that you want to align.

2. If an axis title was selected, choose Selected Axis Title from the Format menu. If a chart title was selected, open the Format menu and choose Selected Chart Title. If a text box was selected, choose Text Box from the Format menu.

3. Select the Alignment tab.

NOTE *If the Alignment tab isn't displayed, click the Cancel button, select something outside the text that you want to format, and redo steps 1 through 3.*

4. Select the options you want.

TIP *Quickly change the horizontal alignment of selected chart titles and text boxes by choosing Align Left, Center, or Align Right from the Formatting toolbar.*

Configuring a Chart for Printing

A chart may look just dandy on your Mac's display, but you may also want to print the chart and preserve as much of the fancy formatting. You'll want to consider the following guidelines to set up a chart for printing:

- If your chart is embedded in a worksheet, it can be configured so that it will print on the page by sizing and moving the chart with the mouse in page break view. Do this by selecting the worksheet outside the chart area and choosing Page Break Preview from the View menu.

- If you are using a chart sheet, you can size and scale the area with the chart, specify how the chart should be placed on the printed page, and then view your work in the preview window. Set printing options for a chart sheet by selecting the tab for the sheet, choosing Page Setup from the File menu, and choosing the options you want from the Chart tab.

- To move and size the chart area of a chart sheet using the mouse, select Custom from the Chart tab and click OK to go back to the chart sheet.

NOTE   *To print an embedded chart without its associated worksheet data, select the chart and follow the preceding instructions relating to chart sheets. The chart area can be moved and sized without having to deal with the Custom option of the Chart tab.*

Adding Error Bars and Trendlines

The following section discusses error bars and trendlines as they might apply to the chart you create.

Using Error Bars

The purpose of errors bars is to graphically display potential error amounts relative to each data marker in a series. For example, positive or negative margins of error could be displayed in the results of a scientific experiment.

Error bars can be added to data series in 2-D area, bar, column, line, XY (scatter), and bubble charts. For XY and bubble charts, error bars can be shown for their x values, y values, or both.

To add error bars to a data series, do the following:

1. Select the data series to which you want to add error bars.

2. Choose Selected Data Series from the Format menu.

3. Choose the options you want from either the X Error Bars tab or the Y Error Bars tab (only the latter applies for a bar chart).

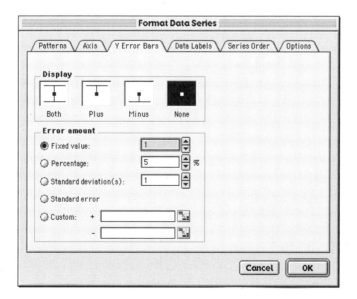

If the worksheet values or formulas related to the data points in the series are modified, the error bars can be adjusted to reflect your changes.

Changing Error Bar Settings

Once you've created an error bar, you can change the settings for it. Any changes you make will affect all of the error bars in the associated data series.

To change the settings, use the following steps:

1. Select the data series with error bars you want to change.

2. Choose Selected Data Series from the Format menu.

3. Select the X Error Bars tab or the Y Error Bars tab, depending on the type of error bars that you want to modify. To choose a different kind of error bar, select the type you want under Display.

If you want to change the method used for determining the error, select the method you want from the Error Amount area. To modify a custom error amount, select Custom. In the plus (+) and minus (–) boxes, define the worksheet range to be used as error amount values or enter the values that you want to use, separated by commas.

Using Trendlines

The purpose of trendlines is to graphically show trends in data and analyze predictions. Such analysis is known as regression analysis. Using this type of analysis, a trendline in a chart can be extended beyond the actual data to predict future values. For example, a chart using a simple linear trendline can be used to forecast ahead eight quarters to display a trend toward increasing profits.

You also can create a moving average, which smoothes out rapid changes in data and displays the pattern or trend more clearly.

Trendlines can be added to data series in unstacked 2-D area, bar, column, line, stock, XY (scatter), and bubble charts. Trendlines cannot be added to data series in 3-D, stacked, radar, pie, surface, or doughnut charts.

If you modify a data series or chart that can't support the associated trendline (by changing the chart type to a pie chart, for example), the trendlines will be lost.

To add a trendline to a data series, do the following:

1. Select the data series to which you want to add a trendline or moving average.

2. Choose Add Trendline from the Chart menu.

3. Select the kind of regression trendline or moving average you want from the Type tab.

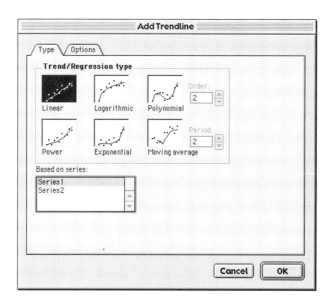

If Polynomial is selected, enter the highest power for the independent variable in the Order box. If Moving Average is selected, enter the number of periods to be used for the calculation of the moving average in the Period box.

Here's some additional information you'll want to consider when you're setting up your chart. If you add a moving average to a scatter chart, the moving average is based on the order of the *x* values plotted in the chart. You may have to sort the *x* values before adding a moving average to get the answers you want.

Showing the R-Squared Value of a Trendline

The R-squared value, also called the *coefficient of determination,* is an indicator with values ranging from 0 to 1 and shows how closely the estimated values of the trendline relate to your actual data. A trendline is most reliable when its R-squared value is at or near 1. To show the R-squared value, follow these steps:

1. Select the trendline whose R-squared value you want to see.

2. Choose Selected Trendline from the Format menu.

3. Choose Display R-Squared Value on Chart from the Options tab.

An R-squared value for a moving average can't be displayed.

Formatting Charts

There are many ways to format your chart in Excel. By using the various features that apply to specific types of charts, you can greatly enhance the look and clarity of the information you present.

We'll explore many of these formatting techniques in the sections that follow.

Modifying the Depth and Width of a 3-D Chart

The chart depth of 3-D charts with axes, the gap depth of 3-D perspective charts, and the gap width in 3-D bar or column charts can be modified. Use the following steps to do this:

1. Select a data series from the 3-D chart that you want to modify.

2. Choose Selected Data Series from the Format menu and select the Options tab.

3. Choose the options you want.

Modifying the Height and Perspective in a 3-D Chart

You can change the height and perspective of a chart depending on the type of 3-D chart and the options selected for it. Here's how:

1. Select the 3-D chart you want to modify.

2. Choose 3-D View from the Chart menu.

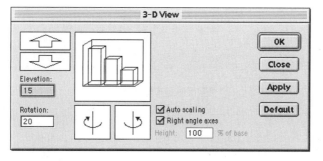

3. Choose the options you want.

When you modify your 3-D chart, you'll want to consider the following:

- ■ The Perspective and Height options are available to be set when the Right Angle Axes check box has been cleared.

- ■ When the Right Angle Axes check box is selected, you can either set the Height option or select the Auto Scaling option.

- ■ The Perspective option cannot be used in 3-D bar charts, for which the Right Angle Axes check box is always selected.

Modifying the Elevation and Rotation of a 3-D Chart

To change the rotation or elevation of a 3-D chart, do the following:

1. Select the 3-D chart you want to change.

2. On the Chart menu, click 3-D View.

3. Select the options you want.

> **NOTE**   *You also can rotate the chart using the mouse. Select the intersection of any two axes to choose the corners of the chart and then drag a corner to change the elevation and rotation of the chart. Hold down the COMMAND key while you're dragging to see the data markers.*

Modifying the Scale of the Value Axis

The scale is used to define the range of values on an axis, the manner in which axis values are shown, the intervals at which values are placed, and the point where one axis crosses another. To change the scale of the value axis, do the following:

1. Select the value axis you want to change.

2. Choose Selected Axis from the Format menu and select the Scale tab.

3. Choose the options you want.

> **NOTE**   *To flip the direction of bars or columns in a bar or column chart, make sure that the Values in Reverse Order check box is selected.*

Modifying the Display Unit of the Value Axis

If your chart values are large numbers, you can make the axis text shorter and easier to read by modifying the display unit of the axis. For example, if the values in your chart range from 1,000,000 to 30,000,000, the numbers can be displayed on the axis as 1 to 30, and a label can be displayed that indicates that the units express millions. This way, those who view your chart will not be confronted by huge numbers, and the presentation will also be easier to digest if the space of the chart is constrained.

To change the display unit of the value axis, do the following:

1. Select the value axis you want to modify.

2. Choose Selected Axis from the Format menu and select the Scale tab.

3. Select the units you want from the Display Units pop-up menu.

4. To display a label that describes the expressed units, choose the Show Display Units Labels on Chart check box.

Modifying the Spacing of
Tick Marks and Labels on the Category Axis

Every category on the category axis is identified by a label and is kept separate from other categories by tick marks. The intervals at which labels and tick marks are displayed can be modified. For 2-D charts, you can choose where you want the value (y) axis to cross the category (x) axis. Use the following steps:

1. Select the category axis you want to modify.

2. Choose Selected Axis from the Format menu and select the Scale tab.

3. Choose the options you want.

When you modify the spacing of tick marks and labels in your chart, you'll want to remember that if your chart has more than one level of category axis labels, the amount of space, or offset, between the levels can be changed.

Modifying Tick Mark Appearance and Placement of Labels

To change the appearance of tick marks and the placement of labels on an axis, do the following:

1. Select the axis with tick marks that you want to modify.

2. Choose Selected Axis from the Format menu and select the Patterns tab.

3. Choose the options you want under Tick Mark Type and Tick Mark Labels.

NOTE *To hide major or minor tick marks, or to hide both kinds, select None. When your chart has more than one level of category axis labels, the amount of space between the levels and the alignment of all of them except the first level can be modified.*

Modifying the Alignment and Spacing of
Multiple-Level Category Labels

When your chart has several levels of category labels, the alignment of all of them except the first level can be changed. You also can change the amount of space between every level of label. Follow these steps:

1. Select the category axis you want to modify.

2. Choose Selected Axis from the Format menu and select the Alignment tab.

3. Modify the label alignment by selecting the position you want from the Alignment pop-up menu. Change the spacing between the levels by choosing a value from the Offset box.

NOTE *The higher the value, the more space there will be between every level.*

Overlapping or Spacing Data Markers in Bar and Column Charts

To modify the overlap or spacing of all data series of the same kind of chart, you only have to choose a single data series. Use the following steps:

1. Select a data series from the chart you want to modify.

2. Choose Selected Data Series from the Format menu and select the Options tab.

3. Change the overlap of the data markers in every category by entering a value between –100 and 100 in the Overlap box. The higher the value, the more the overlap in the category will be. Keep in mind that this box does not exist in 3-D line or bar charts.

4. Change the spacing between categories of data markers by entering a value between 0 and 500 in the Gap Width box.

Note the following:

- The higher the value, the greater the distance between every category.
- Different options exist for different charts.

Rotating the Position of the Slices in a Doughnut or Pie Chart

The order in which data series in pie and doughnut charts are plotted is determined by the way the data is arranged on the worksheet. This procedure can be used to rotate slices in the 360 degrees of a pie or doughnut chart:

1. Select a data series from the pie or doughnut chart that you want to modify.

2. Choose Selected Data Series from the Format menu and select the Options tab.

3. Type a value between 0 and 360 to choose the angle where you want the first slice displayed.

Removing Slices from Pie and Doughnut Charts

You can pull out the slices of only the outer ring in a doughnut chart. To remove slices from pie and doughnut charts, do one of the following:

- Remove all of the slices in a pie chart by selecting the chart and then dragging away from the middle of the chart.
- Remove only a slice from a pie chart by selecting the chart, choosing the slice you want to move, and then dragging it away from the middle of the chart.

- Remove all of the slices in the outer ring of a doughnut chart by selecting the outer ring and dragging away from the middle of the chart.

- Remove only one slice from the outer ring of a doughnut chart by selecting the outer ring, choosing the slice you want to move, and then dragging it away from the chart's center.

Modifying the Hole Size in a Doughnut Chart

To change the hole size in a doughnut chart, do the following:

1. Select a data series from the doughnut chart you want to modify.

2. Choose Selected Data Series from the Format menu and select the Options tab.

3. Type a value between 10 and 90 in the Doughnut Hole Size box to specify the hole's diameter.

Modifying the Size of the Pie-of-Pie or Bar-of-Pie Plot Area

Change the size of a pie-of-pie of bar-of-pie plot area by following these steps:

1. Select a data series from the pie chart you want to modify.

2. Choose Selected Data Series from the Format menu and select the Options tab.

3. Enter a value between 5 and 200 in the Size of Second Plot box to specify the size of the second pie or bar as a percentage of the first pie chart.

NOTE *For example, if you enter 80, that will make the second pie or bar 20 percent smaller than the first one.*

Adding a Picture

You can add an image, such as a bitmap, to certain types of data markers, the chart area, the plot area, the legend of 2-D and 3-D charts, and the walls and floor of 3-D charts. Using the following steps, you also can use a picture for data markers in column, bar, area, bubble, 3-D line, and filled radar charts. To use a picture for any of these, do the following:

1. Select the chart item for which you want to use a picture.

2. Choose the arrow next to Fill Color, select Fill Effect, and then select the Picture tab.

3. Choose Select Picture to choose a picture. Select the picture by double-clicking it. If the picture you want isn't displayed in the list, make sure that the correct file format is selected in the Show pop-up menu.

4. Choose the options you want from the Picture tab.

ORGANIZING YOUR DATA WITH EXCEL 2001

NOTE *The Fill Effects command cannot be used with 2-D line, scatter, or unfilled radar chart markers. If you want to use a picture as the data marker for these types of charts, select the picture from the worksheet or chart sheet or in a picture editing program such as Adobe Photoshop, select Copy from the Edit menu, choose the data series, and then select Paste from the Edit menu.*

Clearing a Picture or Fill Effect from a Data Series

When you remove a picture or fill effect from a data series, all the formatting added to the data series using the Patterns tab of the Selected Data Series dialog box selected from the Format menu will be removed, and the default formatting will be restored.

To clear a picture or fill effect from a data series, do the following:

1. Select the data series you want to modify.

2. Open the Clear submenu from the Edit menu and select Formats.

Clearing a Picture or Fill Effect from a Chart Item

Use the following steps to clear a picture or fill effect from the chart area, the plot area, the legend in 2-D and 3-D charts, and the walls and floor of 3-D charts:

1. Double-click the chart item you want to modify and then select the Patterns tab.

2. Clear the picture or fill effect and bring the object back to its default format by selecting Automatic, under Area. To clear all formatting, including the picture or fill effect, choose None, under Area.

Modifying Colors, Patterns, Lines, Fills, and Borders

Use these steps to modify colors, add a texture or pattern, or change the line width or border style for data markers, the chart area, the plot area, gridlines, axes, and tick marks in 2-D and 3-D charts; trendlines and error bars in 2-D charts; and the walls and floor of 3-D charts:

1. Double-click the chart item you want to change.

2. If necessary, select the Patterns tab and make the modifications you want. To choose a fill effect, select Fill Effects and then choose the options you want from the Gradient, Texture, or Pattern tab.

ORGANIZING YOUR DATA
WITH EXCEL 2001

> **NOTE** *Formatting added to an axis will also be added to the tick marks on that axes. Gridlines are formatted independently of axes.*

Modifying the Size, Color, or Shape of Line, XY (Scatter), or Radar Chart Markers

To modify the size, color, or shape of line, scatter, or radar chart markers, do the following:

1. Select the line with data markers that you want to modify.

2. Choose Selected Data Series from the Format menu and select the Patterns tab.

3. Choose the options you want under Marker.

Modifying Colors in a Surface Chart

Format the colors of a surface chart by following these steps:

1. Add a legend to the surface chart you want to modify if it doesn't already have one.

2. Select the legend once and then select the legend key that stands for the surface level you want to modify.

3. Choose Selected Legend Key from the Format menu and select the Patterns tab.

4. Choose the color you want and then redo steps 2 and 3 for every level you want to format.

> **NOTE** *If you want the legend to be removed, select it and press the DELETE key. The colors you choose will stay in the surface chart even after the legend has been deleted.*

Varying Colors in the Same Data Series

You can vary the colors of data markers in the same data series in doughnut and single-series charts. The colors of slices in pie and doughnut charts are varied by default. Vary the colors by doing the following:

1. Select the data series for which you want to vary the colors.

2. Choose Selected Data Series or Selected Data Point from the Format menu and select the Options tab.

3. Select the Vary Colors by Point check box or the Vary Colors by Slice check box.

Smoothing the Angles of Line Charts

When you use the following steps to soften the jagged edges in a line chart, your data won't be changed. To smooth the angles of line charts, do the following

1. Select the line data series that you want to smooth.

2. Choose Selected Data Series from the Format menu and select the Patterns tab.

3. Choose the Smoothed Line check box.

Adding Up-Down Bars and Drop, Series, and High-Low Lines

Series lines can be applied to connect data series in 2-D stacked bar and column charts. Drop lines can be used in 2-D and 3-D area and line charts. High-low lines and up-down bars are available in 2-D line charts. Stock charts come with high-low lines and up-down bars. To add any of these to a chart, do the following:

1. Select a data series from the chart to which you want to add bars or lines.

2. Choose Selected Data Series from the Format menu and select the Options tab.

3. Choose the option for the type of lines or bars you want.

Saving Excel Data as a Web Page

Like other kinds of Office files, including Word documents and PowerPoint presentations, Excel workbooks can be saved as Web pages that you can put on your personal Web site or publish on the Web site of your company. Publishing your data on the Web is a very efficient way to enable many people to see it at once, considering that hundreds of millions of people across the world currently have some form of Internet access, and that number is growing by leaps and bounds every year.

Before you save your workbook as a Web page or save any of the data in it, make sure your workbook has been saved so you have a version that can be changed if you have to modify your Web page later.

Use the following steps to save any data in your workbook as a Web page:

1. Choose the data you want to be saved as a Web page.

2. Select Save as Web Page from the File menu.

3. Using the folder list and pop-up menu above it, select the folder you want to put your new document in by double-clicking it.

4. Type a name for the document in the Name box.

5. Do one of the following: Select Sheet if you want to save a worksheet as a Web page. If you want to just save the data you selected, choose Selection.

6. Add a title and keywords to the Web page by selecting Web Options and choosing the General tab. Type the title and keywords you want and then click on OK.

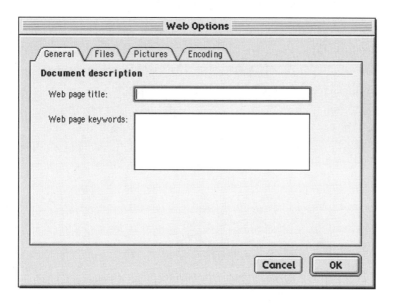

7. Click the Save button.

NOTE   *When a chart is published, it will be saved as a Graphics Interchange Format (.gif) image file in the supporting files folder.*

Saving a Workbook as a Web Page

To save a workbook as a Web page, use the following steps:

1. Select Save as Web Page from the File menu.

2. Using the folder list and pop-up menu above it, select the folder you want by double-clicking it.

3. Type a name for the document in the Name box.

4. Select Workbook.

5. Add a title and keywords by selecting Web Options and choosing the General tab. Then type the title and keywords you want and click OK.

6. Click the Save button.

Automatically Saving Data to a Web Page

To automatically save data to a Web page, do the following:

1. Open the workbook or choose the worksheet data that you want to save as a Web page.

2. Choose Save as Web Page from the File menu.

3. Using the folder list and pop-up menu above it, select the folder you want by double-clicking it.

4. Type a name for the document in the Name box.

5. Choose whether you want the entire workbook, an individual worksheet, or selected data in the worksheet to be saved and select Automate.

6. In the Automate dialog box, select Every Time This Workbook Is Saved and then click OK.

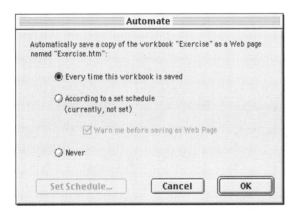

7. Click the Save button.

Configuring a Schedule to Save Data to a Web Page

You can also set up a schedule for saving your worksheet data to your Web page. Here's how:

1. Open the workbook or choose the worksheet data you want to save on a Web page.

2. Choose Save as Web Page from the File menu.

3. Using the folder list and pop-up menu above it, select the folder you want by double-clicking it.

4. Type a name for the document in the Name box.

5. Choose whether you want the entire workbook, a worksheet, or selected data in a worksheet to be saved and then select Automate.

6. Select According to a Set Schedule from the Automate dialog and then choose Set Schedule.

7. Set the options you want in the Recurring Schedule dialog box (see Figure 19-2).

8. Click OK.

9. Click the Save button.

Summary

In this chapter, you learned how to create various kinds of charts and how to modify them for your own purposes. You also learned how to save your Excel data to a Web page.

In the next chapter, you will meet PowerPoint 2001, the multimedia presentation component of Office. You'll be introduced to the application's various features, and you'll learn how to create a simple presentation using text, graphics, and pictures.

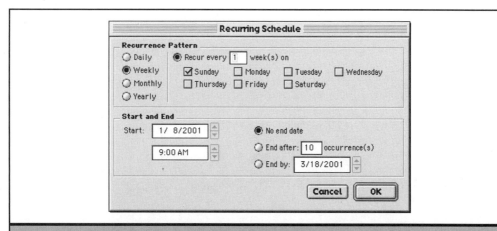

Figure 19-2. *The Recurring Schedule dialog box allows you to define a schedule to automatically save data to a Web page.*

Part V

Mastering PowerPoint 2001

Chapter 20

Introduction to PowerPoint 2001

The fourth member of the Office 2001 family may end up being one of your favorites, although it has been underutilized by most users of this application suite.

PowerPoint 2001 (see Figure 20-1) is a powerful tool for creating presentations, whether it's an innovative proposal you're making before your corporation's impatient board of directors or an elaborate, creative slide show you simply want to put together for family and friends. PowerPoint allows you to create everything from simple presentations with text and graphics to professional-caliber shows with animated GIFs, QuickTime movies, MP3 sound files, and much, much more.

In this chapter, we discuss the new features of PowerPoint, and you'll also learn how to make your first presentation.

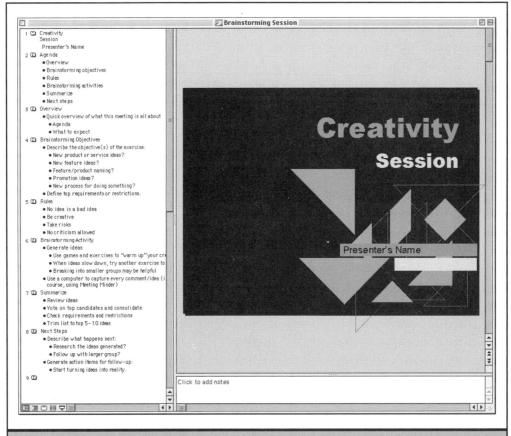

Figure 20-1. *PowerPoint 2001 is the multimedia component of Office 2001.*

PowerPoint's New Features

As for the other Office 2001 applications, Microsoft has added a number of useful features that make PowerPoint easier to use and you more productive.

Before you learn how to use those features, we'll take a brief look at them:

- **Project Gallery Makes You More Productive** The Office 2001 Project Gallery (seen in Figure 20-2) lets you easily find the template or wizard that best suits your project. It will come up every time you launch PowerPoint, and you can open it manually by clicking the File menu and choosing Project Gallery.

- **Documents Can Be Found and Opened Faster** Apple's new Open and Save dialog boxes (shown in Figure 20-3) help you gain easier access to your documents in PowerPoint. You have a number of additional choices. If you click the Shortcuts button, you can access the desktop, network Macs, and your mounted volumes much more efficiently. Or you can click Favorites and access, add to, or remove items from your Favorites folder. You can even click Recent to access documents that you've recently worked on.

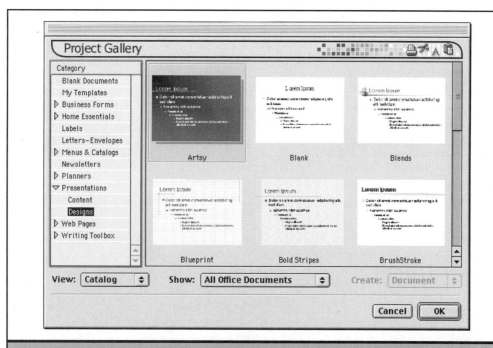

Figure 20-2. *The Project Gallery is an ever-present companion to help you with your PowerPoint presentations.*

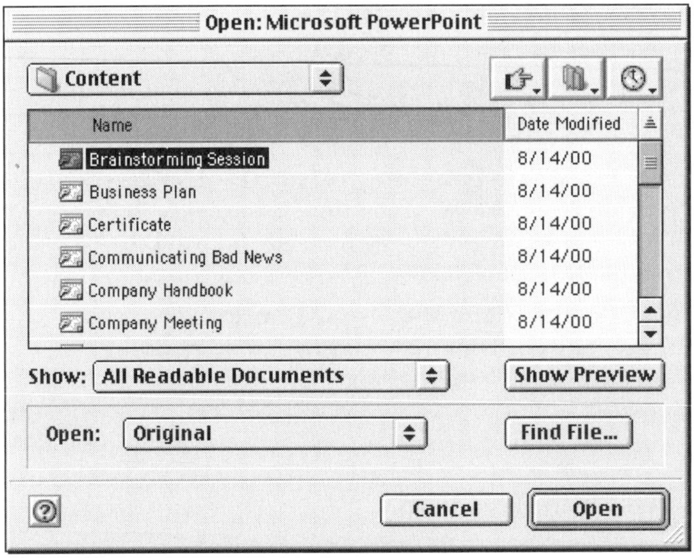

Figure 20-3. *PowerPoint has full support for the newest Open and Save dialog boxes.*

- **Formatting Palette Formats Presentations Faster** PowerPoint fully supports the Office 2001 Formatting Palette (shown in Figure 20-4), which gives you the options you need to easily format your presentation without having to navigate through menus and endless dialog boxes. For example, when you select a block of text, the Formatting Palette allows you to choose many of the most common text formatting options. If you select a drawing object, the Formatting Palette changes to give you options for drawing objects.

- **Slide Finder Locates and Inserts Slides Quickly** The Slide Finder enables you to search through thumbnail or miniature preview images of your slides in a presentation so you can easily examine the slides you have already made, to copy them into a new presentation, for example. The Slide Finder can also be used to add a new slide master or title master to your slides (we'll get to all of these features in this and the next two chapters).

- **Convenient Online Dictionary** The built-in Encarta dictionary is shared by all Office programs and allows you to quickly search for and find the correct definitions of words and paste them into your presentations.

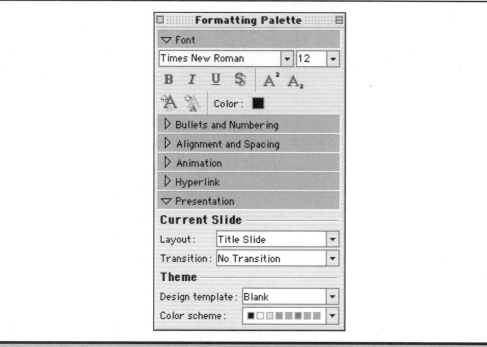

Figure 20-4.   *PowerPoint's Formatting Palette offers one-click access to many of the program's most important features.*

- **Got Euros?**   Just in case you want it, PowerPoint provides full support for displaying, entering, and printing euro currency values.

- **Multiple Slide Values**   PowerPoint 2001 now allows you to use more than one slide master and title master in a presentation. Both can be applied to single or multiple slides at a time, and if it's necessary to copy slides between two different presentations, the program can be configured to copy the slide and title masters with the slides themselves.

- **More Powerful Office Assistant**   The handy-dandy Office Assistant window can now be resized and placed next to the toolbars above the presentation window. This reduces display clutter and gives you more space on your screen for your projects while still giving you the help you need if you choose to accept it. However, if you find the Office Assistant just a little too persistent, then it can be turned off, and you can just refer to PowerPoint's Help menu or table of contents for help (in addition to this book, of course).

■ **Helpful Interactive Advice**   If you decide to keep the Office Assistant as a constant companion, you can use it to improve your presentations by accepting the tips and advice it provides based on the task you're trying to accomplish. All you have to do to see the information is click the light bulb.

■ **AutoFit Your text**   If you're left with a few lines of text that simply won't fit in a text placeholder, PowerPoint can automatically resize the text so that it does fit.

> NOTE   *All features of this type have their limits, and you may find that the text that has been AutoFitted is so small that shortening the material is still a better idea.*

■ **New Normal Three-Pane View**   The new and improved Normal view (shown in Figure 20-5) allows you to see the Slide, Outline, and Notes views all at the same time in their own adjustable panes, so you can view all elements of your project at once.

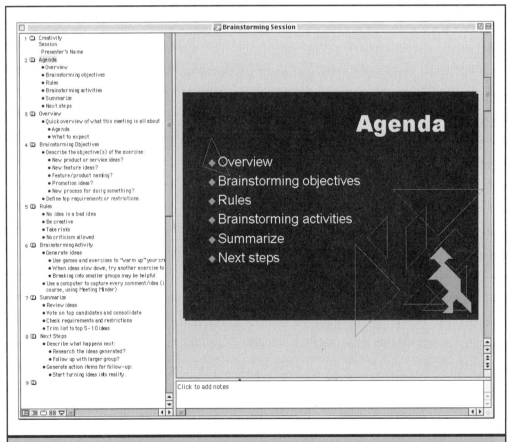

Figure 20-5.   *The three-pane view of PowerPoint helps you view and create your presentations.*

- **Grayscale Output**   Slides can now be seen and printed in true grayscale or black-and-white. You don't have to have a color printer at hand for best output.

- **Powerful Table Tools**   PowerPoint's new table tools allow you to easily create and format tables in your slides. The Insert Table tool can now be used in much the same manner as it is in Word.

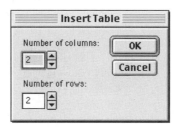

Once you specifiy the number of columns and rows, all you have to do is click and drag to draw the table boundaries and cell partitions. In addition, individual cells can be given the exact height and width that you choose.

- **Graphical Bullets**   New graphical bullets can make your slides look more stylish and appealing. They can replace the standard font-based bullets. Many different kinds of bullets are included with PowerPoint, and you also can import your very own customized bullets if you choose to do so.

- **Numbered Lists**   Lists with numbers, the same as you employ in your Word documents, can now also be formatted automatically in PowerPoint. Whenever you change the number of items in a list, the program will automatically renumber the list for you.

- **Follow-Up Flags**   You can now create reminders that will alert you in Entourage when you have to begin working on a presentation again.

- **New Templates for Content and Design**   Many different, fancy, new templates are now available for use in your PowerPoint presentations.

- **New Clip Gallery**   PowerPoint's new Clip Gallery (shown in Figure 20-6) allows you to organize pictures into custom categories, assign keywords to pictures, and put images in your presentation. The Clip Gallery can be left open in a smaller window so it doesn't disturb your creativity while you produce your presentation. It can also store sounds and movies.

- **Support for Digital Cameras and Scanners**   This feature mirrors the one available in Word. You can scan your artwork directly into PowerPoint from many TWAIN-compatible scanners and digital cameras. That way, you don't have to make a separate trip to an image-editing program to receive and export the artwork.

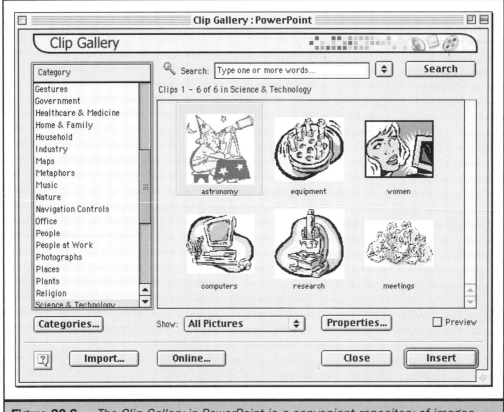

Figure 20-6. *The Clip Gallery in PowerPoint is a convenient repository of images and sounds.*

■ **Animated GIFs** PowerPoint now allows you to use animated GIF pictures to add motion to your presentations. This is particularly helpful if you plan on using your PowerPoint presentation on a Web site.

■ **PowerPoint at (in) the Movies** The new PowerPoint Movie format lets you save a presentation as a QuickTime movie and display it using any QuickTime-compatible movie player, regardless of computing platform. PowerPoint movies can be controlled just like normal presentations: by clicking to move to the next slide or clicking hyperlinks and action buttons. PowerPoint can also save the individual text, graphics, and objects on your slides, so all elements of the presentation are available if you need to edit them again.

■ **Save as Web Page** Your presentations can be shared across the Internet or local network when you save them as Web pages. PowerPoint's outline component will automatically be transformed into a table of contents to allow people to more easily navigate through a presentation on the Web.

- **Better Compatibility with Browsers**   Your Web-based presentations can take full advantage of the advanced features found in Microsoft Internet Explorer 4.0 or Netscape Navigator 4.0 or later, while still remaining compatible with older browsers, such as Internet Explorer 3.0 and Netscape Navigator 3.0.

- **Navigation Bar in Web Presentations**   The Outline pane will automatically be transformed into a table of contents to help the visitors to your Web site easily navigate through a Web presentation.

- **Exit Animations**   PowerPoint supports exit animations that allow you to add more style to the transitions between each of your slides. New animation options also enable clear control over entry and exit animation effects, sound, order, and timing.

- **QuickTime Transitions**   By adding full support for QuickTime, you can use PowerPoint QuickTime transitions to move between slides in a presentation. This helps you give your project a real "movie" feel.

- **Customizing Web Pages**   You can quickly change the way Web pages are generated and formatted by PowerPoint, using the Web Options dialog box (see Figure 20-7). Just access the Preferences dialog box from the Edit menu and click the General tab and then the Web Options button to get to this feature. For example, you can specify the format for saving graphics to be used with Web pages. In addition, you can use design templates to create Web pages of a professional quality. You can also preview your Web page in your browser with the Web Page Preview command (found on the File menu) without having to save and close your document.

- **Automatic File and Link Management**   PowerPoint automatically manages your companion files, such as graphics. This eliminates confusion and mistakes in your presentations. If you create a Web page, all supporting files will be stored in a file folder that has the same name as the main .htm file. If you save your presentation to a different location, the program will check the links, and those that aren't working will be fixed immediately.

- **International Text Encoding**   If you create Web pages that are meant to be viewed across the world, files will be saved using the necessary international text encoding, enabling users of any language to see the correct characters.

PowerPoint's View Options

A new, exclusive feature of Microsoft PowerPoint is the ability to have several different views available to aid you while you are creating or working on a presentation. The two main views that you use in the program are Normal view and Slide Sorter view.

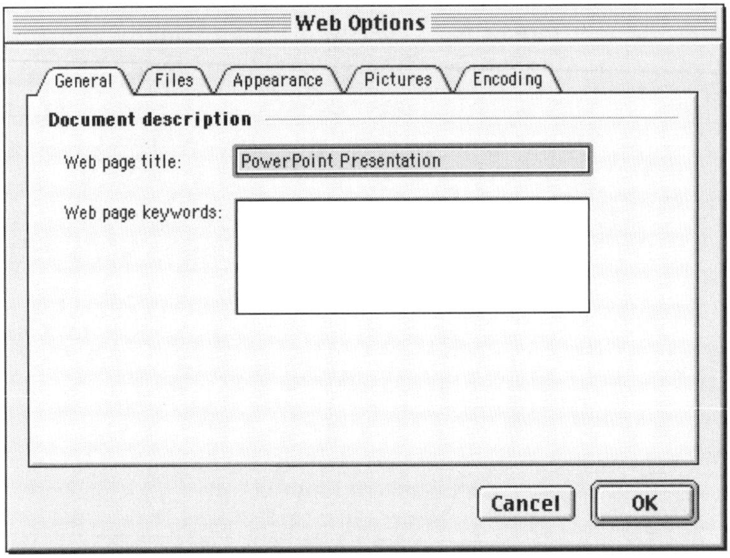

Figure 20-7. *Choose the options for your PowerPoint Web pages here.*

To move among them, all you have to do is click the buttons at the lower left of the PowerPoint window.

Normal View

Normal view, also called Tri-Pane view, is the default view for looking at content in PowerPoint. The three panes are the Outline pane, the Slide pane, and the Notes pane. These panes allow you to work on all aspects of your presentation in one place.

> TIP   *To adjust the size of the panes, simply click the mouse on one of the pane borders and drag it to the size you want. The change takes effect interactively, as you continue to move the borders.*

Here's a brief description of each of the three panes:

- **Outline Pane**   The Outline pane can be used to organize and develop the content of your presentation. You can reformat the text as you like, and you can rearrange bullet points, paragraphs, and slides. You do not, however, see the way the text will actually appear, just the content.

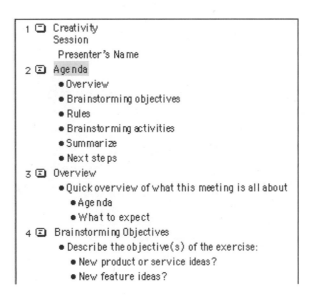

- **Slide Pane**   The Slide pane lets you see how your text looks on each slide. Graphics, movies, and sounds can be added to each slide, and you can also create hyperlinks, and add animations to the individual slides.

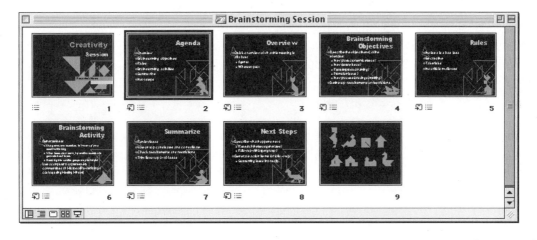

- **Notes Pane**   The Notes pane (shown in Figure 20-8) allows you to add speaker notes or information to share with an audience. If you need graphics in your notes, the notes must be added in the Notes Page view.

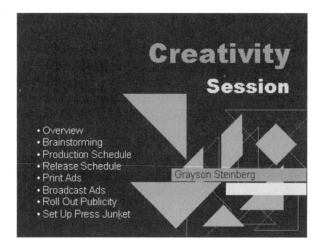

Slide 1: We are only covering the broad outlines of this production. The information here is meant purely as a starting point. We expect that the production and creative team will become more familiar with the project as the script is finalized.

Slide 2: We assume here that the writer's strike will not be a factor in getting this production started, so we're hoping to have ongoing changes in the shooting script.

Slide 3: We need to wrap our locations within 12 weeks, so we will have to hustle to get production started.

1

Figure 20-8. *Add additional information about your slides here.*

> NOTE   *These three panes will appear only in Normal view when you save your presentation as a Web page. The one change will be that the contents of the Outline pane will change to a table of contents for the Web page.*

Other Viewing Options

If the three-pane viewing scheme isn't your cup of tea, or if you need to see your presentation from a different point of view, there are two other choices. Each of these viewing options can be selected directly from the View menu.

Here's a brief description of the other view options available in PowerPoint:

- **Slide Sorter View**   This view allows you to see all the slides of your presentation on the screen at the same time, displayed as miniature or thumbnail versions of the real thing. This option makes it much easier to add, delete, and move slides; add timings; and use animated transitions between each slide. Animations can also be shown on multiple slides by selecting the ones you want to preview and then clicking Animation Preview on the Slide Show menu.

- **Presentation in Slide Sorter View**   While you are in the process of putting together your presentation, you can start your slide show and preview your masterpiece any time you want simply by clicking Slide Show.

Creating a Presentation

Now that you have an idea of all the nifty things you can do with PowerPoint, no doubt you'll want to try your first presentation. In the following pages, you'll go through the steps involved in creating several types of simple presentations. In this and the next two chapters, you'll see how to fine-tune those presentations with text formatting, drawings, and pictures.

Creating a Presentation Using a Wizard

The easiest way to get started is to use the Project Gallery to select a wizard and let it guide you the rest of the way. Here's how to create a presentation based on existing content and design:

1. Double-click the PowerPoint icon to open the program.

2. If the Project Gallery isn't open, choose Project Gallery from the File menu to bring it up.

3. In the Project Gallery, choose Blank Documents from the Category list, double-click AutoContent Wizard (which can also be accessed from the top of the Gallery window), and then follow the instructions. At that point,

PowerPoint will open a sample presentation to which you can add your own words and pictures.

4. Choose the what kind of presentation you want. There are several categories you can choose from and several choices within each category. Then click Next.

5. Choose the way your presentation will be delivered: on-screen, black-and-white or color overheads, or 35mm slides. Click Next again.

6. Add the information you want on your title slide and click Finish.

7. Modify the sample presentation to make it exactly as you want it . For example, you can type text in the place of the sample text, add or remove slides, and add pictures or any other items that will improve the quality of your presentation.

8. Name your presentation (such as Rockoid Presentation) in the Save As dialog box and choose a location to store the file.

9. Click Save. That's it. The end result will be a polished presentation, ready for distribution or printing.

Creating a Presentation from a Template

Microsoft Office provides a number of useful design templates that offer a convenient starting point for formatting a presentation.

You can create a presentation based on a design template by following these steps:

1. Launch PowerPoint and, if it's not open, choose Project Gallery from the File menu.

2. In the Project Gallery, click Presentations in the Category list.

3. Select Designs.

4. Choose whatever design you want in the right pane and then click OK, or double-click the chosen design template to open it.

> NOTE   *If you want to view a list of designs instead of just seeing tiny thumbnails, select List from the View pop-up menu.*

5. Choose a layout for your title slide. Figure 20-9 shows a sample of one layout.

6. Type the title and add any other content you want, such as bullets and pictures, to the title slide.

7. Click New Slide and then choose a layout for the next slide.

8. Add the content you want.

9. Repeat steps 6 through 8 for every new slide you create.

10. After you have finished, open the File menu and select Save As.

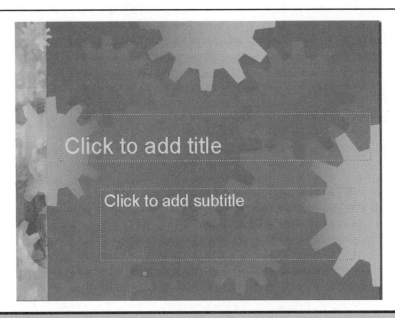

Figure 20-9.   *This is just one of the possible layout templates you can use in PowerPoint.*

11. Give your presentation a name in the Save As dialog box and select a location for the completed file.

12. Click Save to store your finished presentation.

> **TIP**   *If you are doing a long presentation, it's a good idea to save regularly as the project progresses. That way, if your Mac crashes or you suffer a power outage, you won't lose the work you've already done.*

Creating a Presentation from a Previous Presentation

If you've already created a design that you like, you can easily use an existing presentation as the basis for a new one. Simply follow these steps:

1. With PowerPoint open, choose Project Gallery from the File menu if it's not already open.

2. Select Presentations from the Category list in the Project Gallery.

3. Click Content and then choose the presentation you want to use as the basis for the new presentation (see Figure 20-10). PowerPoint will open an untitled copy of the original presentation. If the project is a unique design that has not been added to the Project Gallery, make sure it is added.

Figure 20-10. *PowerPoint lets you base a new presentation on one that already exists.*

NOTE *To get the best results, you'll probably want to use a document formatted with heading styles, as in Microsoft Word. Slides can be created more efficiently if PowerPoint uses these styles.*

4. Click each slide in turn in the Outline pane and make the changes you want. The actual slide will not appear, just an outline of it.

5. When you're done creating the presentation, choose Save As from the File menu.

6. Give your new presentation a name and specify a location for the file.

7. Click Save to store your new presentation.

Creating a Presentation from an Existing Outline

Another option is to build your presentation from an existing outline, whether in Word or PowerPoint. Here's how to set up a presentation in this fashion:

1. With PowerPoint running, choose Open from the File menu.

2. Select All Outlines from the Show pop-up menu.

3. After you've found the outline you want, double-click it in the Open dialog box. The imported outline will appear in the program. Every major heading will appear as an individual slide title, and every point will appear as body text.

4. Edit and format each slide as you prefer.

5. When your presentation is complete, choose Save As from the File menu.

6. Give the presentation a name in the Save As dialog box and then specify the location for the file.

7. Click Save to store the project.

Starting a Presentation from Scratch

If you do not want to rely on an existing presentation, template, wizard, or outline, you can just start your project from scratch and format it in the way you like. Here's what to do:

1. With PowerPoint open, go to the File menu and select New Presentation.

2. Choose a design from the New Slide dialog box (see Figure 20-11); a blank presentation will appear.

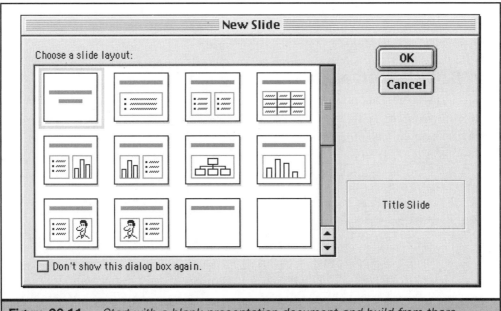

Figure 20-11.   *Start with a blank presentation document and build from there.*

3. Select the layout you want for your title slide in the New Slide dialog box and click OK.

4. Type the title and add any other content you want, such as pictures and bullets, on the title slide. Text can be added in either the Slide pane or the Outline pane.

5. For each additional slide in the presentation, select New Slide from the Standard toolbar.

6. Choose a layout for this new slide and click OK.

7. Repeat steps 4 through 6 for every new slide you create.

8. Modify the presentation to make it look the way you want.

9. When the job is done, choose Save As or Save from the File menu.

10. Give the presentation a name and specify its location on your hard drive.

11. Click Save to finish the project.

Sounds pretty easy, doesn't it? Now it's time to actually add some of the extra elements we've mentioned, such as text, pictures, bullets, and numbering.

Formatting Text and Paragraphs

Adding and formatting text involves many of the same steps that you learned in Microsoft Word 2001. You can either select what you need from menus or use the handy Formatting Palette. In the following pages, we'll discuss some of the text enhancements you can add to your PowerPoint slides.

Adding Bullets and Numbering

Bullets and numbers are very useful when you have long lists of items and you don't want your audience to become confused. It's very easy to add bullets and numbers to any kind of presentation.

1. Select the text or placeholders to which you want to add bullets or numbers.

2. Do one of the following:

   ■ To add bullets, click the Bullets button on the Formatting Palette (see Figure 20-12).

   ■ To add numbers, click the Numbering button on the Formatting Palette.

3. To change the appearance of bullets, select the text or placeholders with the bullet characters you want to change. Then click the disclosure triangle next to Bullets and Numbering on the Format palette. Select the character you want to use from the Style pop-up menu on the Formatting Palette (if you want to use one of the default bullet characters).

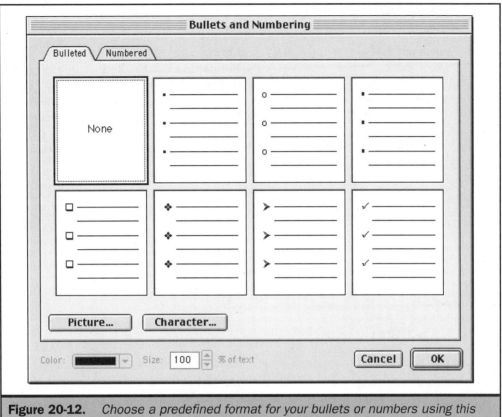

Figure 20-12.   *Choose a predefined format for your bullets or numbers using this dialog box.*

If you want a different bullet character, choose a font and character by clicking Character. In addition, you can even use a picture as a bullet: just select Picture from the Insert menu and then locate and double-click the picture you want.

4. To remove bullets or numbers entirely, select the text containing them and toggle the appropriate button on the Formatting toolbar.

Changing the Size and Color

If you want to change the size or color of bullets or numbers, do the following:

1. Select the text or placeholders with the bullets or numbers characters for which you want to change the size or color.

2. Select Bullets and Numbering from the Format menu and then click the tab for the type of list you want to modify.

3. Click the Customize button.

4. To change the size of the bullets or numbers, type a percentage in the Size box.

5. To change the color of the bullets or numbers, click the Color button in the Bullets and Numbering section of the Formatting Palette. If you want to use the default color, click Automatic. If you prefer to change to a color in the color scheme, select one of the eight colors below Automatic. If you want a color that isn't in the color scheme, click More Colors. In the dialog box that comes up, choose Crayon Picker, select the color that you want, and click OK.

Formatting a Numbered List

To change the style and starting number of a list, do this:

1. Choose the text or placeholder for which you want to change the numbering style or starting number.

2. Select Bullets and Numbering from the Format menu.

3. Choose the style of list you want from the Numbered tab.

4. To change the number or letter with which the list starts, click the Customize button and then choose that letter or number from the Start At list.

A numbered list can also be started this way:

1. Press DELETE to get rid of any bullets at the beginning of the line.

2. Type a number 1, letter a, or roman numeral I or i followed by a period or closing parenthesis; then press the SPACEBAR.

3. Type the text you want after the letter or number and then press RETURN to begin a new line. The numbering will continue automatically unless you choose otherwise.

If you want to change the default settings for bullets or numbering on all your slides, make the changes on the slide master. We'll discuss slide masters in more detail in Chapter 21.

If you just need to change the default settings for bullets or numbering for one slide, choose the options you want from Bullets and Numbering on the Format menu.

NOTE   *If you use a picture as a bullet character, its color can't be changed using the regular procedure just described. Instead, choose another bullet character picture or open it in a graphics program, change the colors, save the picture, and then put it back in as a bullet in PowerPoint. Also remember that a bullet's size directly relates to the text size. The size of the bullet can be increased or decreased by increasing or decreasing the font size of the text next to the bullet.*

Adding Pictures and Graphics

Any sort of image, whether it is a photo or a piece of clip art, can greatly enhance your presentation for your audience; people will probably respond better to seeing something on a screen rather that simply reading. It is very simple to add pictures to your presentation.

PowerPoint supports QuickTime graphics filters as well as its own native filters. That means that any graphics file type supported by your version of QuickTime will also be supported by PowerPoint, allowing you to insert almost any popular graphics file type into your presentation. PowerPoint supports the following graphics file types:

- Device Independent Bitmap (DIB)
- Encapsulated PostScript File (EPSF)
- Enhanced Windows Metafile (EMF)
- FlashPix (FPX)
- Graphics Interchange Format (GIF)
- Joint Photographic Experts Group (JPEG)
- Macintosh Paint (PNTG)
- Macintosh Picture (PICT)
- Photoshop Document (PSD, 8BPS)
- Portable Network Graphics (PNG)
- QuickTime Image Format (QTIF)
- Silicon Graphics Incorporated (SGI)
- Tagged Image File Format (TIFF)
- Targa (TGA)
- Windows Bitmap (BMP)
- Windows Metafile (WMF)

This is how you insert clip art or a picture from the Clip Gallery:

1. Bring up the slide to which you want to add clip art or a picture.
2. Select Clip-Art from the Picture submenu of the Insert menu.
3. Choose the category and then the image that you want.
4. Click Insert.

Inserting an imported picture is a bit more complicated. Here's how you do it:

1. Bring up the slide to which you want to add a picture. If you want to add the picture to all the slides in your presentation, add it to the slide master. If you want to put the picture in all the title slides, add it to the title master.

2. Using Normal view, select Picture from the Insert menu and then choose From File from the Picture submenu.

3. Find the folder where the picture you want to insert is located.

4. Click the picture (see Figure 20-13).

5. Depending on how you want to handle your picture, do one of the following:

   ■ If you want to embed the picture into your slide, click Insert.

   ■ If you want to link the picture in your presentation to the picture file on your hard drive, select the Link to File check box. Keep in mind that although the linked object in the destination file will be updated whenever its source is updated, the linked object won't become part of the destination file.

NOTE *Pictures can also be added to your notes pages. If you want to add a picture to a notes page, from the View menu choose Notes Page and then select the picture you want to add.*

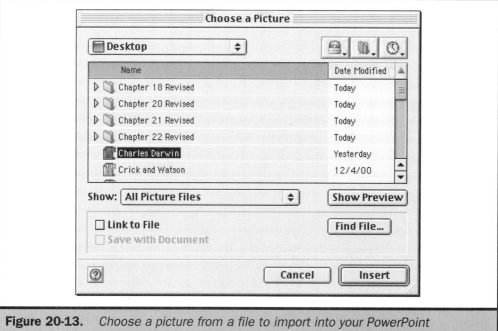

Figure 20-13. *Choose a picture from a file to import into your PowerPoint presentation.*

Importing Pictures from a Scanner or Digital Camera

If you want, you can even import a picture from a scanner or a digital camera. To do this, your scanner or digital camera has to be connected to your Mac and either be TWAIN-compatible or support Adobe Photoshop plug-ins. You also should double-check that you have installed the necessary Photoshop plug-in or the driver software that supports TWAIN.

Remember that some devices come with more than one software program. If you don't know which program to use, check the documentation that came with the product or contact the manufacturer.

CAUTION
TWAIN is a protocol that allows various programs to acquire images from such products as scanners and digital cameras. Not all such products come with TWAIN drivers, and not all TWAIN drivers will work with Office. If you have a problem getting your input device to work, you may want to check the documentation that came with the product or call the manufacturer for additional advice.

Here's how to import a picture from a scanner or digital camera:

1. Bring up the slide to which you want to add a picture.

2. Put the picture inside the scanning device (or just make sure your camera is working).

3. From the Insert menu, choose Picture and then select From Scanner or Camera.

4. In the From Scanner or Camera dialog box, select the name of your scanner or digital camera in the Device pop-up menu and click Acquire. At that point, PowerPoint will launch the program that came with your device. To scan a picture or retrieve it from a digital camera, follow the instructions for capturing artwork in that program.

5. Once the image is on your slide, make any changes using the tools found on the Picture toolbar.

Adding Graphics

Microsoft PowerPoint provides a number of graphics tools, similar to the ones provided in Microsoft Word. Here's a brief look at the options. We'll explore them in more detail in Chapter 21.

Text Boxes

Callouts, labels, and other kinds of text can be added to your graphics through text boxes. After you have put a text box in your presentation, you have many options available to improve it using the Drawing toolbar, just as with any other drawing object. You can even add text to an AutoShape just like you can to a normal text box.

AutoShapes

PowerPoint comes equipped with a number of premade AutoShapes for use in your slide shows. These AutoShapes can be resized, rotated, flipped, or made into more complex shapes by combining them with other figures such as circles and squares. Several kinds of shapes, including basic ones, lines, parts of flowcharts, stars and banners, and callouts are available through the AutoShapes button on the Drawing toolbar, when you add an Autoshape to a presentation.

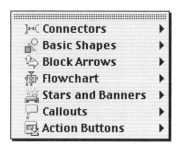

Lines, Curves, and Freeforms

The Curve, Freeform, and Scribble functions can be used to draw lines and curves by clicking the Lines button on the Drawing toolbar. If you want greater control over how you draw your curves, use the Curve button instead. If you want a specific shape, such as one without jagged lines or sharp direction changes, use the Freeform button. The Scribble function can be used to make your drawing object look like it was made with a pen. Whatever shape you draw will be almost identical to what you draw on the screen.

NOTE *Creating computer art isn't always easy or intuitive. But with a little practice, and the use of the shapes available in PowerPoint, you'll be able to make some pretty sophisticated designs in short order.*

WordArt Drawing Objects

You can insert decorative text by clicking Insert WordArt on the Drawing toolbar. Figure 20-14 shows the WordArt Gallery that appears. You can create shadowed, skewed, rotated, and stretched text, as well as text that has been fitted to predefined shapes. Because a special text effect is a drawing object, you can also use other buttons on the Drawing toolbar to change the effect—for example, you can fill a text effect with a picture. To choose a picture, select one from the Picture submenu of the Insert menu.

Viewing Slide Shows

Once you have finished creating your masterpiece, you'll want to see it on the screen as a completed slide show. To do this, click Slide Show at the lower left of the PowerPoint

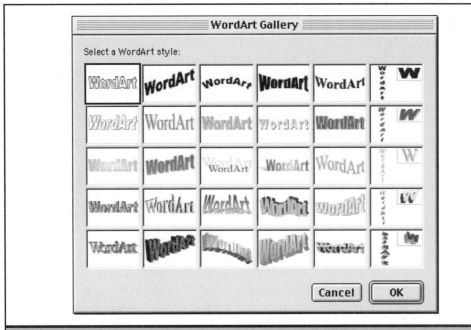

Figure 20-14.   *WordArt is another way to add artistic effects to a PowerPoint presentation.*

window. Then choose View Show from the Slide Show menu. From the View menu, select Slide Show.

You can configure a slide show for viewing in three different ways. You will see these options whenever you click Set Up Show on the Slide Show menu.

■ **Presented by a Speaker (Full Screen)**   This option allows you to see a full-screen presentation (filling your entire display), which is the most common method, with a speaker directing the show. The presenter will have complete control over the show and can run it automatically or manually, stop it to add meeting minutes or action items, and even record narration as the show continues. This mode can also be used to project a slide show onto a larger screen.

■ **Browsed by an Individual (Window)**   This option can be used for a smaller-screen presentation, such as one browsed by a person over a company's network or the Internet. The presentation will appear in a smaller window, with commands at your disposal for moving through the show and for editing, copying, and printing slides. In this mode, you can move the PAGE UP and PAGE DOWN keys or the scroll bar to move among slides. Another program can also be started at the same time, and the Web toolbar can be displayed so you can browse through other presentations and Office documents.

MASTERING
POWERPOINT 2001

■ **Browsed at a Kiosk (Full Screen)**   This option is similar to the "Presented by a Speaker" option. It's best for a self-running presentation, such as one that occurs at a trade show or convention. If you have a booth, kiosk, or other location where you need to run a slide show without constantly watching over it, the presentation can be configured so that most menus and commands are unavailable to the end user (for security and convenience); it restarts automatically after each showing.

Fonts in Your Slide Show

The message you're trying to present in your slide show is greatly affected by the font you use to display it. For example, you'll probably want to use a more formal font, such as Times New Roman, for a presentation to a company's board of directors or to present a serious message, while you might use a "fun" font like Comic Sans MS to present your slide show to friends or family.

Here are some guidelines for using fonts to their maximum advantage in PowerPoint:

CAUTION   *For a presentation to look the way you want when played on another computer, make sure the other computer has the same fonts available. Otherwise, save the presentation as a QuickTime movie to make it self-contained.*

■ Serif fonts like Times New Roman and Palatino are easier to read when you have large amounts of text, but sans serif fonts, like Arial (or Helvetica) and Verdana, are cleaner and work better for titles or headlines or brief text passages.

■ If your presentation is designed for Web or slide viewing, use fonts that look good online, regardless of platform. These types of fonts include Arial, Times New Roman, and Verdana, or the common Mac fonts: Helvetica and Times Roman.

■ Font colors should contrast sharply with the background to ensure that people can read them. Bold and italics should be used only for emphasis; overusing them reduces their effectiveness.

■ All fonts have their own individual personalities, so make sure you are consistent. If you use a lot of different fonts, your message may seem less consistent to the audience—it may look more like a ransom note. Don't use more than three or four fonts in a single presentation.

Tips and Tricks to Improve Your Slide Show

If you're presenting your slide show on your Mac, it's often a good idea to add special visual, sound, or animation effects. However, don't use too many special effects in your presentations. Use effects such as animations and transitions only to emphasize your main ideas; don't distract your audience with the effects themselves.

A computer-based presentation can be delivered in a number of different ways, as described earlier. Here are some guidelines to consider when using various types of effects.

Music, Sound, and Video

Adding music or sound to a transition or animation can help the audience to stay focused on your presentation. Videos can also be used as part of a commercial or training film for your company. Just remember: as with any other effect, don't use too many of these types of effects, because they can distract the audience and reduce the effectiveness of your slide show. They can also make the presentation seem less professional, as if you were choosing form over substance.

Animations and Transitions

Animations are special sound or visual effects that can be added to text or other objects such as charts and pictures. Because your audience reads words and characters from left to right (unless a foreign language that uses a different order is selected), you could design animations so that your points appear from the left. Then if you want to emphasize a main idea, the animation could enter your presentation from the right. A shift like this will get the attention of your audience, reinforce the point, and keep the audience from getting confused about a subject.

Transitions are special effects that smooth the movement between slides in your presentation; for instance, fades, dissolves, or wipes are common transitions. You can select from a number of PowerPoint and QuickTime transitions. A transition effect can be used to show that a new section of a presentation has begun or to emphasize a specific slide. You will learn more about transitions and how to use them in Chapter 22.

Pace and Rehearsing

How fast or slow your presentation goes will affect what the audience does in response. If you go too fast, you might end up tiring the audience or even confusing people, and if you go too slowly, you risk boring your audience or just losing attention. PowerPoint lets you fine-tune the pace before you actually present your slide show.

When rehearsing, you should also consider the visual impact of your slides on the audience. If you have too many words or pictures on a single slide, the audience could be distracted or confused. If you use too much text, try getting rid of words that aren't necessary or split a large, complicated slide into two or three slides and increase the size of the fonts on each one.

Voice Narration

If you include narration in your slide show, people who missed the original presentation will be able to access it with commentary included, and you will be able to have a copy for later review. Voice narration also helps when you need to explain a complicated process that may be difficult to describe in written text, or when you want to reemphasize important points that might be missed. In addition, because narrated presentations are generally self-running, narration makes them better for use on the Internet.

Methods of Showing Presentations

PowerPoint provides many different ways of showing your presentations. They are all described in the paragraphs that follow.

NOTE *Many of the techniques summarized here will be described in more detail in the next two chapters. They are presented here for information only.*

On the Screen

You can use the special effects and features found in PowerPoint to make your online presentation much more pleasing to the eye. Everything from slide transitions to movies to sounds can be used to enhance your show. Once you decide to use a computer to let people see your slide show, there are a number of options for setting it up.

■ **Self-Running Presentation** If you're going to be using a presentation at a trade show or convention, it might be a good idea to set up as self-running. Most of the controls won't be available to sneaky passers-by who might get the urge to disrupt your slide show by changing it. A self-running presentation will start over again every time it is complete or when it's been idle on a manually advanced slide for more than five minutes. This is the Kiosk mode described earlier.

■ **PowerPoint Movies** The new PowerPoint Movie format lets you save a slide show as a QuickTime movie and present it using any QuickTime-compatible movie player. This allows your presentation to be viewed cross-platform, without the need to have PowerPoint or a PowerPoint viewer installed on the viewer's machine. PowerPoint movies can be modified just like any standard presentation, and you can click to move on to the next slide or click hyperlinks and action buttons. The program can also save the individual text, graphics, and objects on your slides so that the movie file can be opened later for editing. You will learn more about this in Chapter 22.

Overhead Transparencies

You can print your slides as black-and-white or color transparencies and use them with an overhead projector. The slides can be designed in either landscape or portrait format.

Printouts

Your presentation can be configured so it will look professional both on the screen in color and when it is printed in grayscale or black-and-white on a laser printer.

You can preview your slide show and transform its look so that it will appear exactly as you want when it is printed in black-and-white. To adjust the colors so they print well in black-and-white, open the Standard toolbar and choose Grayscale from the View menu.

35mm Slides

Your electronic slides can be converted into 35mm slides by a service bureau. They can then be viewed in a standard slide projector. Assuming that you live in the United States, the Genigraphics service can prepare your slide. To take advantage of this extra-cost feature, open the File menu and choose Send To; then click Genigraphics and follow the instructions in the Genigraphics Wizard.

Internet Presentations

Your slide shows can be shared across the Internet if you save them as Web pages and publish them on the Web or the intranet of your company. As already mentioned, the outline pane will be converted automatically into a table of contents to help users navigate through your slide show.

Notes, Handouts, and Outlines

You can give audiences smaller versions of your slides printed two, three, or six to a page to help support your slide show. You can also print your speaker notes for the audience. To accomplish this, follow these steps:

1. With PowerPoint open, choose the File menu, select Print, and choose Microsoft PowerPoint from the pop-up menu.

2. Select Handouts or Notes Pages from the Print What pop-up menu (see Figure 20-15).

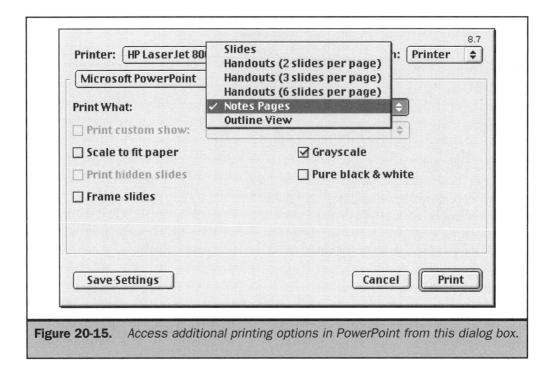

Figure 20-15. *Access additional printing options in PowerPoint from this dialog box.*

While you're creating your slide show, you can print your outline, including slide titles and main points. Also, you can send your slide images and notes to Word for further editing. Just open the File menu, select Send To and choose Microsoft Word from the submenu. Then you can use the various sophisticated formatting features of Word to improve the appearance of your slides.

PowerPoint Keyboard Shortcuts

As with all Office programs, PowerPoint offers a liberal sprinkling of keyboard shortcuts. They are listed in the following sections.

General PowerPoint Actions

Shortcut	Action
COMMAND-N	Start a new presentation.
COMMAND-SHIFT-P	Open the Project Gallery.

Shortcut	Action
COMMAND-M	Insert a new slide.
COMMAND-D	Make a copy of the selected slide in Outline view, Slide Sorter view, or in the Outline pane in Normal view (works only with text boxes).
COMMAND-SHIFT-D	Make a copy of the selected slide in Notes Page view, or if the mouse is in the Slide pane or Notes pane in Normal view (works only with text boxes).
COMMAND-O	Open a presentation.
COMMAND-W	Close a presentation window.
COMMAND-P	Print a presentation.
COMMAND-S	Save a presentation.
COMMAND-Q	Quit PowerPoint.
COMMAND-F	Find text, formatting, and special items.
COMMAND-H	Replace text, specific formatting, and special items.
SHIFT-OPTION-F7	Open the Encarta dictionary.
COMMAND-OPTION-L	Check spelling.
COMMAND-K	Insert a hyperlink (works only in text boxes).
ESC	Cancel an action.
COMMAND-Z	Undo an action.
COMMAND-Y	Redo or repeat an action.
COMMAND-click	Display a contextual menu.

Changing Views

Shortcut	Action
COMMAND-G	Show or hide guides.
SHIFT-click View button (button in the middle in the row of five at the bottom of the window)	Switch from Normal view to Master view.

Copying Objects and Text

Shortcut	Action
DELETE	Delete a character from the left.
COMMAND-DELETE	Delete a word from the left.
DEL (old-style Mac USB keyboards found on the original iMacs and Power Mac G3s and G4s do not have this key)	Delete a character from the right.
COMMAND-DEL (old-style Mac USB keyboards found on the original iMacs and Power Mac G3s and G4s do not have this key)	Delete a word from the right.
COMMAND-X	Delete the selected object.
COMMAND-C	Copy the selected object.
COMMAND-V	Paste the cut or copied object.
COMMAND-D	Duplicate the selected object.
COMMAND-Z or F1	Undo the last action.

Moving Through Text

Shortcut	Action
LEFT ARROW	Move a character to the left.
RIGHT ARROW	Move a character to the right.
UP ARROW	Move one line up.
DOWN ARROW	Move one line down.
COMMAND or OPTION-LEFT ARROW	Move one word to the left.
COMMAND-RIGHT ARROW	Move one word to the right.
END (old-style Mac USB keyboards found on the original iMacs and Power Mac G3s and G4s do not have this key)	Move to the end of the line.
HOME	Move to the beginning of the line.

Shortcut	Action
COMMAND-UP ARROW	Move up one paragraph.
COMMAND-DOWN ARROW	Move down one paragraph.
COMMAND-END (old-style Mac USB keyboards found on the original iMacs and Power Mac G3s and G4s do not have this key)	Move to the end of the text box.
COMMAND-HOME	Move to the beginning of the text box.
OPTION-RETURN	Move to the next title or body text placeholder.

Selecting Text and Objects

Shortcut	Action
SHIFT-RIGHT ARROW	Select one character to the right.
SHIFT-LEFT ARROW	Select one character to the left.
COMMAND-SHIFT-RIGHT ARROW	Select to the end of a word.
COMMAND-SHIFT-LEFT ARROW	Select to the beginning of a word.
SHIFT-UP ARROW	Select one line up.
SHIFT-DOWN ARROW	Select one line down.
TAB or SHIFT-TAB until the object you want is selected	Select an object.
COMMAND-A	Select all objects (Slide view). Select all slides (Slide Sorter view). Select all text (Outline view).

Character and Paragraph Formats

Shortcut	Action
COMMAND-SHIFT-F	Use the arrow keys to change the font.
COMMAND-SHIFT->	Increase the size of a font.
COMMAND-SHIFT-<	Decrease the size of a font.

Shortcut	Action
COMMAND-T	Change the formatting of characters (select Font from the Format menu).
SHIFT-F3	Change the case of letters.
COMMAND-B	Make a character bold.
COMMAND-U	Underline characters.
COMMAND-I	Make characters italic.
COMMAND-= (equal sign)	Add subscripts.
COMMAND-SHIFT	Add superscripts.
COMMAND-SPACEBAR	Remove the style of a font (such as bold or superscript) and effects. This does not alter font size or color.
COMMAND-SHIFT-C	Copy formats.
COMMAND-SHIFT-V	Paste formats.
COMMAND-E	Center the paragraph.
COMMAND-J	Justify the paragraph.
COMMAND-L	Left align the paragraph.
COMMAND-R	Right align the paragraph.

Working in Windows and Dialog Boxes

Shortcut	Action
COMMAND-W	Close an open window.
SHIFT-TAB	Move to previous text box (only when no text is selected).
The arrow keys	Move between options in a list.
The first letter of the option name	Move to an option in a selected list.
RETURN	Perform the action assigned to a default button in a dialog box.
ESC	Cancel the command and close the dialog box.
LEFT ARROW or RIGHT ARROW	Move a single character to the left or right.

Working in an Outline

Shortcut	Action
OPTION-SHIFT-LEFT ARROW	Promote the paragraph.
OPTION-SHIFT-RIGHT ARROW	Demote the paragraph.
OPTION-SHIFT-UP ARROW	Move up selected paragraphs.
OPTION-SHIFT-DOWN ARROW	Move down selected paragraphs.
OPTION-SHIFT-1 (on the numeric keypad)	Show heading level 1.
OPTION-SHIFT-+ (plus sign on the numeric keypad)	Expand text under a heading.
OPTION-SHIFT-- (minus sign on the numeric keypad)	Collapse text under a heading.
OPTION-SHIFT-9 (on the numeric keypad)	Reveal all text and headings.

NOTE *The same keys can be used in both the Slide pane and Outline pane to promote and demote paragraphs or move them up and down.*

Slide Show Summary

Shortcut	Action
N, RETURN, PAGE DOWN, RIGHT ARROW, DOWN ARROW, ENTER, or the SPACEBAR (or click the mouse)	View the next animation or go to the next slide.
P, PAGE UP, LEFT ARROW, UP ARROW, or DELETE	Go to the previous animation or slide.
<number>-RETURN	Go to slide *<number>*.
B or . (period)	Show a black screen or go back to the slide show from the black screen.
W or , (comma)	Show a white screen or go back to the slide show from a white screen.

Shortcut	Action
S or + (plus sign)	Stop or restart an automatic slide show.
ESC, COMMAND-. (period) or - (hyphen)	End the slide show (doesn't work in Kiosk mode).
E	Stop on-screen annotations (while a slide show is in progress).
H	Go to the next hidden slide if the slide following it is hidden.
T	Set new timings while rehearsing (while still preparing your slide show).
O	Use original timings while rehearsing (while still preparing your slide show).
M	Use mouse-click to advance through the slide show while rehearsing.
COMMAND-P	Redisplay the hidden pointer and/or convert the pointer to a pen.
COMMAND-A	Hide the pointer and button immediately.
COMMAND-U	Hide the pointer and button in 15 seconds.
A or = (equal sign)	Show or hide the arrow pointer.
Hold down CONTROL and click the mouse	Display contextual menu.

Summary

Overall, PowerPoint is a very efficient program with lots of clever options. It can easily be used to create simple presentations, whether they're for the office or for your own purposes. You can also create highly complex presentations using animation, transitions, and sound to give them a movie-like sheen.

In the next chapter, you'll learn more about the most sophisticated features of PowerPoint, including how to add tables and animated GIFs to a presentation, as well as how to publish your creation on the Internet.

Chapter 21

Advanced PowerPoint Techniques

Y ou've learned the fundamentals of creating a simple presentation with text and graphics in PowerPoint, but there is still so much more you can do with the program to spruce up your slide show. After all, you wouldn't want to bore your audience (it'd be a killer for that innovative idea you're presenting to your company's board of directors). A series of special effects and other features, including tables and animated GIFs, can really enhance the quality of your presentation if used correctly.

In this chapter, you will learn how to use many of the advanced features of PowerPoint, features that will give your presentation a professional spit and polish, greatly enhancing its impact whether the presentation is made for home or business.

Tables, Equations, and Charts

Perhaps you thought you could use tables, equations, and charts only in Microsoft Word or Excel. However, you can access a similar set of features in PowerPoint, so you don't have to go through the process of importing them from those programs.

TIP
Another way to quickly access these extra features is to choose a slide layout that specifies a chart or table. That way, all you have to do is double-click the icon in the PowerPoint slide to access the extra program you need.

Creating a Table

Here's how to create a basic table:

1. Choose Insert Table from the Insert Menu or select the icon from the Standard toolbar. The Insert Table dialog box appears.

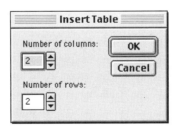

2. Enter the number of columns and rows you want in your table (don't fret; you can change the figures later).

3. Click OK to create a blank table.

4. Type your text in the table.

NOTE *PowerPoint has a slide layout with a placeholder for a table. If you want to use this layout, from the Format menu, select Slide Layout; then select Table Layout and click Apply.*

A Look at PowerPoint's Advanced Table Creation Features

When you create your table, you'll see the Table and Borders toolbar (shown in Figure 21-1), which gives you a host of options with which to spruce up your simple tables.

1. Do one of the following: If the Tables and Borders toolbar hasn't yet appeared, choose Tables and Borders from the Standard toolbar.

2. If the Tables and Borders toolbar is displayed, click Draw Table. Once you have done this, the pointer will transform into a pencil.

3. Drag from one corner to its diagonal opposite to form the outer boundaries of the table. Then drag again to create the boundaries for the rows and columns.

4. If you want to eliminate a line, select Eraser, move it over the line you want to delete, and click the line.

5. After you are done setting up the table, choose a cell and then begin typing. You can now work with a PowerPoint table in much the same way you would in Microsoft Word (see Chapter 13).

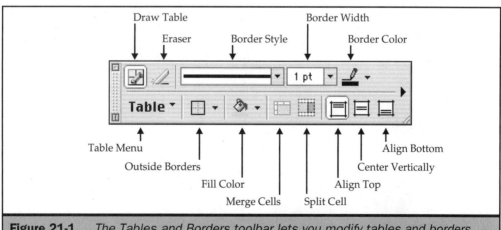

Figure 21-1. *The Tables and Borders toolbar lets you modify tables and borders.*

The table toolbar has all sorts of functions you can use to make your table look better:

- Click the Border Style icon to create lines and the Border Width pop-up menu to specify line thickness.

- Click the Border Color arrow at the right of the Border Width icon to give the border a color.

- Use the Table menu on the toolbar to insert and delete columns and rows, as well as to split and merge cells within your table.

- Click the All Borders button to add a border around your table.

- Click the Paint Bucket to add a fill color and the down arrow at its right to choose the color you want.

- Click the remaining icons to merge and split cells and to set the way text aligns within a cell—at the top of the cell, centered, or at the cell's bottom.

Creating a Chart

If you would prefer something more visually stimulating than a mostly text-based table, you can create a chart with a colorful graph. Here's how you create a chart in PowerPoint:

1. Select Chart from the Insert menu. When you do this, a chart with sample data will be opened in Microsoft Graph (as shown in Figure 21-2).

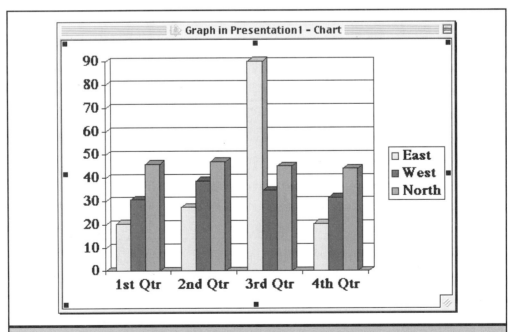

Figure 21-2. *Microsoft Graph lets you create graphs easily without complex steps.*

PowerPoint has slide layouts with placeholders for charts. If you want to use any of these layouts, open the Format menu, select Slide Layout, and then choose a layout from the slide layout dialog box with a chart placeholder.

2. Click the datasheet window.

3. To get rid of the sample data and replace it with you own, type the text you want. Press RETURN to move the cursor down, SHIFT-RETURN to move it up, TAB to move it right, and SHIFT TAB to move it left. You can also use the cursor arrow keys.

4. To get back to PowerPoint, where you can move and size the chart, select Quit and Return to Presentation from the File menu in Microsoft Graph.

Adding Extras to Your Charts

If you want to change the colors, patterns, lines, fills, borders, or pictures in your charts, do the following:

1. Select the chart you want to modify and it will be opened in Microsoft Graph.

NOTE *If Microsoft Graph isn't installed on your Mac, Excel will be opened instead, but many of the features to modify your tables are the same.*

2. Choose the chart item that requires modification.

3. Select the options you want from the Patterns tab. If you want to have a fill effect, select Fill Effect and then choose the options you want from the Gradient, Texture, Pattern, or Picture tabs.

4. Open the File menu in Microsoft Graph or Excel and select Quit and Return to Presentation to return to PowerPoint and see your changes.

Once the chart is set up as you prefer, you can work with it in much the same way you do in Graph or Excel. Chapters 14 and 19 cover those subjects in more detail.

Creating an Organization Chart

Of course, a mostly visual chart may not be the best approach if you need to explain and show a lot of things at the same time. If you want to illustrate the structure of a company or the way a product relates to other products to accomplish a specific purpose, you will want to consider creating an organization chart. Here's how:

1. With PowerPoint open, display the slide to which you want to add an organization chart.

2. Select the Picture submenu from the Insert menu and then choose Organization Chart (the result is shown in Figure 21-3). This action will launch the Organization Chart application that comes with Office.

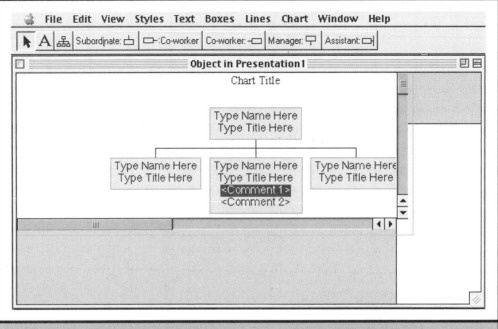

Figure 21-3. *Organization charts are a means of visually organizing information.*

3. Choose Styles from the Group Styles menu to begin your chart.

4. Select Levels from the Edit menu to select various aspects of your chart and move them around.

5. Continue formatting your chart to meet your needs.

6. When you're done, choose Quit and Return to Presentation from the Organization Chart.

NOTE *PowerPoint has a slide layout with a placeholder for an organization chart. To use this layout, choose Slide Layout from the Standard toolbar, select the Organization Chart layout, and then click Apply.*

Creating an Equation

PowerPoint can also access Microsoft's Equation Editor program. This can come in handy if you need to show a mathematical formula in your presentation, perhaps to illustrate the mixture of chemicals required to get a reaction to something in the creation of a drug or to show how much money your project is *really* going to cost your company.

Use the following steps to insert an equation into your presentation:

1. Open the slide to which you want to add an equation.

2. Select Object from the Insert menu.

3. Choose Microsoft Equation 3.0 from the Object Type list. If the program isn't available, use the Value Pack Installer on your Office 2001 CD to install Microsoft Equation Editor.

> **NOTE** *The normal installation of Office 2001 doesn't include the Equation Editor, so a trip to the Value Pack is going to be necessary if the program hasn't been installed previously.*

4. Create and modify the equation using the Equation Editor tools and menus (see Figure 21-4).

5. Click a symbol and type the values or text at the right of the pointer to build your equation as needed.

6. Choose Quit from the Equation Editor's File menu to get back to PowerPoint where your equation will be inserted.

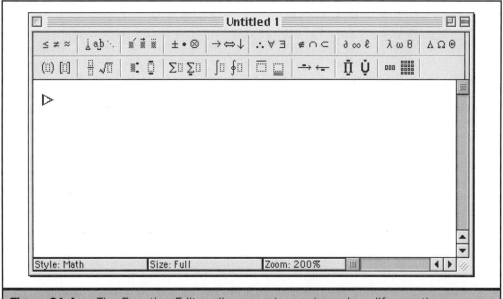

Figure 21-4.   *The Equation Editor allows you to create and modify equations.*

Publishing Your Presentation on the Web

The idea of presenting your slide show on the Web probably sounds enticing, especially if you want to impress a certain group of people with your skills, as well as with the information you present. Considering that the Web reaches millions of people across the world, even though it may not be the gold mine it once was, it is a useful and efficient way for you to reach business contacts and potential contacts.

To save your presentation as a Web page, do the following:

1. Open the presentation that you want to save as a Web page.

2. Select Save as Web Page from the File menu.

3. Click Web Options and change the options of your Web presentation if you wish to do so.

4. Click Save.

PowerPoint will now create a file formatted as filename.htm and a companion filename_files folder that contains the individual files that make up your presentation, including slides and graphics. If you want to see your presentation in a browser, open the main file.

If you want to move the presentation to a different location on your drive or another volume, make sure you transfer both the main file and its companion folder. Otherwise, the Web page won't be displayed properly on your Mac or on the Web when it's published.

Changing Screen Size for Web Presentations

If you want to change the target screen size of your Web presentation to make it more accommodating for people using different platforms, resolutions, and monitors, do the following:

1. Select Preferences from the Edit menu.

2. Choose Web Options from the General tab.

3. Click the Pictures tab in the Web Options dialog box.

4. Select a screen size from the Screen Size pop-up menu under Target Monitor.

NOTE   *The typical display size of the iMac is 800×600 pixels; larger screens and PC-based displays use 1024×768 and larger. However, you want to choose settings for the smallest possible monitor those viewing the site are likely to use. Consider the iMac display size as the bare minimum, and consider whether a 640×480 display might be suitable.*

Once you have made these basic changes in the setup of your presentation, you can work with your Web page presentation in PowerPoint in much the same way you work with Web pages in Word—you can change the title, view the language in which the page is encoded, choose start and search pages, view your presentation in a Web browser before you publish it, and more.

Using Animated GIFs

Animated GIFs are a series of rapidly displayed individual images often used on Web pages to provide animation effects, in the same way as in a cartoon (though in a far more limited way, of course). If you have an animated GIF that will really suit your presentation, use it to improve the effect of your slide show on your audience.

Here's how you insert an animated GIF on a slide:

1. Open the slide to which you want to add an animated GIF picture.

2. If you want to use an animated GIF picture from the Clip Gallery, select Clip Art from the Picture submenu of the Insert menu, or click Insert Clip Art on the Drawing toolbar; then choose All Motion Clips in the Show pop-up menu. Otherwise, you can retrieve an animated GIF from a file. To do this, select the Picture submenu from the Insert menu and then choose From File.

NOTE   *Most of the available motion clips require a custom installation of additional clip art from the Value Pack. The Value Pack is covered in detail in Chapter 2.*

3. To choose an animated GIF from the Clip Gallery in step 2, select the picture that you want to add to your slide and then click the Insert button. To use an animated GIF from outside the program, find the folder containing the picture you want and click its name.

NOTE   *Keep in mind that your animated GIFs will be in motion only when your slide show is being presented, not when you're working on it in Normal or Slide Sorter view. The pictures will also play if you save your presentation as a Web page and view it in a Web browser.*

4. To see how the animated GIF picture will appear in the slide show, select Slide Show from the lower left of the Microsoft PowerPoint window.

CAUTION   *You can't crop or change the fill, border, shadow, or transparency of an animated GIF picture by using PowerPoint's Picture toolbar without removing the animation. Such changes have to be made in a program that can edit animated GIFs before you insert the file on the slide.*

Creating Hyperlinks

Hyperlinks are useful clickable objects that can help people navigate through a presentation more easily, especially if you publish it on the Web. In the following section, you will learn how to create several types of hyperlinks.

Creating a Hyperlink to a Custom Show or Location

The first type of hyperlink we'll look at puts another presentation or location a click away. Here's how to create this sort of hyperlink:

1. Select the text or object that you want to set as the hyperlink.

2. Select Action Settings from the Slide Show menu.

3. On the Mouse Click tab, select Hyperlink To (see Figure 21-5).

4. To add a link to a slide within your presentation, select Slide and then choose the slide to which you want to link in the Hyperlink to Slide dialog box that appears. To link to a custom show in your presentation instead, choose Custom Show and select the custom show from the Link to Custom Show dialog box that appears.

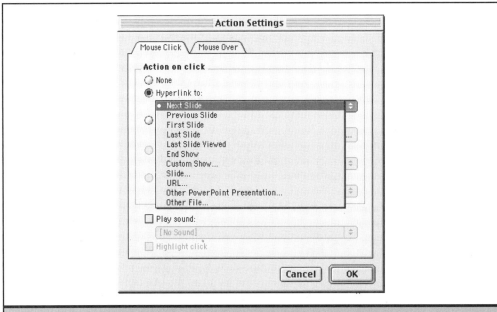

Figure 21-5. *Use the Action Settings dialog box to create various kinds of hyperlinks.*

NOTE *You can use a custom show to place a specific presentation within a more general presentation. Instead of having to create multiple, almost identical presentations for different people, slides can be given different names and grouped together differently for each new presentation.*

5. If your link is designed to go to a slide at the end of the custom show, select the Show and Return check box.

6. After you've made the modifications you want, click OK.

7. To see how the hyperlink will work in the slide show, preview it by selecting Slide Show in the lower left of the PowerPoint window.

Creating a Hyperlink to an Existing Presentation, File, or Web Page

You can create a hyperlink to any kind of existing file, such as a Word document, PowerPoint presentation, Excel workbook, or even another Web page. Here's how:

1. Select the text or object you want to use as the hyperlink.

2. Click Insert Hyperlink on the Standard toolbar.

3. Choose the Document tab in the Insert Hyperlink dialog box (shown in Figure 21-6); then click Select. Using the list and the pop-up menu above it, locate and click the file to which you want to link.

4. To display a tip when the mouse pointer rests on the hyperlink, click ScreenTip and then type in the text that you want. If you don't enter anything, then the path or URL of the file will be used.

5. After you've made your modifications, click OK.

TIP *You will automatically create a hyperlink to link to an existing Web page if you type the URL on a slide or in the outline. For example, if you type **www.rockoids.com** on a slide, the hyperlink will be created automatically.*

6. To see how the hyperlink will work in the slide show, preview it by selecting Slide Show in the lower left of the PowerPoint window.

NOTE *You can also link to files in your Favorites folder or recently opened files by selecting Favorites or Recent Documents from the Favorites tab.*

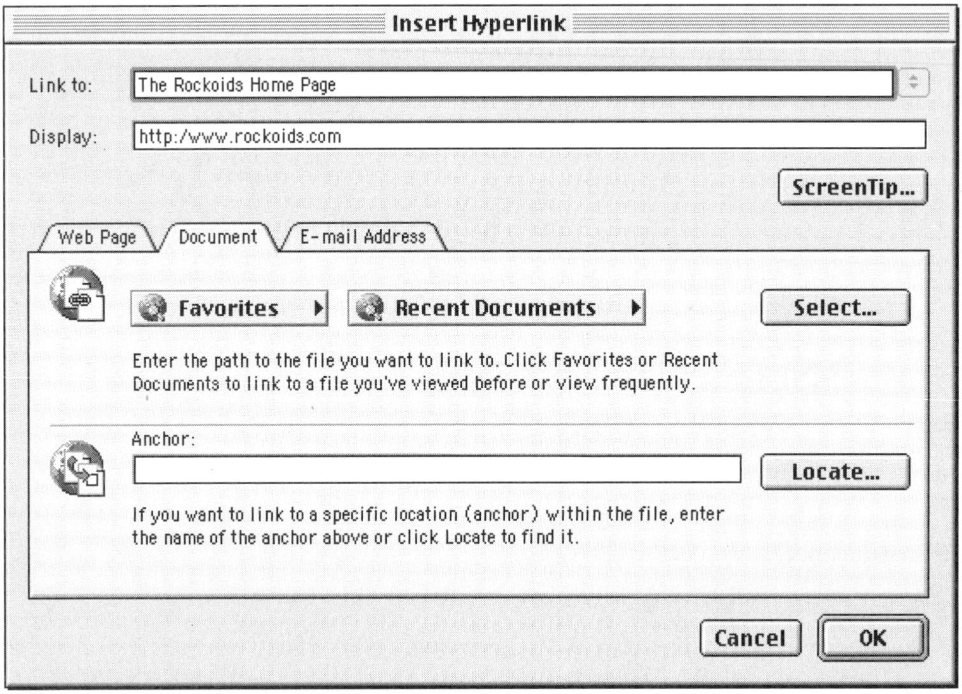

Figure 21-6.   *The Document tab lets you modify your hyperlinks.*

Creating a Hyperlink to a Slide in Another Presentation

Use the following steps to create a hyperlink to a slide in a presentation other than the one you're working in:

1. Select the text or object you want to use as the hyperlink.

2. Click Insert Hyperlink on the Standard toolbar.

3. Select the Document tab in the Insert Hyperlink dialog box and then click Select.

4. Find and choose the presentation file containing the slide you want to link to and click the Open button.

5. Select Locate and then find the title of the slide that you want. You may need to click the triangle next to Slide Titles to view the whole list.

6. To display a tip when the mouse pointer rests on the hyperlink, choose Screen Tip and type whatever text you want. If you don't enter a tip, the title of the slide will be used.

7. After you've made the modifications you want, click OK.

8. To see how the hyperlink will work in the slide show, preview it by selecting Slide Show in the lower left of the PowerPoint window.

Creating a Hyperlink to an E-Mail Address

Just as in any Web page, whenever a hyperlink to an e-mail address is clicked, an e-mail message will be created with the proper address in the To: line in the user's e-mail software. In the case of a fellow Microsoft Office user, that will be Entourage.

To make this possible, do the following:

1. Select the text or object you want to use as the e-mail address.

2. Click Insert Hyperlink on the Standard toolbar.

3. Select the E-mail Address tab (seen in Figure 21-7) in the Insert Hyperlink dialog box.

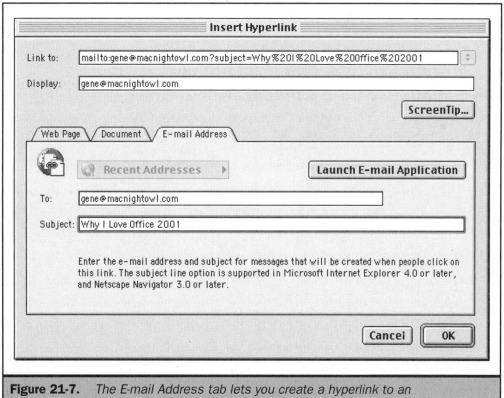

Figure 21-7.   *The E-mail Address tab lets you create a hyperlink to an e-mail address.*

4. In the To box, type the e-mail address to which you want to link or select Recent Addresses and then choose an address from the list. If you need to look up an address in your e-mail program, click Launch E-mail Application. If Entourage is installed, that will be the program that's launched.

5. Type the subject of the e-mail message in the Subject box.

NOTE   *E-mail address hyperlinks that use the subject line option work properly only if the page is viewed in Microsoft Internet Explorer 4.0 or later or Netscape Navigator 3.0 or later.*

6. To assign a tip that will be displayed when the mouse pointer rests on the hyperlink, select Screen Tip and type whatever text you want. If a tip is not specified, the e-mail address and subject line will be used.

7. After you've made the modifications you want, click OK.

8. To see how the hyperlink will work in the slide show, preview it by selecting Slide Show in the lower left of the PowerPoint window.

TIP   *You also can create a hyperlink to an e-mail address by directly typing it on a slide or in an outline. For example, a hyperlink will be created automatically if you simply type gene@macnightowl.com on a slide (if you want my name in your hyperlink).*

Adding Action Buttons and Hyperlinks to Self-Running or Web Presentations

Action buttons are premade buttons that appear to be pushed in when they are clicked during a slide show. Such buttons make it easy to navigate directly to another slide in your presentation.

Here's how to create action buttons:

1. Choose the slide to which you want to add buttons. To put these buttons on every slide, open the View menu, choose the Master submenu, and then select Slide Master.

NOTE   *If you want the same action buttons to be on every slide, you must place them on the slide master.*

2. From the Slide Show menu, select Action Buttons and then choose the button you want.

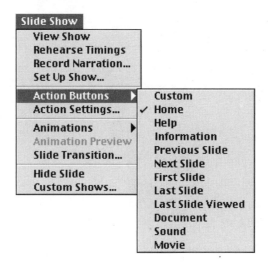

3. To add a button with a predefined size, click the slide. To change the button's size, drag the shape until the button is the size you want. To keep the width-to-height ratio the same, hold down the SHIFT key while dragging.

4. When the Action Settings dialog box appears, either click OK to accept the proposed hyperlink in the Hyperlink To list or choose the link you want.

Adding and Modifying
Color Schemes and Backgrounds

Whether you're publishing your presentation on the Web or simply displaying it on an overhead projector, the colors you have to work with may not be suitable. If not, you can create and change color schemes in a number of ways.

Color Schemes

The following pages explain how to work with color schemes on your slides.

Creating or Changing a Color Scheme
Using the Crayon Picker

Follow these steps to create or change a color scheme:

1. From the Format menu, select Slide Color Scheme. The dialog box shown in Figure 21-8 appears.

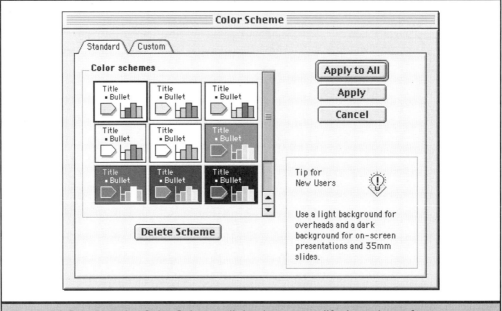

Figure 21-8. *Use the Color Scheme dialog box to modify the colors of your presentation.*

2. To create a new color scheme, select the Standard tab, find a color scheme that meets your requirements, and then select the Custom tab. To modify an existing color scheme, select the Custom tab right away.

3. Select the color that you want to modify under Scheme Colors and then click Change Color.

4. Select Crayon Picker from the Color Picker dialog box (shown in Figure 21-9) and then select the color you want.

5. Repeat steps 3 and 4 for any colors you want to modify.

6. To save your color scheme with the presentation, click Add As Standard Scheme.

7. To add the new color scheme to the current slide only, choose Apply. To add the new color scheme to all of the slides in the presentation, click Apply to All.

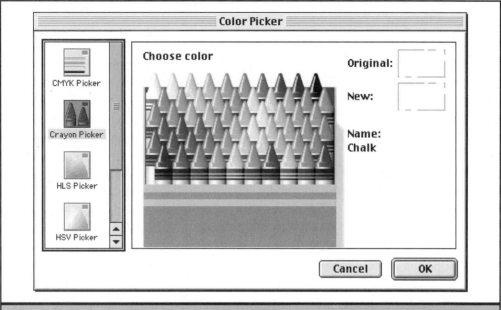

Figure 21-9. *The Color Picker dialog box allows you to change color schemes.*

Creating or Modifying a Color Scheme Using Other Color Schemes

A number of color models are used in PowerPoint to enhance the look of your document, but you can create or modify a color scheme with the existing information to produce many variations. Here's how it's done.

1. Select Slide Color Scheme from the Format menu.

2. To create an entirely new color scheme, select the Standard tab, choose a color scheme that meets your requirements, and then select the Custom tab. To modify an existing color scheme, just select the Custom tab right away.

3. Select the color that you want to modify under Scheme Colors and then click Change Color.

4. Choose a color model from the Color Picker dialog box. Figure 21-10 shows the CMYK model selected.

NOTE   *The CMYK color model is based on four colors—cyan, magenta, yellow, and black—commonly used in the printing industry. (K is used to indicate "black" because B could be confused with "blue"). Another color model, RGB (red, green, blue), is employed by computer monitors and TVs to display color.*

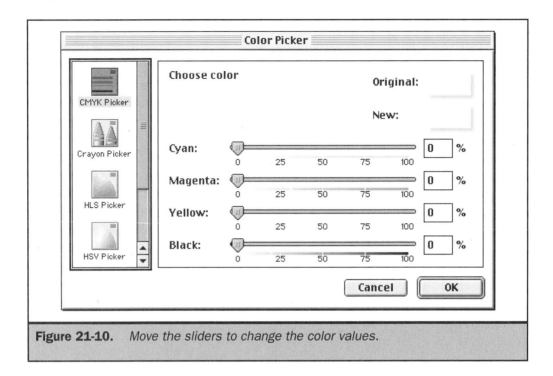

Figure 21-10. *Move the sliders to change the color values.*

5. Drag the sliders to adjust the colors as you want; then click OK. You will see the New color displayed as you modify it to your liking.

6. Repeat steps 3 through 5 for every color that you want to modify.

7. Select Add As Standard Scheme if you want to save your color scheme with the presentation.

8. To add the new color scheme to only the current slide, click Apply. If you want to add the new color scheme to all the slides in the presentation, click Apply to All.

NOTE *You can use the Eyedropper tool to select any color on a slide and apply it to a color scheme. For example, if you want to modify the color of text, be sure that the Color Picker dialog box is open, hold down the OPTION key to change the pointer to an Eyedropper, click the CMYK button, choose the color you want, and then click OK. There are also HLS, RSV, and RGB buttons, which allow you to make different color selections. The available color selections will vary depending on the imaging model you select.*

Adding the Color Scheme of One Slide to Another

Do the following to apply the color scheme of one slide to another:

1. In Slide Sorter view, select a slide with the color scheme you want use.

2. Click the Format Painter on the Standard toolbar once to recolor one slide or click twice to recolor more than one.

3. Choose the slide or slides to which you want to add the color scheme.

4. If you're going to recolor more than one slide, press the ESC key after you're done to cancel the Format Painter. If you click once to recolor only one slide, the Format Painter will be canceled automatically when you're done.

> **TIP** *Color schemes can also be applied between two presentations. To do this, open both of them, open the Window menu, select Arrange All, and then follow the steps just listed.*

Creating or Modifying a Color Scheme to be Used in a Web Browser

Although the Web is a highly flexible means of getting your presentations to the widest possible audience, it has some severe limitations, particularly in your choices of color. You'll want to limit your selection to Web-safe colors to avoid viewing problems on the part of your visitors who may use other computing platforms.

1. Select Slide Color Scheme from the Format menu.

2. To create a new color scheme, choose the color scheme that best meets your requirements from the Standard tab; then select the Custom tab. To modify an existing color scheme, just select the Custom tab.

3. Select the color that you want to modify under Scheme Colors and then select Change Color.

4. Choose HTML Picker from the Color Picker dialog box.

5. Drag the slider of each color that you want to modify; then click OK.

6. Repeat steps 3 through 5 for any color you want to change.

7. To save your color scheme with the presentation, choose Add as Standard Scheme.

8. To add the new color scheme to only the current slide, click Apply. To add the new color scheme to every slide in the presentation, click Apply to All.

> **NOTE** *To drag the slider to a predefined color that most Web browsers can display, select the Snap to Web color check box. If you happen to know the hexadecimal value used to describe a color, you can enter its value in the HTML box.*

Backgrounds

Another way to change the appearance of your slide is to adjust the background color or pattern. The next few pages describe how to accomplish this.

Modifying the Background Color of a Slide

Do the following to change the background color of a slide:

1. From the Format menu, select Background to display the Background dialog box.

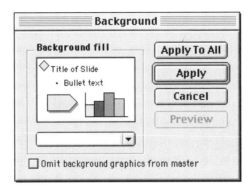

2. Click the down arrow in the box below Background Fill. To modify the color scheme, choose one of the eight colors under Automatic.

 If you want to modify a color that isn't in the color scheme, select More Colors. Choose Crayon Picker from the Color Picker dialog box, select the color you want, and click OK. To return the background to its default color, choose Automatic.

3. To change only the current slide, click Apply. To change all the slides and the slide master, click Apply to All.

Applying or Modifying a Shaded Slide Background

If you want to add or change the shaded background or apply a gradient for a special effect, follow these steps:

1. Select Background from the Format menu.
2. Click the down arrow below Background Fill; select Fill Effects and choose the Gradient tab.
3. Choose the options you want and click OK.
4. To change only the current slide, click Apply. To change all the slides and the slide master, click Apply to All.

Applying or Modifying a Textured Slide Background

A textured background is another way to give dimension to your presentation. Just follow these steps to perform this task:

1. Select Background from the Format menu.

2. Click the down arrow below Background Fill; then choose Fill Effects and select the Texture tab.

3. Choose the texture you want or select Other Texture and find the texture you want; then click OK.

4. To change only the current slide, click Apply. To change all the slides and the slide master, click Apply to All.

Applying or Modifying a Patterned Slide Background

Another way to add dimension to your presentation is to create a background with patterns. Here's how it's done:

1. Select Background from the Format menu.

2. Click the down arrow below Background Fill; then choose Fill Effects and select the Texture tab.

3. Select the options you want and click OK.

4. To change only the current slide, click Apply. To change all the slides and the slide master, click Apply to All.

Applying or Modifying a Slide Background Picture

You can also put a photo or other picture in the background of a slide. Here's how it's done:

1. Select Background from the Format menu.

2. Click the down arrow below Background Fill; then choose Fill Effects and select the Picture tab.

3. Choose Select Picture, locate the folder with the picture that you want, select the file name, and then click OK.

4. To change only the current slide, click Apply. To change all the slides and the slide master, click Apply to All.

Notes and Handouts

Notes and handouts are very useful for emphasizing key points to the audience. They can also help your audience to stay focused while you're making your presentation because they'll have something to guide them through the process.

Adding Notes Pages

Here's how you type notes while working on your presentation:

1. Select Notes Page from the View menu. The notes box appears as shown in Figure 21-11.

2. Click within the notes box and then type your notes for the current slide. To make your view of the notes box larger, click the Zoom box.

3. Use the scroll bar to move to other slides to which you want to add notes.

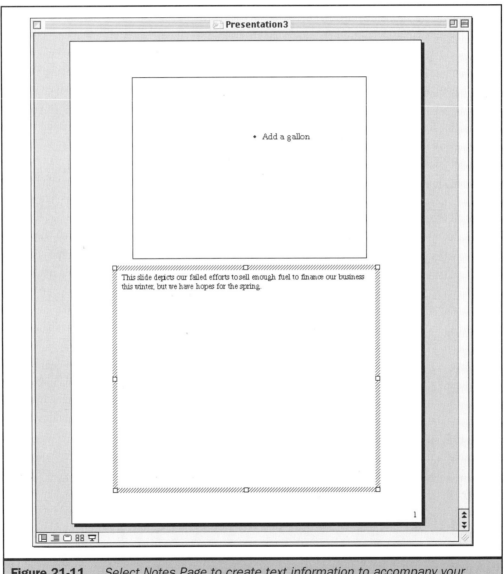

Figure 21-11.   *Select Notes Page to create text information to accompany your presentation.*

Creating Handouts

Use the following steps to create handouts:

1. From the View menu, select the Master submenu and choose Handout Master. The additional toolbars that appear help you format this feature (see Figure 21-12).

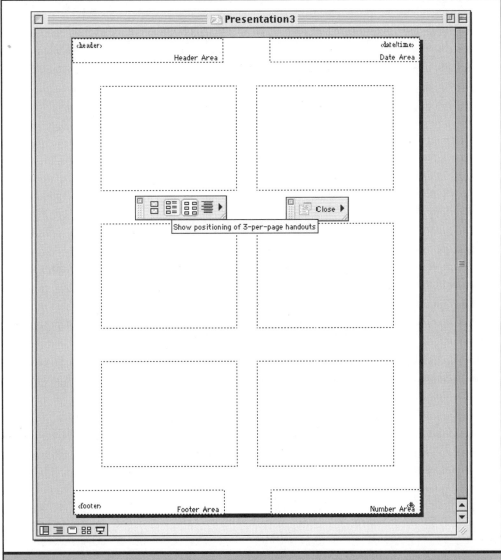

Figure 21-12.   *The Handout Master allows you to add material to your presentation.*

2. Enter the items that you want on the handout master, such as art, text, headers, footers, date, time, and page number. These items will appear only on the handouts, and no changes will be made to the slide master.

3. Select Close on the Handout Master toolbar.

4. Choose the slide numbers you want on the handout from the Handout Master toolbar.

5. Select Print from the File menu.

6. If your dialog box has a pop-up menu, choose Microsoft PowerPoint from it. (If your dialog box does not have this pop-up menu, just go to the next step.)

7. Select the slides numbers you want to have on the handout from the Print What pop-up menu. Then click Print.

NOTE   *If want to modify any of your notes or an outline in Word, select the note, then simply open the File menu, choose Send To, and then choose Microsoft Word.*

Hiding Notes and Outlines

Sometimes, you may be working on a Web presentation that contains notes, and you may not want to have your notes visible as a distraction. To hide the Notes pane, do one of the following:

■ Open the File menu; then choose the Save as Web Page command. On the Appearance tab of the Web Options dialog box, uncheck the Include Slide Notes check box and then resave your presentation.

■ When viewing your presentation on the Web, click Notes.

If it's the Outline pane that you want to hide, simply toggle Show/Hide Outline.

NOTE   *The Notes pane won't be displayed if you are viewing slides with no notes on them. In addition, the Outline pane won't be displayed if you are viewing a presentation with only one slide.*

Changing the Colors in the Notes and Outline Panes

If you want to change the colors in the Notes and Outline panes in your Web presentation, do the following:

1. Select Preferences from the Edit menu.

2. Choose Web Options from the General tab.

3. Select the Appearance tab and choose the background and text colors you want from the Colors list.

Printing

You can print parts of your presentation if you choose to do so. Printing your notes can be useful if you want others to read them while you're presenting your slide show, and printing your outline allows you to pull your thoughts together and figure out exactly how you want to format your slide show.

Printing Specific Slides, Handouts, Notes Pages, or Outline Pages

Here's how to print selections from your presentation:

1. Choose Print from the File menu.

2. Select Microsoft PowerPoint from the General pop-up menu. If the dialog box does not include such a pop-up menu, just go to the next step.

3. Select the item you want to print in the Print What box.

4. Choose General from the pop-up menu. Again, if the dialog box does not include this pop-up menu, just go to the next step.

5. Type the slide numbers you want printed in the From and To boxes.

NOTE   *If you want to print slides noncontinuously, create a custom show (you'll learn about these later in the chapter in "Creating Custom Shows") with just the slides you want to print; then print the custom show.*

Printing an Outline

Whenever an outline is printed, character formatting, such as bold or italic, will appear, even if it's hidden in the Outline pane in Normal view.

To print an outline, follow these steps:

1. Open the presentation you want to print.

2. To print only the title slides, choose Collapse All from the Outlining toolbar. To print all levels of text, select Expand All from the Outlining toolbar. To add headers and footers to your printed outline, choose Header and Footer from the View menu, select the Notes and Handouts tab (see Figure 21-13), and choose all the options you want; the headers and footers will be applied to the handouts and notes pages in addition to the printed outline.

3. Choose Print from the File menu.

4. Select Microsoft PowerPoint from the General menu. (If the dialog box doesn't have such a pop-up menu, just go to the next step.)

5. Choose Outline View from the Print What pop-up menu; then select any other options you want.

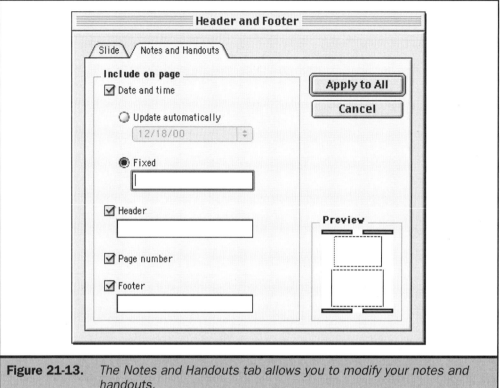

Figure 21-13.   *The Notes and Handouts tab allows you to modify your notes and handouts.*

6. If you can't locate the Outlining toolbar (see Figure 21-14), choose the View menu, select Toolbars, and choose Outlining.

> TIP   *The size of your outline text on the printout can be changed by modifying the magnification of the Outline pane. To do this, click the Outline pane, then the Standard toolbar, select the arrow next to the Zoom box, and then choose the required magnification.*

Printing Slides, Notes, and Handouts

Here's how to print your slides, notes, or handouts:

1. Select Print from the File menu.

2. Select Microsoft PowerPoint from the General pop-up menu. (If the dialog box does not include such a pop-up menu, just go to the next step.)

3. Choose the item you want to print from the Print What pop-up menu. If you want to print frames around your slides, select the Frame Slides check box.

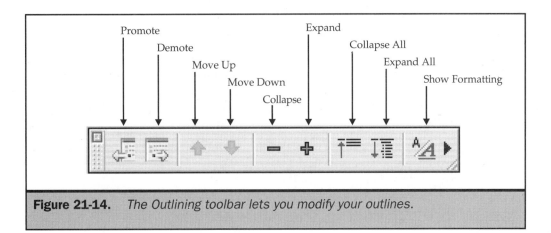

Figure 21-14. *The Outlining toolbar lets you modify your outlines.*

Configuring the Slide Size and Orientation for Printing

You may want your slides printed horizontally on the page (landscape style) instead of vertically (portrait style), or you may want them printed in a different size. If so, here are the steps to follow:

1. Select Page Setup from the File menu. The dialog box shown in Figure 21-15 appears.

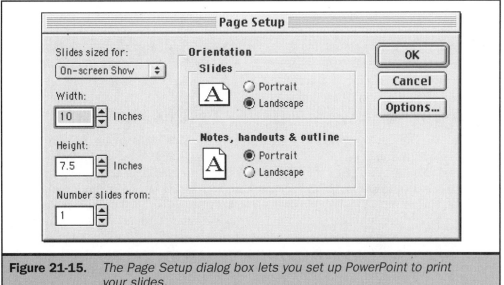

Figure 21-15. *The Page Setup dialog box lets you set up PowerPoint to print your slides.*

NOTE *Some printer options available to you depend on the kind of printer you have.*

2. To change the size, choose the option you want from the Slides Sized For pop-up menu. If you choose Custom, type the measurements you want in the Width and Height boxes.

3. To set the orientation of the slides, select Portrait or Landscape from the Slides options. All slides in a presentation must use the same orientation.

4. Select Portrait or Landscape from the Notes, Handouts, and Outline options. These three items can be printed, for example, in portrait orientation even if landscape orientation is selected for your slides.

Previewing and Changing the Appearance of Slides Printed in Black-and-White

Printing slides in black-and-white is essential if you don't have a color printer. You'll want to change the contents of your slide to show black and white, and gray, to represent the colors in between. To do that, follow these directions:

1. Choose Grayscale View from the Standard toolbar to preview your slides in grayscale.

2. Press the CONTROL key while in grayscale view and select the object whose grayscale settings you want to change; a contextual menu appears.

3. On the contextual menu, select Grayscale Settings and choose the option you want.

TIP *More than one object can be modified at a time: hold down the SHIFT key when you select each object and then select an option. Grayscale options can also be mixed on the same slide.*

Flagging Presentations for Follow-Up

If you are working on a presentation, but you can't finish it right away, it can be flagged for follow-up. Doing this automatically creates a task in the Tasks list of Microsoft Entourage and pops up a reminder at the specified date and time.

When this alert appears, the presentation for which you set the reminder will be listed in the Reminders window. At that point, you can dismiss the reminder from the window, extend the time so that you're reminded again, or open the presentation.

If a flagged presentation is renamed later, Entourage will still be able to find it. However, if a flagged presentation is deleted, moved to a network volume, or moved to another volume on your Mac, Entourage won't be able to locate it and therefore can't display the reminder.

Flagging a Presentation

Follow these steps to flag a presentation for follow-up:

1. Open the presentation you want to flag for follow-up.

2. Select Flag for Follow Up from the Standard toolbar or the Tools menu to display the following dialog box.

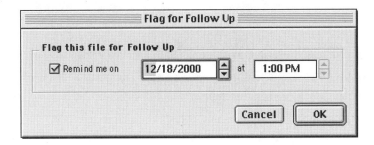

3. Select the Remind Me check box and enter the date and time you want to be reminded; then click OK.

4. Select Save from the File menu to save your changes.

Marking a Presentation as Complete

After you have followed up, a flagged presentation can be marked as complete. Here's how to do this:

1. Choose Open Item when the Reminders window comes up.

2. Choose the Complete check box in the Flagged Document window.

3. Select Save.

NOTE   *If you can't locate the Reminders window, choose Flag for Follow Up, set the reminder for the current date and time, click OK, and then click the No button so the Reminders window can be opened.*

Changing the Reminder Date and Time

If you want to change the reminder date for your flagged presentation, do the following:

1. Open the presentation that has the reminder that you want to modify.

2. Select Flag for Follow Up from the Standard toolbar.

3. Enter a new reminder date and time.

4. Click OK.

Templates

Templates are useful if you create similar kinds of presentations often and you don't want to always have to create the formatting and text for scratch. Templates are especially helpful if your basic layout was complicated to set up.

Creating a Content Template

A content template contains text as well as formatting. Here's how to create a content template:

1. Open an existing presentation or template to use as a basis for your new template.

2. Modify the presentation or template to meet your requirements.

3. Choose Save As from the File menu.

4. Type a name for your content template in the Name text box.

5. Select Design Template from the Format pop-up menu; then click Save. To access your new content template, open the Project Gallery from the File menu, select My Templates from the Category list, and then choose your template.

In addition, you can attach templates to the AutoContent Wizard, to make them available with all the other presentations in the wizard.

Creating a Design Template

If you want to only use the formatting and design of a presentation for a template, and not the text, you can do that as well. Here's how to create a design template:

1. Open an existing presentation or use a design template to create a presentation to use as a foundation for your new design template.

2. Modify the design or presentation so that it meets your requirements.

3. Select Save As from the File menu.

4. Type a name for your design template in the Name text field.

5. Select Design Template from the Format pop-up menu, make sure that your new template is saved in the Templates directory, and click Save.

Whenever you want to open your new design template, open the File menu and choose Project Gallery, choose My Templates from the Category list, and select the template.

If none of the design templates are what you want, or if want to set up a presentation with a unique appearance, start with a blank presentation. To do this, open the File menu, select Project Gallery, choose Blank Documents from the Category list, and select PowerPoint Presentation.

Modifying the Default Blank Presentation

If you always use a certain color scheme, or if you want your company's logo to show up in every presentation, you may want to modify the default format of the blank presentation. Here's how:

1. Open an existing presentation or create a new one.

2. Modify the presentation to meet your requirements.

3. Select Save As from the File menu.

4. Choose Design Template from the Format pop-up menu.

5. Find the Microsoft Office 2001 folder and open the Template subfolder.

6. Type **Blank Presentation** in the Name box; then click Save.

7. Click Replace to replace the existing blank presentation if a message appears asking whether you want to do so.

CAUTION   *You could, if you want, make a copy of your blank presentation and put it elsewhere on your Mac, in case you want to restore it later on without having to reinstall Office.*

Advanced Slide Show Techniques

The following pages present additional tools and methods you can use to make more effective presentations in PowerPoint.

Microsoft PowerPoint Viewer 98

Microsoft PowerPoint Viewer 98 for the Mac is great for running slide shows on computers that don't have PowerPoint installed. The viewer can be downloaded from Microsoft's Web site. If you have Internet access, you can reach this site by choosing Help on the Web from the Help menu and then selecting Free Downloads.

Microsoft PowerPoint Viewer 98 is a freely distributed program. However, because it is designed to support only the features of the older version of the program, it does not provide playback of advanced PowerPoint features such as exit animations, graphical bullets, QuickTime transitions, and animated GIFs; but the basic elements of your presentation will otherwise be present.

NOTE: If you intend your presentation to be viewed in PowerPoint Viewer 98, you'll want to consider simplifying the formatting so that those who see your presentation won't be missing key elements that might otherwise be present.

Creating Custom Shows

When you create a Custom Show, you are building a separate presentation using a subset of your slides. Here's how it's done:

1. Select Custom Shows from the Slide Show menu and then choose New. The Define Custom Show dialog box appears.

2. Choose the slides you want in the custom show from the Slides in Presentation pane; then click the Add button. Hold the down the SHIFT key to add multiple slides as you click each one.

3. To modify the order in which the slides appear, choose a slide in the Slides in Custom Show list; then click one of the arrows to move the slide up or down in the list.

4. Type a name in the Slide Show Name box and then click OK.

5. To preview a custom show, select its name in the Custom Shows dialog box and then click Show.

Creating Agenda Slides

You can easily create a special slide that lists agenda items or the main sections of your presentation. An agenda slide allows you to jump to each section of your presentation and then, when you reach the end of the section, return automatically to the agenda slide. You can consider it an introduction slide if you want.

Follow these steps to create an agenda slide:

1. Open the completed presentation to which you want to add an agenda slide.

2. Set up a custom show for each section of your presentation.

3. Create a new slide to serve as your agenda slide and then put it where you want it to make its appearance in the presentation.

4. Enter the title of each custom show on the agenda slide.

5. Set up a hyperlink from each agenda item to its custom show. Choose the duration and then select Action Settings from the Slide Show menu.

6. In that dialog box, choose Hyperlink To, select Custom Show, and then select the slide to which you want to jump. To get back to the agenda slide after the final slide of the custom show, select the Show and Return check box.

7. Repeat steps 5 and 6 for every item on the agenda slide.

Typing Notes or Meeting Minutes During a Slide Show

You can also add notes or minutes of your meeting during the slide presentation. Here's how it's done:

1. Click the mouse button and hold down the CONTROL key at the same time; then select Meeting Minder from the contextual menu.

2. Type your notes or minutes.

Writing or Drawing (Annotating) Slides During a Slide Show

During the course of the slide show, you can also write or draw additional items on slides. Follow these steps to do it:

1. Hold down the CONTROL key and at the same time click the mouse; then select Pen from the contextual menu.

2. Hold down the mouse button while writing or drawing on your slide.

Keep in mind that the pointer will remain a pen until you select one of the other commands from the Pointer Options menu. In addition, annotations will be erased when you move to another slide. If you return to the slide, your annotations will not be there.

Setting Up a List of Action Items During a Presentation

An action item is a series of steps that will be performed during a slide presentation; consider it similar to a macro. Here's how it's done:

1. Hold down the CONTROL key and at the same time click the mouse. Choose Meeting Minder from the contextual menu and then select the Action Items tab.

2. Enter the information for the first action item and then click Add.

3. Repeat step 2 for each action item and then click OK. Your action items will appear on a new slide at the end of your slide show.

Sending Meeting Minutes or Action Items Created During a Slide Show to a Word Document

To send meeting minutes or action items created during a slide show to a Word document, select Meeting Minder from the Tools menu and then choose Export to Word. At that point, a new document containing your minutes or action items will be opened by Word.

If a slide show is going on at the time, hold down the CONTROL key and at the same time click the mouse; then select Meeting Minder from the contextual menu.

Showing a Hidden Slide During a Slide Show

You want to hide a slide that's part of your presentation in order to speed up the flow or customize it for a particular audience. But when you need to display the slide again, you'll need to perform either of the following:

- Hold down the CONTROL key and select the slide just before the hidden one, click Go, and then select Hidden Slide. This command will be available only if the next slide is hidden.

- Hold down the CONTROL key and select any slide in a presentation, click Go, select By Title, and then choose the slide you want. Hidden slides are identified by numbers in parentheses.

Configuring a Slide Show to Run on a Second Monitor

You can run your slide show on the full screen of a second monitor while your presentation is shown in Normal view on another monitor. This can let you see your outline and notes while your audience sees only the slides.

> **NOTE**   *To use this feature, the computer on which the main presentation runs must have a second monitor. If you have a PowerBook, you can connect it to another monitor using the VGA port found on most Apple PowerBooks (the iBook doesn't offer such support, alas). However, when you connect from a desktop Mac, you must have not just a second display, but a second graphic card as well, though some older Power Macs already have internal video and separate graphic cards. ProMax Systems, which packages Mac systems for the desktop video market, also sells a line of graphic cards that support two separate monitors.*

Here's how to set up your slide show to run on two monitors:

1. Select Set Up Show from the Slide Show menu.
2. Choose Screen in the Set Up Show dialog box and choose the monitor on which you want the slide show to appear from the ones displayed.

Configuring a Slide Show to Run in a Continuous Loop

If you want to set up your slide show to run continuously—for example, for a kiosk presentation—here's how:

1. Select Set Up Show from the Slide Show menu.
2. Choose the Loop Continuously Until Esc check box.

3. If you want to set up a self-running slide show, such as one that might be used at a trade show, select Browsed at a Kiosk (Full Screen) in the Set Up Show dialog box. This will make the slide show loop and will also prevent users from changing the slide show.

Modifying the Annotation Pen Color Before Beginning a Slide Show

An annotation pen color is used to generate the annotations on your slide. Depending on the colors used, you may want to change the pen's color to make it more visible. Here's how:

1. Select Set Up Show from the Slide Show menu.

2. Choose the color you want in the Pen color box.

Modifying the Annotation Pen Color During a Slide Show

To change the annotation pen color during a slide show, do one of the following:

■ Hold down the CONTROL key and at the same time click the mouse; then choose Pointer Options from the contextual menu, select Pen Color, and choose the color you want.

■ If the Slide Navigator scroll bar is displayed, select Slide Show Controls, choose Point Options, select Pen Color, and then choose the color you want.

Jumping to a Specific Slide

To move immediately to a specific slide, do the following: In Normal view, drag the vertical scroll bar across the Slide pane until you reach the number of the slide that you want. If you're in the Outline pane, click the slide number. In Slide Sorter view, double-click the slide. If your slide show is playing, hold down the CONTROL key and at the same time click the mouse, select Go from the contextual menu, select By Title, and then choose the title of the slide you want to go to. Alternatively, if you know the number of the slide you want to see, simply type it and press RETURN. If the Slide Navigator is displayed, you can drag the horizontal scroll bar to see the thumbnails.

Copying a Slide from One Presentation to Another

You can easily copy a slide from one presentation to another. Here's how:

1. Display the slide that will appear before the one you want to insert.

2. Select Slides from File on the Insert menu.

3. Select the presentation from which you want to copy a slide from the Choose a File dialog box.

4. Choose Select Slides and then click the Open button.

5. Choose the slide or slides you want to copy, select Insert, and then click Done. If you want to copy an entire presentation, select Insert All and then click Done.

If the Multiple Masters feature is activated, you can retain the master format of the copied slides by selecting the Keep Design of the Original Slide or Slides check box and clicking choosing Done. If this feature isn't activated, this option will not appear.

Changing the Slide Master or Title Master

Here's how to modify the slide or title master:

1. Choose one of the slides associated with the master you want to modify.

2. From the View menu, choose Master and then select Slide Master or Title Master.

3. Make the modifications you want. For example, you can change the font, the color or size of the text, or the bullet character or insert a picture or text box.

CAUTION   *Make sure you don't delete or add any characters in the placeholder text.*

4. Click Close on the Master toolbar.

Applying or Reapplying the Master Format to a Presentation

A master format is one used to set up the overall look of your presentation. Here's how to use this feature:

1. Open the presentation and choose the slides to which you want to apply or reapply the master format.

2. Select Apply Design Template from the Format menu.

3. From the Choose a File dialog box, choose the template that you want to add or reapply to the presentation.

4. To add the master format to only the selected slides, choose Apply to Selected Slides and then click Apply.

Any items you added to the slide master, such as pictures or text boxes, will not be removed when the design template is added.

Making an Object Appear on All Slides in a Presentation

You can easily make an object appear on all slides in your presentation. Here's how:

1. Choose one of the slides that uses the slide master to which you want to add an object.

2. From the View menu, select Master and choose Slide Master.

3. Add the object to the slide master.

4. Click Close on the Master toolbar to go back to your slide. If this toolbar is not visible, select Slide Master from the Master submenu of the View menu, and it will appear.

If your presentation uses a title master and you want the object to appear on all title slides, you will have to add the object to the title master as well.

If objects don't show up on a certain slide, choose the Format menu and select Background and be sure that the Omit Background Graphics from Master check box isn't checked.

Turning Multiple Master Formats On or Off

For your presentation to use more than one master format, you must select the Enable Multiple Designs per Presentation check box on the Advanced tab of the Preferences dialog box, which can be accessed from the Edit menu. If you want to use only one master format, make sure this check box is cleared.

> **NOTE** *To retain the master format of slides that you insert in your presentation from another one, make sure that the Keep Design When Copying Slides Between Presentations check box is selected. If you choose to apply the master format of the current presentation to inserted slides, make sure this check box is cleared.*

Viewing a Miniature of a Slide

To view a miniature or thumbnail of a slide, select Slide Miniature from the View menu. If this option is not available, increase the zoom to a point where most of your slide can't be seen. If there are animations or transitions on a slide, you can preview them simply by clicking the slide miniature or choosing Animation Preview from the Slide Show menu.

Summary

In this chapter, you learned about many of the advanced features of PowerPoint, including how to add animated GIFs and prepare presentations to be published on the Web. Once you've tried these features, you'll see how easy it is to give your presentations a highly professional look and feel.

In the next chapter, you will learn how to add QuickTime movies to your presentations as well as transitions, MP3 sound files, and other special effects.

Chapter 22

Creating QuickTime Movies with PowerPoint

Now that you've created a basic presentation with some nice effects and graphics, you may think you're got a masterpiece in front of you, something that's sure to wow your company's board of directors. Yet you still think your slide show needs something more, something that will blow your audience completely out of the water. In that case, there are many ways you can spruce up your presentation by adding special effects, including sound files and videos and even QuickTime movies.

Apple's QuickTime is definitely one of the company's most popular "Think Different" ideas. Over 100 million copies of the various versions of this software have been acquired either on a new Mac or via a download. Because QuickTime works under Windows as well as on Macs, QuickTime has rapidly become a standard. In fact, major motion picture companies have used QuickTime for distribution of their movie trailers. Among the most popular was the *Star Wars: Episode One* trailer, and it should be no surprise to learn that one of the brilliant special effects supervisors who worked on that film, John Knoll, is himself a Mac advocate and one of the original authors of Adobe Photoshop.

When Microsoft built Office 2001, the company decided to exploit Mac technologies to a greater extent in the program. One of Microsoft's best ideas was to include the ability to save PowerPoint presentations in QuickTime format. The lets you take advantage of QuickTime technologies, and also makes it possible for anyone with a copy of QuickTime to view your presentation.

In this chapter, you'll discover how easily you can put QuickTime and PowerPoint to work together to give your presentation an extra touch of professionalism.

Special Effects

As already mentioned in previous chapters, PowerPoint offers many different kinds of special effects and enhancements that you can use to make your slide show better and more appealing (especially to the eyes of impatient executives). The following sections show you how to add various kinds of effects to your presentation.

Adding Music and Sounds

To add music or sound effects to your presentation, just follow these steps:

1. Bring up the slide to which you want to add sounds or music.

2. From the Insert menu, select Movies and Sounds and choose Sound from Gallery.

3. In the Clip Gallery dialog box that appears (see Figure 22-1), choose the sound you want.

4. If you want to get a sound from another location, when you select Movies and Sounds, choose Sound from File, find the folder with the sound you want, and double-click it (or click the name once and then the Insert button). A sound icon will appear on the slide.

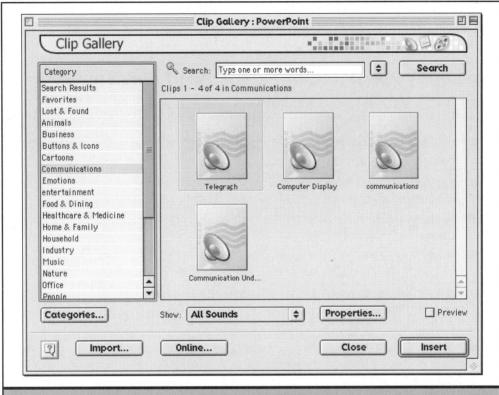

Figure 22-1.   *You can select many different types of sounds from PowerPoint's Clip Gallery.*

NOTE   *You can also use sounds from a CD or that you record with a sound-editing program. If you are using prerecorded sounds, check copyright restrictions before using material that may be presented in a public presentation. You probably won't get permission to use material from a commercial recording, but there are royalty-free music CDs designed to work with such projects.*

5. After you've selected a sound, you'll be presented with a dialog box with two options. If you want the sound to play automatically whenever you go to the slide, click Yes. If you want the sound to play only when you click a sound icon during a slide show, click No.

NOTE   *Click the Preview button in the dialog box to listen to the sound before you insert it.*

6. Double-click the sound icon to preview the sound in Normal view.

MASTERING
POWERPOINT 2001

NOTE *You can modify play settings to loop the sound—in other words, to play it over and over again continuously—or to add an animation effect to your sound. You'll learn more about these options later in this chapter in "Animations."*

Reference: Types of Sound Files PowerPoint Supports

PowerPoint can support a pretty good array of sound files, so you have great flexibility in choosing sound clips for your presentation. Here's the list:

- **Audio Interchange File Format (AIF, AIFF, AIFC)**   This is the sound format used for audio CDs.

- **Apple QuickTime Movie Sound (MOV, MOOV)**   This format is the one used for sounds saved in Apple's QuickTime software.

- **Apple System Sound (SFIL)**   This is the sound file used by your Mac's system sounds.

- **Apple System Resource Sound (RSRC, rsrc)**   This is the format used when a sound file is embedded into a program, such as the System file.

- **CCITT A-Law (European Telephony) Audio Format (ALAW)**   This is a sound encoding and audio compression scheme supported by Windows and Web phones.

- **CCITT U-Law (US Telephony) Audio Format (AU, SND, ULAW)**   Intended originally as a phone-communications standard, this is another sound encoding and audio compression scheme supported by Windows and Web phones.

- **Microsoft Windows Media Audio (ASF)**   This format is used with Microsoft's Windows Media Player.

- **Microsoft Windows Waveform (WAVE, WAV)**   This is the standard sound format used in the Windows platform.

- **MPEG Layer 3 Audio (MP3)**   This is the sound format for compressing large sound files, made infamous by the Internet music file sharing utility Napster (see Figure 22-2), which has been slapped with multimillion dollar lawsuits over copyright infringement by some of the world's largest record companies.

- **Musical Instrument Digital Interface (MIDI, MID, KAR)**   This is the popular music format that was first supported by the Mac way back when, which is why so many musicians embraced the platform early on. These days, even fairly inexpensive keyboards have MIDI support.

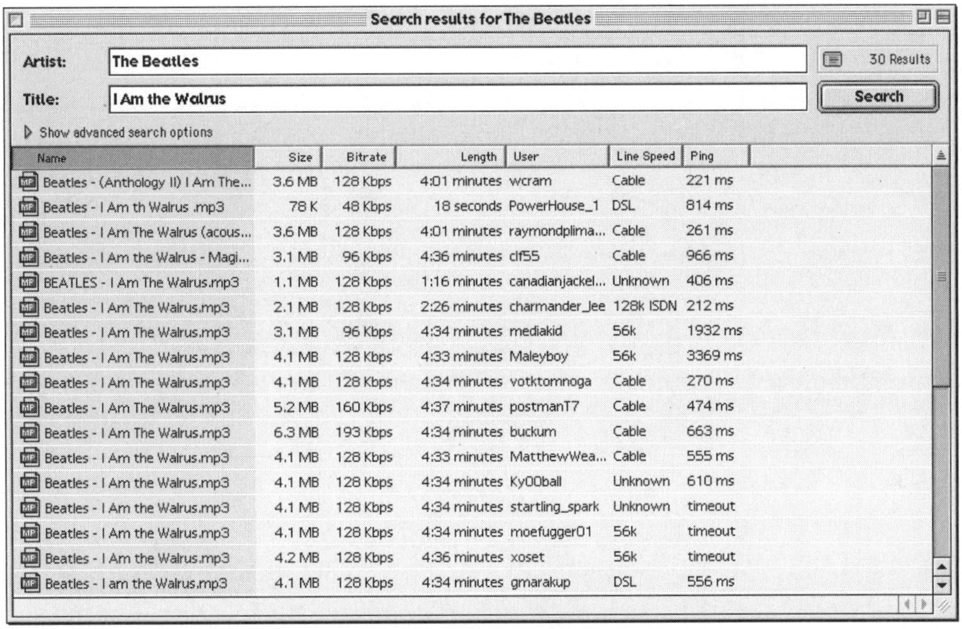

Figure 22-2.   *The controversial Napster software allows you to share MP3 music files with music lovers all over the world.*

Inserting a CD Audio Track

Among the sound formats supported is AIFF, used on your conventional audio CD, which means, of course, that you can add a track from a CD to your presentation.

1. Display the slide to which you want to add a CD audio track.
2. Put the CD you want to use in your CD-ROM or DVD-ROM drive.
3. Select Movies and Sounds from the Insert menu and choose Play CD Audio Track from the submenu.
4. Choose the track and timing options you want from the Play Options dialog box (see Figure 22-3) and click OK. A CD icon will appear on the slide.

NOTE   *You will, of course, have to play your CD in advance (you can use the AppleCD Audio Player on most recent Macs) to make sure you've selected the proper track and the beginning and end point for the selected track. By default the Play Options dialog box will list the total time for the selected track.*

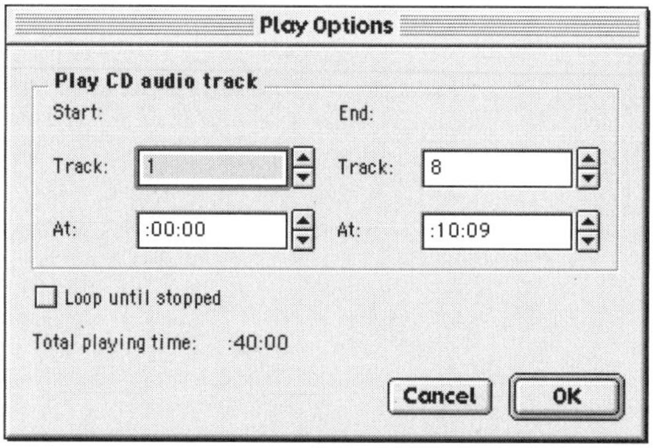

Figure 22-3.   *You can add audio tracks from CDs to your presentation.*

5. When you make your selection, you'll see a dialog box with two choices. If you want the CD to play automatically when you move to the slide, click Yes; if you want the CD to play only when you click the CD icon during a slide show, click No.

6. Double-click the CD icon to preview the music in Normal view.

Adding Videos to Your PowerPoint Presentation

Of course, what's the point of having the ability to use QuickTime movies unless you actually insert a movie into you presentation? Here's how it's done:

CAUTION   *As with any third-party file, if your presentation is meant to be viewed publicly or by business contacts, make sure that you have the right to use the video clip in your presentation. This is likely to be out of the question with a commercial video, but you can obtain clips that are meant to be used by anyone who downloads or orders them, much the same as clip art.*

1. Display the slide to which you want to add a video.

2. From the Insert menu, select Movies and Sounds.

3. To add a video from the Clip Gallery, select Movie from Gallery and then choose the video you want in the Clip Gallery dialog box (see Figure 22-4). To insert a video from another place, select Movie From File, find the folder that contains the video you want, and double-click the video.

Figure 22-4. *PowerPoint's Clip Gallery is a repository for your movie clips.*

4. After you select a movie to insert into your presentation, a dialog box appears giving you two choices. If you want the movie to play automatically when you move to the slide, click Yes; if you want the movie to play only when you click the movie during a slide show, click No.

5. Double-click the movie in Normal view to preview it.

NOTE *Just as with sound files, you can change the play settings of a movie file for the desired effect. For example, you can loop the movie or add animation effects to it.*

Reference: Types of Movie Files PowerPoint Supports

You can use videos in any of several popular formats with your PowerPoint presentations. This gives you great flexibility in choosing source material.

Here's a list of the formats supported:

■ **QuickTime (or MoviePlayer) Movies**   These are movies that are saved in the QuickTime format.

■ **QuickTime VR Movies**   The QuickTime VR format lets you see all sides of an image, providing a 3D-like effect. You need a version of QuickTime that supports the feature, however. The latest versions support QuickTime VR; on older versions of QuickTime, VR software must be installed separately, if it's not already on your Mac.

■ **MPEG Videos**   These types of videos require the QuickTime MPEG extension, or QuickTime 4.0 or later, which incorporates the software in one package.

■ **Video for Windows**   Also known as Movie Clips or Audio Video Interleave (AVI) files, this is the primary format used for movies under Windows. Microsoft's Windows Media Player software is available on the Mac, if you want to see movies in this format.

CAUTION

The movies you insert into your presentation are not actually copied to it; otherwise, file size would be huge. Instead, a link is established to the original file, in the same fashion as page layout programs link to graphics inserted in a document. If your presentation will be shown on a computer different from the one you develop it on, make you sure you copy the movie file when you copy the presentation; otherwise, only the empty frame will appear. Note, though, that if you save your presentation as a QuickTime movie (which puts it all in one file), you can include the original PowerPoint presentation data as part of your file (the option is available when you click the Adjust Settings radio button).

Configuring Sound and Video Options in Your Slide Show

To me the needs your specific project, you will want to adjust the sound and video options. Here's how:

1. Click the icon of the sound or video for which you want to set options.

2. Select the Animations from the Slide Show menu, choose the Custom option, and then select the Options tab in the Custom Animation dialog box (see Figure 22-5). The following options are available:

   ■ **Play Using Animation Order**   This choice plays your animations in the sequence you describe on the Order and Timing tab.

   ■ **While Playing**   This option lets you choose whether to play your slide show or pause it while your animation is playing.

   ■ **Stop Playing**   This option lets you decide whether to stop playing the presentation after the current slide or after a certain number of slides.

   ■ **Loop Until Stopped**   If you select this option, your animations will keep playing over and over again until you click to bring them to a halt.

   ■ **Hide While Not Playing**   This option hides your animations when they aren't being played.

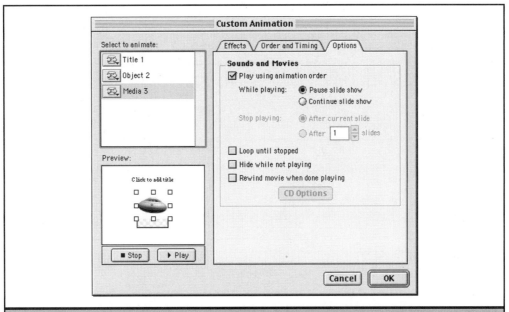

Figure 22-5.   *The Options tab of the Custom Animation dialog box lets you choose options to modify.*

■ **Rewind Movie When Done Playing**   If you select this option, PowerPoint will return to the beginning of your movie after it is done playing or in the background, when it isn't playing.

3. Choose the options you want, then click OK.

NOTE   *If you want, you can animate a sound icon or video. For example, you can have a sound icon fly in from the left side of a slide and begin to play during an animation sequence. You'll learn more about how to do this in "Animations," later in this chapter.*

Recording Voice Narration

Another way to give your presentation a professional veneer is to give it voice narration.

NOTE   *To use the narration feature, you need a microphone for your Mac. Also, make sure that you don't have any other sound recording programs open, such as a speech recognition program, when you add narration to your slides.*

Here's how to add narration to your presentation:

1. Select Record Narration from the Slide Show menu. A dialog box listing the amount of free disk space and the number of minutes that can be recorded will appear (see Figure 22-6).

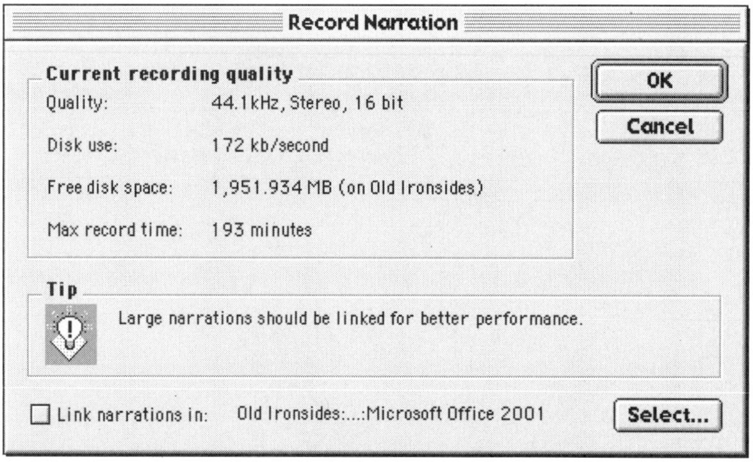

Figure 22-6. Use the Record Narration dialog box to record voice narrations for your presentation.

2. To put the narration on your slides as an embedded object, just click OK and begin recording. If you want to keep your files short, choose the Link Narrations In check box to insert the narration as a linked file; then click OK to start recording.

NOTE *For effective narration, use a shooting script or notes. That way, your timing and content will be more accurate. You should also do a few test runs to make sure the narration runs all right.*

3. Go through the slide show and record the narration as you go along.

4. After the show is complete, click Stop and choose one of the options in the dialog box that appears. To save the timings along with the narration, click Yes. To save only the narration, click No.

A sound icon will appear in the lower-right corner of each slide containing a narration. Whenever the slide show is being played, the narration will automatically be played with the show.

NOTE *If you want to play your show without narration, open the Slide Show menu and select the Show Without Narration check box.*

If narration is linked, the location where the narration file is saved can be changed. For example, if you have a large file, you might want to save it to another hard drive that has extra capacity. To do this, open the Slide Show menu, choose Record Narration, and click Select. Also, remember that you must copy the narration file if you show your presentation on another computer, unless they're both accessing it from a network; otherwise, the narration won't be available when the presentation is played.

Pausing or Stopping Voice Narration While Recording

You don't have to record your narration straight through. Even experienced actors need to stop to catch their breath or rest (unless they're doing a play, of course, when there's no rest for the weary).

NOTE   *In the radio broadcasting industry, a switch to turn off a mike is sometimes called a "cough switch" for obvious reasons. Although some broadcasters, such as Howard Stern, don't mind making unpleasant noises on the air because it's part of their act, when I worked in radio we tried to create the illusion that we never did such mundane things.*

To pause or stop the presentation, do the following:

1. When you're recording your narration, hold down the CONTROL key and at the same time click the mouse; then choose Pause Narration from the contextual menu.

2. To begin recording again, reopen the contextual menu and choose Resume Narration.

Recording a Sound or Comment on One Slide

You can limit your narration or comments to a single slide, rather than have them span the entire presentation.

To record a sound or comment on one slide, follow these steps:

1. Display the slide to which you want to add sound.

2. Select Movies and Sounds from the Insert menu and choose Record Sound. A control panel appears.

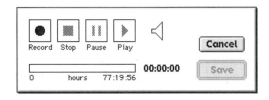

3. Click the Record button to begin recording.

4. Click the Stop button when you are done recording and then choose Save.

5. Type a name for the sound in the Name box and then click OK. A sound icon will appear on the slide.

Animations

Animating various elements of your presentation is a great way to spruce it up without adding elaborate videos and sounds that might overshadow the main points of your slide show. Animations can provide an effective enhancement to your slide show without going overboard.

Animating Objects and Text

You do not have to be a professional graphic artist to add some basic animations to your presentation. Just follow these steps to animate objects and text:

1. Display the slide that contains the text or objects that you want to animate; select Normal view from the View menu.

2. Select Animations from the Slide Show menu and then choose Custom.

3. In the Select to Animate list, choose the text or object that you want to animate.

4. Select the Effects tab and choose the options you want (see Figure 22-7). The following options are available:

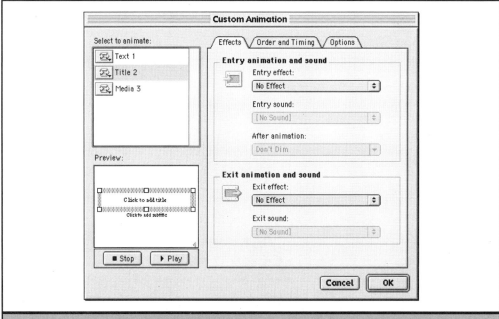

Figure 22-7.   *Use the Effects tab to specify the way you want your animation to look.*

■ **Entry Animation and Sound**   Choose an effect from the pop-up menu to use at the beginning of your slide.

■ **Exit Animation and Sound**   Pick an effect to use at the end of your animated slide.

5. Repeat steps 3 and 4 for every block of text or object that you want to animate. You can also select the objects as a group and apply the same animation settings to the entire batch.

6. When you're finished selecting your effects settings, click the Order and Timing tab (see Figure 22-8).

7. To modify the order of animation, which controls what frame appears and when, choose the entry or exit animation for the object under Animation Order and move it up or down in the list by the clicking one of the arrows.

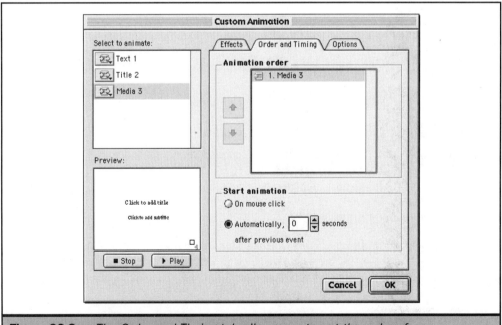

Figure 22-8.   *The Order and Timing tab allows you to set the order of your animation.*

8. Choose the entry or exit animation for the object to set the timing for it and then do one of the following:

■ If you want to begin the animation when you click the mouse button, select On Mouse Click.

■ If you want the animation to begin automatically, select Automatically After and enter the number of seconds you want as a gap between the previous animation and the one following it.

9. If text or an AutoShape with text inside is being animated, choose the Options tab and select the text entry options you want. Here are the choices:

■ **Text Entry Options**   These options allow you to decide how text enters an animation (at once, by word, by letter), how bullets are grouped (all at once, first level, second level, third level, fourth level, fifth level), whether you want the actions to occur in reverse order, and whether you want to animate an attached shape.

■ **Text Exit Options**   These choices allow you to specify how text exits an animation, how bullets are grouped, whether the actions to occur in reverse order, and whether an attached shape animates. The options are the same as for text entry.

10. Select Play to preview your animations.

NOTE   *A good way to create basic animations is to select the object you want to animate while in Normal view, select Animation from the Slide Show menu, and choose the specific option you want.*

To preview your animations while in Slide view, select Animation Preview from the Slide Show menu. A slide miniature will appear, and the animation will play inside it. If you want to replay the animation, click the slide miniature.

Animating Chart Elements

You aren't limited to animating PowerPoint slides. The elements of a chart created in Microsoft Graph or Excel can be animated as well. Once you have animated these charts, you can insert them into PowerPoint to enhance the look and feel of your presentation.

Use the following steps to animate Graph or Excel charts:

1. From the Insert menu, choose Chart.

2. After the chart is inserted in your presentation, select Animations from the Slide Show menu and choose the Options tab.

3. Specify the way you want the chart animated.

4. Select the Order and Timing tab.

5. To modify the order of animation, choose the entry or exit animation for the chart under Animation Order and then move the item up or down in the list by clicking one of the arrows.

6. Choose the entry or exit animation for the object to set its timing and then do one of the following:

   ■ If you want the animation to begin when you click the mouse button, select On Mouse Click.

   ■ If you want the animation to begin automatically, choose Automatically After and enter the number of seconds you want as a gap between the previous animation and the one following it. The timing you set will also be the time between each animated element of the chart.

7. Select the entry or exit effects you want by choosing the Effects tab. The choices are described in the previous section. Click Play below the preview window to preview the effects of your animation settings.

Integrating Sounds and Movies with Your Animation

The animation settings of PowerPoint can be used to integrate sounds or movies during the course of your presentation. Follow these steps:

1. Display the sound or movie you want to animate.

2. Select Animations from the Slide Show menu and choose the Custom option; then select the Options tab in the Custom dialog box.

3. Specify the way you want the movie or sound to be controlled.

4. Select the Order and Timing tab.

5. Choose the entry or exit animation for the sound or movie (the media) to modify the order of events under Animation Order and then click one of the arrows to move the animation up or down in the list.

6. Choose the entry or exit animation for the movie or sound to set the timing and then do one of the following:

   ■ If you want the movie or sound to begin when you click the mouse button, select On Mouse Click.

   ■ If you want the movie or sound to begin automatically, choose Automatically After and then enter the number of seconds you want as a gap between the previous animation and the one following it.

Adding Sound Effects to Animations

Another way to enhance your animations is to insert sound effects, which gives them life and vigor.

Follow these steps to add sound effects to animations:

1. With your presentation document in Normal view, display the slide to which you want to add a sound effect.

2. Select Animations from the Slide Show menu; then choose the Custom option and select the Effects tab in the Custom dialog box.

3. Under Select to Animate, choose the object to which you want to add a sound effect and then select an option under Entry Sound or Exit Sound.

4. Repeat steps 2 and 3 for each object to which you want to add a sound effect.

NOTE   *If you want to use a sound file as a sound effect, select Other Sound from the Entry Sound or Exit Sound pop-up menu.*

Adding Visual Effects to the Beginning or End of an Animation

Special effects are the hallmark of a motion picture, and adding some extra effects in your PowerPoint presentations can go a long way towards enhancing their visual appeal and impact to your audience. PowerPoint is outfitted with dozens of special animated effects, such as the ability to make an object in your slide fly into the picture and fly out again.

You can add a special visual effect to the start or end of your animation. Just follow these steps:

1. With the presentation document in Normal view, display the slide to which you want to add a visual effect.

2. Select Animations from the Slide Show menu; then choose the Custom option and select the Effects tab in the Custom dialog box.

3. Under Select to Animate, choose the object to which you want to add an effect; then select an option under Entry Animation And Sound or Exit Animation And Sound.

NOTE   *If you don't choose an option, the object will simply stay on the screen by default.*

4. From the pop-up menus choose the effects or sounds you want to add.

5. To test your effect, click the Play button.

6. Repeat steps 1 through 5 for every object or slide to which you want to add an effect.

Timings and Transitions

When you set the timing for a slide, you are configuring the amount of time that passes between the end of one slide and the beginning of the next. Setting a particular timing is useful if a specific amount of time needs to pass between two slides.

NOTE *If you're going to have to constantly stop your slide show to explain key points or clarify information, setting the exact timing may not be important.*

Transitions, such as fades and wipes, are a neat way to move between slides. Transitions are special effects that use the same concept as employed in videos to make the process of switching between slides smooth (and sometimes they look really cool, too).

CAUTION *Although transitions can enhance your presentation, too many may distract your audience from focusing on the main points of your presentation.*

In this section, you will learn how to configure timings and create transitions.

Setting Slide Show Timings Manually

To set slide show timings, follow these steps:

1. Choose the slide or slides for which you want to configure timings and switch to either Normal or Slide Sorter view.

2. Select Slide Transition from the Slide Show menu. The dialog box shown in Figure 22-9 appears.

3. In the Advance section, select Automatically After; then enter the number of seconds you want the slide to appear on the screen.

4. Click Apply to add the timing just to the selected slides.

NOTE *Click Apply to All if you want to add the timing to all of your slides.*

5. Repeat steps 1 through 4 for every slide for which you want to change the timing. To see the effect of these timings, select Slide Show in the lower left of the PowerPoint window.

NOTE *If you want the next slides to appear either when you click the mouse button or automatically after a set number of seconds, whichever comes first, select both the On Mouse Click and Automatically After check boxes. If you have a self-running presentation and you want to keep viewers from using the action buttons connected to hyperlinks to get to the next slide, clear both of these check boxes.*

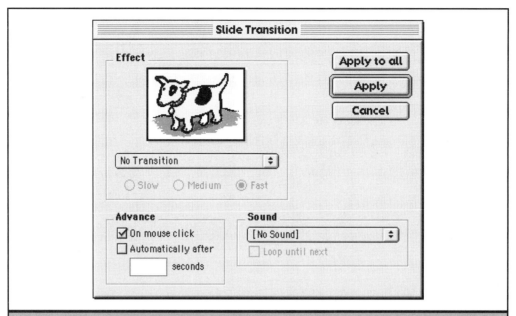

Figure 22-9. *Use the Slide Transition dialog box to set timings and add transitions to your presentation.*

Setting Slide Timings Automatically When Rehearsing

Before finishing your presentation, you'll want to do, as they say in show business, a run through, so that you can make sure everything works as expected. When you're rehearsing your presentation, you can set slide timings automatically. Here's how:

1. Select Rehearse Timings from the Slide Show menu to begin the show in rehearsal mode.

2. To figure out how long a slide remains on the screen, keep a close eye on the timing in the lower right of the PowerPoint window; then use the RIGHT ARROW key to go to the next slide when the duration is what you want.

3. Upon reaching the end of the slide show, select Yes to accept the timings or No to try again.

NOTE *If the same slide will be displayed more than one time, such as in a custom show, the last timing is the one recorded by PowerPoint.*

Adding Transitions

Now that you've configured the timings for your slides, the next step is to add transitions. Here's how:

1. Choose the slide or slides to which you want to add a transition; switch to Normal or Slide Sorter view.

2. Select Slide Transition from the Slide Show menu.

3. Choose the transition you want from the pop-up menu in the Slide Transition dialog box (shown in Figure 22-9) and then select any other options you want (such as adding sounds to your transitions).

4. If you prefer a QuickTime transition, which accesses features directly from Apple's QuickTime software, choose Select QuickTime Transition from the pop-up menu and select your transition from the list in the Select Effect dialog box.

5. When you've selected the appropriate effect, you are returned to the Slide Transition dialog box. To add the transition to the currently selected slide only, click Apply. To add the transition to every slide, click Apply to All.

6. Repeat steps 1 through 5 for every slide to which you want to add a transition. To see these transitions in action, select Animation Preview from the Slide Show menu.

Creating a Custom Transition

You do not have to use the standard range of transitions; you can also make your own variations on the theme to fit your needs. Using the Gradient Wipe QuickTime transition, you can select an image from your own library to use as a matte or backdrop for this transition, or you can create an image on your own with a graphics program such as Adobe Illustrator.

NOTE   *A matte is, in this context, a background image used for your transition.*

Here's how to create a custom transition:

1. Select Slide Transition from the Slide Show menu.

2. Choose Select QuickTime Transition from the pop-up menu in the Effect section of the Slide Transition dialog box (see Figure 22-10).

3. In the Select Effect dialog box, select Gradient Wipe.

4. Click the Matte preview window.

5. Locate the image you want to use as your new Gradient Wipe matte in the Open dialog box that appears and then select Open. Locate and select the image, then click OK.

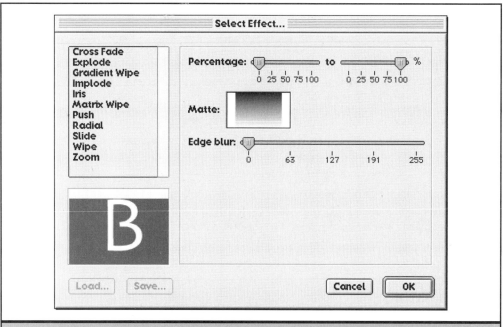

Figure 22-10. *You can create your own custom transitions by clicking the Matte preview window from this screen.*

For best results in creating a custom transition, use a two-color image such as a black-and-white image. This prevents conflict with the colors from which you may want to choose for your slide.

PowerPoint QuickTime Movies

Besides being able to add various special effects to your presentation and animate those effects and other objects, you can also transform your presentation into a QuickTime movie, which can be modified and edited just like any other movie file. In this section, you learn how to save a presentation as a PowerPoint movie and then edit it to meet your needs.

Saving a Presentation as a PowerPoint Movie

After your presentation is finished, it doesn't take long to set it up as a PowerPoint movie. Just follow these steps to save a presentation as a PowerPoint movie:

1. Select Make Movie from the File menu.

2. To adjust PowerPoint movie options, select Adjust Settings from the Save dialog box; then click Next.

3. Choose the options you want in the Movie Options dialog box (shown in Figure 22-11) and then click OK. The following choices are available:

- **Optimization**   Click the pop-up menu to change the quality of the movie. You have several choices that allow you to trade off between file size and picture quality.

- **Movie Dimensions**   Change the screen size for your movie; 640×480 pixels is standard for a movie, but you can also choose from the present screen size or a custom setting if you want a different image size, such as the wide-screen view that is popular these days.

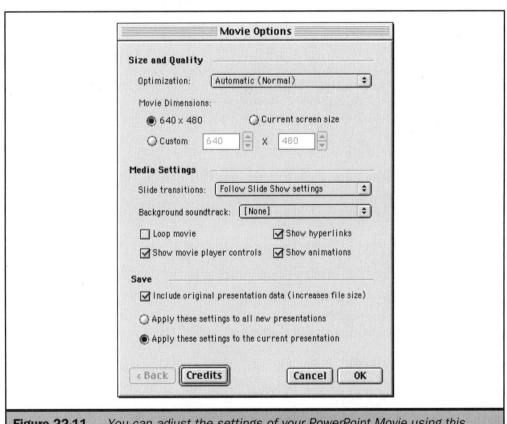

Figure 22-11.   *You can adjust the settings of your PowerPoint Movie using this dialog box.*

■ **Media Settings**   You can add slide transitions from a pop-up menu, add a background soundtrack from a pop-up menu, have the movie play over and over again using looping, display the movie player controls, show hyperlinks, and play animations.

You will probably want to include movie player controls, at the very least, so that the viewer can turn the presentation on or off or pause it in the same fashion as any other QuickTime movie.

■ **Save**   You can select an option to include the original presentation data in the saved file, which makes editing your movie in PowerPoint easier if you want to change it later. You can also choose an option to apply your settings to all new presentations or just the current one.

The option to include the presentation data will, of course, greatly increase file size, but it also makes the file totally self-contained, so that anyone viewing the presentation doesn't have to have the linked files at hand.

4. Type in a name for your movie in the Name box. If your movie is going to be viewed on a Windows-based computer, select the Append File Extension check box to automatically add the .mov extension that Window needs to properly associate a QuickTime viewer program with the file.

5. Click Save to store your completed movie.

Adding Credits to a PowerPoint Movie

Credits are a big deal in show business, and they're no doubt also a big deal to those who worked on your presentation. Even if you did it all by yourself, you'll want to add the appropriate credits.

Follow these steps to add credits to your PowerPoint movie:

1. Select Make Movie from the File menu.

2. Choose Adjust Settings from the Save dialog box and then click Next.

3. Click the Credits button and then type the movie credits you want in the text boxes (as illustrated in Figure 22-12).

If you want to modify any other movie settings set previously, click the Back button.

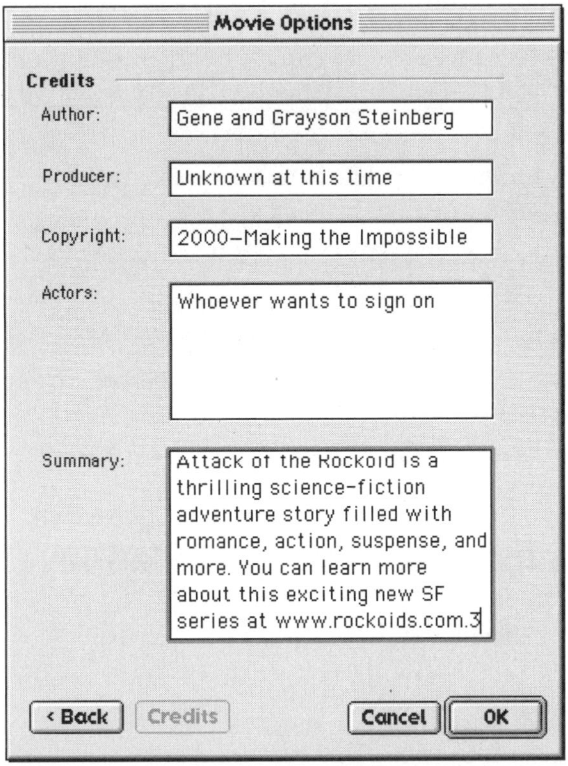

Figure 22-12.   *You can create credits for PowerPoint movies as shown here.*

Looping the Playback of a PowerPoint Movie

Would you like your movie to play over and over again? Follow these steps to play your PowerPoint Movie over again automatically:

1. Select Make Movie from the File menu.

2. Choose Adjust Settings from the Save dialog box and then click Next.

3. Select the Loop Movie check box under Media Settings. Click OK.

Modifying the Screen Size of a PowerPoint Movie

The screen size you select affects the way your presentation appears on a specific computer display or on a TV monitor. Here's how to change the size of the screen in a PowerPoint movie:

1. Select Make Movie from the File menu.

2. Choose Adjust Settings from the Save dialog box and then click Next.

3. In the Size and Quality section, do one of the following:

   - To set the movie resolution to 640×480 pixels, which is the standard resolution for VGA monitors on Macs and PCs, select 640×480.

   - To configure the movie dimensions to match your current screen size, choose Current screen size.

   - To make your movie dimensions any size from 100×100 pixels to 2000×2000 pixels, select Custom and enter any dimensions in that range that you want.

Displaying or Hiding PowerPoint Movie Player Controls

Do you want movie player controls to appear in your presentation? If you do, you give the person who views that movie an extra measure of control.

Here's how to show or hide the movie player controls in the program:

1. Select Make Movie from the File menu.

2. Choose Adjust Settings from the Save dialog box and then click Next.

3. Select or clear the Show Movie Player Controls check box under Media Settings. Normally you'll want to leave the controls on.

Modifying Default PowerPoint Movie Options

If you plan on making a number of PowerPoint movies, you can save time in preparing custom configurations if you adjust the default configuration to your needs.

Here's how to change the default options for your movie:

1. Select Preferences from the Edit menu.

2. Choose the General tab and then select Movie Options, which brings up the same dialog box you saw in Figure 22-11.

3. Select the settings you want as the defaults for the options.

4. Choose Apply These Settings to All New Presentations and then click OK. From here on, those settings will apply to all the new movies you create in PowerPoint, unless you change them by selecting Adjust Settings when you are making a movie.

Slide Show Effects

In addition to the special effects that you can add to your presentation to make it more interesting, there are enhancements that you can add to improve the slide show itself. This section covers some of the more interesting possibilities.

Configuring a Macro to Run During a Slide Show

As you learned in Chapter 15, a macro is a series of prerecorded actions that can be used to automate various activities. They are especially useful for tasks that you have to do over and over again. Macros let you sit back, relax, and have your computer do the work for you. They can be created in the Visual Basic Editor that comes with Office 2001. Once you have a macro created for your slide show, use the following steps to insert it:

NOTE   *Unlike Word, PowerPoint is not able to record and play back user actions, so the feature here is less useful than the one in Word, unless you are willing to learn how to use the Visual Basic Editor to write your own.*

1. Select the text or object on the slide on which you want to use a macro.
2. Choose Action Settings (see Figure 22-13) from the Slide Show menu.

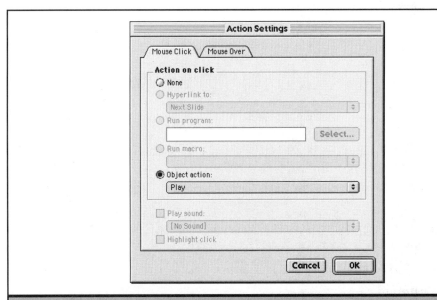

Figure 22-13.   *Use the Action Settings dialog box to add hyperlinks and macros to your presentation.*

3. To run the macro by clicking the selected object during the slide show, select the Mouse Click tab. To run the macro by moving the mouse pointer over the object, choose the Mouse Over tab.

4. Select Run Macro and then choose the macro you want.

5. Make any modifications you want. You can create hyperlinks to a file or slide, or run a program when the action is triggered.

6. Select Slide Show at the lower left of the PowerPoint window to preview your macro in action during the slide show. If you use macros in your presentation, you must use PowerPoint to run your slide show because the PowerPoint Viewer does not have the ability to run macros.

Configuring a Program to Open During a Slide Show

Because Office 2001 programs are configured by Microsoft to talk to each other, you can configure your slide show so that it will open any of the Office programs, plus any others you have, in your presentation. For example, you might link a presentation to your Word or Excel document, to provide additional information about a certain item or bit of data.

NOTE   *This feature requires that the program be present on or at least accessible from the computer where the slide is viewed. The program itself, of course, can't be embedded in the presentation.*

Follow these steps to open a program during a slide show:

1. Choose the text or object you want to use to open the program on the slide.

2. Select Action Settings from the Slide Show menu.

3. To open the program by clicking the selected object during the slide show, choose the Mouse Click tab. To open the program by moving the mouse pointer over the object, select the Mouse Over tab.

4. Choose Run Program and then type the path for the program that you want opened. If you don't know the path, click Select, find the program, and then click OK.

5. Make any other modifications you want to your setup.

6. Select Slide Show in the lower left of the PowerPoint window to preview the way the program will be opened when the slide show is running.

Configuring an OLE Object to Open During a Slide Show

OLE, short for Object Linking and Embedding, is Microsoft's method for enabling you to link to objects or items created in other programs that support this technology. An example would be the ability to access an object from another Office program.

NOTE   *Most of the programs that support this technology are Microsoft's. Other OLE-enabled programs will mention OLE support in their help menus or other documentation.*

Follow these steps to configure an OLE object to open during a slide show:

1. Choose the OLE object you want opened on the slide.

2. Select Action Settings from the Slide Show menu.

3. If you want the OLE object opened when it is clicked during a slide show, select the Mouse Click tab. If you want the OLE object to open when the mouse pointer is moved over it, choose the Mouse Over tab.

4. Select Object Action and then choose Open or Edit.

5. Select Slide Show in the lower left of the PowerPoint window to preview the way the OLE object will be opened when the slide show is running.

Using Action Settings in PowerPoint

Action settings allow you to exploit hyperlinks in your presentations. For example, you can specify a hyperlink for text or an object by using Insert Hyperlink or the Mouse Click tab in the Action Settings dialog box. You can also use the Mouse Over tab, configuring the hyperlink so that a sound plays when the mouse pointer rests on the text or object during the slide show. If the hyperlink is an object, the object can be highlighted when the pointer rests on it.

To use hyperlinks in PowerPoint, follow these steps:

1. Bring up the Action Settings dialog box from the Slide Show menu.

2. Click on the Mouse Click or Mouse Over tab.

3. Click the Hyperlink To button.

4. Choose the slide, URL, text or object you want to use as the hyperlink and then select Action Settings from the Slide Show menu.

5. Choose Hyperlink To on the Mouse Click tab and then select the hyperlink you want from the pop-up menu.

6. If you created a hyperlink with the Insert Hyperlink option in step 2, choose the text or object to which you want to assign an action; then select Action Settings from the Slide Show menu.

7. If you want to have a sound play when the pointer rests on the text or object, choose the Play Sound check box on the Mouse Over tab and then choose the sound you want from the pop-up menu.

8. To have text highlighted when the pointer rests on it, choose Highlight When Mouse Over on the Mouse Over tab.

Troubleshooting PowerPoint Movies

If you follow the steps presented in this chapter, you should be able to make your PowerPoint presentations run with a minimum of fuss and bother. But sometimes things don't work as planned. Fortunately, the solutions to these problems usually aren't difficult to come by:

- **PowerPoint Movie Doesn't Play**   To play PowerPoint movies correctly, you must have QuickTime version 3.0 or later. Make sure that the latest version of QuickTime is installed on your Mac when you are viewing your movies. The latest version of QuickTime is always available for downloading from Apple's Web site at http://www.apple.com/quicktime; both Mac and Windows versions are available from the site. In addition, if you intend to use the file on a Windows computer, you need to make sure the .mov file extension is added, so Windows knows what the file is.

- **Can't Edit PowerPoint Movies**   To edit your PowerPoint movies, you must have the original presentation files in addition to the movie file. One quick way to include these files is to embed them in your movie file. This option can be enabled by selecting Include Original Presentation Data (which increases the size of the file) in the Movie Options dialog box.

- **Can't Find Make Movie Command**   You need to have Mac OS version 8.5 or later and QuickTime version 3.0 or later installed on your Mac to use the Make Movie command. As mentioned earlier in this section, QuickTime can be downloaded directly from Apple's Web site.

- **PowerPoint Movie File Is Too Big**   You can make your PowerPoint Movie file smaller by leaving the Include Original Presentation Data check box unchecked in the Movie Options dialog box; just remember that you need those files to edit your movie. You can also reduce the screen size of your PowerPoint movie in the same dialog box and then resave the movie. You can optimize the size of your PowerPoint movie by selecting Size from the Optimization pop-up menu in the Movie Options dialog box. Finally, you can reduce the number of elements in your presentation that consume the most file space, such as CD-quality soundtracks, narration, high-resolution pictures, and animations. It's the eternal trade-off between size and quality.

- **PowerPoint Movie Is Played Too Slowly**   You can optimize your movie for smooth playback by selecting Smooth Playback from the Optimization pop-up menu in the Movie Options dialog box. You can also reduce the dimensions of your movie and resave it. If you have a slower Mac (and not all of us have the latest and greatest), you'll want to reduce the quality levels to allow a wider variety of viewers to see the presentation in all its glory.

- **Images Don't Look Right**   You can optimize your PowerPoint movie for image quality by selecting Quality from the Optimization pop-up menu in the Movie Options dialog box.

NOTE   *If your presentation will be seen by people in a variety of situations, test it on different computers, if possible, to make sure that everyone can see the movie with a reasonable amount of quality.*

- **Hyperlinks and Action Settings Won't Work**   Be sure that the Show Hyperlinks option is selected in the Movie Options dialog box. In addition, note that hyperlinks and action settings can't be used with QuickTime transitions in PowerPoint movies. Be sure that QuickTime transitions are not set in the Slide Transition dialog box for any of your slides, and be sure that the Follow Slide Show setting is selected from the Slide Transitions pop-up menu in the Movie Settings dialog box. Also, keep in mind that PowerPoint movies don't support all action settings. For example, if a movie is designed to play when one of your slides is selected, the movie will also play automatically when the slide is viewed in PowerPoint Movie format.

Summary

In this chapter, you learned how you can add special effects, such as sound files and videos, to enhance your presentation. You also learned how to set timings, add transitions, and transform your presentation into a PowerPoint QuickTime movie.

MASTERING
POWERPOINT 2001

Index

T

X

INTERNATIONAL CONTACT INFORMATION

AUSTRALIA
McGraw-Hill Book Company Australia Pty. Ltd.
TEL +61-2-9417-9899
FAX +61-2-9417-5687
http://www.mcgraw-hill.com.au
books-it_sydney@mcgraw-hill.com

CANADA
McGraw-Hill Ryerson Ltd.
TEL +905-430-5000
FAX +905-430-5020
http://www.mcgrawhill.ca

GREECE, MIDDLE EAST,
NORTHERN AFRICA
McGraw-Hill Hellas
TEL +30-1-656-0990-3-4
FAX +30-1-654-5525

MEXICO (Also serving Latin America)
McGraw-Hill Interamericana Editores S.A. de C.V.
TEL +525-117-1583
FAX +525-117-1589
http://www.mcgraw-hill.com.mx
fernando_castellanos@mcgraw-hill.com

SINGAPORE (Serving Asia)
McGraw-Hill Book Company
TEL +65-863-1580
FAX +65-862-3354
http://www.mcgraw-hill.com.sg
mghasia@mcgraw-hill.com

SOUTH AFRICA
McGraw-Hill South Africa
TEL +27-11-622-7512
FAX +27-11-622-9045
robyn_swanepoel@mcgraw-hill.com

UNITED KINGDOM & EUROPE
(Excluding Southern Europe)
McGraw-Hill Education Europe
TEL +44-1-628-502500
FAX +44-1-628-770224
http://www.mcgraw-hill.co.uk
computing_neurope@mcgraw-hill.com

ALL OTHER INQUIRIES Contact:
Osborne/McGraw-Hill
TEL +1-510-549-6600
FAX +1-510-883-7600
http://www.osborne.com
omg_international@mcgraw-hill.com